business

3E

accounting
economics
management
marketing
finance

JEFF MADURA

Florida Atlantic University

THOMSON

SOUTH-WESTERN

Australia · Canada · Mexico · Singapore · Spain · United Kingdom · United States

THOMSON
SOUTH-WESTERN

Introduction to Business, 3e
Jeff Madura

VP/Editorial Director:
Jack Calhoun

VP/Editor-in-Chief:
Michael P. Roche

Sr. Publisher:
Melissa Acuña

Sr. Acquisitions Editor:
Steve Hazelwood

Developmental Editor:
Mardell Toomey

Marketing Manager:
Nicole Moore

Production Editor:
Amy McGuire

Manufacturing Coordinator:
Diane Lohman

Compositor:
G & S Typesetters

Printer:
Transcontinental Printing, Inc.
Beauceville, QC

Design Project Manager:
Rik Moore

Internal Designer:
Kim Torbeck, Imbue Design

Cover Designers:
Kim Torbeck, Imbue Design
Rik Moore

Cover Photo Sources:
PhotoDisc, Inc.
Rik Moore

Photography Manager:
John Hill

Photo Researchers:
Darren Wright
Sam A. Marshall

Library of Congress
Control Number: 2002115369

Package ISBN: 0-324-18626-6
Book ISBN: 0-324-27222-7

Loose-Leaf Package ISBN:
0-324-20016-1
Loose-Leaf ISBN: 0-324-20071-4

Non-Infotrac Package ISBN:
0-324-20070-6
Non-Infotrac Loose-Leaf Package ISBN:
0-324-20072-2

To Mary

Brief Contents

Contents

Chapter 3 Business Ethics and Social Responsibility 65

Chapter 5   Assessing Industry Conditions   133

Chapter 6   Assessing Global Conditions   157

Chapter 9   Improving Productivity and Quality   259

Chapter 14   Promoting Products   443

Chapter 19 Managing Risk 609

Chapter 20 Synthesis of Business Functions 635

Preface

An Introduction to Business course can have a major impact on the career direction and success of students, whether they major in business, the sciences, or liberal arts. Regardless of their major, students normally pursue a career that is in a business setting. For example, students who major in science commonly work for biotechnology firms, and can benefit from an understanding of business. Students who select journalism as a major often work for media and publishing firms and, therefore, benefit from an understanding of business. Business concepts such as creating ideas, leadership, teamwork, and quality control are relevant to most students regardless of the career that they choose.

An Introduction to Business course provides the foundation of business knowledge that can enable students to utilize their talents in the business world. It also provides an overview of the different business topics, allowing students who major in business to determine the field of business (management, marketing, etc.) they would like to pursue.

WHAT MAKES THIS TEXT UNIQUE?

- Approach and Focus
  - Focus on a Business Plan and Decision-Making
  - Focus on Key Concepts
- New and Enhanced Content
  - All Updated Content
  - Expanded Coverage of Topics
  - Examples Everywhere
- Engaging Pedagogy
  - Value-Added Student Tutorials
  - Small Business Applications
  - Valuation Emphasis
  - Practical, Real-World Applications and Team-Building Exercises
  - Focus on Learning Skills Endorsed by AACSB and SCANS
  - Reinforcement of Key Concepts
- The Supplements Package
  - Supplements for Instructors
  - Supplements for Students

APPROACH AND FOCUS

Focus on a Business Plan and Decision-Making

The first chapter of this text provides a brief overview of business planning for all functions of a business. This overview not only serves as an outline for a business plan, but also serves as an outline for the text. In each chapter, the key concepts are applied to a business plan so students recognize how the concepts are used to make business decisions.

Each part of the text represents a key component of the business plan. Part I explains how to establish a business, choose a specific form of business organization, and develop a set of ethics guidelines for the business. Part II describes how the business environment (economic, industry, and global conditions) can affect the performance of the business. Parts III and IV focus on the management of a business, while Part V focuses on the marketing, and Part VI explains the financial management of the business. Part VII discusses other business topics.

When students complete each of these parts, they should be capable of applying the key concepts to create or revise the business plan for a particular business. The final chapter of the text integrates many of the key business functions described throughout the text, helping students to "pull it all together."

Focus on Key Concepts

This textbook prepares students for the business world by focusing on business concepts, without dwelling on definitions. Its application of business concepts to decision-making allows students to appreciate the dilemmas faced by businesses. Some of the key business concepts include:

- How the objectives of a firm's managers and its stockholders may cause conflict.

- How a firm's executives frequently face ethical dilemmas.

- How a firm's decision to expand may be dependent on economic conditions.

- How a firm's decision to expand overseas may depend on the foreign competition.

- How compensation schemes to motivate managers sometimes backfire.

- How a firm's product quality can be measured through feedback from customers.

- How a firm can improve its marketing with the use of the Internet.

- How a firm's financing decisions can affect its risk.

- How the decisions made within the various departments of a business are integrated.

NEW AND ENHANCED CONTENT

All Updated Content

The text is completely revised and designed to emphasize the events and technology changes that have had a major impact on businesses over the past year. More attention is given to business ethics as a result of the Enron and WorldCom scandals and reports that the executives of some firms have misreported their financial condition to their employees and stockholders. This text covers the responsibilities of firms to their employees and stockholders, and emphasizes the recent conflicts between executives and the stockholders of some firms. It also explains the controls that should be established by firms to ensure that executives behave in a manner that serves the firm's employees and stockholders rather than themselves. Where appropriate, the text also covers the impact of September 11th on businesses.

Expanded Coverage of Topics

The following business concepts have become more crucial to the success of a business over time, and therefore are given extra attention in this new edition:

- e-commerce
- e-marketing
- conflicts of interest between managers and subordinates and strategies to resolve those conflicts
- entrepreneurship
- supply chain management
- the merging of internet businesses with traditional businesses,
- the euro

This edition provides comprehensive treatment of key business topics while also addressing exciting, current topics that are certain to appeal to students. Every effort has been made to create a balance of enough coverage of important concepts without burdening students with too much information that is covered in subsequent business courses.

Examples Everywhere

Virtually every concept discussed in the text is followed by an example for further clarification. Many examples are based on real-world people, companies and events, including the Enron scandal, September 11th, and many e-commerce applications.

ENGAGING PEDAGOGY

Value-Added Student Tutorials

In-Text Study Guide

Answers are in an appendix at the back of the book.

18. A production process where employees go to the position of the product, rather than waiting for the product to come to them, is a(n):
    a) assembly line.
    ...ch process.

23. A strategy of deleg is referred to as:
    a) routing.
    b) dispatching.
    c) deintegration

In-Text Study Guide

Found at the end of each chapter, the *In-Text Study Guide*, as prepared by Janelle Dozier, serves as a study guide *without the additional cost*. Segments focus on test preparation, with at least 10 true/false and 25 multiple-choice questions per chapter. Answers to these questions, along with page references for where the answers can be found, are provided in Appendix C of the text. *In-Text Study Guide* questions are repeated in a separate section of the test bank for instructors who want to provide an incentive for students to work through the questions.

Self-Scoring Exercises

Self-Scoring Exercises are provided throughout the text to prepare students for the business world. These exercises allow students to discover their own strengths and weaknesses when making business decisions.

self-scoring exercise

The Frazzle Factor

Read each of the following statements, and rate yourself on a scale of 0 to 3, giving the answer that best describes how you generally feel (3 points for always, 2 points for often, 1 point for sometimes, and 0 points for never). Answer as honestly as you can, and do not spend too much time on any one statement.

Am I Angry?
___ 1. I feel that people around me make too many irritating mistakes.
___ 2. I feel annoyed because I do good work or perform well in school, but no one appreciates it.
___ ...en people make me an...ell them off.

Xtra! CD-ROM

New to this edition, and packaged with every new text, this *Xtra! CD-ROM* includes the digitized end-of-part *Integrative Video Cases*, self-assessment quiz questions, as prepared by Fernando Rodriguez, of Miami Dade Community College, and "Investing in a Business" Flash Presentation to walk students through researching a company, as well as the texts' PowerPoint® presentation. This CD-ROM provides students with additional support in preparing for exams and reinforcing key topics.

Small Business Applications

Continuing Example of College Health Club

College Health Club presents dilemmas faced by the owner, Sue Kramer, a young entrepreneur to whom students can relate. Students can put themselves in Sue's

position and figure out how they would resolve the various dilemmas she encounters when managing her small business. Students' problem-solving skills and critical thinking abilities are strengthened as they learn some of the challenges and potential rewards of owning a small business. *College Health Club* also increases the relevance of chapter material by demonstrating how concepts discussed in each chapter are applied to making real business decisions.

It's Your Decision

This end-of-chapter exercise gives students an opportunity to provide their opinions and advice on how the small business, College Health Club (discussed in every chapter) should be managed. Questions prompt the students to make managerial decisions for College Health Club about issues discussed in the chapter.

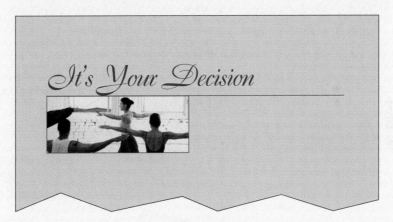

Small Business Survey

Small Business Survey provides a reality-based picture of small business decision-making. The surveys cover various topics, including the typical background of board members at a small business, and how CEOs of small business use their time to manage employees.

Campus.com

Students are put in the position of owners of a small business called *Campus.com*, which sells information about college campuses to prospective students over the Internet. They are asked to make decisions about how to apply business concepts covered within each part of the text. By the end of the semester, they will have completed a business plan for this small business. Students can utilize the accompanying *Business Plan Booklet and CD-ROM* templates to build their business plan. This project offers the opportunity for students to work in teams and to develop their communication skills by sharing their ideas with their team or with the class.

Running Your Own Business

An alternative business plan project is the *Running Your Own Business* project. Students are allowed to create their own business idea. At the end of each part of the text, students are guided step-by-step through issues and decisions they would face in running their own business. They develop a business plan as they go through the chapters of the text. At the end of the school term, students can convert their accumulated answers into a formal business plan. Students utilize the accompanying *Business Plan Booklet and CD-ROM* to build their business plan. This exercise can enable students to improve their writing and speaking skills as they communicate their ideas.

Business Plan Booklet and CD-ROM

A *Business Plan Booklet and CD-ROM* are tied to both the *Campus.com* and *Running Your Own Business* end-of-part projects. These templates provide pre-designed documents for students to fill in so that they can complete their business plans for these projects. This *Business Plan Booklet and CD-ROM*, packaged with every new text, provides the electronic templates for the *Campus.com* and *Running Your Own Business* business plans.

Cases

Short cases present real-world scenarios for students to analyze and make decisions about the direction of a business. The cases cover businesses such as Burton Snowboards, Valassis, and JIAN.

End-of-Chapter Video Cases

Video cases at the end of each chapter bring a real business into the classroom, where students can discuss the situation faced by the business and the results of the action the business decided to take.

Video Case: Motivating Employees at Valassis Communications, Inc.

Valassis Communications, Inc., creates the promotional newspaper inserts for 58 million households. It uses a pay-for-performance system that rewards employees for high performance. The company rewards employees both for individual achievements and for team achievements. The team awards are tied to the performance of the firm overall. In this way, the employees benefit whenever shareholders of the firm benefit.

Questions

1. How is Valassis's reward system related to pectancy theory"?

2. How does Valassis use positive reinforcen

3. Is Valassis's success due entirely to monet wards, or are there other reasons for emp faction at the firm?

End-of-Part Integrative Video Cases

Two new video cases are now found at the end of each part, *Integrative Video Case*. The *Integrative Video Case* features interviews with small business owners that provide a wide variety of scenarios involving decision-making. The end-of-part exercises that accompany these videos integrate content studied in the individual chapters of that part, helping students "pull it all together." These video cases are also available digitized on the *Xtra! CD-ROM* so students can view these in, or out of class.

Valuation Emphasis

The Coca-Cola Company Annual Report Project

The Coca-Cola Company Annual Report Project, at the end of each chapter, allows students to play the role of stockholders of The Coca-Cola Company. It enables students to recognize how a real firm's business decisions affect its value, and therefore affect the return to its shareholders. Updated questions for the most recent Coca-Cola Company annual report are found on the text's web site at http://madura.swlearning.com.

Specific questions show students how to access recent news about Coca-Cola and to monitor Coca-Cola's value (its stock price). This exercise can be done *individually or in teams*, and can allow students to develop analytical and communication skills by explaining the relationship between the firm's decisions and the stock's value over the semester.

The Stock Market Game

This end-of-part feature puts students in the position of shareholders. Each student selects a stock in which he or she would like to invest, tracks the firm's stock price throughout the school term, and investigates how that firm manages its business operations.

- allows students to witness how a firm's value is affected by its decisions

- explains how the student can retrieve the annual report and news stories of the firm selected

- allows students to monitor the change in the stock's price over the school term, so that they can determine which stock performs the best over the term.

THE STOCK MARKET GAME

Go to **http://finance.yahoo.com.** and che[ck] continuously by Yahoo! Finance.

Check Your Stock Portfolio

1. What is the value of your stock port[folio]

2. What is your return on your investm[ent]

3. How did your return compare to th[e] you whether your stock portfolio's p[erformance]

- allows students to develop analytical and communication skills by explaining the relationship between the firm's decisions and the stock's value over the semester.

- this exercise can be done individually or in teams

The stock market contest allows students to simulate the management of a stock portfolio. It keeps track of the portfolio as the student trades over time, and determines the market value of the portfolio on a daily basis. The last part includes a project that allows the student to determine the performance of their investments, and to identify the business decisions that caused the performance to change.

Investing in a Business

This end-of chapter feature sends students out to real-companies web sites to research and answer questions about how the chapter concepts can affect the firm's business. This exercise shows students how they can learn more about a firm by exploring its web site. The

Investing in a Business

Using the annual report of the firm in which you would like to invest, complete the following:

1 Does the firm appear to recognize that its employees are the key to its success?

2 Does the firm empower its workers? Does it encour-

Xtra! CD-ROM includes a flash presentation, which guide students through this exercise by using Krispy Kreme, as an example, demonstrating where information can be found on that company's web site. This presentation as prepared by Charlie T. Cook, Jr., of the University of West Alabama can serve as a tutorial of this applications based end-of-chapter feature.

Practical, Real-World Applications and Team-Building Exercises

Your Career in Business

Each part concludes with a section that helps students better understand various business majors and professions and think about the career they might pursue.

Students will have increased understanding of various business majors offered by colleges and universities as they directly relate to each part.

Students will understand the primary emphasis of the courses that are required of the various business majors described in each part.

Students will learn about the various careers that they can pursue depending on their particular major, including a job description and the salary range.

Cross-Functional Teamwork

Cross-Functional Teamwork boxes explain the need for managers of different functional areas to make decisions as a team in order to increase a firm's value, illustrating to students how and why various areas need to work together.

cross functional teamwork:

olved in Total

h ongoing product as-
oduct materials are
omer has purchased
TQM requires an in-
ey management
ng the proper types
fficient (low-cost)
ng that the product
rds.

customer satisfaction, and obtaining feedback from customers on how to improve the product. When marketing managers receive a similar criticism about a product from many customers, they should contact the production managers, who may redesign the product. This interaction between management and marketing functions is shown in Exhibit 9.7.

The financing function is indirectly affected, as changes in expenses or revenue resulting from TQM may alter th   t of new financi   firm needs.

Global Business

Global Business boxes in each chapter show how global realities impact every area of business and emphasize how decisions to pursue international opportunities can enhance the firm's value.

Increasing Value with Technology

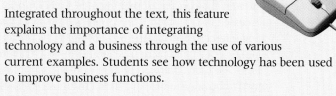

Integrated throughout the text, this feature explains the importance of integrating technology and a business through the use of various current examples. Students see how technology has been used to improve business functions.

Business Online

Web site links related to the text's main concepts are cited and described in each chapter. All links shown in the text are listed on our web site, where students can link directly to each site, without having to key in the full address.

FOCUS ON LEARNING SKILLS ENDORSED BY AACSB AND SCANS

This text offers several features and exercises that allow students to build their learning skills that are endorsed by the American Association of Collegiate Schools of Business (AACSB) and by the Secretary's Commission of Achieving Necessary Skills (SCANS). In particular, this text emphasizes the development of four skills:

- Decision-making and Planning
- Teamwork
- Technology
- Communication

Decision-making is the focus of every chapter. Teamwork is emphasized within the *Cross-functional Teamwork* feature. Technology is emphasized within several features of the text, including *Increasing Value With Technology*, and *Business Online*.

All four of the skills are emphasized in the exercises. For example, students are challenged to be creative by forming their own business idea. The cases and other end-of-chapter exercises frequently put students in positions in which they must make business decisions. Various exercises allow teams so that students can work together to resolve business dilemmas. Some of the exercises require students to communicate their views through a written report or a presentation.

EXERCISE	Decision-Making	Teamwork	Technology	Communication
Students as Managers:				
It's Your Decision	✔	✔		✔
Cases	✔			✔
Video Cases	✔			✔
Students as Stockholders:				
Coca-Cola Project	✔			✔
The Stock Market Game	✔			✔
Investing in a Business			✔	✔
Students as Owners of Their Own Business:				
Campus.com	✔	✔	✔	✔
Running Your Own Business	✔	✔		✔

Reinforcement of Key Concepts

Many of the features just described reinforce the key concepts in each chapter. This leads to better understanding on the part of the student. In turn, instructors have more flexibility to focus on current events and class discussion exercises.

To illustrate how this text can ensure a clear understanding through reinforcement, consider the concept of making a decision on how to promote a product, which is discussed in Chapter 15. *Increasing Value with Technology* boxes discuss electronic shopping offered by firms. The *Small Business Survey* section in that chapter discusses the opinions of small businesses about the skills that are necessary to be successful in sales. The *Global Business* section in that chapter explains why promotion strategies need to be adjusted to appeal to customers in foreign countries. The *College Health Club* section in that chapter explains the dilemma of a health club that is considering various strategies to promote its services. The *Investing in a Business* exercise in that chapter asks students to determine how the firm that they decided to invest in at the beginning of the term promotes its products. The *Case* in that chapter illustrates the decisions involved in promoting a product on a web site. The *Video Case* illustrates promotion strategies for Red Roof Inn. The *Business Online* feature in that chapter observes the promotion strategies of Amazon.com. The *Coca-Cola Company Annual Report Project* in that chapter enables students to determine the ways in which The Coca-Cola Company promotes its products. Finally, the In-Text Study Guide in that chapter allows students to test their understanding of promotion strategies. Students are consistently empowered to make decisions as if they were managers of a firm.

Every key concept in the text can be reinforced with one or more of the text features just described. While instructors may vary in their emphasis of features in this text to reinforce each concept, they have a variety of features available to them.

THE SUPPLEMENTS PACKAGE

SUPPLEMENTS FOR INSTRUCTORS!

We know how vital the supplement package is to the success of your Introduction to Business course, so we're pleased to provide an extensive package to accompany *Introduction to Business, 3e.*

Instructor's Manual

The Instructor's Manual, prepared by Francis H. Dong of DeVry University, includes chapter outlines, discussion questions for boxed material in the text, suggestions for research topics, suggestions for guest speakers, and solutions to end-of-chapter materials.

New to this edition!

- Detailed guidance on how to roll out *The Stock Market Game.*
- Sample syllabi
- The "Questions Students Always Ask" are included for each chapter
- Suggestions for using the videos

This instructor's manual provides excellent support for all instructors and is especially ideal for someone teaching from this textbook for the first time.

Test Bank

The Test Bank, prepared by Debora Gilliard, of Metropolitan State College, includes over 2,000 true/false, multiple-choice, and essay questions. Each question notes the text page reference and difficulty level. Questions from the in-text study guide are included in a separate section.

ExamView Testing Software

ExamView Testing Software contains all of the questions in the printed test bank. This program is an easy-to-use test creation software compatible with Microsoft Windows. Instructors can add or edit questions, instructions, and answers; and select questions by previewing them on the screen, selecting them randomly, or selecting them by number. Instructors can also create and administer quizzes online, whether over the Internet, a local area network (LAN), or a wide area network (WAN).

PowerPoint® Presentation Slides

PowerPoint Presentation Slides, prepared by Jude Rathburn, of the University of Wisconsin, Milwaukee, are available to qualified adopters. The slides that accompany Introduction to Business include custom presentations that contain chapter outlines and key exhibits from the text.

New to this edition!

- More slides, more color, more graphics, more excitement!

End-of-Chapter Videos

Video cases at the end of each chapter bring a real business into the classroom, where students can discuss the situation faced by the business and the results of the action the business decided to take.

End-of-Part Integrative Videos

Two new video cases are now found at the end of each part, *Integrative Video Case*. The *Integrative Video Case* features interviews with small business owners that provide a wide variety of scenarios involving decision-making. The end-of-part exercises that accompany these videos integrate content studied in the individual chapters of that part, helping students "pull it all together." These video cases are also available digitized on the Xtra! CD-ROM so students can view these in, or out of class.

Instructor's Resource CD-ROM (IRCD)

All instructor supplements are contained in one easy-to-find location. The IRCD includes electronic files of the instructor's manual, test bank, ExamView® Testing Software and PowerPoint®.

Teaching Transparencies

Full-color Acetate Transparencies of key text exhibits are provided for qualified adopters.

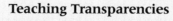

Loose-Leaf Version of Introduction to Business

If you prefer to teach the topics in a different order, you should look into the loose-leaf version of *Introduction to Business, 3e*. This provides instructors with more flexibility of topical coverage for customizing their course.

SUPPLEMENTS FOR STUDENTS!

Business Plan Booklet and CD-ROM

A *Business Plan Booklet and CD-ROM* are tied to both the *Campus.com* and *Running Your Own Business* end-of-part projects. These templates provide pre-designed documents for students to fill in so that they can complete their business plans for these projects. This *Business Plan Booklet and CD-ROM,* packaged with every new text, provides the electronic templates for the *Campus.com* and *Running Your Own Business* business plans.

Xtra! CD-ROM

New to this edition, and packaged with every new text, this Xtra! CD-ROM includes the digitized end-of-part Integrative Video Cases, self-assessment quiz questions, as prepared by Fernando Rodriguez, of Miami Dade Community College, and "Investing in a Business" Flash Presentation to walk students through researching a company, as well as the texts PowerPoint® presentation. This CD-ROM provides students with additional support in preparing for exams and reinforcing key topics.

InfoTrac® College Edition (ICE)

Every new copy of the text is packaged with InfoTrac® College Edition, free of charge! ICE is a fully searchable database that gives users access to full-text articles from more than 900 periodicals.

WebTutor™ on Blackboard® or WebCT™

Instructors can harness the power of the Internet to deliver a course online utilizing WebCT™ or BlackBoard®. *WebTutor™* offers a rich collection of content designed specifically for this edition. *WebTutor®* offers in-depth content, concept presentations, instructor customization, flashcards, Internet links, email, and much more! *WebTutor™* also offers instructors the course management tools in which they need such as gradebook, and assessment features.

Web Site

A text support Web Site at
http://madura.swlearning.com
offers many resources
for both instructors and students. Instructors can access downloadable supplement materials, while students can access interactive quizzes, crossword puzzles, chapter links, career-related links, PowerPoint and updated questions for *The Coca-Cola Company Annual Report Project* related to its most recent annual report.

ACKNOWLEDGEMENTS

The author and the entire South-Western/Thomson publishing team are grateful to the reviewers whose feedback was so important to the success of this current edition. They are:

Sally L. Andrews
Linn-Benton Community College

Janet Caruso
Briarcliffe College

Francis H. Dong
DeVry University

Douglas Dorsey
Manchester Community College

Jay Ebben
University of Wisconsin

Brenda Eichelberger
Portland State University

Chris W. Grevesen
DeVry College of Technology

Bruce E. Guttman
Katharine Gibbs School

Nathan Himelstein
Essex County College

Jennifer Howe
North Carolina State College

Daryl Kerr
University of North Carolina at Charlotte

Rodney D. Merkle
Indian Hills Community College

Jim McGowen
SouthWestern Illinois College

Stephen Peters
Walla Walla Community College

Michael R. Potter
Devry University

Jude Rathburn
University of Wisconsin-Milwaukee

Marvin Recht
Butler University

Dennis Shannon
Southwestern Illinois College

We also are very grateful to all of the supplement preparers listed below:

Charlie T. Cook
University of West Alabama

Francis H. Dong
Devry University

Dr. Janelle Dozier, PhD

Debora Gilliard
Metropolitan State College

Jude Rathburn
University of Wisconsin, Milwaukee

Fernando Rodriguez
Miami Dade Community College

Oliver Schnusenberg
St. Joseph's University

Finally, the author wishes to express his gratitude to the publishing team at South-Western who helped to ensure a quality final product:

Steve Hazelwood
Acquisitions Editor

Mardell Toomey
Developmental Editor

Nicole Moore
Marketing Manager

Amy McGuire
Production Editor

Rik Moore
Cover Design, Design Project Manager

Kim Torbeck
Cover and Internal Design

And a special thanks to **John Hill, Darren Wright** *and* **Rik Moore** *for their excellent work on the photos.*

ABOUT THE AUTHOR

Jeff Madura is the SunTrust Professor of Finance at Florida Atlantic University. He has written several other textbooks as well, including *International Financial Management* and *Financial Market and Institutions*. He has had articles on business published in numerous journals, including *Journal of Financial and Quantitative Analysis, Journal of Banking and Finance, Journal of Business Research, Financial Review, Journal of Financial Research, Columbia Journal of World Business, Journal of International Money and Finance,* and *Journal of Business Strategies*. He has received awards for teaching and research and has served as a consultant for many businesses. He has served as Director for the Southern Finance Association and the Eastern Finance Association and has also served as President of the Southern Finance Association.

Part I

Organization of a Business

A business is created to provide products or services to customers. The first step in understanding how businesses operate is to recognize their most important functions and how a business is initially organized. Part I, which contains Chapters 1 through 3, provides this background. Chapter 1 describes key business functions and explains how to develop a plan for a new business. Chapter 2 describes the possible forms of business ownership that the creators of a new business can select. It also explains how the potential reward and the risk to business owners are dependent on the form of ownership selected. Chapter 3 describes the ethical and social responsibilities of owners who establish a business and of employees who are hired to manage the business. This chapter is included in Part I because a business should recognize its ethical and social responsibilities as soon as it is established. Overall, Part I explains the main decisions that owners must make when they create a new business. These decisions serve as a foundation for other decisions that are made by employees as the business develops. Consequently, these initial decisions affect the performance of the firm and ultimately its value.

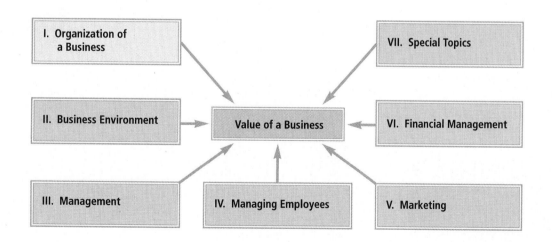

I. Organization of a Business		VII. Special Topics
II. Business Environment	Value of a Business	VI. Financial Management
III. Management	IV. Managing Employees	V. Marketing

All businesses, including that of Britney Spears, must decide how to produce their product, how to promote their product, how to finance their expenses, and how to assess their financial performance.

The Learning Goals of this chapter are to:

1 Identify the key stakeholders that are involved in a business.

2 Describe the key functions of a business.

3 Explain how to develop a business plan.

Chapter 1

Planning a Business

A business (or firm) is an enterprise that provides products or services desired by customers. According to the U.S. Labor Department, more than 800,000 businesses are created in the United States every year. Along with large, well-known businesses such as The Coca-Cola Company and IBM, there are many smaller businesses that provide employment opportunities and produce products or services that satisfy customers. What do Britney Spears, a bungee-jumping company, your local dentist, the New York Yankees organization, your plumber, and your favorite restaurant have in common? They are all businesses that provide products or services desired by customers. Consider the business established by Britney Spears. She produces music that is desired by customers and packages that music into a CD. When Britney creates her next CD, some of her more important business decisions are:

▶ What type of music should she produce? [Product decision]

▶ How should the music be produced? [Production decision]

▶ How should the music that is produced be promoted? [Promotion decision]

▶ How should she obtain funds to finance the cost of producing the music? [Financing decision]

Regarding the decision about the type of product (music) to produce, Britney wants to produce music that utilizes her talent and is also desired by potential customers. Her production decision involves determining the instruments, the sound system, and the backup vocals to be used for each song. Thus, each song is a component of the product that she produces. Her promotion decision is intended to increase the demand for her CDs. An effective promotion strategy will result in a higher level of sales of her CDs. Her promotion decision will also affect the expenses associated with promoting her product. Her financing decision will affect the financing expenses.

All businesses must make these types of decisions, whether the product produced is music, cell phones, shoes, computers, or jewelry. This chapter introduces the key types of decisions made by a business, which represent the different parts of this text. Whether these decisions are made by Britney Spears's business or by any other business, they are made in a manner that maximizes the firm's value.

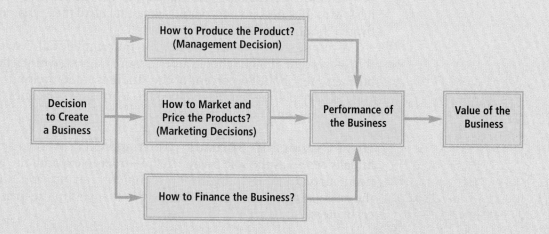

The goal of any business is to provide products or services that customers desire. Many businesses, such as Dell Computer, The Gap, Ford Motor Company, and Motorola, develop products for customers. Others, such as American Airlines and Hilton Hotels, provide services rather than products. Common types of service organizations include travel agencies and health care, law, and accounting firms. Some firms, such as IBM, Microsoft, and AT&T, provide both products and services. Managing a business that provides services can be as challenging and rewarding as managing a business that provides products.

KEY STAKEHOLDERS IN A BUSINESS

1

Identify the key stakeholders that are involved in a business.

stakeholders people who have an interest in a business; the business's owners, creditors, employees, suppliers, and customers

Every business involves transactions with people. Those people are affected by the business and therefore have a stake in it. They are referred to as **stakeholders,** or people who have an interest (or stake) in the business. Five types of stakeholders are involved in a business:

▶ Owners

▶ Creditors

▶ Employees

▶ Suppliers

▶ Customers

Each type of stakeholder plays a critical role for firms, as explained next.

Owners

entrepreneurs people who organize, manage, and assume the risk of starting a business

Every business begins as a result of ideas about a product or service by one or more people, called **entrepreneurs,** who organize, manage, and assume the risk of starting a business. Entrepreneurship is the act of creating, organizing, and managing a business. Today, more than 8 million people in the United States are entrepreneurs. Entrepreneurs are critical to the development of new business because they create new products (or improve existing products) desired by consumers.

People will be willing to create a business only if they expect to be rewarded for their efforts. The rewards of owning a business come in various forms. Some people are motivated by the chance to earn a large income. Others desire to be their own boss rather than work for someone else. Many people enjoy the challenge or the prestige associated with owning a business. Most business owners would agree that *all* of these characteristics motivated them to start their own business.

A recent survey by the Center for Entrepreneurial Leadership found that 69 percent of high school students were interested in starting their own business. Yet about 86 percent of the students rated their business knowledge as very poor to fair. People need to learn how a business operates before they set out to create a business.

How Ownership Spreads An entrepreneur who creates a business initially serves as the sole owner. Yet, in order to expand, the business may need more funding than the entrepreneur can provide. Consequently, the entrepreneur may allow other people to invest in the firm and become co-owners.

Charles Harris and Evan Betzer are co-owners of Stoneworth Financial, LLC, an investment banking firm founded the day after the co-owners were laid off from Enron. While thousands of careers collapsed with Enron, dozens of exciting new enterprises are now being created.

AP Photo/ Richard Carson

When the ownership of the firm is shared, the proportion of the firm owned by the existing owners is reduced. Consider a bakery that two people created with a $100,000 investment each. Each person owns one-half of the firm. They can obtain more funds by allowing a third person to invest in the firm. If the third person invests $100,000, each of the three people will own one-third of the firm. Any profits (or earnings) of the firm that are distributed to the owners will be shared among three owners. By accepting investment from more owners, however, the firm may be able to expand its business so that the original owners benefit despite their decreased share of ownership.

stock certificates of ownership of a business

stockholders (shareholders) investors who become partial owners of firms by purchasing the firm's stock

Many firms have grown by issuing stock to other investors; that is, they essentially sell a portion of the ownership to these investors. The **stock** received by investors is a certificate representing ownership of the specific business. The investors who purchase stock are called **stockholders** (or **shareholders**) of those firms. The funds received by a firm that issues stock can be used to expand the business. Large firms such as Cisco Systems, IBM, and General Motors now have millions of stockholders, but when they were created, they were small businesses.

When a firm's performance improves, its value may increase as well, as reflected in a higher stock price for those who own the stock. Stockholders can sell their stock to other investors whenever they want. They benefit when a firm performs well because they will be able to sell the stock at a higher price than they paid for it if the firm's value rises. As an extreme example, stockholders of Dell Computer have doubled their investment in some years because Dell performed so well. At the other extreme, stockholders who owned the stock of firms such as Enron and Global Crossing at the time these firms went bankrupt lost their entire investment.

A firm has a responsibility to the stockholders who have invested funds. It is expected to invest those funds in a manner that will increase its performance and value. Consequently, it should be able to provide the stockholders with a decent return on their investment. However, some firms perform much better than others, so investors must carefully assess a firm's potential performance before investing in its stock.

Creditors

Firms typically require financial support beyond that provided by their owners. When a firm is initially created, it incurs expenses before it sells a single product or service. Therefore, it cannot rely on cash from sales to cover its expenses. Even firms that have existed for a long time, such as Little Caesars Pizza, Disney, and Nike, need financial support as they attempt to expand. A fast-growing business such as Little Caesars Pizza would not generate sufficient earnings to cover new investment in equipment or buildings.

creditors financial institutions or individuals who provide loans

Many firms that need funds borrow from financial institutions or individuals called **creditors,** who provide loans. Bank of America, SunTrust Bank, and thousands of other commercial banks commonly serve as creditors for firms. Firms that borrow from creditors pay interest on their loans. The amount borrowed represents the debt of the firm, which must be paid back to the creditors along with interest payments over time. Large firms such as General Motors and DuPont have billions of dollars in debt.

Creditors will lend funds to a firm only if they believe the firm will perform well enough to pay the interest on the loans and the principal (amount borrowed) in the future. The firm must convince the creditors that it will be sufficiently profitable to make the interest and principal payments.

Employees

Employees of a firm are hired to conduct the business operations. Some firms have only a few employees; others, such as General Motors and IBM, have more than 200,000 employees. Those employees who are responsible for managing job assignments of other employees and making key business decisions are called **managers.** The performance of a firm is highly dependent on the decisions of its managers. Although managers' good decisions can help a firm succeed, their bad decisions may cause a firm to fail.

managers employees who are responsible for managing job assignments of other employees and making key business decisions

Goals of Managers   The goal of a firm's managers is to maximize the firm's value and, therefore, to maximize the value of the firm's stock. Maximizing firm value is an obvious goal for many small businesses since the owner and manager are often the same. In contrast, most stockholders of a publicly traded firm do not work for the firm. They rely on the firm's managers to maximize the value of the stock held by stockholders. The following statements from recent annual reports illustrate the emphasis firms place on maximizing shareholder value:

"We are not promising miracles, just hard work with a total focus on why we're in business: to enhance stockholder value."

—Zenith Electronics

"We believe that a fundamental measure of our success will be the shareholder value we create over the long term."

—Amazon.com

"Everything we do is designed to build shareholder value over the long haul."

—Wal-Mart

"We create value for our share owners, and that remains our true bottom line."

—The Coca-Cola Company

Maximizing the firm's value encourages prospective investors to become shareholders of the firm.

To illustrate how managers can enhance a firm's value, consider the case of Dell Computer, which created an efficient system for producing computers. This resulted in low costs and allowed Dell to provide high-quality computers at low prices. Over time, Dell's sales increased substantially, as did its profits. The ability of Dell's managers to control costs and sell computers at low prices satisfied not only its customers but also its owners (shareholders).

Suppliers

Firms commonly use materials to produce their products. For example, automobile manufacturers use steel to make automobiles, while home builders need cement, wood siding, and many other materials. Firms cannot complete the production process if they cannot obtain the materials. Therefore, their performance is partially dependent on the ability of their suppliers to deliver the materials on schedule.

Customers

Firms cannot survive without customers. To attract customers, a firm must provide a desired product or service at a reasonable price. It must also ensure that the products or services produced are of adequate quality so that customers are satisfied. If a firm cannot provide a product or service at the quality and price that customers desire, customers will switch to the firm's competitors. Motorola and Saturn (a division of General Motors) attribute some of their recent success to recognizing the types of products that consumers want. These firms also are committed to quality and to pricing their products in a manner that is acceptable to customers.

Summary of Key Stakeholders

Firms rely on entrepreneurs (owners) to create business ideas and possibly to provide some financial support. They rely on other owners and creditors to provide additional financial support. They rely on employees (including managers) to produce and sell their products or services. They rely on suppliers to provide the materials needed for production. They rely on customers to purchase the products or services they produce. The president of Goodyear Tire and Rubber Company summarized the relationship between a firm and its stakeholders in a recent annual report: "Last year I reaffirmed our values—protecting our good name, focusing on customers, respecting and developing our people [employees], and rewarding investors."

Interaction among Stakeholders   The interaction among a firm's owners, employees, customers, suppliers, and creditors is illustrated in Exhibit 1.1. Managers decide how the funds obtained from owners, creditors, or sales to customers should be utilized. They use funds to pay for the

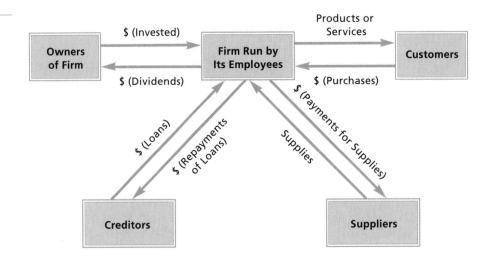

resources (including employees, supplies, and machinery) needed to produce and promote their products. They also use funds to repay creditors. The money left over is profit. Some of the profit (or earnings) is retained and reinvested by the firm. Any remaining profit is distributed as **dividends,** or income that the firm provides to its owners.

dividends income that the firm provides to its owners

CREATING A BUSINESS IDEA

To create a business idea, entrepreneurs must determine what products or services are desired by customers. To be successful, a business needs to achieve a **competitive advantage,** or unique traits that make its products more desirable than those of competitors. Some businesses create a competitive advantage by offering products similar to their competitors' products but at a lower price. Other businesses attempt to provide a product that is of higher quality than those produced by competitors. Some other businesses offer more convenient services.

competitive advantage unique traits that make a business's products more desirable than those of its competitors

Steps Involved in Creating a Business

To create a business idea, entrepreneurs take four key steps identified next.

Identify a Competitive Advantage   First, entrepreneurs must recognize their own experience or skills so that they can identify the type of business they can create that may have a competitive advantage over others. For example, people with excellent writing skills may consider being an author or establishing a publishing business. People with computer skills may consider a business in software development or computer repair. People with carpenter skills may establish their own home repair business.

Differentiate the Product   The second step is for entrepreneurs to determine how they can distinguish their product or service from others that are already offered. For example, an entrepreneur who establishes a home repair company must determine what that business can offer that

Starting a Business This website provides guidance on starting a business.

e-business

U.S. Small Business Administration

http://www.sba.gov/starting

other existing home repair companies do not. Perhaps it can specialize in one type of repair that other home repair firms in the area do not offer, such as roof repair. Before finalizing their business idea, entepreneurs should ask why no other business has provided the product or service that they think would be successful. Perphaps other businesses have tried to specialize in roof repair and found that demand for roof repair service in the area is insufficient to support a business.

Determine the Necessary Resources   The third step is to determine the resources that are needed to implement the idea. The resources may include employees, a workspace that will have to be purchased or leased, and machinery.

Assess the Feasibility of the Idea   The fourth step is to determine whether the business idea is feasible. That is, will it generate a sufficient amount of profits to make the investment in the business worthwhile? An entrepreneur must estimate the profits that would be earned from this type of business. The revenue will be based on the price charged per product or service and the number of products or services that will be sold per period. The expenses occur as a result of obtaining the resources that are needed to provide the product or service. The difference between the revenue and the expenses is the profit, which is subject to taxes. Some businesses fail simply because the entrepreneurs overestimated the revenue that would be generated or underestimated the expenses. In other words, if the entrepreneurs had estimated the revenue and expenses properly, they might have realized that the business idea was not feasible. Then, they could have revised the business idea in a manner that would make it feasible.

Success Stories about Creating a Business

The following successful entrepreneurs detected a desire by consumers for something that they had the skills to offer:

1 Domino's Pizza (of Ann Arbor, Michigan) is a classic example of a business that started with little funding. It was established when Tom Monaghan (a college dropout) and his brother bought a bankrupt pizza parlor in 1960. Tom had to borrow the $500 that he needed to invest in the firm. Later, he bought his brother's interest in the business. Domino's Pizza now generates sales of about $1 billion per year.

2 Jeremy's Micro Batch Ice Cream (of Philadelphia, Pennsylvania) has applied the microbrewery concept to ice cream: it makes ice cream in small quantities and sells it in limited editions. The owner, Jerry Kraus, created the business idea for a class project when he was a student at the University of Pennsylvania.

3 Glow Dog, Inc. (of Concord, Massachusetts), sells light-reflective clothing for pets. The owner, Beth Marcus, thought of this business idea when she was walking her dog at night and realized that the dog was not visible to passing motorists. After just two years in business, her firm averaged annual sales of more than $1 million.

A successful business does not require a great invention, but may simply focus on making life more convenient for customers. For example, many lunch delivery businesses in downtown areas of cities are successful because of their convenience, not their food.

Entrepreneurs must recognize that some of their business ideas will likely fail. Nevertheless, they can learn from their failures. Many business ideas are revisions of a previous business idea that failed. For example, many restaurant businesses have failed in one location, but succeeded when they were moved to a different location.

Impact of Technology on the Creation of Businesses

Technology has contributed to the creation of many successful businesses in recent years. **Technology** can be defined as knowledge or tools used to produce products and services. An important subset of technology, **information technology,** involves the use of information to produce products and services. It includes the use of computers to transfer information among departments within a firm and the use of the Internet to provide customers with information.

Information technology accounts for only about 8 percent of the total output produced in the United States, but it represents more than one-third of the growth in the U.S. output produced. A recent study by the U.S. Commerce Department estimates that about half of all U.S. workers will soon be employed in industries that produce information technology. It also found that information technology has reduced the cost of producing products and resulted in lower prices of products. Furthermore, workers in the technology industries earn about $53,000 per year on average versus $30,000 for workers in other industries.

A related type of technology is **electronic business (e-business),** also referred to as **electronic commerce (e-commerce),** which is the use of electronic communications to produce or sell products and services. E-business includes both business transactions, such as sales of products over the In-

technology knowledge or tools used to produce products and services

information technology technology that enables information to be used to produce products and services

electronic business (e-business) or electronic commerce (e-commerce) use of electronic communications, such as the Internet, to produce or sell products and services

Almost all businesses have changed how they conduct business and have derived new benefits as a result of technology. Here, a wig shop owner is shown using a laptop computer to track her year-to-date sales.

© Cat Gwyn/ CORBIS

ternet, and interactions between a firm and its suppliers over the Internet. In fact, many people use the terms *information technology* and *e-commerce* interchangeably. A study by the University of Texas estimates that e-business generates about $301 billion in revenue and creates 1.2 million jobs annually.

An example of a successful e-business idea is Amazon.com, which enables customers to purchase books and other products online (over the Internet). Amazon.com's creativity is not the product (books) but an alternative method of reaching customers. Its customers use the Internet to have their book orders delivered to them rather than having to go to a retail bookstore. Several other firms have applied the same idea to their own businesses. Computer firms now sell computers over the Internet, toy manufacturers sell toys over the Internet, and automobile manufacturers sell automobiles over the Internet. Hotels, airlines, and cruiselines allow customers to make reservations over the Internet.

Exhibit 1.2 describes some of the successful firms that have been created to capitalize on e-business. Notice that these businesses started out very small and were created to offer a product or service that was not being provided by other firms. Thus, these new businesses were created to accommodate the needs or preferences of customers. As these e-businesses were created, many existing firms recognized that they should develop their own e-business to satisfy their customers. Thus, the innovations of some e-businesses transformed the way that all firms conduct business.

Many firms applied e-business to facilitate their existing operations. The Internet allows for easier communication from the firm to the consumer, from the firm to another firm, and from the consumer to the firm. Information flows freely between firms and consumers, avoiding the delays and disrupted business transactions that used to occur when the two parties were not available at the same time to communicate. A survey by the firm

Exhibit 1.2

Successful Internet Businesses

Business Name	Business Description	How the Business Was Created
1. Amazon.com	This online bookseller is frequently cited as an Internet success story. Customers can purchase books and music and participate in auctions at its website. Amazon's innovative bookselling idea allows the company to offer popular titles at deeply discounted prices due to low overhead costs.	Jeff Bezos founded the company in 1994. Bezos quit his job as vice president of a Wall Street firm, moved to Seattle, and started the business in his garage. When Amazon.com opened for business in July 1995, Bezos himself frequently dropped off the packages at the post office. Bezos's estimated net worth (value of his house and other assets after paying off any debts) is now $10 billion.
2. Yahoo!	This Internet search engine is the most visited site on the Web. It has evolved to offer a wide variety of other products to attract users. Free e-mail, Web page hosting, and custom-designed start-up pages are just a few of the options available. Revenues are generated through advertising sales.	David Filo and Jerry Yang were Ph.D. students at Stanford who had put together an electronic directory of their favorite websites. It was essentially a list of their bookmarks that they titled Yahoo! (which stands for Yet Another Hierarchical Officious Oracle). The site was generating so much traffic that the students dropped out of school and launched their company in 1995. Each of the founders now has a net worth of nearly $4 billion.
3. eBay	eBay is an online auction service that enables users to sell goods to each other. The person-to-person services attract a wide variety of goods, most of them used. Sellers develop a reputation, which creates some level of trust and excuses eBay from any responsibility. The company profits by charging fees based on the sale price.	The company evolved out of a method that Pierre Omidyar devised to help his girlfriend collect Pez candy dispensers. By 1996, the volume of goods traded forced Omidyar to quit his job at General Magic and devote all his time to the company. The company has been profitable since 1996.

KPMG found that 87 percent of firms are using e-business to improve their efficiency. Firms are also using e-business to complement rather than replace their traditional operations. Consumers who want to use traditional channels to make orders can still do so, while other consumers can communicate their orders electronically. Thus, even if a firm is not classified as an Internet company, it can still use e-business to enhance its value.

Although the use of the Internet to serve consumers has attracted considerable attention, the Internet is also having an important impact on the way businesses serve other businesses (referred to as "business-to-business e-commerce" or "B2B e-commerce"). Business-to-business e-commerce might be used, for example, when a firm needs construction work to repair its facilities, wants an outside firm to conduct seminars to improve relationships among employees, or requires specific supplies for its production process. The firm can request bids online from several businesses that may meet its needs and then select the firm that submits the best bid. This process is much easier and faster than calling various firms and waiting for return phone calls. Furthermore, having to send a message online forces the bidders to specify their bids in writing.

Business-to-business e-commerce has already reduced the expenses associated with transactions between firms and is expected to reduce them even further once all firms take full advantage of the technology. In particular, firms that rely on other businesses for supplies, transportation services, or delivery services can reduce their expenses substantially by using business-to-business e-commerce.

2

Describe the key functions of a business.

KEY FUNCTIONS OF A BUSINESS

The five key functions involved in operating a business are management, marketing, finance, accounting, and information systems. These five functions are the focus of this text because they must be conducted properly if a business is to be successful. Each of the functions is briefly introduced here and will be thoroughly discussed in other chapters. College students who pursue a business degree can usually major in any one of these five business functions.

Management is the means by which employees and other resources (such as machinery) are used by the firm. **Marketing** is the means by which products (or services) are developed, priced, distributed, and promoted to customers. **Finance** is the means by which firms obtain and use funds for their business operations. **Accounting** is the summary and analysis of the firm's financial condition and is used to make various business decisions. **Information systems** include information technology, people, and procedures that provide appropriate information so that the firm's employees can make business decisions.

management means by which employees and other resources (such as machinery) are used by the firm

marketing means by which products (or services) are developed, priced, distributed, and promoted to customers

finance means by which firms obtain and use funds for their business operations

accounting summary and analysis of the firm's financial condition

information systems include information technology, people, and procedures that work together to provide appropriate information to the firm's employees so they can make business decisions

Interaction among Business Functions

Most business decisions can be classified as management, marketing, or finance decisions. Examples of these types of decisions are provided in Exhibit 1.3. Notice from this exhibit that management decisions focus on the use of resources, marketing decisions focus on the products, and finance decisions focus on obtaining or using funds.

A firm's earnings (or profits) are equal to its revenue minus its expenses. The effect that each type of business decision has on a firm's earnings is illustrated in Exhibit 1.4. Since management decisions focus on the utilization of employees and other resources, they affect the amount of production expenses incurred. Since marketing decisions focus on strategies that will make the product appealing to customers, they affect the firm's revenue. Marketing decisions also influence the amount of expenses incurred in distributing and promoting products. Since finance decisions focus on how funds are obtained (borrowing money versus issuing stock), they influence the amount of interest expense incurred. As the management, marketing, and finance decisions affect either a firm's revenue or expenses, they affect the earnings and value of the firm.

Although some decisions focus on only one function, many decisions require interaction among management, marketing, and finance. For example, production managers of a cell phone manufacturer receive sales projections from the marketing managers to determine how much of the product to produce. The finance managers must receive the planned production volume from the production managers to determine how much funding is needed.

Exhibit 1.3

Common Business Decisions

Management Decisions
1. What equipment is needed to produce the product?
2. How many employees should be hired to produce the product?
3. How can employees be motivated to perform well?

Marketing Decisions
1. What price should be charged for the product?
2. Should the product be changed to be more appealing to customers?
3. Should the firm use advertising or some other strategy to promote its product?

Finance Decisions
1. Should financial support come from the sale of stock or from borrowing money? Or a combination of both?
2. Should the firm attempt to obtain borrowed funds for a short-term period (such as one year) or a long-term period?
3. Should the firm invest funds in a new business project that has recently been proposed (such as expansion of its existing business or development of a new product), or should it use these funds to repay debt?

Exhibit 1.4

How Business Decisions Affect a
Firm's Earnings

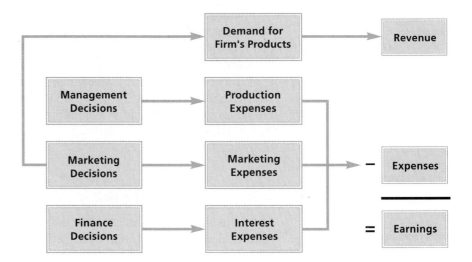

How Some Business Functions Enhance Decision Making

Proper business decisions rely on accounting and information systems.

Accounting Managers of firms use accounting to monitor their operations and to report their financial condition to their owners or employees. They can also assess the performance of previous production, marketing, and finance decisions. They may even rely on accounting to detect inefficient uses of business resources that can be eliminated. Consequently, a firm's accounting function can be used to eliminate waste, thereby generating higher earnings.

Information Systems Firms use information systems to continually update and analyze information about their operations. This information can be used by the firm's managers to make business decisions. In addition, the information can be used by any employee within the firm who has access to a personal computer. For example, FedEx uses information on its computer system to track deliveries and determine when packages will arrive at their destination.

3

Explain how to develop
a business plan.

business plan a detailed description of the proposed business, including a description of the product or service, the types of customers it would attract, the competition, and the facilities needed for production

DEVELOPING THE BUSINESS PLAN

A **business plan** is a detailed description of the proposed business, including a description of the product or service, the resources needed for production, the marketing needed to sell the product or service, and the financing required. When entrepreneurs create a business idea, they develop a business plan that demonstrates how the business functions just described can be applied to make the business successful.

Entrepreneurs commonly show their plan to those investors who may be willing to serve as partial owners. They also present their plan to creditors (such as commercial banks) that may be willing to provide business loans. Thus, the business plan should be clear and must convince others that the business will be profitable. If investors do not believe in the business plan, they will be unwilling to invest funds in the business. If creditors do not believe in the plan, they will not supply any loans. In that case, the entrepreneurs would have to rely only on their own funds, which might not be sufficient to support the business.

The business plan is not needed just when the entrepreneur is raising funds to support the opening of the business. The plan will be used as a guide to making business decisions throughout the life of the business. It provides a sense of direction for the business's future development. The success or failure of any firm is partially dependent on its business plan. A complete business plan normally includes an assessment of the business environment, a management plan, a marketing plan, and a financial plan, as explained in detail next.

Assessment of the Business Environment

The business environment surrounding the business includes the economic environment, the industry environment, and the global environment.

Economic Environment The economic environment is assessed to determine how demand for the product may change in response to future economic conditions. The demand for a product can be highly sensitive to the strength of the economy. Therefore, the feasibility of a new business may be influenced by the economic environment.

Industry Environment The industry environment is assessed to determine the degree of competition. If a market for a specific product is served by only one or a few firms, a new firm may be able to capture a significant portion of the market.

One must also ask whether a similar product could be produced and sold at a lower price, while still providing reasonable earnings. A related question is whether the new business would be able to produce a higher-quality product than its competitors. A new business idea is more likely to be successful if it has either a price or a quality advantage over its competitors.

Global Environment The global environment is assessed to determine how the demand for the product may change in response to future global conditions. The global demand for a product can be highly sensitive to changes in foreign economies, the number of foreign competitors, exchange rates, and international trade regulations.

Management Plan

A management plan, which includes an operations plan, focuses on the proposed organizational structure, production, and human resources of the firm.

Organizational Structure   An organizational structure identifies the roles and responsibilities of the employees hired by the firm. The organizational structure of a new factory is more complicated than that of a pizza delivery shop. If the owner plans to manage most of the operations, the organizational structure is simple. Some businesses begin with the owner assuming most responsibilities, but growth requires the hiring of managers. Even if the owners initially run the business, they should develop plans for the future organizational structure. A job description for each employee should be included, along with the estimated salary to be paid to each employee.

Production   Various decisions must be made about the production process, such as the site (location) of the production facilities and the design and layout of the facilities. The location decision can have a major effect on a firm's performance because it influences both the cost of renting space in a building and the revenue generated by the business.

The proposed design and layout of the facilities should maximize the efficiency of the space available. This proposal should contain cost estimates on any machinery or equipment to be purchased. The cost estimates for factories are normally more complicated than those for retail stores.

Human Resources   Human resources (employees) are critical to the success of a firm. A business must set up a work environment that will motivate the employees. It must also develop a plan for monitoring and evaluating employees and for compensating them. By monitoring and compensating employees properly, the business can ensure that the employees are striving to maximize its performance.

Marketing Plan

A marketing plan focuses on the target market, as well as product characteristics, pricing, distribution, and promotion.

customer profile Characteristics of the typical customer (based on gender, age, hobbies, and so on)

target market Customers who fit the customer profile

Target Market   The **customer profile,** or characteristics of the typical customer (based on gender, age, hobbies, and so on), should be identified. This helps to determine the **target market,** which consists of customers who fit the customer profile. A paperback book of fiction for adults has a much larger target market than a book for young children, for example.

Product Characteristics   The characteristics of the product should be described, with an emphasis on what makes the product more desirable than similar products offered by competitors. A product may be desirable because it is easier to use, is more effective, or lasts longer. Any competitive advantage of this product over similar products should be identified.

Pricing   The proposed price of the product should be stated. Prices of similar products sold by competitors should also be mentioned. The price will influence the demand for the product.

Distribution The means by which the product will be distributed to the customers should be described. Some products are sold to customers directly, while others are distributed through retail outlets.

Promotion The means by which the product will be promoted should be described. The promotion strategy should be consistent with the customer profile. For example, products that appeal to college students may be advertised in student newspapers.

Financial Plan

The financial plan determines the means by which the business is financed. It also attempts to demonstrate that the creation of the business is feasible.

Financing The creation of a business requires funds to purchase machinery and materials, rent space, hire employees, and conduct marketing. Most firms rely heavily on funding from the entrepreneurs who established them. If the entrepreneurs do not have sufficient funds to create their business, they may borrow funds from relatives or friends. Once a business grows and establishes a track record of good performance, it may be able to borrow funds from financial institutions. To obtain a loan from a financial institution (such as a commercial bank), the firm will need to present a detailed business plan. The lending institution assesses the business plan to determine whether the business is likely to be successful, and therefore deserves a loan. A business might consider issuing stock only after demonstrating adequate performance for several years.

Feasibility Entrepreneurs should assess the feasibility of a potential business before they invest their money and time in creating it. They can assess the business's feasibility by calculating its expected earnings (profits). Earnings are measured as revenue minus expenses, as shown in Exhibit 1.4. The expected revenue to be generated by a business is based on the sales volume (number of units sold) times the price per unit. A firm's revenue is influenced by its marketing decisions. Expenses can be categorized as operating expenses or interest expenses. Operating expenses can be broadly defined as the expenses associated with business operations, such as production and marketing expenses. Therefore, operating expenses are dependent on the production and marketing decisions. Interest expenses are the interest payments made to creditors from which funds were borrowed. The interest expenses are dependent on the financial decision of how much money to borrow.

When revenue exceeds total expenses, earnings are positive. Entrepreneurs will seriously consider establishing a business only if it is expected to generate positive earnings over time, as those earnings will provide the return on their investment. Entrepreneurs should also consider the risk of a business, which can be measured as the uncertainty of the future earnings. The less uncertainty surrounding the future earnings, the more desirable is the business.

Summary of a Business Plan

The key parts of a business plan are summarized in Exhibit 1.5. This text is designed so that each part of the text represents a part of the business plan. The description and proposed ownership of the business are discussed in

Exhibit 1.5

Contents of a Typical Business Plan

I.   DESCRIPTION AND OWNERSHIP OF PROPOSED BUSINESS
   ▶ Describe the product (or service) provided by the proposed business.

II.   ASSESSMENT OF THE BUSINESS ENVIRONMENT
   ▶ *Economic Environment:* Describe the prevailing economic conditions and the exposure of the firm to those conditions.
   ▶ *Industry Environment:* Describe the competition in the industry and the general demand for the product in the industry.
   ▶ *Global Environment:* Describe the prevailing global conditions that relate to the business, such as foreign markets where the business may sell products in the future or obtain supplies.

III.   MANAGEMENT PLAN
   ▶ *Organizational Structure:* Describe the organizational structure and show the relationships among the employee positions. This structure should also identify the responsibilities of each position in overseeing other positions and describe the specific tasks and salaries of managers and other employees.
   ▶ *Production Process:* Describe the production process, including the site, design, and layout of the facilities needed to produce a product. Also, describe the planned amount of production per month or year.

IV.   MANAGING EMPLOYEES
   ▶ Describe the work environment used to motivate employees and the plans for training, evaluating, and compensating employees.

V.   MARKETING PLAN
   ▶ *Target Market:* Describe the profile (such as the typical age and income level) of the customers who will purchase the product and therefore make up the target market. (Who will buy the product?)
   ▶ *Product Characteristics:* Explain desirable features of the product. (Why will customers buy the product?)
   ▶ *Pricing:* Describe how the product will be priced relative to competitors' products. (How much will customers pay for the product?)
   ▶ *Distribution:* Describe how the product will be distributed to customers. (How will customers have access to the product?)
   ▶ *Promotion:* Describe how the product will be promoted to potential customers. (How will customers be informed about the product?)

VI.   FINANCIAL PLAN
   ▶ *Funds Needed:* Estimate the amount of funds needed to establish the business and to support operations over a five-year period.
   ▶ *Feasibility:* Estimate the revenue, expenses, and earnings of the proposed business over the next five years. Consider how the estimates of revenue, expenses, and earnings of the proposed business may change under various possible economic or industry conditions.

VII.   TECHNOLOGY AND INSURANCE
   ▶ *Technology:* Determine what technology is needed to run the business efficiently.
   ▶ *Insurance:* Determine what insurance is needed to protect against business risk.

Part I of the text. The assessment of the business environment is discussed in the chapters in Part II. The management plan is discussed in Part III, and managing employees is described in Part IV. The marketing plan is discussed in Part V. The financial plan is covered in Part VI. Technology needs and protection against risk are examined in Part VII. Thus, the key concepts discussed in each part of the text can be applied to develop a specific part of the business plan.

The business plan can be changed over time in response to changing conditions in the business environment. Consider a business that initially focused on producing classroom chairs and selling them to schools. If the business decides to make other furniture such as office desks and chairs, it will have to change its management plan to allow for more production space, revise its production process, hire more workers, and perhaps even revise its organizational structure. It will also alter its marketing plan to focus its sales on offices as well as schools. It will alter its financial plan to obtain additional funding to support the additional production and marketing tasks. Thus, business planning is not confined to the creation of the business, but must be ongoing as the plans are revised.

increasing value with technology

ONLINE RESOURCES FOR STARTING A BUSINESS

Starting a small business can be a difficult process. Business publications and the Small Business Administration (SBA) have been the usual sources for advice. Financing has primarily been available through local financial institutions and has been relatively difficult to obtain.

The Internet has made this process much easier. A variety of sites provide advice about starting a business. Information on government grants, advice about specific industries, business plan templates, and discussions of legal issues are readily available.

Yahoo!'s Small Business site (**http://smallbusiness .yahoo.com**) is a good place to find links to more specific information. American Express (**http://americanexpress .com/smallbusiness**) provides information about building a business. The SBA (**http://www.sbaonline.sba.gov**) offers information about government programs and other relevant information for small businesses.

Obtaining financing is crucial to beginning any business, and there are sites to facilitate this process, too. Quicken Small Business (**http://www.quicken.com/ small_business**) matches entrepreneurs with lenders. Once a questionnaire has been completed, the site offers advice on the most appropriate financing. It also provides a list of interested banks and the appropriate applications. Garage.com (**http://www.garage.com**) targets start-up companies in the high-tech sector and matches the companies with venture capitalists. The Elevator (**http://www .thelevator.com**) also matches entrepreneurs with investors and does not restrict itself to high-tech firms. The Internet is always changing, so the sites listed here may become obsolete. Nevertheless, a simple search for small business resources will find numerous sites with much information.

Business planning software is another tool that entrepreneurs can use to ease the start-up process. A good business plan is a complex document that is demanded by lenders and potential investors and can provide a valuable guide for the business. It details the nature of the company, the competition, and a forecasted financial analysis. In the past, putting a business plan together was both time-consuming and expensive. Today, business plan software can make the process much easier.

Most of the software packages contain a collection of options, which can be used to create a thorough business plan. The best packages incorporate many of the following capabilities:

▶ *Business Plan Outlines* Packages normally offer one or more outlines of business plans that can be altered to fit most businesses. Some packages take entrepreneurs through a series of questions in order to create a tailor-made plan.

▶ *Text Generation* Much of the information that goes into a business plan is standardized. Business plan software can insert such text directly into the plan, making the appropriate substitutions for company names and products. Once in place, the text can be edited as needed.

▶ *Forecasting* Any business plan software packages should include the ability to create consistent projections. The software package should be able to predict sales and costs in various ways (for example, using percentage growth models, market share models, or values that are individually specified by the planner) and should ensure that interrelated data are consistent. For example, when the planner changes values in a table of projected market shares, forecasted sales in other parts of the document should automatically be updated.

▶ *Graphics* Business plan software offers the ability to create charts of several different types (bar charts, pie charts, line charts) and should also allow users to draw other common charts, such as organizational charts.

▶ *Supplementary Documents* A number of business plan packages offer supplementary documents, such as disclosure agreements, which are often used in conjunction with business plans, although not necessarily as part of the document.

A few hours on the computer are now all that is needed to gather information and apply for financing. Prior to the advances in technology described here, this process might have taken weeks. The result has been a rise in the number of small businesses and a more competitive environment as the barriers to entry have decreased.

ASSESSING A BUSINESS PLAN

Many business ideas that seem reasonable at first may not be undertaken because the entrepreneur has various concerns after developing the business plan. Some concerns may relate to the potential revenue to be generated by the business. Perhaps the potential demand for the product or service is highly uncertain. Other concerns may relate to the expense of producing the product or service. For example, the entrepreneur may believe that the costs of production may be too high. Any concerns about the revenue or the expenses raise questions about the potential profitability. If the business idea does not have much potential for profit, the entrepreneur may decide to search for alternative business ideas.

Even if the estimated costs of the business are too high, this does not necessarily mean that the business idea should be completely discarded. Perhaps one or more aspects of the proposed business need to be changed to make the idea feasible. For example, establishing a video store in a business district may not be feasible because of the high costs of renting space in that location. Establishing the store in a location where rents are lower may significantly reduce the cost, but the firm's revenue may also be affected. An entirely new assessment of the expenses and the revenue should be conducted after changing the proposed location or any other part of the business plan for a specific business.

College Health Club: Business Planning at College Health Club

Many of the key concepts in this text are applied to one small business (a health club) in a feature that appears in every chapter. The applications demonstrate how business decisions are made and how they are related. They also show that even the smallest business must make decisions about all types of business functions.

Sue Kramer recently graduated with a degree in business from Texas College in Dallas, Texas. She has always wanted to own and manage a business. Throughout her college years, she belonged to Energy Health Club, a 20-minute drive from the college campus. She noticed that many other students from Texas College were members of this club. She also knew other students who wanted to join a health club, but lived on campus and did not have a car. There was a health club called Magnum Club in the shopping mall just across the street from the college, but it was very expensive and focused on personal training. Magnum Club recently closed those facilities and moved to a downtown location far from Texas College.

For some time, Sue has considered opening a health club next to the Texas College campus that would cater to students. Shortly after graduation, Sue distributed a survey to hundreds of students at the college to determine whether they would be interested in joining a health club and what types of facilities and equipment they would desire. Now that Magnum Club has moved, there are no health clubs very close to campus. The shopping center where Magnum Club was located is a perfect location for a health club catering to students because students frequently go to stores in that center.

The space where Magnum Club was located is available for rent. In addition, Magnum purchased new equipment when it moved downtown, so it has offered to lease its old exercise and weight machines that are already set up at its former facilities to Sue for $600 per month, or $7,200 per year.

Sue has accumulated savings of $20,000 over the years. She and her husband have calculated that the income from his job will cover their normal household expenses, so Sue has developed a business plan for a health club. Some of the key features of her business plan are described below.

The propietor of this sporting goods store is enjoying the rewards of owning a small business. All successful businesses begin with a sound business plan.

© CORBIS

Business Idea

The business is a health club called College Health Club (CHC) that will be located in a shopping mall just across from the Texas College campus. It will sell memberships on an annual basis. The health club should appeal to the students because it is convenient and would be affordable to them.

Management Plan

▶ *Production Process:* The business will provide its members with health club services, such as access to exercise machines, weight machines, and aerobics classes. It will rent the exercise and weight machines that were previously owned by Magnum Club for $7,200 per year. It will rent the space in the shopping mall across from the Texas College where Magnum Club was located. The rent expense for the facilities will be $5,000 per month, or $60,000 per year. Utility expenses are estimated to be $700 per month, or $8,400 for the first year.

▶ *Organizational Structure:* Sue Kramer will be the president of CHC and will also manage CHC. She will not require a salary as manager of the business, as she wants to limit the salary expenses in the first few years.

Managing Employees

Sue will hire some part-time employees who are majoring in exercise science at Texas College. Typically, one or two employees will be working whenever the health club is open. Sue will train the employees. The total salary expense of CHC is estimated to be $4,000 per month, or $48,000 during the first year.

Marketing Plan

▶ *Target Market:* CHC will primarily target students at Texas College, but will also attempt to attract nonstudents who live nearby. The main competitor is Energy Club, but that is a 20-minute drive from the campus. Based on her survey of students about their interest in joining a health club, Sue is very confident that a minimum of 200 students will become members in CHC's first year of business. Her best guess is that 300 students will become members in CHC's first year. She expects that the membership will grow each year.

▶ *Pricing:* The price for an annual membership will be $500, which is less than the prices of most health clubs in the area.

▶ *Promotion:* CHC will advertise in the Texas College newspaper and use other promotion methods. Sue estimates that the cost of promoting CHC will be $300 per month, or $3,600 for the first year.

Financial Plan

▶ *Funding:* Sue will invest $20,000 in the business. She expects that she will need an additional $40,000 to run the business. Diane Burke, a relative of Sue's, has offered to lend the business $40,000 if she believes that the business plan is feasible. She will charge an interest rate of 10 percent on the loan. If Sue accepts the funds as a loan, she will have to pay Diane interest of $4,000 at the end of each year (computed as $40,000 × 10%).

▶ *Revenue:* CHC's main source of revenue will be the annual membership fees. Sue estimates that there will be 300 paid memberships over the first year. Since the membership fee is $500, CHC should receive a total of $150,000 in revenue (estimated as $500 × 300 members). The revenue is expected to increase yearly as the number of members increases.

▶ *Expenses:* The monthly expenses expected to be incurred by CHC are summarized in Exhibit 1.6. The expenses are segmented into operating expenses, which result from operating the business, and interest expenses, which are incurred as a result of financing the business. CHC's main operating expenses will be the cost of renting the facilities, salaries, utility expenses, the cost of renting the exercise and weight machines, marketing expenses, and the cost of insuring the business. The total expenses in the first year are expected to be $142,000. The annual expenses are expected to be stable over time.

Exhibit 1.6

Expected Monthly Expenses of CHC

	Monthly Expenses	Total Expenses in First Year
Operating Expenses		
Rent facilities	$5,000	$60,000
Salaries	4,000	48,000
Utilities	700	8,400
Rent exercise and weight machines	600	7,200
Marketing expenses	300	3,600
Liability insurance	800	9,600
Miscellaneous	100	1,200
Total Operating Expenses		$138,000
Interest expenses		4,000
Total Expenses		$142,000

▶ *Earnings.* CHC's earnings (before taxes) in the first year are derived by subtracting the annual expenses from the annual revenue, as shown in Exhibit 1.7. Since the total revenue should increase over time (due to an increase in memberships) while the expenses remain stable, the earnings should increase over time. The earnings generated by CHC will be reinvested to support future expansion of the existing club or the possible establishment of an additional health club near a different college campus.

Exhibit 1.7

Expected Performance of CHC in the First Year

Revenue	$150,000
Total operating expenses	−138,000
Interest expenses	−4,000
Earnings before Taxes	**$8,000**

SUMMARY

1 The key stakeholders in a business are owners, creditors, employees, suppliers, and customers. The owners invest in the firm, while creditors lend money to the firm. Employees are hired to conduct the firm's business operations efficiently in order to satisfy the owners. Suppliers provide the materials that the firm needs to produce its product. The firm's revenue is generated by selling products or services to customers.

2 The key functions in operating a business are management, marketing, finance, accounting, and information systems. Management decisions determine how the firm's resources are allocated. Marketing decisions determine the product to be sold, along with the pricing, distribution, and promotion of that product. Finance decisions determine how the firm obtains and invests funds. Business decisions are improved as a result of accounting and information systems. Accounting is used to monitor performance and detect inefficient uses of resources in order to improve business decisions. Information systems provide the firm's employees with information that enables them to improve business decisions.

3 A business plan forces an owner of a proposed business to specify all the key plans for the business. The business plan normally consists of (1) an assessment of the business environment; (2) a management plan that explains how the firm's resources are to be used; (3) a marketing plan that explains the product pricing, distribution, and promotion plans; and (4) a financial plan that demonstrates the feasibility of the business and explains how the business will be financed.

Even after the business is established, the business plan is continually revised in response to changes in market conditions, competition, and economic conditions. The parts of this text are organized so that each part represents a part of the business plan. The chapters in each part will cover the concepts that are necessary to develop that part of the business plan.

KEY TERMS

accounting   13
business plan   15
competitive advantage   8
creditors   6
customer profile   16
dividends   8
electronic business (e-business)   10

electronic commerce
   (e-commerce)   10
entrepreneurs   4
finance   13
information systems   13
information technology   10
management   13

managers   6
marketing   13
stakeholders   4
stock   5
stockholders (shareholders)   5
target market   16
technology   10

Review & Critical Thinking Questions

1. Describe the roles of the five key stakeholders in a business.

2. Explain how and why the ownership of a business may spread.

3. List and briefly describe the four key steps used by entrepreneurs to create a business idea.

4. What is information technology? Why has information technology recently received so much attention in business?

5. If you were to start your own business, what key functions would be needed to operate the business? Discuss some decisions made by each function.

6. What is a business plan? Why should a business plan be very clear and precise? Explain what is included in a business plan.

7. Discuss the economic, industry, and global environments and how they may affect the business environment.

8. What are the three major plans within a business plan?

9. Explain why business plans are closely reviewed by creditors or investors. Are business plans only needed when raising support for the opening of the business? Explain.

10. Describe the elements included in a marketing plan.

11. Give a brief description of a typical financial plan for starting a new business.

12. Explain some of the concerns an entrepreneur may have when starting a new business.

Discussion Questions

1. Assume you are in a rock band that performs at the college you attend. Is a product or a service being provided? Is the management function more or less important than the marketing function for your band?

2. You are planning to open your own record store in a local mall. Discuss this statement: "The customer is king."

3. Assume you are about to launch a business. You believe employees do not work as hard as owners do; therefore, you do not need them. In addition, you do not believe in keeping financial records and will therefore not need an accountant for your business. Discuss.

4. You have just opened a small pizzeria in your hometown. Since you put up all the funds yourself, you did not develop a business plan for the pizzeria. Discuss the possible disadvantages of this action.

5. How could a potential firm use the Internet to plan its business? How could a firm use the Internet to promote its business once it is established?

6. Wal-Mart is planning to open a new store in your local area. Since Wal-Mart is nationally known, is it necessary for this store to have a marketing plan designed for this particular location?

Even after a business is established, the business plan is continually revised in response to changes in market conditions, competition, and the economy. A successful business continually evaluates the business environment.

© Getty Images/ Photo Disc

It's Your Decision: **Business Planning at CHC**

1. Why would Sue attempt to obtain funds from a creditor rather than allow a second owner to invest equity funds?
2. Assume that the enrollment at Texas College is expected to grow by 10 percent each year. How will this affect CHC's estimated earnings?
3. How does Sue's marketing plan affect CHC's expenses and revenue?
4. How does Sue's production plan affect CHC's expenses and revenue?
5. Explain how the production plan is dependent on the marketing plan. That is, explain why the decisions as to how much equipment to have and how much space to rent are dependent on the decision regarding the degree to which the health club is marketed.
6. CHC's performance can be measured by its earnings (before taxes), which are equal to its revenue minus expenses. CHC's revenue and expenses are subject to uncertainty. How will CHC's earnings before taxes be affected if revenue is less than expected? How will CHC's earnings before taxes be affected if expenses are more than expected?
7. A health club differs from manufacturing firms in that it produces a service rather than products. To produce their products, most manufacturing firms require machinery as well as production facilities. Do you think that small manufacturing firms would typically require more or less financing than a health club? Explain.

Investing in a Business

The following exercise allows you to apply the key concepts covered in each chapter to a firm in which you are interested.

If you had funds available right now to purchase the stock of a firm, which stock would you purchase? Record the price of that stock by reviewing today's stock quotations in your local paper or in *The Wall Street Journal*. Your instructor may explain how to find these quotes. If the stock was issued by a large U.S. firm, it is probably listed on the New York Stock Exchange (NYSE). Otherwise it may be on the American Stock Exchange (AMEX) or on the over-the-counter exchange, which includes Nasdaq.

Record the following information:

▶ Name of the stock _____

▶ Today's date _____

▶ Present stock price per share _____

▶ Annual dividend per share _____

▶ Standard & Poor's (S&P) 500 index _____

The stock quotations provide the price and dividend information for each stock.

The S&P 500 index is based on the stock prices of 500 large firms. It indicates the general level of stock prices and is quoted in the section of the newspaper that provides stock price quotations. It also serves as a benchmark with which you can compare your stock's performance at the end of the term. For each chapter, "Investing in a Business" will allow you to determine how the key concepts apply to that firm. You will need the firm's annual report, which can often be found on the firm's website or can be ordered by calling or writing to the firm's shareholder relations department. Addresses of many firms are available at your local library. For your information, Appendix A (near the end of this text) provides a background on investing in stocks.

You should also monitor how the price of your stock moves over time in response to specific conditions. This will help you recognize the factors that can affect the firm's stock price (and therefore its value). At the end of the school term, the "Investing in a Business" project at the end of the last chapter will help you determine the performance of your investment.

THE STOCK MARKET GAME

Many firms are owned by individuals such as yourself who buy stock. When individuals buy stock, they become partial owners of the firm, but they must rely on the firm's managers to manage the firm. Investors attempt to invest in firms that have much potential to perform well in the future. If a firm's performance improves, its value increases, and its stock price should increase as well. Here is an opportunity for you to test your skills at selecting stocks.

Instructions

Assume you have $100,000 to invest. Decide how you want to allocate your $100,000 among stocks. You can invest all your money in one stock or in as many as five stocks. At the end of the semester, students can compare their stock portfolios to determine whose portfolio increased the most. You can easily monitor your portfolio by following the instructions below.

First, go to **http://www.yahoo.com**, and click on "Sign Up" (it's free) and follow the instructions provided. After registering, click on "Continue to Yahoo!" and then click on the Finance icon at the top of the page. This will direct you to **http://finance.yahoo.com**. Obtain stock ticker symbols for any stock in which you may wish to invest by using "Symbol Lookup." Click on "Symbol Lookup" and type in the name of the firm for which you want a ticker symbol. A list of symbols will appear; choose the one that represents the firm in which you are interested. By clicking on the symbol, information about the stock, including the stock's price, will appear.

To create your portfolio of stocks on **http://finance.yahoo.com**:

▶ Click on "Create" (near "Portfolios" on the screen).

▶ Then click on "Track Your Current Holdings."

▶ In the name box, type in a name for your portfolio.

▶ Insert the stock symbols for the stocks in which you wish to invest.

▶ Scroll down to the bottom of the screen and click on "Continue."

▶ You will see your ticker symbols listed. Insert the number of shares as well as the current price per share.

▶ Then click on "Finished"

At any time during the semester, you can check the current value of your stock portfolio by going to **http://finance.yahoo.com** and clicking on the name of your portfolio (which is now listed on the screen near "Portfolios"). Notice that just below the area in which your stock values are shown, links to news items for each of these stocks are provided. At any time, you can review the news items to determine why the value of a specific stock changed substantially. Your professor may provide additional instructions on the rules of the stock market game for your class.

Case: Planning a New Business

Mike Cieplak has just created an idea for a business. He wants to provide lessons to people on how to use the Internet and e-mail. He believes that this idea will work because many people (especially older people) do not know how to use the Internet. He will provide hands-on experience and will also show people how to do searches for information, how to buy products on-line, and how to use other online services. He will also teach people how to create a website.

Mike knows that many people need this service, which is why he thinks this business will be successful. He also knows that he needs a business plan so that he can make this business run efficiently. In particular, he wants to make people aware of his business. He must also decide where he will provide the lessons and what price he will charge for his services.

Mike is currently finishing his studies at a university and will not start this business full-time until he receives his degree in about three months. Mike does not believe he will need much money to run this business, but the amount of money he will need is partially dependent on his other business decisions within his business plan.

Questions

1. What are the key decisions that Mike must make when developing his management plan? Relate these decisions to his business.

2. What are the key decisions that Mike must make when developing his marketing plan? Relate these decisions to his business.

3. What are the key decisions that Mike must make when developing his financial plan? Relate these decisions to his business.

4. What do you think will determine whether Mike's business is successful?

Video Case: Business Planning by Yahoo!

Yahoo!'s original owners were students who created informational websites as a hobby. They realized how valuable this service was to people and turned their hobby into a business. Yahoo has become a very successful business over a short period of time. It has expanded the information it provides on its website to include stock quotations, sports, weather, yellow pages, and business news. Its popularity has generated revenue from firms that pay Yahoo! to advertise their products on its website. Yahoo! is continually changing its website to provide additional information. It attempts to offer whatever information customers want so that it will become even more popular and attract even more advertising revenue. It relies on customer feedback to determine what customers like about its website. It receives a substantial amount of immediate feedback every day in the form of e-mail from its customers.

Questions

1. What do you think Yahoo!'s business plan is regarding its production of a service and how it generates revenue?

2. Given that Yahoo!'s business plan seems to be working, why is it still necessary for Yahoo! to focus on continual improvement based on feedback from its customers?

3. Why might Yahoo!'s business plan change over time?

Internet Applications

1. *http://www-3.ibm.com/services/learning/conf*

What are some of the upcoming technical conferences that IBM is hosting in the United States? How do you think these conferences benefit IBM? How do you think these conferences benefit IBM's customers and employees? Do you think establishing a website such as this one would be useful for a company that is just starting up operations? Why or why not?

2. *http://www.bplans.com*

What is some advice provided by experts in the "Starting a Business" section? Do you find this advice useful? Do you think it will aid you in starting your own busi-

ness? What software packages are available to help you write a business plan? Do you think you might purchase some of that software if you ever consider starting your own business? Why or why not?

3. *http://www.businessplans.org*

View some of the sample business plans provided on this website. Does reading these plans provide you with a better sense of the information contained in a business plan? Do you see any differences between business plans written for product- versus sevice-oriented companies?

The Coca-Cola Company Annual Report Project

 Questions for the current year's annual report are available on the text website at **http://madura.swlearning.com.**

You are probably familiar with the product Coca-Cola. The producer of that product is The Coca-Cola Company. At the end of each chapter in this book are questions related to The Coca-Cola Company's annual report. *Fortune* magazine recently conducted a survey of leading executives and named The Coca-Cola Company as America's most admired corporation. Thus, this exercise will provide you with some insights into the operations of one of the world's most successful business organizations.

The following questions apply concepts presented in this chapter to The Coca-Cola Company. Go to The Coca-Cola Company website **(http://www.cocacola.com)** and find the "Letter to Share Owners" in the company's 2001 annual report.

Questions

1 Why do you think The Coca-Cola Company's main goal is to satisfy its stockholders?

2 In the "Letter to Share Owners," what was the focus of The Coca-Cola Company's management in 2001? How does the Chairman feel about the future?

3 How did the mutually constructive relationship with bottlers benefit The Coca-Cola Company in 2001? Provide specific examples.

4 When is The Coca-Cola Company unbeatable? How does that benefit The Coca-Cola Company's share owners?

5 Go to **http://hoovers.com** and locate the NEWS CENTER. Key in The Coca-Cola Company in the space provided, click on "Search," and review the recent news stories about the firm. Summarize any (at least one) recent news story about The Coca-Cola Company that applies one or more of the key concepts within this chapter of the text.

In-Text Study Guide

Answers are in an appendix at the back of the book.

True or False

1. Creditors organize, manage, and assume the risks of the business. *F*

2. The goal of a firm's management is to maximize the firm's value, which is in the best interests of the firm's owners. *T*

3. A firm must satisfy its customers by providing the products or services that customers desire at a reasonable price. *T*

4. Dividend payments are made to repay loans from creditors. *F*

5. A firm's earnings (or profits) are equal to its revenue plus its expenses. *F*

6. Firms use information systems primarily to determine how to finance their businesses. *F*

7. Managers use accounting to monitor and assess the performance of a business. *T*

8. A business plan is intended to provide information for potential investors or creditors of a proposed business. *F*

9. Assessing the business environment includes information from industry, economic, and global environments. *T*

10. A marketing plan focuses on various decisions that must be made about the production process, such as site location and design and layout of the facilities. *T*

Multiple Choice

11. An enterprise that provides products or services that customers desire is a(n):
    a) institution.
    b) philanthropy.
    c) market.
    d) agency.
    e) business.

12. The five types of stakeholders involved in a business include all of the following except:
    a) owners.
    b) creditors.
    c) couriers.

    d) employees.
    e) customers.

13. Most business owners would agree that the following characteristics motivated them to start their own business except:
    a) earning large incomes.
    b) being their own boss.
    c) challenge.
    d) prestige associated with owning a business.
    e) risk.

14. The stakeholders of a firm include all of the following except:
    a) owners.
    b) creditors.
    c) employees.
    d) suppliers.
    e) government officials.

15. When an entrepreneur allows other investors to invest in the business, they become:
    a) creditors.
    b) brokers.
    c) employees.
    d) sponsors.
    e) stockholders.

16. A certificate of ownership of a business is a:
    a) bond.
    b) stock.
    c) mutual fund.
    d) co-article.
    e) contract.

17. Many firms that need funds borrow from financial institutions or individuals called:
    a) debtors.
    b) creditors.
    c) collateral.
    d) joint ventures.
    e) investors.

In-Text Study Guide

Answers are in an appendix at the back of the book.

18. Employees responsible for making key business decisions are:
    a) stockholders.
    b) owners.
    c) managers.
    d) business agents.
    e) creditors.

19. All of the following describe the products or services provided by successful firms except:
    a) obsolete.
    b) reasonably priced.
    c) adequate quality.
    d) desired by customers.
    e) customer satisfying.

20. Entrepreneurs need to find a product or service that has a(n):
    a) market edge.
    b) competitive advantage.
    c) structural incentive.
    d) economic niche.
    e) consumer linkage.

21. Which of the following statements is false about e-business and information technology?
    a) E-businesses are successful if they are large.
    b) E-business innovations affect the way all firms do business.
    c) Over one-third of U.S. growth involves information technology.
    d) Technology workers have higher earnings than other workers.
    e) E-business can complement traditional operations.

22. The function of business by which products are created, priced, distributed, and promoted to customers is:
    a) finance.
    b) information systems.
    c) accounting.
    d) management.
    e) marketing.

23. The expenses associated with transactions between firms has been reduced by:
    a) accounting transaction systems
    b) systems engineering
    c) environmental assessments
    d) business-to-business e-commerce
    e) feasibility studies

24. The function of business responsible for the efficient use of employees and other resources (such as machinery) is:
    a) finance.
    b) accounting.
    c) management.
    d) information systems.
    e) marketing.

25. The business function that focuses on strategies to make the product more appealing to customers and improve the firm's revenue is:
    a) production.
    b) marketing.
    c) manufacturing.
    d) personnel.
    e) finance.

26. The function of business that gathers information about a firm and then provides that information to management for use in decision making is known as:
    a) management.
    b) information systems.
    c) economics.
    d) finance.
    e) marketing.

27. The function of business that summarizes the firm's financial condition and is used to make various business decisions is:
    a) accounting.
    b) information systems.
    c) production.
    d) marketing.
    e) management.

In-Text Study Guide

Answers are in an appendix at the back of the book.

28. _____ is the business function that is responsible for obtaining the necessary funds to be used by the firm.
    a) Finance
    b) Marketing
    c) Accounting
    d) Information systems
    e) Management

29. Managers rely on _____ to detect the inefficient use of resources
    a) owners
    b) creditors
    c) marketing research
    d) marketing mix studies
    e) accounting data

30. The purpose of an industry business environmental assessment is to determine the:
    a) degree of competition.
    b) inflation rate.
    c) unemployment rate.
    d) population growth.
    e) economic growth.

31. Management, marketing, and finance are key parts of a(n):
    a) accounting plan.
    b) production strategy.
    c) inventory plan.
    d) business plan.
    e) information systems plan.

32. The management plan that identifies the roles and responsibilities of the employees hired by the firm is the:
    a) unity of command.
    b) division of work.
    c) degree of specialization.
    d) organizational structure.
    e) standardization concept.

33. A marketing plan focuses on all the following except:
    a) financing the business.
    b) a profile of typical customers.
    c) product characteristics.

d) pricing of the product.
e) distribution of the product.

34. The _____ identifies the characteristics of the typical customer.
    a) stockholders' report
    b) customer profile
    c) Dun & Bradstreet report
    d) credit report
    e) production schedule

35. A plan that demonstrates why the business is feasible and proposes how the business should be financed is the:
    a) production report.
    b) marketing plan.
    c) financial plan.
    d) human resource plan.
    e) bottom-up plan.

36. The uncertainty of future earnings is:
    a) capitalization.
    b) incentive.
    c) risk.
    d) hazard.
    e) venture finance.

37. A business plan is a detailed description of the proposed business that includes all of the following except:
    a) description of the business.
    b) types of customers it would attract.
    c) competition.
    d) facilities needed for production.
    e) monetary and fiscal policy.

business decisions

The Learning Goals of this chapter are to:

1 Explain how business owners select a form of business ownership.

2 Explain how the potential return and risk of a business are affected by its form of ownership.

3 Describe methods of owning existing businesses.

Chapter 2

Selecting a Form of Business Ownership

When entrepreneurs establish a business, they must decide on the form of business ownership. There are different types of business ownership, and the type that is chosen can affect the profitability, risk, and value of the firm.

Consider the case of a bicycle rental company, which was recently created by three entrepreneurs. The entrepreneurs want to use a form of business ownership that gives each of them equal ownership. They want to limit their liability and would like easy access to funding if they need it. They also want to consider how they might obtain the ownership of other bike rental businesses if they decide to expand in other locations.

The entrepreneurs creating the bicycle rental company must decide:

▶ What are the advantages of each type of business ownership?

▶ What are the disadvantages of each type of business ownership?

▶ How will the form of business ownership they choose affect the return on their investment?

▶ How will the form of business ownership they choose affect their risk?

▶ What methods can be used to obtain ownership of existing businesses?

The business ownership decision determines how the earnings of a business are distributed among the owners of the business, the degree of liability of each owner, the degree of control that each owner has in running the business, the potential return of the business, and the risk of the business. These types of decisions are necessary for all businesses. This chapter explains how the business ownership decisions by the bicycle rental company or any other firm can be made in a manner that maximizes the firm's value.

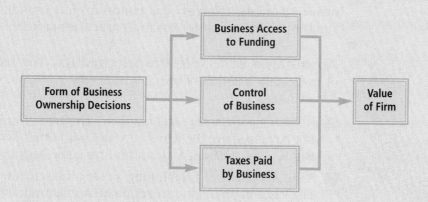

35

1

Explain how business owners
select a form of business
ownership.

POSSIBLE FORMS OF BUSINESS OWNERSHIP

Entrepreneurs choose one of three possible forms of business ownership:

▶ Sole proprietorship

▶ Partnership

▶ Corporation

Sole Proprietorship

sole proprietorship a business
owned by a single owner

sole proprietor the owner of a
sole proprietorship

A business owned by a single owner is referred to as a **sole proprietorship.** The owner of a sole proprietorship is called a **sole proprietor.** A sole proprietor may obtain loans from creditors to help finance the firm's operations, but these loans do not represent ownership. The sole proprietor is obligated to cover any payments resulting from the loans but does not need to share the business profits with creditors.

Typical examples of sole proprietorships include a local restaurant, a local construction firm, a barber shop, a laundry service, and a local clothing store. About 70 percent of all firms in the United States are sole proprietorships. But because these firms are relatively small, they generate less than 10 percent of all business revenue. The earnings generated by a sole proprietorship are considered to be personal income received by the proprietor and are subject to personal income taxes imposed by the Internal Revenue Service (IRS).

Characteristics of Successful Sole Proprietors

Sole proprietors must be willing to accept full responsibility for the firm's performance. The pressure of this responsibility can be much greater than any employee's responsibility. Sole proprietors must also be willing to work flexible hours. They are on call at all times and may even have to substitute for a sick employee. Their responsibility for the success of the business encourages them to continually monitor business operations. They must exhibit strong leadership skills, be well organized, and communicate well with employees.

Many successful sole proprietors had previous work experience in the market in which they are competing, perhaps as an employee in a competitor's firm. For example, restaurant managers commonly establish their own restaurants. Experience is critical to understanding the competition and the behavior of customers in a particular market.

Advantages of a Sole Proprietorship

The sole proprietor form of ownership has the following advantages over other forms of business ownership:

1 *All Earnings Go to the Sole Proprietor* The sole proprietor (owner) does not have to share the firm's earnings with other owners. Thus, the rewards of establishing a successful firm come back to the owner.

2 *Easy Organization* Establishing a sole proprietorship is relatively easy. The legal requirements are minimal. A sole proprietorship need not establish a separate legal entity. The owner must register the firm with the state, which can normally be done by mail. The owner may also need to apply for an occupational license to conduct a particular type of business. The specific license requirements vary with the state and even the city where the business is located.

3 *Complete Control*   Having only one owner with complete control of the firm eliminates the chance of conflicts during the decision-making process. For example, an owner of a restaurant can decide on the menu, the prices, and the salaries paid to employees.

4 *Lower Taxes*   Because the earnings in a proprietorship are considered to be personal income, they may be subject to lower taxes than those imposed on some other forms of business ownership, as will be explained later in this chapter.

Disadvantages of a Sole Proprietorship   Along with its advantages, the sole proprietorship has the following disadvantages:

1 *The Sole Proprietor Incurs All Losses*   Just as sole proprietors do not have to share the profits, they are unable to share any losses that the firm incurs. For example, assume you invest $10,000 of your funds in a lawn service and borrow an additional $8,000 that you invest in the business. Unfortunately, the revenue is barely sufficient to pay salaries to your employees, and you terminate the firm. You have not only lost all of your $10,000 investment in the firm but also are liable for the $8,000 that you borrowed. Since you are the sole proprietor, no other owners are available to help cover the losses.

unlimited liability no limit on the debts for which the owner is liable

2 *Unlimited Liability*   A sole proprietor is subject to **unlimited liability,** which means there is no limit on the debts for which the owner is liable. If a sole proprietorship is sued, the sole proprietor is personally liable for any judgment against that firm.

3 *Limited Funds*   A sole proprietor may have limited funds available to invest in the firm. Thus, sole proprietors have difficulty engaging in airplane manufacturing, shipbuilding, computer manufacturing, and other businesses that require substantial funds. Sole proprietors have limited funds to support the firm's expansion or to absorb temporary losses. A poorly performing firm may improve if given sufficient time. But if this firm cannot obtain additional funds to make up for its losses, it may not be able to continue in business long enough to recover.

4 *Limited Skills*   A sole proprietor has limited skills and may be unable to control all parts of the business. For example, a sole proprietor may have difficulty running a large medical practice because different types of expertise may be needed.

Partnership

partnership a business that is co-owned by two or more people

partners co-owners of a business

general partnership a partnership in which all partners have unlimited liability

limited partnership a firm that has some limited partners

limited partners partners whose liability is limited to the cash or property they contributed to the partnership

general partners partners who manage the business, receive a salary, share the profits or losses of the business, and have unlimited liability

A business that is co-owned by two or more people is referred to as a **partnership.** The co-owners of the business are called **partners.** The co-owners must register the partnership with the state and may need to apply for an occupational license. About 10 percent of all firms are partnerships.

In a **general partnership,** all partners have unlimited liability. That is, the partners are personally liable for all obligations of the firm. Conversely, in a **limited partnership,** the firm has some **limited partners,** or partners whose liability is limited to the cash or property they contributed to the partnership. Limited partners are only investors in the partnership and do not participate in its management, but because they have invested in the business, they share its profits or losses. A limited partnership has one or more **general partners,** or partners who manage the business, receive a salary, share the profits or losses of the business, and have unlimited liability. The

Runi Madiprajitno and Tom Moffit hold samples of their new Moovitz caffeinated candy. Their business partnership also includes a third partner, Monica Sentoso.

AP Photo/The Capital Times, Mike DeVries

earnings distributed to each partner represent personal income and are subject to personal income taxes imposed by the IRS.

Advantages of a Partnership The partnership form of ownership has three main advantages:

1. *Additional Funding* An obvious advantage of a partnership over a sole proprietorship is the additional funding that the partner or partners can provide. Therefore, more money may be available to finance the business operations. Some partnerships have thousands of partners, who are all required to invest some of their own money in the business. This type of partnership has much potential for growth because of its access to substantial funds.

2. *Losses Are Shared* Any business losses that the partnership incurs are spread across all of the partners. Thus, a single person does not have to absorb the entire loss. Each owner will absorb only a portion of the loss.

3. *More Specialization* With a partnership, partners can focus on their respective specializations and serve a wide variety of customers. For example, an accounting firm may have one accountant who specializes in personal taxes for individuals and another who specializes in business taxes for firms. A medical practice partnership may have doctors with various types of expertise.

Disadvantages of a Partnership Along with its advantages, the partnership has the following disadvantages:

1. *Control Is Shared* The decision making in a partnership must be shared. If the partners disagree about how the business should be run, business and personal relationships may be destroyed. Some owners of firms do not have the skills to manage a business.

2. *Unlimited Liability* General partners in a partnership are subject to unlimited liability, just like sole proprietors.

3 *Profits Are Shared*   Any profits that the partnership generates must be shared among all partners. The more partners there are, the smaller the amount of a given level of profits that will be distributed to any individual partner.

S-Corporations

> **S-corporation** a firm that has 75 or fewer owners and satisfies other criteria. The earnings are distributed to the owners and taxed at the respective personal income tax rate of each owner.

A firm that has 75 or fewer owners and satisfies other criteria may choose to be a so-called **S-corporation.** The owners of an S-corporation have limited liability (like owners of corporations), but they are taxed as if the firm were a partnership. Thus, the earnings are distributed to the owners and taxed at the respective personal income tax rate of each owner. Some state governments also impose a corporate tax on S-corporations. Many accounting firms and small businesses select the S-corporation as a form of ownership.

Limited Liability Company (LLC)

> **limited liability company (LLC)** a firm that has all the favorable features of a typical general partnership but also offers limited liability for the partners

A type of general partnership called a **limited liability company (LLC)** has become popular in recent years. An LLC has all the favorable features of a typical general partnership but also offers limited liability for the partners. It typically protects a partner's personal assets from the negligence of other partners in the firm. This type of protection is highly desirable for partners, given the high frequency of liability lawsuits. The assets of the company (such as the property or machinery owned by the company) are not protected. Although S-corporations may also provide liability protection, various rules may restrict the limited liability of some partners of S-corporations. An LLC is not subject to such stringent rules.

An LLC must be created according to the laws of the state where the business is located. The precise rules on liability protection vary among the states. Numerous general partnerships (including many accounting firms) have converted to LLCs to capitalize on the advantages of a partnership, while limiting liability for their owners.

Comparison of a Proprietorship with a Partnership

A general comparison of a proprietorship and a partnership can illustrate how your earnings and losses will be affected by the form of business you choose. Exhibit 2.1 shows the earnings of your business over four years if you are the sole proprietor, versus the earnings if you are a co-owner (partner) in a partnership. In the first two years when the business incurs losses, your loss is larger if you are the sole owner of the business rather than a co-owner. In the next two years, however, when the business generates positive earnings, your gain is larger if you are the sole owner of the business. As the comparison illustrates, being the sole owner offers a relative advantage when the business performs well, but it is a relative disadvantage when the business incurs losses.

Corporation

> **corporation** a state-chartered entity that pays taxes and is legally distinct from its owners

A third form of business is a **corporation,** which is a state-chartered entity that pays taxes and is legally distinct from its owners. Although only about 20 percent of all firms are corporations, corporations generate almost 90 percent of all business revenue. Exhibit 2.2 compares the relative contributions to business revenue made by sole proprietorships, partnerships, and corporations.

Exhibit 2.1

Your Portion of Earnings (or Losses) on a Proprietorship versus a Partnership

Year	Total Business Earnings (or Loss)	Earnings to a Sole Owner	Earnings to One Partner
1	−$40,000	−$40,000	−$20,000
2	−$20,000	−$20,000	−$10,000
3	+$40,000	+$40,000	+$20,000
4	+$80,000	+$80,000	+$40,000

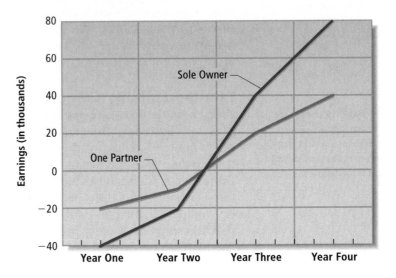

Exhibit 2.2

Relative Contributions to Business Revenue of Sole Proprietorships, Partnerships, and Corporations

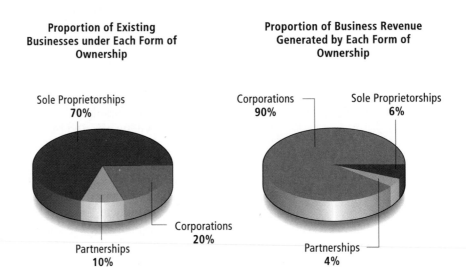

Proportion of Existing Businesses under Each Form of Ownership

Sole Proprietorships 70%

Partnerships 10%

Corporations 20%

Proportion of Business Revenue Generated by Each Form of Ownership

Corporations 90%

Sole Proprietorships 6%

Partnerships 4%

charter a document used to incorporate a business. The charter describes important aspects of the corporation.

bylaws general guidelines for managing a firm

To form a corporation, an individual or group must adopt a corporate **charter,** or a document used to incorporate a business, and file it with the state government. The charter describes important aspects of the corporation, such as the name of the firm, the stock issued, and the firm's operations. The people who organize the corporation must also establish **bylaws,** which are general guidelines for managing the firm.

Since the shareholders of the corporation are legally separated from the entity, they have limited liability, meaning that they are not held personally

business online

Becoming a Corporation   This website enables you to incorporate your business online.

e-business

http://www.bizfilings.com/

Business Filings Incorporated.

responsible for the firm's actions. The most that the stockholders of a corporation can lose is the amount of money they invested.

The stockholders of a corporation elect the members of the board of directors, who are responsible for establishing the general policies of the firm. One of the board's responsibilities is to elect the president and other key officers (such as vice-presidents), who are then given the responsibility of running the business on a day-to-day basis.

If the board of directors becomes displeased with the performance of the key officers, the board has the power to replace them. Similarly, if the stockholders become displeased with the performance of members of the board, the stockholders can replace the directors in the next scheduled election. In some corporations, one or a few individuals may serve as a stockholder, as a member of the board of directors, and as a key officer of the firm. The chief executive officer of a business commonly serves as the chair of the board.

How Stockholders Earn a Return on Their Investment   Stockholders can earn a return on their investment in a firm in two different ways. First, they may receive dividends from the firm, which are a portion of the firm's recent earnings over the last three months that are distributed to stockholders. Second, the stock they hold may increase in value. When the firm becomes more profitable, the value of its stock tends to rise, meaning that the value of stock held by owners has increased. Thus, they can benefit by selling that stock for a much higher price than they paid for it.

In the late 1990s, stock prices of many firms more than doubled. When stockholders invest in a stock, however, they also face the risk that the stock

Stockholders can earn money in the form of dividends or if the value of the stock increases.

© Getty Images / Eye Wire

price may decline. In the 2000–2002 period, the performance of firms was generally weak, and stock prices of many firms declined by more than 50 percent. Some firms failed, causing investors in the firms' stock to lose 100 percent of their investment.

Privately Held versus Publicly Held Corporations People become owners of a corporation by purchasing shares of stock. Many small corporations are **privately held,** meaning that ownership is restricted to a small group of investors. Some well-known privately held firms include L. L. Bean, Enterprise Rent-A-Car, and Rand McNally and Company. Most large corporations are **publicly held,** meaning that shares can be easily purchased or sold by investors.

privately held ownership is restricted to a small group of investors

publicly held shares can be easily purchased or sold by investors

Stockholders of publicly held corporations can sell their shares of stock when they need money, are disappointed with the performance of the corporation, or simply expect that the stock price will not rise in the future. Their stock can be sold (with the help of a stockbroker) to some other investor who wants to invest in that corporation.

Although virtually all firms (even Ford Motor Company) were privately held when they were created, some of these firms became publicly held when they needed funds to support large expansion. The act of initially issuing stock to the public is called **going public.** Recently, well-known firms such as Barnesandnoble.com, United Parcel Service (UPS), and Prodigy have gone public to raise funds.

going public the act of initially issuing stock to the public

Publicly held corporations can obtain additional funds by issuing new common stock. This means that either their existing stockholders can purchase more stock, or other investors can become stockholders by purchasing the corporation's stock. By issuing new stock, corporations may obtain whatever funds are needed to support any business expansion. Corporations that wish to issue new stock must be able to convince investors that the funds will be utilized properly, resulting in a reasonable return for the investors.

Shares of the AT&T Wireless Group were created through the biggest initial public offering in U.S. history.

AP Photo/ Richard Drew

Advantages of a Corporation   The corporate form of ownership offers the following advantages:

1 *Limited Liability*   Owners of a corporation have limited liability (as explained earlier), whereas sole proprietors and general partners typically have unlimited liability.

2 *Access to Funds*   A corporation can easily obtain funds by issuing new stock (as explained earlier). This allows corporations the flexibility to grow and to engage in new business ventures. Sole proprietorships and partnerships have less access to funding when they wish to finance expansion. To obtain more funds, they may have to rely on their existing owners or on loans from creditors.

3 *Transfer of Ownership*   Investors in large, publicly traded companies can normally sell their stock in minutes by calling their stockbrokers or by selling it online over the Internet. Conversely, owners of sole proprietorships or partnerships may have some difficulty in selling their share of ownership in the business.

Disadvantages of a Corporation   Along with its advantages, the corporate form of ownership has the following disadvantages:

1 *High Organizational Expense*   Organizing a corporation is normally more expensive than creating the other forms of business because of the necessity to create a corporate charter and file it with the state. Some expense may also be incurred in establishing bylaws. Issuing stock to investors also entails substantial expenses.

2 *Financial Disclosure*   When the stock of a corporation is traded publicly, the investing public has the right to inspect the company's financial data, within certain limits. As a result, firms may be obligated to publicly disclose more about their business operations and employee salaries than they would like. Privately held firms are not forced to disclose financial information to the public.

3 *Agency Problems* Publicly held corporations are normally run by managers who are responsible for making decisions for the business that will serve the interests of the owners. Managers may not always act in the best interests of stockholders, however. For example, managers may attempt to take expensive business trips that are not necessary to manage the business. Such actions may increase the expenses of running a business, reduce business profits, and therefore reduce the returns to stockholders. When managers do not act as responsible agents for the shareholders who own the business, a so-called **agency problem** results. There are many examples of high-level managers who made decisions that were in their best interests, at the expense of shareholders. One of the most blatant examples occurred at Enron, Inc., which went bankrupt in 2001. Agency problems are less likely in proprietorships because the sole owner may also serve as the sole manager and make most or all business decisions.

agency problem when managers do not act as responsible agents for the shareholders who own the business

4 *High Taxes* Since the corporation is a separate entity, it is taxed separately from its owners. The annual taxes paid by a corporation are determined by applying the corporate tax rate to the firm's annual earnings. The corporate tax rate is different from the personal tax rate. Consider a corporation that earns $10 million this year. Assume that the corporate tax rate applied to earnings of corporations is 30 percent this year (the corporate tax rates can be changed by law over time). Thus, the taxes and after-tax earnings of the corporation are as follows:

Earnings before Tax = $10,000,000
　　　Corporate Tax = 　3,000,000 (computed as 30% × $10,000,000)
　Earnings after Tax = $7,000,000

If any of the after-tax earnings are paid to the owners as dividends, the dividends represent personal income to stockholders. Thus, the stockhold-

Agency problems are less likely in proprietorships where a single owner or partners also manage the business and make most of the business decisions.

Getty Images/ Photo Disc

Exhibit 2.3

Illustration of Double Taxation

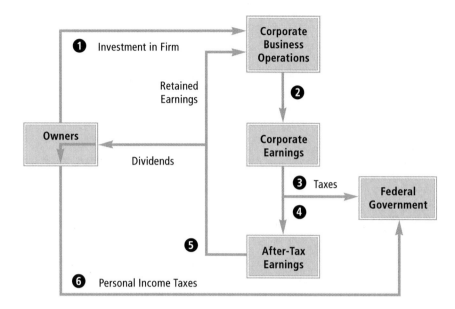

ers will pay personal income taxes on the dividends. Continuing with our example, assume that all of the $7 million in after-tax earnings is distributed to the stockholders as dividends. Assume that the personal tax rate is 20 percent for all owners who will receive dividends (personal tax rates depend on the person's income level and can be changed by law over time). The actual dividend income received by the stockholders after paying income taxes is as follows:

$$
\begin{aligned}
\text{Dividends Received} &= \$7,000,000 \\
\text{Taxes Paid on Dividends} &= \underline{1,400,000} \quad \text{(computed as 20\%} \times \$7,000,000) \\
\text{Income after Tax} &= \underline{\underline{\$5,600,000}}
\end{aligned}
$$

Since the corporate tax was $3,000,000 and the personal tax was $1,400,000, the total tax paid as a result of the corporation's profits was $4,400,000, which represents 44 percent of the $10,000,000 profit that the corporation earned.

As this example shows, owners of corporations are subject to double taxation. First, the corporation's entire profits from their investment are subject to corporate taxes. Then, any profits distributed as dividends to individual owners are subject to personal income taxes. Exhibit 2.3 shows the flow of funds between owners and the corporation to illustrate how owners are subject to double taxation.

To recognize the disadvantage of double taxation, consider what the taxes would have been for this business if it were a sole proprietorship or partnership rather than a corporation. The $10,000,000 profit would have been personal income to a sole proprietor or to partners and would have been subject to personal taxes. Assuming a personal tax rate of 20 percent, the total tax would be $2,000,000 (computed as 20 percent × $10,000,000), or less than half of the total amount that a corporation that earned the same profit and its stockholders together would pay. Even if the personal income tax rate of a sole proprietor or a partner was higher than 20 percent, the taxes paid by a corporation and its stockholders would probably still be higher. A comparison of the tax effects on corporations and sole proprietorships is provided in Exhibit 2.4.

Exhibit 2.4

Comparison of Tax Effects on Corporations and Sole Proprietorships

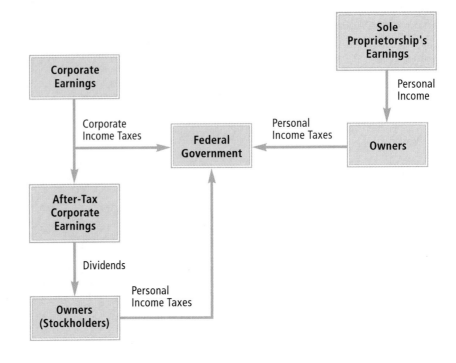

One way that a corporation may reduce the taxes paid by its owners is to reinvest its earnings (called "retained earnings") rather than pay the earnings out as dividends. If owners do not receive dividends from a corporation, they will not be subject to personal taxes on the profits earned by the corporation. This strategy makes sense only if the corporation can put the retained earnings to good use.

When stockholders of a corporation sell their shares of stock for more than they paid for them, they earn a **capital gain,** which is equal to the price received from the sale of stock minus the price they paid for the stock. The stockholders must pay a capital gains tax on the capital gain, however. Thus, whether stockholders receive income from selling the stock at a gain or from receiving dividend payments, they are subject to taxes.

capital gain the price received from the sale of stock minus the price paid for the stock

Comparing Forms of Business Ownership

No single form of business ownership is ideal for all business owners. An individual setting up a small business may choose a sole proprietorship. Some people who decide to co-own a small business may choose a partnership. If they wish to limit their liability, however, they may decide to establish a privately held corporation. If this corporation grows substantially over time and needs millions of dollars to support additional business expansion, it may convert to a publicly held corporation so that it can obtain funds from stockholders.

How a Business's Ownership Can Change Over Time As an example of how the optimal form of ownership for a specific business can change over time, consider the history of PC Repair Company, which specializes in repairing personal computers. The owner, Ed Everhart, started his business in Columbus, Ohio, in 1983. He initially used his garage as work space to fix customers' computers. Since he was the sole owner at that

increasing value with technology

ORGANIZING YOUR BUSINESS BY USING THE INTERNET

The decision on the form of business ownership can have long-term implications for taxes, liability, and control of the business. For these reasons, it should not be made lightly and will usually require a lawyer. Unfortunately, good legal advice does not come cheap. Therefore, entrepreneurs should familiarize themselves with the issues involved in organizing their businesses prior to retaining legal counsel. In recent years, the Internet has become an excellent place for finding out about such issues.

Perhaps the best starting point for learning more about business organization is the Small Business Administration (SBA). The SBA's home page (http://www.sbaonline.sba.gov/), pictured in Exhibit 2.5, represents an excellent starting point for further research. Among the resources offered are the following:

▶ Information on local SBA offices.

▶ Access to the Service Corps of Retired Executives (SCORE), consisting of over 10,000 retired business-people who have volunteered to help small businesses for free.

▶ SBA publications. As illustrated (Exhibit 2.6), the range of topics covered by the publications is enormous, and each can be copied directly to the entrepreneur's computer at no charge.

All of these services are also available through local SBA offices, but the entrepreneur can reach them far more quickly over the Internet.

In addition to government agencies, such as the SBA, many private organizations provide information and serv-

Exhibit 2.6   List of SBA Publications on the Internet

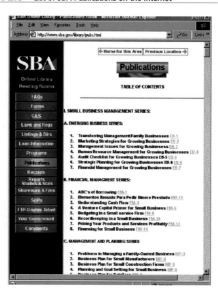

ices to small businesses just setting up. Many of these organizations, such as The Company Corporation (Exhibit 2.7), allow corporations and other forms of businesses to be set up entirely over the Internet. A particularly attractive feature of these services is their low cost—often hundreds or thousands of dollars less than using a lawyer. The entrepreneur is cautioned, however, that "undoing" the wrong form of ownership can often be expensive. Therefore, unless the entrepreneur has extensive knowledge of various forms of ownership, establishing a long-term relationship with a local attorney is generally prudent.

Exhibit 2.5   The Small Business Administration's Home Page

Exhibit 2.7   The Company Corporation Home Page

time, his business was a proprietorship. By 1989, the business had grown, and Ed wanted to open a computer repair shop downtown. He needed more funds to purchase a shop and hire employees. He asked a friend, Maria Rosas, if she wanted to become a partner by investing funds in the firm and working for the business. She agreed, so the business was converted from a proprietorship to a partnership. From Ed's point of view, the main benefit was that Maria could invest money that would help the business grow. In addition, she had good computer repair skills. The main disadvantage was that he was no longer the sole decision maker, but he and Maria usually agreed on how to run the business.

By 1996, the business had grown even more. Ed and Maria wanted to establish three more computer repair shops in Columbus, so they obtained funds from eight friends who served as limited partners. These limited partners invested in the business because they expected that it would flourish and provide them with a good return on their investment. In 2003, Ed and Maria wanted to expand their business throughout Ohio, but they needed a substantial amount of funds to do so. They decided to issue stock to the public, with the help of a financial institution. Their stock offering raised $20 million, although about $1.5 million of the proceeds went to pay expenses associated with the stock offering. At this time, the ownership of the business was converted from a partnership to a corporation. The corporate form of ownership allowed the business to expand. With the establishment of several repair shops throughout Ohio, the firm now had the potential to generate large earnings. The organization was also much more complex than when the business was a proprietorship. Ed and Maria still made the business decisions, but they were now accountable to hundreds of other investors who were part-owners of the business. Thus, by 2003 PC Repair Company had changed considerably since its beginnings in a garage 20 years earlier.

2 HOW OWNERSHIP CAN AFFECT RETURN AND RISK

Explain how the potential return and risk of a business are affected by its form of ownership.

When business owners assess a possible investment in any business, they consider both the potential return and the risk from that type of investment. The potential return and the risk from investing in a business are influenced by its form of ownership. Thus, entrepreneurs should consider how the form of ownership affects the potential return and the risk when deciding on the optimal form of ownership for their business.

Impact of Ownership on the Return on Investment

The return on investment in a firm is derived from the firm's profits (also called "earnings" or "income"). As described earlier, when a firm generates earnings, it pays a portion to the IRS as income taxes. The remaining (after-tax) earnings represent the return (in dollars) to the business owners. However, the dollar value of a firm's after-tax earnings is not necessarily a useful measure of the firm's performance unless it is adjusted for the amount of the firm's **equity,** which is the total investment by the firm's stockholders. For this reason, business owners prefer to measure a firm's profitability by computing its **return on equity (ROE),** which is the earnings as a proportion of the equity:

equity the total investment by the firm's stockholders

return on equity (ROE) earnings as a proportion of the firm's equity

cross functional teamwork:

Sources of Risk across Business Functions

A firm relies on the management of resources (including human resources and other resources such as machinery), marketing, and finance functions to perform well. Poor performance can normally be attributed to poor management of resources, poor marketing, or poor financing, as explained next.

If resources are not properly managed, the firm will incur excessive expenses. The following are typical mistakes that can cause excessive production expenses:

1 Hiring more employees than necessary, which results in high operating expenses.

2 Hiring fewer employees than necessary, which prevents the firm from achieving the desired volume or quality of products.

3 Hiring employees who lack proper skills or training.

4 Investing in more equipment or machinery than necessary, which results in high operating expenses.

5 Investing in less equipment or machinery than necessary, which prevents the firm from achieving the desired volume or quality of products.

The following are typical marketing mistakes that can cause poor performance:

1 Excessive spending on marketing programs.

2 Ineffective marketing programs, which do not enhance the firm's revenue.

The following are typical finance mistakes that can cause poor performance:

1 Borrowing too much money, which results in a high level of interest expenses incurred per year.

2 Not borrowing enough money, which prevents a firm from investing the necessary amount of funds to be successful.

Since business decisions are related, a poor decision in one department can affect other departments. For example, a computer manufacturer's production volume is based on the forecasted demand for computers by the marketing department. When the marketing department underestimates the demand, the manufacturer experiences shortages.

$$\text{Return on Equity} = \frac{\text{Earnings after Tax}}{\text{Equity}}$$

For example, if the stockholders invested \$1 million in a firm and its after-tax earnings last year were \$150,000, its return on equity last year was:

$$\text{ROE} = \frac{\$150,000}{\$1,000,00}$$

$$= .15, \text{ or } 15\%$$

Thus, the firm generated a return equal to 15 percent of the owners' investment in the firm.

As a real-world application, the return on equity for The Children's Place Retail Stores, Inc., for 2001 is derived in Exhibit 2.8. Notice that The Children's Place generated earnings before taxes of about \$75 million. Of this amount, \$29 million (38 percent) was used to pay corporate taxes. The remaining \$46 million represents after-tax earnings. Given the total investment (equity) in The Children's Place of about \$217 million, the after-tax earnings represent a return of about 21 percent (computed as \$46 million divided by \$217 million).

If a firm like The Children's Place wants to expand internationally, it needs a substantial amount of funds to support the expansion. This is possible only by issuing stock to a large group of stockholders. By using the \$217 million provided by stockholders to open new stores, The Children's Place now has expanded to 520 retail stores. The large amount of equity

Exhibit 2.8

Return on Equity for The Children's Place

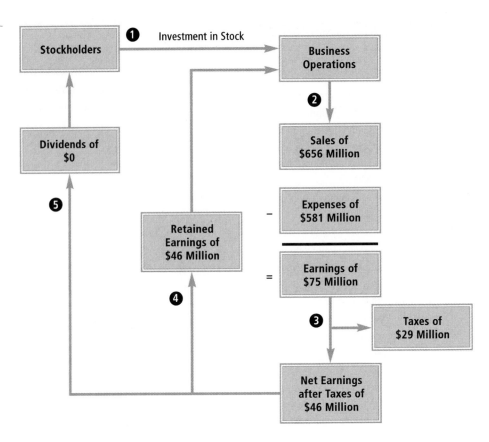

Return on Equity (ROE)
Given that The Children's Place equity was about $217 million, its ROE was:

$$ROE = \frac{\text{Earnings after Taxes}}{\text{Equity}}$$

$$= \frac{\$46 \text{ million}}{\$217 \text{ million}}$$

$$= 21\%$$

that The Children's Place obtained as a result of choosing the corporate form of ownership has enabled it to grow and generate a large amount of sales and earnings. If The Children's Place had chosen the partnership form of ownership, its growth would have been limited.

However, access to a large amount of equity is beneficial only if the firm can put the equity to good use. If a firm has more equity than it can use, its performance will be weak. Consider the situations of Firms A and B. Firm A is a partnership and Firm B is a corporation.

	Firm A (Partnership)	Firm B (Corporation)
Earnings after taxes last year	$15 million	$15 million
Owners' equity	$100 million	$300 million
Return on equity	15%	5%

self-scoring exercise

Do You Have the Skills Necessary to Succeed in Business?

According to the U.S. Department of Labor, achieving success in the workplace, now and in the future, will require that a person possess three enabling skills as a foundation for the five functional skills required in the business environment. Answer each of these three basic questions:

1. Do you believe you possess the basic reading, speaking, listening, and mathematics skills required for future learning?

2. Do you believe you possess the intellectual skills for effective decision making and problem solving?

3. Do you believe you possess the affective skills required for you to cooperate with others and achieve effective sociability?

If you answered yes to each question, you have the basic skills needed to enable you to master five functional skills in the business environment. How do you rate yourself in each of these five functional skill areas? In the blank before each skill, place the number from 1 (very good) to 5 (needs improvement) that reflects your self-rating.

_____ 1. Resource management skills, such as human resource management, time management, and financial resources management.

_____ 2. Information management skills, such as identifying and interpreting information.

_____ 3. Personal interaction skills, such as teamwork, negotiation, and working with customers.

_____ 4. Systems behavior and performance skills, such as anticipating consequences of behavior and cause-and-effect relationships.

_____ 5. Technology utilization skills, such as selecting, using, maintaining, and/or troubleshooting technology.

If you rated yourself a 4 or 5 on any of the five functional skills, you may want to talk with your instructor or the university's career and counseling office about specific opportunities that will enable you to strengthen those skills.

risk the degree of uncertainty about a firm's future earnings

Notice that the firms had the same dollar value of earnings after taxes. However, the corporation has three times the equity investment of the partnership. The return on equity is much higher for the partnership than for the corporation because the partnership achieved the same level of earnings with a smaller equity investment.

Impact of Ownership on Risk

The **risk** of a firm represents the degree of uncertainty about the firm's future earnings, which reflects an uncertain return to the owners. A firm's future earnings are dependent on its future revenue and its expenses. Firms can experience losses if the revenue is less than expected or if the expenses are more than expected. Some firms that experience severe losses ultimately fail. In these cases, the owners may lose most or all of the funds they invested in the firms.

Since sole proprietorships tend to be small businesses with very limited funds, they are generally riskier than larger businesses such as partnerships and corporations. Consider a sole proprietorship that has revenue of $200,000 and expenses of $300,000 this year. It needs $100,000 of equity to cover its loss. If it has only $60,000, it cannot cover the loss. If the business had another owner, it would have more equity and might be able to cover its loss.

The limited funding of sole proprietorships also means that they are not able to diversify their business. If their single line of business experiences problems, they are highly susceptible to failure. An event such as a workers' strike in a supplier firm or reduced demand for the type of products they produce can result in failure. In contrast, a larger firm that sells a diversified product line may not be severely affected by events that adversely affect only one of its products. The death or retirement of a key manager can also have a great impact on a sole proprietorship. Larger businesses typically have several employees in high-level positions who can make key decisions, so no one person is irreplaceable.

When deciding on ownership, the following trade-off should be obvious. The greater the number of owners, the larger the amount of funds that can be accessed, but the larger the number of people who share in the performance of the business. Thus, a sole proprietorship can reduce its risk by converting to a partnership so that it can access more funds. A partnership can reduce its risk by converting to a corporation so that it can access more funds.

College Health Club: Business Ownership at CHC

One of the decisions that Sue Kramer needs to make as part of her business plan is the appropriate form of business ownership for College Health Club (CHC). Diane Burke, a relative of Sue's, has offered a loan of $40,000 if she believes that the business plan is feasible. Diane is willing to provide the funds as a 10-year loan and will charge an interest rate of 10 percent. If Sue accepts the funds as a loan, then she will be the sole owner of CHC. However, she will have to pay Diane interest of $4,000 at the end of each year (computed as $40,000 × 10%).

Alternatively, Diane is willing to provide the funds as an equity investment. This would make her an owner of the firm. In this case, Diane's investment would be two-thirds of the total investment in the firm, and she would receive two-thirds of the proceeds when the business is sold, perhaps several years from now.

Sue compares the expected performance of CHC for the two forms of ownership as follows:

Expected Performance of CHC in the First Year if Sue Kramer Accepts Borrowed Funds versus an Equity Investment from Diane		
	Performance if . . .	
	Sue Borrows Funds and Is the Sole Owner of CHC	**Sue Allows Diane to Be a Part-Owner of CHC**
Revenue	$150,000	$150,000
Total operating expenses	138,000	138,000
Interest expenses	4,000	0
Earnings before taxes	$8,000	$12,000

In each year, CHC's earnings would be $4,000 higher if she accepts the funds as an equity investment rather than a loan, because she would avoid the interest expense. This is the advantage of the partnership form of ownership. In addition, any losses incurred by CHC would be shared if she allows Diane to be a partner.

If Sue uses the partnership form, however, she would receive only one-third of the proceeds when the business is sold, and Diane would receive the remainder. In addition, Sue would have to share the decision making with Diane. With the proprietorship form of ownership, Sue would receive the entire proceeds if she sells the business someday. Furthermore, she would have complete control. She believes that she can run CHC better by herself than if other partners are involved in the business decisions.

After weighing the advantages and disadvantages of a sole proprietorship versus a partnership, Sue decides that the proprietorship is the more desirable form of ownership. She risks losing more of her own money as the sole proprietor, but she is willing to take that risk because she is confident that her business will be successful.

Sue does not even consider the corporation form of ownership at this point because she is just starting a very small business. If she ever decides to expand the business by allowing for additional owners, the partnership form would be more appropriate than the corporation form. She would consider forming a corporation only if she plans to expand her health clubs throughout Texas.

OBTAINING OWNERSHIP OF AN EXISTING BUSINESS

Some people become the sole owners without starting the business. The following are common methods by which people become owners of existing businesses:

▶   Assuming ownership of a family business

▶   Purchasing an existing business

▶   Franchising

Assuming Ownership of a Family Business

Many people work in a family business and after a period of time assume the ownership of it. This can be an ideal way to own a business because its performance may be somewhat predictable as long as the key employees continue to work there. Major decisions regarding the production process and other operations of the firm have been predetermined. If the business has historically been successful, a new owner's main function may be to ensure that the existing operations continue to run efficiently. Alternatively, if the business is experiencing poor performance, the new owner may have to revise management, marketing, and financing policies.

Purchasing an Existing Business

Businesses are for sale on any given day in any city. They are often advertised in the classified ads section of local newspapers. Businesses are sold for various reasons, including financial difficulties and the death or retirement of an owner.

People considering the purchase of an existing business must determine whether they have the expertise to run the business or at least properly monitor the managers. Then they must compare the expected benefits of the business with the initial outlay required to purchase it. The seller of the business may provide historical sales volume, which can be used to estimate the future sales volume. However, the prospective buyer must be cautious when using these figures. In some businesses such as dentistry and hair styling, personal relationships between the owner and customers are critical. Many customers may switch to competitors if the ownership changes. For these types of businesses, the historical sales volume may substantially overestimate future sales. For other, less personalized businesses such as grocery stores, a change of ownership is not likely to have a significant effect on customer preferences (and therefore on sales volume).

Franchising

franchise an arrangement whereby a business owner allows others to use its trademark, trade name, or copyright, under specific conditions

franchisor a firm that allows others to use its trade name or copyright, under specified conditions

franchisee a firm that is allowed to use the trade name or copyright of a franchise

A **franchise** is an arrangement whereby a business owner (called a **franchisor**) allows another (the **franchisee**) to use its trademark, trade name, or copyright, under specified conditions. Each individual franchise operates as an independent business and is typically owned by a sole proprietor. Thus, a new business is created using the trademark and name of the existing franchisor.

Franchises like Mailboxes, Etc. are usually owned by a single proprietor or franchisee.

Franchises in the United States number over 500,000, and they generate more than $800 billion in annual revenue. Some well-known franchises include McDonald's, Thrifty Rent-a-Car System, Mail Boxes Etc., Dairy Queen, Super 8 Motels Inc., TGI Fridays, Pearle Vision, Inc., and Baskin-Robbins. The costs of purchasing a franchise can vary significantly, depending on the specific trademarks, technology, and services provided to the franchisees.

Types of Franchises   Most franchises can be classified as a distributorship, a chain-style business, or a manufacturing arrangement.

In a **distributorship,** a dealer is allowed to sell a product produced by a manufacturer. For example, Chrysler and Ford dealers are distributorships.

In a **chain-style business,** a firm is allowed to use the trade name of a company and follows guidelines related to the pricing and sale of the product. Some examples are McDonald's, CD Warehouse, Holiday Inn, Subway, and Pizza Hut.

In a **manufacturing arrangement,** a firm is allowed to manufacture a product using the formula provided by another company. For example, Microsoft might allow a foreign company to produce its software, as long as the software is sold only in that country. Microsoft would receive a portion of the revenue generated by that firm.

Advantages of a Franchise   The typical advantages of a franchise are as follows:

1 *Proven Management Style*   Franchisees look to the franchisors for guidance in production and management. McDonald's provides extensive training to its franchisees. The management style of a franchise is already a proven success. A franchise's main goal is to duplicate a proven business in a particular location. Thus, the franchise is a less risky venture than a new type of business, as verified by a much higher failure rate for new businesses.

---

distributorship a type of franchise in which a dealer is allowed to sell a product produced by a manufacturer

chain-style business a type of franchise in which a firm is allowed to use the trade name of a company and follows guidelines related to the pricing and sale of the product

manufacturing arrangement a type of franchise in which a firm is allowed to manufacture a product using the formula provided by another company

2 *Name Recognition*   Many franchises are nationally known because of advertising by the franchisor. This provides the franchisee with name recognition, which can significantly increase the demand for the product. Therefore, owners of Holiday Inn, Pizza Hut, and other franchises may not need to spend money on advertising because the franchises are already popular with consumers.

3 *Financial Support*   Some franchisees receive some financial support from the franchisor, which can ensure sufficient start-up funds for the franchisee. For example, some McDonald's franchisees can receive funding from McDonald's. Alternatively, franchisees can purchase materials and supplies from the franchisor on credit, which represents a form of short-term financing.

Disadvantages of a Franchise   Two common disadvantages of franchising are as follows:

1 *Sharing Profits*   In return for services provided by the franchisor, the franchisee must share profits with the franchisor. Annual fees paid by the franchisee may be 8 percent or more of the annual revenue generated by the franchise.

2 *Less Control*   The franchisee must abide by guidelines regarding product production and pricing, and possibly other guidelines as well. Consequently, the franchisee's performance is dependent on these guidelines. Owners are not allowed to revise some of the guidelines.

Though decision making is limited, owners of a franchise still make some critical decisions. They must decide whether a particular franchise can be successful in a particular location. In addition, even though the production and marketing policies are somewhat predetermined, the owners are responsible for managing their employees. They must provide leadership and motivation to maximize production efficiency. Thus, a franchise's performance is partially dependent on its owners and managers.

The Popularity of Business-to-Business Franchises   Franchises that serve other businesses (called business-to-business or B2B franchises) have grown substantially in the last few years. In particular, many franchises focus on providing hiring services, consulting services, and training services for firms. These types of franchises are popular because they normally require a smaller initial investment than many other franchises such as hotels and restaurants. Many B2B franchises can be operated by computer from a home office and therefore can be started with an investment of between $30,000 and $100,000. In contrast, restaurant franchises may require an investment of $150,000 or more. In addition, a B2B franchise can use computer technology instead of employees to do some of the work, such as sorting résumés and offering training with animated computer files. Furthermore, since a B2B franchise interacts with other businesses, less weekend work may be required than with restaurant franchises, which commonly operate seven days a week.

College Health Club: **Considering a Franchise at CHC**

Another decision that Sue Kramer needs to make as part of her business plan is the best way to establish her health club business. Rather than start her own health club, she could acquire an existing business. She is aware that a health club is for sale, but it is not near the Texas College campus. Recall that she wants to establish a health club near the Texas College campus because her target market is the set of students at the college. Thus, the only way that she can achieve her business idea is to establish a new health club rather than purchasing an existing health club.

Sue has also learned that a national health club chain is selling a health club franchise near a corporate office complex about 25 miles from Texas College. If Sue were to purchase that franchise instead of establishing her own health club, the national chain would train her to run the club, and she would receive a percentage of the revenue it generates. This franchise is likely to be successful because the chain has a national reputation. Although Sue would be assuming less risk by purchasing a franchise, she would not have complete control over the club. She would prefer to have control over a health club and also would prefer not to share any profits that it earns. Therefore, she decides to start her own club rather than purchase the franchise.

Ownership of Foreign Businesses Opportunities in foreign countries have encouraged many entrepreneurs in the United States to establish foreign businesses in recent years. A common way for an entrepreneur to establish a foreign business is to purchase a franchise created by a U.S. firm in a foreign country. For example, McDonald's, Pizza Hut, and KFC have franchises in numerous foreign countries. The potential return on these franchises may be higher than in the United States if there is less competition.

Another popular way for U.S. entrepreneurs to own a foreign business is to purchase a business that is being sold by the foreign government. During the 1990s, many governments in Eastern Europe and Latin America sold a large number of businesses that they had owned. They also encouraged more competition among firms in each industry. Entrepreneurs recognized that many businesses previously owned by the government were not efficiently managed. Consequently, many businesses were perceived as having relatively low values, thus enabling some entrepreneurs to purchase the businesses at low prices. However, these businesses were subject to a high degree of risk because the foreign environment was unstable. Since most of the businesses in these countries had been managed by their respective governments, the rules for privately owned businesses were not completely established. The tax rates that would be imposed on private businesses were uncertain. The degree of competition was also uncertain, as firms were now free to enter most industries.

Given the uncertainties faced by new businesses in these foreign countries, some entrepreneurs made agreements with existing foreign firms rather than establishing their own business. For example, suppose that an entrepreneur recognizes that various household products will be popular in some Latin American countries but prefers not to establish a firm there because of uncertainty about tax rates and other government policies. The entrepreneur may make an agreement with an existing firm that distributes related products to retail stores throughout Latin America. This firm will earn a fee for selling the household products produced by the entrepreneur. This example is just one of many possible arrangements that allow U.S. entrepreneurs to capitalize on opportunities in a foreign country without owning a business there.

global business

SUMMARY

1 When starting a new business, entrepreneurs must select from among three forms of ownership:

▶ A sole proprietorship, owned by a single person who often manages the firm as well.

▶ A partnership, composed of two or more co-owners who may manage the firm as well. A partnership can allow for more financial support by owners than a sole proprietorship, but it also requires that control and profits of the firm be shared among owners.

▶ A corporation, which is an entity that is viewed as separate from its owners. Owners of a corporation have limited liability, while owners of sole proprietorships and partnerships have unlimited liability.

2 The return and the risk from investing in a business are dependent on the form of business ownership. The return on equity is higher if a business can use a limited amount of equity. Sole proprietorships have the potential to generate a high return to the owners because there is only one owner. However, they are generally more risky because of their limited funding, among other reasons. A business can reduce its risk by allowing additional owners, but the trade-off is that its profitability is spread among all the owners.

3 The common methods by which people can obtain ownership of existing businesses are as follows:

▶ Assuming ownership of a family business

▶ Purchasing an existing business

▶ Franchising

Assuming the ownership of a family business is desirable because a person can normally learn much about that business before assuming ownership. Many people are not in a position to assume a family business, however. Before purchasing an existing business, one must estimate future sales and expenses to determine whether making the investment is feasible. Franchising may be desirable for people who will need some guidance in running the firm. However, the franchisee must pay annual fees to the franchisor.

KEY TERMS

agency problem   44
bylaws   40
capital gain   46
chain-style business   54
charter   40
corporation   38
distributorship   54
equity   48
franchise   53
franchisee   53

franchisor   53
general partners   37
general partnership   37
going public   42
limited liability company (LLC)   38
limited partners   37
limited partnership   37
manufacturing arrangement   54
partners   37
partnership   37

privately held   42
publicly held   42
return on equity (ROE)   48
risk   51
S-corporation   38
sole proprietor   36
sole proprietorship   36
unlimited liability   37

Review & Critical Thinking Questions

1. What are the key differences among a sole proprietorship, a partnership, and a corporation?

2. List and briefly describe the advantages and disadvantages of a sole proprietorship.

3. Distinguish between a general partnership and a limited partnership.

4. What is an S-corporation? What are the advantages of an S-corporation?

5. What is a limited liability company (LLC)? What are the differences between an S-corporation and a limited liability company?

6. How can stockholders earn a return on their investment?

7. Identify and explain the differences between privately held and publicly held corporations.

8. List and briefly describe the advantages and disadvantages of a corporation.

9. Explain why stockholders are concerned that managers may

not always act in their best interests.

10. Explain the difference between the corporate tax rate and the personal tax rate.

11. Describe a franchise and identify its advantages and disadvantages.

12. What are B2B franchises? Provide some examples of B2B franchises. Why are B2B franchises popular?

Discussion Questions

1. Assume you are a management consultant. For each of the following situations, recommend an appropriate form of business ownership:

   a. Four physicians wish to start a practice together, and each wants to have limited liability.

   b. A friend wants to open her own convenience store.

   c. An entrepreneur wants to acquire a large U.S. steel business.

   d. Five friends want to build an apartment complex and are not concerned about limited liability.

2. What basic steps should be undertaken to organize a corporation in your state?

3. Discuss and give examples of what you believe is the most common form of business ownership in your hometown.

4. Assume you are starting your own business. What decisions do you have to make concerning the type of ownership and control of your business?

5. Discuss the advantages and disadvantages of starting your own business compared to buying a franchise.

6. You are operating a sole proprietorship with a single product line, men's hair shampoo. Explain how a recession would affect your business versus a business with a more diversified product line.

It's Your Decision: Ownership at CHC

1. One advantage of a partnership is that it allows partners to focus on their respective specializations. Should this advantage cause Sue Kramer to search for a partner for her health club business?
2. How will CHC be taxed, given that Sue plans to be the sole owner?
3. What is an advantage for Sue of starting her own health club instead of operating a franchise health club?
4. Explain how Sue's decision to be the sole owner will affect her marketing and production plans. How might the marketing and production plans be different if she had invited several investors to invest substantial amounts of equity in her business?
5. A health club differs from manufacturing firms in that it produces a service rather than products. Why might Sue need other partners if she had established a manufacturing firm instead of a health club?

Investing in a Business

Using the annual report of the firm in which you would like to invest, complete the following:

1 Each annual report contains an income statement, which discloses the firm's earnings before taxes, its taxes, and its earnings after taxes over the most recent year. Search for the table called "Income Statement" and determine your firm's earnings before taxes, taxes paid, and earnings after taxes last year. What proportion of your firm's earnings were eventually paid as taxes?

2 Is your firm involved in franchising? If so, describe its franchises. Check its website to obtain franchise information.

3 Describe any conditions mentioned in the annual report that expose the firm to risk.

4 Explain how the business uses technology to provide information about its form of business ownership. For example, does it use the Internet to disclose the form of business ownership it uses?

5 Go to **http://hoovers.com** and locate the NEWS SEARCH. Type in the name of the firm in the space provided, and review the recent news stories about the firm. Summarize one recent news story about the firm that applies to one or more of the key concepts in this chapter.

Case: Deciding the Type of Business Ownership

Paul Bazzano and Mary Ann Boone are lifelong friends and have decided to go into business. They are not sure what form of business ownership and control to use. Paul would like to invest his savings of $25,000, but he does not want to take an active role in managing the day-to-day operations of the business. Mary Ann is a self-starter, enjoys cooking and baking, and has a vast number of pizza recipes. An existing pizza business is for sale for $50,000. Paul and Mary Ann both like the idea of investing in a business. Mary Ann has $5,000 she would like to contribute and believes that buying an existing business has certain advantages. She likes the idea that Paul will not be an active owner and that she will have full control of the pizza operation.

The existing business has sales of $150,000 and generates earnings after taxes of $32,500. Mary Ann be-

lieves the business can be expanded and foresees future growth by expanding into different locations throughout the Boston area. She projects two more stores in the next five years.

Questions

1 What form of business ownership would you recommend for this business?

2 Would Mary Ann's form of ownership be any different from Paul's?

3 How could Paul and Mary Ann determine the return on their investment after their first year of business? Assume that Paul and Mary Ann can borrow the remaining $20,000 needed to finance the purchase when answering this question.

4 Describe the risk of this business.

Video Case: Business Organization at Second Chance Body Armor

Richard Davis was shot while he was working at a pizza restaurant. When he recovered, he thought of a way to create a bulletproof vest that would be so flexible that it could be worn all day. He decided to turn this idea into a business (called Second Chance Body Armor) that would produce vests that would enhance the safety of police officers around the country. He began the firm as a sole proprietorship and started with just $70. Any revenue that he received was used to pay for marketing the concealable body armor that he created. Once law enforcement agencies learned of his product, they began to order it. Consequently, Second Chance Body Armor

became a success. In time, the firm hired many employees and converted into a corporation.

Questions

1 Why do you think Richard Davis initially began his firm as a sole proprietorship?

2 When Richard Davis started his firm, how could he have benefited from creating a partnership with a few other owners? What would have been a disadvantage of using this form of business ownership instead of a sole proprietorship?

3 Why do you think Richard Davis decided to convert his sole proprietorship into a corporation?

Internet Applications

1. *http://www.ibm.com*

Find the "Financials" section under "Investors." What were IBM's most recent quarterly earnings (total and per share)? Compute IBM's return on equity (ROE) for the last quarter. How does a corporate website such as IBM's allow investors to evaluate the performance of a company? What other information do you think a website such as this could provide to help investors evaluate corporate performance?

2. *http://www.sba.gov/starting/index.faqs.html*

What different forms of ownership are implied in the suggested alternatives to financing a business? Which form of ownership do you think most new businesses will choose? Why? What are the advantages and disadvantages of each form of ownership mentioned in the "Startup Kit"?

3. *http://sbdc.deltacollege.org/startup/ownership.html*

What are the advantages and disadvantages of franchising for an entrepreneur? Would you personally consider a franchise for your business? Why or why not? What criterion of ownership would be most important to you in selecting a form of ownership for your business? Explain.

The Coca-Cola Company Annual Report Project

 Questions for the current year's annual report are available on the text website at **http://madura.swlearning.com.**

The following questions apply concepts presented in this chapter to The Coca-Cola Company. Go to The Coca-Cola Company website (**http://www.cocacola.com**) and find the index for the 2001 annual report.

Questions

1 Why do you think The Coca-Cola Company is organized as a corporation rather than a sole proprietorship or a partnership?

2 Click on "Share-Owner Information." According to the annual report, The Coca-Cola Company has increased its dividend 40 years in a row. Why might this be an advantage to shareholders?

3 Click on "Financial Highlights." What was the market value of Coca-Cola common stock at the end of 1981? What was it at the end of 2001?

4 Do you think a global company such as The Coca-Cola Company would experience more or fewer agency conflicts than a corporation operating solely within the United States?

5 Go to **http://hoovers.com** and locate the NEWS CENTER. Key in The Coca-Cola Company in the space provided, click on "Search," and review the recent news stories about the firm. Summarize any (at least one) recent news story about The Coca-Cola Company that applies one or more of the key concepts within this chapter of the text.

In-Text Study Guide

Answers are in an appendix at the back of the book.

True or False

1. The legal requirements for establishing a sole proprietorship are very difficult. F

2. One advantage of sole proprietorships is that this form of ownership provides easy access to additional funds. F

3. Limited partners are investors in the partnership and participate in the management of the business. F

4. The limited liability feature is an advantage of owning a sole proprietorship. F

5. When a corporation distributes some of its recent earnings to stockholders, the payments are referred to as capital gains. F

6. If the board of directors becomes displeased with the performance of the key officers, the board has the power to replace them. T

7. Publicly held corporations can obtain additional funds by issuing new common stock. T

8. Publicly held corporations are required to disclose financial information to the investing public. T

9. To incorporate a business, one must adopt a corporate charter and file it with the state government where the business is to be located. F

10. The form of ownership of a firm should not be changed unless there are major tax advantages. F

11. Distributorships, chain-style businesses, and manufacturing arrangements are all common types of franchises. T

Multiple Choice

12. When entrepreneurs establish a business, they must first decide on the form of:
    a) divestiture.
    b) global expansion.
    c) joint venture.
    d) ownership.

13. The following are possible forms of business ownership except for a:
    a) sole proprietorship.
    b) partnership.
    c) bureaucracy
    d) corporation.

14. Joe wants to form his own business. He wants to get started as quickly and inexpensively as possible and has a strong desire to control the business himself. He is confident he will be successful and wants to keep all the profits himself. Joe's goals indicate he would probably choose to operate his business as a(n):
    a) limited partnership.
    b) limited liability company.
    c) S-corporation.
    d) franchise.
    e) sole proprietorship.

15. A business owned by a single owner is referred to as a:
    a) partnership.
    b) sole proprietorship.
    c) limited partnership.
    d) corporation.
    e) subchapter S-corporation.

16. A disadvantage of a sole proprietorship is that:
    a) sole proprietors have very little control over the operations of the business.
    b) sole proprietors have unlimited liability.
    c) it is more difficult and expensive to establish than other forms of business.
    d) its earnings are subject to higher tax rates than other forms of business.
    e) sole proprietors are required to share the firm's profits with employees.

17. Partners have unlimited liability in a:
    a) general partnership.
    b) corporation.
    c) limited partnership.
    d) cooperative.

18. In a limited partnership:
    a) all partners have limited liability.
    b) the partnership exists only for a limited time period, or until a specific task is accomplished.
    c) the limited partners do not participate in management of the company.
    d) the partners agree to operate in a limited geographic area.
    e) no more than 75 partners may invest in the company at any one time.

19. When two or more people, having complementary skills, agree to co-own a business, this agreement is referred to as a:
    a) partnership.
    b) sole proprietorship.
    c) cooperative.
    d) corporation.
    e) joint venture.

20. A firm that has 75 owners or less and also meets other criteria may choose to be a so-called:
    a) cooperative.
    b) proprietorship.
    c) joint venture.
    d) S-corporation.
    e) bureaucracy.

21. A general partnership that protects a partner's personal assets from the negligence of other partners is called a:
    a) limited liability company.
    b) cooperative.
    c) private corporation.
    d) master limited partnership.
    e) protected partnership.

22. A corporation is:
    a) easier to form than other types of businesses.
    b) a state-chartered entity that is legally distinct from its owners.
    c) a business that is owned and operated by a government agency.
    d) a form of business that is legally exempt from paying taxes on earnings.
    e) simply another term for a large sole proprietorship.

23. A corporate charter contains general guidelines for managing the company called:
    a) rules of order.
    b) bylaws.
    c) indenture agreements.
    d) control procedures.
    e) disclosure clauses.

24. Important aspects of a corporation, such as the name of the firm, information about the stock issued, and a description of the firm's operations, are contained in a:
    a) mission.
    b) policy.
    c) charter.
    d) plan.
    e) venture.

25. The members of the board of directors of a corporation are chosen by the corporation's:
    a) president and chief executive officer.
    b) creditors.
    c) general partners.
    d) stockholders.
    e) charter members.

26. When ownership of a small corporation is restricted to a small group of investors, it is:
    a) publicly held.
    b) government owned.
    c) bureaucratic.
    d) privately held.
    e) perfectly competitive.

27. When a corporation's shares can be easily purchased or sold by investors, it is:
    a) publicly held.
    b) privately held.
    c) institutionalized.
    d) monopolized.
    e) franchised.

In-Text Study Guide

Answers are in an appendix at the back of the book.

28. People become owners of a corporation by purchasing:
    a) shares of stock.
    b) corporate bonds.
    c) retained earnings.
    d) inventory.
    e) accounts receivable.

29. Agency problems are least likely in:
    a) sole proprietorships.
    b) limited liability companies.
    c) general partnerships.
    d) publicly-held corporations.
    e) privately-held corporations

30. When stockholders of a corporation sell shares of stock for more than they paid for them, they receive a:
    a) dividend.
    b) premium.
    c) capital gain.
    d) discount.
    e) stock option.

31. The return on investment in a firm is derived from the firm's ability to earn:
    a) assets.
    b) liabilities.
    c) profits.
    d) expenses.

32. The total amount invested in a company by its owners is called:
    a) the corporate margin.
    b) equity.
    c) working capital.
    d) the stock premium.
    e) treasury stock.

33. The degree of uncertainty about future earnings, which reflects an uncertain return to the owners, is known as:
    a) certainty.
    b) profits.
    c) risk.
    d) equity.
    e) dividends.

34. An arrangement whereby business owners allow others to use their trademark, trade name, or copyright under specified conditions is a:
    a) franchise.
    b) labor union.
    c) bureau.
    d) joint venture.
    e) cartel.

35. A business that is allowed to use the trade name of a company and follows guidelines related to the pricing and sales of the products is a:
    a) joint venture.
    b) monopoly.
    c) chain-style business.
    d) sole proprietorship.

36. All of the following are common types of franchise arrangements except:
    a) business agencies.
    b) chain-style businesses.
    c) manufacturing arrangements.
    d) distributorships.

37. Sharing profits and less control of the business ownership are two common disadvantages of:
    a) sole proprietorships.
    b) downsizing.
    c) divestiture.
    d) franchising.

38. Advantages of business-to-business franchises include all of the following except:
    a) tax advantages.
    b) smaller initial investment.
    c) ability for home-based work.
    d) substitution of computer technology for employees.

business decisions

All businesses, including cruise lines, need to determine their ethical and social responsibilities.

The Learning Goals of this chapter are to:

1 Describe the responsibilities of firms to their customers.

2 Describe the responsibilities of firms to their employees.

3 Describe the responsibilities of firms to their stockholders and creditors.

4 Describe the responsibilities of firms to the environment.

5 Describe the responsibilities of firms to their communities.

6 Explain the costs that firms incur in fulfilling their social responsibilities.

Chapter 3

Business Ethics and Social Responsibility

A firm's employees should practice business ethics, which involves following a set of principles when conducting business. Each firm has a social responsibility, which is the firm's recognition of how its business decisions can affect society. The term *social responsibility* is sometimes used to describe the firm's responsibility to its community and to the environment. However, it may also be used more broadly to include the firm's responsibility to its customers, employees, stockholders, and creditors. Although the business decisions a firm makes are intended to increase its value, the decisions must not violate its ethics and social responsibilities.

Golden Cruise Lines offers 7-day and 14-day cruises to various tropical islands. Like many cruise lines, it hires employees from the Philippines and other Asian and Latin American countries, where wages are very low. It re-lies on funding from large investors and from loans by commercial banks.

Golden Cruise Lines is reassessing its corporate responsibilities, in light of recent media attention paid to cruise lines that have not fulfilled their corporate responsibilities. Some cruise lines were recently criticized because of (1) using misleading advertising with their customers, (2) mistreatment of employees hired from less-developed countries, (3) inability to provide a decent return to investors, (4) inability to repay their debts, and (5) discharge of waste into the sea. To ensure that it meets its corporate responsibilities, Golden Cruise Lines decides to develop a formal code of ethics. Specifically, it must decide:

▶ what is its responsibility to customers?

▶ what is its responsibility to employees?

▶ what is its responsibility to its investors?

▶ what is its responsibility to creditors?

▶ what is its responsibility to the environment and community?

Golden Cruise Lines' responsibility to its customers influences customer loyalty and, therefore, affects the revenue that it generates. Its relationship with employees influences the effort they will exert on various tasks, which can also affect the revenue generated.

All businesses must recognize their responsibilities to their stakeholders and make decisions that reflect these responsibilities. This chapter explains how decisions about ethical and social responsibilities by Golden Cruise Lines or any other firm can be made in a manner that maximizes the firm's value.

Business Ethics and Social Responsibility → Business Decisions → Firm's Earnings → Value of Firm

RATIONALE FOR ETHICAL DECISIONS

Business decisions should be guided by business ethics. Managers or other employees are sometimes tempted to make business decisions that would improve their situation, but at the expense of customers, employees, owners, creditors, or the environment. Such unethical decisions will ultimately give the business a bad reputation and will adversely affect the firm's performance over time.

Several examples of common unethical business decisions are provided in the first column of Exhibit 3.1. Note that each decision results in a benefit to one or more of the employees who made the decision, but has an adverse effect on other stakeholders or on the environment. In every example, the firm's reputation will be damaged. If the customers were adversely affected, they may avoid purchasing products from the firm in the future. If other

Exhibit 3.1

Examples of Unethical Decisions

Unethical Decision	Benefit to:	Adverse Effect on:
1. An employee of a car dealership tries to sell a car at the sticker price to any customers who are not aware that the usual selling price is at least $2,000 less than the sticker price. The employee is paid on commission and will receive a higher income if the customer pays a higher price.	Employee selling the car	Customer
2. An employee of a computer company who is paid on commission attempts to sell a much more expensive computer to a customer than the customer needs.	Employee selling the computer	Customer
3. A manager hires a friend, even though the friend is not the most qualified applicant for the job.	Manager	Other applicants for the job
4. An employee who is the buyer of supplies at a manufacturing plant buys most supplies from a supplier who sends him tickets to the Super Bowl each year. This supplier charges 20 percent more than another supplier. Since the cost of supplies is so high, the firm's earnings are lower.	Employee who is assigned to buy supplies	Other suppliers and the firm's shareholders
5. A manager of a firm attempts to avoid paying some employees for some hours worked so that she can reduce her expenses and possibly earn a higher bonus for keeping expenses low.	Manager	Other employees
6. The president of a firm uses most of this year's earnings to purchase a private jet for the firm. The jet supposedly was obtained for business purposes, but the president uses it to fly to golf outings and other forms of entertainment for himself. Consequently, a smaller amount of dividends is distributed to the shareholders who own the firm.	President	Firm's shareholders
7. An employee of a factory saves himself time by putting several pollutants into the garbage rather than disposing of them properly.	Employee	Environment
8. The manager of a factory decides to close it and build a new factory in her hometown, where she wants to live. Expenses will be higher at the new factory, but the manager will be able to move back to her hometown.	Manager	Community and the firm's shareholders

Exhibit 3.2

Columbia's Stock Price after Overbilling

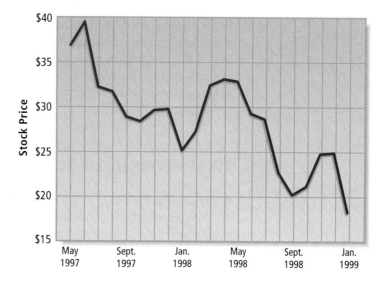

Exhibit 3.3

Sunbeam's Stock Price after It Was
Accused of Overstating Its Earnings

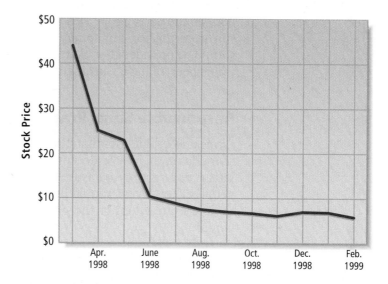

employees were mistreated, the firm may have difficulty hiring employees in the future. If investors or creditors were damaged, the firm may be unable to obtain funding in the future. If the environment was damaged, the firm may be subject to severe penalties imposed by the government.

Impact of Unethical Practices on Firm Value

Unethical business practices can adversely affect a firm's value. As an illustration, consider the case of Columbia Hospital, which was accused of overbilling for its hospital services in 1998. It experienced numerous employee resignations, and its value (as measured by its stock price) declined substantially, as shown in Exhibit 3.2.

As a related example, Sunbeam used unusual accounting practices that appeared to overstate its earnings. In June 1998, it was alleged that Sunbeam's earnings were overstated to enhance the compensation of its high-level managers (their pay was tied to performance). Once the allegations were publicized, many investors who held Sunbeam's stock sold the stock. This caused the stock price to decline substantially, as shown in Exhibit 3.3.

Given the potential damage that can result from unethical behavior, firms should attempt to prevent their employees from making unethical decisions. In general, some form of monitoring may be needed to ensure that a firm's decision makers maintain their responsibilities to their stakeholders and to the environment. This chapter describes these responsibilities and discusses how firms can ensure that the decision makers will uphold them.

1 RESPONSIBILITY TO CUSTOMERS

Describe the responsibilities of firms to their customers.

A firm's responsibility to customers goes beyond the provision of products or services. Firms have a **social responsibility** when producing and selling their products, as discussed next.

social responsibility a firm's recognition of how its business decisions can affect society

Responsible Production Practices

Products should be produced in a way that ensures customer safety. Products should carry proper warning labels to prevent accidents that could result from misuse. For some products, information on possible side effects should be provided. For example, Tylenol gelcaps, Nyquil cough syrup, and Coors beer all have warning labels about possible adverse effects.

Responsible Sales Practices

Firms need guidelines that discourage employees from using overly aggressive sales strategies or deceptive advertising. They may also use customer satisfaction surveys to ensure that customers were treated properly by salespeople. The surveys should be conducted after customers make a purchase to determine whether the product worked as the salesperson said that it would.

labels about toxic plants

to increase profits through sales strategies

give honest advice

Food labeling allows consumers to make informed decisions about the quality and nutritional content of food they purchase. In this way, the FDA regulates food companies' responsibility to their customers.

The Bristol-Myers Squibb Pledge

TO THOSE WHO USE OUR PRODUCTS. . .
We affirm Bristol-Myers Squibb's commitment to the highest standards of excellence, safety and reliability in everything we make. We pledge to offer products of the highest quality and to work diligently to keep improving them.

TO OUR EMPLOYEES AND THOSE WHO MAY JOIN US. . .
We pledge personal respect, fair competition and equal treatment. We acknowledge our obligation to provide able and humane leadership throughout the organization, within a clean and safe working environment. To all who qualify for advancement, we will make every effort to provide opportunity.

TO OUR SUPPLIERS AND CUSTOMERS. . .
We pledge an open door, courteous, efficient and ethical dealing, and appreciation of their right to a fair profit.

TO OUR SHAREHOLDERS. . .
We pledge a companywide dedication to continued profitable growth, sustained by strong finances, a high level of research and development, and facilities second to none.

TO THE COMMUNITIES WHERE WE HAVE PLANTS AND OFFICES. . .
We pledge conscientious citizenship, a helping hand for worthwhile causes, and constructive action in support of civic and environmental progress.

TO THE COUNTRIES WHERE WE DO BUSINESS. . .
We pledge ourselves to be a good citizen and to show full consideration for the rights of others while reserving the right to stand up for our own.

ABOVE ALL, TO THE WORLD WE LIVE IN. . .
We pledge Bristol-Myers Squibb to policies and practices which fully embody the responsibility, integrity and decency required of free enterprise if it is to merit and maintain the confidence of our society.

How Firms Ensure Responsibility toward Customers

A firm can ensure responsibility toward its customers by following these steps:

business responsibilities a set of obligations and duties regarding product quality and treatment of customers, employees, and owners that a firm should fulfill when conducting business

1 *Establish a Code of Responsibilities*   Firms can establish a code of **business responsibilities** that sets guidelines for product quality, as well as guidelines for how employees, customers, and owners should be treated. The pledge (from an annual report) by Bristol-Myers Squibb Company in Exhibit 3.4 is an example of a code of ethics and responsibilities. Many firms distribute a booklet on ethics and responsibilities to all their employees.

The code of responsibilities is not intended to cover every possible action by a firm that would be unfair to customers. Nevertheless, it serves as a guide for the firm to consider when expanding its business. For example, consider a firm that implements a code that emphasizes safety for customers. Whatever the firm may produce in the future, it should always ensure that the products are not harmful. Thus, this code does not force the firm to produce any particular product, but simply ensures that any product will be tested to ensure that it is safe for customers. If another provision of the code is honest communication with customers, then the advertising of all of the firm's products should conform to these guidelines. Although some government laws prohibit blatantly false advertising, this type of provision within a code of ethics and responsibilities would prevent advertising that is deceptive although not blatantly false. To the extent that the code can enhance a firm's image and credibility, it may enhance the firm's value.

2 *Monitor Complaints*   Firms should make sure that customers have a phone number that they can call if they have any complaints about the quality of the product or about how they were treated by employees.

The firm can attempt to determine the source of the complaint and ensure that the problem does not occur again. Many firms have a department that receives complaints and attempts to resolve them. This step may involve assessing different parts of the production process to ensure that the product is produced properly. Or it may require an assessment of particular employees who may be violating the firm's code of responsibilities to its customers.

3 *Obtain and Utilize Customer Feedback*   Firms can ask customers for feedback on the products or services they recently purchased, even if the customers do not call to complain. This process may detect some other problems with the product's quality or with the way customers were treated. For example, automobile dealers such as Saturn send a questionnaire to customers to determine how they were treated by salespeople. Customers may also be asked whether they have any complaints about the automobile they recently purchased. Once the firm is informed of problems with either production defects or customer treatment, it should take action to correct these problems.

Role of Consumerism

consumerism the collective demand by consumers that businesses satisfy their needs

Specific groups of consumers are also calling for firms to fulfill their responsibilities toward customers. **Consumerism** is the collective demand by consumers that businesses satisfy their needs. Consumer groups became popular in the 1960s and have become increasingly effective as they have grown.

Role of the Government

In addition to the codes of responsibility established by firms and the wave of consumerism, the government attempts to ensure that firms fulfill their responsibility to customers through various laws on product safety, advertising, and industry competition.

Government Regulation of Product Safety   The government protects consumers by regulating the quality of some products produced by firms. For example, the Food and Drug Administration (FDA) is responsible for testing food products to determine whether they meet specific requirements. The FDA also examines new drugs that firms have recently developed. Because potential side effects may not be known immediately, the FDA tests some drugs continually over several years.

Government Regulation of Advertising   The federal government has also established laws against deceptive advertising. Nevertheless, it may not be able to prevent all unethical business practices. Numerous examples of advertising could be called deceptive. It is difficult to know if a product is "new and improved." In addition, a term such as "lowest price" may have different meanings or interpretations.

Government Regulation of Industry Competition   Another way the government ensures that consumers are treated properly is to promote competition in most industries. Competition between firms is beneficial to consumers, because firms that charge excessive prices or produce goods of unacceptable quality will not survive in a competitive environ-

Exhibit 3.5

Key Antitrust Laws

▶ **Sherman Antitrust Act (1890)** Encouraged competition and prevented monopolies.
▶ **Clayton Act (1914)** Reinforced the rules of the Sherman Antitrust Act and specifically prohibited the following activities because they reduced competition:
  ▶ *Tying agreements* Forced firms to purchase additional products as a condition of purchasing the desired products.
  ▶ *Binding contracts* Prevented firms from purchasing products from a supplier's competitors.
  ▶ *Interlocking directorates* The situation in which the same person serves on the board of directors of two competing firms.
▶ **Federal Trade Commission Act (1914)** Prohibited unfair methods of competition; also called for the establishment of the Federal Trade Commission (FTC) to enforce antitrust laws.
▶ **Robinson-Patman Act (1936)** Prohibited price policies or promotional allowances that reduce competition within an industry.
▶ **Celler-Kefauver Act (1950)** Prohibited mergers between firms that reduce competition within an industry.

ment. Because of competition, consumers can avoid a firm that is using deceptive sales tactics.

monopoly a firm that is the sole provider of goods or services

A firm has a **monopoly** if it is the sole provider of goods or services. It can set prices without concern about competition. However, the government regulates firms that have a monopoly. For example, it regulates utility firms that have monopolies in specific locations and can control the pricing policies of these firms.

In some industries, firms negotiated various agreements to set prices and avoid competing with each other. The federal government has attempted to prevent such activity by enforcing antitrust laws. Some of the more well-known antitrust acts are summarized in Exhibit 3.5. All of these acts share the objective of promoting competition, with each act focusing on particular aspects that can influence the degree of competition within an industry.

The trucking, railroad, airline, and telecommunications industries have been deregulated, allowing more firms to enter each industry. In addition, banks and other financial institutions have been deregulated since 1980 and now have more flexibility on the types of deposits and interest rates they can offer. They also have more freedom to expand across state lines. In general, deregulation results in lower prices for consumers.

2

Describe the responsibilities of firms to their employees.

RESPONSIBILITY TO EMPLOYEES

Firms also have a responsibility to their employees to ensure their safety, proper treatment by other employees, and equal opportunity.

Employee Safety

Firms ensure that the workplace is safe for employees by closely monitoring the production process. Some obvious safety precautions are to check machinery and equipment for proper working conditions, require safety glasses or any other equipment that can prevent injury, and emphasize any special safety precautions in training seminars.

Firms that create a safe working environment prevent injuries and improve the morale of their employees. Many firms now identify workplace safety as one of their main goals. Dow Chemical Company has developed a pledge of no accidents and no injuries to its employees. Levi Strauss

Companies have a responsibility to ensure safe working conditions for their employees. Safety concerns will affect company policies, practices and expenditures.

© CORBIS

& Company imposes safety guidelines not only on its U.S. facilities but also on Asian factories where some of its clothes are made. Starbucks Coffee Company has developed a code of conduct in an attempt to improve the quality of life in coffee-producing countries.

Owners of a firm recognize that the firm will incur costs in meeting responsibilities such as employee safety. The firm's efforts to provide a safe working environment represent a necessary cost of doing business.

Proper Treatment by Other Employees

Firms are responsible for ensuring that employees are treated properly by other employees. Two key issues concerning the treatment of employees are diversity and the prevention of sexual harassment, which are discussed next.

Diversity In recent years, the workforce has become much more diverse. More women have entered the job market, and more minorities now have the necessary skills and education to qualify for high-level jobs. Exhibit 3.6 shows the proportions of various job categories held by women, African Americans, and Hispanics.

Many firms have responded to the increased diversity among employees by offering diversity seminars, which inform employees about cultural diversity. Such information can help employees recognize that certain statements or behavior may be offensive to other employees.

The following statement from a recent annual report of General Motors reflects the efforts that have been made by many firms to encourage diversity:

"Internally, we are working to create an environment where diversity thrives. We are trying to remove barriers that separate people and find new ways to engage teams to maximize productivity and profitability. This is being done through communication, teamwork, mutual support, and pulling together to achieve common objectives. Our challenge is to seek a diverse population in leadership roles with a wide range of backgrounds, views, and experiences to ensure we capture diverse perspectives to meet and exceed customer expectations."

Johnson & Johnson, The Coca-Cola Company, IBM, Merrill Lynch, Sara Lee Corporation, and many other firms have made major efforts to promote

Exhibit 3.6

Proportion of Women and Minorities in Various Occupations

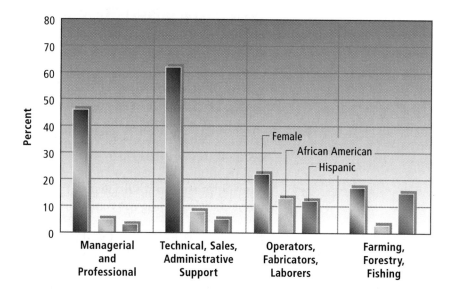

diversity. Rockwell International has a diversity task team that developed guidelines for workforce diversity planning in each of its businesses. Xerox has improved its workplace diversity in recent years.

sexual harassment unwelcome comments or actions of a sexual nature

Prevention of Sexual Harassment   Another workplace issue is **sexual harassment,** which involves unwelcome comments or actions of a sexual nature. For example, one employee might make unwelcome sexual advances toward another and use personal power within the firm to threaten the other employee's job status. Firms attempt to prevent sexual harassment by offering seminars on the subject. Like diversity seminars, these seminars can help employees recognize that some statements or behavior may be offensive to other employees. These seminars are not only an act of responsibility to employees but also can improve a firm's productivity by helping employees get along.

Equal Opportunity

Employees who apply for a position at a firm should not be subjected to discrimination because of their national origin, race, gender, or religion. The Civil Rights Act of 1964 prohibits such forms of discrimination. The act is enforced by a federal agency known as the Equal Employment Opportunity Commission (EEOC). Beyond the federal guidelines, many firms attempt to ensure equal treatment among applicants for a position by assigning someone to monitor the hiring process. The concept of equal treatment applies not only to the initial hiring of an employee but also to annual raises and promotions within the firm.

affirmative action a set of activities intended to increase opportunities for minorities and women

Many firms and government agencies implement **affirmative action** programs. Some people expect affirmative action programs to ensure equal treatment among prospective and existing employees. Other people expect these programs to establish quotas, which would designate specific positions for minorities or women. Most people would agree that affirmative action programs have good intentions, but quotas may be viewed as a form of reverse discrimination.

Denny's (a restaurant business) was charged with racial discrimination in 1993. That same year, it began implementing a program to promote diversity. In recent years, Denny's has increased both its minority management and the number of franchises owned by African Americans.

How Firms Ensure Responsibility toward Employees

Firms can ensure that their responsibility toward employees will be fulfilled by taking the following steps.

Code of Responsibility   A firm's responsibility toward its employees should be disclosed in its code of responsibilities. As with the responsibilities toward customers, the code will not attempt to spell out the recommended behavior in every situation, but it can offer some guidance for the decisions made by the firm. For example, the code may state that hiring decisions should be made without any form of bias. The firm should establish a hiring procedure that satisfies this provision. The procedure may specify that an ad describing the main duties of the job position be placed in the local newspaper for two weeks before anyone is hired. Doing this will help to ensure that the most qualified person is hired for the job. Thus, the procedure is implemented in a manner that is consistent with the firm's responsibility of hiring without any form of bias.

Grievance Policy   To ensure that employees receive proper treatment, many firms establish a grievance policy for employees who believe they are not being given equal opportunity. A specific person or department is normally assigned to resolve such complaints. This procedure is similar to that used to address customer complaints. By recognizing the complaints, the firm attempts both to resolve them and to revise its procedures to prevent further complaints.

A good example of a firm that has made an effort to resolve employee complaints is Marriott, which has implemented three strategies. First, it has set up a mediation process, in which a neutral person outside the firm (called a mediator) assesses the employee complaint and suggests a solution. The mediator does not have the power to enforce a final judgment but may help the employee and the firm resolve the conflict.

Second, Marriott offers a toll-free number for employees to call if they believe they were subjected to discrimination, harassment, or improper firing. Marriott begins to investigate the complaint within three days of the call. Third, Marriott allows the employee to voice complaints in front of a panel of other employees who determine whether the employee's complaints are valid, based on Marriott's existing guidelines.

Marriott's procedure for resolving employee complaints has shown positive results. EEOC investigations of employee complaints against Marriott declined by 50 percent in the year after the procedure was implemented and by 83 percent in the next year. Since more employee complaints are resolved within the firm, employees are more satisfied with their jobs and focus on satisfying customers.

The cost of attempting to listen to every employee complaint can be substantial for a firm, however. Furthermore, some of the complaints may not be valid. Firms must attempt to distinguish between complaints that are valid and those that are not and then focus on resolving the valid complaints.

Conflict with Employee Layoffs

Some business decisions are controversial because although they improve the firm's performance, they may adversely affect employees and the local community. Consider the following example, which reflects a common

Global Ethics U.S. firms typically have a code of ethics that provides guidelines for their employees. However, these guidelines may be much more restrictive than those generally used in some foreign countries. Consider a U.S. firm that sells supplies to foreign manufacturers. The employees of this firm may be subject to rules that prevent them from offering payoffs ("kickbacks") to any employees of the manufacturing companies that order the firm's supplies. Competitors based in other countries, however, may offer payoffs to employees of the manufacturing companies. In some countries, this type of behavior is acceptable. Thus, the U.S. supplier is at a disadvantage because its employees are required to follow a stricter code of ethics. This is a common ethical dilemma that U.S. firms face in a global environment. The employees of U.S. firms must either ignore their ethical guidelines or be at a disadvantage in certain foreign countries.

Another ethical dilemma that U.S. firms may face involves their relationship with certain foreign governments. Firms that conduct business in foreign countries are subject to numerous rules imposed by the local government. Officials of some foreign governments commonly accept bribes from firms that need approval for various business activities. For example, a firm may need to have its products approved for safety purposes, or its local manufacturing plant may need to be approved for environmental purposes. The process of approving even minor activities could take months and prevent the firm from conducting business. Those firms that pay off government officials may receive prompt attention from the local governments. Employees of Lockheed Martin were charged with bribing Egyptian government officials to win a contract to build new aircraft. Executives of IBM's Argentina subsidiary were charged with bribing Argentine government officials to generate business from the government.

A recent assessment of foreign countries by the U.S. Commerce Department and intelligence agencies detected numerous deals in which foreign firms used bribes to win business contracts over U.S. competitors. Many of these foreign firms are located in France, Germany, and Japan, as well as in some less-developed countries.

Many U.S. firms attempt to follow a worldwide code of ethics that is consistent across countries. This type of policy reduces the confusion that could result from using different ethical standards in different countries. Although a worldwide code of ethics may place a U.S. firm at a disadvantage in some countries, it may also enhance the firm's credibility.

---

dilemma that many firms face. As your firm's business grew, you hired more employees. Unfortunately, demand for your product has declined recently, and you no longer need 20 of the employees that you hired over the last two years. If you lay off 20 employees, you will reduce your expenses substantially and satisfy your stockholders. However, you may be criticized for not serving employees' interests. This situation is unpleasant because the layoffs may be necessary (to cut expenses) for your firm to survive. If your firm fails, all your other employees will be out of work as well.

This dilemma has no perfect solution. Many firms may do what's best for the business, while attempting to reduce the adverse effects on their employees. For example, they may help laid-off employees find employment elsewhere or may even attempt to retrain them for other jobs within the firm.

Describe the responsibilities of firms to their stockholders and creditors.

RESPONSIBILITY TO STOCKHOLDERS

Firms are responsible for satisfying their owners (or stockholders). Employees may be tempted to make decisions that satisfy their own interests rather than those of the owners. For example, some employees may use the firm's money to purchase computers for their personal use rather than for the firm.

How Firms Ensure Responsibility

Managers of a firm monitor employee decisions to ensure that they are made in the best interests of the owners. Employee compensation may be directly tied to the firm's performance. For example, a firm may provide its top managers with some of the firm's stock as partial compensation. If the managers make decisions that lead to a high level of performance, the value of the firm's stock should increase, and therefore the value of the stock held by the managers should increase. In this way, employees benefit directly when they make decisions that maximize the value of the firm.

Conflicts in the Efforts to Ensure Responsibility

Tying employee compensation to the firm's performance can resolve some conflicts of interest, but create others. Some top managers who have received stock have later reported an artificially high performance level for the firm in a period when they wanted to sell their stock holdings. This allowed them to sell their stock at a relatively high price. Rather than improving the firm's performance, these managers manipulated the financial reporting to exaggerate the firm's performance. When investors decide whether to buy stock, they commonly rely on information disclosed by the firm to determine whether its stock would be a good investment.

There are many cases in which a firm has misled its existing and prospective investors by neglecting to mention relevant information that would have made its stock less desirable. In addition, there are many cases in which a firm has exaggerated its estimates of its revenue or earnings. When a firm misleads investors by creating an overly optimistic view of its potential performance, it can cause investors to pay too much for the stock. The stock's price will likely decline once the firm's true financial condition becomes apparent.

In January 2001, the chief executive officer (CEO) of Oracle Corporation sold 29 million shares of his holdings of Oracle stock. During the next few months, the firm disclosed that its earnings for the first quarter of 2001 would be lower than expected, and the stock price declined in response. Oracle's stockholders alleged that the CEO knew this information and sold his stock holdings before disclosing the bad news. That is, the investors who purchased the shares that were sold by the CEO claimed that they paid a much higher price than they should have paid for the stock and consequently incurred large losses on their investment.

One of the most blatant examples of a firm's managers misleading its existing and prospective stockholders is the case of Enron, Inc. Enron was one of the fastest-growing firms in the 1990s. Nevertheless, it created misleading financial statements, which led investors to believe that it was performing better than it really was. Consequently, some investors were fooled into paying much more for the stock than they should have during the 1999–2000 period. While Enron was creating such an optimistic view of its financial condition, some of its top managers were selling their holdings of Enron stock. Thus, they were dumping their shares while the price was high—before investors recognized that Enron's financial condition was much weaker than reported. While Enron's top managers earned large gains on their stock holdings, the investors who purchased Enron stock at this time lost most or all of their investment. In November 2001, Enron filed for bankruptcy, and the stock essentially became worthless. Thus, the top managers of Enron who were able to sell their stock at a high price (before bad news was disclosed) benefited at the expense of other stockholders.

Former Enron executives Jeffrey Skilling (center), Sherron Watkin, and Jeffrey McMahon are sworn in prior to testifying before the Senate Commerce Committee's hearing on Enron. The Enron scandal represents a total departure from any code of ethics and responsibility toward the company's former stockholders and employees.

AP Photo/ Ron Edmonds

In 2002, executives at other firms, including Global Crossing and Im-Clone, were accused of attempting to sell their holdings of their firm's stock before disclosing unfavorable information about the firm to the public. The initial intent of tying employee compensation to the firm's value was to ensure that employees would serve the interests of stockholders, but the practice has enabled some managers to benefit at the expense of stockholders. In June 2002, WorldCom admitted that it had overstated earnings by $3.8 billion in the previous five quarters. Some of WorldCom's top managers received much higher compensation as a result of the overstated earnings.

Investors have become much more suspicious of the financial reports provided by firms now that they are aware of the unethical reporting by some firms. Some firms have taken the initiative to reduce suspicion by providing more complete financial statements that are also more understandable and more readily interpreted.

How Stockholders Ensure Responsibility

shareholder activism active efforts by stockholders to influence a firm's management policies

In recent years, there has been much **shareholder activism,** or active efforts by stockholders to influence a firm's management policies. Stockholders have been especially active when they are dissatisfied with the firm's executive salaries or other policies.

institutional investors financial institutions that purchase large amounts of stock

The stockholders who have been most active are **institutional investors,** or financial institutions that purchase large amounts of stock. For example, insurance companies invest a large portion of the insurance premiums that they receive in stocks. If institutional investors invest a large amount of money in a particular stock, the return on their investment is highly dependent on how that firm performs. Since many institutional investors commonly invest $10 million or more in a single firm's stock, they pay close attention to the performance of any firm in which they invest.

If an institutional investor believes the firm is poorly managed, it may attempt to meet with the firm's executives and express its dissatisfaction. It may even attempt to team up with other institutional investors who also own a large proportion of the firm's stock. This gives them more negotiating power because the firm's executives are more likely to listen to institutional investors who collectively hold a large proportion of the firm's stock.

Exhibit 3.7

Impact of Executive Salaries on a Firm's Performance

	Firm C	Firm D
Revenue	$200,000,000	$200,000,000
−Expenses (except executive salaries)	−150,000,000	−150,000,000
−Executive salaries expense	−30,000,000	−5,000,000
=Profits	=$20,000,000	=$45,000,000

The institutional investors do not attempt to dictate how the firm should be managed. Instead, they attempt to ensure that the firm's managers make decisions that are in the best interests of all stockholders.

Conflict with Excessive Executive Compensation

A firm's managers can attempt to satisfy its stockholders by ensuring that funds invested by the stockholders are put to good use. If these funds are used to cover unnecessary expenses, the firm's profits are reduced, which reduces the return that stockholders receive on their investment. A major concern of stockholders is the salaries paid to the firm's CEO and other executives. The following example illustrates the potential effect that excessive executive salaries can have on a firm's performance (and therefore on the returns to stockholders).

Consider two firms called Firm C and Firm D, which are in the same industry and have similar revenue and expenses, as shown in Exhibit 3.7. Assume that the only difference is that Firm C pays its top five executives a total of $30 million in annual salary, while Firm D pays its top five executives a total of $5 million. As shown in Exhibit 3.7, the annual profits of Firm D are $25 million higher than those of Firm C. This difference can be attributed to Firm C's higher executive salary expenses. Thus, the stockholders of Firm C receive a smaller return than the stockholders of Firm D.

CEO compensation has increased substantially over recent decades. In 1980, the average compensation of CEOs was about 42 times the average compensation of employees. In 1990, it was about 85 times the average salary of employees. In 2000, it was more than 500 times the average salary of employees.

Some customers and stockholders may argue that firms paying executives such high salaries are not meeting their social responsibilities. These firms may be serving the interests of the executives and not the stockholders who own the firm. Although it may be possible to justify very high compensation for CEOs who have been successful, it is difficult to justify such compensation for CEOs whose companies have performed poorly. In 2001, the compensation of many CEOs increased even though the earnings or stock price of their firm declined. The compensation paid to CEOs is partially influenced by the size of the firm. CEOs of larger firms tend to earn higher salaries, even when their firm performs poorly.

RESPONSIBILITY TO CREDITORS

Firms are responsible for meeting their financial obligations to their creditors. If a firm is experiencing financial problems and is unable to meet its obligations, it should inform its creditors. Sometimes creditors are willing to

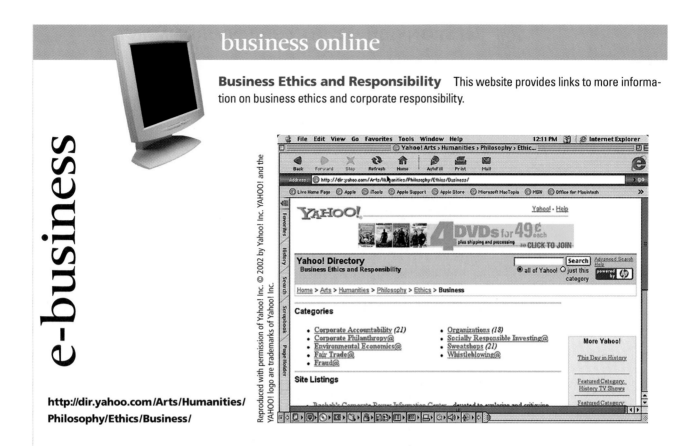

business online

Business Ethics and Responsibility This website provides links to more information on business ethics and corporate responsibility.

e-business

http://dir.yahoo.com/Arts/Humanities/
Philosophy/Ethics/Business/

extend payment deadlines and may even offer advice on how the firm can improve its financial condition. A firm has a strong incentive to satisfy its responsibility to creditors. If the firm does not pay what it owes to creditors, it may be forced into bankruptcy.

How Firms Violate Their Responsibility

Some firms violate their responsibility to creditors by providing misleading financial information that exaggerates their financial condition. For example, Enron's financial reporting misled its creditors as well as its stockholders. Enron received some loans from creditors that it would not have received if the creditors had known of its weaknesses. Specifically, Enron did not disclose some of its debt. Creditors would have been concerned about extending more credit if they had fully understood how much debt Enron already had. By hiding some debt, Enron was able to more easily borrow funds. Then, in November 2001, it went bankrupt because it could not cover the payments on all of its debt. Many creditors lost hundreds of millions of dollars because of the large amount of credit they provided to Enron that would never be paid back. Although creditors recognize the possible risk that a business will fail and be unable to repay its loans, they were angry that Enron used unethical financial reporting methods to obtain loans. While some firms have received bad publicity for distorting their financial condition, others have taken the initiative to give creditors more detailed and clear financial information.

Describe the responsibilities of firms to the environment.

RESPONSIBILITY TO THE ENVIRONMENT

The production processes that firms use, as well as the products they produce, can be harmful to the environment. The most common abuses to the environment are discussed next, along with recent actions that firms have taken to improve the environment.

Air Pollution

Some production processes cause air pollution, which is harmful to society because it inhibits breathing. For example, the production of fuel and steel, as well as automobile use, increases the amount of carbon dioxide in the air.

How Firms Prevent Air Pollution   Automobile and steel firms have reduced air pollution by changing their production processes so that less carbon dioxide escapes into the air. For example, firms such as Honeywell and Inland Steel spend substantial funds to reduce pollution. Ford Motor Company has formulated an environmental pledge, which states that it is dedicated to developing environmental solutions and intends to preserve the environment in the future.

How the Government Prevents Air Pollution   The federal government has also become involved by enforcing specific guidelines that call for firms to limit the amount of carbon dioxide caused by the production process. In 1970, the Environmental Protection Agency (EPA) was created to develop and enforce pollution standards. In recent years, pollution control laws have become more stringent.

The response of oil companies to disastrous spills is well publicized and serves as an indicator of these companies' sense of responsibility to society and the environment.

© Getty Images / Photo Disc

Land Pollution

Land has been polluted by toxic waste resulting from some production processes. A related form of land pollution is solid waste, which does not deteriorate over time. As a result of waste, land not only looks less attractive but also may no longer be useful for other purposes, such as farming.

How Firms Prevent Land Pollution   Firms have revised their production and packaging processes to reduce the amount of waste. They now store toxic waste and deliver it to specified toxic waste storage sites. They also recycle plastic and limit their use of materials that would ultimately

Exhibit 3.8

Monsanto's Stock Price after Receiving Bad Publicity about Its Effects on the Environment

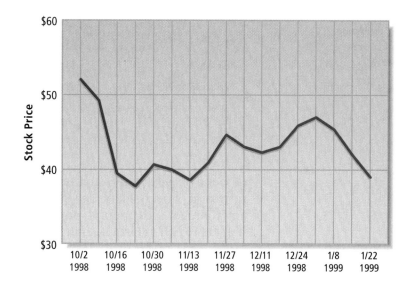

become solid waste. Many firms have environmental programs that are designed to reduce damage to the environment. For example, Homestake Mining Company recognizes that its mining operations disturb the land, so it spends money to minimize any effect on the environment. PPG Industries restructured its production processes to generate about 6,000 fewer tons of waste in a single year. Kodak recycles more than a half-billion pounds of material a year and also supports a World Wildlife Fund environmental education program. IBM typically spends more than $30 million a year for environmental assessments and cleanup. ChevronTexaco and DuPont spend hundreds of millions of dollars every year to comply with environmental regulations. Rockwell International has reduced its hazardous waste by more than 50 percent in recent years.

As an example of how a lack of responsibility can adversely affect a firm's value, consider the case of Monsanto. In 1998, when Monsanto received bad publicity about the damaging effects of its operations on the environment, many investors sold their holdings of Monsanto stock. Consequently, Monsanto's value (as measured by its stock price) declined as shown in Exhibit 3.8.

Conflict with Environmental Responsibility

Although most firms agree that a clean environment is desirable, they may disagree on how much responsibility they have for improving the environment. Consider two firms called Firm A and Firm B, which have similar revenue and expenses. Firm A, however, makes a much greater effort to clean up the environment; it spends $10 million, while Firm B spends $2 million. The profit of each firm is shown in Exhibit 3.9. Firm A has an annual profit of zero, while Firm B has an annual profit of $8 million. If you could invest in the stock of either Firm A or Firm B, where would you invest your money? Most investors desire to earn a high return on their money. Although they recognize that a firm may have some environmental cleanup expenses, they do not want those expenses to be excessive. Therefore, most investors would prefer to invest in Firm B rather than Firm A.

Firm A could attempt to recapture its high environmental cleanup expenses by charging a higher price for its product. In this way, it may be able

Exhibit 3.9

Effect of Environmental
Expenses on Business
Performance

	Firm A	Firm B
Revenue	$90,000,000	$90,000,000
Total operating expenses	−80,000,000	−80,000,000
Environmental cleanup expenses	−10,000,000	−2,000,000
Profit	0	$8,000,000

to spend heavily on the environment, while still generating a reasonable return for its stockholders. This strategy makes the customers pay for its extra environmental cleanup. A problem, however, is that if Firm A charges a higher price than Firm B, many customers will switch to Firm B so that they can pay the lower price.

As this example illustrates, there is a limit to how much firms can spend on improving the environment. Firms have a responsibility to avoid damaging the environment, but if they spend excessively on environmental improvement, they will not satisfy most of their customers or owners.

Although firms have increased their efforts to clean up the environment, they do not necessarily agree with the guidelines imposed by the government. Oil refineries that are losing money remain open to avoid the cleanup that the EPA would require if they closed down. Some refineries would pay about $1 billion for cleanup costs because of the EPA's strict guidelines. Firms have questioned many other environmental guidelines imposed by the EPA.

 RESPONSIBILITY TO THE COMMUNITY

Describe the responsibilities of firms to their communities.

When firms establish a base in a community, they become part of that community and rely on it for customers and employees. Firms demonstrate their concern for the community by sponsoring local events or donating to local charities. For example, SunTrust Bank, IBM, and many other firms have donated funds to universities. Bank of America has provided loans to low-income neighborhoods and minority communities.

Conflict with Maximizing Social Responsibility

The decisions of a firm's managers that maximize social responsibility could conflict with maximizing firm value. The costs involved in achieving such a goal will have to be passed on to consumers. Thus, the attempt to maximize responsibility to the community may reduce the firm's ability to provide products at a reasonable price to consumers.

Many companies support charitable organizations that promote nutrition, education, performing and visual arts, or amateur athletics. Even though this social support requires a considerable financial commitment, the firm can gain from an enhanced image in the eyes of the consumers to whom it sells its products. In a sense, the charitable support not only can help society but also can be a valuable marketing tool to improve the firm's image. Consequently, both society and stockholders can benefit from the charitable donations. If a company identifies a charitable cause that is closely related to its business, it may be able to simultaneously contribute to

increasing value with technology

ETHICAL MISCONDUCT

Information technology has greatly increased the potential for ethical misconduct in a variety of areas. Recent studies indicate that many employees believe that playing computer games, pirating company software for personal use, and sending personal e-mail are not unethical.

The integration of company systems allows more employees to have access to confidential books and records. A well-publicized breach of ethics was disclosed when the Internal Revenue Service revealed that celebrity returns had been accessed unnecessarily by a number of employees. In another incident, an employee of Texas Instruments provided information to an investor chat line on the Internet. The employee did not realize that the information was private company information and that disclosing it may have violated regulations of the Securities and Exchange Commission.

Another area of concern is the protection of company information. According to a recent survey by the American Society for Industrial Security, U.S. companies lose about $250 billion annually due to theft of intellectual property. In the past, companies were primarily concerned about protecting product formulas. Now, marketing strategies and business strategies must also be protected.

A number of methods have been developed to combat ethics violations. Some are as simple as establishing a written policy regarding the appropriate use of e-mail, copying software, and accessing data. More complex methods must be used to guard against the theft of intellectual property. Computer security procedures must be developed and continually examined to protect against theft of information.

society and maximize the firm's value. For example, a running shoe manufacturer may sponsor a race, or a tennis racket manufacturer may sponsor a tennis tournament.

Apple and IBM invest substantial funds in local education programs. Not only is this investment helpful to the communities but it also results in computer sales to schools. Home Depot donates to community programs that use much of the money for housing projects. Many Checkers restaurants have been located in inner-city areas. They not only provide jobs to many minorities but also have been profitable.

One of the best examples of a firm that has demonstrated its social responsibility in a manner that has also enhanced its performance is The Coca-Cola Company. It initiated a 10-year, $60 million sponsorship of Boys & Girls Clubs of America—the largest amount of funds donated by a firm to a specific cause. The sponsorship involves several events, such as basketball and golf tournaments, and after-school reading sessions. Coca-Cola's name will be promoted at the events, which can help attract new young customers to its products.

As another illustration of how a firm may benefit from its attention to its social responsibilities, consider the case of Nike. During 1998, Nike was criticized for poor working conditions in its manufacturing plants in Asia. In 1999, Nike hired a former executive of Microsoft to help increase its concern for its social responsibilities. This created a more favorable public perception of Nike. Home Depot has demonstrated a responsibility toward its communities that has increased its name recognition. In particular, it responded to the September 11 destruction of the World Trade Center by providing supplies and equipment to the rescue effort. Ace Hardware has established a foundation that has given more than $20 million to the communities that it serves. During the September 11 crisis, it donated three tractor-trailer loads of tools and equipment that could be used by relief workers to clean up the damage.

As an example of community and social responsibility, the M&M/Mars candy company recently sold red, white and blue M&Ms with the profits donated to the American Red Cross Disaster Relief Fund.

Photo by M&M/Mars/Getty Images

Dow Chemical Company has created a Community Advisory Panel, which identifies community needs and ensures that Dow gives to its communities. Its recent community acts include funding education programs in South America where it conducts some of its business, supporting a Habitat for Humanity homebuilding project in Korea, and funding a new art center in West Virginia.

SUMMARY OF BUSINESS RESPONSIBILITIES

Firms have many responsibilities to customers, employees, the environment, the community, stockholders, and creditors that must be recognized when doing business. The general concern of firms about ethics and social responsibility can be illustrated with the following quotations from recent annual reports:

"A comprehensive annual ethics training program heightens the awareness of our employees and provides guidelines to resolve issues responsibly."

—Rockwell International

"Boise Cascade is committed to protecting the health and safety of our employees, being a responsible corporate citizen in the communities in which we operate, and providing active stewardship of the timberlands under our management."

—Boise Cascade

"We . . . believe that to create long term value for shareholders, we must also create value in our relationships with customers, employees, suppliers and the communities in which we operate."

—Briggs & Stratton

Most firms have procedures in place to ensure that their social responsibilities are satisfied. They also enforce codes that specify their responsibilities. Prudential Securities has created a position called "Corporate Values

self-scoring exercise

Assessing the Ethical Standards of the Firm Where You Work

Think about the organization you currently work for or one you know something about and complete the following Ethical Climate Questionnaire. Use the scale below and write the number that best represents your answer in the space next to each item.

To what extent are the following statements true about your company?

Completely false	Mostly false	Somewhat false	Somewhat true	Mostly true	Completely true
0	1	2	3	4	5

_____ 1. In this company, people are expected to follow their own personal and moral beliefs.

_____ 2. People are expected to do anything to further the company's interests.

_____ 3. In this company, people look out for each other's good.

_____ 4. It is very important to follow the company's rules and procedures strictly.

_____ 5. In this company, people protect their own interests above other considerations.

_____ 6. The first consideration is whether a decision violates any law.

_____ 7. Everyone is expected to stick by company rules and procedures.

_____ 8. The most efficient way is always the right way in this company.

_____ 9. Our major consideration is what is best for everyone in the company.

_____ 10. In this company, the law or ethical code of the profession is the major consideration.

_____ 11. It is expected at this company that employees will always do what is right for the consumer and the public.

To score the questionnaire, first add up your responses to questions 1, 3, 6, 9, 10, and 11. This is subtotal number 1. Next, reverse the scores on questions 2, 4, 5, 7, and 8 (5 = 0, 4 = 1, 3 = 2, 2 = 3, 1 = 4, 0 = 5). Add the reverse scores to form subtotal number 2. Add subtotal number 1 to subtotal number 2 for an overall score.

Subtotal 1 _____ + Subtotal 2 _____ = Overall Score _____ .

Overall scores can range from 0 to 55. The higher the score, the more the organization's culture encourages ethical behavior.

Officer" to ensure that its social responsibilities are fulfilled.

Some firms may make more of an effort to follow ethical standards than others. The first Self-Scoring Exercise allows you to assess the ethical standards of the firm where you work. Employees may vary in their perception of what behavior is ethical. The second Self-Scoring Exercise provides a variety of situations that would probably be perceived as unethical by some people but as acceptable by others.

Business Responsibilities in an International Environment

When firms compete in an international environment, they must be aware of cultural differences. Firms from some countries do not necessarily view certain business practices such as payoffs to large customers or to suppliers as unethical. This makes it difficult for other firms to compete for international business. Nevertheless, firms typically attempt to apply their ethical guidelines and corporate responsibilities in an international setting. By doing so, they establish a global reputation for running their business in an ethical manner.

6

Explain the costs that firms incur in fulfilling their social responsibilities.

THE COST OF FULFILLING SOCIAL RESPONSIBILITIES

A summary of possible expenses incurred as a result of social responsibilities is provided in Exhibit 3.10. Some firms incur large expenses in all areas of social responsibility. For example, automobile manufacturers such as Ford Motor Company and General Motors must ensure that their production of automobiles does not harm the environment. Second, they must ensure that all employees in their massive workforces are treated properly. Third, they must ensure that they deliver a safe and reliable product to their customers.

In recent years, many new government regulations have been imposed to create a cleaner environment and ensure that firms do not neglect other

self-scoring exercise

Assessing Whether Specific Situations Are Ethical

The purpose of this exercise is to explore your opinions about ethical issues faced in organizations. The class should be divided into 12 groups. Each group will randomly be assigned one of the following issues:

1. Is it ethical to take office supplies from work for home use? Make personal long-distance calls from the office? Use company time for personal business? Or do these behaviors constitute stealing?

2. If you exaggerate your credentials in an interview, is it lying? Is lying to protect a co-worker acceptable?

3. If you pretend to be more successful than you are to impress your boss, are you being deceitful?

4. How do you differentiate between a bribe and a gift?

5. If there are slight defects in a product you are selling, are you obligated to tell the buyer? If an advertised "sale" price is really the everyday price, should you divulge the information to the customer?

6. Suppose you have a friend who works at the ticket office for the convention center where Shania Twain will be appearing. Is it cheating if you ask the friend to get you tickets so that you won't have to fight the crowd to get them? Is buying merchandise for your family at your company's cost cheating?

7. Is it immoral to do less than your best in work performance? Is it immoral to accept workers' compensation when you are fully capable of working?

8. What behaviors constitute emotional abuse at work? What would you consider an abuse of one's position of power?

9. Are high-stress jobs a breach of ethics? What about transfers that break up families?

10. Are all rule violations equally important? Do employees have an ethical obligation to follow company rules?

11. To what extent are you responsible for the ethical behavior of your co-workers? If you witness unethical behavior and don't report it, are you an accessory?

12. Is it ethical to help one work group at the expense of another group? For instance, suppose one group has excellent performance and you want to reward its members with an afternoon off. The other work group will have to pick up the slack and work harder if you do this. Is this ethical?

Once your group has been assigned its issue, you have two tasks:

1. First, formulate your group's answer to the ethical dilemmas.

2. After you have formulated your group's position, discuss the individual differences that may have contributed to your position. You will want to discuss the individual differences presented in this chapter as well as any others that you believe affected your position on the ethical dilemma.

Your instructor will lead the class in a discussion of how individual differences may have influenced your positions on these ethical dilemmas.

social responsibilities. Normally, all the firms in an industry will raise their prices to cover the expenses associated with following new government regulations. For example, restrictions on cutting down trees resulted in higher expenses for paper companies. These companies raised their prices to cover these higher expenses. Maintaining social responsibilities is necessary but costly, and customers indirectly pay the expenses incurred.

Cost of Lawsuits

When assessing the expense involved in dealing with customer or employee complaints, firms normally consider the cost of hiring people to resolve the complaints. However, they must also consider the cost of defending against possible lawsuits by customers and employees. Customers suing firms for product defects or deceptive advertising and employees suing their firms for discrimination are common practices today.

A number of expenses can be associated with a lawsuit. First, the court may fine a firm that is found guilty. Some court-imposed fines have amounted to several million dollars. Second, some lawsuits are settled out-of-court, but the settlement may require the firm to make some payment to customers or employees. Third, a firm may incur substantial expenses when hiring an attorney. Many lawsuits continue for several years, and the expenses of the attorney (or a law firm) for a single case may exceed $1 million. Fourth, an indirect cost of a lawsuit is the decline in demand for a firm's product because of bad publicity associated with the lawsuit. This results in less revenue to the firm. Even when firms establish and enforce a comprehensive code of social responsibility, they do not necessarily avoid lawsuits. They must recognize this when estimating the expenses involved in social responsibility. Consider the situation in June 1993, when the media announced that some customers had found syringes in their Pepsi cans.

Exhibit 3.10

Possible Expenses Incurred as a Result
of Social Responsibilities

Responsibility to:	Expenses Incurred as a Result of:
Customers	Establishing program to receive and resolve complaints Conducting surveys to assess customer satisfaction Lawsuits by customers (product liability)
Employees	Establishing program to receive and resolve complaints Conducting surveys to assess employee satisfaction Lawsuits by employees based on allegations of discrimination
Stockholders	Disclosing financial information periodically Lawsuits by stockholders based on allegations that the firm's managers are not fulfilling their obligations to stockholders
Environment	Complying with governmental regulations on environment Complying with self-imposed environmental guidelines
Community	Sponsoring community activities

cross functional teamwork:

Ethical Responsibilities across Business Functions

The perception of a firm's ethical standards is dependent on its team of managers. The ethical responsibilities of a firm's managers vary with their specific job assignments. Production managers are responsible for producing a product that is safe. They should also ensure that the production process satisfies environmental standards.

Marketing managers are responsible for marketing a product in a manner that neither misrepresents the product's characteristics nor misleads consumers or investors. Marketing managers must communicate with production managers to ensure that product marketing is consistent with the production. Any promotion efforts by marketing managers that make statements about product quality should be assessed by production managers to ensure accuracy.

Financial managers are responsible for providing accurate financial reports to creditors or investors who may provide financial support to the firm. They rely on information from production and marketing managers when preparing their financial reports.

A firm earns a reputation for being ethical by ensuring that ethical standards are maintained in all business functions. If some members of its team of managers are unethical, the entire firm will be viewed as unethical.

After this announcement, other customers reported similar findings. This not only caused potential product liability lawsuits but also caused some consumers to switch to other soft drinks. Within two weeks of the first claim, several people were arrested on tampering charges. One person was even caught on videotape placing a syringe in a Pepsi can. It became clear that the product was not defective but that people were claiming a defect to win large cash settlements through lawsuits. Although the conclusion in this case was favorable, PepsiCo spent millions of dollars attempting to determine whether the claims were valid and then convincing the public that the claims were false.

Firms must recognize that they will incur some expenses arising out of customer or employee claims (whether the claims are valid or not). They may also incur expenses from purchasing product liability insurance to cover potential lawsuits. In some businesses (such as specific medical fields), a major expense to the firm is liability insurance. The threat of liability lawsuits may even discourage entrepreneurs from establishing some types of businesses.

College Health Club: **Social Responsibility Decisions at CHC**

As a college student, Sue Kramer always had an interest in the social responsibility of businesses. Now that she is establishing the College Health Club (CHC), she can apply her beliefs about social responsibility to her own business. Sue recognizes that being socially responsible may reduce her firm's earnings or result in higher prices to her customers because attending to many social responsibilities can increase expenses. Sue's goal is to develop strategies for satisfying CHC's social responsibilities in a manner that can still maximize the firm's value.

Sue identifies the following specific responsibilities of CHC to her customers, employees, environment, and community:

▶ *Responsibility to Customers* Sue plans to spend some of her time talking with customers at the health club to determine whether the customers (members) are satisfied with the facilities that CHC offers. She also plans to send out a survey to all the members to obtain more feedback. Furthermore, she offers a money-back guarantee if the customers are not satisfied after a two-week trial period.

Sue's efforts are intended not only to fulfill a moral responsibility but also to increase the firm's memberships over time. In the health club business, the firm's reputation for satisfying the customer is important. Many customers choose a health club because of referrals by other customers. Therefore, Sue hopes that her efforts will identify ways in which she can make CHC more appealing to potential members. She also wants to show her interest in satisfying the existing members.

▶ *Responsibility to Employees* Sue started the business with herself as the only full-time employee. However, she has one part-time employee (Lisa Lane) and expects to hire more employees over time as the number of memberships increases. Sue plans to pay employee wages that are consistent with those of other health clubs in the area. She also plans to have employees who are diverse in gender and race. Her goal is not just to demonstrate her willingness to seek diversity but also to attract diversity among customers as well. For example, she wants her health club to have a somewhat even mix of males and females and believes that an even mix of employees over time might attract an even mix of customers.

▶ *Responsibility to the Environment* Since the health club is a service, no production process is involved that could damage the environment. However, Sue will establish recycling containers for cans of soft drinks consumed at CHC.

▶ *Responsibility to the Community* Sue feels a special allegiance to Texas College, which she has attended over the last four years. She has volunteered to offer a free seminar on health issues for the college students. She believes that this service will not only fulfill her moral responsibility but also allow her to promote her new health club located next to the college campus. Therefore, her community service could ultimately enhance the value of CHC.

▶ *Summary of CHC's Social Responsibilities* In general, Sue is developing strategies that will not only satisfy social responsibilities but also retain existing customers and attract new customers. She has created the following pledge, which she will use as a guideline when making various business decisions:

Pledge of Social Responsibilities at CHC

Sue Kramer, owner of CHC, recognizes her firm's responsibility to its customers, its employees, its owners, its creditors, and the environment. CHC intends to offer its customers excellent service at reasonable prices. It will consider feedback from customers and attempt to continually improve its services to satisfy customers. It will offer its employees a safe working environment and equal opportunities without bias. The firm will be managed in a manner that will maximize the value of the business for any owners who are invited to invest in the firm over time. CHC recognizes its responsibility to make timely payments on debt owed to creditors. It also pledges to conduct its business in a manner that will not harm the environment. By satisfying customers, employees, and creditors, CHC should establish a good reputation and attract more customers in the future.

SUMMARY

1 The behavior of firms is molded by their business ethics, or set of moral values. Firms have a responsibility to produce safe products and to sell their products without misleading the customers. They ensure social responsibility toward customers by establishing a code of ethics, monitoring customer complaints, and asking customers for feedback on products that they recently purchased.

2 Firms have a responsibility to provide safe working conditions, proper treatment, and equal opportunity for employees. They can satisfy their responsibility toward employees by enforcing safety guidelines, offering seminars on diversity, and establishing a grievance procedure that allows employees to report any complaints.

3 Firms have a responsibility to satisfy the owners (or stockholders) who provided funds. They attempt to ensure that managers make decisions that are in the best interests of stockholders.

4 Firms have a responsibility to maintain a clean environment when operating their businesses. However, they incur expenses when attempting to fulfill their environmental responsibility.

5 Firms have a social responsibility to the local communities where they attract customers and employees. They provide donations and other benefits to these communities.

6 When firms fulfill their social responsibilities, they may incur substantial expenses. These expenses are ultimately passed on to the customers because the prices firms charge for their products are influenced by the expenses they incur.

KEY TERMS

affirmative action   73
business responsibilities   69
consumerism   70

institutional investors   77
monopoly   71
sexual harassment   73

shareholder activism   77
social responsibility   68

Review & Critical Thinking Questions

1. Define business ethics and describe an ethical situation in which you had to distinguish between right and wrong.

2. Identify the entities to which firms have a social responsibility. Briefly describe the social responsibility a firm has to each entity.

3. How can tying employee compensation to a firm's performance resolve some conflicts of interest? How can tying employee compensation to a firm's performance create other conflicts of interest?

4. Identify the actions a firm can take to ensure that if fulfills its social responsibility to its customers.

5. What is the purpose of a code of responsibilities?

6. How can a business fulfill its social responsibility to its customers and still earn a profit?

7. Explain the role the government plays in ensuring that firms become socially responsible to customers.

8. What is the purpose of a grievance policy?

9. Briefly describe a firm's social responsibility to its community and the environment.

10. Describe the most common abuses of the environment and explain how businesses can prevent them.

11. How does a business's responsibility to its community affect product prices? Are firms that maximize their social responsibility to the community able to maximize shareholder value? Why or why not?

12. Identify and explain the conflicting objectives that often challenge a manager's responsibility.

13. Identify expenses that a firm may incur when assuming social responsibility for customers and employees.

Discussion Questions

1. Assume that you are a manager. Broadly speaking, how would your firm's business ethics and social responsibility affect your decision making? What effect would these issues have on the organization's bottom line (earnings)?

2. Assume that you are a manager. What are your ethical responsibilities to the following: (a) employees, (b) stockholders, (c) customers, and (d) suppliers?

3. You are an employee at XYZ Corp. You just discovered that a manager deliberately neglected to include a large expense in the company's last annual report. The manager also told you that he plans to sell some of the stock he owns in the firm soon. How does this manager benefit at the expense of other employees? What are the ethical implications of his actions?

4. How could a firm use the Internet to promote the business ethics and social responsibility it practices?

5. You are an advertising manager for a pharmaceutical company. You have just left a meeting that informed you about truth in labeling laws. Would you be obligated to disclose the ingredients in your product, especially if that product has a potential side effect?

6. Discuss the pros and cons of affirmative action programs and how they affect business recruiting and selection efforts. Do you think they constrain or aid businesses?

It's Your Decision: Ethics at CHC

1. Sue was recently asked if she wants to sell aerobics clothing in her health club. A clothing firm has the clothing produced in Asia and would sell it to her customers at a reasonable price and still earn a profit. Sue has heard that this firm hires children to make the clothing under poor working conditions. Should Sue sell this clothing at CHC?

2. Based on the information in the previous question, what is Sue's social responsibility (if any) to prevent improper treatment of employees in other countries?

3. Sue has several friends at Texas College who would like a part-time job at the health club. However, she knows that CHC would perform better if she hires part-time students who are majors in exercise science. Does Sue have a social responsibility to hire her friends?

4. Do you think a services firm like a health club has different social responsibilities than a manufacturing firm has?

Investing in a Business

Using the annual report of the firm in which you would like to invest, complete the following:

1 Many firms disclose their policies on ethics and social responsibilities within their annual reports. Does your firm mention any specific policies that encourage employees' ethical behavior? Does the firm give any specific examples of how it accomplishes these goals?

2 Describe your firm's policies on its social responsibility toward its community and the environment. Does the firm give any specific examples of how it accomplishes these goals?

3 Explain how the business uses technology to enhance its business ethics and social responsibility. For example, does it use the Internet to provide information regarding its business practices? Does it provide a place for customer complaints on the Internet?

4 Go to **http://hoovers.com** and locate the NEWS SEARCH. Type in the name of the firm in the space provided, and review the recent news stories about the firm. Summarize any (at least one) recent news story about the firm that applies to one or more of the key concepts in this chapter.

Case: Responsibilities to Employees

David Thomas, a supervisor in the bearings department at the ABC Corporation, a rollerblade manufacturer, manages a nonunion plant where the work atmosphere appears to be a "good ol' boy" system. He desires to give preference to males by giving them the better jobs and newer equipment, and favoritism is often extended to them. Currently, there are no females in management positions throughout the plant. Females tend to occupy token positions, often starting out as clerk-typists or file clerks, and few female employees advance into higher positions. Presently, twenty people work in Mr. Thomas's department; only two are female. All perform the same job; skills, responsibility, and authority are the same. Males are paid $10.50 per hour; females with the same seniority earn $7.50 per hour. Working conditions throughout the department are often unsanitary, and neglect on the supervisor's part has made the department unsafe. Recently, many complaints have been made from Mr. Thomas's employees concerning the poor working conditions. Mr. Thomas is a profit maximizer with a bottom-line orientation and often ignores any safety policy directive that comes from top management.

In his office, Mr. Thomas has pinups on every wall. On his desk are sexually explicit slogans that some females have found offensive. His language tends to be off-color and is often upsetting to many people throughout the plant.

Mr. Thomas has just received a memo. He has been asked by the company president to attend a meeting on the firm's responsibilities. The memo reads, "The company is going in a new direction. We would like your input on responsibility issues that this company should adopt." Mr. Thomas's immediate reaction is, "This company has always been a profit-maximizing firm and should not concern itself with any social issues because they constrain and impact the bottom line of the company's operations." Thus, he refuses to attend the meeting.

Questions

1 Is Mr. Thomas ignoring any responsibility issues in his department operations?

2 Is Mr. Thomas correct in saying that the ABC Corporation should be a profit-maximizing firm at all costs?

3 Is Mr. Thomas discriminating against females and, if so, in what areas?

4 What are the potential costs to the firm as a result of Mr. Thomas's actions?

Video Case: Social Responsibility at Ben & Jerry's Ice Cream

Ben & Jerry's Ice Cream began as a small business and has grown into an international corporation. Its mission statement includes provisions about (1) producing a good product for its customers, (2) providing an economic reward (profits) to its shareholders, and (3) fulfilling its social responsibility. These three goals have no particular order. Ben & Jerry's believes that it should not focus on any one goal but should achieve all three goals.

Ben & Jerry's directs 7.5 percent of its pretax profits to a foundation, which donates money to specific charitable organizations. In another effort to fulfill its social responsibility, Ben & Jerry's works with small businesses, as its owners remember that it was once a small business. It relies on small businesses for some of the materials used in its production process.

Ben & Jerry's has proved that it can achieve its economic mission while fulfilling its social mission. Its social commitment has enhanced Ben & Jerry's reputation, increased its name recognition, and stimulated demand for its ice cream. Thus, the company's social mission has enhanced its profits and therefore is aligned with its economic mission.

Questions

1 Why do you think Ben & Jerry's has a social mission?

2 Does the firm's social mission conflict with its economic mission?

3 Do you think the shareholders disapprove of Ben & Jerry's social mission?

Internet Applications

1. *http://www.pg.com/about_pg/sectionmain.jhtml*

Find Procter & Gamble's latest "Sustainability Report." How does P&G define "sustainability"? What are some initiatives and programs that P&G conducts regarding the environment? Has P&G won any environmental awards? Overall, do you think P&G is an environmentally responsible company? Why or why not?

2. *http://www.pg.com/about_pg/sectionmain.jhtml*

Find Procter & Gamble's "Values and Code of Conduct." Briefly summarize the information contained in this document. Based on this information, do you think P&G is fulfilling its social responsibility to its employees? Why or why not? What do you think is the purpose of the "Code of Conduct"?

3. *http://www.nautilus.org/cap/index.html*

What is "Beyond Good Deeds"? How does the report seek to improve corporate accountability? Describe some of the global standards and guidelines on the website. Overall, do you think the project helps to improve corporate accountability? Why or why not?

The Coca-Cola Company Annual Report Project

 Questions for the current year's annual report are available on the text website at **http://madura.swlearning.com.**

The following questions apply concepts presented in this chapter to The Coca-Cola Company. Go to The Coca-Cola Company website (**http://www.cocacola.com/**) and find the index for the 2001 annual report.

Questions

1. Click on "Operations Review." Do you think The Coca-Cola Company has an advantage over other large companies with respect to its impact on the environment?

2. Click on "Our Building Blocks." In what sense does The Coca-Cola Company provide a global brand? How does the company use the Internet and other marketing programs to connect with its customers?

3. Do you think The Coca-Cola Company's sense of social responsibility, such as investing in countries with poor economic performance or responding to the attacks of September 11, conflicts with the goal of satisfying shareholders?

4. Look at the "Letter to Share Owners." Why is the financial health of The Coca-Cola Company's bottling partners important? Provide some examples of relationships The Coca-Cola Company has with its bottling partners.

5. Go to **http://hoovers.com** and locate the NEWS CENTER. Key in The Coca-Cola Company in the space provided, click on "Search," and review the recent news stories about the firm. Summarize any (at least one) recent news story about The Coca-Cola Company that applies one or more of the key concepts within this chapter of the text.

In-Text Study Guide

Answers are in an appendix at the back of the book.

True or False

1. The responsibility of firms toward customers can be enforced by specific groups of consumers. T

2. The government protects consumers by regulating the quality of some products that firms produce. T

3. Deregulation results in lower prices for consumers. T

4. The Clayton Act is intended to restrict competition. F

5. U.S. firms that conduct business in foreign countries are not subject to the rules enforced by the local government. F

6. In recent years, stockholders have been active in trying to influence a firm's management practices. T

7. An attempt by a firm to maximize social responsibility to the community may reduce the firm's ability to provide products at a reasonable price to consumers. T

8. In recent years, pollution laws have become less stringent. F

9. Employees commonly sue firms for product defects or deceptive advertising. F

10. Marketing managers are primarily responsible for providing accurate financial information to creditors and investors. F

Multiple Choice

11. The recognition of how a firm's business decisions can affect society is its:
    a) moral code.
    b) social responsibility.
    c) conservation policies.
    d) recycling program.
    e) consumer bill of rights.

12. A firm's _____ is measured by its stock price, which can be negatively affected by unethical business practices:
    a) value
    b) revenue
    c) bond rating
    d) risk
    e) return on equity

13. Many U.S. firms provide guidelines of behavior to employees through a code of:
    a) reciprocity.
    b) cartel arrangements.
    c) kickback arrangements.
    d) technical production manuals.
    e) responsibilities and ethics.

14. Firms can ensure responsibility to customers by:
    a) safe manufacturing techniques.
    b) proper disposal of toxic waste.
    c) employee diversity programs.
    d) soliciting feedback about products.
    e) full financial disclosure.

15. _____ represents the collective consumer demand that businesses satisfy their needs.
    a) Conservationism
    b) Consumerism
    c) Social responsibility
    d) Business ethics
    e) Recycling

16. The act that prohibits unfair methods of competition is the:
    a) Humphrey Act.
    b) Civil Rights Act of 1964.
    c) Federal Trade Commission Act.
    d) Garn Act.
    e) Reagan Antitrust Act.

17. Tying agreements, binding contracts, and interlocking directorates are prohibited by the:
    a) Clayton Act.
    b) Sherman Antitrust Act.
    c) Robinson-Patman Act.
    d) Celler-Kefauver Act.
    e) Federal Trade Commission Act.

18. The act that prohibits mergers between firms that reduce competition within an industry is the:
    a) Robinson-Patman Act.
    b) Celler-Kefauver Act.
    c) Federal Trade Commission Act.

    d) Clayton Act.

    e) Sherman Antitrust Act.

19. Which of the following represents legislation passed to prevent firms from entering into agreements to set prices and avoid competition?

    a) affirmative action laws

    b) deregulation codes

    c) antitrust laws

    d) consumerism laws

    e) Food and Drug Administration Act

20. If a firm is the sole provider of a good or service, it is a(n):

    a) unsuccessful organization.

    b) sole proprietorship.

    c) deregulated firm.

    d) institutional investor.

    e) monopoly.

21. The following industries have been deregulated, allowing more firms to enter the industry, except for:

    a) trucking.

    b) railroads.

    c) airlines.

    d) boating.

    e) telecommunications.

22. The act that prohibits price differences on promotional allowances that reduce competition within an industry is the:

    a) Celler-Kefauver Act.

    b) Robinson-Patman Act.

    c) Clayton Act.

    d) Sherman Antitrust Act.

    e) Federal Trade Commission Act.

23. The act that encourages competition and prevents monopolies is the:

    a) Deregulation Act.

    b) Federal Trade Commission Act.

    c) Robinson-Patman Act.

    d) Celler-Kefauver Act.

    e) Sherman Antitrust Act.

24. Unwelcome comments or actions of a sexual nature are examples of:

    a) business as usual.

    b) sexual harassment.

    c) equal employment opportunities.

    d) workplace diversity.

    e) deregulation.

25. Which of the following terms describes a set of activities intended to increase opportunities for minorities and women?

    a) affirmative action

    b) Americans with Disabilities Act

    c) minimum wage law

    d) antitrust action

    e) consumerism

26. The act that prohibits discrimination due to national origin, race, gender, or religion is the:

    a) Clayton Act.

    b) Sherman Antitrust Act.

    c) Federal Trade Commission Act.

    d) Civil Rights Act of 1964.

    e) Robinson-Patman Act.

27. One example of a firm's attempt to ensure the proper and equal treatment of all employees is the establishment of a:

    a) labor contract.

    b) strike.

    c) grievance procedure.

    d) walkout.

    e) lockout.

28. The firm's management is responsible for satisfying its:

    a) union demands.

    b) owners or stockholders.

    c) business agents.

    d) competition.

    e) friends.

In-Text Study Guide

Answers are in an appendix at the back of the book.

29. If a firm exaggerates its estimates of revenues or earnings:
    a) investors pay too much for the stock.
    b) stock value initially declines.
    c) equity is diluted.
    d) insider trading is occurring.
    e) the stock is illiquid.

30. Tying employee compensation to firm performance can lead to:
    a) lack of employee motivation.
    b) resolution of all conflicts of interest within the firm.
    c) enhanced ethical behavior by employees.
    d) excessive turnover.
    e) manipulation of financial reporting.

31. An active role by stockholders in influencing a firm's management policies is called:
    a) empowerment.
    b) reengineering.
    c) self-managed teams.
    d) quality circles.
    e) shareholder activism.

32. Shareholder activism is most commonly practiced by:
    a) customers.
    b) chief executive officers.
    c) institutional investors.
    d) managers.
    e) the government.

33. Assuming everything else is the same, a firm that pays higher executive salaries will experience a _____ rate of return on the stockholders' investment than a firm that pays lower executive salaries.
    a) more stable
    b) lower
    c) higher
    d) steadier
    e) more erratic

34. Firms are responsible to their creditors by meeting their:
    a) dividend payments.
    b) financial obligations.
    c) retained earnings.
    d) stockholders' equity.
    e) treasury stock.

35. If a firm fails to meet its responsibilities to _____, it may be forced into bankruptcy.
    a) its employees
    b) the environment
    c) the government
    d) its creditors
    e) its owners

36. Enron's main ethical breach was:
    a) improper disposal of toxic waste
    b) sex discrimination
    c) misleading financial reporting
    d) unsafe products
    e) violation of antitrust laws

37. A firm's decision to maximize its social responsibilities may conflict with its responsibility to:
    a) monopolize the marketplace.
    b) provide safe products for customers.
    c) maximize the opportunities for women and minorities.
    d) maximize the firm's value for stockholders.
    e) follow government regulations.

38. Most firms have procedures in place as well as codes to ensure individual employee accountability. This is a part of their:
    a) program network.
    b) division of work.
    c) local area network.
    d) social responsibility.
    e) recycling program.

Part I

Summary

Organization of a Business

The success of a business may depend on the initial decisions that are made by its owners when it is established. The first set of decisions is made within the business plan (Chapter 1), which requires management, marketing, and financial plans. The management plan consists of decisions about production, organizational structure, and employee job descriptions. Management policies are discussed in more detail in Parts III and IV. The marketing plan consists of pricing, distribution, and promotion decisions and is discussed in more detail in Part V. The financial plan consists of financing decisions and business investment decisions, which are discussed in detail in Part VI.

In addition to the business plan, owners who establish a new business must select the proper form of ownership (Chapter 2). The possible forms of ownership are sole proprietorships, partnerships, and corporations. This decision is based on various characteristics of the business, such as the potential liability of the business and the amount of funds needed to support the business.

Owners of a new business also need to establish their ethical and social responsibilities (Chapter 3) and provide guidelines for proper treatment of customers, employees, stockholders, and creditors. Overall, the business plan, form of business ownership, and ethical guidelines establish a foundation that can be used by the firm's managers to make future decisions.

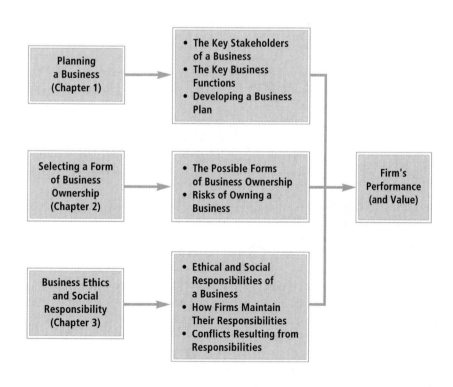

DEVELOPING A BUSINESS PLAN FOR CAMPUS.COM

Following is a business idea called Campus.com that has been created for you. It is your job to develop a business plan for the business during the school term, applying many of the key concepts discussed in each chapter. At the end of each part, questions will guide your development of a portion of the plan that relates to that part. By the end of the school term, you will have developed a complete business plan for Campus.com. This exercise will not only enhance your understanding of business concepts but will also demonstrate how the concepts are integrated; it can also enhance your teamwork and communication skills.

Your instructor will tell you whether you will be developing the business plan by yourself or as part of a team. There is no single perfect method for developing the business, so your (or your team's) business plan may vary from the plans created by other students (or student teams). However you develop the business plan, your method should be based on logical business concepts discussed in the chapters.

As you (or your team) answer the questions at the end of each part, you can insert your answers in the Business Plan booklet or on the Business Plan CD-ROM that are supplied with the text. Once you (or your team) complete the questions at the end of each part, you will have completed the business plan for Campus.com and will be ready to implement your plan.

Business Idea (related to Chapter 1)

Campus.com will provide an information service for high school students who are assessing different colleges to which they may apply. It will provide information on the lifestyles at any college that they select. High school students might find this service useful for several reasons. First, many books compare academic requirements at colleges but provide very limited information on student lifestyles. Second, some high school students do not rely on the lifestyle information in these books because they question whether the authors really understand students. Third, students do not necessarily want to purchase an entire volume on all colleges across the country just to obtain information on the few colleges to which they may apply. Fourth, students recognize that the material in these books can become outdated.

For these reasons, the business of Campus.com can satisfy high school students. The business does not require any physical facilities initially. It requires a website that provides information to high school students who wish to purchase the information. The website will show an index of all colleges. Customers will click on those colleges for which they want information. They must submit a credit card number and will be charged $1 for each college that they select. They will receive immediate information on their computer about the campus lifestyles of each college selected.

The main expenses for Campus.com are the creation of the website and gathering information about every college campus from reliable sources. Initially, this information will be gathered by ordering back issues of campus newspapers for the last year and then summarizing the campus activities for each college. In addition, the plan is to send a brief survey to about 30 students at each school (offering $20 to each respondent who fills out the survey), asking them to answer general questions about the activities and to rate the campus in terms of its sports activities, entertainment on campus, and nightlife. You hope to receive responses from at least 20 students before you summarize the information for each college. The information will be updated every three months by paying some of the same students who filled out the first survey to fill out an updated survey. Thus, the information that you provide to customers is frequently updated, which is an advantage over any books they could buy in stores.

Ownership (related to Chapter 2)

Decide what is the optimal form of business ownership for this firm, and indicate that form in your business plan for Campus.com. To answer this question, consider whether you would prefer to be the sole owner of Campus.com or to invite other individuals into the firm to form a partnership. If you are working with a team of students, you already have a partnership. In your business plan, explain why you selected the form of ownership you chose for Campus.com. What are the advantages of forming a partnership for this firm? What are the disadvantages of forming a partnership?

Main Sources of Revenue and Expenses

The success of this business is highly dependent on your revenue and expenses. What will be the main source of your revenue? What will be the main source of your expenses? Should you pay yourself a salary, or will you reinvest any earnings in the firm? Summarize your comments in your business plan for Campus.com.

Responsibility to Customers, Employees, and Owners (related to Chapter 3)

Describe the mission of the business as part of your business plan for Campus.com. Include statements on how the business will fulfull its responsibilities to its customers, its employees, and its owners.

Communication and Teamwork

Your instructor may ask you (or your team) to hand in and/or present the sections of your business plan that relate to this part of the text. As you build the plan at the end of each part of the text, you can continue to use the Business Plan booklet or CD-ROM.

Integrated Video Case: Finding Sources of Financing

"We'll Show you the Money" features different businesses every week that create work and wealth. The video illustrates that entrepreneurs with a good idea can obtain financing by using other people's money. The key ingredient to obtaining financing is to have a solid idea and to communicate that idea with enthusiasm. For example, the Jagged Edge, a clothing store for climbers, obtained financing because of the market's potential for growth; the clothing store, run by Lori Davis, was able to obtain financing because of her background in the industry. General advice from a bank featured in this video to entrepreneurs is to have a good package, including reasonable projections and a fallback plan if things don't go as expected.

Questions

1 Explain how the funding obtained by businesses relates to other business functions.

2 Why might a business plan be critical to obtain financing?

3 What form of business ownership did the two companies mentioned in the clip have? How do you think the form of business ownership relates to the amount of financing a business can obtain from an outside source?

Integrated Video Case: Selecting the Management Team and Form of Organization

 Founded by Robert Redford with money obtained from his salary for the movie "Butch Cassidy and the Sundance Kid" and other investors, Sundance Catalog became a mail order business located in Utah before mail order businesses gained popularity. Larry Rosenthal, the CEO of Sundance Catalog, initially helped to write the business plan and obtain funding for the company. Sundance Catalog is associated with name recognition; Robert Redford is associated with environmental support and support of the arts. Sundance catalog stands for environmental responsibility, support of the arts, creativity, and responsible business.

Questions

1 How can Sundance's corporate responsibility affect its profitability?

2 Explain how Sundance's form of corporate responsibility might change if it became a large corporation and spread its business throughout the United States.

3 How can Sundance's corporate responsibility affect its financing?

THE STOCK MARKET GAME

 Go to **http://finance.yahoo.com** and check your portfolio balance, which is updated continuously by Yahoo! Finance.

Check Your Stock Portfolio Performance

1 What is the value of your stock portfolio today?

2 What is your return on your investment? (This return is shown on your balance.)

3 How did your return compare to those of other students? (This comparison tells you whether your stock portfolio's performance is relatively high or low.)

Changing Your Stock Portfolio

At the end of each of the following parts, you will be prompted to assess the performance of your portfolio since you created it at the beginning of the school term. At this point, you should decide whether you want to change your portfolio. You can change it at any time throughout the semester. You should consider changing the portfolio if you no longer wish to hold one or more of the stocks in which you invested. If you do not want to change your portfolio, however, you can leave it as is.

RUNNING YOUR OWN BUSINESS

The following exercise allows you to apply the key concepts covered in each chapter to a business that you would like to create for yourself. Applying these concepts to a business in which you are interested enables you to recognize how these concepts are used in the business world. Since this part focused on the organization of a business, you will be asked specific questions about the organization of a business of your choice. Chapter 1 focused on the creation of a business idea, so the first questions will ask you to create your own business idea. Give this some serious thought because you will be developing specific details about your business idea at the end of each part. In Chapter 1, you learned how a college student developed a health club business. One could develop numerous types of small businesses without necessarily being a business expert. If you do not have any ideas initially, consider the types of businesses that are in a shopping mall. Or consider the firms that produce and sell products to those businesses. You might look through the yellow pages to find other types of small businesses.

The "Running Your Own Business" exercise at the end of each part will apply the key concepts in the chapters in that part to the business that you create. You can record good business ideas in the Business Plan booklet or on the Business Plan CD-ROM that are supplied with the text. By developing a business idea, you may actually implement it someday. Alternatively, you may realize from developing your idea why such a business could fail, which may lead you to alternative business ideas.

When developing your business idea, try to create a business that will require you to hire at least a few employees in the future. By doing this, you will find it easier to apply the concepts related to managing employees in later chapters.

1 Describe in general terms the type of business that you would like to create.

2 Explain in general terms how your business would offer some advantage over competing firms.

3 Explain whether your business will be a sole proprietorship, a partnership, or a corporation. Why did you make this decision?

4 Describe the risk of your business. That is, explain what conditions could result in lower revenue or higher expenses than you expect.

5 Describe the ethical dilemmas (if any) that you might face in your business. How do you plan to handle these situations?

6 What types of social responsibilities would your business have toward your employees, customers, or community? What, if any, special policies would you establish to take better care of your employees, customers, or community?

7 Explain how your business would use the Internet to provide relevant information to its customers, employees, and shareholders. Would it use the Internet to fulfill some of its social responsibilities? How?

Part II

Business Environment

The success of a firm is partially dependent on its environment. Although managers of a firm cannot control the business environment, they can attempt to make business decisions that benefit from that environment or that offer protection against adverse conditions. To do this, they need to understand how the business environment affects their firm.

A firm is exposed to three different aspects of the business environment: (1) economic conditions, (2) industry conditions, and (3) global conditions. Chapter 4 describes how economic conditions affect a firm's performance. It also explains how government policies affect firms indirectly by influencing economic conditions. Chapter 5 explains how a firm's performance is affected by industry conditions, and Chapter 6 explains how it is affected by global conditions.

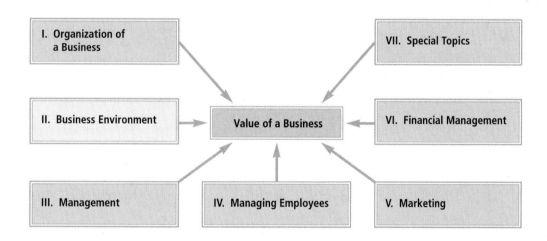

All businesses, including ZanyBrainy, need to determine their exposure to economic conditions.

The Learning Goals of this chapter are to:

Identify the macroeconomic factors that affect business performance.	**4**
Explain how market prices are determined.	**5**
Explain how the government influences economic conditions.	**6**

Chapter 4

Assessing Economic Conditions

4

Economic conditions reflect the level of production and consumption for a particular country, area, or industry. **Macroeconomic conditions** reflect the overall U.S. economy; **microeconomic conditions** are more focused on the business or industry of concern. This chapter focuses on the macroeconomic factors, and the following chapter focuses on microeconomic (industry) factors.

Economic conditions can affect the revenue or expenses of a business and therefore can affect the value of that business. Consider the case of Zany-Brainy, which sells children's toys. Although the demand for its toys has grown substantially over time, the demand tends to be stronger when the economy is strong and customers have more income to buy toys. Its sales declined recently when the economy weakened. When the demand for its toys is high, ZanyBrainy generates a high level of revenue, and its business performance is high. When the demand for its toys is low, its performance tends to be weaker. ZanyBrainy anticipates the demand for its toys in the near future so that it can ensure that it has a large enough supply of toys to accommodate the future demand. Since its demand is dependent on economic conditions, the amount of toys that it will sell is dependent on economic conditions. In addition, government policies can affect economic conditions and must be considered as well. Thus, ZanyBrainy must determine:

▶ How will prevailing economic conditions affect the demand for its toys?

▶ How will prevailing government policies affect the economy and therefore, affect the demand for its toys?

These types of assessments are necessary for all businesses. Although every business is not affected in the same manner by changing economic conditions, most businesses are affected to some degree. This chapter explains how the assessment of the economic environment by ZanyBrainy or any other firm can be conducted in a manner that maximizes the firm's value.

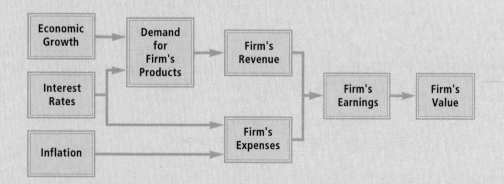

Televisions on the floor of the New York Stock Exchange broadcast Federal Reserve Chairman Alan Greenspan as he testifies before the Senate Banking Committee that the economy is on its way to full recovery.

AP Photo/ Richard Drew

1

Identify the macroeconomic factors that affect business performance.

MACROECONOMIC FACTORS THAT AFFECT BUSINESS PERFORMANCE

The performance of most firms is highly dependent on three macroeconomic factors:

▶ Economic growth

▶ Inflation

▶ Interest rates

Economic Growth

economic growth the change in the general level of economic activity

A critical macroeconomic factor that affects business performance is **economic growth,** or the change in the general level of economic activity. When U.S. economic growth is higher than normal, the total income level of all U.S. workers is relatively high, so there is a higher volume of spending on products and services. Since the demand for products and services is high, firms that sell products and services should generate higher revenue. When economic growth is negative for two consecutive quarters, the period is referred to as a **recession.**

recession two consecutive quarters of negative economic growth

Whereas high economic growth enhances a firm's revenue, slow economic growth results in low demand for products and services, which can reduce a firm's revenue. The potential impact of slower economic growth is reflected in the following statements:

"Our caution stems largely from the macroeconomic environment, in which some forecasts are for slower growth."

—Hewlett-Packard

"[The company] expects to experience significant fluctuations in future [performance] due to . . . general economic conditions."

—Amazon.com

Exhibit 4.1

Trend of Gross Domestic
Product (GDP)

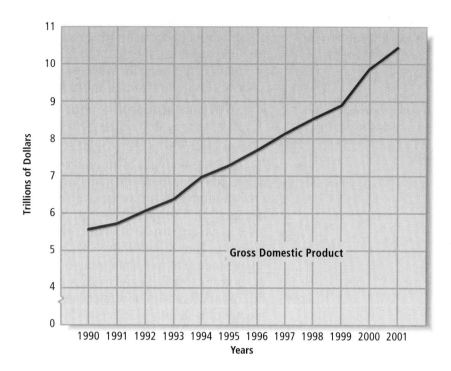

General Motors and Ford Motor Company commonly shut down some factories in response to low economic growth.

Indicators of Economic Growth Two common measures of economic growth are the level of total production of products and services in the economy and the total amount of expenditures (also called **aggregate expenditures**). The total production level and total aggregate expenditures in the United States are closely related, because a high level of consumer spending reflects a large demand for products and services. The total production level is dependent on the total demand for products and services.

Businesses can monitor the U.S. total production level by keeping track of the **gross domestic product (GDP),** which is the total market value of all final products and services produced in the United States. The GDP is reported quarterly in the United States. The trend of GDP is shown in Exhibit 4.1. Notice that GDP was stagnant during the early 1990s but has grown substantially since then. Economic growth is commonly interpreted as the percentage of change in the GDP from one period (such as a quarter) to another. Businesses tend to monitor changes in economic growth, which may signal a change in the demand for their products or services.

An alternative indicator of economic growth is the unemployment level. Businesses may monitor various unemployment indicators because they can indicate whether economic conditions are improving. The four different types of unemployment are as follows:

▶ **Frictional unemployment** (also referred to as *natural unemployment*) represents people who are between jobs. That is, their unemployment status is temporary, as they are likely to find employment soon. For example, a person with marketable job skills might quit her job before finding a new one because she believes she will find a new job before long.

▶ **Seasonal unemployment** represents people whose services are not needed during some seasons. For example, ski instructors may be unemployed in the summer.

aggregate expenditures the total amount of expenditures in the economy

gross domestic product (GDP) the total market value of all final products and services produced in the United States

frictional unemployment people who are between jobs

seasonal unemployment people whose services are not needed during some seasons

cyclical unemployment people who are unemployed because of poor economic conditions

structural unemployment people who are unemployed because they do not have adequate skills

▶ **Cyclical unemployment** represents people who are unemployed because of poor economic conditions. When the level of economic activity declines, the demand for products and services declines, which reduces the need for workers. For example, a firm may lay off factory workers if the demand for its product declines.

▶ **Structural unemployment** represents people who are unemployed because they do not have adequate skills. For example, people who have limited education may be structurally unemployed.

Of the four types of unemployment, the cyclical unemployment level is probably the best indicator of economic conditions. When economic growth improves, businesses hire more people and the unemployment rate declines. Unfortunately, determining how much of the unemployment level is cyclical can be difficult. Some people assume that when the unemployment rate changes, the change is primarily due to economic cycles. A lower unemployment rate may be interpreted as an indicator of increased economic growth. Conversely, a higher unemployment rate is commonly interpreted as a sign of reduced economic growth. The trend of U.S. unemployment is shown in Exhibit 4.2. Notice that the U.S. unemployment level was at its peak in 1992, when U.S. economic conditions were weak, but it declined in the middle and late 1990s when economic growth was strong. From 2000 to 2002, as the economy weakened, the unemployment level turned upward.

Many other indicators of economic growth, such as the industrial production index, new housing starts, and the personal income level, are compiled by divisions of the federal government and reported in business magazines and newspapers.

Exhibit 4.2

Trend of U.S. Unemployment

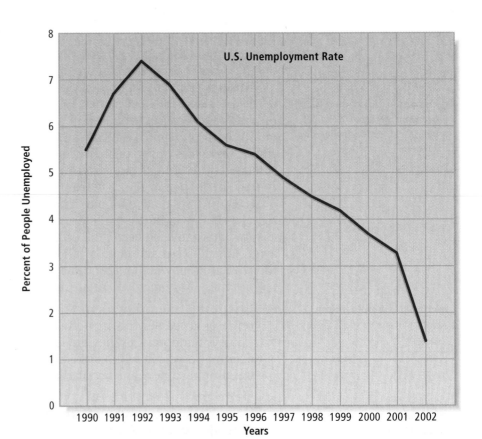

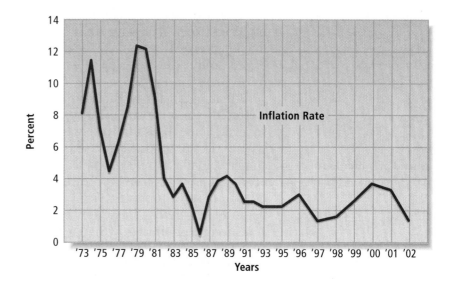

Sensitivity of a Firm to Economic Growth   Some firms are more sensitive than others to economic conditions because the demand for their product is more sensitive to such conditions. For example, the demand for the product (food) provided by McDonald's is not very sensitive to economic conditions because people still purchase McDonald's food even when the economy is weak. In contrast, the demand for new automobiles is more sensitive to economic conditions. When the economy is weak, the demand for new automobiles declines. Ford Motor Company experienced negative profits during the 1991–1992 period and the 2001–2002 period when the U.S. economy was weak, but earned high profits in the late 1990s during strong economic conditions.

Inflation

inflation the increase in the general level of prices of products and services over a specified period of time

Inflation is the increase in the general level of prices of products and services over a specified period of time. The inflation rate can be estimated by measuring the percentage change in the consumer price index, which indicates the prices on a wide variety of consumer products such as grocery products, housing, gasoline, medical services, and electricity. The annual U.S. inflation rate is shown in Exhibit 4.3. Notice that the inflation rate was generally higher in the 1970s than in more recent years, which was partially attributed to an abrupt increase in oil prices then.

Inflation can affect a firm's operating expenses from producing products by increasing the cost of supplies and materials. Wages can also be affected by inflation. A higher level of inflation will cause a larger increase in a firm's operating expenses. A firm's revenue may also be high during periods of high inflation because many firms charge higher prices to compensate for their higher expenses.

Types of Inflation   Inflation may result from a particular event that increases the costs of production. For example, when oil prices rise, gasoline prices increase and the costs of transporting products increase. Firms that incur higher costs from transporting their products increase their prices to cover the higher costs. This situation, when firms charge higher prices due to higher costs, is referred to as **cost-push inflation.** For example, beverage producers such as PepsiCo and Anheuser-Busch raised prices when the cost

cost-push inflation the situation when higher prices charged by firms are caused by higher costs

of aluminum (used to make cans) increased. Procter & Gamble raised prices on paper towels following an increase in the cost of pulp (used in the production process). In contrast, advances in information technology have reduced production costs for some products in recent years, thereby minimizing cost-push inflation.

Inflation can also be caused by strong consumer demand. Consider a situation in which consumers increase their demand for most products and services. Some firms may respond by increasing their prices. This situation, when prices of products and services are pulled up because of strong consumer demand, is referred to as **demand-pull inflation.** In periods of strong economic growth, strong consumer demand can cause shortages in the production of some products. Firms that anticipate shortages may raise prices because they are confident they can sell the products anyway.

Strong economic growth may place pressure on wages as well as prices. Strong economic growth may mean fewer unemployed people, so workers may negotiate for higher wages. Firms may be more willing to provide higher wages to retain their workers when no other qualified workers are available. As firms pay higher wages, production costs rise, and firms may attempt to increase their prices to recover the higher expenses.

demand-pull inflation the situation when prices of products and services are pulled up because of strong consumer demand

Interest Rates

Interest rates represent the cost of borrowing money. Businesses closely monitor interest rates because they determine the amount of expense a business will incur if it borrows money. If a business borrows $100,000 for one year at an interest rate of 8 percent, the interest expense is $8,000 (computed as .08 × $100,000). At an interest rate of 15 percent, however, the interest expense would be $15,000 (computed as .15 × $100,000). Imagine how the interest rate level can affect firms such as General Motors, which has borrowed more than $1 billion at any time. An interest rate in-

Zero percent financing signs seen everywhere as a result of General Motors' campaign to "Keep America Rolling" after the September 11 terrorist attacks. This incentive war was a great boon to the economy but has also resulted in very low profits for automakers.

AP Photo/ Paul Warner

Exhibit 4.4

Effect of Interest Rates on Interest Expenses and Profits

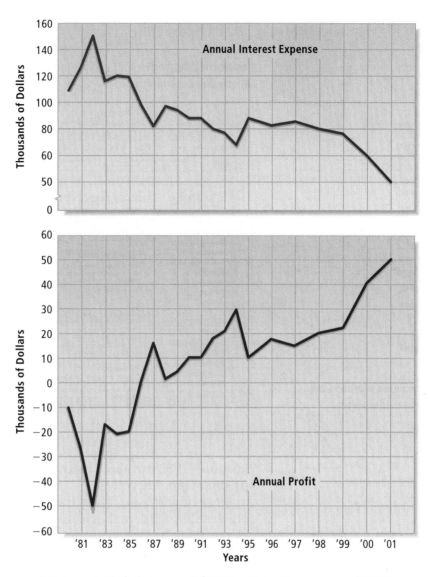

Note: Assume that the firm's revenue equals $400,000 and its operating expenses equal $300,000.

crease of just 1 percent on $1 billion of borrowed funds results in an extra annual interest expense of $10 million.

Changes in market interest rates can influence a firm's interest expense because the loan rates that commercial banks and other creditors charge on loans to firms are based on market interest rates. Even when a firm obtains a loan from a commercial bank over several years, the loan rate is typically adjusted periodically (every six months or year) based on the prevailing market interest rate at that time.

Exhibit 4.4 illustrates the annual interest expense for a reputable U.S. firm that borrows $1 million from a bank each year and earns $100,000 in annual profits before paying its interest expense. The interest expenses are adjusted each year according to the interest rate prevailing in the United States during that year. As this exhibit shows, interest rates can significantly influence a firm's profit. Notice that the firm incurred much higher interest expenses in the early 1980s than in the 1990s and early 2000s. Because the interest rate in 1982 was about twice as high as in 2001, the interest

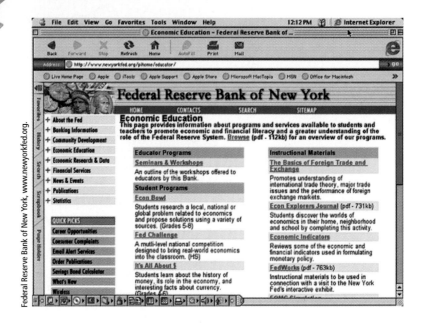

e-business

business online

Economic Impact   This website provides tutorials about how economic conditions can affect business performance.

http://www.ny.frb.org/
pihome/educator/

expense in 1982 was about twice the expense incurred in 2001 for the same amount of funds borrowed.

Since interest rates affect the cost of financing, some possible projects considered by the firm that would be feasible during periods of low interest rates may not be feasible during periods of high interest rates. That is, the project may not generate an adequate return to cover financing costs. Consequently, firms tend to reduce their degree of expansion when interest rates are high.

Interest rates affect a firm's revenue as well as its interest expenses. For example, when interest rates rise, the cost of financing the purchase of new homes increases. Therefore, the demand for new homes typically declines, and firms that build homes experience a decline in business. In addition, firms such as Caterpillar and Weyerhaeuser that produce equipment and construction products experience a decline in business. This explains why firms involved in the construction industry are highly influenced by interest rate movements.

Summary of Macroeconomic Factors
That Affect a Firm's Performance

A summary of how the three macroeconomic factors affect a firm's performance is provided in Exhibit 4.5. The firm's revenue is affected by economic growth, which influences the demand for the firm's products. Its revenue and operating expenses are affected by inflation. Its interest expenses are affected by interest rate movements.

Exhibit 4.5

How Macroeconomic Factors Affect a
Firm's Profits

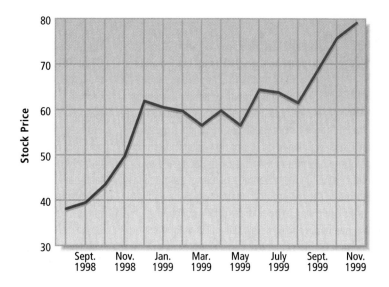

College Health Club: **Impact of Economic Conditions on CHC**

As Sue Kramer develops her business plan for College Health Club (CHC), she needs to recognize the exposure of her business to economic conditions. Based on expected economic conditions, she anticipates that she will have 300 memberships over the first year. If economic conditions weaken, however, some students will probably lose their part-time jobs in the local community and will not be able to afford a health club membership. If the economy weakens, Sue expects that there will be only 260 memberships. Conversely, if the economy strengthens, she expects that there will be 340 memberships in the first year. She therefore determines CHC's revenue for each of these three scenarios as shown in row 3 of the following table. Assuming that CHC's expenses would not be affected, CHC's earnings would be as shown in row 6.

	Present Economic Conditions	If the Economy Weakens	If the Economy Strengthens
(1) Price per membership	$500	$500	$500
(2) Number of members in first year	300	260	340
(3) Revenue in first year = (1) × (2)	$150,000	$130,000	$170,000
(4) Operating expenses	$138,000	$138,000	$138,000
(5) Interest expenses	$4,000	$4,000	$4,000
(6) Earnings before taxes = (3) − (4) − (5)	$8,000	−$12,000	$28,000

As the table shows, CHC's revenue will be lower when economic conditions are weaker. Since most of CHC's expenses (such as rent) are fixed, any change in revenue has a direct effect on earnings. Thus, if a weaker economy causes CHC's revenue to be lower, CHC's earnings will also be lower. A weaker economy could even force Sue to lower the membership price, which could also reduce revenue.

Capitalizing on Global Economic Conditions The demand for a firm's products is dependent on the economic growth where the products are sold. Given the mature economy of the United States, its potential for economic growth is limited. Less-developed countries, however, have much greater potential for economic growth because they have not yet taken full advantage of existing technology. Furthermore, the governments of many less-developed countries are trying to accelerate their economic growth by encouraging more business development by entrepreneurs. Many of these governments have also allowed U.S. firms to enter their markets. These U.S. firms are attempting to capitalize on the changing economic and political conditions in less-developed countries by selling their products there.

The Coca-Cola Company is among many U.S. firms that have targeted countries with high potential for economic growth. Its sales have increased substantially in Brazil, Chile, East Central Europe, North Africa, and China. The Coca-Cola Company's increased sales in these countries can be attributed in part to economic growth, which increases the amount of consumer spending. It can also be attributed to reductions in government restrictions imposed on U.S. firms that desire to conduct business in these countries.

Other U.S. firms are planning major expansion in less-developed countries to capitalize on the changes in economic and political conditions. General Motors plans to expand in various Asian markets, including China, India, and Indonesia, where the potential for economic growth is strong.

U.S. firms that attempt to capitalize on economic growth in foreign countries can be adversely affected if these countries experience a recession. If a U.S. firm diversifies its business among several different countries, however, a recession in any single foreign country should not have a major effect on the firm's worldwide sales.

HOW MARKET PRICES ARE DETERMINED

2

Explain how market prices are determined.

The performance of firms is affected by changes in the prices they charge for products (which influence their revenue) and the prices they pay for supplies and materials (which influence their operating expenses). The prices of products and supplies are influenced by demand and supply conditions.

The following framework uses demand and supply conditions to explain how prices of products change over time. The market price of a product is influenced by the total demand for that product by all customers. It is also affected by the supply of that product produced by firms. The interaction between demand and supply determines the price, as explained in detail next.

Demand Schedule for a Product

demand schedule a schedule that indicates the quantity of a product that would be demanded at each possible price

The demand for a product can be shown with a **demand schedule,** or a schedule that indicates the quantity of the product that would be demanded at each possible price. Consider personal computers as an example. Assume that the demand schedule for a particular type of personal computer is as shown in the first and second columns in Exhibit 4.6 for a given point in time. If the price is relatively high, the quantity demanded by consumers is relatively low. For example, if the price is $3,000, only 8,000 of these computers will be demanded (purchased) by consumers. At the other extreme, if the price is $1,000, a total of 25,000 of these computers will be demanded by customers. The quantity of personal computers demanded is higher when the price is lower.

Exhibit 4.6

How the Equilibrium Price Is Determined
by Demand and Supply

If the Price of a Particular Computer Is:	The Amount of These Computers Demanded by Consumers Will Be:	The Amount of These Computers Supplied (Produced) by Firms Will Be:
$3,000	8,000	30,000
2,500	14,000	24,000
2,000	18,000	18,000
1,500	22,000	16,000
1,000	25,000	10,000

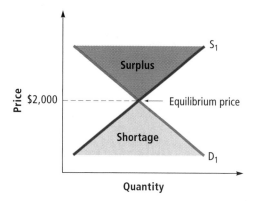

The graph in Exhibit 4.6, which is based on the table, shows the relationship between the price of a computer and the quantity of computers demanded by consumers. The demand curve (labeled D_1) shows that as the price decreases, the quantity demanded increases.

Supply Schedule for a Product

supply schedule a schedule that indicates the quantity of a product that would be supplied (produced) by firms at each possible price

The supply of a product can be shown with a **supply schedule,** or a schedule that indicates the quantity of the product that would be supplied (produced) by firms at each possible price. Assume that the supply schedule for the type of personal computer already discussed is as shown in the first and third columns of Exhibit 4.6 for a given point in time. When the price at which the personal computer can be sold is relatively high, firms will produce a large supply of this computer. For example, if the price is $3,000, 30,000 of these computers will be produced. Firms are willing to produce the computers at this price because they will earn a high profit if they can sell the computers at such a high price.

At the other extreme, if the price of computers is only $1,000, only 10,000 of these computers will be produced. The quantity supplied is much smaller at a low price because some firms will be unwilling to produce the computers if they can sell them for only $1,000. If some firms' actual cost of producing the computers is above this price of $1,000, these firms will be unwilling to produce the computers.

The graph accompanying Exhibit 4.6, which is based on the table, shows the relationship between the price of a computer and the quantity of computers supplied (produced) by firms. The supply curve (labeled S_1) shows that as price increases, the quantity of computers supplied increases.

A group of visitors to a Porsche and Audi dealership demonstrates North American desires for foreign-made cars, TVs and clothes.

AP Photo/ Keith Srakocic

Interaction of Demand and Supply

The interaction of the demand schedule and supply schedule determines the price. Notice from Exhibit 4.6 that at relatively high prices of computers (such as $3,000), the quantity supplied by firms exceeds the quantity demanded by customers, resulting in a so-called **surplus** of computers. For example, at the price of $3,000 the quantity supplied is 30,000 units and the quantity demanded is 8,000 units, resulting in a surplus of 22,000 units. This surplus occurs because consumers are unwilling to purchase computers when the price is excessive.

surplus the situation when the quantity supplied by firms exceeds the quantity demanded by customers

When the price of a computer is relatively low, the quantity supplied by firms will be less than the quantity demanded by customers, resulting in a so-called **shortage** of computers. For example, at a price of $1,000, the quantity demanded by customers is 25,000 units, while the quantity supplied by firms is only 10,000 units, causing a shortage of 15,000 units.

shortage the situation when the quantity supplied by firms is less than the quantity demanded by customers

Notice from Exhibit 4.6 that at a price of $2,000, the quantity of computers supplied by firms is 18,000 units, and the quantity demanded by customers is also 18,000 units. At this price, there is no surplus and no shortage. The price at which the quantity of a product supplied by firms equals the quantity of the product demanded by customers is called the **equilibrium price.** This is the price at which firms normally attempt to sell their products.

equilibrium price the price at which the quantity of a product supplied by firms equals the quantity of the product demanded by customers

At any price above the equilibrium price, the firms will be unable to sell all the computers they produce, resulting in a surplus. Therefore, they would need to reduce their prices to eliminate the surplus. At any price below the equilibrium price, the firms will not produce a sufficient quantity of computers to satisfy all the customers willing to pay that price (resulting in a shortage). The firms could raise their price to correct the shortage.

The demand and supply concepts just applied to a particular type of computer can also be applied to every product or service that firms produce. Each product or service has its own demand schedule and supply schedule, which will determine its own equilibrium price.

Exhibit 4.7

How the Equilibrium Price Is Affected by a
Change in Demand

If the Price of a Particular Computer Is:	The Quantity of These Computers Demanded by Consumers Was:	But the Quantity of These Computers Demanded by Consumers Will Now Be:
$3,000	8,000	18,000
2,500	14,000	24,000
2,000	18,000	28,000
1,500	22,000	32,000
1,000	25,000	35,000

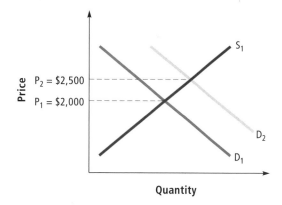

Effect of a Change in the Demand Schedule

As time passes, changing conditions can cause a demand schedule or a supply schedule for a specific product to change. Consequently, the equilibrium price of that product will also change. Reconsider the previous example and assume that computers become more desirable to potential consumers. Assume that the demand schedule for the computer changes as shown at the top of Exhibit 4.7. At any given price, the quantity demanded is now 10,000 units higher than it was before the computer became more popular. The graph accompanying Exhibit 4.7 shows how the demand curve shifts outward from D_1 to D_2.

Now consider the effect of this change in the demand schedule on the equilibrium price of computers. Assuming that the supply schedule remains unchanged, the effect of the change in the demand schedule on the equilibrium price is shown in Exhibit 4.7. At the original equilibrium price of $2,000, the quantity of computers demanded is now 28,000, while the quantity of computers supplied is still 18,000. A shortage of computers occurs at that price. At a price of $2,500, however, the quantity of computers supplied by firms equals the quantity of computers demanded by customers. Therefore, the new equilibrium price is $2,500. The graph at the bottom of Exhibit 4.7 confirms that the shift in the demand schedule from D_1 to D_2 causes the new equilibrium price of computers to be $2,500.

The graph illustrating the effect of a shift in the demand schedule on the equilibrium price of a product can be supplemented with simple logic. When a product becomes more popular, consumers' demand for that product increases, resulting in a shortage. Under these conditions, firms

Exhibit 4.8

How the Equilibrium Price Is Affected by a
Change in Supply

If the Price of a Particular Computer Is:	The Quantity of These Computers Supplied by Firms Was:	But the Quantity of These Computers Supplied by Firms Will Now Be:
$3,000	30,000	36,000
2,500	24,000	30,000
2,000	18,000	24,000
1,500	16,000	22,000
1,000	10,000	16,000

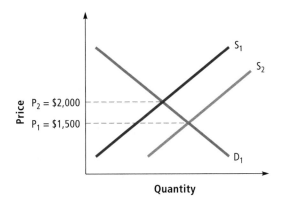

recognize that they can sell whatever amount they produce at a higher price. Once the price is raised to the level at which the quantity supplied is equal to the quantity demanded, the shortage is corrected.

Effect of a Change in the Supply Schedule

Just as the demand for a product may change, so may the supply. A change in the supply can also affect the equilibrium price of the product. To illustrate this effect, reconsider the original example in which the equilibrium price of computers was $2,000. Now assume that improved technology allows firms to produce the computer at a lower cost. In this case, firms will be willing to produce a larger supply of computers at any given price, which reflects a change in the supply schedule.

Assume that as a result of the improved technology (lower production costs), the supply schedule changes as shown in Exhibit 4.8. At any given price, the quantity supplied is now 6,000 units higher than it was before the improved technology. The graph accompanying Exhibit 4.8 shows how the supply schedule shifts outward from S_1 to S_2.

Now consider the effect of this change in the supply schedule on the equilibrium price of computers. Assuming that the demand schedule remains unchanged, the effect of the change in the supply schedule on the equilibrium price is shown in Exhibit 4.8. At the original equilibrium price of $2,000, the quantity of computers demanded is 18,000, while the quantity of computers supplied (produced) is now 24,000. A surplus of computers occurs at that price. At a price of $1,500, however, the quantity of computers supplied by firms equals the quantity of computers demanded by consumers. Therefore, the new equilibrium price is $1,500. The graph at the bottom of Exhibit 4.8 confirms that the shift in the supply schedule from S_1 to S_2 causes the new equilibrium price of computers to be $1,500.

The graph illustrating the effect of a shift in the supply schedule on the equilibrium price of a product can be supplemented with simple logic. When improved technology allows firms to produce a product at a lower cost, more firms will be willing to produce the product. This results in a larger supply produced, which causes a surplus. Firms recognize that the only way they will be able to sell all that is supplied (produced) is to lower the price of the product. Once the price is lowered to the level at which the quantity supplied is once again equal to the quantity demanded, the surplus is eliminated.

Effect of Demand and Supply on the General Price Level

The discussion so far of demand and supply has focused on one product to show how the equilibrium price of that product might change. Now consider how the general price level for all products might change. The general price level is an average of prices of all existing products and services. If the total (aggregate) demand by consumers for all or most products suddenly increases (perhaps because of an increase in the income level of most consumers), the general level of prices could rise. The general price level may also be affected by shifts in the supply schedules for all goods and services. If the supply schedule of all or most products suddenly decreases (perhaps because of increasing expenses when producing the products), the general level of prices should rise.

FACTORS THAT INFLUENCE MARKET PRICES

Thus far, examples have illustrated how the demand by customers or the supply produced by firms can change, causing a new market price. Shifts in the demand schedule or the supply schedule can be caused by several factors, some of which are identified next.

Consumer Income

Consumer income determines the amount of products and services that individuals can purchase. A high level of economic growth results in more income for consumers. When consumers' income rises, they may demand a larger quantity of specific products and services. That is, the demand schedules for various products and services may shift out in response to higher income, which could result in higher prices.

Conversely, when consumers' income level declines, they may demand a smaller quantity of specific products. For example, in the early 1990s, the average income level in the United States declined substantially in specific areas where firms relied on government contracts (such as for building missiles and so on). The federal government's cutbacks on such expenditures resulted in less work for firms in specific regions of the country. As income declined, the demand for new homes in these areas declined, causing a surplus of new homes. The firms that were building new homes were forced to lower their prices because of the surplus.

Consumer Preferences

As consumer preferences (or tastes) for a particular product change, the quantity of that product demanded by consumers may change. There are numerous examples of products whose prices rose in response to increased demand. For example, the price of a scalped ticket at a sold-out event such as a concert, the World Series, or the Super Bowl may easily exceed $300.

When a product becomes less popular, the demand for the product declines. The resulting surplus may force firms to lower their prices to sell what they produce. For example, when specific clothes become unpopular, clothing manufacturers sell these clothes at discounted prices just to eliminate the surplus.

Production Expenses

Another factor that can affect equilibrium prices is a change in production expenses. When firms experience lower expenses, they are willing to supply (produce) more at any given price (as explained earlier). This results in a surplus of the product, forcing firms to lower their price to sell all that they have produced. For example, the prices of musical compact discs have declined every year since they were first introduced.

When expenses of firms increase, the opposite result occurs. For example, insurance companies that had insured South Florida homes in the early 1990s incurred high expenses in the aftermath of Hurricane Andrew. Some of these companies decided that they would no longer supply this insurance service in South Florida. Those companies that were still willing to provide insurance were able to raise their prices.

3

Explain how the government influences economic conditions.

GOVERNMENT INFLUENCE ON ECONOMIC CONDITIONS

The federal government can influence the performance of businesses by imposing regulations or by enacting policies that affect economic conditions. Since the regulations tend to vary by industry, they are discussed in the chapter on the industry environment. To influence economic conditions, the federal government implements monetary and fiscal policies, which are discussed next.

Monetary Policy

money supply demand deposits (checking accounts), currency held by the public, and traveler's checks

In the United States, the term **money supply** normally refers to demand deposits (checking accounts), currency held by the public, and traveler's checks. This is a narrow definition, as there are broader measures of money supply that count other types of deposits as well. Regardless of the precise definition, any measure of money represents funds that financial institutions can lend to borrowers.

Federal Reserve System the central bank of the United States

monetary policy decisions on the money supply level in the United States

The U.S. money supply is controlled by the **Federal Reserve System** ("the Fed"), which is the central bank of the United States. The Fed sets the **monetary policy,** which represents decisions on the money supply level in the United States. The Fed can easily adjust the U.S. money supply by billions of dollars in a single day. Because the Fed's monetary policy affects the money supply level, it affects interest rates. When the Fed affects interest rates with its monetary policy, it directly affects a firm's interest expenses. Second, it can affect the demand for the firm's products if those products are commonly purchased with borrowed funds.

How the Fed Can Reduce Interest Rates

The Fed maintains some funds outside the banking system, which are not loanable funds. These funds are not available to firms or individuals who need to borrow. The Fed can use these funds to purchase Treasury securities held by individuals and firms. These purchases provide individuals and firms with new funds, which they deposit in their commercial banks. Consequently, the money supply increases because the commercial banks and other financial institutions can loan out these funds. In other words, the Fed's action increases the supply of loanable funds. Assuming that the demand for loanable funds remains unchanged, the increase in the supply of loanable funds should cause interest rates to decrease. The impact of the supply of loanable funds on interest rates is discussed in more detail in the Chapter 17 appendix. By reducing interest rates, the Fed may be able to stimulate economic growth. The lower borrowing rates may entice some consumers and firms to borrow more funds and spend more money, which can result in higher revenue and earnings for businesses.

How the Fed Can Increase Interest Rates

When the Fed reduces the U.S. money supply, it pulls funds out of commercial banks and other financial institutions. This reduces the supply of funds that these financial institutions can lend to borrowers. Assuming that the demand for loanable funds remains unchanged, the decline in the supply of loanable funds should cause interest rates to rise. The higher interest rates increase the cost of borrowing and thus tend to discourage consumers and firms from borrowing. The Fed raises interest rates when it wants to reduce the degree of spending in the United States. The Fed might do this because an excessive amount of spending can cause a higher degree of inflation. Therefore, when the Fed raises interest rates, in order to reduce spending, it is actually trying to reduce the level of inflation.

Fiscal Policy

fiscal policy decisions on how the federal government should set tax rates and spend money

Fiscal policy involves decisions on how the federal government should set tax rates and spend money. These decisions are relevant to businesses because they affect economic growth and therefore can affect the demand for a firm's products or services.

Revision of Personal Income Tax Rates

Consider a fiscal policy that reduces personal income taxes. With this policy, people would have higher after-tax incomes, which might encourage them to spend more money. Such behavior reflects an increase in the aggregate demand for products and services produced by businesses which would improve the performance of businesses.

Revision of Corporate Taxes

Fiscal policy can also affect a firm's after-tax earnings directly. For example, assume the corporate tax rate is reduced from 30 percent to 25 percent. If a specific corporation's before-tax earnings are $10 million, its taxes would have been $3 million (computed as 30% × $10,000,000) at the old tax rate. Now, however, at a corporate tax rate of 25 percent, its taxes are $2.5 million (computed as 25% × $10,000,000). Therefore, the corporation's after-tax earnings are now $500,000 higher, simply because the corporate taxes are $500,000 lower.

Revision in Excise Taxes

excise taxes taxes imposed by the federal government on particular products

Excise taxes are taxes imposed by the federal government on particular products. These taxes raise the cost of producing these goods. Consequently, manufacturers tend to incorporate the tax into the price they charge for the products. Thus, consumers indirectly incur the tax. The tax may also discourage consumption of these goods by indirectly affecting the price. Excise taxes are imposed on various products, including alcohol and tobacco.

Revision in the Budget Deficit

federal budget deficit the situation when the amount of federal government spending exceeds the amount of federal taxes and other revenue received by the federal government

The fiscal policy set by the federal government dictates the amount of tax revenue generated by the federal government and the amount of federal spending. If federal government spending exceeds the amount of federal taxes, a **federal budget deficit** results.

When the federal government receives less revenue than it spends, it must borrow the difference. For example, if the federal government plans to spend $900 billion but receives only $700 billion in taxes (or other revenue), it has $200 billion less than it desires to spend. It must borrow $200 billion to have sufficient funds for making its expenditures (as shown in Exhibit 4.9). If the federal government needs to borrow additional funds, it creates a high demand for loanable funds, which may result in higher interest rates (for reasons explained earlier).

In the 1998–2000 period, the federal government spent less funds than it received, which resulted in a small surplus. Under these conditions, the government's budget policy does not place upward pressure on interest rates. In 2001, the tax revenue received by the U.S. government declined because income levels declined as the economy weakened. In addition, the U.S. government spent more money in 2001 due to expenses associated with the September 11 tragedy and the subsequent war. Therefore, the U.S. government experienced a budget deficit in 2001. The increase in government spending in the 2001–2002 period was offset by the reduction in spending by consumers and businesses, however, demand for loanable funds remained relatively low, as did interest rates.

Summary of Government Influence on Economic Factors

Exhibit 4.10 provides a summary of how the federal government can affect the performance of firms. Fiscal policy can affect personal tax rates and therefore influence consumer spending behavior. It can also affect corpo-

---

Exhibit 4.9

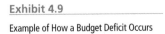

Example of How a Budget Deficit Occurs

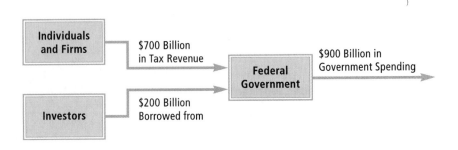

Exhibit 4.10

How Government Policies Affect Business
Performance

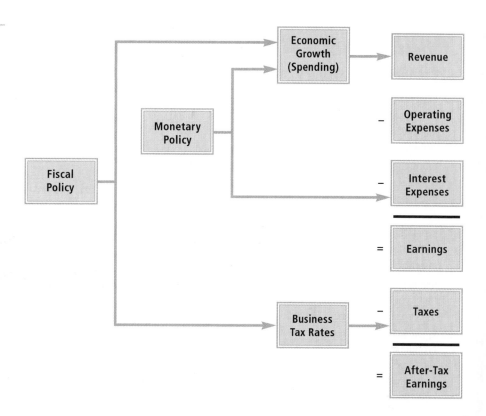

rate tax rates, which influence the earnings of firms. Monetary policy can
affect interest rates, which may influence the demand for a firm's product
(if the purchases are sometimes paid for with borrowed funds). By influencing interest rates, monetary policy also affects the interest expenses that
firms incur.

Dilemma of the Federal Government

The federal government faces a dilemma when attempting to influence economic growth. If it can maintain a low rate of economic growth, it can prevent inflationary pressure caused by an excessive demand for products. A
restrictive monetary or fiscal policy may be used for this purpose. A restrictive monetary policy leads to low growth in the money supply over time,
which tends to place upward pressure on interest rates. This discourages
borrowing and therefore can reduce total spending in the economy. A restrictive fiscal policy results in high taxes and low government spending.

Although restrictive monetary and fiscal policies may keep inflation
low, a critical trade-off is involved. The unemployment rate may be higher
when the economy is stagnant. The federal government can use a more
stimulative policy (such as low tax rates or a monetary policy designed to
reduce interest rates) to boost economic growth. Although these policies increase economic growth, they may also cause higher inflation.

Rarely is a consensus reached on whether the government should use
a stimulative or restrictive policy at a given point in time. During the late
1990s, the federal government used stimulative monetary policies because
inflation was very low and was not expected to be a serious problem. This
monetary policy helped to increase economic growth during that period. As

cross functional teamwork:

Economic Effects across Business Functions

Since managers of a firm have different responsibilities, they assess different aspects of the economic environment. Managers who focus on production monitor the changes in economic conditions that could affect the firm's production costs. They tend to monitor inflationary trends, or changes in the price levels of specific supplies or equipment that they purchase.

Marketing managers attempt to forecast sales of their products and assess economic conditions that affect the demand for the products, such as economic growth. They may also monitor interest rates if the products are commonly purchased with borrowed funds because the demand for these products may increase in response to a reduction in interest rates. Since the firm's production volume is dependent on the forecasted demand for the product, it is influenced by economic conditions.

Marketing managers assess economic conditions because their marketing decisions can be affected by the strength of the economy. Some of a firm's products (such as necessities and relatively inexpensive products) may be marketed more heavily when economic conditions are weak because these products may be more popular at that time. Conversely, the firm may market its expensive products more heavily when economic conditions are more favorable.

The firm's financial managers monitor the economic conditions that affect the cost of financing. They tend to focus on interest rates because the firm's financing expenses are directly affected by changes in interest rates.

When different types of managers forecast economic conditions so that they can make business decisions, they should work as a team. Otherwise, a forecast of some economic conditions may vary across managers, which may cause their business decisions to be different. For example, if the marketing managers of an automobile manufacturer expect low interest rates, they will expect a high sales volume, which will require a large production of automobiles. However, if the production managers expect high interest rates, they will expect a lower level of sales and will be concerned that a large production volume could cause excessive inventories.

Some firms assign one person or department to develop the forecasts of all economic conditions, which the managers use in all business functions. In this way, all managers make decisions according to the same forecasts of economic conditions.

the economy weakened, in the early 2000s, stimulative monetary policies were used in an effort to increase economic growth.

Managers of firms commonly attempt to forecast how future fiscal and monetary policies will affect economic conditions. Then they use this information to predict the demand for the firm's product, its labor and material costs, and its interest expenses. To illustrate, assume an automobile manufacturer forecasts that next year's interest rate on consumer loans will decrease by 2 percent. This forecast of interest rates will be used to forecast the demand for the firm's automobiles. Lower interest rates will probably lead to higher demand, because more consumers will be willing to finance their purchases of new automobiles. Assume that the firm believes that for every 1 percent decrease in interest rates, demand for its automobiles will increase by 3 percent. Thus, it anticipates a 6 percent increase in sales volume in one year.

College Health Club: CHC's Exposure to Economic Conditions

A business plan should include a discussion of how the firm's performance is exposed to economic conditions. The business plan of College Health Club (CHC) discussed this topic as follows:

Business Plan of CHC

CHC's membership is exposed to local economic conditions. If a weaker economy causes some students to lose their part-time jobs, in the local area, the number of memberships is likely to decline. Consequently, CHC's revenue and earnings would decline. A stronger economy would allow for more part-time jobs in the local area and would likely result in more memberships at CHC. Consequently, CHC's revenue and earnings would increase.

SUMMARY

1 A firm's performance is highly dependent on three macroeconomic factors: (1) economic growth, (2) inflation, and (3) interest rates. A high level of economic growth tends to increase the overall demand for a firm's products and services. Inflation affects the costs of supplies and wages, which represent the firm's operating expenses. Higher inflation tends to cause higher operating expenses. Interest rates affect the firm's interest expenses. An increase in interest rates will typically result in higher interest expenses for the firms

2 Market prices are determined by demand and supply conditions. The demand for a product is influenced by consumer income and preferences. Higher consumer income generally results in a higher demand for products. The amount of a product produced is influenced by production expenses. Firms will supply products to the market only if the market price is sufficiently high to more than cover expenses.

3 The federal government influences macroeconomic conditions by enacting monetary or fiscal policies. Its monetary policy affects the amount of funds available at commercial banks and other financial institutions and therefore affects interest rates. Its fiscal policy affects the taxes imposed on consumers, which can influence the amount of spending by consumers and therefore affect the performance of firms. Fiscal policy is also used to tax the earnings of firms.

KEY TERMS

Review & Critical Thinking Questions

1. List and briefly describe macro-economic factors that affect business performance.

2. Describe the four different types of unemployment and explain which type a college graduate would face upon entering the job market.

3. Why should firms be concerned with changes in interest rates?

4. What are the two basic determinants of market prices? How are shortages and surpluses corrected in the marketplace?

5. Define and explain price equilibrium for businesses and consumers. What is the effect on the equilibrium price when there is a surplus or shortage?

6. Briefly describe three factors that influence market prices.

7. Explain the effect of demand and supply on the general price level in the economy.

8. Define monetary policy. Who is responsible for regulating monetary growth in the United States?

9. Describe how the Fed can reduce interest rates. How can the Fed increase interest rates?

10. Distinguish between macroeconomics and microeconomics. Are fiscal policy decisions of a macroeconomic or microeconomic nature?

11. Discuss the two primary responsibilities of the federal government in establishing economic policies. What does it mean to have a budget deficit?

Discussion Questions

1. In your community, do businesses and housing show signs of economic growth or evidence of decay? What effect do these conditions have on inflation and interest rates?

2. Discuss the current interest rate environment. Do you think interest rates are likely to increase or decrease in the near future?

3. How could a firm use the Internet to assess the current level of some macroeconomic factors that may affect business performance, such as economic growth and inflation? How could a firm use the Internet to determine the demand for its products?

4. Assume that you are a manager in a plant that produces rollerblades. What factors would you consider in determining the price for this product?

5. When college students are given federal grants (such as Pell Grants) that cover some education expenses, does this reflect a form of fiscal policy or monetary policy? Explain your answer.

6. Discuss the effects of a federal government budget deficit. How could a budget deficit affect borrowing by firms and households?

It's Your Decision: **Economic Exposure at CHC**

1. Would the business performance of CHC be more exposed to economic growth in the United States as a whole or to economic growth in the local area? Why?

2. Assume that the federal government is expected to raise income taxes for all people, regardless of income level. How could this change in tax policy affect the performance of CHC?

3. Would CHC's business performance be more exposed to inflation in the United States as a whole or in the local area? How could CHC's future expenses be affected by inflation?

4. Explain how marketing at CHC could be affected by economic conditions. Then explain how the amount of aerobics classes and other health club services produced could be affected by economic conditions.

5. A health club differs from manufacturing firms in that it produces a service rather than products. Consider Local Video, Inc., which manufactures video games that are primarily

sold to the students at Texas College. Is this manufacturing firm more exposed than CHC to the overall economic conditions in the United States? Now consider Tex, Inc., which produces video games for adults throughout the United States. Is Tex, Inc., more exposed to the overall economic conditions in the United States than CHC is? Explain.

Investing in a Business

Using the annual report of the firm in which you would like to invest, complete the following:

1 Was your firm's performance affected by economic growth last year? If so, how? Are these trends expected to continue? What does your firm plan to do about the economic conditions it faces?

2 Was your firm's performance affected by inflation or interest rates last year? If so, how?

3 Explain how the firm uses technology to assess its economic environment. For example, does it use the Internet to assess the economic environment?

Case: Impact of Economic Conditions

Gold Autoparts, Inc., produces automobile parts which are purchased by various automobile manufacturers that are building new cars. Gold has had some success in selling its parts to automobile manufacturers because they do not have to produce those parts if they can rely on Gold to do so.

Gold has recently created a website that lists all of its parts and the prices charged for them. The automobile manufacturers can order parts online, and Gold tries to fill these orders quickly.

Gold attempts to anticipate when orders will increase so that it can produce enough parts to fill orders. It realizes that the demand for its auto parts is dependent on economic conditions that affect the demand for new cars. When demand for new cars increases, more new cars are produced, and there is greater demand for Gold's parts.

Tom Gold, president of Gold Autoparts, expects that economic growth will increase this year. He expects that interest rates will be relatively low over the next year. He also expects that foreign car manufacturers will introduce many new types of cars into the U.S. market. At this time, Gold Autoparts focuses its business on U.S. automobile manufacturers.

Questions

1 How will Gold Autoparts, Inc., be affected if economic growth increases as expected?

2 How will Gold Autoparts be affected if interest rates decline as expected?

3 How might the introduction of many new cars by foreign car manufacturers affect Gold's business?

4 Overall, do you think conditions will cause an increase or decrease in the demand for Gold's auto parts?

Video Case: Exposure to Weak Economic Conditions

Linda Russell's CollectionCenter faced a dilemma. Major job sources in Wyoming—oil, gas, coal, uranium, and timber—were in trouble, a trouble especially deep in the area around Rawlins, location of Russell's collection and credit-reporting agency. Rawlins was experiencing a very weak economy, which reduced the ability of customers to pay their bills.

Russell takes a gentle approach to debt collection, with a philosophy of helping people figure out ways to pay what they owe, rather than browbeat them. The approach had been working well.

CollectionCenter had strengths: a team of skilled, dedicated people and a reputation for outstanding service. The team included Russell's husband, Jerry, a lawyer with an outside practice who served as CollectionCenter's executive vice president.

The Russells huddled with some of the team and collection and credit-reporting managers. It was agreed that CollectionCenter would shrink and die if its territory didn't expand. Input was solicited from everyone on the team, and the company moved into Wyoming's two largest cities, Casper and Cheyenne, buying existing agencies there.

"We were off and running," says Linda Russell, "but we found we were in real need of more expertise in the rapidly changing world of computers with which we had to deal."

Since then, the company has expanded farther, to Ft. Collins and Grand Junction in Colorado and Salt Lake City, Utah. Its team has increased from 12 to 69.

Questions

1 Explain why the revenue generated by Linda Russell's CollectionCenter may decline when the local economy is weak, while the expenses of the CollectionCenter do not decline.

2 Explain how expansion of the CollectionCenter business into other locations can reduce the firm's exposure to the economic conditions of Rawlins, Wyoming. Would expansion into new locations where the economic conditions were similar to Rawlins, Wyoming, be a useful strategy for the CollectionCenter? Explain.

3 Assume that the one executive of the CollectionCenter suggested that the entire firm be moved to Salt Lake City, where the economic conditions are presently more favorable than all other regions. Is this an appropriate strategy to prevent any adverse effects of economic conditions over the next several years?

Internet Applications

1. *http://www.federalreserve.gov/policy.htm*

Briefly describe the Federal Open Market Committee (FOMC) and explain its role. When is the next scheduled meeting of the committee? Have you heard any news coverage regarding the type of action the FOMC might take at this meeting? How is the type of information provided on this website useful for decision making by a business?

2. *http://www.worldbank.org*

What is the World Bank? What is its purpose? Click on "Data and Statistics." What is some economic information provided on this website for the United States? How could this information be used by companies to make business decisions?

The Coca-Cola Company Annual Report Project

Questions for the current year's annual report are available on the text website at **http://madura.swlearning.com.**

The following questions apply concepts presented in this chapter to The Coca-Cola Company. Go to The Coca-Cola Company website (**http://www.cocacola.com**) and find the index for the 2001 annual report.

Questions

1 Find "Impact of Inflation and Changing Prices" in the consolidated financial statements. How could inflation affect The Coca-Cola Company's future profitability? What does The Coca-Cola Company generally do to counteract inflationary effects?

2 Find "Euro Conversion" in the consolidated financial statements. Did the management of The Coca-Cola Company experience any problems associated with the introduction of the euro, the new European currency? Does the management of The Coca-Cola Company expect any future problems?

3 Click on "Selected Market Results" under "Operations Review." Given that it is impossible to predict future economic conditions, what might be a general strategy of a large firm such as The Coca-Cola Company to insulate against shifts in the economic environment of any particular country?

4 Find the "Interest Income and Interest Expense" section in the consolidated financial statements. How were The Coca-Cola Company's interest income and interest expenses affected by the interest rate environment in 2001? How does this compare to the year 2000?

5 Go to **http://hoovers.com** and locate the NEWS CENTER. Key in The Coca-Cola Company in the space provided, click on "Search," and review the recent news stories about the firm. Summarize any (at least one) recent news story about The Coca-Cola Company that applies one or more of the key concepts within this chapter of the text.

In-Text Study Guide

Answers are in an appendix at the back of the book.

True or False

1. Macroeconomics is focused on a specific business or industry of concern. F

2. When the U.S. economic growth is lower than normal, the total income level of all U.S. workers is relatively high. F

3. Economic growth represents the change in the general level of economic activity. T

4. The total amount of expenditures in the economy is known as aggregate expenditures. T

5. Structural unemployment refers to workers who lose their jobs due to a decline in economic conditions. F

6. A higher level of inflation will cause a larger decrease in a firm's operating expenses. F

7. Inflation is usually measured as the percentage change in gross domestic product. F

8. The demand for a product can be shown with a demand schedule, which indicates the quantity of the product that would be demanded at each possible price. T

9. The Federal Reserve System sets the monetary policy that determines the money supply in the United States. T

10. The Fed affects interest rates by changing the supply of funds banks can loan. T

Multiple Choice

11. _____C_____ conditions reflect the overall performance of the nation's economy.
    a) Microeconomic
    b) Multi-economic
    c) Macroeconomic
    d) Proto-economic
    e) Supraeconomic

12. All of the following are examples of macroeconomic concerns except:
    a) a drop in the nation's gross domestic product.
    b) an increase in the rate of inflation.
    c) a strike by workers at a local bakery.

    d) an increase in the amount of cyclical unemployment.
    e) an increase in the rate of interest charged on bank loans.

13. The total market value of all final goods and services produced in the United States is known as:
    a) gross domestic product.
    b) aggregate expenditures.
    c) fiscal output.
    d) the production quota.
    e) aggregate supply.

14. Jan is currently between jobs, but she has marketable job skills and is confident she will find work in the near future. Jan's current situation would be an example of _____ unemployment.
    a) seasonal
    b) structural
    c) functional
    d) frictional
    e) cyclical

15. The type of unemployment that represents people who are unemployed because of poor economic conditions is:
    a) functional unemployment.
    b) cyclical unemployment.
    c) seasonal unemployment.
    d) structural unemployment.
    e) general unemployment.

16. The type of inflation that requires firms to increase their prices to cover increased costs is referred to as:
    a) demand-pull inflation.
    b) stagflation.
    c) cost-push inflation.
    d) disequilibrium.
    e) unemployment.

17. The prices firms pay for supplies or materials directly influence their:
    a) operating expenses.
    b) operating revenue.
    c) dividends.
    d) stockholders' equity.
    e) economic assets.

In-Text Study Guide

Answers are in an appendix at the back of the book.

18. An increase in the general level of prices of products and services over a specified period of time is called:
    a) inflation.
    b) stagflation.
    c) unemployment.
    d) disinflation.
    e) equilibrium.

19. _____ represent the cost of borrowing money.
    a) Discount factors
    b) Depreciation rates
    c) Inflation premiums
    d) Dividends
    e) Interest rates

20. Over the next several years, economic growth in less-developed nations is:
    a) unlikely to occur due to lack of natural resources in most of these countries.
    b) likely to occur, but at a much slower rate than growth in the United States.
    c) likely to be greater than the growth in the United States, thus providing U.S. firms with important market opportunities.
    d) unlikely to occur because of the anti-growth attitudes of their governments.
    e) likely to be quite rapid, but U.S. firms are unlikely to benefit since they view the opportunities in less-developed countries as being too risky.

21. A typical demand schedule shows that:
    a) as price decreases, quantity demanded will also decrease.
    b) as price decreases, quantity demanded will increase.
    c) quantity supplied can never be less than quantity demanded.
    d) the total quantity of goods consumers want to buy will fall during periods of inflation.
    e) a firm can always increase its revenue by increasing the prices it charges for its products.

22. A supply schedule shows:
    a) the relationship between quantity supplied and quantity demanded.

b) how the quantity firms supply in the market affects their total profits.
    c) the quantity firms are willing to supply at each possible price.
    d) the average cost of supplying various quantities of a good.
    e) the relationship between the amount of labor and other inputs the firm employs and the quantity of output the firm can produce.

23. At the equilibrium price for a good, the:
    a) firms in the market are maximizing their total revenue.
    b) consumers in the market have spent all of their income.
    c) firms in the market are maximizing their total output.
    d) firms in the market are just breaking even.
    e) quantity demanded by consumers equals the quantity supplied by firms.

24. If the market price of a good is above the equilibrium price:
    a) a surplus will exist, which will put downward pressure on prices.
    b) the supply curve will shift to the right as firms rush to take advantage of the high price.
    c) the demand curve will shift to the left as consumers decrease the quantity they buy.
    d) the government will intervene to force the price downward.
    e) a shortage will exist, which will force the price even higher.

25. If the market price is below the equilibrium price:
    a) quantity demanded will exceed quantity supplied, resulting in a shortage.
    b) quantity demanded will exceed quantity supplied, resulting in a surplus.
    c) quantity supplied will exceed quantity demanded, resulting in a shortage.
    d) quantity supplied will exceed quantity demanded, resulting in a surplus.
    e) the supply curve will shift to the left and the demand curve will shift to the right.

26. An increase in the demand for a product is likely to cause:
    a) a matching decrease in supply.

In-Text Study Guide

Answers are in an appendix at the back of the book.

b) an increase in the equilibrium price.
c) the supply curve to shift to the right.
d) a decrease in the equilibrium price.
e) the government to attempt to increase production quotas.

27. If consumer incomes increase, the effect on consumer decisions about how much they want to buy can be shown by:
a) shifting the demand curve outward (to the right).
b) shifting the supply curve outward.
c) shifting the demand curve inward (to the left).
d) moving downward to the right along the demand curve.
e) shifting the supply curve inward.

28. The _____ of the United States is defined as the total amount of demand deposits, currency held by the public, and traveler's checks.
a) financial wealth
b) financial reserves
c) money supply
d) total banking assets
e) gross domestic product

29. The central bank of the United States, where the money supply is controlled and regulated, is the:
a) Federal Reserve System.
b) Senate.
c) Department of Congress.
d) Council of Economic Advisers.
e) Board of Directors.

30. A major effect of the Federal Reserve's monetary policies is to bring about changes in the:
a) stock of gold held by the government to back the money supply.
b) income tax rates paid by households and businesses.
c) size of the federal budget deficit.
d) amount the government spends to finance social programs.
e) interest rates banks charge when they make loans.

31. Which of the following is the best example of the federal government's use of fiscal policy?
a) The Federal Reserve places new regulations on the nation's banks that require them to make more loans to minorities and women.

b) The U.S. Treasury announces that it has redesigned the nation's paper money to make the bills more difficult to counterfeit.
c) The government cuts taxes during an economic downturn.
d) The president appoints a new commission to look into concerns about how pollution is damaging the environment.
e) The Federal Reserve gives banks more funds to enable them to make more loans.

32. Taxes that the federal government imposes on particular products are called:
a) excise taxes.
b) import taxes.
c) export taxes.
d) quotas.
e) embargoes.

33. When the amount of federal government spending exceeds the amount of federal taxes, the result is a so-called:
a) trade deficit.
b) federal budget deficit.
c) balance of payments.
d) price equilibrium.
e) opportunity cost.

34. Restrictive monetary and fiscal policies may keep inflation low, but the critical trade-off is that they may also cause:
a) disinflation.
b) environmental problems.
c) massive crime.
d) unemployment.
e) higher inflation.

35. The government can prevent inflationary pressure caused by an excessive demand for products by maintaining a low rate of:
a) fiscal policies.
b) economic growth.
c) monetary policies.
d) unemployment.
e) savings.

business decisions

The Learning Goals of this chapter are to:

1 Identify the industry characteristics that influence business performance.

2 Explain why some firms are more exposed to industry conditions.

3 Explain how a firm can compete within its industry.

Chapter 5

Assessing Industry Conditions

Just as a firm is affected by macroeconomic conditions, it is also affected by microeconomic conditions related to the firm and its respective industry.

Consider the case of Dunham Golf Course, which has benefited from the dramatic increase in the popularity of golf. In recent years, the demand for golf services has increased substantially. In response to the increase in demand, many new golf courses have been established. Consequently, the competition among golf courses has increased. Like all golf courses, the Dunham Golf Course is subject to industry conditions. Its revenue is directly affected by the demand for its golf services, which is dependent on industry conditions. To cope with industry conditions, it must determine:

▶ What industry characteristics will influence its business performance?

▶ How sensitive is its revenue to industry conditions?

▶ What can it do to compete more effectively within its industry?

These types of decisions are necessary for all businesses. This chapter explains how the assessment of the industry environment by the Dunham Golf Course or any other firm can be conducted so that it maximizes the firm's value.

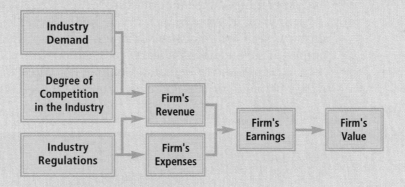

1 INDUSTRY CHARACTERISTICS THAT INFLUENCE BUSINESS PERFORMANCE

Identify the industry characteristics that influence business performance.

The performance of the firm can be highly dependent on the following industry characteristics:

▶ Industry demand
▶ Industry competition
▶ Labor environment
▶ Regulatory environment

Industry Demand

Over a given time period, a specific industry can perform much better than others because the total demand for the industry's products (called **industry demand**) is high. The industry demand for baby clothes is highly dependent on the number of children that are born. The industry demand for hotels in Florida during the winter is partially dependent on the weather in the northern states. In cold winters, more tourists travel to Florida. Therefore, it would be a mistake for a firm to conclude that it will perform well over the next year just because economic conditions in the United States are favorable.

As industry demand changes, so does the performance of firms in the industry. For example, the performance levels of DaimlerChrysler, Ford Motor Company, and General Motors are related over time because they are similarly affected by industry conditions. These firms experienced relatively poor performance in the early 1990s when the economy was weak and the demand for new automobiles was low. They performed much better in the mid- and late-1990s when the demand for new automobiles increased. When the economy slowed during the 2001–2002 period, their performance declined again.

Industry demand can change abruptly and therefore is monitored closely by a firm's managers. It can be affected by changes in consumer income levels or preferences. For example, consumer preferences have substantially increased the demand for minivans in recent years, which has favorably affected DaimlerChrysler and other manufacturers of minivans. Consumer preferences have also recently increased the demand for athletic footwear, which has favorably affected Nike, Reebok International, and other athletic shoe manufacturers.

Just as an increase in industry demand is beneficial to firms in that industry, a decline in industry demand has adverse effects. The following examples illustrate how industry competition can change in response to a change in industry demand. Compaq benefited from the increased industry demand for computers in the mid-1990s. As new firms recognized

Toyota President Fijio Cho displays the automaker's new compact car "ist" during its launching in Tokyo in 2002. The four-seater is a new model intended to attract more customers.

AP Photo/ Katsumi Kasahara

Industry demand resulted in increased bicycle and bicycle accessories sales that have occurred across generations.

(c) Getty Images / Photo Disc

the large industry demand and entered the computer industry, however, Compaq faced more intense competition and ultimately was acquired by Hewlett-Packard.

As a second example, consider the case of Bell Sports Corporation, which was once the largest producer of motorcycle helmets. In the early 1990s, it experienced a decline in business because the demand for these helmets leveled off. As demand for bicycles increased, Bell switched its production process to make bicycle helmets instead. However, other firms also recognized the popularity of bicycles and began to compete in this market. In response to the intense competition in the bicycle helmet industry, Bell began to produce other bicycle accessories, such as child seats, safety lights, and car racks. In this way, it diversified its product line so that it was not completely reliant on its bicycle helmet business.

Industry Competition

Each industry is composed of various firms that compete against each other for the customers who want their products. The level of competition varies across industries. When a firm faces more competition in its industry, it will typically be less profitable. A firm's sales as a proportion of the total market (called **market share**) are normally higher when it faces little competition. In addition, a firm can charge a higher price without losing its customers if it faces little competition. Total revenue is dependent on the quantity (Q) of units sold and the price (P) per unit:

market share a firm's sales as a proportion of the total market

$$\text{Revenue} = Q \times P$$

A firm that faces little competition can sell a high quantity at a high price and therefore generate a high level of revenue.

A high degree of competition has the opposite effect. First, it can reduce each firm's market share, thereby reducing the quantity of units sold by each firm in the industry. Second, a high degree of competition may force each firm in the industry to lower its price to prevent competitors from taking away its business. For example, when some phone services lowered their rates on long-distance calls in 2001–2002, all phone services were forced to follow that strategy in order to retain their customers.

College Health Club: **Impact of Competition on CHC**

As Sue Kramer develops her business plan for College Health Club (CHC), she must assess the competition. Currently, CHC's main competitor is Energy Health Club, which is a 20-minute drive from the college campus. Sue expects that she will achieve her initial goal of 300 members by the end of the first year. However, she recognizes that a competing health club could be established near the college campus at any time. She attempts to estimate how CHC's earnings would be affected this year if a new health club opens. Assuming that a new health club would charge about the same price for a membership, she believes that CHC might attract only 250 members instead of 300 members. The potential impact of a new competitor on CHC's performance is shown in the following table.

	Present Conditions (No New Competiton)	If a Competing Health Club Is Established near the Campus
(1) Price per membership	$500	$500
(2) Number of members in first year	300	250
(3) Revenue in first year $= (1) \times (2)$	$150,000	$125,000
(4) Operating expenses	$138,000	$138,000
(5) Interest expenses	$4,000	$4,000
(6) Earnings before taxes $= (3) - (4) - (5)$	$8,000	−$17,000

Since CHC's expenses are mostly fixed, any effect of a decline in memberships on revenue has a direct impact on earnings. Given the exposure of CHC's performance to a new competitor, Sue recognizes that she will need to develop strategies to retain her members if a new health club is established nearby.

Labor Environment

Some industries have specific labor characteristics. The cost of labor is much higher in industries such as health care that require specialized skills. Unions may also affect the cost of labor. Some manufacturing industries, particularly those in the northern states, have labor unions, and labor costs in these industries are relatively high. Industries that have labor unions may also experience labor strikes. Understanding the labor environment within an industry can help a firm's managers estimate the labor expenses the firm will incur.

Regulatory Environment

The federal government may enforce environmental rules or may prevent a firm from operating in particular locations or from engaging in particular types of business. Although all industries are subject to some form of government regulation, some industries face especially restrictive regulations. Automobile and oil firms have been subject to increased environmental regulations. Firms in the banking, insurance, and utility industries have been subject to regulations on the types of services they can provide. Thus, an entrepreneur who wishes to enter any industry must recognize all the regulations that are imposed on that industry.

Firms that are already operating in an industry must also monitor industry regulations because they may change over time. For example, recent reductions of regulations in the banking industry have allowed banks more freedom to engage in other types of business. Some banks have attempted to capitalize on the change in regulations by offering new services.

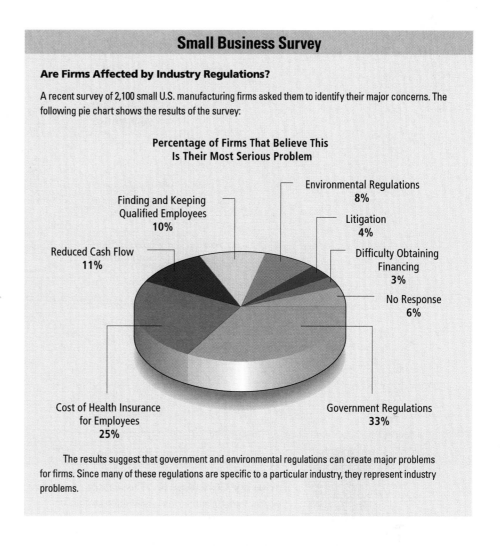

Small Business Survey

Are Firms Affected by Industry Regulations?

A recent survey of 2,100 small U.S. manufacturing firms asked them to identify their major concerns. The following pie chart shows the results of the survey:

Percentage of Firms That Believe This Is Their Most Serious Problem

Environmental Regulations
8%

Litigation
4%

Difficulty Obtaining Financing
3%

No Response
6%

Government Regulations
33%

Cost of Health Insurance for Employees
25%

Reduced Cash Flow
11%

Finding and Keeping Qualified Employees
10%

The results suggest that government and environmental regulations can create major problems for firms. Since many of these regulations are specific to a particular industry, they represent industry problems.

In addition, firms must be aware of regulations aimed at promoting competition within an industry. For example, the U.S. Justice Department attempts to prevent price-fixing, in which two or more firms in the same industry set prices. In the early 1990s, U.S. airlines were forced to provide millions of dollars in discounts to passengers to settle a price-fixing lawsuit.

Summary of Industry Characteristics

All of the industry characteristics just identified must be considered to determine their impact on a firm's performance. The means by which these characteristics affect a firm's profits are shown in Exhibit 5.1. Changes in industry demand and competition affect the demand for a firm's products and therefore affect its revenue. Since these industry characteristics influence the quantity of products that the firm produces, they also affect operating costs, such as manufacturing and administrative expenses. Any changes in the labor and regulatory environments typically affect a firm's expenses. The overall effect on profits is dependent on the impact each individual characteristic has on either the firm's revenue or expenses. The potential impact of industry demand and competition on a firm's performance can be confirmed by consulting any business periodical that discusses how a particular industry performed recently.

Exhibit 5.1

Industry Effects on a Firm's Performance

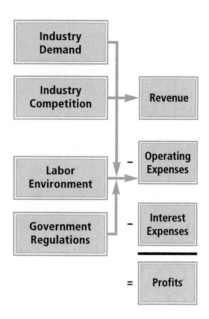

business online

Industry Conditions   This website provides information about changes in business activity for various industries within each state.

U.S. Department of Labor

http://stats.bls.gov/eag/

SOURCES OF INDUSTRY INFORMATION

Although a firm can attempt to monitor its industry's characteristics, it may also rely on other sources for industry information. The following sources provide useful information about the characteristics of each industry:

1 *Value Line*   The Value Line Investment Survey provides valuable information about numerous publicly traded companies, including financial characteristics, forecasts of earnings, and general information about the respective industries.

2 *Standard and Poor's*   The Standard and Poor's Industry Outlook provides industry data and assessments for several different industries. A firm can use this source to forecast the industry demand, competition, labor environment, and regulatory environment.

EXPOSURE TO INDUSTRY CONDITIONS

2

Explain why some firms are more exposed to industry conditions.

The exposure of a firm to a given industry's conditions is dependent on its particular characteristics. Some firms are more exposed to industry conditions, causing their performance to be more dependent on prevailing industry conditions. Two of the key characteristics that affect a firm's exposure to industry conditions are the firm's market share and the firm's focus on its main industry.

Firm's Market Share

The degree to which a firm is affected by a change in industry conditions is dependent on its market share, or its share of total sales in the industry (or market). A firm that controls a larger share of the market will normally benefit more from an increase in industry demand. For example, Hewlett-Packard benefits more than small firms from an increase in the demand for fax machines.

A line of Hewlett-Packard shareholders wait to get into a shareholders meeting. The proxy fight over the $21 billion acquisition of Compaq Computer Corporation by HP gave individual investors a rare chance to directly influence the fate of the two companies.

AP Photo/ Paul Sakuma

Exhibit 5.2

Influence of Market Share on Exposure to Industry Conditions

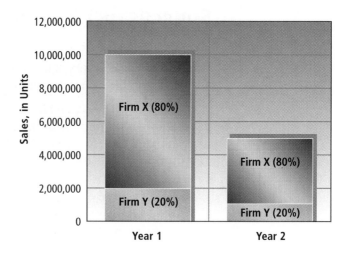

Firms that have the most market share, however, are also hurt more than smaller firms when industry demand declines. Exhibit 5.2 illustrates how firms with a larger market share are affected more by changes in industry demand. It assumes that an industry has just two firms: Firm X with 80 percent market share and Firm Y with 20 percent market share. In Year 1, total industry sales were equal to 10,000,000 units. In Year 2, however, total industry sales declined to 5,000,000 units. Assuming that each firm's market share remained unchanged, Firm X's sales declined by 4,000,000 units in Year 2 whereas Firm Y's sales declined by only 1,000,000 units.

A firm does not have much control over the industry demand. Nevertheless, it may attempt to forecast industry demand, which may allow it to forecast the demand for its own product. For example, assume that a firm expects industry demand to equal 5,000,000 units over the next year. If its market share is 20 percent, its forecast of the demand for its product is as follows:

$$\text{Demand for Firm's Product} = \text{Firm's Market Share} \times \text{Industry Demand}$$
$$= \quad 20\% \quad \times \ 5{,}000{,}000 \text{ Units}$$
$$= \ 1{,}000{,}000 \text{ Units}$$

If changing conditions cause industry demand to decline, the forecasted demand for the firm's product should be revised. For example, if the forecasted industry demand from the previous example is revised to 4,000,000 units, the demand for the firm's product would be only 800,000 units (computed as 20% × 4,000,000 units).

Firm's Focus on Its Main Industry

Firms that focus all of their business on one industry are generally more exposed to the industry's conditions. For example, Smith Corona Corporation, which focused its business on producing typewriters and word processors, was highly exposed to any changes in the total demand for these office machines. When the demand for these machines declined due to increased use of computers, Smith Corona filed for bankruptcy.

As another example of the impact of industry conditions, consider the case of Motorola. It attempted to capitalize on the telecommunications boom in 2000 by expanding its production facilities for telecommunications equipment and devices. In 2001, however, there was a major downturn in the telecommunications industry, causing a decline in the total demand for telecommunications equipment. In addition, many new firms had entered the industry, which increased the degree of competition within the industry. Motorola lost some of its market share because of the increased competition. Because of the decline in the industry demand and the intensified competition, Motorola's sales declined by more than 20 percent. Furthermore, it incurred expenses from expanding its production facilities to prepare for growth that failed to occur. Many other firms in the telecommunications industry experienced similar problems as a result of these industry conditions.

Firms in the computer industry experienced similar effects during 2001. Not only did the industry demand for computers decline, but fierce competition among the firms forced them to lower their prices to maintain their share of the market. Consequently, they not only sold fewer computers, but earned a smaller profit on each computer that they sold because of the low price charged per computer.

Exhibit 5.3 compares changes in performance among industries. It shows the monthly percentage changes in stock indexes for four broadly defined industries during a recent period. If the general performance levels of all industries were the same, the four trends would be identical. The four trends vary substantially. Thus, a firm's performance is dependent on the industry that it serves.

Reducing Exposure through Diversification A firm may desire to reduce its exposure to the possibility of poor conditions in its respective industry. One solution is to diversify its businesses across several different industries. For example, consider the case of Westin Company, which manufactured electronic components that are used only by auto manufacturers. When the automobile industry experienced weak demand, the demand for Westin's components declined. To reduce its exposure to the automobile industry, Westin began to produce electronic components for computer firms

Exhibit 5.3

Comparison of Performance across Industries

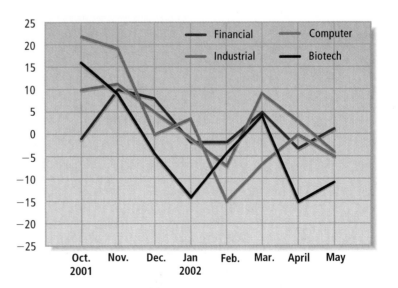

and construction companies. Its business is now somewhat sensitive to the level of activity in the computer and construction industries, but it is less sensitive to the activity in the automobile industry. When Westin anticipates a large decline in demand in the automobile industry, it adjusts its operations to produce and sell more components in the computer and construction industries. In this way, it can reduce any adverse effects that could be caused by a decline in any particular industry.

Ford Motor Company has diversified by producing a variety of trucks along with its cars. When demand for its cars is stagnant, it may still benefit from an increase in demand for trucks. Seagrams Company traditionally focused on sales of alcoholic beverages, but its performance was adversely affected by the decline in demand for alcoholic drinks. It responded by producing nonalcoholic beverages to reduce its risk of poor performance because of exposure to a single industry. Exxon (now ExxonMobil) benefited from diversifying into the petrochemical businesses because the performance of its oil business was highly exposed to changes in the market price of crude oil. DuPont produces a wide variety of products, including nylon, coatings, pharmaceuticals, polyester, and specialty fibers. Dow Chemical Company has diversified across chemicals, plastics, and energy products. Wal-Mart has recently diversified its retail business by becoming a retailer of groceries.

The following comments from a recent annual report from Textron (a large diversified firm) confirm the potential benefits of diversification:

"Textron's presence in diverse industries helps achieve balance and stability in a variety of economic environments by providing insulation from business and industry cycles. More specifically, we were able to maintain consistent growth . . . because the growth of our Aircraft, Automotive, Industrial and Finance businesses more than offset the downturns in the Systems and Components segment."

Exhibit 5.4 compares the average return on equity for two related industries and for a combination of those two industries. Notice how a diversified combination of the two industries creates a more stable return on

Exhibit 5.4

How Diversification Can Influence the Return on Equity

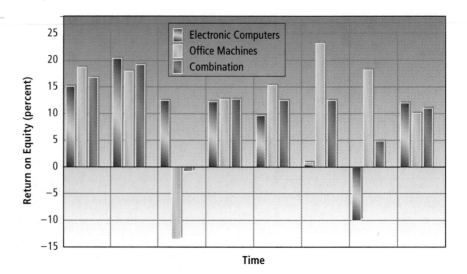

investment than either individual industry over time. In a period when one industry performs poorly, the other industry may perform well.

Although diversification can effectively reduce a firm's exposure to one industry, firms should only diversify across industries in which they have sufficient expertise. During the 1980s, many firms diversified across industries completely unrelated to their expertise. Many of these unrelated businesses performed poorly and were sold by the firms during the 1990s. For example, Chrysler (now DaimlerChrysler) entered the corporate aircraft business, military defense business, and car rental business. It lost its focus by attempting to engage in too many different businesses and incurred higher expenses than expected.

College Health Club: CHC's Exposure to Industry Conditions

As Sue Kramer develops her business plan for College Health Club (CHC), she needs to assess the exposure of her business to industry conditions. The general demand for health club services has increased over time. Sue is confident that the strong demand will continue because people are more conscious about staying in shape. Within the health club industry, the types of services desired can change significantly over time. For example, there are fads for specific types of aerobic classes and weight machines. Regardless of the fads, Sue thinks that she can adjust her classes and machines to satisfy changes in consumer preferences.

Sue has no plans to diversify her business, as she believes she should focus on what she knows best. Nevertheless, she hopes to diversify her sources of revenue over time by selling some products to members of her health club. She plans to sell vitamin supplements and workout clothing and may even offer health therapy services someday.

3

Explain how a firm can compete within its industry.

COMPETING WITHIN AN INDUSTRY

Intense competition can separate the performance of the well-managed firms in an industry from that of the poorly managed firms. When the airlines industry became more competitive, some of the poorly managed airlines failed. The well-managed airlines captured some of the market share lost by those that failed. Similarly, when the banking industry became more competitive and many commercial banks failed, the well-run commercial banks were able to capture some of the market share lost by those that failed.

Given the influence of industry competition on a firm's performance, a firm should perform two tasks:

▶ Assess the competitors.

▶ Develop a competitive advantage.

Assess the Competitors

segments subsets of a market that reflect a specific type of business and the perceived quality

Every firm should be able to identify its competitors and measure the degree of competition. Each industry has **segments,** or subsets that reflect a specific type of business and the perceived quality. Thus, an industry can be narrowly defined by segmenting the industry according to type of business and quality. Segmenting the industry in this way helps identify the main competitors so that they can be assessed.

Segmenting by Type of Business Within an industry, some firms may focus on specific types of customers. For example, in the car rental industry, some firms (such as National Car Rental Systems) focus heavily on business customers, while others (such as Hertz) are more evenly split between businesses and individuals on vacation. The furniture industry has segments such as outdoor furniture, bedroom furniture, and office furniture. The degree of competition within each segment may vary. There may be heavy competition in bedroom furniture but little competition in outdoor furniture. A firm that focuses only on the production of outdoor furniture is not concerned with the demand for office furniture. Therefore, it is helpful for a firm to narrowly define its industry before assessing the degree of competition.

Segmenting by Perceived Quality Once the firm defines its industry by the type of business, it should assess the different quality segments that exist. Exhibit 5.5 shows different quality segments (based on customer perceptions) in the market for small cars. Each type of car in this market is represented by a point. Some cars, such as the BMW and the Corvette, are perceived to have high quality (measured according to engine size and other features that customers desire) and a relatively high price. Other cars have a moderate quality level and a lower price, such as the Toyota Celica. The Ford Escort and the Chevy Cavalier represent cars in a lower quality and price segment. Because each consumer focuses only on one particular market segment, the key competitors are within that same segment. For example, the Escort and Cavalier are competitors within the low-priced segment. The Escort is not viewed as a competitor to the higher-priced cars.

Many firms create products that are designed for different population segments. Firms commonly expand by producing different types of the same product, which are offered to various segments. General Motors produces the Cavalier for the low-priced, small-car segment, the Firebird for the moderate-priced segment, and the Corvette for the high-priced segment. A firm may produce a high-quality product for consumers who can afford to pay a high price and a low-quality product for consumers who are less concerned about quality and more concerned about price. Tire companies such as Goodyear and Michelin produce tires that fit the high-priced and low-priced segments. Beer producers such as Anheuser-Busch and Miller Brewing produce different types of beer to satisfy high-priced

Exhibit 5.5

Identifying Industry Segments

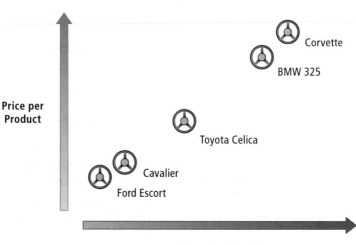

and low-priced segments. Most airlines provide first-class (high-priced) and coach (low-priced) seats to satisfy different segments.

Anticipating Changes in Competition   The competitors within an industry segment change over time. New firms may enter the market; others that were in the market but were unsuccessful may exit. Many competing firms in the same market attempt to expand. It is not unusual for every firm competing within a specific industry segment to share the same goal of increasing market share. Yet, all competitors within an industry segment cannot increase their market share at the same time. When some competitors gain market share, other competitors lose.

As an illustration of how a firm assesses its competition, consider the following statements made by Amazon.com in a recent annual report:

"The retail book market is extremely competitive. The Company's current or potential competitors include various online booksellers . . . , a number of indirect competitors that specialize in online commerce, . . . and publishers, distributors and retail vendors of books, music, and videotapes, including Barnes & Noble Inc. . . . The Company believes that the principal competitive factors in its market are . . . convenience, price, accessibility, customer service, quality . . . reliability, and speed of fulfillment. . . . The company believes that competition in the online commerce market will intensify in the future."

To understand how firms can be affected by changes in competition, consider the airline industry. In recent years, many new airlines began servicing specific routes. They attracted customers by offering low airfares. In response, some existing airlines reduced their airfares to discourage customers from switching to the new airlines. In general, the existing airlines were adversely affected by the new competition in two ways. First, their sales of airline tickets declined, as some customers switched to the new airlines. Second, the prices of many airline tickets were reduced to match the prices of new competitors. Both effects resulted in a decline in the revenue of the existing airlines, as well as a decline in their earnings. Recent annual reports by airlines, such as Delta Air Lines, confirm the adverse effects of increased competition. These effects intensified after the terrorist attacks on September 11, 2001, as many people chose to avoid flying. Thus, the airlines were competing for a smaller number of passengers.

Firms in various other industries have also acknowledged that they have been adversely affected by more intense competition. Kellogg Company has said that it was adversely affected by increased competition in the cereal industry. Federal Express claimed that its earnings were hurt by fierce competition in the express mail industry.

Develop a Competitive Advantage

Once a firm has identified and assessed its key competitors, it must search for ways to increase or at least maintain its market share. A firm must assess its specific industry segment to determine whether it has a competitive advantage. The following characteristics could create a competitive advantage for a firm:

► Low-cost production

► Better quality

► Product differentiation

increasing value with technology

COMPETITIVE ADVANTAGE

Advances in information technology are changing many industries, including the retail grocery industry. A few firms in that industry are building competitive advantages through state-of-the-art technology.

Grocery stores have typically been labor-intensive. In the past, cashiers entered every item and inventory was taken manually. Most stores have converted to scanners, which reduce the time required to check out a customer and allow the store to track the inventory electronically. The firms that committed to this technology early have prospered while others have lagged behind.

Many other advances are occurring as the grocery industry goes through a transition. Kroger Company is one of the firms that have adopted advanced self-scanning technology. With self-scanners, a store can open additional checkouts even when it is not adequately staffed. Customers come in waves to grocery stores, creating long lines at peak periods and overstaffing problems during nonpeak times. Self-scanning can help remedy this problem and lower costs.

Grocers and other retailers have also been using other advances in technology to create effective frequent-shopper programs. Customers of Schultz Sav-O are able to log on to a web page and access targeted discounts by entering their frequent-shopper account numbers. Sav-O customizes the discounts based on customer purchase histories. The system creates strong customer loyalty and enables the store to effectively evaluate its incentive program.

Retailers are also using data mining techniques to identify products that are purchased together. Data mining involves the search and analysis of large volumes of data for important information. Once a grocer identifies products that are purchased together, marketing and placement can improve sales. For instance, a study revealed that beer and diapers were frequently purchased together. Marketers surmised that fathers were purchasing beer on their late night diaper run. This led some stores to increase sales by placing high-margin beer near the diapers.

Low-Cost Production   If a firm can produce a product of similar quality at a lower cost, it can price the product lower than its competitors. This should enable that firm to attain a larger market share. For example, assume that a firm can produce high-quality outdoor furniture at a lower price than the other firms in the high-priced segment. This may allow the firm to charge a lower price and thereby capture a larger share of the high-priced outdoor furniture market. The low production cost may result from efficient management of the firm's employees (human resources) and its production process.

Some firms attempt to achieve a price advantage even when they do not have a cost advantage. For example, an entrepreneur may notice that the only gas station in a populated area has set high prices on its gasoline. The entrepreneur may consider establishing a new gas station in the area, with lower prices as its competitive advantage. However, the existing gas station may lower its gas prices in response to the new competitor. In this example, the entrepreneur's competitive advantage may be eliminated unless it has a cost advantage.

Airlines commonly attempt to achieve a price advantage over their competitors by advertising special fares on various routes over a particular period. The objective is to attract a higher demand by pulling customers away from other airlines. In many cases, other airlines respond by lowering their airfares by the same amount. If some of the airlines are less efficient, however, they may not be able to continue the low fares for a long period of time (because their costs may exceed the fares charged). Thus, the more efficient firms may drive the inefficient competitors out of the industry.

Better Quality   If a firm can produce a product of better quality without incurring excessive costs, it has a competitive advantage over other competitors in the same price range. For example, in the low-priced outdoor furniture market, one firm may be perceived to produce higher-quality furniture than other firms. If its furniture is priced about the same as others in its segment, its superior quality creates a competitive advantage within the low-priced outdoor furniture segment.

Various characteristics may cause a product to be of better quality. It may be easier to use, last longer, or provide better service. The specific characteristics that determine perceived quality vary among products. For soft drinks, quality may be measured by taste. For outdoor furniture, quality may be measured by durability. For computers, quality may be measured by ease of use, the service provided, and processing speed. By achieving higher quality, a firm can satisfy customers to a greater degree.

Product Differentiation   Firms commonly attempt to identify particular needs of some customers so that they can differentiate their product (or service) to satisfy those needs. For example, some contact lenses are made for permanent wear. Other lenses must be cleaned daily because some customers cannot wear lenses permanently. A third type of lens is disposable for those customers who are unable to keep the lenses clean and frequently need new lenses. Rarely can a particular product serve all customers, because customers desire different features in a given product.

Computer firms tend to differentiate their computers in ways that attract customers with specific preferences. Computers vary in power, size (some are portable), warranty, and service. They are also made to allow for replaceable components so that the product can precisely fit customers' needs.

Customer preferences for each particular type of service also vary, allowing firms in each service industry to differentiate their service. Some travel agencies specialize in cruise vacations. Others focus on international travel packages. The choice of a travel agent may be dependent on specific customer needs.

As time passes, customer preferences for a particular product's features can change. Firms must attempt to recognize these changes in the industry so that they can revise the products they offer. Failure to adapt can result in a reduction in the firm's market share. For several years, IBM conducted business without paying close attention to changes in industry conditions (such as a preference by many business customers for personal rather than mainframe computers). During that time, it did not keep pace with changes in the industry. General Motors was also slow to react to changes in customer preferences in the automobile industry. These firms improved their performance once they recognized the importance of responding to changes in customer preferences.

Firms commonly use *SWOT analysis* to develop a competitive advantage. The acronym SWOT stands for strengths, weaknesses, opportunities, and threats. Thus, in SWOT analysis, the firm assesses its own strengths and weaknesses, as well as external opportunities and threats. For example, Amazon.com may consider its strengths to include the creativity of its employees and its ability to apply technology. Its weakness may be its lack of traditional retail outlets to sell books (although that is also a strength because Amazon.com can avoid intermediaries). Its opportunities may be the potential market for other related products (in addition to books) online and the potential growth in the demand for online services in foreign

cross functional teamwork:

Industry Effects across Business Functions

Managers of a firm have different responsibilities and therefore assess different aspects of the industry environment. Production managers monitor changes in labor costs in a particular industry when anticipating how their production costs may change. They monitor changes in the industry's technology, because their production costs will be influenced by the level of technology. They also monitor regulatory changes in the industry that could require revisions to the production process. Such revisions may also affect the cost of production. Production managers may also monitor the level of industry demand so that they can determine the proper volume of products for their firm to produce.

Marketing managers monitor new competitors in the industry to become aware of the features of competing products. The managers consider this industry information when they search for strategies to make their product superior to those sold by competitors. Marketing man-

agers must obtain production cost information from production managers when deciding how to make their product superior.

Financial managers monitor the industry environment to determine how much money they can afford to borrow. If the competition in the industry is intense, the firm may lose its market share to other competitors. Therefore, a firm should limit its debt so that it is capable of covering future interest payments on that debt. Financial managers should obtain information from the marketing managers about the intensity of competition in the industry so that they can determine the amount of funds that will be available (from sales) to cover future interest payments.

In general, the industry environment can affect a firm's production, marketing, and finance functions in different ways. The overall assessment of potential industry effects requires input from each function.

countries. Its threats may include specific competitors that are creating similar online book businesses that provide the same type of services for consumers. SWOT analysis can help direct a firm's future business by using the firm's strengths to capitalize on opportunities, while reducing its exposure to threats. For example, if Amazon.com believes that one of its strengths is its technology, it may attempt to improve that technology to make its direct sales of books to customers even more convenient. Thus, even if competitors attempt to copy its existing business, Amazon.com will have advanced technology that allows it to offer better service than the competitors.

Assessing the Industry Environment from a Global Perspective When U.S. firms engage in international business, they must consider the segments within the foreign countries of concern. A specific product that is classified in a specific segment in the United States may be classified in a different segment in other countries. A product that is perceived as an inexpensive necessity in the United States may be perceived as an expensive luxury product in less-developed countries. U.S. firms may revise the quality and price of their products to satisfy a particular market segment. For example, Procter & Gamble produces a wide variety of household products that U.S. consumers may view as basic necessities.

Yet, those products are not affordable to consumers in some less-developed countries. Rather than ignore those countries, Procter & Gamble has revised its product and pricing strategies to fit the country of concern. As the company stated in a recent annual report: "In some countries where incomes are low, striking this balance between quality and price requires us to market a diaper that offers more basic features, at a substantially lower price, than the premium diaper we sell in many countries." This example illustrates how a firm's assessment of market segment can vary across countries and how its product and pricing strategies may need to be revised in accordance with each foreign country's characteristics.

global business

SUMMARY

1 The main industry characteristics that influence business performance are

▶ industry demand,

▶ industry competition,

▶ labor environment, and

▶ regulatory environment.

Industry demand and the degree of industry competition affect the demand for a firm's products or services and therefore affect the firm's revenue. The labor and regulatory environments typically affect the firm's expenses. Since a firm's profits equal its revenue minus its expenses, its profits are influenced by these industry factors.

2 A firm is more exposed to an industry's conditions when it has a large market share and focuses most of its business within that industry. As the industry's conditions change, most of the firm's business will be affected. Firms can reduce their exposure to industry conditions by diversifying their business across industries.

3 A firm can battle the competition by assessing its main competitors and then attempting to develop a competitive advantage. To identify its main competitors, it must recognize the segment of the industry that it serves. It can develop a competitive advantage within that industry segment through efficient production (which allows it to charge a lower price), better quality, or product differentiation.

KEY TERMS

industry demand   134

market share   135

segments   143

Review & Critical Thinking Questions

1. Identify and explain the main characteristics of the automobile industry that can influence business performance.

2. Explain why the cost of labor in some industries, such as the health-care industry, is so high.

3. Why is government regulation more restrictive in some industries than in others? Provide specific examples.

4. What outside resources are available to help a firm monitor the industry in which it operates?

5. Discuss what happens to a firm that has a large market share in an industry in which demand suddenly increases.

6. Why is a firm facing less competition in its industry more profitable?

7. Identify the steps a firm should take before deciding to compete in a specific industry.

8. How are existing firms in an industry affected when a new firm with a competitive advantage enters the industry?

9. List some characteristics that could create a competitive advantage for a firm.

10. What are the basic industry characteristics that influence business performance?

11. Distinguish between the responsibilities of a marketing manager and a financial manager in monitoring a particular industry.

Discussion Questions

1. Do you believe business enterprise should be regulated by the federal government or that the marketplace should determine prices? Discuss.

2. A group is discussing how competitive forces can be preserved within the marketplace of a free enterprise system. What are your views on the issue?

3. How can a firm use the Internet to determine how its competitors are performing and how they are affected by industry conditions?

4. Assume that you are a production manager in the automobile industry. Do you think your operation should be labor-intensive or capital- (machinery) intensive? Discuss.

5. Consider a car that has typically been classified in the low-price segment, but has been unable to compete there because it is priced higher than the other cars in that segment. What alternative strategies are possible for the car as it is redesigned for the next year?

It's Your Decision: Industry Exposure at CHC

1. Explain how the increased popularity of exercise videos and portable weight machines will affect the number of CHC's memberships, its revenue, and its earnings.
2. How could Sue differentiate her services to maintain her customers (mostly students) even if a new competitor enters the market?
3. How might the degree of competition affect the amount of marketing CHC requires? How might the degree of competition affect the amount of aerobics classes and other health club services produced at CHC?
4. Assuming that the estimated expenses in the first year are $142,000, determine how CHC's estimated earnings before taxes are affected by the following possible industry scenarios:

If a Competing Health Club Is Established within _____ Miles of CHC	Expected Membership at CHC in the First Year	Earnings before Taxes at CHC in the First Year
4	280	_____
7	290	_____
10	294	_____

Explain the relationship between the proximity of the competitor and CHC's expected earnings.

5. A health club differs from manufacturing firms in that it produces a service rather than products. As with most service firms, CHC's main competition would come from competitors based in the same area. Explain why manufacturing firms may be more exposed to competitors that are located far away.

Investing in a Business

Using the annual report of the firm in which you would like to invest, complete the following:

1 Describe the competition within your firm's industry. If the annual report does not contain information, try to find a magazine or newspaper article that discusses the competitive environment within your firm's industry. How successful is your firm compared with its competitors?

2 Was your firm's performance affected by industry conditions last year? If so, how?

3 Explain how the business uses technology to assess its industry environment. For example, does it use the Internet to assess the industry environment? Does it use the Internet to assess the performance of its competitors?

4 Go to **http://hoovers.com** and locate the NEWS SEARCH. Type in the name of the firm in the space provided, and review the recent news stories about the firm. Summarize any (at least one) recent news story about the firm that applies to one or more of the key concepts in this chapter.

Case: Impact of Industry Conditions

Phoenix Shoes has recently established a shoe store that sells high-quality, high-priced shoes to customers of all ages. Its main source of revenue, however, is the sale of children's shoes. Its store is located in a large shopping mall. The store has been very successful in the year that it has been open. However, Stephanie Scheck, the owner of Phoenix Shoes, is worried about the following industry conditions.

First, she is concerned that the general demand for high-quality shoes could decline because parents may not be so willing to purchase high-quality shoes for children who quickly grow out of them. She is also concerned because published surveys suggest that parents are shifting their preference toward casual footwear for their children. Phoenix has focused on formal footwear.

Second, Stephanie is concerned about a new competitor shoe business at the other end of the mall that sells relatively low-quality shoes at low prices.

Third, Stephanie is concerned about another new competitor shoe business that sells high-quality shoes online through its website. The quality of these shoes is similar to that of Phoenix's shoes, but they are priced at 10 percent less.

Stephanie recognizes that the store's future performance is influenced by industry conditions that affect the general demand for its products, as well as its market share within its industry. She wants to assess how Phoenix might be affected by the recent industry conditions and how it can protect its market share.

Questions

1 How can Stephanie Scheck attempt to protect Phoenix's market share, given the shift in preference toward more casual footwear?

2 Will the demand for shoes at Phoenix be affected by the new shoe business at the other end of the shopping mall? If so, how can Phoenix protect its market share?

3 Will the demand for shoes at Phoenix be affected by the new online shoe business? If so, how can Phoenix protect its market share?

4 Is there any way that Phoenix could expand its product line to increase its revenue?

Video Case: World Gym's Position in the Fitness Industry

World Gym Showplace Square in San Francisco was created to serve customers who prefer a fitness center between the high-end (luxury fitness centers) and the low-end fitness centers. Its facilities were established in a busy area where many people work. There was a strong demand for fitness facilities in the area, but little competition. World Gym set a price that was lower than its competitors' prices. In this way, it encouraged customers to try its services. Its membership increased from 500 to 2,500 in the first year and now is about 8,000. As new competitors (such as Gold's Gym) entered the market, World Gym responded by improving its facilities and lowering prices. Thus, it encouraged its customers to continue their membership rather than switching to other fitness facilities.

Questions

1 Explain how World Gym is focused on a specific market segment.

2 Explain how World Gym used pricing to attract demand.

3 Why do you think World Gym responded with lower prices and improved facilities when new competitors entered the area?

Internet Applications

1. *http://www.activemedia-guide.com/ industry_profile_cp.htm*

Click on an industry of your choice, such as "Entertainment." What is the industry environment of this industry? What are some of the issues firms operating in this industry face, and what are some of the industry trends? Describe any international aspects of the industry. What type of firm do you think would be highly exposed to industry conditions? Why? What type of firm do you think would be able to compete successfully in this industry? Why?

2. *http://www.census.gov/econ/www*

Click on the "Services" category and review the latest economic data available for the various subsectors. How could businesses utilize this information to compete more effectively within their industry? Do you think the economic data available are favorable? Why or why not?

3. *http://www.bls.gov/lpc/home.htm*

What is the industry productivity program? What types of news releases are available as part of this program from the Department of Labor? View the "Most Requested Statistics." Why do you think these statistics are the most requested?

The Coca-Cola Company Annual Report Project

 Questions for the current year's annual report are available on the text website at **http:// madura.swlearning.com**

The following questions apply concepts learned in this chapter to The Coca-Cola Company. Go to The Coca-Cola Company website (**http://www.cocacola.com**) and find the index for the 2001 annual report.

Questions

1. Look at "Selected Market Results" under "Operations Review." How does The Coca-Cola Company's average annual five-year growth rate in U.S. unit case volume compare with the rest of the industry?

2. Study the "Worldwide Volume" section under "Operations Review." Do you think The Coca-Cola Company's competition varies by specific products (Coca-Cola, Sprite, Minute Maid, etc.) that it sells? Do you think The Coca-Cola Company views tap water as a major competitor? Why?

3. Click on "Selected Market Results."

   a. What is The Coca-Cola Company's current market share of sales of nonalcoholic ready-to-drink beverages on a worldwide basis?

   b. What is its market share of the nonalcoholic ready-to-drink beverage market in Mexico? In China? In Germany?

4. Click on "Selected Market Results." By how much did the increase in The Coca-Cola Company's Great Britain unit case volume exceed the growth of the Great Britain soft-drink industry?

5. Go to **http://hoovers.com** and locate the NEWS CENTER. Key in The Coca-Cola Company in the space provided, click on "Search," and review the recent news stories about the firm. Summarize any (at least one) recent news story about The Coca-Cola Company that applies one or more of the key concepts within this chapter of the text.

In-Text Study Guide

Answers are in an appendix at the back of the book.

True or False

1. A firm can safely conclude that it will perform well over the next year if there are favorable economic conditions in the United States. F
2. Total revenue is dependent on the quantity of units sold and the expenses of producing those units. F
3. A firm that faces a high degree of competition can sell a low-quality product at a high price and thereby generate a high level of profit. F
4. The cost of labor is high in industries that require specialized skills. T
5. All industries are subject to some form of government regulation. T
6. Market share refers to an individual firm's sales expressed as a proportion of the total industry sales. T
7. Firms that focus all of their business in one industry are generally less exposed to the industry's conditions. F
8. Typically, a firm will have less ability to predict industry's demand than to control it. F
9. Diversification can reduce a firm's exposure to poor performance in a particular industry. T
10. Improved product quality can create a competitive advantage for a firm. T

Multiple Choice

11. An industry characteristic that influences business performance is:
    a) social responsibility.
    b) competition.
    c) machinery.
    d) inflation throughout the United States.
    e) gross domestic product.

12. As industry demand changes, so does the _____ of firms in the industry.
    a) performance
    b) business ethics

c) consumerism
d) conservationism
e) regulatory environment

13. Over a given time period, a specific industry with strong total demand can perform better than industries experiencing relatively weak demand. This performance difference is due to differences in:
    a) industry supply.
    b) market share.
    c) equilibrium price.
    d) industry demand.
    e) industry conditions.

14. Industry demand is commonly affected by changes in consumer preferences and:
    a) consumer ethics.
    b) consumer income levels.
    c) labor supply schedules.
    d) activity level of labor unions.
    e) production technology advancements.

15. Monitoring changes in market tastes and preferences can enable a firm to stay in touch with changes in consumer demands. This strategy will enable a firm to maintain or improve its:
    a) technology schedule.
    b) social responsibility.
    c) business ethics.
    d) market share.
    e) equilibrium salary schedule.

16. Total revenue is the result of multiplying the selling price of the product times the:
    a) quantity of units sold.
    b) quantity of units produced.
    c) quantity of labor hours used.
    d) quality demanded by consumers.
    e) quantity of government regulations.

17. A firm can charge a higher price without losing its customers if it does not have much:
    a) production.
    b) competition.

In-Text Study Guide

Answers are in an appendix at the back of the book.

c) marketing.

d) advertising.

e) industry demand.

18. Labor costs are often higher in industries that have:

a) labor unions.

b) unemployment.

c) savings.

d) demand schedules.

e) interest expense.

19. According to the text, industry regulations have recently been reduced in the:

a) automobile industry.

b) chemical industry.

c) oil industry.

d) banking industry.

e) steel industry.

20. Managers will monitor changes in labor costs in order to control:

a) marketing costs.

b) macroeconomics.

c) production costs.

d) social responsibility.

e) industry demand.

21. The performance of a firm can be highly dependent on the following industry characteristics except for:

a) regulatory environment.

b) labor environment.

c) industry competition.

d) industry demand.

e) gross domestic product.

22. Changes in industry demand and competition affect both the demand for a firm's products and the firm's:

a) location.

b) customer service.

c) revenue.

d) recycling.

e) segmentation.

23. A firm's share of total sales in the industry is called its:

a) industry demand.

b) regulatory environment.

c) market share.

d) economic segment.

e) competitive advantage.

24. Two of the key characteristics that affect a firm's exposure to industry conditions are the firm's market share and the firm's focus on its:

a) recycling.

b) downsizing.

c) main industry.

d) fringe market.

e) labor union.

25. The demand for a firm's product equals the firm's market share multiplied by:

a) industry demand.

b) gross national product.

c) gross domestic product.

d) inflation rate.

e) unemployment rate.

26. A firm may attempt to conduct an industry forecast; however, it does not have much control over:

a) revenue.

b) production costs.

c) production schedules.

d) industry demand.

e) employee hiring.

27. To reduce its exposure to the possibility of poor conditions in its respective industry, a firm needs to:

a) diversify.

b) socialize.

c) privatize.

d) commercialize.

e) increase its size.

28. During the 1980s, many firms diversified across industries completely unrelated to their:

a) business ethics.

b) expertise.

In-Text Study Guide

Answers are in an appendix at the back of the book.

   c) management styles.
   d) social responsibility.
   e) goal of high performance.

29. Another name for subsets in an industry that reflect a specific type of business and the perceived quality is:
   a) demographics.
   b) marketing.
   c) sales.
   d) segments.
   e) economics.

30. A firm must assess its specific industry segment to determine whether it has a(n):
   a) forecast.
   b) competitive advantage.
   c) industry condition.
   d) cost differential.
   e) shift in supply.

31. After a firm identifies a specific industry, it can segment that industry by:
   a) level of employees.
   b) scrap reworked.
   c) labor environment.
   d) conservationism.
   e) quality segments.

32. Once a firm has identified and assessed its key competitors, it must search for ways to increase or at least maintain its:
   a) labor environment.
   b) regulatory environment.
   c) market share.
   d) competition.
   e) social costs.

33. Even if a firm does not have a cost advantage, it may still create a(n):
   a) inflation advantage.
   b) condition advantage.
   c) monopoly advantage.
   d) price advantage.
   e) ethics advantage.

34. Since a particular product or service cannot serve all customers, firms attempt to _____ their products or services.
   a) diffuse
   b) differentiate
   c) target
   d) consolidate
   e) diversify

35. Firms commonly use a _____ analysis to develop a competitive advantage.
   a) SWOT
   b) SPUR
   c) SNAP
   d) STEP
   e) SPOT

Most businesses, including Starbucks, should consider how they might be exposed to the international environment, and how they can capitalize on international opportunities.

The Learning Goals of this chapter are to:

1 Explain the motives for U.S. firms to engage in international business.

2 Describe the global opportunities that have encouraged U.S. firms to pursue international business.

3 Describe how firms conduct international business.

4 Explain how foreign characteristics can influence a firm's international business.

5 Explain how exchange rate movements can affect a firm's performance.

Chapter 6

Assessing Global Conditions

Many U.S. firms have capitalized on opportunities in foreign countries by engaging in international business. The amount of international business has grown in response to the removal of various international barriers. Even small U.S. firms are now engaging in international business by purchasing foreign supplies or by selling their products in foreign countries.

International economic conditions affect a firm's revenue and expenses and therefore affect its value. To illustrate how the international environment can affect the value of a business, consider the case of Starbucks, which is well-known in the United States for its coffee business. In recent years, Starbucks has expanded into foreign countries. Its expansion has been successful so far,

and there are many foreign locations that are being considered for future expansion. Since expansion of business into foreign countries can be very expensive, Starbucks wants to carefully assess whether to expand and where to expand. The performance of the Starbucks business in a foreign country is dependent on the country's cultural characteristics (whether its coffee appeals to the local people), and financial characteristics (the cost of establishing a Starbucks shop). In addition, the performance is affected by economic conditions in the country, since the demand for coffee is influenced by the income level of the local people.

Specifically, Starbucks must determine:

▶ What methods might it use to increase its business?

▶ What foreign characteristics influence its level of business in foreign countries?

▶ How is its international business affected by exchange rates?

All firms that conduct international business must address these types of questions. These firms commonly strive to increase their international business, because an increase in the foreign demand for their products results in higher revenue and earnings. By understanding the foreign characteristics that influence its level of international business, Starbucks can attempt to offer its product to foreign customers. This chapter explains how the assessment of the global environment by Starbucks or any other firm can be conducted in a manner that maximizes the firm's value.

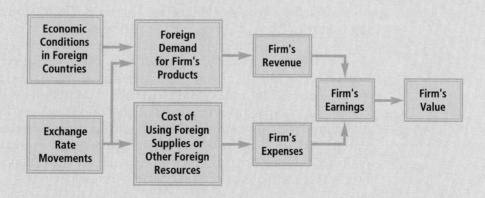

1

Explain the motives for U.S. firms to engage in international business.

MOTIVES TO ENGAGE IN INTERNATIONAL BUSINESS

A firm may have several possible motives for engaging in international business. The following are some of the more common motives:

▶ Attract foreign demand

▶ Capitalize on technology

▶ Use inexpensive resources

▶ Diversify internationally

Attract Foreign Demand

Some firms are unable to increase their market share in the United States because of intense competition within their industry. Alternatively, the U.S. demand for the firm's product may decrease because of changes in consumer tastes. Under either of these conditions, a firm might consider foreign markets where potential demand may exist. Many firms, including DuPont, IBM, and PepsiCo, have successfully entered new foreign markets to attract new sources of demand. Wal-Mart Stores has recently opened stores in numerous countries, including Mexico and Hong Kong. Boeing (a U.S. producer of aircraft) recently received orders for jets from China Xinjiang Airlines and Kenya Airways.

During the 1990s, Avon Products opened branches in 26 different countries, including Brazil, China, and Poland. McDonald's is now in more than 80 different countries and generates more than half of its total revenue from foreign countries. Blockbuster Entertainment has hundreds of stores in Asia. Hertz has expanded its agencies in Europe and in other foreign markets. Amazon.com has expanded its business by offering its services in many foreign countries.

Exhibit 6.1 shows how The Coca-Cola Company's business has expanded globally over time. Now the company has a significant presence in almost every country. It expanded throughout Latin America, Western Europe, Australia, and most of Africa before 1984. Since then, it has expanded into Eastern Europe and most of Asia.

Capitalize on Technology

Many U.S. firms have established new businesses in the so-called developing countries (such as those in Latin America), which have relatively low technology. AT&T and other firms have established new telecommunications systems in developing countries. Other U.S. firms that create power generation, road systems, and other forms of infrastructure have extensive business in these countries. Ford Motor Company and General Motors have attempted to capitalize on their technological advantages by establishing plants in developing countries throughout Asia, Latin America, and Eastern Europe. IBM is doing business with the Chinese government to capitalize on its technology. Amazon.com can capitalize on its technology advantage by expanding in foreign countries where technology is not as advanced.

Exhibit 6.1

The Coca-Cola Company's Global
Expansion

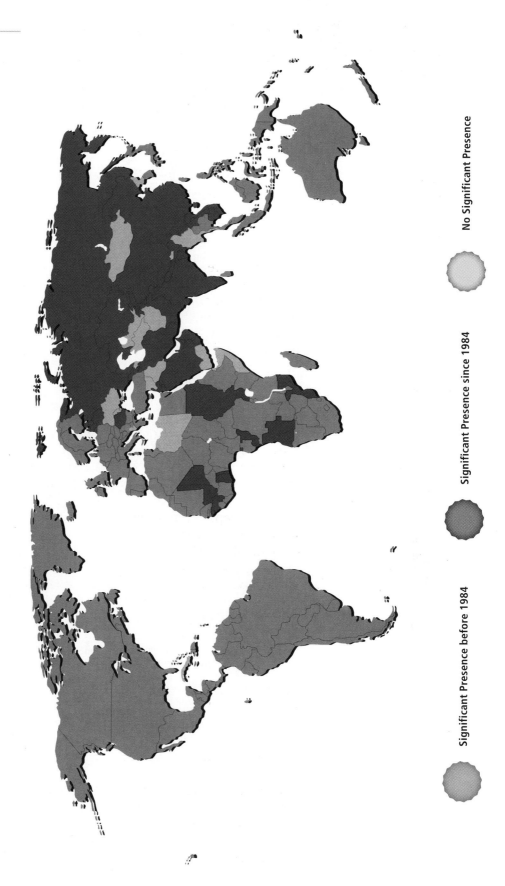

No Significant Presence

Significant Presence since 1984

Significant Presence before 1984

Exhibit 6.2

Approximate Hourly Compensation Costs
for Manufacturing across Countries

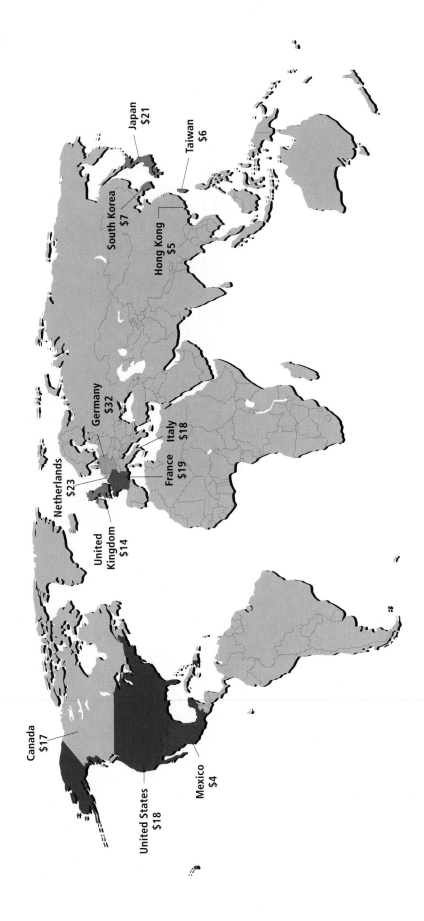

Use Inexpensive Resources

Labor and land costs can vary significantly among countries. Firms often attempt to set up production at a location where land and labor are inexpensive. Exhibit 6.2 illustrates how hourly compensation (labor) costs can vary among countries. The costs are much higher in the developed countries (such as the United States and Germany) than in other countries (such as Mexico or Taiwan). Numerous U.S. firms have established subsidiaries in countries where labor costs are low. For example, Converse has shoes manufactured in Mexico. Dell Computer has disk drives and monitors produced in Asia. General Electric, Motorola, Texas Instruments, Dow Chemical, and Corning have established production plants in Singapore and Taiwan to take advantage of lower labor costs. Many firms from the United States and Western Europe have also established plants in Hungary, Poland, and other parts of Eastern Europe, where labor costs are lower. General Motors pays its assembly-line workers in Mexico about $10 per day (including benefits) versus about $220 per day for its assembly-line workers in the United States.

Diversify Internationally

When all the assets of a firm are designed to generate sales of a specific product in one country, the profits of the firm are normally unstable. This instability is due to the firm's exposure to changes within its industry or within the economy. The firm's performance is dependent on the demand for this one product and on the conditions of the one economy in which it conducts business. The firm can reduce such risk by selling its product in various countries.

Because economic conditions can vary among countries, U.S. firms that conduct international business are affected less by U.S. economic conditions. A U.S. firm's overall performance may be more stable if it sells its product in various countries, so that its business is not influenced solely by the economic conditions in a single country. For example, the demand for PepsiCo's products in Mexico might decline if the Mexican economy is weak, but at the same time economic growth in Brazil, the Netherlands, and Spain might result in a higher overall demand for PepsiCo's products.

Exhibit 6.3 shows how DuPont has diversified its business across countries. Because DuPont has achieved geographic diversification, it is not as exposed to the economic conditions in the United States. Of course, it is somewhat exposed to economic conditions in the foreign countries where it conducts its business.

Combination of Motives

Many U.S. firms engage in international business because of a combination of the motives just described. For example, when 3M Company engages in international business, it attracts new demand from customers in foreign countries. Second, it is able to capitalize on its technology, which is often more advanced than the technology available to local firms in these countries. Third, it is able to use low-cost land and labor in some countries. Finally, it is able to diversify its business among countries. It has also reduced its exposure to U.S. economic conditions by increasing its international business over time.

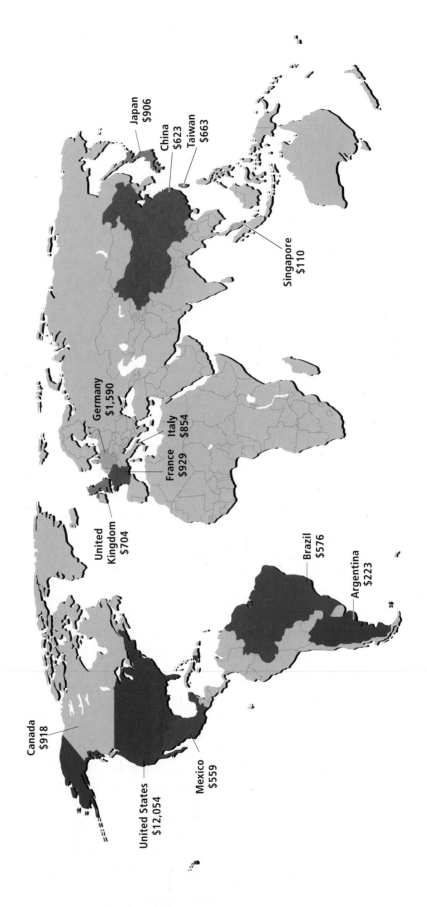

Exhibit 6.3

DuPont's Geographic Diversification (measured by annual sales in millions of dollars)
Source: 2001 annual report.

Japan $906

China $623

Taiwan $663

Singapore $110

Germany $1,590

Italy $854

France $929

United Kingdom $704

Brazil $576

Argentina $223

Canada $918

United States $12,054

Mexico $559

General Electric is another example of a major firm that has expanded internationally in recent years. It has substantial business in Europe. Its sales have also increased in Latin America and the Pacific Basin. Wal-Mart is another firm that has been motivated by the reasons just described to expand into foreign countries.

2

Describe the global opportunities that have encouraged U.S. firms to pursue international business.

GLOBAL OPPORTUNITIES

Changes in global, economic, and political conditions have created opportunities for U.S. firms to more easily pursue international business.

Opportunities in Europe

Over time, economic and political conditions can change, creating new opportunities in international business. Three events have had a major impact on opportunities in Europe: (1) the Single European Act, (2) the removal of the Berlin Wall, and (3) the inception of the euro.

Single European Act   In the late 1980s, industrialized countries in Europe agreed to make their regulations more uniform and to remove many taxes on goods traded between these countries. This agreement, supported by the Single European Act of 1987, was followed by a series of negotiations among the countries to begin phasing in policies that achieved uniformity by 1992. As a result, firms in a given European country now have greater access to supplies from firms in other European countries.

Many firms, including European subsidiaries (branches) of U.S.-based multinational corporations, have capitalized on the agreement by attempting to penetrate new markets. Before the Single European Act, some subsidiaries conducted business only in their host countries because taxes and other barriers discouraged them from pursuing opportunities in neighboring countries. As these barriers were reduced in the late 1980s, firms began to enter new markets. By producing more of the same product and distributing it across European countries, firms are now better able to achieve economies of scale (that is, their cost per unit declines as the quantity produced increases). General Motors is one of many firms that was able to increase its efficiency by streamlining manufacturing operations as a result of the reduction in barriers.

A busy industrial shipyard suggests increasing international business in response to the removal of various international barriers.

© Getty Images/ Photo Disc

Removal of the Berlin Wall In 1989, another historic event occurred in Europe when the Berlin Wall separating East Germany from West Germany was removed. This was symbolic of new relations between East Germany and West Germany and was followed by the reunification of the two countries. In addition, it created momentum to encourage free enterprise in all Eastern European countries and privatization of businesses that had been owned by the government (discussed later in this chapter). A key motive for pursuing opportunities in Eastern Europe was the unavailability of many products there. The Coca-Cola Company, Reynolds Metals Company, General Motors, and numerous other firms aggressively pursued expansion in Eastern Europe as a result of the shift toward free enterprise.

While the Single European Act of 1987 and the momentum toward free enterprise in Eastern Europe offered new opportunities to firms, they also posed new risks. As the Single European Act removed cross-border barriers, it exposed firms to additional competition. As in other historical examples of deregulation, the more efficient firms have benefited at the expense of less efficient firms.

Inception of the Euro In 1999, several European countries adopted the euro as their currency for business transactions between these countries. The euro was phased in as a currency for other transactions during 2001 and had completely replaced the currencies of the participating countries by 2002. The introduction of the euro allows firms (including European subsidiaries of U.S.-based corporations) to engage in international transactions using only one currency and has eliminated the transactions costs incurred from exchanging currencies. Although the full effects are not yet known, the use of a single currency in many European countries should definitely encourage more trade among those countries. In addition, the use of a single currency in most of Europe allows for a single monetary policy among the participating European countries. Thus, firms assessing economic conditions in Europe can focus on one monetary policy rather than the country-specific monetary policies that were prevalent before 1999.

Opportunities in Latin America

Like Europe, Latin America offers more business opportunities now because of a reduction in restrictions.

NAFTA As a result of the North American Free Trade Agreement (NAFTA) of 1993, trade barriers between the United States and Mexico (and Canada as well) have been eliminated. Some U.S. firms have attempted to capitalize on this by exporting previously restricted goods to Mexico. Other firms have established subsidiaries in Mexico to produce their goods at a lower cost than is possible in the United States and then sell the goods in the United States. The removal of trade barriers essentially has allowed U.S. firms to penetrate product and labor markets that previously were not accessible.

The removal of trade barriers between the United States and Mexico also allows Mexican firms to export some products to the United States that were previously restricted. Thus, U.S. firms that produce these goods are now subject to competition from Mexican exporters. Given the low cost of labor in Mexico, some U.S. firms have lost some of their market share. The effects should normally be most pronounced in the labor-intensive industries.

Within a month after the NAFTA accord, the momentum for free trade continued with a GATT (General Agreement on Tariffs and Trade) accord. This accord was the conclusion of trade negotiations from the so-called Uruguay Round that had begun seven years earlier. It called for the reduction or elimination of trade restrictions on specified imported goods over a 10-year period across 117 countries. It also led to the creation of the World Trade Organization, which now has 140 member countries. The accord enabled firms to more easily penetrate foreign markets.

Removal of Investment Restrictions Many Latin American countries have made it easier for U.S. firms to engage in direct foreign investment there (direct foreign investment is discussed in more detail later in this chapter). They allow U.S. firms more ownership rights if they acquire a local company. In particular, U.S. firms with technological advantages have been able to capitalize on their comparative advantages in Latin America. The flow of direct foreign investment into Latin America has not only been beneficial to the U.S. firms, but has improved the level of technology there.

Opportunities in Asia

Many U.S. firms have identified Asia as having tremendous business potential because of its large population base. Nevertheless, they had difficulty pursuing growth opportunities in Asia because of excessive restrictions on investment there. Some of the restrictions were explicit policies, while others were implicit (major bureaucratic delays).

Removal of Investment Restrictions During the 1990s, many Asian countries reduced the restrictions they had imposed on investment by U.S. firms. Consequently, these firms were able to more easily acquire companies in Asia or negotiate licensing agreements with Asian companies without government interference.

Since the reduction in restrictions, U.S. firms such as PepsiCo, The Coca-Cola Company, Apple Computer, and International Paper have increased their international business in Asia. In particular, many U.S. firms view China as the country with the most potential for growth. General Motors, Ford Motor Company, Procter & Gamble, and AT&T have invested billions of dollars in China to capitalize on the expected growth.

Impact of the Asian Crisis In 1997, several Asian countries including Indonesia, Malaysia, and Thailand experienced severe economic problems. Many local companies went bankrupt, and concerns about economic conditions in these countries caused outflows of funds. These outflows left limited funds to support the economy. The so-called Asian crisis lingered into 1998 and adversely affected numerous U.S. firms that conducted business in these countries.

At the same time, however, the crisis also created international business opportunities. The values of local firms were depressed, and governments of the Asian countries reduced restrictions on acquisitions, which allowed firms from the United States and other countries to pursue acquisitions in the Asian countries. Thus, the crisis created opportunities for some U.S. firms to purchase local companies at a relatively low cost, improve their efficiency, and benefit from future expected economic growth. For example, during the Asian crisis in 1997–1998, South Korea's large conglomerate firms (called *chaebols*) experienced financial problems and began to sell many of their business units to obtain cash. Several U.S. firms such as General Electric, Procter & Gamble, and The Coca-Cola Company acquired business units in Asia during this period.

FOREIGN EXPANSION IN THE UNITED STATES

Just as U.S. firms have expanded into foreign countries, foreign firms have expanded into the United States. Some foreign firms have established new subsidiaries in the United States, such as Toyota (expanded its Kentucky plant), Mitsubishi Materials (built a silicon plant in Oregon), and Honda (expanded its Ohio plant). Other foreign firms such as Sony have acquired firms in the United States. Many foreign firms have spent hundreds of millions of dollars to develop or expand their U.S. businesses. Since foreign firms have expanded into the United States, even those U.S. firms that only sell their products domestically are subject to foreign competition.

Foreign Competition

In some industries, such as the automobile, camera, and clothing industries, many foreign firms offer their products in the United States. Thus, the U.S. firms in these industries must compete against the foreign firms for the U.S. market share. In industries with little foreign competition, the U.S. firms compete only among themselves. For example, service industries such as accounting and hairstyling normally are not exposed to much foreign competition because foreign firms cannot easily offer these services.

Most industries in the United States are susceptible to foreign competition. Some foreign firms control a significant share of the U.S. market for the following reasons. Some countries, such as China, Mexico, and Thailand, have extremely low labor costs. The production costs of foreign firms in these countries can be especially low for labor-intensive industries, such as clothing. Competing in these industries is difficult for U.S. firms because production expenses are higher in the United States.

A second reason why foreign firms are successful in the United States is that some foreign-made products may be perceived as having higher quality than U.S.-made products. For example, at one time many U.S. consumers considered Japanese automobiles to be of higher quality than U.S. automobiles. Although this general perception of the automobile industry has changed, some foreign products (such as furniture, watches, and wine) are still considered to be of higher quality and therefore more desirable.

3

Describe how firms conduct international business.

HOW FIRMS CONDUCT INTERNATIONAL BUSINESS

Firms engage in various types of international business. Some of the more popular types are:

▶ Importing

▶ Exporting

▶   Direct foreign investment (DFI)

▶   Strategic alliances

Importing

importing the purchase of foreign products or services

Importing involves the purchase of foreign products or services. For example, some U.S. consumers purchase foreign automobiles, clothing, cameras, and other products from firms in foreign countries. Many U.S. firms import materials or supplies that are used to produce products. Even if these firms sell the products locally, they can benefit from international business. They import foreign supplies that are less expensive or of a higher quality than alternative U.S. supplies.

tariff a tax on imported products

Factors That Influence the Degree of Importing   The degree to which a firm imports supplies is influenced by government trade barriers. Governments may impose a **tariff** (or tax) on imported products. The tax is normally paid directly by the importer, who typically passes the tax on to consumers by charging a higher price for the product. Thus, the product may be overpriced compared with products produced by firms based in that country. When governments impose tariffs, the ability of foreign firms to compete in those countries is restricted.

quota a limit on the amounts of specific products that can be imported

Governments can also impose a **quota** on imported products, thereby limiting the amounts of specific products that can be imported. This type of trade barrier may be even more restrictive than a tariff because it places an explicit limit on the amount of a specific product that can be imported.

In general, trade barriers tend to both discourage trade and protect specific industries from foreign competition. As described earlier, however, many trade barriers have been removed in Europe and in many Asian countries. In addition, since 1993 when NAFTA removed many restrictions on trade among Canada, Mexico, and the United States, U.S. firms have had more opportunities to expand their businesses in Canada and Mexico. At the same time, however, they are also more exposed to competition from foreign firms within the United States.

Striking South African workers demand minimum payments for laid-off workers in an attempt to force the government to slow tariff reductions. As firms diversify internationally, they can become vulnerable to global changes within a particular industry or within various world economies.

AP Photo / Obed Zilwa

Most of the product from this raisin cleaning factory in Kabul, Afghanistan, is exported to Russia to make alcoholic beverages.

AP Photo/ Kamran Jebreili

Exporting

exporting the sale of products or services (called exports) to purchasers residing in other countries

Exporting is the sale of products or services (called exports) to purchasers residing in other countries. Many firms, such as DuPont, Intel, and Zenith, use exporting as a means of selling products in foreign markets. Many smaller firms in the United States also export to foreign countries.

Trend of U.S. Exports and Imports   The trend of U.S. exports and imports is shown in Exhibit 6.4. Notice that the amount of U.S. exports and imports more than quadrupled between 1980 and the early 2000s, reflecting the increased importance of international trade.

balance of trade the level of exports minus the level of imports

trade deficit the amount by which imports exceed exports

The U.S. **balance of trade,** which is also shown in Exhibit 6.4, is equal to the level of U.S. exports minus the level of U.S. imports. A negative balance of trade is referred to as a **trade deficit** and means that the United States is importing (purchasing) more products and services from foreign countries than it is selling to foreign countries. The U.S. trade deficit has been consistently negative since 1980 and has grown in recent years.

How the Internet Facilitates Exporting   Many firms use their websites to identify the products that they sell, along with the price for each product. This allows them to easily advertise their products to potential importers anywhere in the world without mailing brochures to various countries. In addition, they can add to their product line and change prices by simply revising the website. Thus, importers can keep abreast of an exporter's product information by monitoring the exporter's website periodically.

Firms can also use their websites to accept orders online. Some products such as software can be delivered from the exporter to the importer directly over the Internet in the form of a file that lands in the importer's computer. Other products must be shipped, but the Internet makes it easier to track the shipping process. The importer can transmit its order for products via e-mail to the exporter. The exporter's warehouse then fills the order. When the products are shipped from the warehouse, an e-mail message is sent to

Exhibit 6.4

Trend of U.S. Exports and Imports

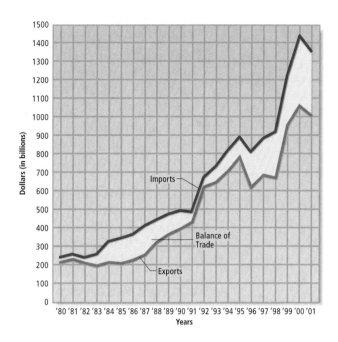

the importer and to the exporter's headquarters. The warehouse may even use technology to monitor its inventory of products so that suppliers are automatically notified to send more supplies when the inventory is reduced to a specific level. If the exporter uses multiple warehouses, the Internet allows them to work as a network so that if one warehouse can not fill an order, another warehouse will.

Direct Foreign Investment (DFI)

direct foreign investment (DFI) a means of acquiring or building subsidiaries in one or more foreign countries

Many firms engage in **direct foreign investment (DFI),** which is a means of acquiring or building subsidiaries in one or more foreign countries. For example, Ford Motor Company has facilities in various countries that produce automobiles and sell them in those locations. Blockbuster Video has stores in various countries that rent videos to customers in those countries. A U.S. firm may either build a subsidiary in a foreign country or acquire an existing foreign firm and convert that into its subsidiary. Many U.S. firms acquire foreign firms to expand internationally. They most commonly acquire firms in Canada and the United Kingdom but have recently increased their acquisitions in countries such as Brazil, the Czech Republic, and Hungary. Direct foreign investment is feasible in a variety of situations, including the following:

1 A firm that has successfully exported to a foreign country desires to reduce its transportation costs. It establishes a subsidiary in the foreign country that manufactures the product and sells it in that country. Kellogg Company uses this strategy and has production plants in 19 different countries, including China and India. Nike initially subcontracted with factories in Taiwan and Korea to produce athletic shoes and then sold the shoes in Asian countries. It then began to export shoes to Europe and South America. Nike expanded its production facilities in foreign countries so that it could produce shoes to be sold in Europe.

2 A firm that has been exporting products is informed that the foreign government will impose trade barriers. Therefore, the firm establishes a subsidiary that can manufacture and sell products in that country. In this way, it avoids the trade barriers.

3 A foreign country is desperately in need of advanced technology and offers a U.S. firm incentives, such as free use of land, to establish a subsidiary in that country. The foreign country also expects that the firm will employ some local workers.

4 A U.S. firm believes that it can substantially reduce its labor costs by shifting its production facilities to a developing country where labor and land are less expensive.

Although DFI can often be feasible, firms should conduct a thorough analysis of the costs and benefits before investing. Once funds are spent on DFI, the decision cannot easily be reversed because the foreign facilities would have to be sold at a loss in most cases.

Strategic Alliances

strategic alliance a business agreement between firms whereby resources are shared to pursue mutual interests

joint venture an agreement between two firms about a specific project

U.S. and foreign firms commonly engage in **strategic alliances,** which are business agreements that are in the best interests of the firms involved. Various types of international alliances between U.S. firms and foreign firms can be made. One type is a **joint venture,** which involves an agreement between two firms about a specific project. Joint ventures between U.S. and non-U.S. firms are common. The U.S. firm may produce a product and send it to a non-U.S. firm, which sells the product in that country. The non-U.S. firm is involved because it knows the culture of that country and is more capable of selling the product there.

In another type of joint venture, two firms participate in the production of a product. This type of joint venture is common in the automobile industry. The automakers in the United States are involved in a variety of ventures with foreign manufacturers. General Motors dealerships and Ford Motor Company dealerships sell cars manufactured by firms in France, Japan, and South Korea. RJR Nabisco has engaged in joint ventures with some food producers in some of the former Soviet republics. This gives Nabisco access to local production facilities and skilled workers. These joint ventures reflect the improved commercial relations with the former Soviet republics that have led to a major change in attitude by U.S. companies about doing business in those areas.

international licensing agreement a type of alliance in which a firm allows a foreign company (called the "licensee") to produce its products according to specific instructions

Another type of alliance is an **international licensing agreement,** in which a firm allows a foreign company (called the "licensee") to produce its products according to specific instructions. Many U.S. beer producers engage in licensing agreements with foreign firms. The foreign firm is given the technology to produce the products. As the foreign firm sells the products, it channels a portion of revenue to the licensing firm. The advantage of licensing is that the firm is able to sell its product in foreign markets without the costs involved in exporting or direct foreign investment. One disadvantage, however, is that the foreign firm shares the profits from products sold in the foreign country.

How the Internet Facilitates Licensing
Some firms with international reputations use their brand name to advertise products over the Internet. They then license manufacturers in foreign countries to produce some of their products subject to their specifications. For example, Mesa Company set up a licensing agreement with a manufacturer in Indonesia to

manufacture its product, which Mesa advertises over the Internet. When Mesa receives orders for its product from customers in Asia, it relies on this manufacturer to produce and deliver the products ordered. This expedites the delivery process and may even enable Mesa to have the products manufactured at a lower cost than if it produced them itself.

4 HOW FOREIGN CHARACTERISTICS INFLUENCE INTERNATIONAL BUSINESS

Explain how foreign characteristics can influence a firm's international business.

When a firm engages in international business, it must consider the following characteristics of foreign countries:

▶ Culture

▶ Economic system

▶ Economic conditions

▶ Exchange rates

▶ Political risk

Culture

Because cultures vary, a firm must learn a foreign country's culture before engaging in business there. Poor decisions can result from an improper assessment of a country's tastes, habits, and customs. Many U.S. firms know that cultures vary and adjust their products to fit the culture. For example, McDonald's sells vegetable burgers instead of beef hamburgers in India. PepsiCo (owner of Frito Lay snack foods) sells Cheetos without cheese in China because Chinese consumers dislike cheese, and it has developed a shrimp-chip to satisfy consumers in Korea. Beer producers sell nonalcoholic beer in Saudi Arabia, where alcohol is not allowed.

Nonverbal Communications in Different Cultures Nonverbal behavior can only be interpreted within a specific cultural context. Here are five common nonverbal behaviors and how they are interpreted in different countries or geographic areas. Caution is always the better part of valor in using nonverbal behaviors outside your native land.

▶ *Withholding eye contact:*
  ▶ In the United States, it indicates shyness or deception.
  ▶ In Libya, it is a compliment to a woman.
  ▶ In Japan, it is done in deference to authority.
▶ *Crossing legs when seated:*
  ▶ In the United States, it is done for comfort.
  ▶ In Arab countries, it is an insult to show the soles of the feet.

▶ *Displaying the palm of the hand:*
  ▶ In the United States, it is a form of greeting, such as a wave or handshake.
  ▶ In Greece, it is an insult.
▶ *Joining the index finger and thumb to make an O:*
  ▶ In the United States, it means "okay."
  ▶ In Mediterranean countries, it means "zero" or "the pits."
  ▶ In Japan, it means money.
  ▶ In Tunisia, it means "I'll kill you."
  ▶ In Latin America, it is an obscene gesture.
▶ *Standing close to a person while talking:*
  ▶ In the United States, it is an intrusion, and the speaker is viewed as pushy.
  ▶ In Latin America and southern Europe, it is the normal spatial distance for conversations.

global business

Economic System

A firm must recognize the type of economic system used in any country where it considers doing business. A country's economic system reflects the degree of government ownership of businesses and intervention in business. A U.S. firm will normally prefer countries that do not have excessive government intervention.

Although each country's government has its own unique policy on the ownership of businesses, most policies can be classified as capitalism, communism, or socialism.

capitalism an economic system that allows for private ownership of businesses

Capitalism   **Capitalism** allows for private ownership of businesses. Entrepreneurs have the freedom to create businesses that they believe will serve the people's needs. The United States is perceived as a capitalist society because entrepreneurs are allowed to create businesses and compete against each other. In a capitalist society, entrepreneurs' desire to earn profits motivates them to produce products and services that satisfy customers. Competition allows efficient firms to increase their share of the market and forces inefficient firms out of the market.

U.S. firms can normally enter capitalist countries without any excessive restrictions by the governments. Typically, though, the level of competition in those countries is high.

communism an economic system that involves public ownership of businesses

Communism   **Communism** is an economic system that involves public ownership of businesses. In a purely communist system, entrepreneurs are restricted from capitalizing on the perceived needs of the people. The government decides what products will be produced and in what quantity. It may even assign jobs to people, regardless of their interests, and sets the wages to be paid to each worker. Wages may be somewhat similar, regardless of individual abilities or effort. Thus, workers do not have much incentive to excel because they will not be rewarded for abnormally high performance.

In a communist society, the government serves as a central planner. It may decide to produce more of some type of agricultural product if it recognizes a shortage. Since the government is not concerned about earning profits, it does not focus on satisfying consumers (determining what they want to purchase). Consequently, people are unable to obtain many types of products even if they can afford to buy them. In addition, most people do not have much money to spend because the government pays low wages.

Countries in Eastern Europe, such as Bulgaria, Poland, and Romania, had communist systems before 1990. During the 1990s, however, government intervention in these countries declined. Prior to the 1990s, communist countries restricted most U.S. firms from entering, but as they began to allow more private ownership of firms, they also allowed foreign firms to enter.

socialism an economic system that contains some features of both capitalism and communism

Socialism   **Socialism** is an economic system that contains some features of both capitalism and communism. For example, governments in some so-called socialist countries allow people to own businesses and property and to select their own jobs. However, these governments are highly involved in the provision of various services. Health-care services are run by many governments and are provided at a low cost. Also, the governments of so-

cialist countries tend to offer high levels of benefits to unemployed people. Such services are indirectly paid for by the businesses and the workers who earn income. Socialist governments impose high tax rates on income so that they have sufficient funds to provide all their services.

Socialist countries face a trade-off when setting their tax policies, though. To provide a high level of services to the poor and unemployed, the government must impose high tax rates. Many businesses and workers in socialist countries, however, would argue that the tax rates are excessive. They claim that entrepreneurs may be discouraged from establishing businesses if the government taxes most of the income to be earned by the business. Entrepreneurs thus have incentive to establish businesses in other countries where taxes are lower. But if the government uses a low tax rate, it may not generate enough tax revenue to provide the services.

A socialist society may discourage not only the establishment of new businesses but also the desire to work. If the compensation provided by the government to unemployed workers is almost as high as the wages earned by employed workers, unemployed people have little incentive to look for work. The high tax rates typically imposed on employed people in socialist countries also discourage people from looking for work.

Comparison of Socialism and Capitalism In socialist countries, the government has more influence because it imposes higher taxes and can spend that tax revenue as it chooses. In capitalist countries, the government has less influence because it imposes lower taxes and therefore has less funds to spend on the people. Businesses and highly skilled workers generally prefer capitalist countries because there is less government interference.

Even if a capitalist country is preferred, people may disagree on how much influence the government should have. For example, some people in the United States believe that the government should provide fewer services to the unemployed and the poor, which would allow for lower taxes. Other people believe that taxes should be increased so that the government can allocate more services to the poor.

Many countries exhibit some combination of capitalism and socialism. For example, the governments of many developed countries in Europe (such as Sweden and Switzerland) allow firms to be privately owned but provide various services (such as health care) for the people. Germany's government provides child-care allowances, health care, and retirement pensions. The French government commonly intervenes when firms experience financial problems.

European countries have recently attempted to reduce their budget deficits as part of a treaty supporting closer European relations. This may result in less government control because the governments will not be able to spend as much money.

Privatization Historically, the governments of many countries in Eastern Europe, Latin America, and the Soviet Bloc owned most businesses, but in recent years they have allowed for private business ownership. Many government-owned businesses have been sold to private investors. As a result of this so-called **privatization,** many governments are reducing their influence and allowing firms to compete in each industry. Privatization allows firms to focus on providing the products and services that people desire and forces the firms to be more efficient to ensure survival. Thousands

privatization the sale of government-owned businesses to private investors

of businesses in the former Soviet Bloc have been privatized. Some U.S. firms have acquired businesses sold by the governments of the former Soviet republics and other countries. Privatization has provided an easy way for U.S. firms to own businesses in many foreign countries.

Privatization in many countries, such as Brazil, Hungary, and the countries of the former Soviet Bloc, is an abrupt shift from tradition. Most people in these countries have not had experience in owning and managing a business. Even those people who managed government-owned businesses are not used to competition because the government typically controlled each industry. Therefore, many people who want to own their own businesses have been given some training by business professors and professionals from capitalist countries such as the United States. In particular, the MBA Enterprise Corps, headquartered at the University of North Carolina, has sent thousands of business students to less-developed countries.

Even the industrialized countries have initiated privatization programs for some businesses that were previously owned by the government. The telephone company in Germany has been privatized, as have numerous large government-owned businesses in France.

Economic Conditions

To predict demand for its product in a foreign country, a firm must attempt to forecast the economic conditions in that country. The firm's overall performance is dependent on the foreign country's economic growth and on the firm's sensitivity to conditions in that country, as explained next.

Economic Growth Many U.S. firms have recently expanded into smaller foreign markets because they expect that economic growth in these countries will be strong, resulting in a strong demand for their products. For example, Heinz has expanded its business throughout Asia. General Motors, Procter & Gamble, AT&T, Ford Motor Company, and Anheuser-Busch plan new direct foreign investment in Brazil. The Coca-Cola Company has expanded in China, India, and Eastern Europe.

The primary factor influencing the decision by many firms to expand in a particular foreign country is the country's expected economic growth, which affects the potential demand for their products. If firms overestimate the country's economic growth, they will normally overestimate the demand for their products in that country. Consequently, their revenue may not be sufficient to cover the expenses associated with the expansion.

In addition, foreign countries may experience weak economies in some periods, which can adversely affect firms that serve those countries. For example, during the Asian crisis of 1997–1998, Asian economies were weak, and U.S. firms with business in Asia, such as Nike and Hewlett-Packard, experienced a decline in the demand for their products. In 2001–2002, worldwide economic conditions were generally weak, and many U.S. companies that served foreign countries were adversely affected. Economic conditions in the United States were also weak. Consequently, firms with business diversified across different countries were not insulated from the weak economic conditions because these conditions existed in most countries during this period. For example, DuPont, Nike, 3M, and Hewlett-Packard experienced lower-than-expected revenue because of weak European economies in the 2001–2002 period. To illustrate the impact of global economic conditions, consider the comments made by Dell Computer in a recent annual report:

"During 2002, worldwide economic conditions negatively affected demand for the Company's products and resulted in declining revenue and earnings. . . . The Company believes that worldwide economic conditions will improve. However, if economic conditions continue to worsen, or if economic conditions do not improve as rapidly as expected, the Company's revenue and earnings could be negatively affected."

Sensitivity to Foreign Economic Conditions   A U.S. firm's exposure to a foreign country's economy is dependent on the proportion of the firm's business conducted in that country. To illustrate, compare the influence of Canada's economy on two U.S. firms (Firm X and Firm Y), as shown in Exhibit 6.5. Assume that Firm X typically generates 20 percent of its total revenue from selling its products in Canada and 80 percent of its total revenue from the United States. Firm Y typically generates 60 percent of its total revenue from Canada and 40 percent of its total revenue from the United States. A weak economy in Canada will likely have a more negative effect on Firm Y because it relies more on its Canadian business.

Some U.S. firms, such as The Coca-Cola Company, Dow Chemical, and ExxonMobil, generate more than half of their total revenue from foreign countries. Nevertheless, they are not heavily influenced by any single foreign country's economy because their international business is scattered across many countries. The Coca-Cola Company, for example, conducts business in more than 200 foreign countries. The demand for The Coca-Cola Company's soft drink products may decline in some countries where the weather is cooler than normal, but this unfavorable effect can be offset by a higher demand for Coca-Cola's products in other countries where the weather is warmer than normal.

Exchange Rates

Countries generally have their own currency. The United States uses dollars ($), the United Kingdom uses British pounds (£), Canada uses Canadian dollars (C$), and Japan uses Japanese yen (¥). As mentioned earlier, twelve European countries recently adopted the euro (€) as their currency. Exchange rates between the U.S. dollar and any currency fluctuate over time. Consequently, the number of dollars a U.S. firm needs to purchase foreign supplies may change even if the actual price charged for the supplies by the foreign producer does not. When the dollar weakens, foreign currencies strengthen; thus, U.S. firms need more dollars to purchase a given amount

Exhibit 6.5

Comparing the Influence of the Canadian Economy on Two U.S. Firms

U.S. Firm	Total Annual Revenue	Proportion of Canadian Business	Proportion of U.S. Business	Annual Revenue from Canadian Business	Annual Revenue from U.S. Business
Firm X	$100,000,000	20%	80%	$20,000,000	$80,000,000
Firm Y	10,000,000	60%	40%	6,000,000	4,000,000

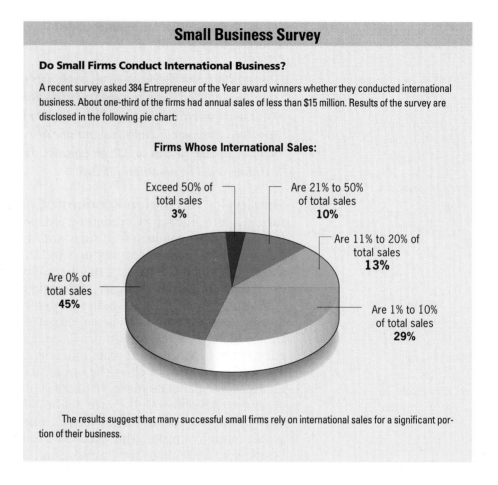

Small Business Survey

Do Small Firms Conduct International Business?

A recent survey asked 384 Entrepreneur of the Year award winners whether they conducted international business. About one-third of the firms had annual sales of less than $15 million. Results of the survey are disclosed in the following pie chart:

Firms Whose International Sales:

Exceed 50% of total sales
3%

Are 21% to 50% of total sales
10%

Are 11% to 20% of total sales
13%

Are 0% of total sales
45%

Are 1% to 10% of total sales
29%

The results suggest that many successful small firms rely on international sales for a significant portion of their business.

of foreign supplies. Exchange rate fluctuations can also affect the foreign demand for a U.S. firm's product because they affect the actual price paid by the foreign customers (even if the price in dollars remains unchanged).

Political Risk

political risk the risk that a country's political actions can adversely affect a business

Political risk is the risk that a country's political actions may adversely affect a business. Political crises have occurred in many countries throughout Eastern Europe, Latin America, and the Middle East. U.S. firms are subject to policies imposed by the governments of the foreign countries where they do business. As an extreme form of political risk, a foreign government may take over a U.S. firm's foreign subsidiary without compensating the U.S. firm in any way. A more common form of political risk is that the foreign government imposes higher corporate tax rates on foreign subsidiaries. The exposure of multinational companies to political risks is clearly emphasized in a recent annual report of Dell Computer:

"The Company's future growth rates and success are dependent on continued growth and success in international markets. . . . The success and profitability of the Company's international operations are subject to numerous risks and uncertainties, including local economic and labor conditions, political instability, unexpected changes in the regulatory environment, trade protection measures, tax laws, and foreign currency exchange rates."

cross functional teamwork:

Managing International Business across Business Functions

When a firm plans to conduct business in a foreign country, it should request input from its managers across various departments. The production managers may assess a country according to the expenses associated with production and therefore may focus on the following questions:

1. What is the cost of hiring the necessary labor?
2. What is the cost of developing a new facility?
3. What is the cost of purchasing an existing facility?
4. Does the country have access to the necessary materials and technology?

The answers to these questions are dependent on the specific part of the country where the firm is considering locating its facility.

The marketing managers may assess a country according to the potential revenue to be earned from selling a product in that country and therefore may focus on the following questions:

1. What is the foreign demand for the firm's product?
2. What changes need to be made in the product to satisfy local consumers?
3. What types of marketing strategies would be effective in that country?
4. What is the cost of marketing the product in that country?

The financial managers may assess a country according to the costs of financing any business conducted in that country and therefore may focus on the following questions:

1. Is it possible to obtain a local loan in that country?
2. What is the interest rate charged on local loans?
3. Should the firm use some of its retained earnings from its domestic business to support any foreign business?
4. How would the firm's earnings increase as a result of doing business in the foreign country?

Because of these cross functional relationships, the decision to establish a business in a foreign country must consider input across departments. The production department cannot properly estimate the production costs in a specific country until the marketing department determines whether the product must be revised to satisfy the local consumers. Also, the financial managers cannot estimate the earnings from this business until they receive estimates of revenue (from the marketing department), production expenses (from the production department), and marketing expenses (from the marketing department).

Firms must understand how government characteristics could affect their businesses in foreign countries. For example, some governments impose a tax on funds sent by a subsidiary to the parent firm (headquarters) in the home country. They may even prevent the funds from being sent for a certain period of time. Government-imposed taxes on business earnings and environmental laws vary among countries. By increasing costs, these laws can affect the feasibility of establishing a subsidiary in a foreign country. Stringent building codes, restrictions on the disposal of production waste materials, and pollution controls are examples of regulations that may force subsidiaries to incur additional costs. Many European countries have recently imposed tougher anti-pollution laws as a result of severe pollution problems.

During the 1990s, several U.S. firms were adversely affected by political risk. A McDonald's restaurant in China was given an eviction notice from the Beijing city government, which ignored the firm's 20-year agreement to use the land. Some U.S. firms operating in Russia were surprised to learn that they had to pay a wage tax on all salaries over the minimum salary and a large social security tax. Governments of various foreign countries have failed to honor agreements with U.S. automobile manufacturers.

5

Explain how exchange rate
movements can affect a
firm's performance.

How Exchange Rate Movements Can Affect Performance

International trade transactions typically require the exchange of one currency for another. For example, if a U.S. firm periodically purchases supplies from a British supplier, it will need to exchange U.S. dollars for the British currency (pounds) to make the purchase. This process is shown in Exhibit 6.6.

Generally, the exchange rate between a given currency and the U.S. dollar fluctuates daily. When the exchange rate changes, U.S. firms involved in international trade are affected. The impact of exchange rate movements on a U.S. firm can be favorable or unfavorable, depending on the characteristics of the firm, as illustrated by the following examples.

Impact of a Weak Dollar on U.S. Importers

Assume that the value of the pound (£) at a given point in time is $2.00. That is, each dollar is worth one-half of a British pound. If a U.S. firm needs £1,000,000 to purchase supplies from a British supplier, it will need $2,000,000 to obtain those pounds, as shown:

$$\text{Amount of \$ Needed} = (\text{Amount of £ Needed}) \times (\text{Value of £})$$
$$= £1,000,000 \times \$2.00$$
$$= \$2,000,000$$

appreciates strengthens in value

Now assume that the pound **appreciates** (or strengthens in value) against the dollar. This also means that the dollar weakens (is worth less) against the pound. For example, assume the pound is now equal to $2.02 instead of $2.00. Now the U.S. firm needs $20,000 more to obtain the pounds than it needed before the pound appreciated. Thus, the cost of the supplies has increased for the U.S. firm as a result of the appreciation in the British pound (a weaker dollar). This illustrates why a weak dollar adversely affects U.S. firms that frequently import supplies.

Impact of a Strong Dollar on U.S. Importers

depreciates weakens in value

Now consider a situation in which the pound **depreciates,** or weakens in value against the dollar. This also means that the dollar strengthens against the pound. For example, assume the pound's value was $2.00, but has

Exhibit 6.6

Example of Importing by a U.S. Firm

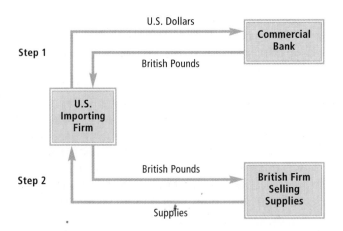

business online

Exchange Rate Quotations   This website provides updated exchange rate quotations for currencies around the world.

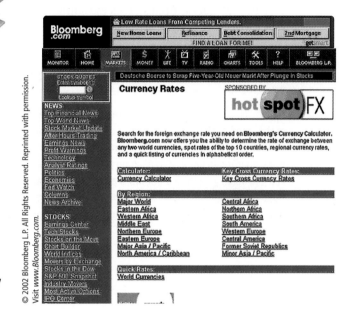

e-business

http://www.bloomberg.com/
markets/currency.html

increasing value with technology

MOVING TECHNOLOGY ACROSS BORDERS

Technologies that are highly effective in one country may have to be modified substantially before they are suitable for another country. A good example of the challenges of moving technology across borders can be found in the case of AucNet, the satellite used-car auctioning system.

AucNet was developed in the mid-1980s in Japan as a substitute for traditional used-car auctions. It used laser disk and later satellite technology to permit dealers from around the country to view the used cars that were going to be sold. Dealers could also view the results of inspections conducted by AucNet's team of on-site inspectors. After they had been given the opportunity to study the cars, dealers were then able to participate in online auctions.

Participating in such auctions offered dealers two major advantages: they did not have to go to the auction sites, and they did not have to take their vehicles to the auction sites. As a result of its innovative approach, the company became a major force in the Japanese used-car business, participating in the sale of over a million cars during its first 10 years of operation.

In 1995, AucNet entered the U.S. market, first in the Atlanta area and then expanding to California. The used cars were typically much older, however, so a simple inspection of a vehicle could not guarantee its actual condition. Also, used-car dealers in the United States were less specialized than those in Japan and therefore were interested in a broader range of cars.

In attempting to address these problems, AucNet U.S.A., Inc., took two key steps: (1) it chose to focus on the high-priced market segment of cars, and (2) it increased the scope of its inspection program. Specifically, whereas the Japanese inspections had been almost entirely cosmetic, inspectors of U.S. operations checked 120 specific items, both cosmetic and mechanical, and took each vehicle on a test drive. The final rating of each vehicle was then determined using custom-designed inspection software. In addition, a digital camera was used to take three photos of each car, which could then be downloaded by potential bidders. These changes were deemed necessary to make AucNet's approach attractive to the U.S. market.

changed to $1.90 over the last month. If the U.S. firm needs to obtain £1,000,000, it will be able to purchase the pounds for $100,000 less than was needed before the pound depreciated. The firm's payment has declined by 5 percent because the pound's value has declined by 5 percent.

This example shows how the depreciation of a foreign currency against the dollar (a stronger dollar) reduces the expenses of a U.S. firm that is purchasing foreign supplies. This explains why a strong dollar favorably affects U.S. firms that frequently import supplies.

College Health Club: CHC's Exposure to Global Conditions

College Health Club (CHC) sells its services locally, and its competitors are local. Therefore, global conditions do not have a direct effect on its business. However, Sue Kramer, the president of CHC, plans to purchase vitamin supplements from Mexico and sell them at the club. The price charged to her is 100 Mexican pesos per jar. She plans to order just one case containing 200 jars initially and will order more after these jars are sold. The present exchange rate of the peso is $.08, but Sue wants to know how a change in the exchange rate will affect the price that she will pay in dollars. Her calculations of the potential exchange rate effects are shown in the following table.

	If the Exchange Rate Is $.08	If the Exchange Rate Is $.09
(1) Number of jars ordered	200	200
(2) Purchase price per jar in Mexican pesos	100 pesos	100 pesos
(3) Exchange rate	$.08	$.09
(4) Purchase price per jar in dollars	$8.00	$9.00
(5) Total purchase price = (1) × (4)	$1,600.00	$1,800.00

A case of vitamin supplements will cost $200 more if the value of the peso increases by $.01 by the time the bill is paid. Sue plans to sell the jars to CHC's members for $12 per jar. Therefore, CHC's profit from selling these jars will be reduced if the value of the peso increases.

Exchange rates for foreign currencies are shown by each country's name and flag symbol. When a firm engages in international business, the exchange rate is an important determining factor in making business decisions.

© Getty Images/ Photo Disc

Actual Effects of Exchange Rate Movements on U.S. Importers

To illustrate how exchange rate movements can affect firms engaged in international business, actual exchange rate movements of the British pound (£) are shown at the top of Exhibit 6.7. The amount of dollars paid by a U.S. importer that owes £1,000,000 every quarter to a British supplier is shown at the bottom of Exhibit 6.7. Notice that the pound depreciated substantially in some periods, such as 1981–1984, 1991–1993, and 2001. In other periods, such as 1985–1987 and 2002, the pound appreciated. When the pound appreciated, the amount of dollars needed to buy British imports increased. Conversely, when the pound depreciated, the amount of dollars needed to buy British imports declined. Exhibit 6.7 illustrates how the expenses of a U.S. importing firm are highly sensitive to changes in the value of the pound.

The exchange rates of currencies of less-developed countries fluctuate more than those of developed countries. For example, the Mexican peso depreciated by 45 percent during the month of December 1994. Consequently, U.S. firms that do business in less-developed countries are exposed to wide swings in exchange rates.

Impact of a Weak Dollar on U.S. Exporters

Just as exchange rate movements can affect U.S. importing firms, they can also affect U.S. firms that export products to other countries. The effect of a weak dollar will be examined first, followed by the effect of a strong dollar.

Exhibit 6.7

How Exchange Rate Movements Can Affect the Price of Imports

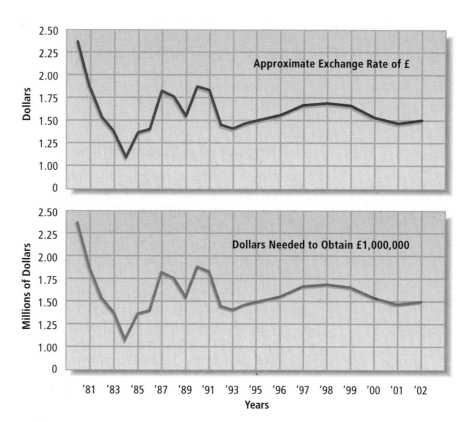

Exhibit 6.8

Example of Exporting by a U.S. Firm

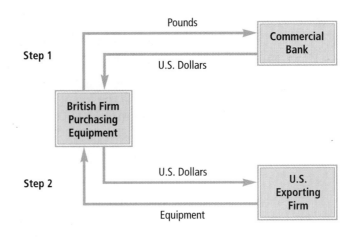

Consider how a U.S. firm that exports equipment to a British firm is affected by a weak dollar. The exporting process is shown in Exhibit 6.8. If the U.S. exporter wants to receive U.S. dollars for its equipment, the British firm must first exchange its currency (pounds) into dollars at a commercial bank (Step 1 in Exhibit 6.8). Then the British firm uses these dollars to purchase the equipment of the U.S. exporting firm (Step 2).

If the dollar weakens, the British firm can obtain the dollars it needs with fewer pounds. Therefore, it may be willing to purchase more equipment from the U.S. exporting firm. The U.S. firm's revenue will rise in response to a higher demand for the equipment it produces. Therefore, its profits should increase as well.

As this example shows, a weak dollar can result in higher revenue and profits for U.S. firms that frequently export their products. U.S. exporting firms tend to benefit from a weak dollar because their prices are perceived as inexpensive by foreign customers who must convert their currencies into dollars. A weak dollar favorably affects U.S. firms that export heavily because foreign demand for the products they export increases substantially when the dollar is weak.

Impact of a Strong Dollar on U.S. Exporters

Now consider a situation in which the value of the pound depreciates against the dollar. As the pound's value declines, the British firm must exchange more British pounds to obtain the same amount of dollars as before. That is, it needs more pounds to purchase equipment from the U.S. firm. Consequently, it may reduce its purchases from the U.S. firm and perhaps will search for a British producer of the equipment to avoid having to obtain dollars.

As this example shows, a strong dollar can result in lower revenue for U.S. firms that frequently export their products. A strong dollar adversely affects U.S. exporting firms because the prices of their exports appear expensive to foreign customers who must convert their currencies into dollars. When the dollar strengthens, U.S. exporting firms such as Procter & Gamble and Boeing are adversely affected.

Hedging against Exchange Rate Movements

hedge action taken to protect a firm against exchange rate movements

U.S. firms commonly attempt to **hedge,** or protect against exchange rate movements. They can hedge most effectively when they know how much of a specific foreign currency they will need or will receive on a specific date in the future.

Hedging Future Payments in Foreign Currencies   Consider a firm that plans to purchase British supplies and will need £1,000,000 in 90 days to pay for those supplies. It can call a large commercial bank that exchanges foreign currencies and request a so-called **forward contract,** which provides that an exchange of currencies will occur for a specified exchange rate at a future point in time. In this case, the forward contract will specify an exchange of dollars for £1,000,000 in 90 days. In other words, the firm wants to purchase pounds 90 days forward.

forward contract provides that an exchange of currencies will occur at a specified exchange rate at a future point in time

forward rate the exchange rate that a bank will be willing to offer at a future point in time

spot exchange rate the exchange rate quoted for immediate transactions

The bank will quote the so-called **forward rate,** or the exchange rate that the bank will be willing to offer at a future point in time. The forward rate is normally close to the **spot exchange rate,** which is the exchange rate quoted for immediate transactions. Assume that the bank quotes a 90-day forward rate of $1.80 for the British pound. If the firm agrees to this quote, it has agreed to a forward contract. It will lock in the purchase of £1,000,000 in 90 days for $1.80 per pound, or $1,800,000 for the £1,000,000. Once the firm hedges its position, it has locked in the rate at which it will exchange currencies on that future date, regardless of the actual spot exchange rate that occurs on that date. In this way, the U.S. firm hedges against the possibility that the pound will appreciate over that period.

Hedging Future Receivables in Foreign Currencies   U.S. firms can also hedge when they expect to receive a foreign currency in the future. For example, consider a U.S. firm that knows it will receive £1,000,000 in 90 days. It can call a commercial bank and negotiate a forward contract in which it will provide the £1,000,000 to the bank in exchange for dollars. Assuming that the 90-day forward rate is $1.80 (as in the previous example), the firm will receive $1,800,000 in 90 days (computed as $1.80 × £1,000,000). By using a forward contract, this firm locks in the rate at which it can exchange its pounds for dollars, regardless of the spot exchange rate that occurs on that date. In this way, the U.S. firm hedges against the possibility that the pound will depreciate over the period of concern.

Limitations of Hedging   A major limitation of hedging is that it not only prevents unfavorable exchange rate effects but also favorable rate effects. For example, reconsider the initial example in which the firm locks in the purchase of pounds 90 days ahead at a forward rate of $1.80. If the actual spot exchange rate in 90 days is $1.70, the firm would have been better off without the hedge. Nevertheless, it is obligated to fulfill its forward contract by exchanging dollars for pounds at the forward exchange rate of $1.80. This example illustrates why many U.S. firms hedge only when they expect that their future international business transactions will be adversely affected by exchange rate movements.

How Exchange Rates Affect Foreign Competition

Many U.S. firms compete with foreign firms in the U.S. market. Exhibit 6.9 shows a common situation in the United States. RCA is a U.S. firm that sells televisions in the U.S. market. It competes with many foreign competitors

Exhibit 6.9

How Exchange Rates Affect the Degree of Foreign Competition

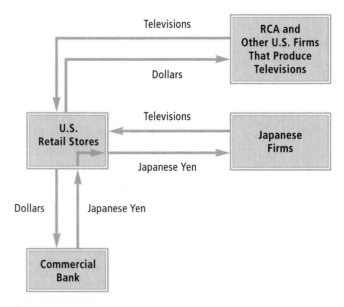

Scenario	Result
1. Japanese yen depreciates against the dollar.	U.S. retail stores can purchase Japanese televisions with fewer dollars, so the demand for Japanese televisions increases (and therefore the demand for U.S. televisions decreases).
2. Japanese yen appreciates against the dollar.	U.S. retail stores must pay more dollars to purchase Japanese televisions, so the demand for Japanese televisions decreases (and therefore the demand for U.S. televisions increases).

that export televisions to the United States. Retail stores purchase televisions from RCA as well as other firms.

Assume that the stores mark up the price of each television by 20 percent. When these stores purchase Japanese televisions, they convert dollars to Japanese yen (the Japanese currency). If the value of the yen depreciates against the dollar, the store needs fewer dollars to purchase the Japanese televisions. If it applies the same markup, it can reduce its price on the Japanese televisions. Therefore, increased foreign competition (due to depreciation of one or more foreign currencies) may cause RCA to lose some U.S. business.

If the foreign currency appreciates against the dollar, the foreign competitors may be unable to compete in the United States because the prices of imported products will rise. Using our example, if the Japanese yen appreciates, the retail store will need more dollars to purchase the Japanese televisions. When applying its markup, it will need to increase its price on the Japanese televisions. Therefore, U.S. firms such as RCA may gain more U.S. business.

SUMMARY

1 The main reasons why U.S. firms engage in international business are to

▶ attract foreign demand,

▶ capitalize on technology,

▶ use inexpensive resources, or

▶ diversify internationally.

The first two reasons reflect higher revenue, while the third reason reflects lower expenses. The fourth reason reflects less risk by reducing exposure to a single economy.

2 Global opportunities for U.S. firms have expanded as a result of the reduction of trade barriers in Europe, Latin America, and Asia. The reduction in trade barriers has made it easier for U.S. firms to engage in international business in those regions.

3 The primary ways in which firms conduct international business are:

▶ importing,

▶ exporting,

▶ direct foreign investment, and

▶ strategic alliances.

Many U.S. firms have used all of these strategies.

4 When firms sell their products in international markets, they assess the cultures, economic systems and conditions, exchange rate risk, and political risk in those markets. A country's economic conditions affect the demand by its citizens for the firm's product. The larger the proportion of the firm's total sales generated in a specific foreign country, the more sensitive is the firm's rev-

enue to that country's economic conditions.

5 Exchange rate movements can affect U.S. firms in various ways, depending on their characteristics. U.S. importers benefit from a strong dollar. U.S. exporters benefit from a weak dollar but are adversely affected by a strong dollar. U.S. firms competing with foreign firms that export to the U.S. market are adversely affected by a strong dollar, because the products exported by foreign firms appear inexpensive to U.S. consumers when the dollar is strong.

KEY TERMS

appreciates   178
balance of trade   168
capitalism   172
communism   172
depreciates   178
direct foreign investment
    (DFI)   169
exporting   168

forward contract   183
forward rate   183
hedge   183
importing   167
international licensing
    agreement   170
joint venture   170
political risk   176

privatization   173
quota   167
socialism   172
spot exchange rate   183
strategic alliance   170
tariff   167
trade deficit   168

Review & Critical Thinking Questions

1. Explain why a business may want to sell its product or service in a foreign country.

2. Discuss why foreign competitors may have an advantage over U.S. firms.

3. In which areas of the world have changes in economic and political conditions created opportunities for U.S. firms to more easily pursue interna-

tional business? Provide specific examples.

4. What are tariffs and quotas? Explain how tariffs and quotas affect the price of imports.

5. Distinguish exporting from importing. Can a business such as DuPont be involved in both exporting and importing? How?

6. What is direct foreign investment (DFI)? Why should a

company be particularly careful when engaging in DFI?

7. Identify and explain the various types of international alliances between U.S. firms and foreign firms.

8. Explain the difference between a direct foreign investment and a strategic alliance undertaken by an international business.

9. Identify and briefly describe the foreign characteristics that can influence international business investments.

10. Explain the differences between capitalism, communism, and socialism.

11. Why must a firm assess economic conditions before entering a foreign market? What determines a U.S. firm's exposure to a foreign country's economy?

12. Explain why many U.S. firms may increase their foreign acquisitions in response to exchange rate movements.

Discussion Questions

1. Discuss the advantages and disadvantages of foreign ownership in the United States. Are there any types of businesses that should not be sold to a foreign investor?

2. Assume you are a business entrepreneur. Do you support free trade among nations, or do you believe that there should be tariffs and quotas on imported goods? How would each position affect the U.S. economy?

3. How could a firm use the Internet to attract foreign demand? How could a firm use the Internet to access the current level of exchange rates?

4. How could a U.S. firm use the Internet to facilitate exporting?

5. Do you think Americans should buy U.S.-produced goods and services or foreign goods and services? Does either practice affect the U.S. balance of trade? Comment.

6. Discuss the implications of a stronger dollar in relation to other foreign currencies for 1) an exporter, and 2) someone who is planning to travel to a foreign country. Are there differences between the two parties?

It's Your Decision: Global Exposure at CHC

1. CHC may purchase exercise machines that are produced in Chile. How will the cost of the machines be affected by the value of the Chilean peso?

2. Why is CHC's business performance somewhat insulated from global conditions?

Investing in a Business

Using the annual report of the firm in which you would like to invest, complete the following:

1 Describe the means (if any) by which the firm engages in global business. Does it export? Does it import? Does the firm have foreign subsidiaries overseas? Joint ventures?

2 In what foreign countries does the firm do business? Is the firm seeking to expand into new foreign markets? How does its overseas sales growth compare with its domestic sales growth?

3 Does the firm's annual report specifically mention foreign firms as a source of competition?

4 Was the firm's performance affected by exchange rate movements last year? If so, how?

5 Explain how the business uses technology to assess the global environment in which it operates. For example, does it use certain websites to determine its exchange rate risk? Does it use the Internet to determine its global competition?

6 Go to **http://hoovers.com** and locate the NEWS SEARCH. Type in the name of the firm in the space provided, and review the recent news stories about the firm. Summarize any (at least one) recent news story about the firm that applies to one or more of the key concepts in this chapter.

Case: Global Expansion by Linton Records

Linton Records is a U.S. producer of recordings of soul music, which are sold in the United States and exported to Europe. A year ago, the company entered into a joint venture with a distributor in London to retail its records. It is planning to import British rock into the United States, as it has just entered into a strategic alliance with this distributorship. Sales are expected to increase 20 percent a year over first-year sales of £12.5 million. Linton receives payment for its exports in British pounds. The dollar has been weakening against the British pound.

Linton Records has learned that its product line will be subject to a tariff on goods imported into Europe. The tariff is related to the European Union, the common market alliance that includes many European countries. The company has expressed concern because it believes that political intervention disrupts the free flow of trade as it exists in the United States.

Management is developing a strategic alliance with a French manufacturer to produce compact discs for the entire operation. The company expects to cut production costs by 25 percent because of the French firm's advanced technology. In this strategic alliance, the French manufacturer will buy all its raw materials from a company in Bonn, Germany. In addition to the distributorship in London, Linton Records plans to open new markets in six different countries in Western Europe in the future.

Questions

1. Discuss the primary reasons why Linton Records may benefit from its international business.

2. How will Linton Records be affected if the dollar weakens further?

3. Should music imported by U.S. firms from England be subjected to a tariff?

Video Case: Global Business by ETEC

Enforcement Technology (ETEC) uses technology to manufacture the AutoCite system for parking enforcement. It sells its technology to parking enforcement agencies in the United States so that they can monitor parking meters. In recent years, it has received orders from parking enforcement agencies in foreign countries. When ETEC creates an AutoCite system for a foreign agency, it must adjust the technology to fit the system used in that country. For example, Australian agencies require much more information on parking tickets than U.S. agencies

do, so the AutoCite system had to be adjusted to allow for this information.

Questions

1. Why is it so important for ETEC to adjust its product to satisfy various types of customers (parking enforcement agencies) in different countries?

2. Do you think that ETEC's performance is highly exposed to U.S. economic conditions? Explain.

3. Do you think ETEC's performance is highly exposed to exchange rate fluctuations?

Internet Applications

1. *http://www.worldbank.org*

What type of information is provided on this website? How do you think this information is useful for companies operating in a global environment or competing with foreign companies? What online databases are available from the World Bank? What are some publications available from the World Bank?

2. *http://www.imf.org*

Click on "About the IMF." What is the IMF, and how is it useful for companies competing in an international

environment? Select a country and summarize some of the recent news articles and information available for that country.

3. *http://www.exchangerate.com*

Find the most recent exchange rates for (1) the Australian dollar, (2) the euro, and (3) the British pound. Find the charts for three European currencies and view their recent movements. Do European currencies appear to move in the same direction? If so, why do you think that happens? If not, why not?

The Coca-Cola Company Annual Report Project

Questions for the current year's annual report are available on the text website at **http://madura.swlearning.com.**

The following questions apply concepts presented in this chapter to The Coca-Cola Company. Go to The Coca-Cola Company website (**http://www.cocacola.com**) and find the index for the 2001 annual report.

Questions

1 Study the "2001 Worldwide Unit Case Volume By Operating Segment" section. Do you think The Coca-Cola Company's products have achieved a global presence?

2 Click on "Selected Market Results."

   a. In terms of 2001 annual growth rates, what are The Coca-Cola Company's major successes?

   b. Where do you think there are major opportunities for The Coca-Cola Company to increase annual growth rates?

3 Find the "Financial Risk Management" section in the consolidated financial statements. In some situations, The Coca-Cola Company may receive cash inflows from foreign countries that can be affected by exchange rate changes.

   a. How does it measure these currency fluctuations?

   b. How does it hedge against these currency fluctuations?

4 Click on "Operations Review." How many servings of The Coca-Cola Company's products does the average resident of Latin America consume in a year?

5 Go to **http://hoovers.com** and locate the NEWS CENTER. Key in The Coca-Cola Company in the space provided, click on "Search," and review the recent news stories about the firm. Summarize any (at least one) recent news story about The Coca-Cola Company that applies one or more of the key concepts within this chapter of the text.

In-Text Study Guide

Answers are in an appendix at the back of the book.

True or False

1. An important reason U.S. firms establish new businesses in less-developed countries is to capitalize on technological advantages. _T_

2. The best way for a firm to stabilize its profits over time is to focus its efforts on producing and selling one specific product in one specific country. _F_

3. Land and labor costs can vary significantly among countries. _T_

4. U.S. firms that provide services are more likely to face strong foreign competition than firms that produce manufactured goods. _F_

5. A tax placed on imported goods is called a tariff. _T_

6. Competition among firms is usually more intense in communist economies than it is in capitalist economies. _F_

7. A key advantage of socialist economies is the emphasis on keeping tax rates as low as possible. _F_

8. A firm's performance in a foreign country is dependent on that country's economic growth. _T_

9. If firms overestimate the economic growth in a particular country, they will normally overestimate the demand for their products in that country. _T_

10. The values of most currencies are not allowed to change relative to the dollar. _F_

Multiple Choice

11. A country that has relatively low technology is termed a(an):
    a) least-favored nation.
    b) post-communist country.
    c) pre-industrial nation.
    d) backward nation.
    e) developing country. ⟵

12. All of the following are important reasons why U.S. firms engage in international business except to:
    a) attract foreign demand.
    b) capitalize on technology.
    c) take advantage of lower taxes in socialist economies.
    d) use inexpensive labor and natural resources available in less-developed countries.
    e) diversify internationally.

13. A major reason U.S. firms want to achieve international diversification is that it:
    a) exposes them to cultural diversity.
    b) enables them to take big tax write-offs.
    c) helps them stabilize profits, thus reducing their risk.
    d) allows them to acquire more advanced technology.
    e) allows them to offer stock to foreign investors, thus increasing their financial base.

14. Which of the following was not a motive for the Single European Act?
    a) reduction of trade barriers
    b) opening of new markets
    c) increased efficiency
    d) increased tax revenue from tariffs
    e) economies of scale

15. With the implementation of NAFTA in 1993:
    a) most trade restrictions between the United States, Canada, and Mexico were removed.
    b) European nations began using a common currency.
    c) U.S. firms were encouraged to invest in the less-developed nations of Asia, Central America, and Africa.
    d) the World Bank was given the authority to set interest rates on international business loans.
    e) countries were no longer allowed to have trade deficits continue for more than three years.

16. A number of European nations recently agreed to share a common currency known as the:
    a) gifspen.
    b) francmarc.
    c) European pound.
    d) euro.
    e) NAFTA.

In-Text Study Guide

Answers are in an appendix at the back of the book.

17. As a result of NAFTA, some U.S. firms have lost market share to Mexican firms. This effect tends to be most pronounced in:
    a) the public sector.
    b) labor-intensive industries.
    c) professional services firms.
    d) states bordering Mexico.
    e) high-technology industries.

18. Many U.S. firms view _____ as the country with the most potential for growth:
    a) the United States itself
    b) Mexico
    c) China
    d) Germany
    e) Indonesia

19. The purchase of foreign supplies by IBM is an example of:
    a) direct foreign investment.
    b) exporting.
    c) importing.
    d) international licensing.
    e) a joint venture.

20. The U.S. government just imposed a numerical limit on the amount of widgets that may be imported, which is called a:
    a) quota.
    b) tariff.
    c) call rate.
    d) exchange factor.
    e) limit order.

21. A negative balance of trade is referred to as a:
    a) trade deficit.
    b) trade surplus.
    c) favorable balance of payments.
    d) direct investment.
    e) hedge.

22. The sale of film produced by Kodak in the United States to Chinese firms is an example of:
    a) direct foreign investment.
    b) exporting.
    c) importing.

23. When a firm in one country acquires or builds a subsidiary in another country, it is engaging in:
    a) arbitrage.
    b) a joint venture.
    c) foreign aid.
    d) a forward contract.
    e) direct foreign investment.

24. A(n) _____ is a strategic alliance in which a firm allows a foreign company to produce its products according to specific instructions.
    a) international cartel
    b) international licensing agreement
    c) joint venture
    d) international limited partnership
    e) limited liability contract

25. Under _____ the government owns most businesses and decides what products to produce and in what quantity.
    a) socialism
    b) capitalism
    c) communism
    d) dualism
    e) pluralism

26. In a _____ economy, businesses are privately owned and profit-seeking entrepreneurs are free to start businesses they believe will serve the people's needs.
    a) capitalist
    b) communist
    c) feudalist
    d) mercantilist
    e) pluralist

27. _____ is an economic system that allows some private ownership of businesses and property but also has an active government sector and high tax rates to support the government's programs.
    a) Socialism
    b) Capitalism
    c) Feudalism

d) international licensing.
e) a joint venture.

In-Text Study Guide

d) Mercantilism

e) Dualism

28. In recent years, governments of many nations have sold government-owned and -operated businesses to private investors. This process is known as:
    a) public disinvestment.
    b) privatization.
    c) repatriation.
    d) democratization.
    e) public capitalization.

29. The political risks to a U.S. firm operating in a foreign country include all of the following, except:
    a) inflation of the currency.
    b) higher tax rates for foreign subsidiaries.
    c) taking over U.S. companies without compensation.
    d) strict pollution controls.
    e) eviction from property.

30. The dollar weakens against the British pound if the value of the pound:
    a) depreciates.
    b) sells off.
    c) softens.
    d) appreciates.
    e) declines.

31. If the dollar depreciates relative to the Japanese yen:
    a) Japanese goods will seem cheaper to American importers.
    b) gold will flow from the United States to Japan.
    c) American goods will seem less expensive to Japanese consumers.
    d) the dollar must appreciate relative to some other Asian currency.
    e) the U.S. government will have to intervene to increase the value of the dollar.

32. One disadvantage of hedging is that it:
    a) is illegal in many foreign countries.
    b) requires businesses to pay additional taxes on their earnings.
    c) is considered unethical behavior by some investors.
    d) prevents not only unfavorable, but also favorable, changes in exchange rates.
    e) greatly increases the risk of doing business in foreign countries.

33. A _____ states an exchange of currencies that will occur at a specified exchange rate at some future point in time.
    a) reserve clause
    b) forward contract
    c) limit order
    d) market order
    e) fixed time exchange contract

34. When businesses take action to lock in a specific exchange rate for a future international transaction in order to reduce risk, their strategy is referred to as:
    a) rate fixing.
    b) trading on reserve.
    c) selling short.
    d) hedging.
    e) trading on margin.

35. If you plan to convert dollars to obtain Japanese yen today, you would pay the:
    a) spot rate.
    b) open market rate.
    c) discount rate.
    d) hedge rate.
    e) forward rate.

Part II

Summary

Business Environment

A firm is exposed to economic conditions (Chapter 4), industry conditions (Chapter 5), and global conditions (Chapter 6). The economic conditions that affect a firm's performance are economic growth, inflation, and interest rates. Economic growth influences the demand for products and services produced by firms. Inflation influences the production expenses of materials, machinery, or employees. Interest rates influence the demand for products that are typically purchased with borrowed funds. They also influence the cost of financing. In general, a firm's performance is improved as a result of strong economic growth, low inflation, and low interest rates.

The industry conditions that affect a firm's performance are the demand for a specific type of product (industry demand), the industry competition, the labor environment, and the regulatory environment. A firm's performance is typically improved when industry demand is high, industry competitors are weak, the supply of available labor is high, and regulations do not impose excessive restrictions.

The global conditions that affect a firm's performance are economic conditions in foreign countries and exchange rates. A U.S. firm's performance may be improved when the foreign countries where it sells some of its products experience a high rate of economic growth. A U.S. firm may also benefit from a weak dollar if it exports products or from a strong dollar if it imports products.

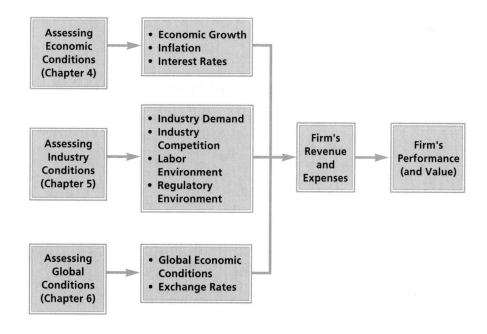

ASSESSING THE BUSINESS ENVIRONMENT WITHIN THE BUSINESS PLAN FOR CAMPUS.COM

Exposure to Economic Conditions (related to Chapter 4)

In your business plan for Campus.com, explain whether and how the firm's performance may be affected if economic conditions change. For example, would the demand for Campus.com's services be affected if economic conditions deteriorate? Why?

Industry Segments (related to Chapter 5)

In your business plan, identify the various segments of the industry that Campus.com could target. The business was initially created to serve high school students who are about to graduate. Could the business offer different levels of service to its main market (high school students) and charge higher prices for some types of services?

Competition (related to Chapter 5)

In your business plan for Campus.com, describe any existing competition for its product, including services that provide general information about colleges throughout the United States.

Global Conditions (related to Chapter 6)

Describe in the business plan how Campus.com could expand outside the United States. In this part of the plan, identify the logical choice of a foreign country that Campus.com could target.

Communication and Teamwork

You (or your team) may be asked by your instructor to hand in and/or present the section of your business plan that relates to this part of the text.

Integrative Video Case: Social Responsibility and Communication (Ben & Jerry's)

Ben Cohen and Jerry Greenfield founded the ice cream company Ben & Jerry's in 1978 in Burlington, Vermont, with a $12,000 investment, a $5 correspondence course in ice cream making, and a rock salt ice cream maker. Today, Ben & Jerry's is affected by many uncontrollable external factors, including demographics and target markets, economic factors, regulatory constraints, competition, and technology. Ben & Jerry's is generally considered to be an environmentally responsible company. The company has illustrated that it is possible to prosper economically with a strong commitment to the environment.

Questions

1 Explain Ben & Jerry's exposure to industry conditions. Why does the company view itself as insulated from economic factors like low economic growth and inflation?

2 Do you think Ben & Jerry's is also affected by global conditions? Do you think some of the global characteristics Ben & Jerry's is subject to in foreign countries are similar to the economic conditions in the U.S.?

3 Explain the importance to a firm of understanding its exposure to industry conditions. How does this affect its business planning?

Integrative Video Case: Confronting the Competition (Renegade Animation)

Renegade Animation was founded in 1992 by two former employees of Warner Bros. In their first year of operations, Renegade's sales were approximately $1.2 million, largely due to a Super Bowl spot designed for Nike. Today, Renegade has four employees and is very competitive in the animation industry due to several competitive advantages.

2 How might the degree of competition affect Renegade Animation's business decisions?

3 Do you think Renegade Animation would be affected by economic conditions such as economic growth and inflation? Do you think it would be affected by the labor environment in its industry? Explain.

Questions

1 What is Renegade Animation's competitive edge? Explain how Renegade Animation attempted to distinguish itself from the competition.

THE STOCK MARKET GAME

Go to **http://finance.yahoo.com** and check your portfolio balance, which is updated continuously by Yahoo! Finance.

Check Your Stock Portfolio Performance

1 What is the value of your stock portfolio today?

2 What is your return on your investment? (This return is shown on your balance.)

3 How did your return compare to those of other students? (This comparison tells you whether your stock portfolio's performance is relatively high or low.)

Keep in mind that you can change your portfolio at any time during the school term.

Explaining Your Stock Performance

Stock prices are frequently influenced by the economic environment, including economic, industry, and global conditions. Review the latest news about some of your stocks on Yahoo! Finance by clicking on "Symbol Lookup" and typing the ticker symbol of your stock.

1 Identify one of your stocks whose price was affected (since you purchased it) as a result of the business environment (the main topic in this part of the text).

2 Identify the specific changes in the business environment (interest rate movements, industry competition, etc.) that caused the stock price to change.

3 Did your stock's price increase or decrease in response to changes in the business environment?

RUNNING YOUR OWN BUSINESS

1 How would the performance of your business be affected by economic conditions in the local area? How would it be affected by economic conditions across the United States? How would your company be affected by global economic events?

2 How would the performance of your business be affected by an increase in interest rates?

3 Describe the main competitors that would be competing against your business. Would it be easy for additional competitors to enter your market? Could you effectively expand your business?

4 How would the performance of your business be affected by industry conditions? Explain.

5 What competitive advantage of your business can be affected by industry conditions? Explain.

6 Explain whether your business would benefit from importing any supplies from foreign countries.

7 Will your business attempt to export any products to foreign countries? Identify which countries could be targeted. Will your business compete against foreign competitors?

8 Explain how the performance of your business would be affected in any way by exchange rate movements.

9 How could your business use the Internet to assess its competition, its industry environment, and its global environment?

YOUR CAREER IN BUSINESS: PURSUING A MAJOR AND A CAREER IN ECONOMICS

If you are very interested in the topics covered in this section, you may want to consider a major in economics. Some of the more common courses taken by economics majors are summarized here.

Common Courses for Economics Majors

▶ *Principles of Macroeconomics*   Focuses on the economy as a whole, inflation, and the impact of government policies on economic conditions.

▶ *Principles of Microeconomics*   Focuses on how firms set prices and determine how much to produce.

▶ *Intermediate Macroeconomics*   Analyzes the trade-offs resulting from government policies.

▶ *Intermediate Microeconomics*   Focuses on profits, wages, and the market structure.

▶ *International Economics*   Focuses on the comparison of different economies, international trade and capital flows, and the development of emerging economies.

▶ *Labor Economics*   Focuses on the relationships between firms and their employees, including the role of labor unions.

▶ *Mathematical Economics*   Explains how mathematics can be used to solve economic problems.

▶ *Econometrics*   Applies statistical models to assess economic relationships.

▶ *Urban Economics*   Emphasizes economic development and the environment within urban areas.

▶ *Managerial Economics*   Examines how economic theories can be used in making managerial decisions related to production and pricing.

▶ *Money and Banking*   Focuses on money, the banking system, and credit, as well as on the impact of monetary policy on economic conditions.

▶ *Industrial Economics*   Focuses on economic concepts related to industry, including pricing, competition, and market share.

Careers in Economics

The following websites provide information about common job positions, salaries, and careers for students who major in economics:

▶ Job position websites:

http://jobsearch.monster.com	Information on jobs in Finance, Economics, Government, or Policy.
http://careers.yahoo.com	Information on jobs in Banking, Mortgage Loans, or Government.
http://collegejournal.com/ salarydata	Information on jobs in Banking or Financial Services.

Some of the job positions described in these websites may require work experience or a graduate degree.

Part III

Management

anagement is the use of human and other resources in a manner that best achieves the firm's objectives. Four key components of management are (1) understanding the characteristics necessary for managers to be effective, (2) assigning job responsibilities, (3) managing the process by which products are produced, and (4) monitoring and improving the quality of the products produced. Chapter 7 explains how managers can be more effective, and Chapter 8 explains how job responsibilities are assigned. Chapter 9 describes how the resources used in the production process can be allocated to achieve efficiency and quality.

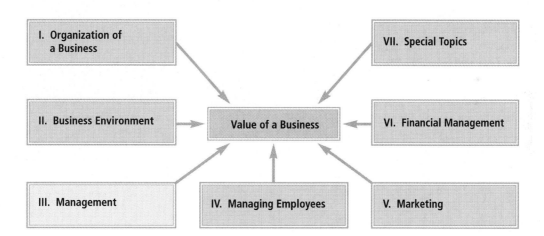

- I. Organization of a Business
- II. Business Environment
- III. Management
- IV. Managing Employees
- V. Marketing
- VI. Financial Management
- VII. Special Topics

Value of a Business

All businesses, including GoldRush Casino, need to determine the necessary skills and tasks of their managers.

The Learning Goals of this chapter are to:

1 Identify the levels of management.

2 Identify the key functions of managers.

3 Describe the skills that managers need.

4 Describe methods that managers can use to utilize their time effectively.

Chapter 7

Managing Effectively

Management involves the utilization of human and other resources (such as machinery) in a manner that best achieves the firm's plans and objectives. According to a recent survey by Shareholder Surveys, shareholders ranked good management and long-term vision as the two most important characteristics of a firm. Consider the situation of GoldRush Casino, which just recently opened. The casino offers slot machines, blackjack tables, roulette wheels, and other methods of gambling. It also plans to provide entertainment. GoldRush must decide:

▶ What levels of management will it need to manage the casino?

▶ What functions will be required of the managers who manage the casino?

▶ What skills will the managers need?

▶ How can the casino ensure that the

managers use their time efficiently?

The decision about the levels of management needed to manage the casino will affect the expense of running its business. The decision about the functions is necessary to ensure that the managers can complete all the required tasks. The decision about the managers' skills is needed to ensure that the managers are capable of completing all the necessary tasks. The decision about how the managers should use

their time is necessary to get the most work out of the managers so that the firm does not need to hire too many managers.

The types of decisions described above are necessary for all businesses. This chapter explains how GoldRush or any other firm can determine the necessary levels, functions, skills, and efficiency for its managers that will maximize its value.

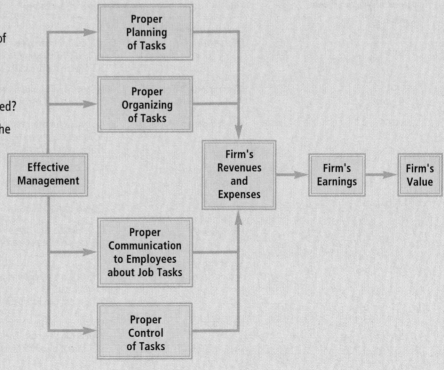

Identify the levels of management.

top (high-level) management managers in positions such as president, chief executive officer, chief financial officer, and vice-president who make decisions regarding the firm's long-run objectives

middle management managers who are often responsible for the firm's short-term decisions

supervisory (first-line) management managers who are usually highly involved with the employees who engage in the day-to-day production process

LEVELS OF MANAGEMENT

Employees who are responsible for managing other employees or other resources serve as managers, even if their official title is different. The functions of managers vary with their respective levels within the firm. **Top (high-level) management** includes positions such as president, chief executive officer (who commonly also serves as president), chief financial officer, and vice-president. These managers make decisions regarding the firm's long-run objectives (such as three to five years ahead).

Middle management is often responsible for the firm's short-term decisions, as these managers are closer to the production process. Middle managers resolve problems and devise new methods to improve performance. Middle management includes positions such as regional manager and plant manager.

Supervisory (first-line) management is usually highly involved with the employees who engage in the day-to-day production process. Supervisors deal with problems such as worker absenteeism and customer complaints. Supervisory management includes positions such as account manager and office manager. The types of functions that each level of management conducts are summarized in Exhibit 7.1.

The relationships among top, middle, and supervisory managers can be more fully understood by considering a simple example. Exhibit 7.2 shows the responsibilities of all managers in light of a firm's new plans to expand production and increase sales. The middle and top managers must make production, marketing, and finance decisions that will achieve the new plans. The supervisory managers provide specific instructions to the new employees who are hired to achieve the higher production level.

Exhibit 7.1

Comparison of Different Levels of Management

Title	Types of Decisions
Top Management	
President	1) Should we create new products?
	2) Should we expand?
	3) How can we expand? Through acquisitions?
Chief Financial Officer	1) Should more funds be borrowed?
	2) Should we invest available funds in proposed projects?
Vice-President of Marketing	1) Should an existing product be revised?
	2) Should our pricing policies be changed?
	3) Should our advertising strategies be changed?
Middle Management	
Regional Sales Manager	1) How can we boost sales in a particular city?
	2) How can complaints from one of our largest customers be resolved?
	3) Should an additional salesperson be hired?
Plant Manager	1) Should the structure of the assembly line be revised?
	2) Should new equipment be installed throughout the plant?
Supervisory Management	
Account Manager	1) How can workers who process payments from various accounts be motivated?
	2) How can conflicts between two workers be resolved?
Supervisor	1) How can the quality of work by assembly-line workers be assessed?
	2) How can assembly-line tasks be assigned across workers?
	3) How can customer complaints be handled?

Exhibit 7.2

Comparison of Responsibilities among Managers

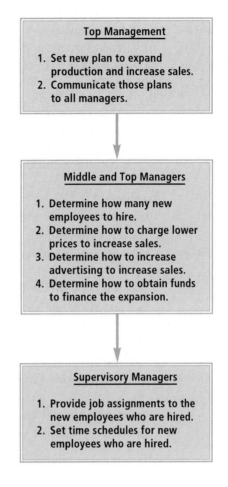

Top Management

1. Set new plan to expand production and increase sales.
2. Communicate those plans to all managers.

Middle and Top Managers

1. Determine how many new employees to hire.
2. Determine how to charge lower prices to increase sales.
3. Determine how to increase advertising to increase sales.
4. Determine how to obtain funds to finance the expansion.

Supervisory Managers

1. Provide job assignments to the new employees who are hired.
2. Set time schedules for new employees who are hired.

2

Identify the key functions of managers.

FUNCTIONS OF MANAGERS

Most managerial functions can be classified into one of the following categories:

▶ Planning

▶ Organizing

▶ Leading

▶ Controlling

Planning

planning the preparation of a firm for future business conditions

mission statement a description of a firm's primary goal

The **planning** function represents the preparation of a firm for future business conditions. As the first step in the planning process, the firm establishes its **mission statement,** which describes its primary goal. For example, here is the mission statement of Bristol-Myers Squibb:

"The mission of Bristol-Myers Squibb is to extend and enhance human life by providing the highest quality health and personal care products."

Most mission statements are general, like that of Bristol-Myers. The mission of General Motors is to be the world's leader in transportation products, and the mission of Ford Motor Company is to be the world's leading consumer company providing automotive products and services.

strategic plan identifies a firm's main business focus over a long-term period, perhaps three to five years

Strategic Plan

The **strategic plan** identifies the firm's main business focus over a long-term period. The strategic plan is more detailed than the mission statement and describes in general terms how the firm's mission is to be achieved. For example, if a firm's mission is to produce quality computer products, its strategic plan might specify the particular computer products to be produced and the manner in which they will be sold (retail outlets, Internet, etc.).

The strategic plan typically includes goals and strategies that can be used to satisfy the firm's mission. For example, a recent annual report of Bristol-Myers Squibb listed the following among its main goals and strategies:

Goals:

"Leadership in each product category and in each geographic market in which we compete. We aim to achieve number one or number two position with increasing market shares."

"Superior customer satisfaction by providing the highest quality products and services to our customers. We will strive to be rated number one or two with continuous improvement as rated by our customers."

"Superior steady shareholder returns, as measured by a number one or two competitive position in economic performance within our industry."

"An organization which is committed to winning through teamwork, empowerment, customer focus, and open communications."

Strategies:

"Our mission and goals will be achieved by adhering to the following core strategies:

- ▶ *Achieve unit growth fueled internally by new products, geographic expansion, and marketing innovation, and externally through acquisition, joint venture and licensing agreements.*
- ▶ *Dedicate ourselves to being recognized as the best in research and development across our businesses . . .*
- ▶ *Achieve continuous improvement in our cost structure . . .*
- ▶ *Attract, develop, motivate, and retain people of the highest caliber. The company's reporting, reward and recognition systems will be built around attainment of the goals identified above."*

Once a firm specifies its mission, it can develop plans to achieve that mission.

tactical planning smaller-scale plans (over one or two years) that are consistent with the firm's strategic (long-term) plan

Tactical Planning

High-level and middle managers also engage in **tactical planning,** or smaller-scale plans (over one or two years) that are consistent with the firm's strategic (long-term) plan. Tactical planning normally focuses on a short-term period, such as the next year or so. To develop their tactical plan, managers of AT&T and other firms assess economic conditions, the general demand for various products, the level of competition among firms producing those products, and changes in technology. They use their vision to capitalize on opportunities in which they have some advantages over other firms in the industry. If a firm's strategic plan is to increase its market share by 20 percent, its tactical plans may focus on increasing sales in specific regions that have less competition. As time passes,

cross functional teamwork:

Interaction of Functions to Achieve the Strategic Plan

The development of a strategic plan requires interaction among the firm's managers who are responsible for different business functions. Recall that the strategic plan of Bristol-Myers Squibb mentioned earlier includes goals of increased market share, customer satisfaction, and continuous improvement. The firm's strategies to achieve those goals include the creation of new products, continuous improvement in cost structure (high production efficiency), and retaining good employees.

The management function of Bristol-Myers Squibb can help achieve the firm's goals by assessing the needs of consumers so that the firm can create new products. It can also attempt to assess customers' satisfaction with existing products and use marketing strategies to increase the market share of these products. The financing function of Bristol-Myers Squibb can help achieve the firm's goals by determining the level of borrowing that will be sufficient to support the firm's operations.

Since the business functions are related, a strategic plan can be implemented only when the interaction among business functions is recognized. A strategic plan that focuses on increased sales will likely require more production and financing. The table below shows some common ways that the goals of a strategic plan can be achieved by each function.

How Various Business Functions Are Used to Achieve the Strategic Plan

Function	Typical Goals or Strategies That Can Be Achieved by This Function
Management	High production efficiency
	High production quality
	Customer satisfaction
	Employee satisfaction
Marketing	Innovation (new products)
	Increase market share of existing products
	Customer satisfaction
Finance	Reduce financing costs
	Efficient use of funds

additional tactical planning will be conducted in accordance with the strategic plan.

operational planning establishes the methods to be used in the near future (such as the next year) to achieve the tactical plans

Operational Planning   Another form of planning, called **operational planning,** establishes the methods to be used in the near future (such as the next year) to achieve the tactical plans. Continuing our example of a firm whose tactical plan is to increase sales, the operational plan may specify the means by which the firm can increase sales. That is, the operational plan may specify an increase in the amount of funds allocated to advertising and the hiring of additional salespeople.

The goals of operational planning are somewhat dependent on the firm's long-term goals. For example, a firm's top managers may establish a goal of 12 percent annual growth in sales over the next several years. The firm's salespeople may be asked to strive for a 1 percent increase in total sales per month during the upcoming year. Their month-to-month goals are structured from the long-term goals established by top management.

policies guidelines for how tasks should be completed

procedures steps necessary to implement a policy

contingency planning alternative plans developed for various possible business conditions

When firms engage in operational planning, they must abide by their **policies,** or guidelines for how tasks should be completed. For example, a policy on the hiring of employees may require that a specific process be followed. Policies enforced by firms ensure that all employees conduct specific tasks in a similar manner. The policies are intended to prevent employees from conducting tasks in a manner that is inefficient, dangerous, or illegal.

Most policies contain **procedures,** or steps necessary to implement a policy. For example, a policy for hiring may specify that an ad is to be placed in the local newspaper for so many days and that the criteria for the job must be disclosed in the ad. These procedures are intended to prevent abuses, such as a manager hiring a friend or relative who is not really qualified for the job. Without procedures, managers could make decisions that conflict with the company's goals.

As another example, a firm may implement procedures for air travel to ensure that employees use airlines that have relatively low prices and that they fly second class. These procedures are intended to prevent managers from incurring excessive travel expenses.

Contingency Planning Some of a firm's plans may not be finalized until specific business conditions are known. For this reason, firms use **contingency planning;** that is, they develop alternative plans for various possible business conditions. The plan to be implemented is contingent on the business conditions that occur. For example, a firm that produces sports equipment may plan to boost its production of rollerblades in response to recent demand. At the same time, however, it may develop an alternative plan for using its resources to produce other equipment instead of rollerblades if demand declines. It may also develop a plan for increasing its production if the demand for its rollerblades is much higher than expected.

Some contingency planning is conducted to prepare for possible crises that may occur. For example, airlines may establish contingency plans in the event that various problems arise, as illustrated in Exhibit 7.3.

The September 11 crisis prompted many firms to develop a contingency plan in the event of a future crisis. Some firms established backup production plans in case their normal facilities are not functioning properly. Other firms have identified backup office space that can be used if their normal offices are destroyed or otherwise are unusable. Many firms have also attempted to back up their information files and store them at an alternative location.

Relationships among Planning Functions The relationships among the planning functions are shown in Exhibit 7.4. Notice how the tactical plan is dependent on the strategic plan and the operational plan is

Exhibit 7.3

Illustration of Contingency Planning

Situation	Contingency Plan
Overbooked reservations	To reduce the number of customers who need that flight, offer customers who are willing to be bumped (wait for next flight) a free round-trip ticket to the destination of their choice in the future.
Minor airplane repair needed	Have airline engineers available at each major airport in the event that a minor repair is needed.
Major airplane repair needed	If the airplane is not suitable for flying, attempt to reroute the passengers who were supposed to be on that plane by reserving seats for them on other flights.

Exhibit 7.4

How Planning Functions Are Related

Example

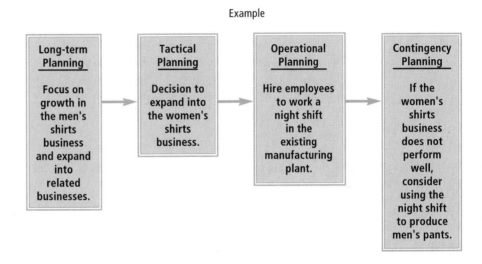

based on the tactical plan. The contingency plan offers alternatives to consider instead of the operational plan in specific situations (such as higher or lower demand for the product than anticipated).

To fully understand how these plans fit together, assume that your firm produces men's shirts and that your strategic plan specifies goals of expanding into related products. In this case, your tactical plan may focus on producing one other product along with men's shirts, such as women's shirts. The operational plan will specify the changes in the firm's operations that are necessary to produce and sell women's shirts. Specifically, the plan will determine how much more fabric must be purchased each month, how the women's shirts will be priced, and where they will be sold. A contingency plan can also be prepared in the event that excessive competition develops in the market for women's shirts. If this occurs, the contingency plan may be to expand into different products, such as men's pants.

College Health Club: **Planning at CHC**

As Sue Kramer plans to open College Health Club (CHC), she develops the following plans for the business:

▶ *Strategic Plan* The main objective of the business is to provide quality health club services, which should attract more members over time. The success of the health club is dependent on the number of memberships. In the long run, a goal is to apply the CHC business idea elsewhere by establishing health clubs near other colleges and universities.

This will involve identifying other colleges and universities that do not have a convenient health club for the students nearby. Consider establishing health clubs next to those campuses that would focus on serving the students. The membership fee should be affordable to students.

▶ *Tactical Plan* To achieve the strategic plan of establishing new health clubs near other colleges, the following tactical plan will be implemented. Conduct an informal survey of friends who are currently attending other colleges or universities nearby to determine whether they have convenient access to a health club next to the campus. The initial focus should be on colleges and universities that are within 50 miles because overseeing the establishment of a new health club will be easier if it is not far away.

▶ *Operational Plan* For any college or university whose students are not being served by a local health club or by facilities on campus, determine the potential benefits and costs of starting a new health club. The potential benefits are dependent on the number of students who might join a new health club. Determine the number of students who live on campus, and conduct an informal survey to estimate how many might be interested in joining a new health club if one is established. The costs of establishing a new health club are dependent on the cost of rental space near that college campus. Use the local newspaper to determine the cost of rental space at shopping centers near the campus. If a new health club appears to be feasible, consider the possible sources of financing that would be needed.

Organizing

organizing the organization of employees and other resources in a manner that is consistent with the firm's goals

The **organizing** function involves the organization of employees and other resources in a manner that is consistent with the firm's goals. Once a firm's goals are established (from the planning function), resources are obtained and organized to achieve those goals. For example, employees of Daimler-Chrysler are organized among assembly lines to produce cars or trucks in a manner consistent with the company's goals.

The organizing function occurs continuously throughout the life of the firm. This function is especially important for firms that frequently restructure their operations. Organizational changes such as the creation of a new position or the promotion of an employee occur frequently. These changes may even necessitate revisions of job assignments of employees whose job positions have not changed.

To illustrate the importance of the organizing function, consider a construction company that builds homes. The general contractor assigns tasks to the employees. From the laying of the foundation to painting, most tasks must be completed in a particular order. Since all tasks cannot be completed simultaneously, the contractor has workers working on different homes. In this way, employees can apply their respective specialties (such as painting, electrical, and so on) to whatever homes are at the proper stage of construction. The organizational structure of a business is discussed in more detail in the following chapter.

Leading

leading the process of influencing the habits of others to achieve a common goal

The **leading** function is the process of influencing the habits of others to achieve a common goal. It may include the communication of job assignments to employees and possibly the methods of completing those assignments. It may also include serving as a role model for employees. The leading should be conducted in a manner that is consistent with the firm's strategic plan.

The leading process influences employees to achieve a common goal.

© Getty Images/ Photo Disc

The leading function involves not only instructions on how to complete a task but also incentives to complete it correctly and quickly. Some forms of leading may help motivate employees. One method is to delegate authority by assigning employees more responsibility. Increased responsibility can encourage employees to take more pride in their jobs and raise their self-esteem. If employees are more actively involved in the production process and allowed to express their concerns, problems can be resolved more easily. Managers who allow much employee feedback may prevent conflicts between management and employees, or even conflicts among employees. To the extent that the leading function can enhance the performance of employees, it will enhance the performance of the firm.

initiative the willingness to take action

For managers to be effective leaders, they need to have **initiative,** which is the willingness to take action. Managers who have all other skills but lack initiative may not be very effective. Some managers who recognize the need to make changes are unwilling to take action because making changes takes more effort than leaving the situation as is, and change may upset some employees. For example, consider a manager who recognizes that the firm's expenses could be reduced, without any adverse effect on the firm, by eliminating a particular department. Nevertheless, this manager may refrain from suggesting any action because it might upset some employees. Managers are more likely to initiate change if they are directly rewarded for suggesting any changes that enhance the firm's value.

Leadership Styles Although all managers have their own leadership styles, styles can be classified generally as autocratic, free-rein, or participative. Managers who use an **autocratic** leadership style retain full authority for decision making; employees have little or no input. For example, if managers believe that one of their manufacturing plants will continue to incur losses, they may decide to close the plant without asking for input from the plant's workers. Autocratic managers may believe that employees cannot offer input that would contribute to a given decision. Employees are instructed

autocratic a leadership style in which the leader retains full authority for decision making

Conflicts with the Goal of a Multinational Corporation As part of their role as leaders, managers should influence other employees to focus on maximizing the firm's value. Sometimes, however, managers are tempted to make decisions that conflict with this goal. For example, a decision to establish a foreign subsidiary (a subsidiary in a foreign country) in one country versus another may be based on the country's appeal to a particular manager rather than on its potential benefits to shareholders. Decisions to expand may be determined by the desires of managers to make their respective divisions grow in order to receive more responsibility and compensation.

The costs of ensuring that managers maximize shareholder wealth (referred to as *agency costs*) are normally larger for multinational corporations than for purely domestic firms, for several reasons. First, multinational corporations that have subsidiaries scattered around the world may experience larger agency problems because monitoring managers of distant subsidiaries is more difficult. Second, managers of foreign subsidiaries who have been raised in different cultures may not follow uniform goals. Third, the sheer size of the larger multinational corporations can also create large agency problems.

Managers of foreign subsidiaries may be tempted to make decisions that maximize the values of their respective subsidiaries. This objective will not necessarily coincide with maximizing the value of the overall firm. Consider the case of Texen, Inc., which produces and sells wallets in the United States. It established a subsidiary in Mexico to produce and sell wallets in South America. Instead, the subsidiary exported the wallets to the United States, thereby taking away some of Texen's U.S. business. The managers of the subsidiary focused on a strategy that would enhance the subsidiary's value without realizing that this strategy could adversely affect Texen, the parent company.

If the U.S. managers of the parent company conduct their function of leading properly, they will communicate the goals that the subsidiary managers should follow. The U.S. managers should ensure that the subsidiary managers understand that a decision that maximizes the value of a subsidiary may be detrimental to the firm overall. Thus, in making decisions, the managers of a subsidiary should always consider the potential impact on other subsidiaries and on the parent.

---

free-rein a leadership style in which the leader delegates much authority to employees

participative a leadership style in which the leaders accept some employee input but usually use their authority to make decisions

to carry out tasks as ordered by autocratic leaders and are discouraged from being creative. In general, employees who desire responsibility are likely to become dissatisfied with such a management style.

Managers who use a **free-rein** (also called "laissez-faire") management style delegate much authority to employees. This style is the opposite extreme from the autocratic style. Free-rein managers communicate goals to employees but allow the employees to choose how to complete the objectives. For example, managers may inform workers in a manufacturing plant that the plant's performance must be improved and then allow the workers to implement an improvement strategy. Employees working under a free-rein management style are expected to manage and motivate themselves daily.

In the **participative** (also called democratic) leadership style, the leaders accept some employee input but usually use their authority to make decisions. This style requires frequent communication between managers and employees. Participative management can allow employees to express their opinions, but it does not pressure employees to make major decisions. For example, managers of a General Motors plant may consider the ideas of assembly-line workers on how to improve the plant's performance, but the managers will make the final decisions.

A comparison of leadership styles is provided in Exhibit 7.5. The optimal leadership style varies with the situation and with employees' experience and personalities. The free-rein style may be appropriate if employees are highly independent, creative, and motivated. An autocratic style may

Managers must continually work together to make decisions related to production, marketing, and finance in order to achieve the business' strategic plan.

© Getty Images/ EyeWire

be most effective for managing employees with low skill levels or high turnover rates. Participative management is effective when employees can offer a different perspective because of their closer attention to daily tasks.

Within a given firm, all three leadership styles may be used. For example, the top management of General Motors may use autocratic leadership to determine the types of automobiles (large versus small cars, luxury versus economy cars, and so on) to design in the future. These plans are made without much employee input because the top managers can rely on recent surveys of consumer preferences along with their own vision of what types of cars will be in demand in the future.

Once top management identifies the types of automobiles to produce, a participative leadership style may be used to design each type of car. That is, top management may establish general design guidelines for a particular type of car to be produced (such as specifying a small economy car) and ask employees for their suggestions on developing this type of car. These employees have experience on specific assembly-line operations and can offer useful input based on various production or quality problems they experienced with other cars. The top managers will make the final decisions after receiving the engineers' proposed designs, which are based on input from

Exhibit 7.5

How Leadership Style Affects Employee Influence on Management Decisions

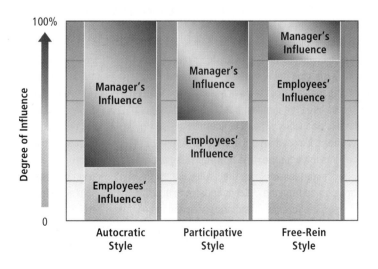

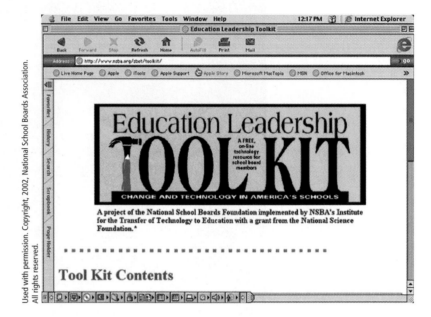

business online

e-business

Leadership and Planning This website provides guidance on leadership and planning.

http://wwwnsba.org/sbot/ toolkit/

global business

Leadership Styles for Global Business When U.S. firms establish subsidiaries in foreign countries, they must determine the type of leadership style to use in those subsidiaries. The firms do not automatically apply the style they use in the United States because conditions in foreign countries may be different. In some countries that have only recently encouraged private ownership of businesses (such as Hungary, Ukraine, and China), people are not accustomed to making decisions that will maximize the value of the business. Many people have had experience only in managing government-owned businesses. In those businesses, management decisions tended to focus on satisfying government goals rather than on maximizing the value of the business. Furthermore, the businesses had little or no competition, so managers could make decisions without concern about losing market share. Now, when U.S. firms establish subsidiaries in such countries, the firms may use a more autocratic leadership style for their subsidiaries. Instructions come from the U.S. headquarters, and the managers of the foreign subsidiaries are responsible for carrying out those instructions. When the managers have problems, they contact U.S. headquarters for advice.

Although many U.S. firms have recently adopted free-rein and participative styles in the United States, they may nevertheless be reluctant to give too much power to managers of some of their foreign subsidiaries. As the managers of the subsidiaries gain experience working for the firm and in a competitive environment, they may be given more power to make decisions.

When a U.S. firm has foreign subsidiaries in several different countries, its choice of a leadership style may vary with the characteristics of the foreign country. For example, it may allow a participative style in industrialized countries where managers are experienced in making business decisions aimed at maximizing the firm's value. The same firm may impose an autocratic style in a country where most business managers are not accustomed to making business decisions in this manner. No one particular leadership style is always appropriate for all countries. The firm must consider the country's characteristics before deciding which leadership style to use. Furthermore, the proper leadership style for any particular country may change over time in response to changes in the country's conditions.

numerous employees. This example reflects a participative style because managers use their authority to decide on the particular type of product to be produced but solicit input from many employees.

After the design of a specific car is completed, managers use a free-rein style for some parts of the production process. For example, a group of employees may be assigned to a set of assembly-line tasks. They may be allowed to assign the specific tasks among themselves. They may also be allowed to rotate their specific jobs to avoid boredom. This example reflects the free-rein style because the employees are allowed to choose how to achieve the firm's objectives.

Controlling

controlling the monitoring and evaluation of tasks

The **controlling** function represents the monitoring and evaluation of tasks. To evaluate tasks, managers should measure performance in comparison with the standards and expectations they set. That is, the controlling function assesses whether the plans set within the planning function are achieved. Standards can be applied to production volume and cost, sales volume, profits, and several other variables used to measure a firm's performance. The controlling function allows for continual evaluation so that the firm can ensure that it is following the course intended to achieve its strategic plan.

The strategic plan of Bristol-Myers Squibb (presented earlier) states that its reward systems will be based on standards set by the goals identified within that plan. An example of how the controlling function can be used to assess a firm's operations is shown in Exhibit 7.6.

Some standards such as profits are general and apply to all departments of a firm. Thus, no single department is likely to be entirely accountable if the firm's profits are not sufficient. Other standards focus on a particular operation of the firm. For example, production volume, production cost per unit, and inventory level standards can be used to monitor production. A specified volume of sales can be used as a standard to monitor the effectiveness of marketing strategies.

The main reason for setting standards is to detect and correct deficiencies. When deficiencies are detected, managers must take corrective action. For example, if labor and equipment repair expenses are too high, the firm will attempt to identify the reason for the high costs so that it can prevent them in the future. If a firm finds that its sales volume is below standards, its managers will determine whether to revise the existing marketing strategies or penalize those employees who are responsible for the deficiency. Deficiencies that are detected early may be more easily corrected.

Exhibit 7.6

Example of the Controlling Function

	Actual Level Last Week	Standards (Expected Level)	Assessment
Sales volume	300 units	280 units	OK
Production volume	350 units	350 units	OK
Labor expenses	$10,000	$9,000	Too high
Administrative expenses	$14,500	$15,000	OK
Equipment repair	$3,000	$1,000	Too high

Exhibit 7.7

Integration of Management Functions

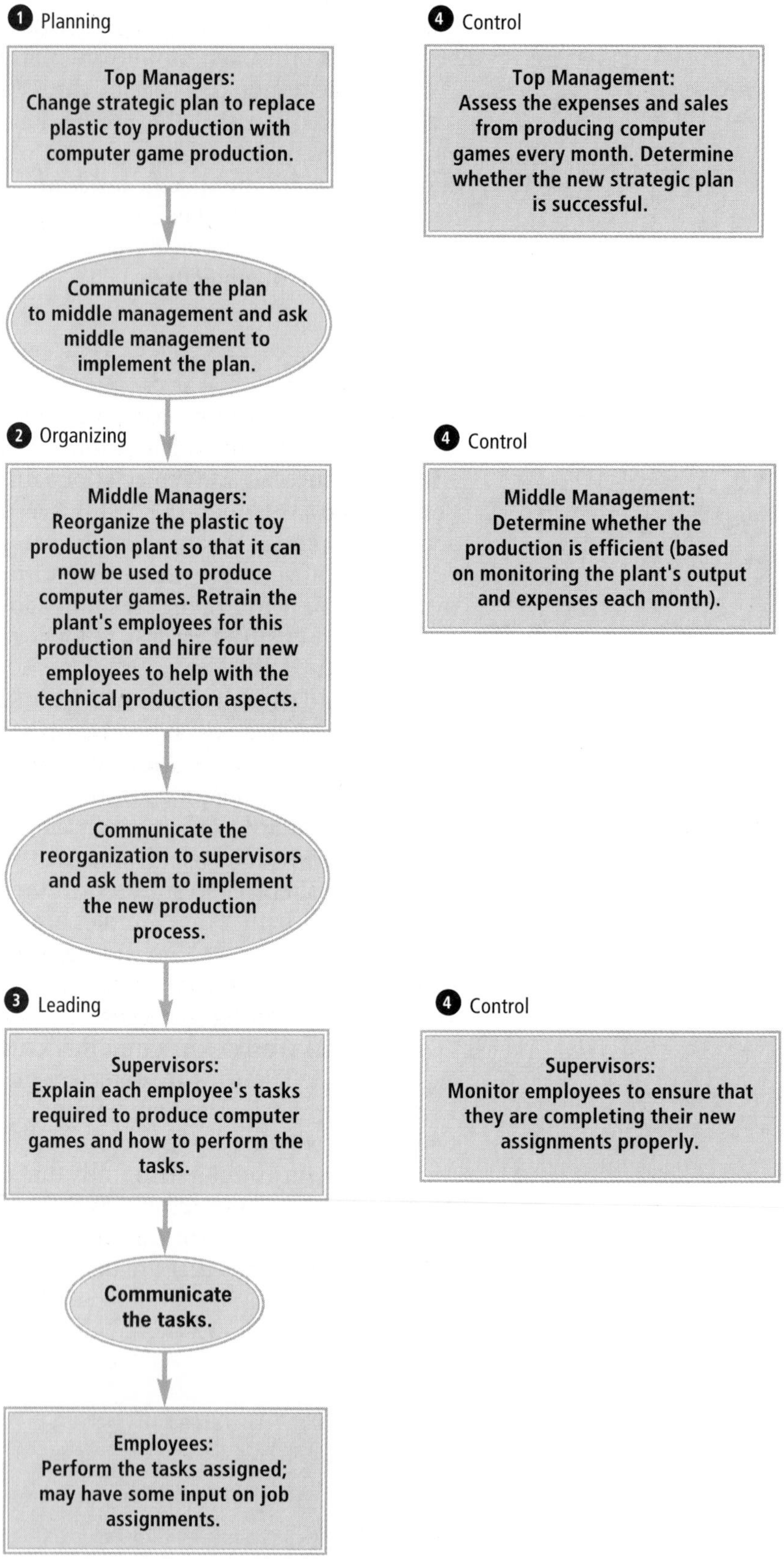

❶ Planning

Top Managers:
Change strategic plan to replace plastic toy production with computer game production.

↓

Communicate the plan to middle management and ask middle management to implement the plan.

❷ Organizing

Middle Managers:
Reorganize the plastic toy production plant so that it can now be used to produce computer games. Retrain the plant's employees for this production and hire four new employees to help with the technical production aspects.

↓

Communicate the reorganization to supervisors and ask them to implement the new production process.

❸ Leading

Supervisors:
Explain each employee's tasks required to produce computer games and how to perform the tasks.

↓

Communicate the tasks.

↓

Employees:
Perform the tasks assigned; may have some input on job assignments.

❹ Control

Top Management:
Assess the expenses and sales from producing computer games every month. Determine whether the new strategic plan is successful.

❹ Control

Middle Management:
Determine whether the production is efficient (based on monitoring the plant's output and expenses each month).

❹ Control

Supervisors:
Monitor employees to ensure that they are completing their new assignments properly.

By identifying deficiencies that must be corrected, the controlling function can help to improve a firm's performance.

In some cases, the standards rather than the strategies need to be corrected. For example, a particular advertising strategy to boost automobile sales may fail when interest rates are high because consumers are unwilling to borrow money to purchase automobiles at those interest rates. The failure to reach a specified sales level may be due to the high interest rates rather than a poor advertising strategy.

Integration of Management Functions

management the utilization of human resources (employees) and other resources (such as machinery) in a manner that best achieves the firm's plans and objectives

To illustrate how the four different functions of **management** are integrated, consider a firm that makes children's toys and decides to restructure its operations. Because of low sales, the top managers create a new strategic plan to discontinue production of plastic toys and to begin producing computer games. This planning function will require the use of the other management functions, as shown in Exhibit 7.7. The organizing function is needed to reorganize the firm's production process so that it can produce computer games. The leading function is needed to provide employees with instructions on how to produce the computer games. The controlling function is needed to determine whether the production process established to produce computer games is efficient and whether the sales of computer games are as high as forecasted.

In a small business, the owner may frequently perform all the management functions. For example, an owner of a small business may revise the strategic plan (planning function), reorganize the firm's production facility (organizing function), assign new tasks to the employees (leading function), and then assess whether all these revisions lead to acceptable results (controlling function).

Role of Technology Technology facilitates the integration of management functions. The planning function may easily involve input from various managers through an online network. Once specific plans are set, they can be immediately communicated to managers at all offices or plants. Next, the managers decide how to achieve the plans that have been established. Then they perform the leading function by offering instructions to their employees. They may provide some general instructions online and other instructions on a more personal level. Finally, an online network can be used to conduct the controlling function. As employees perform their duties, their managers are informed of the amount of output produced, and they relay the information to the top managers who initially established the plans. If the operations are not working according to the plan, this will be detected within the controlling function. Under these circumstances, either the operations or the plan can be modified.

3

Describe the skills that managers need.

MANAGERIAL SKILLS

To perform well, managers rely on four types of skills:

▶ Conceptual skills

▶ Interpersonal skills

▶ Technical skills

▶ Decision-making skills

Conceptual Skills

conceptual skills the ability to understand the relationships among the various tasks of a firm

Managers with **conceptual skills** (also referred to as analytical skills) have the ability to understand the relationships among the various tasks of a firm. They see how all the pieces fit together. For example, top managers of Motorola understand how the production process is related to the marketing and finance functions. Their emphasis is not so much on the precise method of accomplishing any specific task as on having a general understanding of the firm's operations. This enables them to anticipate the potential problems that could arise if, for example, a particular production plant experiences shortages. Managers need conceptual skills to make adjustments when problems like this occur. Managers with good conceptual skills have backup strategies when problems in the production process occur. Such strategies allow the firm to continue using its resources effectively.

Conceptual skills are commonly used by the top-level and middle-level managers who are not directly involved in the production assembly process. These skills are necessary to optimally utilize employees and other resources in a manner that can achieve the firm's goals. Managers with good conceptual skills tend to be creative and are willing to consider various methods of achieving goals.

Interpersonal Skills

interpersonal skills the skills necessary to communicate with customers and employees

Virtually all managers perform tasks that require good **interpersonal skills** (also referred to as communication skills), which are the skills necessary to communicate with customers and employees, as discussed next.

Communication with Customers
Many managers must communicate with customers to ensure satisfaction. They listen to customer complaints and attempt to respond in an acceptable manner. They may also bring other complaints to the attention of top management. Managers lacking good interpersonal skills may ignore customer complaints. Consequently, problems go unnoticed until a sufficient number of dissatisfied customers stop buying the firm's products. By that time, it may be too late for the firm to regain customers' trust.

One of the most important interpersonal skills is the ability to ask good questions. Without this, the real story behind customer or employee dissatisfaction may not be uncovered.

Communication with Employees
Managers need good interpersonal skills when communicating with employees. They must be able to clearly communicate assignments to employees and must communicate with employees who have made mistakes on the job so that they can be corrected. In addition, managers must listen to complaints from employees and attempt to resolve their problems.

Middle- and top-level managers who use good interpersonal skills in communicating with lower management will be better informed about problems within the firm. Interpersonal skills are often used by top and middle managers when they must make decisions based on information provided by other managers. For example, financial managers who develop next year's budget rely on projections of sales volume and prices provided by the marketing department. They also rely on production cost projections provided by the production department. All these managers must communicate with each other because their projections are interrelated.

Supervisory (first-line) management works with employees who engage in the day-to-day production process. Here a manager monitors the work of an employee who works at his drawing board.

© Getty Images/ PhotoDisc

Ford Motor Company has initiated an e-mail newsletter from the chief executive officer (CEO) to all 145,000 employees. The employees are allowed to use e-mail to reply to the CEO. This has encouraged more communication between management and other employees.

Technical Skills

Managers need **technical skills** to understand the types of tasks that they manage. Managers who are closer to the actual production process use their technical skills more frequently than high-level managers. For example, first-line managers of an assembly line of a computer manufacturer must be aware of how computer components are assembled. A technical understanding is important for all managers who evaluate new product ideas or are involved in solving problems.

technical skills skills used to perform specific day-to-day tasks

Decision-Making Skills

decision-making skills skills for using existing information to determine how the firm's resources should be allocated

Managers need **decision-making skills** so that they can use existing information to determine how the firm's resources should be allocated. The types of decisions made by managers vary with the position. The following are some typical decisions regarding the utilization of the firm's resources:

▶ Should more employees be hired?

▶ Should more machinery be purchased?

▶ Should a new facility be built?

▶ Should the assembly-line operation be revised?

▶ Should more supplies be ordered?

▶ Should salaries be adjusted?

These decisions affect either the revenue or the operating expenses of the firm and therefore affect its earnings. Managers who make proper decisions can improve the firm's earnings and thereby increase its value.

Steps for Decision Making   The decision-making process involves several specific stages. First, any possible decisions that are consistent with the firm's strategic plan are identified. Then, information relevant to each possible decision is compiled. Using this information, the costs and benefits of each possible decision are estimated. From these estimates, one or more managers can make and implement the best decision. As time passes, this

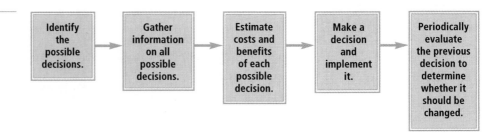

decision should be evaluated to determine if any changes are necessary. The stages of the decision-making process are summarized in Exhibit 7.8.

As an example, consider the task of accommodating increased demand for products at IBM. Managers first think of alternative means of achieving this goal, such as hiring more workers or allowing more overtime for existing workers. Compiling the relevant information, including the cost of adding more workers or allowing more overtime, enables the managers to estimate the costs and benefits of each alternative. Once managers have this information, they can conduct a cost-benefit analysis and select the better alternative. As time passes, the cost of each alternative may change and the managers may reconsider their decisions.

Summary of Management Skills

The various management skills that have been described are summarized in Exhibit 7.9. All of these skills are necessary for managers to be successful.

As an example of how a firm's performance is dependent on the skills of its managers, consider the case of Boston Market. This firm was initially successful, but its managers made several poor decisions about the firm's growth and the pricing of its meals. It then experienced a high degree of management turnover, which resulted in additional poor decisions made by inexperienced managers. In the summer of 1997, its performance declined as a result of the poor management decisions, and so did its value (as measured by its stock price), as shown in Exhibit 7.10.

Skill	Example of How the Skill can be Used by a Firm
Conceptual	Used to understand how the production level must be large enough to satisfy demand and how demand is influenced by the firm's marketing decisions.
Interpersonal	Used to inform employees about the goals of the firm and about specific policies that they must follow; also used to hear complaints from employees or customers and to resolve any conflicts among people.
Technical	Used to understand how components must be assembled to produce a product; also used to understand how machines and equipment should be used.
Decision making	Used to determine whether the firm should expand, change its pricing policy, hire more employees, or obtain more financing; proper decision making requires an assessment of the costs and benefits of various possible decisions that could be implemented.

Exhibit 7.10

Impact of Poor Management on Boston Market's Stock Price

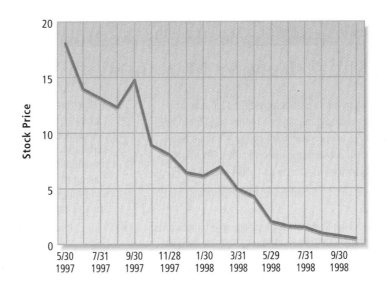

College Health Club: **Using Managerial Skills at CHC**

As Sue Kramer develops her business plan for College Health Club (CHC), she considers what skills she will need to manage the health club. She will use conceptual skills to organize its facilities in a manner that is desirable to customers. She will use interpersonal skills to sell her health club memberships to prospective customers. She will listen to what prospective customers want and then explain to them how CHC may satisfy their needs. She will also use her interpersonal skills to informally get feedback from existing customers about the quality of the services offered. She recognizes that the success of her business is highly influenced by customer satisfaction, since she relies on memberships for most of her revenue. She will use decision-making skills to revise her existing business plan as conditions change over time.

4

Describe methods that managers can use to utilize their time effectively.

time management the way managers allocate their time when managing tasks

HOW MANAGERS MANAGE TIME

Managers have a limited amount of time to spend managing their responsibilities. Therefore, they use **time management,** which refers to the way managers allocate their time when managing tasks. Although there is no single perfect formula for using time efficiently, the following guidelines should be followed:

▶ Set proper priorities.

▶ Schedule long time intervals for large tasks.

▶ Minimize interruptions.

▶ Set short-term goals.

▶ Delegate some tasks to employees.

Each of these guidelines is discussed in turn.

increasing value with technology

SOFTWARE TO IMPROVE MANAGEMENT

Effective management is particularly difficult in a small business where a single manager is responsible for many tasks. Recently, computer software packages have been developed to help managers in several areas. This new category of software, referred to as "MBA-ware" by *PC Magazine,* supports a wide range of activities, including the following:

▶ *Personnel Hiring* Software for screening job applicants, based upon psychological principles, can be used to assess attitudes and potential fit with the company. Software of this type has long been used at a number of well-known companies, such as Mrs. Field's Cookies.

▶ *Personnel Evaluation* Reviewing and evaluating personnel has long been a sensitive task, dreaded by many managers. Software is available that helps managers in constructing and writing reviews, as well as recording employee progress toward goals. Such software can help managers get through the review process and can be extremely valuable in documenting poor performance leading to an employee termination. Such documentation can be extremely valuable if the terminated employee sues his or her former employer.

▶ *General Management* A wide range of software is available to assist managers in day-to-day management activities. Calendar and scheduling software can be used for appointments and for time management. Personnel software can form the basis of a personnel system, keeping track of assorted information such as vacation usage, medical benefits, pension contributions,

and so forth. In addition, some versions of personnel software provide managers with templates for creating complete personnel manuals. Contact management software can help sales personnel keep track of customer calls. Financial software can aid managers in making reasonable projections of future business. A wide range of software supports specific activities, such as creating presentations and business planning.

▶ *Negotiating* A number of software packages have been developed that employ psychological models to help managers devise negotiating strategies for various situations. The software design is based on the principle that different negotiating styles should be employed when dealing with different types of individuals.

▶ *Decision Making* A growing number of software packages are designed to help managers make decisions more rationally. Using tested decision-making techniques, they force managers to identify and prioritize alternatives in such a way that they can be ranked in an internally consistent fashion.

▶ *Creativity* Some software is designed to stimulate managerial creativity. Such packages employ techniques drawn from brainstorming research and may also employ question-and-answer sessions designed to inspire managers with new ideas.

Although it is unlikely that software will ever substitute for managerial experience, more and more managers will undoubtedly use such tools to supplement their own management techniques.

Set Proper Priorities

One of the main reasons for time management problems is that managers lose sight of their role. Consider a regional sales manager who has two responsibilities: (1) resolving any problems with existing sales orders and (2) entertaining new clients. The sales manager may allocate much more time to entertaining because it is more enjoyable. Consequently, problems with sales orders may accumulate. Time management is a matter of priorities. Managers who set priorities according to what is best for the firm, rather than what they enjoy the most, are more successful.

Schedule Long Time Intervals for Large Tasks

Managers may be able to complete large tasks efficiently by scheduling large intervals (blocks) of time to focus on those tasks. Within each block, managers can focus all of their attention on the large task. In general, more work on a large project can be accomplished within one three-hour interval than in three separate one-hour intervals spread throughout a day or a week.

When using short time intervals, managers waste time refreshing their memories on the issue of concern and the potential solutions. They would be more efficient if they could focus on the issue for a longer interval.

The best strategy for a task that requires less than one day of work may be to focus completely on that task until it is done. Short appointments that must be kept during a given day and are unrelated to the large task should be consolidated so that they do not continually break up the time allocated to the large task.

Minimize Interruptions

Virtually all managers are interrupted during the normal working day. Some problems may require immediate attention, but others can be put off until later. Managers should stay focused on the task at hand and avoid un-scheduled interruptions (except for emergencies).

Some managers have a natural tendency to create their own interruptions. For example, they may stop in offices of other employees to socialize. Although socializing during work hours may help reduce stress or boredom, managers should attempt to complete a certain amount of work before taking a social break. In this way, the break is a reward for accomplishing some work, not simply a means of putting off work.

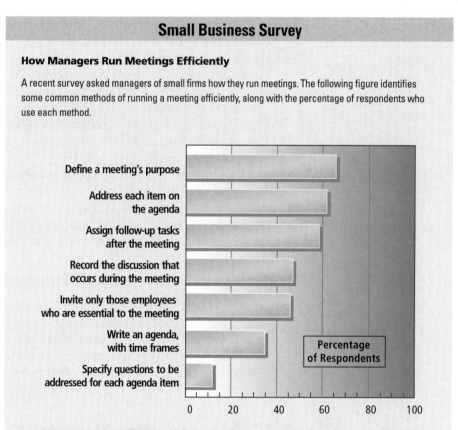

Small Business Survey

How Managers Run Meetings Efficiently

A recent survey asked managers of small firms how they run meetings. The following figure identifies some common methods of running a meeting efficiently, along with the percentage of respondents who use each method.

The results suggest that many managers attempt to keep meetings organized by defining the meeting's purpose and addressing each item on the agenda. However, most managers do not specify questions to be addressed for each agenda item.

Sylvia Woods, outside her restaurant in the Harlem neighborhood of New York, celebrates the restaurant's 40th anniversary. Her restaurant is the largest minority employer in Harlem, with a staff of more than 100.

AP Photo/ Stuart Ramson

Set Short-Term Goals

A common problem for managers is meeting deadlines, especially on large tasks. Managers should set short-term goals so that they can chip away at large tasks. For example, consider a manager who is assigned the task of purchasing a new computer system for the firm. The manager should break down the assignment into smaller tasks, such as (1) obtaining all the relevant information from other employees on the features that the computer system should have (Task A), (2) calling firms that sell computer systems to obtain price quotes (Task B), and (3) visiting firms where similar computer systems are in place to determine how well they work (Task C). Task C cannot be done until Task B is completed, and Task B cannot be done until Task A is completed.

If the assignment must be done in 10 weeks, the manager may set a goal of completing Task A during the first three weeks, Task B during the fourth and fifth weeks, and Task C during the sixth and seventh weeks. This schedule allows a few extra weeks before the deadline in case unexpected problems cause a task to take more time than was planned.

Delegate Some Tasks to Employees

Managers have only so much time to complete the tasks they are assigned. If they can delegate some authority to their employees, they will have more time to be creative. By delegating, managers may even increase the job satisfaction of employees who prefer extra responsibility. However, managers should delegate only those tasks that employees can handle.

College Health Club: Managing Time at CHC

One of the decisions that Sue Kramer needs to make as part of her business plan is how she will use her time. She is not only the owner of College Health Club (CHC) but also its sole manager. Although she will receive some help from part-time employees, she must use her time efficiently to complete numerous tasks each day, such as leading the aerobics classes, responding to prospective customer inquiries, and addressing any concerns by existing customers. Sue's first priority is to conduct the aerobics classes when they are scheduled. When she is not conducting classes, she will deal with any concerns of existing customers, such as a weight machine that is not functioning properly.

Her next priority is to attract new members. She has created a website that provides information about CHC and even allows customers to sign up for a membership online by using a credit card. Prospective customers can also e-mail questions to her. Phone calls are answered by an answering machine, which provides answers to the questions that callers typically ask: the hours CHC is open, directions to CHC, membership information, and the website address. Early in the morning before the club is busy, Sue will deposit any checks from new members at her bank, which is located in the same shopping center as the health club. She will rely on her part-time employees to lead some of the aerobics classes so that she can attend to these other tasks.

SUMMARY

1 The levels of management are

- top (high-level) management, which concentrates on the firm's long-run objectives;
- middle management, which is responsible for intermediate and short-term decisions; and
- supervisory management, which is highly involved with employees who engage in the day-to-day production process.

2 The key functions of management are

- planning for the future (objectives);
- organizing resources to achieve objectives;
- leading employees by providing them with instructions on how they should complete their tasks; and
- controlling, which involves monitoring and evaluating employee tasks.

3 The most important managerial skills needed are

- conceptual skills, which are used to understand relationships among various tasks;
- interpersonal skills, which are used to communicate with other employees and with customers;
- technical skills, which are used to perform specific day-to-day tasks, such as accounting skills to develop financial statements or electrical skills to understand how the wiring of a product is arranged; and
- decision-making skills, which are used to assess alternative choices on the allocation of the firm's resources.

4 Some of the key guidelines for effective time management are to

- set proper priorities in order to focus on the most important job responsibilities;
- schedule long time intervals for large tasks in order to focus on large tasks until the work is done;
- minimize interruptions in order to complete assignments;
- set short-term goals in order to chip away at long-term projects; and
- delegate tasks that employees can complete on their own.

KEY TERMS

Review & Critical Thinking Questions

1. What are the general functions of managers? Briefly describe each function.

2. Discuss the various types of planning functions within a firm. With which type of planning function would the president of a firm most likely be involved?

3. Distinguish between management and leadership. Do you think a person could be an effective manager but an ineffective leader?

4. Describe the different leadership styles. Explain which style would be most appropriate if a manager wanted to consult with an employee before making a decision.

5. Define the concept of management and identify the types of resources that a manager manages for a firm.

6. When U.S. firms establish subsidiaries in foreign countries, management must determine the appropriate leadership style. Discuss the appropriate style for each of the following: an underdeveloped country and an advanced industrialized country.

7. Explain how technology facilitates the integration of management functions.

8. Discuss the different types of skills that a manager should possess. What skills are most important for a supervisor in a machine shop?

9. Explain the stages of decision making for a manager who has just decided to enter a new market with an existing product line.

10. Explain how you would utilize the guidelines for time management for an important project due today.

11. Explain how a manager could handle the task of setting short-term goals for a large project that is due in twenty weeks.

Discussion Questions

1. How do you think the general management functions vary at each level of management within the firm?

2. Assume that you are thinking of becoming a manager. Define management. What are the most important skills you should have to become an effective manager?

3. Discuss how global competition is changing our thinking about managing firms and subsidiaries in foreign countries.

4. How could a firm use the Internet to provide information on its levels of management? How could a firm use the Internet to attract new managers?

5. Have you witnessed examples of effective and ineffective management? Cite some examples of both.

6. Explain the different leadership styles you would use if you were the manager of a project you were doing that involved supervising other employees.

It's Your Decision: **Managing at CHC**

1. Should Sue Kramer pursue her strategic plan of establishing additional health clubs at the same time that she opens CHC?

2. Key tasks of workers at CHC include leading aerobics classes and helping members use the exercise and weight machines. Explain how Sue can influence the performance of her workers through the leading function.

3. Should Sue use an autocratic, free-rein, or participative leadership style, or a combination of styles? Explain.

4. How can Sue use the controlling function at CHC?

5. Explain how the controlling function can be used to assess CHC's marketing and production of health club services.

6. Why does Sue need good interpersonal skills for her business?

7. A health club differs from manufacturing firms in that it produces a service rather than products. Explain why interpersonal skills of employees may be more critical at service firms like CHC than at manufacturing firms. Do employees at manufacturing firms need interpersonal skills?

Investing in a Business

Using the annual report of the firm in which you would like to invest, complete the following:

1 What are the firm's mission and strategic plan?

2 How does the firm intend to achieve its strategic plan? Is it restructuring its operations to achieve its objectives?

3 Explain how the business uses technology to enhance its management function. For example, does it use the Internet to provide information regarding its levels of management and the managerial functions it emphasizes?

4 Go to **http://hoovers.com** and locate the NEWS SEARCH. Type in the name of the firm in the space provided, and review the recent news stories about the firm. Summarize any (at least one) recent news story about the firm that applies to one or more of the key concepts in this chapter.

Case: Applying Management Skills

Maggie Wiltz manages a high-fashion specialty store in Atlanta, Georgia. Her daily activities start one hour before her store normally opens for business. She starts her day by opening the morning mail. Maggie must read numerous memos before the day starts. These memos are typically related to the coming day's business activities.

Half an hour before the store opens, Maggie meets with her employees. Today, she plans to discuss important issues, most notably the fact that sales were off in the first quarter by 10 percent. She also wants to discuss her concern over returned merchandise.

Maggie's employees are relatively new and inexperienced. She believes she should select an appropriate leadership style to fit the situation and elects to use a participative style. Once Maggie starts the meeting, she wants the employees to participate and provide solutions to the problems discussed. The employees cannot offer any reasons why sales are declining, but they do suggest that a quality issue may be involved in the returns of merchandise.

After the store opens, Maggie is frequently interrupted by her employees. Another item on her agenda for the day is a midday luncheon with the Rotary Club, where she is to be the guest speaker. Later in the day, at the close of business, Maggie is to meet with her regional sales manager to discuss the excessive return of merchandise. She intends to provide him with the solutions that resulted from the meeting with her employees. She does not look forward to this meeting.

Questions

1 Define time management. What recommendations could you make to help Maggie improve in this area?

2 Discuss the management functions that Maggie utilizes on her job.

3 Should Maggie have developed a plan of action before her meeting with her employees? If so, what specific plan would you suggest?

4 What management skills is Maggie using in this case? Which management skill is Maggie lacking?

Video Case: Effective Leadership at Vermont Teddy Bear Company

Vermont Teddy Bear Company produces stuffed teddy bears ordered by customers to be sent as gifts to friends or family members. It competes with other firms that send candy, flowers, or other gifts in the mail. Vermont Teddy Bear Company needs a CEO who can provide effective leadership and maintain the firm's success.

Liz Robert (pronounced *Robear*), president and CEO of Vermont Teddy Bear Company, has a special leadership style. She previously was the firm's chief financial officer, a position that required her to pay attention to detail (estimating costs and revenue for the firm). She recognizes that she now needs to use a broad vision when planning the firm's future.

The board of directors was initially concerned that Liz was overly focused on details and would not have the broad vision needed, but she has adapted by focusing on the larger picture when she sets goals for the firm in the future. In addition, she still uses her attention to detail by ensuring that employees are assigned tasks intended to achieve the firm's goals. This reflects leadership because she is influencing the habits of others to achieve a common goal.

Questions

1 What is the potential advantage for Liz of using a participative leadership style that allows other employees to provide input?

2 How can Liz use leadership to improve the value of the firm?

3 When Liz was the chief financial officer, she focused on the revenue and expenses of the firm. Now that she is CEO, she needs conceptual skills to understand the relationships among the various tasks of the firm. Do you think that Liz's previous job helped develop her conceptual skills?

Internet Applications

1. **http://www-1.ibm.com/ibm/history/exhibits/chairmen_1.html**

How many chief executive officers (CEOs) has IBM had in its history? Who currently is the CEO of IBM? What are some of the managerial skills that IBM's CEOs have used? What functions do you think IBM's CEOs have used to develop their key products and innovations?

2. **http://www.sonic.net/~mfreeman/**

What information is available on this website about the various functions of managers (planning, organizing, leading, and controlling)? If you were a manager, would you find this information useful in helping you to manage your organization more effectively? Study the "Mentorship" section. How does the mentorship process work?

3. **http://www.emergingleader.com**

Study some of the featured articles on this site. What are some leadership traits that are commonly mentioned in the featured articles? Relate these traits to the managerial skills mentioned in the text (i.e., conceptual, interpersonal, technical, and decision making). Do you think the importance of these skills varies with the type of company, such as manufacturing versus service companies? Explain.

The Coca-Cola Company Annual Report Project

 Questions for the current year's annual report are available on the text website at **http://madura.swlearning.com**

The following questions apply concepts presented in this chapter to The Coca-Cola Company. Go to The Coca-Cola Company website (**http://www.cocacola.com/**) and find the index for the most recent annual report.

Questions

1 Click on "Letter to Share Owners." How do The Coca-Cola Company's employees forge bonds with customers? Provide an example.

2 Click on "Our Building Blocks." What are the two building blocks on which The Coca-Cola Company success rests? How do these fit into the "leading" role of managers?

3 Study the "Letter to Share Owners" and the "Our Building Blocks" sections. Do you think The Coca-Cola Company uses an autocratic leadership style? Justify your answer.

4 Click on "Letter to Share Owners." How do The Coca-Cola Company's bottling partners fit into the operation? What is The Coca-Cola Company's goal with respect to its bottling partners?

5 Go to **http://hoovers.com** and locate the NEWS CENTER. Key in The Coca-Cola Company in the space provided, click on "Search," and review the recent news stories about the firm. Summarize any (at least one) recent news story about The Coca-Cola Company that applies one or more of the key concepts within this chapter of the text.

In-Text Study Guide

Answers are in an appendix at the back of the book.

True or False

1. Top management is usually highly involved with employees who are engaged in the day-to-day production process. F

2. Planning is the managerial function that influences the habits of others to achieve a common goal. F

3. A firm's mission statement will identify the goals of the firm. T

4. Contingency planning identifies the firm's main business focus over a long-term period. F

5. Leading is the management function that provides employees with the instructions they need to complete a task, as well as incentives to encourage the employees to do the job correctly and quickly. T

6. A U.S. firm with several foreign subsidiaries should vary its leadership style in the different countries, depending upon the characteristics of the foreign country. T

7. The free-rein leadership style is more appropriate than the autocratic style if employees are highly independent, creative, and motivated. T

8. The controlling function of management involves organizing employees and other resources in order to achieve the firm's goals. F

9. In a small business, the owner may frequently perform all the management functions. T

10. Conceptual skills are commonly required by assembly-line employees who are directly involved in the production assembly process. F

Multiple Choice

11. The position of chief financial officer is considered to be a:
    a) supervisory position.
    b) top-management position.
    c) first-line management position.
    d) bottom-line position.
    e) middle management position.

12. Which of the following describes the primary goal of a firm?
    a) tactical plan
    b) mission statement
    c) operating plan
    d) bottom-up plan
    e) contingency plan

13. Middle and high-level managers engage in short-term, small-scale plans that are consistent with the firm's strategic plan. These short-term, smaller-scale plans are known as:
    a) tactical plans.
    b) mission statements.
    c) leadership plans.
    d) bottom-up plans.
    e) contingency plans.

14. The type of planning that identifies the methods used to achieve a firm's tactical plans is called:
    a) operational planning.
    b) mission planning.
    c) strategic planning
    d) contingency planning.
    e) procedure planning.

15. All of the following are typical goals that the management function can help to achieve except:
    a) high production efficiency.
    b) high production quality.
    c) limited competition.
    d) customer satisfaction.
    e) employee satisfaction.

16. The management of a firm would benefit from having _____ in order to effectively handle various possible unexpected business conditions.
    a) interpersonal plans
    b) various leadership styles
    c) strategic plans
    d) tactical management
    e) contingency plans

In-Text Study Guide

Answers are in an appendix at the back of the book.

17. Business firms develop and enforce _____ to prevent employees from conducting tasks in an inefficient, dangerous, or illegal manner.
    a) kickbacks
    b) reciprocity
    c) policies
    d) time management
    e) prioritizing tasks

18. The steps necessary to implement a policy are known as:
    a) contingency plans.
    b) operational goals.
    c) initiative statements.
    d) production standards.
    e) procedures.

19. The leading function of management should be conducted in a manner that is consistent with the firm's:
    a) competition.
    b) strategic plan.
    c) customers.
    d) industry demands.
    e) labor union.

20. When employees have little or no input in decision making, managers use a(n):
    a) free-rein style.
    b) interpersonal communication style.
    c) autocratic leadership style.
    d) participative style.
    e) employee-centered style.

21. Managers who lack initiative may not be very effective even if they possess the necessary:
    a) financial backing.
    b) reciprocity.
    c) support.
    d) skills.
    e) patronage.

22. The style of leadership that is the opposite extreme of the autocratic style is:
    a) free-rein.
    b) authoritative.

c) manipulative.
d) boss-centered.
e) commanding.

23. The type of leadership style that allows employees to express their opinions to their managers is the _____ style.
    a) autocratic
    b) command-oriented
    c) contingency
    d) authoritative
    e) participative

24. The function of management that evaluates employee performance in comparison with established standards is:
    a) planning.
    b) controlling.
    c) organizing.
    d) leading.
    e) time management.

25. The function of management that involves the monitoring and evaluation of tasks is:
    a) planning.
    b) organizing.
    c) controlling.
    d) leading.
    e) motivating.

26. The controlling function requires managers to establish performance standards. All of the following are areas where standards can be applied except:
    a) sales volume.
    b) profits.
    c) production costs.
    d) quality.
    e) number of competing companies.

27. The four functions of management:
    a) must be enacted in the proper sequence.
    b) must be integrated.
    c) are stand-alone, independent functions.
    d) cannot be performed by one individual.
    e) are human functions not compatible with technology.

In-Text Study Guide

Answers are in an appendix at the back of the book.

28. The skills managers use to understand the relationships among the various tasks of the firm are:
    a) interpersonal skills.
    b) technical skills.
    c) decision-making skills.
    d) conceptual skills.
    e) problem-solving skills.

29. The skills that managers need to communicate with customers and employees are:
    a) organizing skills.
    b) control skills.
    c) motivating skills.
    d) conceptual skills.
    e) interpersonal skills.

30. Since they are closer to the production process, first-line managers use their _____ skills more frequently than do high-level managers.
    a) conceptual
    b) interpersonal
    c) decision-making
    d) management
    e) technical

31. Using existing information, managers need _____ to determine how the firm's resources should be allocated.
    a) micro skills
    b) interpersonal skills
    c) technical skills
    d) decision-making skills
    e) autocratic management skills

32. For managers to understand the types of tasks they manage, they must possess:
    a) conceptual skills.
    b) interpersonal skills.
    c) top-management skills.
    d) technical skills.
    e) tactical plans.

33. Which of the following is the first step in making a decision?
    a) gathering information
    b) estimating costs and benefits of each possible decision
    c) identifying the possible decisions
    d) making a decision and implementing it
    e) evaluating the decision to determine whether any changes are necessary

34. All of the following guidelines should be followed when using time management except:
    a) setting proper priorities.
    b) centralizing responsibility.
    c) scheduling long intervals of time for large tasks.
    d) minimizing interruptions.
    e) delegating some tasks to employees.

35. A manager faced with a large task that will take more than one day to complete should:
    a) focus only on this task until it is completed.
    b) take frequent breaks to refresh his/her concentration.
    c) retain sole responsibility for the project.
    d) set short-term goals.
    e) automatically assign the project top priority.

All businesses, including Express Travel Agency, need a strategic plan to guide them in the future.

The Learning Goals of this chapter are to:

1 Explain how an organizational structure may be used by a firm to achieve its strategic plan.

2 Identify methods that can be used to departmentalize tasks.

Chapter 8

Organizational Structure

Each firm should have a strategic plan that identifies the future direction of its business. The responsibilities of its managers should be organized to achieve the strategic plan. Each firm establishes an organizational structure that identifies responsibilities for each job position and the relationships among those positions. The organizational structure also indicates how all the job responsibilities fit together. The organizational structure affects the efficiency with which a firm produces its product and therefore affects the firm's value.

Consider the situation of Express Travel Agency, which has offices in eight different countries that make airline, train, hotel, and cruise reservations for customers. Express Travel Agency must determine:

▶ What kind of organizational structure should it have?

▶ How should the firm's tasks be departmentalized into categories (segmented by type of travel or by location)?

The organizational structure decision determines how many different layers of management the firm will have. Express Travel can reduce expenses by having fewer layers of management, but it also wants to ensure that it has enough employees to cover all necessary tasks. The way Express Travel decides to departmentalize will affect the number of employees needed to complete all tasks and therefore will also affect its expenses. Since these decisions by Express Travel affect the level of its expenses, they also affect the level of its earnings and therefore influence its value.

All business must make the types of decisions described above. This chapter explains how Express Travel Agency or any other firm can establish an organizational structure and departmentalize in a manner that maximizes the firm's value.

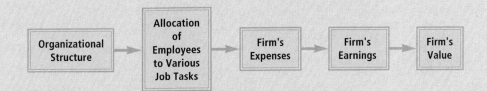

Explain how an organizational structure may be used by a firm to achieve its strategic plan.

organizational structure identifies responsibilities for each job position and the relationships among those positions

organization chart a diagram that shows the interaction among employee responsibilities

chain of command identifies the job position to which each type of employee must report

HOW A FIRM'S ORGANIZATIONAL STRUCTURE ACHIEVES ITS STRATEGIC PLAN

An **organizational structure** identifies responsibilities for each job position and the relationships among those positions. The organizational structure typically varies among firms.

A firm's organizational structure can be illustrated with an **organization chart**, which is a diagram that shows the interaction among employee responsibilities. Exhibit 8.1 provides an example of an organization chart.

Chain of Command

The organizational structure indicates the **chain of command**, which identifies the job positions to which all types of employees must report. The chain of command also indicates who is responsible for various activities. Since employees often encounter problems that require communication with other divisions, it helps to know who is responsible for each type of task.

The president (who also typically holds the position of chief executive officer, or CEO) has the ultimate responsibility for the firm's success. The president normally attempts to coordinate all divisions and provide direction for the firm's business. In most firms, many managerial duties are delegated to other managers. Vice-presidents normally oversee specific divisions or broad functions of the firm and report to the president.

The chain of command can be used to ensure that managers make decisions that maximize the firm's value rather than serve their own interests. For example, some managers may be tempted to hire friends for specific job positions. To the extent that their actions are monitored within the chain of command, they are more likely to make decisions that serve the firm rather than their self-interests. If managers at each level report their key decisions

Exhibit 8.1

Example of an Organization Chart

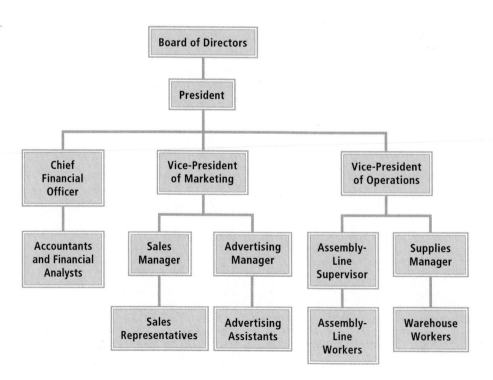

Kennedy Space Center director Roy D. Bridges points to an organization chart showing their new executive team. An organization chart identifies the responsibilities within a company and also shows the relationships among the various positions.

AP Photo/ Peter Cosgrove

to other managers, decisions are subject to scrutiny. This monitoring process is not intended to take away a manager's power, but to ensure that the power is used to serve the goals of the firm.

Authority of the Board of Directors

board of directors a set of executives who are responsible for monitoring the activities of the firm's president and other high-level managers

Each firm has a **board of directors,** or a set of executives who are responsible for monitoring the activities of the firm's president and other high-level managers. Even the top managers of a firm may be tempted to make decisions that serve their own interests rather than those of the firm's owners. For example, the top managers may decide to use company funds to purchase private jets to use when they travel on business. This decision may be driven by their own self-interests. It may result in high expenses, reduce the firm's value, and therefore be detrimental to the firm's owners.

Directors are selected by shareholders and serve as representatives for the shareholders, as confirmed by a quotation from Sears' annual report:

"The board of directors regularly reviews the corporation's structure to determine whether it supports optimal performance and thus serves the best interests of shareholders by delivering shareholder value."

inside board members board members who are also managers of the same firm

outside board members board members who are not managers of the firm

The 1,000 largest U.S. firms have 12 directors on their boards on average. Board members who are also managers of the same firm (such as the CEO) are referred to as **inside board members.** Board members who are not managers of the firm are referred to as **outside board members.** Some firms, including General Electric and PepsiCo, provide directors with stock as partial compensation. This type of compensation may motivate the directors to serve the interests of the firm's shareholders because the board members will benefit if the firm's stock price rises.

Small Business Survey

Who Are the Board Members of Small Firms?

A recent survey asked the CEOs of small firms (with less than $50 million in annual sales) about the background of their outside board members. The results of the survey follow.

Background	Percentage of Firms Whose Board Members Have That Background
Executives of other firms	69%
Major investors in the firm	36%
Retired business executives	30%
Attorneys	29%
Accountants	22%
Bankers	18%
Business consultants	13%
Customers	2%
Others	3%

The results suggest that these firms rely heavily on executives and major investors to serve as their outside board members. The attorneys, accountants, and business consultants who are hired as outside board members typically also perform other duties (such as legal or banking duties) for the firm.

In general, the board focuses on major issues and normally is not involved in the day-to-day activities of the firm. Key business proposals, made by a firm's managers, such as acquisitions or layoffs, must be approved by the board. For example, America Online's decision to merge with Time Warner required board approval. Directors may also initiate changes in a firm. For example, the board may decide that the firm's CEO needs to be replaced or that the firm's businesses should be restructured. Board meetings generally are scheduled every few months or are called when the directors' input is needed on an important issue. Board members of numerous firms have become more active in recent years.

Conflicts of Interest within the Board A board of directors is expected to ensure that top managers serve the interests of the firm rather than their own self-interests, but some directors also face conflicts of interest. As mentioned above, the board normally includes some insiders (employees) of the firm such as the CEO and some vice-presidents. These insiders will not be effective monitors of their own actions. For example, the insiders are not going to complain if the firm's managerial compensation is excessive, because they benefit directly as managers of the firm. In addition, some insider board members are not going to question the decisions of the CEO, because the CEO determines their compensation.

A board of directors may be more willing to take action if most of its members are outside directors (and therefore are not employees of the firm). The outside board members may suggest policies that will benefit shareholders, even if the policies are not supported by the firm's top man-

Exhibit 8.2

Example of How Some Board Members
Are Subject to a Conflict of Interest

Name of Board Member	Job Position	Classified as Inside or Outside Director	Potential Conflict of Interest
Ed Martin	CEO of Gonzaga Co.	Inside	Since the CEO is a key decision maker of Gonzaga Co., he has a potential conflict of interest. A CEO is not an effective monitor of the decisions made by top management.
Lisa Kelly	Vice-President of Finance for Gonzaga Co.	Inside	Since the VP is a key decision maker of Gonzaga Co., she has a potential conflict of interest. A VP is not an effective monitor of the decisions made by top management.
Jerry Coldwell	Vice-President of Operations for Gonzaga Co.	Inside	Since the VP is a key decision maker of Gonzaga Co., he has a potential conflict of interest. A VP is not an effective monitor of the decisions made by top management.
Dave Jensen	Owner of a firm that is the key supplier of parts to Gonzaga Co.	Outside	Dave's company benefits directly from decisions of Gonzaga's top management to buy supplies from his firm. Thus, he is not likely to keep Gonzaga's top managers in line.
Sharon Martin (daughter-in-law of Ed Martin)	Vice-president of a real estate firm that does no business with Gonzaga Co.	Outside	Since Sharon is related to the CEO of Gonzaga, she is not likely to keep Gonzaga's top managers in line.
Karen Chandler	Independent consultant, who does a substantial amount of work for Gonzaga Co.	Outside	Karen relies on Gonzaga Co. for a large portion of her income, and therefore she is not likely to keep Gonzaga's top managers in line.
Terry Olden	Previous CEO of Gonazaga Co., now retired.	Outside	Terry no longer works at Gonzaga Co., but he is close to the top managers. Therefore, he is not likely to keep Gonzaga's top managers in line.
Mary Burke	CEO of a nonprofit health firm that receives large annual donations from Gonzaga Co.	Outside	Since Mary's firm receives donations from Gonzaga Co., she is not likely to keep Gonzaga's top managers in line.

agers. Therefore, shareholders tend to prefer that the board contain more outside directors.

Nevertheless, even outside directors may be subject to a conflict of interests that may inhibit their ability or willingness to make tough decisions for the firm. To illustrate these conflicts, consider the information about the board of directors of Gonzaga Company, shown in Exhibit 8.2. Notice from the exhibit that five of the eight board members are not employees of Gonzaga Company and therefore are outside directors. Yet, those five outside directors have conflicts of interest that may prevent them from making tough decisions about the top management. One of the outside directors is related to the CEO, while the other four outside directors receive money from Gonzaga Company in some form. Therefore, these outside directors will not be effective at representing the interests of Gonzaga's shareholders.

Recall the case of Enron, which distorted its financial statements to make its financial condition look better than it was. A committee from Enron's board was responsible for ensuring that the financial statements were properly checked. Of the six members on that committee, one received

$72,000 per year from a consulting contract with Enron. Two other members were employed by universities that received large donations from Enron. Thus, three of the committee members were subject to a conflict of interest and should not have been on this committee. Such conflicts of interest explain why many of the actions of Enron's top managers were not questioned.

Oversight of the Internal Auditor

internal auditor responsible for ensuring that all departments follow the firm's guidelines and procedures

Many firms employ an **internal auditor,** who is responsible for ensuring that all departments follow the firm's guidelines and procedures. For example, an internal auditor may assess whether employees followed the firm's hiring procedures when filling job positions recently. The internal auditor is not attempting to interfere with managerial decisions, but is simply attempting to ensure that the procedures used to make those decisions are consistent with the firm's guidelines. Although the specific emphasis of an internal auditor varies among firms, some attention is commonly given to ensuring that employees' actions are consistent with the recommended procedures for hiring new employees, evaluating employees, maintaining safety, and responding to customer complaints.

Span of Control

span of control the number of employees managed by each manager

Top management determines the firm's **span of control,** or the number of employees managed by each manager. When an organizational structure is designed so that each manager supervises just a few employees, it has a narrow span of control. Conversely, when it is designed so that each manager supervises numerous employees, it has a wide span of control. When numerous employees perform similar tasks, a firm uses a wide span of control because these employees can be easily managed by one or a few managers. A firm with highly diverse tasks may need more managers with various skills to manage the different tasks, resulting in a narrow span of control.

Exhibit 8.3 illustrates how the span of control can vary among firms. The organizational structure at the top of the exhibit reflects a narrow span of control. Each employee oversees only one other employee. The nature of the business may require highly specialized skills in each position so that employees may focus on their own tasks and not have to monitor a large set of employees. The organizational structure at the bottom of the exhibit reflects a wide span of control. The president directly oversees all the other employees. Such a wide span of control is more typical of firms in which many employees have similar positions that can easily be monitored by a single person.

College Health Club: Span of Control at CHC

One of the decisions that Sue Kramer needs to make as part of her business plan is the appropriate span of control for College Health Club (CHC). She will hire part-time employees to serve the members at CHC. Each employee must be capable of performing three tasks: leading an aerobics class, demonstrating how to use the exercise and weight machines, and showing prospective members around the club. Since each employee must have the same set of diverse skills, a wide span of control is appropriate. No employee needs to report to any other employee. Each of the employees will report to Sue. Since Sue will normally be at the club, she can easily supervise the part-time employees that she hires.

Exhibit 8.3

Distinguishing between a Narrow and a
Wide Span of Control

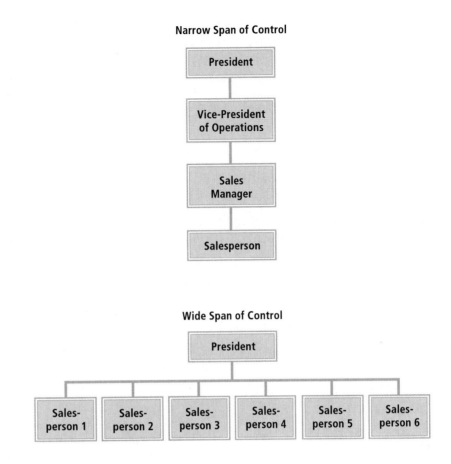

Exhibit 8.3

Distinguishing between a Narrow and a
Wide Span of Control

Organizational Height

The organizational structure can also be described by its height. A tall organizational structure implies that there are many layers from the bottom of the structure to the top. Conversely, a short (or flat) organizational structure implies that there is not much distance from the bottom of the structure to the top because there are not many layers of employees between the bottom and top. Many firms that are able to use a wide span of control tend to have a flat organizational structure because they do not require many layers. Conversely, firms that need to use a narrow span of control tend to have a tall organizational structure with many layers. Notice that in Exhibit 8.3, the organizational structure with the narrow span of control is tall, while the organizational structure with the wide span of control is flat.

Centralization

centralized most authority is
held by the high-level managers

Some firms are **centralized;** that is, most authority is held by the high-level managers. In centralized firms, middle and supervisory managers are responsible for day-to-day tasks and for reporting to the top managers, but they are not allowed to make many decisions.

Decentralization

decentralized authority is spread
among several divisions or
managers

autonomy divisions can make
their own decisions and act
independently

In recent years, many firms have **decentralized,** meaning that authority is spread among several divisions or managers. An extreme form of decentralization is **autonomy,** in which divisions are permitted to make their own

self-scoring exercise

How Decentralized Is Your Company?

Decentralization is one of the key design dimensions in an organization. It is closely related to several behavioral dimensions of an organization, such as leadership style, degree of participative decision making, teamwork, and the nature of power and politics within the organization.

The following questionnaire allows you to get an idea of how decentralized your organization is. (If you do not have a job, have a friend who works complete the questionnaire to see how decentralized his or her organization is.) Which level in your organization has the authority to make each of the following decisions? Answer the questionnaire by circling one of the following:

0 = The board of directors makes the decision.

1 = The CEO makes the decision.

2 = The division /functional manager makes the decision.

3 = A sub-department head makes the decision.

4 = The first-level supervisor makes the decision.

5 = Operators on the shop floor make the decision.

Decision Concerning:		Circle Appropriate Level					
a.	The number of workers required.	0	1	2	3	4	5
b.	Whether to employ a worker.	0	1	2	3	4	5
c.	Internal labor disputes.	0	1	2	3	4	5
d.	Overtime worked at shop level.	0	1	2	3	4	5
e.	Delivery dates and order priority.	0	1	2	3	4	5
f.	Production planning.	0	1	2	3	4	5
g.	Dismissal of a worker.	0	1	2	3	4	5
h.	Methods of personnel selection.	0	1	2	3	4	5
i.	Method of work to be used.	0	1	2	3	4	5
j.	Machinery or equipment to be used.	0	1	2	3	4	5
k.	Allocation of work among workers.	0	1	2	3	4	5

Add up all your circled numbers. Total = _____. The higher your number (for example, 45 or more), the more decentralized your organization. The lower your number (for example, 25 or less), the more centralized your organization.

decisions and act independently. The trend toward decentralization is due to its potential advantages.

Advantages A decentralized organizational structure can improve a firm's performance in several ways. First, decentralization reduces operating expenses because salaries of some employees who are no longer needed are eliminated.

Second, decentralization can shorten the decision-making process because lower-level employees are assigned more power. Decisions are made more quickly if the decision makers do not have to wait for approval from top managers. Many firms, including IBM, have decentralized to accelerate their decision making.

Third, delegation of authority can improve the morale of employees, who may be more enthusiastic about their work if they have more responsibilities. In addition, these managers become more experienced in decision making. Therefore, they will be better qualified for high-level management positions in the future. Decentralization has contributed to innovation at many technology firms, where many managers have become more creative. In addition, decentralization allows those employees who are closely involved in the production of a particular product to offer their input.

Johnson & Johnson is a prime example of a firm that has benefited from decentralization. It has numerous operating divisions scattered among more than 50 countries, and most of the decision making is done by the managers at those divisions. As a result, each unit can make quick decisions in response to local market conditions.

Disadvantages A decentralized organizational structure can also have disadvantages. It could force some managers to make major decisions even though they lack the experience to make such decisions or prefer not to do so. Also, if middle and supervisory managers are assigned an excessive amount of responsibilities, they may be unable to complete all of their tasks.

Proper Degree of Decentralization The proper degree of decentralization for any firm is dependent on the skills of the managers who could be assigned more responsibilities. Decentralization can be beneficial when the managers who are given more power are capable of handling their additional responsibilities. For example, assume that a firm's top managers have previously determined annual raises for all assembly-line workers but now decide to delegate this responsibility to the supervisors who monitor those workers. The supervisors are closer to the assembly line and are possibly in a better position to assess worker performance. Therefore, decentralization may be appropriate. The top managers may still have final approval of the raises that the supervisors propose for their workers.

As a second example, assume that top managers allow assembly-line supervisors to decide what price the firm will bid for a specific business that is for sale. Assembly-line supervisors normally are not trained for this type of task and should not be assigned to it. Determining the proper price to bid for a business requires a strong financial background and should not be delegated to managers without the proper skills.

As these examples demonstrate, high-level managers should retain authority for tasks that require their specialized skills but should delegate authority when the tasks can be handled by other managers. Routine decisions should be made by the employees who are closely involved with the tasks of concern. Decision making may improve because these employees are closer to the routine tasks and may have greater insight than top managers on these matters.

Some degree of centralization is necessary when determining how funds should be allocated to support various divisions of a firm. If managers of each division are given the authority to make this decision, they may request additional funds even though their division does not need to expand.

How Organizational Structure Affects the Control of Foreign Operations A firm that has subsidiaries scattered around the world will find it more difficult to ensure that its managers serve the shareholders' interests rather than their own self-interests. In other words, the firm will experience more pronounced agency problems. First, it is difficult for the parent's top managers to monitor operations in foreign countries because of the distance from headquarters. Second, managers of foreign subsidiaries who have been raised in different cultures may not follow uniform goals. Third, the sheer size of the larger multinational corporations can also create large agency problems.

The magnitude of agency costs can vary with the management style of the multinational corporation. A centralized management style can reduce agency costs because it allows managers of the parent to control foreign subsidiaries and therefore reduces the power of subsidiary managers. However, the parent's managers may make poor decisions for the subsidiary because they are less familiar with its financial characteristics.

A decentralized management style is likely to result in higher agency costs because subsidiary managers may make decisions that do not focus on maximizing the value of the entire multinational corporation. Nevertheless, this style gives more control to the managers who are closer to the subsidiary's operations and environment. To the extent that subsidiary managers recognize the goal of maximizing the value of the overall firm and are compensated in accordance with that goal, the decentralized management style may be more effective.

Given the obvious trade-off between centralized and decentralized management styles, some multinational corporations attempt to achieve the advantages of both styles. They allow subsidiary managers to make the key decisions about their respective operations, but the parent's management monitors the decisions to ensure that they are in the best interests of the entire firm.

The Internet makes it easier for the parent to monitor the actions and performance of foreign subsidiaries. Since the subsidiaries may be in different time zones, it is inconvenient and expensive to require frequent phone conversations. In addition, financial reports and designs of new products or plant sites cannot be easily communicated over the phone. The Internet allows the foreign subsidiaries to e-mail updated information in a standardized format to avoid language problems and to send images of financial reports and product designs. The parent can easily track inventory, sales, expenses, and earnings of each subsidiary on a weekly or monthly basis.

global business

Centralized management of funds can prevent division managers from making decisions that conflict with the goal of maximizing the firm's value.

Effect of Downsizing on Decentralization

As firms expanded during the 1980s, additional management layers were created, resulting in taller organization charts. In the 1990s and early 2000s, however, many firms have attempted to cut expenses by eliminating job positions. This so-called **downsizing** has resulted in flatter organization charts with fewer layers of managers. Continental Airlines, IBM, General Motors, Sears, and many other firms have downsized in recent years.

As some management positions are eliminated, many of those responsibilities are delegated to employees who previously reported to the managers whose positions have been eliminated. For example, Amoco (now part of BP Amoco) eliminated a middle layer of its organizational structure. When managers in the middle of the organization chart are removed, other employees must be assigned more power to make decisions. Thus, downsizing has resulted in a greater degree of decentralization.

Downsizing has also affected each manager's span of control. When many middle managers are eliminated, the remaining managers have more diverse responsibilities. Consequently, the organizational structure of many firms now reflects a wider span of control, as illustrated in Exhibit 8.4.

In addition to removing some management layers and creating a wider span of control, downsizing has also led to the combination of various job responsibilities within the organizational structure. Whereas job assignments traditionally focused on production tasks, more attention is now given to customer satisfaction. Many firms recognize that they must rely on their current customers for additional business in the future and have revised their strategic plan to focus on achieving repeat business from their customers. In many cases, customers would prefer to deal with a single employee rather than several different employees. Consequently, employees are less specialized because they must have diverse skills to accommodate the customers.

downsizing an attempt by a firm to cut expenses by eliminating job positions

Exhibit 8.4

Effect of Downsizing on Span of Control

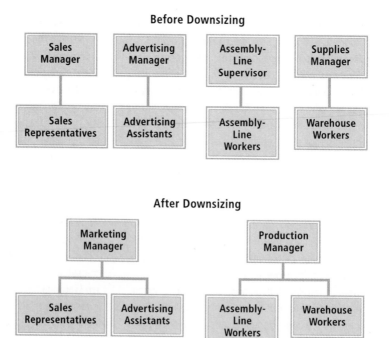

David Lavenda and Izhar Shay's company, Business Layers, specializes in software that automatically sets up computer connections between employees based on the firm's organizational structure.

AP Photo/ Mike Derer

Line versus Staff Positions

The job positions in an organizational structure can be classified as line positions or staff positions. **Line positions** are established to make decisions that achieve specific business goals. **Staff positions** are established to support the efforts of line positions, rather than to achieve specific goals of the firm. For example, managers at Black & Decker who are involved in the production of power tools are in line positions. Employees in staff positions at Black & Decker offer support to the managers who are in line positions. Thus, the staff positions provide assistance to the line positions, and the authority to make decisions is assigned to the line positions.

An organizational structure that contains only line positions and no staff positions is referred to as a **line organization.** This type of organizational structure may be appropriate for a business that cannot afford to hire staff for support, such as a small manufacturing firm.

Most firms need some staff positions to provide support to the line positions. An organizational structure that includes both line and staff positions and assigns authority from higher-level management to employees is referred to as a **line-and-staff organization.**

Exhibit 8.5 depicts a line organization and a line-and-staff organization. The line-and-staff organization in this exhibit includes a director of computer systems, who oversees the computer system, and a director of human resources, who is involved with hiring and training employees. These two positions are staff positions because they can assist the finance, marketing, and production departments but do not have the authority to make decisions that achieve specific business goals.

Creating a Structure That Allows More Employee Input

Firms commonly rely on the input of employees from various divisions for special situations. For this reason, they may need to temporarily adjust their formal organizational structure so that some extra responsibilities may be

line positions job positions established to make decisions that achieve specific business goals

staff positions job positions established to support the efforts of line positions

line organization an organizational structure that contains only line positions and no staff positions

line-and-staff organization an organizational structure that includes both line and staff positions and assigns authority from higher-level management to employees

Exhibit 8.5

Comparison of a Line Organization with a
Line-and-Staff Organization

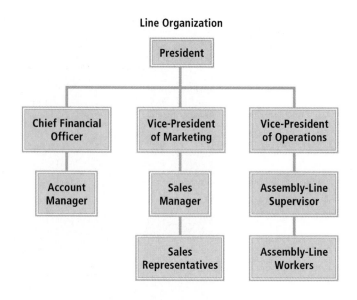

Line Organization

Line-and-Staff Organization

assigned. The following are two common methods for revising the organizational structure to obtain employee input:

▶ Matrix organization

▶ Intrapreneurship

Each of these methods is discussed in turn.

Matrix Organization   Firms are often confronted with special circumstances that require input from their employees. In a **matrix organization,** various parts of the firm interact to focus on specific projects. Because the projects may take up only a portion of the normal work week, participants can continue to perform their normal tasks and are still accountable to the same boss for those tasks. For example, a firm that plans to install a new computer system may need input from each division on the specific functions that division will require from the system. This example is illustrated

matrix organization an organizational structure that enables various parts of the firm to interact to focus on specific projects

Exhibit 8.6

A Matrix Organization for a Special Project to Design a New Computer System

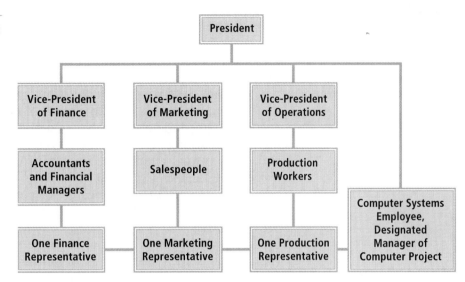

in Exhibit 8.6. As the exhibit shows, the finance, marketing, and production divisions each have one representative on the team; each representative can offer insight from the perspective of his or her respective division. The team of employees will periodically work on the assigned project until it is completed. Some employees may be assigned to two or more projects during the specific period. The lower horizontal line in Exhibit 8.6 shows the interaction among the representatives from different divisions. The manager of this project is a computer systems employee, who will report the recommendations of the matrix organization to the president or to some other top manager.

An advantage of the matrix approach is that it brings together employees who can offer insight from different perspectives. Each participant who is assigned to a specific group (or team) has particular skills that can contribute to the project. By involving all participants in decision making, this teamwork may provide more employee satisfaction than typical day-to-day assignments. Firms such as Intel, IBM, and Boeing commonly use teams of employees to complete specific projects.

One possible disadvantage of a matrix organization is that no employee may feel responsible because responsibilities are assigned to teams of several employees. Therefore, a firm that uses teams to complete various tasks may designate one job position to have the responsibility of organizing the team and ensuring that the team's assignment is completed before the deadline. The person designated as project manager (or team leader) of a specific project does not necessarily have authority over the other participants for any other tasks.

Another disadvantage of the matrix organization is that any time used to participate in projects reduces the time allocated for normal tasks. In some cases, ultimate responsibility is not clear, causing confusion. Many firms eliminated their matrix structure for this reason.

Intrapreneurship   Some firms not only seek input from employees on specific issues but also encourage employees to offer ideas for operational changes that will enhance the firm's value. These firms may even create a special subsidiary within their organizational structure in which particular employees are given the responsibility to innovate. In this way, the costs and benefits of innovation can be estimated separately from the rest of the business operations.

Particular employees of a firm can be assigned to generate ideas, as if they were entrepreneurs running their own firms. This process is referred to as **intrapreneurship,** as employees are encouraged to think like entrepreneurs within the firm. They differ from entrepreneurs, however, in that they are employees rather than owners of the firm. Some employees may even be assigned the responsibility of developing new products or ideas for improving existing products. A potential disadvantage of intrapreneurship is that it can pull employees away from normal, day-to-day production tasks. Nevertheless, it can also allow firms to be more innovative because employees are encouraged to search for new ideas. Many firms, including Apple Computer and 3M Company, have used intrapreneurship to encourage new ideas.

Intrapreneurship is likely to be more successful if employees are rewarded with some type of bonus for innovations that are ultimately applied by the firm. The firm should also attempt to ensure that any ideas that employees develop are seriously considered. If managers shoot down ideas for the wrong reasons (jealousy, for instance), employees may consider leaving the firm to implement their ideas (by starting their own business).

Informal Organizational Structure

All firms have both a formal and an informal organizational structure. The **informal organizational structure** is the informal communications network that exists among a firm's employees. This network (sometimes called the "grapevine") develops as a result of employee interaction over time. Some employees interact because they work on similar tasks. Employees in unrelated divisions often interact in a common lunch area, at social events, or even as a result of a decision that requires input from two different divisions.

Advantages   A firm can benefit from the informal organizational structure in several ways. Employees who need help in performing a task may benefit from others. If employees had to seek help through the formal structure, they would have to go to the person to whom they report. If that particular person is not available, the production process could be slowed. An informal structure may also allow employees to substitute for one another, thereby ensuring that a task will be completed on time. In addition, an informal structure can reduce the amount of manager involvement.

Another advantage of an informal structure is that friendships result from it. Friendships with other employees are a common reason for employee satisfaction with their jobs. It could be the major factor that discourages them from looking for a new job. This is especially true of lower-level jobs that pay low wages. Because friendship can strongly influence employee satisfaction, firms commonly encourage social interaction by organizing social functions.

Yet, another advantage is that informal communication can occur among employees on different levels. This allows information to travel informally from the top down or from the bottom up throughout the organization.

Disadvantages   Along with the advantages just described, an informal structure also has some disadvantages. Perhaps the main disadvantage is that employees may obtain incorrect or unfavorable information about the firm through the informal structure. Even if the information is untrue or is a gross exaggeration, it can have a major impact on employee morale. Un-

intrapreneurship the assignment of particular employees of a firm to generate ideas, as if they were entrepreneurs running their own firms

informal organizational structure an informal communications network among a firm's employees

increasing value with technology

IMPACT OF INFORMATION TECHNOLOGY ON ORGANIZATIONAL STRUCTURE

Advances in technology often bring change to a firm's organizational structure. All parts of a firm use technology, and a wide variety of departments include technology experts among their employees. Technology and the professionals working in the field must support and connect every area of the organization.

The integration of information technology (IT) requires communication among employees. A conscious effort must be made to maintain relationships with the groups each participant represents. IT representatives must communicate the options under consideration and solicit expertise when needed. Other members of the project team or department should inform the ultimate end users about the key issues under consideration and request feedback. These relationships are often overlooked and lost as the immediate challenge of the design overwhelms everything else. Therefore, relationships with other future participants should be maintained through planned communication as the project progresses.

Technology and the knowledge-based economy are not constrained by the physical objects and materials of a firm. Information is flexible and can be structured and organized in a number of different ways. For example, videoconferencing and telecommuting allow members of project teams from different departments to work together regardless of their location or their department. Thus, technology enables departments within a firm to communicate more easily.

These same technologies also allow different companies to communicate with each other. Apple Computer is essentially a computer design and marketing company. All of its production is completed by other firms (outsourced). Yet the different firms that are responsible for bringing an Apple computer to market are able to collaborate and communicate easily.

favorable information that has an adverse impact tends to travel faster and further throughout an informal structure than favorable information does.

METHODS OF DEPARTMENTALIZING TASKS

2

Identify methods that can be used to departmentalize tasks.

departmentalize assign tasks and responsibilities to different departments

When developing or revising an organizational structure, high-level management must first identify all the different tasks and responsibilities that the firm performs. The next step is to **departmentalize** those tasks and responsibilities, which means to assign the tasks and responsibilities to different departments. The best way of departmentalizing depends on the characteristics of the business. By using an efficient method of departmentalizing tasks and responsibilities, a firm can minimize its expenses and maximize its value. The following are four of the more popular methods of departmentalizing:

▶ By function

▶ By product

▶ By location

▶ By customer

Departmentalize by Function

When firms departmentalize by function, they allocate their tasks and responsibilities according to employee functions. The organization chart shown in Exhibit 8.7 is departmentalized by function. The finance, marketing,

Exhibit 8.7

Departmentalizing by Function

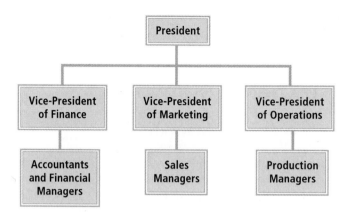

and production divisions are separated. This system works well for firms that produce just one or a few products, especially if the managers communicate across the functions.

Departmentalize by Product

In larger firms with many products, departmentalizing by product is common. Tasks and responsibilities are separated according to the type of product produced. The organization chart shown in Exhibit 8.8 is departmentalized by product (soft drink, food, and restaurant). This type of organizational structure is used by General Motors, which has created divisions such as Buick, Cadillac, and Chevrolet.

Many large firms departmentalize by both product and function, as shown in Exhibit 8.9. The specific divisions are separated by product, and each product division is departmentalized by function. Thus, each product division may have its own marketing, finance, and production divisions. This system may appear to be inefficient because it requires several divisions. Yet, if the firm is large enough, a single division would need to hire as many employees as are needed for the several divisions. Separation by product allows employees to become familiar with a single product rather than having to keep track of several different products.

Departmentalizing by product enables a firm to more easily estimate the expenses involved in the production of each product. The firm can be viewed as a set of separate business divisions (separated by product), and each division's profits can be determined over time. This allows the firm to determine the contribution of each business division to its total profits,

Exhibit 8.8

Departmentalizing by Product

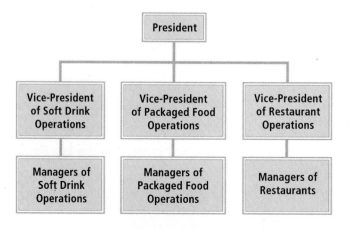

Exhibit 8.9

Departmentalizing by Product and Function

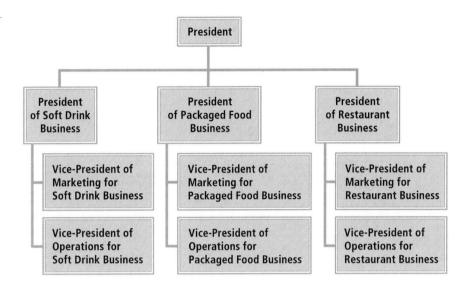

which is useful when the firm is deciding which divisions should be expanded.

For a small or medium-sized firm with just a few products, departmentalizing by product would lead to an inefficient use of employees, resulting in excessive expenses. A single financial manager should be capable of handling all financial responsibilities, and a single marketing manager should be capable of handling all marketing responsibilities. Thus, there is no reason to departmentalize by product.

Departmentalize by Location

Tasks and responsibilities can also be departmentalized by location by establishing regional offices to cover specific geographic regions. This system may be appealing if corporate customers in particular locations frequently purchase a variety of the firm's products. Such customers would be able to

Chinese workers assemble door parts just prior to the "First Chevrolet Off-Line Ceremony" in Shenyang, China. The company is a joint venture between General Motors and China's Jinbei Automotive Corp. It allows General Motors to rely on production in China without revising its organizational structure.

AP Photo/ Eugene Hoshiko

contact the same regional office to place all of their orders. Large accounting firms departmentalize by location in order to be close to their customers.

When a firm is departmentalized by location, it can more easily estimate the expenses incurred at each location. The firm can be viewed as a set of divisions separated by location, with each location generating its own profits. This allows the firm to identify the locations that have been performing well, which may help it determine which locations should attempt to expand their business.

College Health Club: **Departmentalizing Tasks at CHC**

Another decision that Sue Kramer needs to make as part of her business plan is how to departmentalize tasks at College Health Club (CHC). She first considers the main functions of CHC and who will perform these functions. She will decide on the marketing plan that will be implemented to attract new customers. The health club services will be provided by Sue and her part-time employees. Sue will make any future financing decisions for CHC. All services will be provided at one location. Sue needs to departmentalize tasks at CHC so that aerobics classes can be held in one part of the club while members are helped with exercise and weight machines in another area. She decides that she will establish a weekly aerobics schedule and assign a specific employee (or herself) to lead each class. When employees are not leading an aerobics class, they will be assigned to help members use the exercise and weight machines.

Although all health club services are currently provided at one location, Sue may open additional health clubs in the future. She then will departmentalize by location because any part-time employees will be assigned to only one of the health club locations.

Organizational Structure of a Multinational Corporation The organizational structure of a multinational corporation is complex because responsibilities must be assigned not only to U.S. operations but also to all foreign operations. To illustrate, consider General Motors, which has facilities in Europe, Canada, Asia, Latin America, Africa, and the Middle East. It has departmentalized by location, so either a president or a vice-president is in charge of each foreign region. Specifically, a president is assigned to GM of Mexico, a president to GM of Brazil, a vice-president to Asian and Pacific operations, a president to GM of Canada Limited, and a vice-president to Latin American, African, and Middle East operations. In Europe, one vice-president is assigned to sales and marketing, and a second vice-president is assigned to Europe's manufacturing plants. Thus, the European operations are also departmentalized by function.

Even when firms departmentalize their U.S. operations by product or by function, they commonly departmentalize their foreign operations by location. Since some foreign operations are distant from the firm's headquarters, departmentalizing operations in a foreign country by product or function would be difficult. If the foreign operations were departmentalized by product, an executive at the U.S. headquarters would have to oversee each product produced in the foreign country. If the operations were departmentalized by function, an executive at the U.S. headquarters would have to oversee each function conducted at the foreign facility. Normally, executives at the U.S. headquarters cannot easily monitor the foreign operations because they are not there on a daily or even a weekly basis. Consequently, it is more appropriate to assign an executive at the foreign facility the responsibility of overseeing a wide variety of products and functions at that facility.

In recent years, some multinational corporations have begun to select people who have international business experience for their boards of directors. Such directors are better able to monitor the firm's foreign operations. Furthermore, some multinational corporations have become more willing to promote managers within the firm who have substantial experience in international business. Sometimes a corporation will assign employees to its foreign facilities so that they can gain that experience.

global business

cross functional teamwork:

Interaction among Departments

Although the organizational structure formally indicates to whom each employee reports, it still allows interaction among different departments. For example, a firm may departmentalize by function so that one executive is responsible for the management of operations, a second executive is responsible for the marketing function, and a third executive is responsible for the financing function.

Though each function appears independent of the others on the organization chart, executives in charge of their respective functions must interact with the other departments. Exhibit 8.10 shows how the marketing, production, and finance departments rely on each other for information before making decisions. The marketing department needs to be aware of any changes in the production of a product and the volume of the product that will be available before it finalizes its marketing strategies. The production department needs customer satisfaction information as it considers redesigning products. It also needs to receive forecasts of expected sales from the marketing department, which affect the decision of how much to produce. The marketing and production departments provide the finance department with their forecasts of funds needed to cover their expenses. The finance department uses this information along with other information to determine whether it needs to obtain additional financing for the firm.

Exhibit 8.10

Flow of Information across Departments

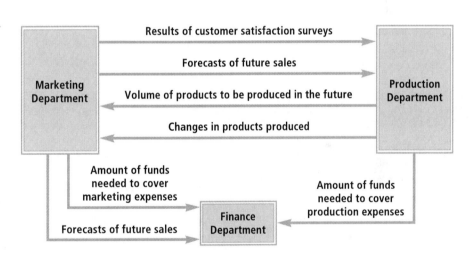

Departmentalize by Customer

Some firms establish separate divisions based on the type of customer. For example, some airlines have a separate reservations division that focuses exclusively on group trips. Computer firms such as IBM have designated some salespeople to focus exclusively on selling computers to school systems. They also have some divisions that focus on online sales to individuals, while others focus on large corporate customers.

SUMMARY

1 The organizational structure of a firm identifies responsibilities for each job position within the firm and the relationships among those positions. The structure enables employees to recognize which job positions are responsible for the work performed by other positions.

Most firms use a line-and-staff organizational structure. However, they may also use a matrix organization

to obtain employee input on various projects. They may also encourage intrapreneurship in which some employees are assigned to create new products or ideas.

2 The main methods of departmentalizing are by

▶ function, in which tasks are separated according to employee functions;

▶ product, in which tasks are separated according to the product produced;

▶ location, in which tasks are concentrated in a particular division to serve a specific area; and

▶ customer, in which tasks are separated according to the type of customer that purchases the firm's products.

KEY TERMS

autonomy 237
board of directors 233
centralized 237
chain of command 232
decentralized 237
departmentalize 245
downsizing 240

informal organizational
 structure 244
inside board members 233
internal auditor 236
intrapreneurship 244
line organization 241
line positions 241

line-and-staff organization 241
matrix organization 242
organization chart 232
organizational structure 232
outside board members 233
span of control 236
staff positions 241

Review & Critical Thinking Questions

1. Define organizational structure. Explain how a firm's organizational structure can affect its value.

2. Explain the following statement: "Generally speaking, no one specific organizational structure is optimal for all firms."

3. Define inside board members and outside board members. What type of compensation may motivate these directors to serve the interests of the firm's shareholders?

4. Why may shareholders prefer that the board of directors contain more outside directors than inside directors? Can there still be conflicts of interest within

the board if it is composed primarily of outside directors?

5. Describe the role of an internal auditor.

6. How would the span of control differ for a firm with numerous employees who perform similar tasks and for a firm with highly diverse tasks?

7. What is decentralization? Explain the advantages and disadvantages of decentralization.

8. Explain the difference between line positions and staff positions within an organization. Provide examples of each.

9. Assume that you are creating a new organizational structure for your firm that allows more em-

ployee input. Identify and explain the two common methods you could use to revise the organizational structure.

10. What is an informal organizational structure? Explain the advantages and disadvantages of an informal organizational structure.

11. Explain why the organizational structure of a multinational corporation that operates a global business is so complex. What methods of departmentalizing are commonly used by multinational corporations?

12. Explain the phase "cross-functional teamwork" and how it relates to interaction among departments.

Discussion Questions

1. You work at a software company that does not have a clearly identifiable chain of command. Over lunch, another manager informs you that he is going to hire his cousin, a software engineer, for a position at your company. "I already know he can do the job. Why should I bother interviewing other employees?" What is wrong with the manager's actions?

2. Assume that you are a high-level manager and are revising the organizational structure of your firm. Identify and explain the main methods for departmentalizing the tasks and responsibilities to the different departments.

3. Assume that you have just been named the project manager for a firm. The project involves employees from various parts of the firm. What type of temporary organizational structure would you recommend and why?

4. Explain the following statement: "Departmentalization is the building block for organizational structure."

5. How could a firm use the Internet to provide information about its organizational structure?

6. Express your opinion of the informal organization. Is it the same as the "grapevine"? Should a manager ever participate in the "grapevine" with employees?

It's Your Decision: Organizational Structure at CHC

1. One alternative span of control Sue could have is to assign the part-time employees to different levels. For example, the student who has been employed at CHC the longest would have the most seniority and could be put in charge of the other students. Would this span of control be more effective at CHC than the wide span of control in which all of the employees will report to Sue? Is any disadvantage associated with giving one of the employees power over the others?

2. Sue may consider hiring a college student majoring in exercise science for an intrapreneurship position during the summer. How could this student help CHC besides as a typical employee?

3. CHC's organizational structure is set up so that each part-time employee will lead aerobics classes, which is essentially a part of production (producing a service). In addition, each part-time employee will show prospective members around the club, which is a marketing function. Explain why assigning integrated tasks to employees may be more effective than assigning each employee just one type of task.

4. Assuming that CHC's total expenses are expected to be $142,000, determine how the club's estimated earnings are affected by the following possible closing times:

If CHC Closes at _____ Each Night	Estimated Annual Salary Expenses Incurred in the First Year	Expected Memberships in the First Year	CHC's Expected Earnings before Taxes in the First Year
11 P.M.	48,000	300	_____
10 P.M.	44,000	290	_____
9 P.M.	40,000	280	_____

Based on this analysis, what time do you think CHC should close each night?

5. A health club differs from manufacturing firms in that it produces a service rather than products. Should manufacturing firms have a narrower span of control than service firms like CHC?

Investing in a Business

Using the annual report of the firm in which you would like to invest, complete the following:

1 Describe the organizational structure of the firm.

2 Does the firm appear to have many high-level managers?

3 Has the firm downsized in recent years by removing middle managers from its organizational structure?

4 Explain how the business uses technology to promote its organizational structure. For example, does it use the Internet to provide information about its organizational structure? Does it provide information regarding the methods of departmentalizing tasks?

5 Go to **http://hoovers.com** and locate the NEWS SEARCH. Type in the name of the firm in the space provided, and review the recent news stories about the firm. Summarize any (at least one) recent news story about the firm that applies to one or more of the key concepts in this chapter.

Case: Creating an Organizational Structure

Janet Shugarts is the president of a barbecue sauce manufacturer in Austin, Texas. A manager in production has come up with a new barbecue recipe that he claims will be the best on the market because it's hot and spicy and has a flavor that the competition cannot match.

Janet has recently received new marketing research information. The research indicates that most Europeans prefer a hot and spicy barbecue sauce. The marketing manager is excited about this new product and believes it can be exported to Western Europe.

Janet has just come out of a meeting with her four managers from production, marketing, finance, and human resources. They have decided to establish a sales office for the barbeque sauce in Paris, France. The plan is to create a project team to set up a production facility within a year in France. The marketing manager will head this project team. He has requested that this subsidiary be decentralized to provide him with an opportunity to make timely decisions in this local market.

Because of this expansion, Janet is planning to increase her existing workforce of 120 employees by 20 percent. She has recently hired a human resource manager to take charge of the recruiting and selection function. A rumor circulating around the plant through the "grapevine" hints that employees may attempt to bring in a union. The human resource manager is alarmed because of his position on the organization chart. His position is listed as a support position; thus, he can only advise and make recommendations to a line manager concerning issues related to recruiting and selection.

Questions

1 Has Janet created an organizational structure? If so, how?

2 Why would the marketing manager request decentralization of authority in Paris, France?

3 Does this organization reflect a line-and-staff organizational structure? If so, explain.

4 What possible disadvantage could result from the decentralization of the marketing function of the foreign sales office?

Video Case: Organizational Structure at JIAN

JIAN creates business software. It wanted to focus on developing additional software and on marketing these products. Because it was a small firm, it intended to focus on tasks that it did well and to avoid problems that could result if it tried to perform all necessary business functions with a small number of employees. Therefore, it decided to use a unique organizational structure that could achieve its objectives. JIAN relies on other firms for its manufacturing and for its employee payroll, benefits, and recruiting functions. Thus, its own em-

ployees can focus entirely on software development and marketing.

Questions

1   Has JIAN departmentalized by product? By function? Explain.

2   Explain how JIAN's unique organizational structure avoids friction between departments.

3   Explain why JIAN's unique organizational structure would be short (flat) rather than tall.

Internet Applications

1.   Go to the website of a company that provides an annual report. Many companies describe their organizational structure in their annual reports. Describe the organizational structure based on the information that you find. Does the structure appear to have many layers? Do tasks appear to be departmentalized? Explain. Alternatively, is the company departmentalized by product, or location, or by customer?

2.   *http://www.metrogis.org/teams/org_structure.shtml*

This is the website for MetroGIS, a voluntary collaboration of organizations in the Minneapolis–St. Paul metropolitan area that use geographic information systems

technology to carry out their business functions. Describe the composition of the board and the coordinating committee. Also discuss the technical advisory team. Does this type of organizational structure indicate a narrow or a wide span of control? Explain.

3.   *http://newsroom.cisco.com/dlls/corp_082301b.html*

Why did Cisco change its organizational structure? What exactly was changed to attain the new structure? How do you think the new organizational structure affects the degree of decentralization at Cisco? Which level of Cisco's organizational structure do you think was most affected by the change?

The Coca-Cola Company Annual Report Project

Questions for the current year's annual report are available on the text website at **http://madura.swlearning.com.**

The following questions apply concepts presented in this chapter to The Coca-Cola Company. Go to The Coca-Cola Company website (**http://www.cocacola.com**) and find the index for the 2001 annual report.

Questions

1 Click on "Selected Market Results." Why do you think The Coca-Cola Company may put a new management team into a foreign country?

2 Download the financial statements from the "Financials Section" and find "Note 12: Restricted Stock, Stock Options and Other Stock Plans." Why may monitoring by institutional investors of The Coca-Cola Company's management be less of a concern than at other companies?

3 Download the financial statements from the "Financials Section" and find the "Investments" section.

a. With which different types of bottlers does The Coca-Cola Company have business relationships? How do the bottlers fit into The Coca-Cola Company's organizational structure?

b. What percentage of worldwide unit case volume do the different types of bottlers produce and distribute?

4 Click on "Operations Review" and "Africa." How could The Coca-Cola Company contribute to people development in Africa? How do you think the company would be able to benefit from these actions in the long run?

5 Go to **http://hoovers.com** and locate the NEWS CENTER. Key in The Coca-Cola Company in the space provided, click on "Search," and review the recent news stories about the firm. Summarize any (at least one) recent news story about The Coca-Cola Company that applies one or more of the key concepts within this chapter of the text.

In-Text Study Guide

Answers are in an appendix at the back of the book.

True or False

1. An organization chart shows the interaction among employee responsibilities. T

2. An organizational structure identifies the responsibilities of each job position and the relationships among those positions. T

3. A company's board of directors normally takes an active role in managing the firm's day-to-day activities. F

4. Inside board members are more likely than outside members to support changes that will benefit the firm's stockholders, especially if the firm's top managers do not support the changes. F

5. An organizational structure that is designed to have each manager supervise just a few employees has a narrow span of control. T

6. In recent years, most firms have attempted to centralize authority in the hands of a few key executives. F

7. Firms will have either a formal organizational structure or an informal organizational structure, but can never have both types of organizational structures at the same time. F

8. An advantage of a firm's informal organizational structure is that it encourages the formation of friendships, which can improve morale and job satisfaction. T

9. Organizing a firm by both product and function is not effective for companies that operate in only one location. F

10. When a firm is departmentalized by location, its expenses involved in each location can be more easily estimated. T

11. Most firms departmentalize their foreign operations by function. F

Multiple Choice

12. The responsibilities of a firm's managers should be organized to achieve the:
    a) grapevine.
    b) formal contingency.
    c) strategic plan.

d) chain of command.
e) bureaucratic organization.

13. The president of a company:
    a) determines which members of the board of directors will be reappointed.
    b) coordinates the actions of all divisions and provides direction for the firm.
    c) directly supervises the actions of all other employees.
    d) seldom delegates managerial duties to other managers.
    e) operates independently of the board of directors.

14. The _____ for a firm identifies the job position to which each type of employee must report.
    a) chain of command
    b) job matrix
    c) staffing chart
    d) flow chart
    e) informal structure

15. The ultimate responsibility for the success of a firm lies with the:
    a) president.
    b) employee.
    c) customer.
    d) competition.
    e) labor union.

16. The outside members of the board of directors of a company are those directors who:
    a) live outside the state in which the corporation received its charter.
    b) are not managers of the firm.
    c) are not stockholders in the firm.
    d) serve on the board without direct compensation.
    e) were appointed by the president of the firm rather than selected by the firm's stockholders.

17. The board of directors has the responsibility of representing the interests of the firm's:
    a) top management.
    b) employees.

c) customers.

d) creditors.

e) shareholders.

18. Members of a firm's board of directors are selected by the firm's:
    a) top management.
    b) management council.
    c) shareholders.
    d) creditors.
    e) employees.

19. Members of the board of directors who are also managers of the same firm are known as:
    a) ex-officio board members.
    b) primary board members.
    c) unelected board members.
    d) inside board members.
    e) organizational board members.

20. Which member of the board of directors would be least likely to have a conflict of interest?
    a) outside director with consulting ties to company
    b) inside director with vice presidential position
    c) the CEO
    d) outside director retired from company
    e) outside director, CEO of another firm

21. The _____ refers to the number of employees managed by each manager.
    a) scope of authority
    b) management ratio
    c) employee limit
    d) span of control
    e) manager-employee multiplier

22. Span of control is determined by:
    a) consultants.
    b) staff.
    c) top management.
    d) employees.
    e) customers.

23. The _____ ensures that all departments follow the firm's guidelines and procedures.
    a) CEO
    b) internal auditor
    c) board of directors
    d) project manager
    e) inside director

24. A firm in which managers have narrow spans of control tends to have:
    a) a tall organizational structure.
    b) very decentralized decision making.
    c) a small number of employees.
    d) very few layers of management.
    e) a very large number of people serving on its board of directors.

25. The strategy of spreading authority among several divisions or managers is called:
    a) centralization.
    b) decentralization.
    c) decision rationing.
    d) abdication of authority.
    e) adjudication of authority.

26. An extreme form of decentralization in which divisions can make their own decisions and act independently is called:
    a) centralization.
    b) autonomy.
    c) span of control.
    d) span of management.
    e) departmentalization.

27. A possible disadvantage of decentralization is that it:
    a) may require inexperienced managers to make major decisions they are not qualified to make.
    b) usually increases the firm's operating expenses.
    c) slows down the decision-making process.
    d) harms employee motivation by forcing them to take on more responsibilities.
    e) prevents employees from making creative decisions.

In-Text Study Guide

Answers are in an appendix at the back of the book.

28. Which of the following is not an advantage of decentralization?
    a) shortens the decision-making process
    b) reduces salary expenses
    c) delegates specialized decisions to low level employees
    d) delegation of authority may improve employee morale
    e) improves employee qualifications for promotion

29. One outcome of the recent downsizing by many corporations during the 1990s was:
    a) an increase in the layers of management.
    b) a narrower span of control for most managers.
    c) decentralization of authority.
    d) increased costs of production.
    e) a big reduction in the importance of the informal organizational structure.

30. Employees who serve in _____ positions provide assistance and support to employees who serve in line positions.
    a) secondary
    b) nominal
    c) reserve
    d) nonlinear
    e) staff

31. Jobs that are established to make decisions that achieve specific business goals are:
    a) staff positions.
    b) line positions.
    c) line-and-staff functions.
    d) temporary jobs.
    e) job placement.

32. Firms use a(n) _____ organization to allow the various parts of a firm to interact as they focus on a particular project.
    a) matrix
    b) quasi-linear
    c) tabular
    d) extracurricular
    e) cellular

33. One possible disadvantage of a matrix organization is that it:
    a) makes it difficult for different departments to communicate with each other.
    b) reduces employee satisfaction by requiring workers to perform monotonous tasks.
    c) reduces the time employees have to perform their normal duties.
    d) puts too much power in the hands of a small number of top managers.
    e) allows top management to make decisions without input from the board.

34. A process whereby particular employees of a firm can be assigned to create ideas as if they were entrepreneurs is referred to as:
    a) staff organization.
    b) intrapreneurship.
    c) co-ownership.
    d) leadership.
    e) line organization.

35. All of the following are common ways of departmentalizing a firm except by:
    a) function.
    b) product.
    c) customer.
    d) time period.
    e) location.

36. It is common for larger firms with many products to departmentalize by:
    a) function.
    b) customer.
    c) manufacturing process.
    d) geographic area.
    e) product.

All businesses, including *NSYNC, need to establish a plan for how they will produce their products.

Chapter 9

The Learning Goals of this chapter are to:

1 Identify the key resources used for production.

2 Identify the factors that affect the plant site decision.

3 Describe how various factors affect the design and layout decision.

4 Describe the key tasks that are involved in production control.

5 Describe the key factors that affect production efficiency.

Improving Productivity and Quality

9

Firms are created to produce products or services. Production management (also called operations management) is the management of the process in which resources are used to produce products or services. The specific process chosen by a firm to produce its products or services can affect its value. Consider the situation of *NSYNC, which is a business that produces music for its customers (fans). *NSYNC must decide:

▶ What human resources and other resources (such as instruments,

speakers, etc.) are needed to produce its music?

▶ At what site (studio) should it produce the music?

▶ What can it do to control the quality of its music?

▶ How can it produce music more efficiently?

The decisions about the human resources needed affect *NSYNC's cost of producing music. Its ability to control its production will affect the quality of the music produced and, therefore, will

affect the demand for its music. If *NSYNC can improve its efficiency, it can reduce its expenses and, therefore, improve its performance.

All businesses must make the types of decisions described above. This chapter explains how *NSYNC or any other firm can make production management decisions in a manner that maximizes the firm's value.

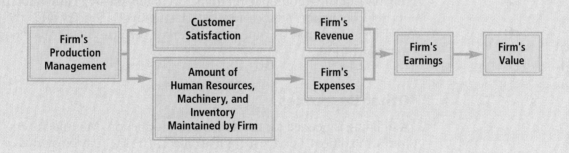

1

Identify the key resources used for production.

production process (conversion process) a series of tasks in which resources are used to produce a product or service

production management (operations management) the management of a process in which resources (such as employees and machinery) are used to produce products and services

RESOURCES USED FOR THE PRODUCTION PROCESS

Whether a firm produces products or services, it needs a **production process** (also called **conversion process**), or a series of tasks in which resources are used to produce a product or service. A process identifies the mixture of resources allocated for production, the assignment of tasks, and the sequence of tasks.

Many possible production processes can achieve the production of a specific product. Thus, effective **production management** (or **operations management**) aims at developing an efficient (relatively low-cost) and high-quality production process for producing specific products and services. Specifically, production management can achieve efficiency by determining the proper amount of materials to use, the proper mix of resources to use, the proper assignments of the tasks, and the proper sequence of the tasks. Production management can contribute to the success of both manufacturing firms and service-oriented firms. For example, the success of Southwest Airlines, a service-oriented firm, is attributed to its low-cost production of air transportation for customers. Thus, the profits and value of each firm are influenced by its production management.

The main resources that firms use for the production process are human resources (employees), materials, and other resources (such as buildings, machinery, and equipment). Firms that produce products tend to use more materials and equipment in their production process. Firms that produce services (such as Internet firms) use more employees and information technology.

Human Resources

Firms must identify the type of employees needed for production. Skilled labor is necessary for some forms of production, but unskilled labor can be used for other forms. Some forms of production are labor-intensive in that they require more labor than materials. The operating expenses involved in hiring human resources are dependent both on the number of employees and on their skill levels. Because of the employee skill level required, an Internet firm incurs much larger salary expenses than a grocery store.

Materials

The materials used in the production process are normally transformed by the firm's human resources into a final product. Tire manufacturers rely on rubber, automobile manufacturers rely on steel, and book publishers rely on paper. Service firms such as travel agencies and investment advisers do not rely as much on materials because they do not engage in manufacturing.

Other Resources

A building is needed for most forms of production. Manufacturers use factories and offices. Service firms use offices. The site may be owned or rented by the firm. Since purchasing a building can be expensive, some firms simply rent the buildings they use. Renting also allows the firm to move at the end of the lease period without having to sell the building. Machinery and equipment are also needed by many manufacturing firms. Technology may also be a necessary resource for manufacturing and service firms.

Combining the Resources for Production

work station an area in which one or more employees are assigned a specific task

assembly line a sequence of work stations in which each work station is designed to cover specific phases of the production process

Managers attempt to utilize the resources just described in a manner that achieves production at a low cost. They combine the various resources with the use of work stations and assembly lines. A **work station** is an area in which one or more employees are assigned a specific task. A work station may require machinery and equipment as well as employees.

An **assembly line** consists of a sequence of work stations in which each work station is designed to cover specific phases of the production process.

business online

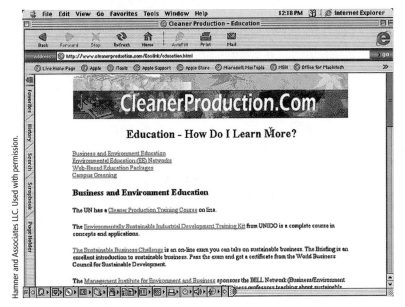

Clean Production   This website provides information about using production processes that maintain a clean environment.

e-business

Hamner and Associates LLC. Used with permission.

http://www.cleanerproduction
.com/ecolink/education.html

The production of a single product may require several work stations, with each station using employees, machinery, and materials. Since the cost of all these resources along with the building can be substantial, efficient management of the production process can reduce expenses, which can convert into higher profits.

An example of a typical production process is shown in Exhibit 9.1. Employees use buildings, machinery, and equipment to convert materials into a product or service. For example, employees of printing firms use machines for typesetting, printing, and binding to produce books. Employees of General Nutrition (GNC) use its manufacturing plant (which is the size of four football fields) to produce more than 150,000 bottles of vitamins per day.

Most production processes are more efficient when different employees are assigned different tasks. In this way, employees can utilize their unique types of expertise to specialize in what they do best.

College Health Club: **Resources Used at CHC**

One of the decisions that Sue Kramer needs to make as part of her business plan is to identify the set of resources that College Health Club (CHC) will need to produce its services. Once she has identified these resources, Sue can estimate the cost of obtaining them. First, human resources will be used to lead aerobics classes and interact with customers. Second, equipment such as weight machines will be provided for customers to use. Third, the health club facility will be available to the customers. The main expenses of providing these resources are salaries to human resources and the rental cost of equipment and the facilities.

Exhibit 9.1

Resources Used in Production

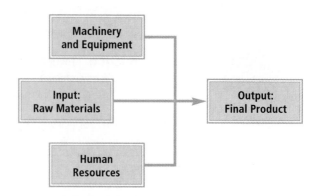

SELECTING A SITE

2

Identify the factors that affect the plant site decision.

A critical decision in production management is the selection of a site (location) for the factory or office. Location can significantly affect the cost of production and therefore the firm's ability to compete against other firms. This is especially true for industrial firms such as Bethlehem Steel and DaimlerChrysler, which require a large investment in plant and equipment.

Factors Affecting the Site Decision

Several factors must be considered when determining the optimal site. The most relevant factors are identified here.

Cost of Workplace Space   The cost of purchasing or renting workplace space (such as buildings or offices) can vary significantly among locations. Costs are likely to be high near the center of any business district where land costs are high. Costs also tend to be higher in certain regions. For example, office rental rates are generally higher in the northeastern states than in other areas. This is one major reason why companies located in northern cities have relocated to the South during the last 10 years.

Cost of Labor   The cost of hiring employees varies significantly among locations. Salaries within a city tend to be higher than salaries outside the city for a given occupation. Salaries are also generally higher in the North than the South for a given occupation. This is another reason why many companies have relocated to the South.

Tax Incentives   Some local governments may be willing to grant tax credits to attract companies to their area. The governments offer this incentive to increase the employment level and improve economic conditions in the area.

Source of Demand   If a firm plans to sell its product in a specific location, it may establish its plant there. The costs of transporting and servicing the product can be minimized by producing at a site near the source of demand.

Access to Transportation   When companies sell products across the nation, they may choose a site near their main source of transportation. They also need to be accessible so that materials can be delivered to them.

Some factories and offices are established near interstate highways, rivers, or airports for this reason.

Supply of Labor   Firms that plan to hire specialized workers must be able to attract the labor needed. They may choose a location where a large supply of workers with that particular specialization exists. For instance, high-tech companies tend to locate near universities where there is an abundance of educated labor.

Evaluating Possible Sites

When a firm considers various sites, it must compare their desirability. First, it may assign a weight to represent the importance of each of the various factors that will influence its decision. Labor-intensive firms would likely place a high weight on the cost of human resources; other firms would be less concerned about this factor.

Once the firm has determined which factors should have the most influence on its decision, it attempts to rate these factors for each possible site. An easy method of comparing alternative sites is to develop a site evaluation matrix, as shown in Exhibit 9.2. Possible sites are listed at the left. Each column identifies a factor that needs to be evaluated. These factors are rated from 1 (outstanding) to 5 (poor). The overall rating assigned to any potential site can be determined by averaging the ratings for that site. If some factors are more important than others, however, they deserve to have a relatively higher influence on the overall ratings.

The site evaluation matrix in Exhibit 9.2 is simplified in that it focuses on only two factors for each city. The land cost is presumed to be the more important factor and has an 80 percent weight. The supply of labor receives the remaining 20 percent weight. The weighted rating shown in Exhibit 9.2 is equal to the rating times the weight of the rating. The weighted ratings for each factor are combined to determine the total rating for each city. For example, the Austin, Texas, site received a land cost rating of 3, which converts to a weighted rating of 2.4 (computed as $3 \times .8$). It also received a supply of labor rating of 1, which converts to a rating of .2 (computed as $1 \times .2$). Its total rating is 2.6 (computed as $2.4 + .2$).

Once the firm determines a rating for each factor, it can derive the total rating for each site considered. Based on the ratings for the four sites in Exhibit 9.2, the Omaha site had the best rating and thus would be selected as the site.

If another firm assessed the same four sites in Exhibit 9.2, it might come to a different conclusion for two reasons. First, it might use different factors

Exhibit 9.2

Example of a Site Evaluation Matrix

| Possible Sites | Land Cost | | Supply of Labor | | |
	Rating	Weighted Rating (80% of Weight)	Rating	Weighted Rating (20% Weight)	Total Rating
Austin, TX	3	2.4	1	.2	2.6
Chicago, IL	4	3.2	2	.4	3.6
Los Angeles, CA	5	4.0	3	.6	4.6
Omaha, NE	1	.8	3	.6	1.4

Selecting a Foreign Production Site The selection of a foreign production site by a U.S. firm is critical because location affects the firm's operating expenses and therefore its earnings. Consider the case of Pfizer, a U.S. firm that produces pharmaceutical and consumer products, including Listerine, Halls cough drops, Clorets mints, Certs mints, and Trident gum. Pfizer has operations in more than 100 countries. Its extensive development of foreign operations was motivated by global demand for its products. Pfizer attempts to offer "every product, everywhere." Consequently, it established production sites that were convenient to the foreign markets where it planned to sell products.

The selection of a production site by any multinational corporation is crucial because costs vary substantially among countries. Annual office rental rates per square foot are more than five times higher in Paris than in Mexico City and more than twice as high in Tokyo as in Paris. The cost of human resources is generally much lower in less-developed countries, but the supply of skilled labor in those countries may be inadequate. Furthermore, consumer demand for products in those countries may be low, so the products would have to be transported to other countries with much higher demand. Multinational corporations must assess the trade-offs involved. If the products are light in weight (and therefore involve low transportation expenses), a multinational corporation might be willing to use facilities in less-developed countries and transport the products to areas where demand is higher.

in its matrix. Second, it might rate the factors differently. For example, one city may have an abundance of people who have computer development skills, but it may not have many people with skills to manage a bank.

Once a particular area (such as a city or county) has been chosen, the precise location must be decided. Some of the factors already mentioned will influence this decision. In addition, factors such as traffic, crime rate, and worker access to public transportation may influence the decision.

College Health Club: Site Selection at College Health Club

The site that Sue Kramer has selected for College Health Club is in a shopping center across the street from the Texas College campus. Since the business will target students at this college who want to join a health club, she has selected a site that is accessible to those students. The cost of rent at this facility is reasonable. The health club also has easy access to labor because it will hire exercise science majors from Texas College to work part-time.

SELECTING THE DESIGN AND LAYOUT

Describe how various factors affect the design and layout decision.

design the size and structure of a plant or office

layout the arrangement of machinery and equipment within a factory or office

Once a site for a manufacturing plant or office is chosen, the design and layout must be determined. The **design** indicates the size and structure of the plant or office. The **layout** is the arrangement of the machinery and equipment within the factory or office.

The design and layout decisions directly affect operating expenses because they determine the costs of rent, machinery, and equipment. They may even affect the firm's interest expenses because they influence the amount of money that must be borrowed to purchase property or machinery.

A study by the management consulting firm Ernst & Young found that firms can improve their profits by using innovative ideas for their plant design and layout. A firm may assign employee teams to identify methods to make its plant design and layout more efficient. Employees may be highly motivated to offer cost-cutting solutions when they realize that their suggestions may prevent layoffs.

Factors Affecting Design and Layout

Design and layout decisions are influenced by the following characteristics.

Site Characteristics   Design and layout decisions are dependent on some characteristics of the site selected. For example, if the site is in an area with high land costs, a high-rise building may be designed so that less land will be needed. The layout of the plant will then be affected by the design.

product layout a layout in which tasks are positioned in the sequence that they are assigned

Production Process   Design and layout are also dependent on the production process to be used. If an assembly-line operation is to be used, all tasks included in this operation should be in the same general area. A **product layout** positions the tasks in the sequence that they are assigned. For example, one person may specialize in creating components, while the next person assembles the components, and the next person packages the product. A product layout is commonly used for assembly-line production.

fixed-position layout a layout in which employees go to the position of the product, rather than waiting for the product to come to them

Alternatively, some products (such as airplanes, ships, or homes) are completely produced in one fixed position, which requires a **fixed-position layout.** The employees go to the product, rather than having the product come to them.

flexible manufacturing a production process that can be easily adjusted to accommodate future revisions

Many firms now use **flexible manufacturing,** a production process that can be easily adjusted to accommodate future revisions. This enables the firm to restructure its layout as needed when it changes its products to accommodate customer demand. Many auto plants use flexible manufacturing so that they can produce whatever cars or trucks are in demand. A flexible layout normally requires that employees have flexible skills. Although employees may have some specialization, they must have other skills so that when the layout of the plant is rearranged, they can focus on the production of other products.

Whatever design and layout are used, they should allow the sequence of tasks to take place efficiently. For example, the production process is commonly completed near the outside of the plant so that the finished products can be easily loaded onto trucks.

Product Line   Most firms produce more than one product or service at their site. Firms with a narrow product line focus on the production of one or a few products, which allows them to specialize. Firms with a broad product line offer a wide range of products.

As market preferences change, demand for products changes. The layout must be revised to accompany these changes. For example, the popularity of sport utility vehicles has caused many automobile manufacturers to allocate more of their layout for the production of these vehicles. The allocation of more space for one product normally takes space away from others, unless the initial design and layout allowed extra space for expansion.

Desired Production Capacity   When planning both design and layout, the firm's desired production capacity (maximum production level possible) must be considered. Most firms attempt to plan for growth by allowing flexibility to increase the production capacity over time. The design

Crystal Warren, left, heats candles as Chot Chot pours hot wax into the molds at the Hot Wax Candle Co. in Greensboro, NY.

AP Photo/ Chuck Burton

of the building may allow for additional levels to be added. The proper layout can open up more space to be used for increased production.

If firms do not plan for growth, they will be forced to search for a new site when demand for their product exceeds their production capacity. When a firm maintains its existing site and develops a second site to expand, it must duplicate the machinery and job positions assigned at the original site. Consequently, production efficiency tends to decrease. To avoid this problem, the firm may relocate to a site with a larger capacity. Reassessing all potential plant sites and developing a new design and layout can be costly, however. Firms can avoid these costs by ensuring that the layout at their initial site allows for growth.

Although having a layout that allows for growth is desirable, it is also expensive. A firm must invest additional funds to obtain additional land or floor space. This investment ties up funds that might be better used by the firm for other purposes. Furthermore, if growth does not occur, the layout will be inefficient because some of the space will continue to be unused.

A firm may achieve greater production capacity without changing its design and layout if employees can do some or all of their work at home.

A worker shovels freshly made butter into the processing line at the Cabot Creamery plant in Cabot, Vermont.

AP Photo/ Toby Talbot

Given the improvements in telecommunications (computer networks, e-mail, and fax machines), employees of some businesses no longer need to be on site. When the employees who work at home need to come in to work, they use work spaces that are not permanently assigned to anyone. For example, a firm may keep an office available with a desk, a computer, and a telephone for any employee who normally works at home but needs to use temporary work space at the firm. This practice is referred to as **hotelling** (or **just-in-time office**). For example, hotelling may be appropriate for salespeople who travel frequently and generally work from a home office.

hotelling (just-in-time office) providing an office with a desk, a computer, and a telephone for any employee who normally works at home but needs to use work space at the firm

College Health Club: **Design and Layout at CHC**

Sue Kramer has organized the production of health club services at College Health Club (CHC) by type of service. Aerobics classes are conducted in one part of the health club, while exercise and weight machines are located in another part. The facilities are large enough to allow for some expansion. The layout of the facilities provides flexibility so that the exercise and weight machines can be rearranged.

A small unit next to CHC's facilities in the shopping center is vacant. Sue could expand the health club by renting this unit as well. The extra rent would be $1,000 per month or $12,000 per year. Sue calculates how this would affect her earnings as follows:

Impact of a Larger Layout on CHC's First-Year Performance

	Performance if . . .	
	CHC Uses the Present Layout	CHC Rents Additional Space
(1) Price per membership	$500	$500
(2) Number of members in first year	300	310
(3) Revenue = (1) × (2)	$150,000	$155,000
(4) Total operating expenses	$138,000	$150,000
(5) Interest expenses	$4,000	$4,000
(6) Earnings before taxes = (3) − (4) − (5)	$8,000	$1,000

She estimates that the extra space would attract an additional 10 members over the first year. As the third column of the table shows, the larger layout would increase CHC's revenue over the first year, but would also result in higher expenses. Sue decides not to rent the unit. If memberships at CHC expand to the extent that the existing facilities are crowded, she may need more space and will inquire about renting another unit at that time.

4

Describe the key tasks that are involved in production control.

production control involves purchasing materials, inventory control, routing, scheduling, and quality control

Production Control

Once the plant and design have been selected, the firm can engage in **production control,** which involves the following:

▶ Purchasing materials

▶ Inventory control

▶ Routing

▶ Scheduling

▶ Quality control

Purchasing Materials

Managers perform the following tasks when purchasing supplies. First, they must select a supplier. Second, they attempt to obtain volume discounts. Third, they determine whether to delegate some production tasks to suppliers. These tasks are discussed next.

Selecting a Supplier of Materials

In selecting among various suppliers, firms consider characteristics such as price, speed, quality, servicing, and credit availability. A typical approach to evaluating suppliers is to first obtain prices from each supplier. Next, a sample is obtained from each supplier and inspected for quality. Then, these suppliers are asked to provide further information on their speed of delivery and their service warranties in case any delivery problems occur. The firm may then try out a single supplier and evaluate its reliability over time.

Alternatively, a firm may initially use a few suppliers and later select the supplier that has provided the best service. Some firms avoid depending on a single supplier so that if any problems occur with one supplier, they will not have a major impact on the firm.

Another consideration in selecting a supplier may be its ability to interact with an Internet-based order system. Many firms now rely on *e-procurement,* or the use of the Internet to purchase some of their materials. This reduces the time that employees must devote to orders and can reduce expenses. A basic system detects the existing level of supplies and automatically orders additional supplies once the quantity on hand falls to a specific level. Some systems are more sophisticated and can handle additional tasks.

Obtaining Volume Discounts

Firms that purchase a large volume of materials from suppliers may obtain a discounted price on supplies while maintaining quality. This practice has enabled firms such as AT&T and General Motors to reduce their production expenses in recent years.

Bread loaves pass through a production line in a Bimbo bread factory in Mexico City. Grupo Bimbo is Mexico's largest bread maker. The bread is delivered fresh daily to thousands of supermarkets, food stores, and restaurants only hours after being baked.

Getty Images/ Photo by Wesley Bocxe/ Liaison

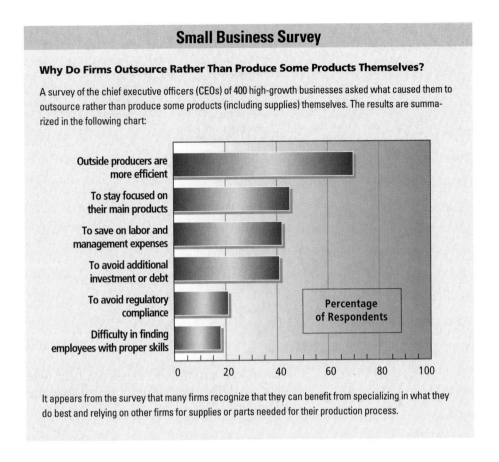

Small Business Survey

Why Do Firms Outsource Rather Than Produce Some Products Themselves?

A survey of the chief executive officers (CEOs) of 400 high-growth businesses asked what caused them to outsource rather than produce some products (including supplies) themselves. The results are summarized in the following chart:

It appears from the survey that many firms recognize that they can benefit from specializing in what they do best and relying on other firms for supplies or parts needed for their production process.

Delegating Production to Suppliers Manufacturers commonly use **outsourcing;** that is, they purchase parts from suppliers rather than producing the parts. Outsourcing can reduce a firm's expenses if suppliers can produce the parts at a lower cost than the firm itself. Some manufacturers have even begun delegating some parts of the production process to suppliers. Consider a manufacturing firm located in a city where wages are generally high. This firm has been ordering several components from a supplier and assembling them at its own plant. It may be better to have the supplier partially assemble the components before shipping them to the manufacturer. Some of the assembly task would thereby be shifted to the supplier. Partial assembly by the supplier may cost less than paying high-wage employees at the manufacturing plant.

Although outsourcing can be beneficial, it places much responsibility on other manufacturing companies. Thus, when a firm outsources, its ability to meet its production schedule depends on these other companies. For this reason, a firm that outsources must be very careful when selecting the suppliers on which it will rely.

The strategy of delegating some production tasks to suppliers is referred to as **deintegration** and is illustrated in Exhibit 9.3. The production process within the plant is no longer as integrated, because part of the production is completed by the supplier before the supplies or components are delivered to the manufacturing plant. Automobile manufacturers have deintegrated their production processes by delegating some production tasks to suppliers or other firms. For example, Ford Motor Company purchases fully

outsourcing purchasing parts from a supplier rather than producing the parts

deintegration the strategy of delegating some production tasks to suppliers

Exhibit 9.3

Effects of Deintegration

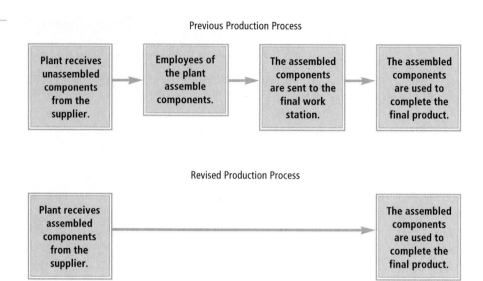

Previous Production Process

| Plant receives unassembled components from the supplier. | → | Employees of the plant assemble components. | → | The assembled components are sent to the final work station. | → | The assembled components are used to complete the final product. |

Revised Production Process

| Plant receives assembled components from the supplier. | → | The assembled components are used to complete the final product. |

assembled automobile seats from Lear Seating. By doing so, it saves hundreds of dollars per automobile because the supplier's cost of labor is lower than Ford's cost.

Inventory Control

inventory control the process of managing inventory at a level that minimizes costs

Inventory control is the process of managing inventory at a level that minimizes costs. It requires the management of materials inventories, work-in-process inventories, and finished goods inventories, as explained next.

Control of Materials Inventories When firms carry excessive inventories of materials, they may need to borrow more funds to finance these inventories. This increases their **carrying costs,** or their costs of maintaining (carrying) inventories. Carrying costs include financing costs as well as costs associated with storing or insuring inventories. Although firms can attempt to reduce their carrying costs by frequently ordering small amounts of materials, this strategy increases the costs involved in placing orders (called **order costs**). Any adjustment in the materials purchasing strategy will normally reduce carrying costs at the expense of increasing order costs, or vice versa.

carrying costs costs of maintaining (carrying) inventories

order costs costs involved in placing orders for materials

A popular method for reducing carrying costs is the **just-in-time (JIT)** system originated by Japanese companies. This system attempts to reduce materials inventories to a bare minimum by frequently ordering small amounts of materials. It can reduce the costs of maintaining inventories. However, it also entails a cost of managerial time required for frequent ordering and a cost of frequent deliveries. In addition, the JIT system could result in a shortage if applied improperly. Nevertheless, U.S. firms such as Applied Magnetics Corporation and Black & Decker Corporation have improved their productivity by effectively using JIT inventory management.

just-in-time (JIT) a system that attempts to reduce materials inventories to a bare minimum by frequently ordering small amounts of materials

materials requirements planning (MRP) a process for ensuring that materials are available when needed

Materials requirements planning (MRP) is a process for ensuring that the materials are available when needed. Normally requiring the use of a computer, MRP helps managers determine the amount of specific materials that should be purchased at any given time. The first step in MRP is to work

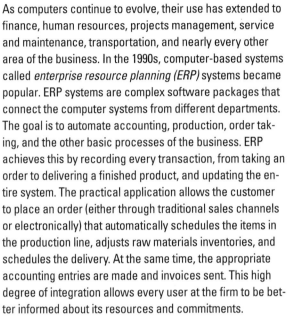

IMPACT OF INFORMATION TECHNOLOGY ON PRODUCTION PROCESSES

As computers continue to evolve, their use has extended to finance, human resources, projects management, service and maintenance, transportation, and nearly every other area of the business. In the 1990s, computer-based systems called *enterprise resource planning (ERP)* systems became popular. ERP systems are complex software packages that connect the computer systems from different departments. The goal is to automate accounting, production, order taking, and the other basic processes of the business. ERP achieves this by recording every transaction, from taking an order to delivering a finished product, and updating the entire system. The practical application allows the customer to place an order (either through traditional sales channels or electronically) that automatically schedules the items in the production line, adjusts raw materials inventories, and schedules the delivery. At the same time, the appropriate accounting entries are made and invoices sent. This high degree of integration allows every user at the firm to be better informed about its resources and commitments.

Integration is the key difference between ERP systems and the mainframe systems that have been used by many large production companies. Mainframe systems offered little flexibility and resulted in firms becoming departmentalized. For instance, different production facilities would each have their own departments for obtaining supplies. Each production facility would order materials according to its own needs, even though all facilities used the same material. The different systems made it difficult to have consolidated knowledge of how much material was purchased, who it was purchased from, and the costs involved. An ERP system puts all of the production facilities on the same platform so that the overall process can be consolidated and costs reduced.

A firm can extend its ERP system to the Internet where customers can access a website to learn which products are available and which have been committed to other customers. The firm may also demand that its suppliers offer the same ability so that supplies can be ordered quickly. This coordination allows the firm to eliminate inventory, improve connections with suppliers, and decrease overall costs.

ERP systems can be expensive, however. The price depends on the complexity of the system and the number of users that will access it. Installation requires data to be reformatted and network systems overhauled.

---

backward from the finished product toward the beginning and determine how long in advance materials are needed before products are completely produced. For example, if computers are to be assembled by a specific date, the computer components must arrive by a specific date before then, which means that they must be ordered even earlier. As the firm forecasts the demand for its product in the future, it can determine the time at which the materials need to arrive to achieve a production level that will accommodate the forecasted demand.

work-in-process inventories
inventories of partially completed products

Control of Work-in-Process Inventories
Firms must also manage their **work-in-process inventories,** which are inventories of partially completed products. Firms attempt to avoid shortages of all types of inventories. The direct consequence of a shortage in raw materials inventory or work-in-process inventory is an interruption in production. This can cause a shortage of the final product, and therefore results in forgone sales.

Control of Finished Goods Inventories
As demand for a firm's product changes over time, managers need to monitor the anticipated supply-demand differential. If an excess supply of a product is anticipated,

a firm can avoid excessive inventories by redirecting its resources toward the production of other products. For example, Ford Motor Company redirects resources away from the production of cars that are not selling as well as expected. Alternatively, a firm that experiences an excess supply of products can continue its normal production schedule and implement marketing strategies (such as advertising) that will increase demand.

If an increase in demand is anticipated, firms become concerned about possible shortages and must develop a strategy to boost production volume. They may schedule overtime for workers or hire new workers to achieve higher levels of production.

When the forecasted demand is underestimated, the firm may not produce a sufficient volume to accommodate all customers. Dell Computer, Apple Computer, and many other firms have experienced severe shortages when they underestimated demand. For this reason, some firms maintain more inventories than their expected volume of sales.

Just as firms attempt to avoid shortages, they also attempt to avoid holding excess inventories of products. When firms produce too much of a product, they are sometimes forced to reduce its price to ensure that they can sell all that they have produced. Sometimes they sell the product at a price below cost just to reduce their excess inventories. Many firms, such as Wal-Mart, Land's End, and Cemex, have reduced their inventory by using computer networks. Changes in inventory level are updated as soon as a customer order is received. IBM refocused its retail sales over the Internet in order to reduce its inventory and lower its costs, as shown in Exhibit 9.4. Its inventory as a percentage of its total assets was cut by more than half over a recent 10-year period.

Routing

routing the sequence (or route) of tasks necessary to complete the production of a product

Routing is the sequence (or route) of tasks necessary to complete the production of a product. Raw materials are commonly sent to various work stations so that they can be used as specified in the production process. A

Exhibit 9.4

Illustration of IBM's Efforts to Minimize Inventory

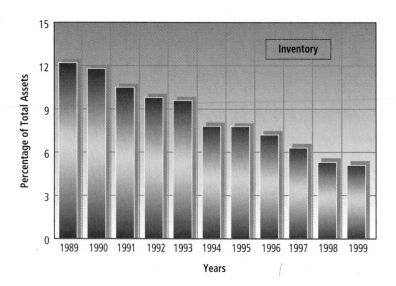

specific part of the production process is completed at each work station. For example, the production of a bicycle may require (1) using materials to produce a bike frame at one work station, (2) assembling wheels at a second work station, and (3) packaging the frames and wheels that have been assembled at a third work station.

The routing process is periodically evaluated to determine whether it can be improved to allow a faster or less expensive production process. General Motors, DaimlerChrysler, and United Parcel Service have streamlined their routing process to improve production efficiency.

Scheduling

scheduling the act of setting time periods for each task in the production process

production schedule a plan for the timing and volume of production tasks

Scheduling is the act of setting time periods for each task in the production process. A **production schedule** is a plan for the timing and volume of production tasks. For example, the production schedule for a bicycle may set a time of two hours for each frame to be assembled and one hour for each wheel to be assembled. Scheduling is useful because it establishes the expected amount of production that should be achieved at each work station over a given day or week. Therefore, each employee understands what is expected. Furthermore, scheduling allows managers to forecast how much will be produced by the end of the day, week, or month. If a firm does not meet its production schedule, it will not be able to accommodate customer orders in a timely fashion and will lose some of its customers.

Impact of Technology on Production Scheduling   Many firms have used technology to improve their production scheduling. For example, Weyerhaeuser (a manufacturer of doors) allows customers to access its website where they can specify the features of the door they desire and receive instant pricing on a door with those features. Consequently, orders are now placed more quickly. In addition, there is less chance of error because the customers specify the desired features themselves rather than

Peapod product selector Bill Brimfield inputs an order with his Palm Pilot device.

Getty Images / Tim Boyle

communicating the information to someone who would then have to communicate the information to the manufacturing department. Deliveries are now almost always on schedule.

Scheduling for Special Projects Scheduling is especially important for special long-term projects that must be completed by a specific deadline. If many related tasks must be completed in a specific sequence, scheduling can indicate when each task should be completed. In this way, managers can detect whether the project is likely to be finished on time. If any tasks are not completed on time, managers must search for ways to make up the time on other tasks.

One method of scheduling tasks for a special project is to use a **Gantt chart** (named after its creator, Henry Gantt), which illustrates the expected timing for each task within the production process. As an example of how a Gantt chart can be applied, assume that a chemical firm must produce 500 one-gallon containers of Chemical Z for a manufacturer. The production process involves creating large amounts of Chemicals X and Y, which are then mixed in a tank to produce Chemical Z. Next, Chemical Z must be poured into gallon containers and then packaged in cases to be delivered. Notice that while the first two tasks can be completed at the same time, each remaining task cannot begin until the previous task is completed.

The bar for each task on the Gantt chart can be marked when that task is completed, as shown in Exhibit 9.5. According to the exhibit, the first four tasks have been completed, so the focus is now on the fifth task.

Another method of scheduling tasks for a special project is the **program evaluation and review technique (PERT),** which schedules tasks in a manner that will minimize delays in the production process. PERT involves the following steps:

1 The various tasks involved in the production process are identified.

2 The tasks are arranged in the order in which they must take place; this sequence may be represented on a chart with arrows illustrating the path or sequence of the production process.

3 The time needed for each activity is estimated.

An example of PERT as applied to the firm's production of Chemical Z is shown in Exhibit 9.6. The production of Chemical X (Task 1) and Chem-

Gantt chart a chart illustrating the expected timing for each task in the production process

program evaluation and review technique (PERT) a method of scheduling tasks to minimize delays in the production process

Exhibit 9.5

Example of a Gantt Chart

Production Tasks	Week 1	Week 2	Week 3	Week 4	Week 5
1. Produce Chemical X.					
2. Produce Chemical Y.					
3. Mix Chemicals X and Y in a tank to produce Chemical Z.					
4. Pour Chemical Z into 500 one-gallon containers.					
5. Package the one-gallon containers into cases.					

Exhibit 9.6

Determining the Critical Path Based on a Sequence of Production Tasks

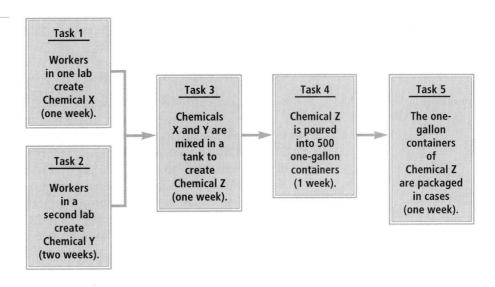

critical path the path that takes the longest time to complete

ical Y (Task 2) can be conducted simultaneously. The mixing of Chemicals X and Y (Task 3) cannot begin until Tasks 1 and 2 are completed.

Each sequence of tasks is referred to as a path. For example, the sequence of Tasks 1, 3, 4, and 5 represents one path. A second path is the sequence of Tasks 2, 3, 4, and 5. The accumulated time for this path is five weeks. The **critical path** is the path that takes the longest time to complete. In our example, the critical path is the sequence of Tasks 2, 3, 4, and 5; that path takes five weeks. It is important to determine the time necessary to complete the steps within the critical path, since the production process will take that long.

Identifying the critical path and calculating the time it requires allows managers to estimate the slack time (extra time) on the other paths and reduce any inefficiencies that can be caused by that slack time. The five-week period has no slack time for the workers involved in the critical path. Since the other path in Exhibit 9.6 has a completion time of four weeks, it has slack time of one week over a five-week period. Therefore, some of the workers assigned to Task 1 may be assigned to help with the second task of the critical path sequence. This may reduce the time necessary to complete the critical path.

The tasks that are part of the critical path should be reviewed to avoid delays or increase production speed. Tasks estimated to take a long time are closely monitored because any delays in these tasks are more likely to cause a severe delay in the entire production process. Furthermore, firms attempt to determine whether these tasks can be performed more quickly so that the critical path is completed in less time.

Managers who oversee special projects recognize that the time necessary for each task may be uncertain. For this reason, they may estimate the longest time for each task to be completed. The critical path represents the sum of the longest times for each task and therefore measures the maximum length of time in which the project would be completed. In our previous example, the expected time of the project was five weeks, but the worst-case time might be seven weeks. That is, the project should be completed in five weeks, but it could take as long as seven weeks if any problems occur (employees call in sick, equipment breaks, and so on). Thus, the managers overseeing the project may guarantee to the customer that the product will be ready in seven weeks. They would be less willing to guarantee five weeks because conditions could delay the production schedule.

Quality Control

quality the degree to which a product or service satisfies a customer's requirements or expectations

Quality can be defined as the degree to which a product or service satisfies a customer's requirements or expectations. Quality relates to customer satisfaction, which can have an effect on future sales and therefore on the future performance of the firm. Customers are more likely to purchase additional products from the same firm if they are satisfied with the quality. Firms now realize that it is easier to retain existing customers than it is to attract new customers who are unfamiliar with their products or services. Thus, firms are increasingly recognizing the impact that the quality of their products or services can have on their overall performance.

quality control a process of determining whether the quality of a product meets the desired quality level

Quality control is a process of determining whether the quality of a product or a service meets the desired quality level and identifying improvements (if any) that need to be made in the production process. Quality can be measured by assessing the various characteristics (such as how long the product lasts) that enhance customer satisfaction. The quality of a computer may be defined by how well it works and how long it lasts. Quality may also be measured by how easy the computer is to use or by how quickly the manufacturer repairs a computer that experiences problems. All of these characteristics can affect customer satisfaction and therefore should be considered as indicators of quality.

The quality of services sold to customers must also be assessed. For example, Amazon.com produces a service of fulfilling orders of books, CDs, and other products ordered over the Internet by customers. Its customers assess the quality of the service in terms of the ease with which they can send an order over the Internet, whether they receive the proper order, and how quickly the products are delivered.

total quality management (TQM) the act of monitoring and improving the quality of products and services provided

The act of monitoring and improving the quality of products and services produced is commonly referred to as **total quality management (TQM),** which was developed by W. Edwards Deming. Among TQM's key guidelines for improving quality are the following: (1) provide managers and

A quality control inspector tests washing machines at the AEG/Electrolux factory in Germany.

Getty Images/ Sean Gallup

cross functional teamwork:

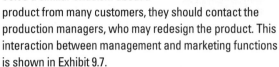

Interaction of Functions Involved in Total Quality Management

Total quality management requires an ongoing product assessment, beginning from the time product materials are ordered and continuing until the customer has purchased and used the product. Consequently, TQM requires an interaction of business functions. The key management functions involved in TQM are ordering the proper types and amounts of supplies, achieving efficient (low-cost) production of the product, and ensuring that the product satisfies the firm's production standards.

The key marketing functions involved in TQM are achieving efficient use of marketing strategies, ensuring customer satisfaction, and obtaining feedback from customers on how to improve the product. When marketing managers receive a similar criticism about a product from many customers, they should contact the production managers, who may redesign the product. This interaction between management and marketing functions is shown in Exhibit 9.7.

The financing function is indirectly affected, as changes in expenses or revenue resulting from TQM may alter the amount of new financing that the firm needs.

Exhibit 9.7

Interaction between Management and Marketing Functions When Implementing Total Quality Management

Management Functions

- **Ordering supplies (inventory management)**
- **Achieving efficient production**
- **Ensuring production standards**

Product is properly produced

Provide feedback on how to improve product

Marketing Functions

- **Achieving efficient use of marketing strategies**
- **Ensuring customer satisfaction**
- **Obtaining customers' suggestions for improvement**

Product is properly marketed and sold

other employees with the education and training they need to excel in their jobs, (2) encourage employees to take responsibility and to provide leadership, and (3) encourage all employees to search for ways to improve the production process. Production quotas are discouraged so that employees can allocate more of their time to leadership and the improvement of the production process. Many firms use teams of employees to assess quality and offer suggestions for continuous improvement.

To ensure that quality is maintained, firms periodically evaluate the methods used to measure product or service quality. They rely on various techniques to assess quality, as described next.

Control by Technology Motorola and many other firms use computers to assess quality. The computers can determine whether each component of a product meets specific quality standards. Computer-controlled machinery has electronic sensors that can screen out defective parts.

global business

Global Quality Standards Firms that conduct international business may attempt to satisfy a set of global quality standards. These standards have been established by the International Standards Organization (ISO), which includes representatives from numerous countries. Firms are not required to meet these standards. By voluntarily meeting them, however, a firm can become certified, which may boost its credibility when selling products to foreign customers, who may be more comfortable if the firm has met the standards.

The certification process commonly costs at least $20,000 and takes at least one year. The standards focus on the design, manufacturing process, installation, and service of a product. Independent auditors review the firm's operations and decide whether to certify the firm. A publication called ISO 9000 specifies the standards for production quality. Another set of standards (called ISO 14000) applies to the environmental effects of the production process.

Firms may also have to meet other standards to sell their products in specific foreign countries. For example, the Japanese government assesses any products that are sold in Japan to ensure that they are safe. Japan's safety standards have discouraged firms based in the United States and other countries from attempting to sell products in Japan. Thus, the standards may serve as a barrier that protects local firms in Japan from foreign competitors.

Dell Computer uses custom configurations to ensure a high level of product quality and thereby fulfill its responsibility to its customers. It relies on its computer network to track its products from the point of initial sales contact to the time the product was sent to the customer, and beyond. Specifically, for a given order, Dell knows the date of the initial query by the customer, the date the order was placed, the date the order was delivered, the dates technical support was requested, and the types of support that were provided. This tracking system offers several benefits. First, Dell can determine the speed at which it fills an order. Second, it has a history of its communications with the customer in case any dispute arises. Third, from the technical support communications, Dell can determine the type of support that was needed. When Dell redesigns its computers in the future, it can take these requests for support into consideration.

Control by Employees Firms also use their employees to assess quality. One person may be assigned to assess components at each stage of the assembly line. Alternatively, a team of employees may be responsible for assessing the quality of products at different stages of the production process. Many firms such as IBM and DaimlerChrysler use a **quality control circle,** which is a group of employees who assess the quality of a product and offer suggestions for improvement. Quality control circles usually allow for more interaction among workers and managers and provide workers with a sense of responsibility.

quality control circle a group of employees who assess the quality of a product and offer suggestions for improvement

Control by Sampling Firms also assess quality by **sampling,** or randomly selecting some of the products produced and testing them to determine whether they satisfy the quality standards. Firms may check one unit per 100 units produced and concentrate specifically on possible flaws that have been detected in previous checks.

sampling randomly selecting some of the products produced and testing them to determine whether they satisfy the quality standards

Control by Monitoring Complaints Quality should be assessed not only when the product is produced but also after it is sold. Some quality deficiencies may not become evident until after customers use the products. The quality of products that have been sold can be assessed by monitoring the proportion of products returned or by tracking customer complaints. Additional customer feedback can be obtained by conducting surveys. Firms can obtain customers' opinions on product quality by sending them a survey months after the sale. For example, Saturn and Toyota commonly survey their customers to determine the level of customer satisfaction. The survey can also ask for feedback on the quality of specific parts or functions of the product. Such surveys tend to be more useful if they ask separate questions about the various aspects that make up quality, including the product itself, its sale, and its servicing.

Correcting Deficiencies   The purpose of the quality control process is not only to detect quality deficiencies but also to correct them. If quality is deficient, the problem was likely caused by one of the following factors: inadequate materials provided by suppliers, inadequate quality of work by employees, or malfunctioning machinery or equipment.

   If inadequate materials caused the quality deficiency, the firm may require the existing supplier to improve the quality or may obtain materials from a different supplier in the future. If the cause is the work of employees, the firm may need to retrain or reprimand those employees. If the cause of quality deficiency is the machinery, the firm may need to to replace the machinery or make repairs.

College Health Club: **Total Quality Management at CHC**

One of the decisions that Sue Kramer needs to make as part of her business plan for College Health Club (CHC) is how to monitor quality. Sue recognizes that CHC will be successful only if its members are satisfied with the health club services it provides. Sue plans to achieve continuous improvement by requesting feedback from CHC's members. She will make survey cards available that ask for members' opinions of the types of weight and exercise machines that are provided, the aerobics classes, and other services. She will record the survey responses and attempt to correct any deficiency that is mentioned.

5

Describe the key factors that affect production efficiency.

production efficiency the ability to produce products at a low cost

benchmarking a method of evaluating performance by comparison to some specified (benchmark) level, typically a level achieved by another company

METHODS TO IMPROVE PRODUCTION EFFICIENCY

Firms strive to increase their **production efficiency,** which reflects a lower cost for a given amount of output and a given level of quality. Managers continually search for ways to manage human and other resources in a manner that improves production efficiency. Firms recognize the need to continually improve because other competitors may become more efficient and take their business away.

   Production efficiency is important to service firms as well as manufacturing firms. For example, airlines need to be efficient in their service of flying passengers from one location to another so that they can achieve low expenses.

   Many firms that set production efficiency goals use **benchmarking,** which is a method of evaluating performance by comparison to some specified (benchmark) level—typically, a level achieved by another company. For example, a firm may set a goal of producing baseball caps at a cost of $3 per cap, which is the average cost incurred by the most successful producer of baseball caps.

increasing value with technology

AGILE MANUFACTURING

Many experts believe we are about to enter a new era in manufacturing: the era of mass customization. What distinguishes mass customization from today's mass production is that factory products will no longer consist of multiple copies of the same item. Instead, product specifications will be fed through information pipelines, and factory equipment will reconfigure itself to produce the exact product desired. Further, experts predict that these customized products will cost about the same as today's mass-produced equivalent.

The techniques needed to create such factories of the future are collectively grouped under the heading of *agile manufacturing* and will depend heavily on information technology. Optical scanning systems combined with telecommunications will be used to get product specifications into the plant. Computer-aided design and computer-aided manufacturing (CAD/CAM) represent the next step. Product specifications, scanned in or drawn by operators, will be translated into instructions for industrial robots and computer-controlled machinery. These pieces of equipment

have great flexibility. Rather than performing a single set of repetitive motions, suitable only for doing the same task over and over again, the equipment will be able to engage in many different activities. This variety of activities will allow a variety of products to be produced.

The U.S. economy is already experiencing some of the benefits of agile manufacturing. A valve maker in Georgia uses CAD/CAM technology to produce customized valves for customers in under three days. In the textile business, agile factories in the United States are able to quickly produce small lots of specialized fabrics to order.

In the near future, agile factories may be the norm in U.S. manufacturing. Experts warn, however, that such factories will not necessarily translate into new manufacturing jobs. The key to achieving agility is automation, so the labor required to run such plants will be limited. Substantial growth, however, is expected in the high-tech jobs associated with designing, building, and maintaining the equipment used in these factories.

---

stretch targets production efficiency targets (or goals) that cannot be achieved under present conditions

The top managers of some firms set production efficiency targets (or goals) that cannot be achieved under present conditions. These targets are referred to as **stretch targets** because they are stretched beyond the ordinary. Stretch targets may be established in response to a decline in the firm's market share or performance. For example, 3M Company created a stretch target that 30 percent of its sales should be derived from sales of products created in the last four years. This target was intended to encourage more development of new products so that 3M did not rely on its innovations from several years ago.

Firms can improve production efficiency through the following methods:

▶ Technology

▶ Economies of scale

▶ Restructuring

Each of these methods is discussed in turn.

Technology

Firms may improve their production efficiency by adopting new technology. New machinery that incorporates improved technology can perform tasks more quickly.

automated tasks are completed by machines without the use of employees

Many production processes have become **automated,** whereby tasks are completed by machines without the use of employees. Since machinery can be less costly than human resources, automation may improve production efficiency. Guidelines for effective automation are summarized in Exhibit 9.8.

Exhibit 9.8

Guidelines for Effective Automation

> To effectively capitalize on the potential benefits from automation, the following guidelines should be considered:
>
> 1. *Plan.* Automation normally does not simply speed up work; instead, it may require the elimination of some production steps. Planning is necessary to decide what type of automation will be most appropriate (computers versus other machinery).
>
> 2. *Use Automation Where the Benefits Are Greatest.* It may not be efficient to evenly allocate automation among all parts of the production process. Some workers will not be able to use a computer for their type of work.
>
> 3. *Train.* To make sure that the automation implemented is effectively utilized, any workers who use new computers or machinery should be trained.
>
> 4. *Evaluate Costs and Benefits over Time.* By assessing the costs and benefits of automation, a firm can decide whether to implement additional automation or revise its existing automation.

Many firms such as Albertson's (a grocery chain) and Home Depot have improved production efficiency with the use of computer technology. For example, computers can keep track of the daily or weekly volume of each type of product that is purchased at the cash register of a retail store. Therefore, the firm does not need an employee to monitor the inventory of these products. The computer may even be programmed to automatically reorder some products once the inventory is reduced to a specified level. Some hospitals use pharmacy robots that stock and retrieve drugs. This technology increases production without additional labor expenses. Numerous manufacturing firms are using more powerful computers that have increased the speed at which various tasks can be completed.

Economies of Scale

economies of scale as the quantity produced increases, the cost per unit decreases

fixed costs operating expenses that do not change in response to the number of products produced

variable costs operating expenses that vary directly with the number of products produced

Firms may also be able to reduce costs by achieving **economies of scale,** which reflect a lower average cost incurred from producing a larger volume. To recognize how economies of scale can occur, consider that two types of costs are involved in the production of a product: fixed costs and variable costs. **Fixed costs** are operating expenses that do not change in response to the number of products produced. For example, the cost of renting a specific factory is not affected by the number of products produced there.

Variable costs are operating expenses that vary directly with the number of products produced. As output increases, the variable costs increase, but the fixed costs remain constant. The average cost per unit typically declines as output increases for firms that incur large fixed costs.

Automobile manufacturers incur a large fixed cost because they have to pay for their large facilities (including all the machinery) even if they do not produce many cars. Therefore, they need to produce a large number of cars to reduce the average cost per car produced.

College Health Club: **Economies of Scale at CHC**

In developing her business plan for College Health Club (CHC), Sue Kramer needs to ensure that she can produce health club services efficiently. By doing so, she can keep expenses low. If CHC is efficient, it will serve a relatively large number of customers at a low cost. Many of CHC's expenses are fixed, meaning that they will not change regardless of the number of members. For example, the rent per month will be the same no matter how many members use the club. Therefore, CHC can achieve production efficiency by providing its services to a large number of members. The cost of providing these services per member can be reduced by increasing the membership.

Sue will attempt to increase the production efficiency of her aerobics classes by offering them at times when more potential customers will want to take them. That way she can increase the number of memberships. In addition, she plans to offer prospective customers a free one-day pass to try the weight and exercise machines. By increasing membership, she will be able to provide services to more members without increasing the cost, thereby achieving economies of scale.

Exhibit 9.9

Relationship between Production Volume and Costs

Quantity of Books Produced	Fixed Cost	Variable Cost ($2 per Unit)	Total Cost	Average Cost per Unit
1,000	$40,000	$2,000	$42,000	$42.00
3,000	40,000	6,000	46,000	15.33
5,000	40,000	10,000	50,000	10.00
10,000	40,000	20,000	60,000	6.00
15,000	40,000	30,000	70,000	4.67
20,000	40,000	40,000	80,000	4.00
25,000	40,000	50,000	90,000	3.60

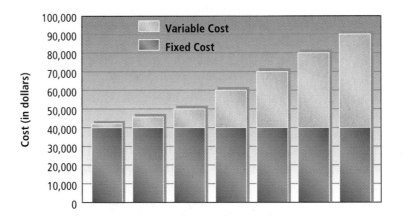

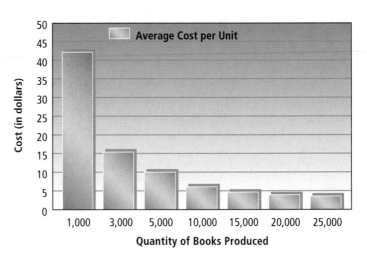

Consider the production of a paperback book that requires some materials (ink and paper) and some manual labor. Assume that a printing company incurs a fixed cost (rent plus machinery) of $40,000 per month. These expenses exist regardless of the number of books printed. Assume that the variable cost of producing each book is $2 per book. The total cost of producing books each month is equal to the fixed cost plus the variable cost. The total cost is estimated for various production levels in Exhibit 9.9. The key measure of production efficiency is the average cost per unit, which is measured as the total cost divided by the number of units produced. Notice how the average cost declines when the production volume increases. This relationship exists because the fixed cost is not affected by the production volume. Therefore, the fixed costs can be spread over a larger production volume. No extra fixed cost is incurred when producing additional products.

Assume that each of the books produced can be sold for $10. Exhibit 9.10 shows the total revenue and total costs for various quantities of books produced. The total revenue is equal to the quantity produced times the price of $10 per book. The profits represent the difference between the total revenue and the total cost. Notice that the firm experiences losses at

Exhibit 9.10

Relationship between Volume and Profitability

Quantity of Books Produced	Total Revenue (= Quantity × Price)	Total Cost	Profits
1,000	$10,000	$42,000	−$32,000
3,000	30,000	46,000	−$16,000
5,000	50,000	50,000	$0
10,000	100,000	60,000	$40,000
15,000	150,000	70,000	$80,000
20,000	200,000	80,000	$120,000
25,000	250,000	90,000	$160,000

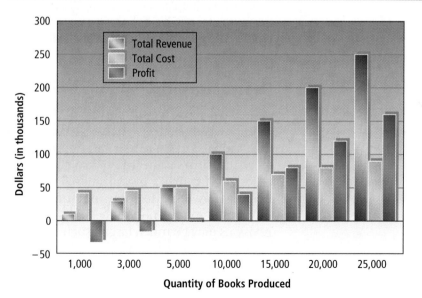

break-even point the quantity of units sold at which total revenue equals total cost

small quantities. This is because the fixed costs are incurred even though the production volume is low. At the quantity level of 5,000 books, the total revenue is equal to the total cost. The quantity of units sold at which total revenue equals total cost is referred to as the **break-even point.** At any quantity beyond 5,000 books, the firm earns profits. The profits are larger for larger quantities produced. This results from the lower average cost incurred from the production of more books.

Some firms strive to achieve a large market share so that they can achieve economies of scale. For example, Dell Computer typically sets a goal to obtain a substantial market share for each of its products. This results in a large production volume so that Dell can achieve economies of scale. One of the largest expenses in the production of computers is the research and development to improve the computers. That expense is incurred whether Dell sells only 20 computers or 50,000 computers. Therefore, the average cost per unit is reduced when Dell produces a large amount of a specific computer.

College Health Club: **Average Cost at CHC**

Sue Kramer wants to ensure that CHC is efficiently managed. Since CHC's expenses are mostly fixed, she recognizes the importance of generating economies of scale. She wants to determine the average cost per member served for various possible levels of membership. Since she expects CHC's total expenses over the first year to be $142,000, she estimates the cost per member served as follows:

Impact of Membership Size on CHC's Average Cost per Member

	If 280 Members Join in the First Year	If 300 Members Join in the First Year	If 320 Members Join in the First Year
(1) Total cost	$142,000	$142,000	$142,000
(2) Number of members	280	300	320
(3) Cost per member = (1)/(2)	$507	$473	$444

If 280 members join, the average cost to CHC per member is $507, which exceeds the annual membership fee of $500. The higher the membership, the lower the average cost to CHC per member. This is why it is so important to attract a large membership at CHC.

Restructuring

restructuring the revision of the production process in an attempt to improve efficiency

reengineering the redesign of a firm's organizational structure and operations

Restructuring involves the revision of the production process in an attempt to improve efficiency. When restructuring reduces the expense of producing products or services, it can improve the firm's profits and therefore increase the firm's value. Many firms also engage in **reengineering,** which is the redesign of a firm's organizational structure and operations. The reengineering may result in some minor revisions, such as changes in the procedures used to take phone messages or to send packages. Alternatively, the revisions may be much larger, such as a new facility or a new assembly-line operation for production.

Reengineering requires that the company forget the old way of doing things and attempt to build the best system from scratch. Delta Air Lines, Hallmark, and many other firms have used reengineering. It requires the efforts of many different types of managers within the firm who are willing to think about the optimal method for production without being forced to focus on the method that is currently being used. Reengineering is normally conducted by obtaining input from employees who understand how the production process works. These employees are likely to recognize any inefficient parts of the process that should be eliminated or revised.

Downsizing

downsizing a reduction in the number of employees

Downsizing When firms restructure, they also typically engage in **downsizing;** that is, they reduce the number of employees. Firms identify various job positions that can be eliminated without affecting the volume or the quality of products produced. Some downsizing occurs as a result of technology because automated production processes replace human resources (as explained earlier). However, numerous firms downsize even when they have no plans to further automate their production process.

In recent years, SBC Communications, American Airlines, Procter & Gamble, Boeing, IBM, and numerous other firms have cut thousands of jobs. A reduction in employees results in a reduction in salary expense. For large firms that eliminate thousands of jobs, the cost savings can exceed $100 million per year. If the jobs can be cut without any other adverse effects, $100 million per year in cost savings should result in an additional $100 million in profit.

corporate anorexia the problem that occurs when firms become so obsessed with eliminating their inefficient components that they downsize too much

Downsizing also has its disadvantages, however. First, costs may be associated with the elimination of job positions, such as costs incurred to find other job positions within the firm or outside it for the employees whose jobs were cut. Second, costs may be associated with training some of the remaining employees whose responsibilities were expanded. Third, if the remaining employees believe their own positions may be cut, their morale may decline, reducing their performance. Fourth, downsizing may result in lower quality, as the remaining employees may be assigned more work and may not detect defects in the production process. Some firms become so obsessed with eliminating their inefficient components that they downsize too much. This is referred to as **corporate anorexia.**

Integration of the Production Tasks

supply chain the process from the beginning of the production process until the product reaches the customer

The production process described in this chapter consists of related tasks, such that each task can be accomplished only after other tasks have been completed. Thus, if any production task breaks down, the entire production schedule is affected. Furthermore, firms are unable to deliver their products to stores or to customers until all production tasks are completed. Therefore, firms monitor the so-called **supply chain,** or the process from the very beginning of the production process until the product reaches the consumer. Firms that produce products identify a site for production, hire employees, set up work stations, and determine the design and layout that will ensure efficient production. To recognize the integration required, consider the following example:

▶ After an automobile manufacturer identifies a site for production—a manufacturing plant where automobiles are to be produced—it hires employees and assigns them to assembly lines.

▶ Machinery and tools (such as special wrenches) are placed along the assembly lines to help the employees assemble the automobiles.

▶ Materials (including steering wheels, seat cushions, engines, and tires) are delivered to different parts of the assembly line so that they can be installed during the production process. The design and layout are structured so that one task is completed before the automobile frame is moved to the next station on the assembly line, and so on. For example, the dashboard may be inserted at one station and the doors and windshield attached at the next station. The dashboard is installed first because inserting a dashboard is more difficult after the doors have been attached.

▶ A sufficient inventory of materials is ordered to accommodate the scheduled production.

▶ Tasks are scheduled so that each person who is assigned a task on the assembly line has enough time to complete it before the automobile frame is moved to the next station. Too much time should not be allocated for a specific task, however, because that would reduce the production volume.

▶ The quality control process takes place at different stations along the assembly line to ensure that each part of the production process is completed according to standards.

How Breakdowns Disrupt the Production Process   To ensure that you understand how the production tasks are integrated, identify the breakdowns that could cause the entire production process to be slowed. This can be accomplished by reviewing the sequence of tasks in order. First, the machinery used by employees in the production process could break down. Does the firm have substitute machinery or tools, or can it quickly purchase new machinery? If it takes a week to replace a machine, a breakdown could disrupt the entire production process for a week. If the dashboard cannot be installed due to a breakdown in machinery, continuing production would be difficult because the dashboard is more easily inserted before some other tasks are completed, as explained earlier.

Second, what if materials needed at different stations along the assembly line do not arrive on time? What if there is no extra inventory of these materials? The production may be stalled. If the manufacturer can easily find an alternative supplier of the materials, the production process is less vulnerable to major problems. If dashboards or other materials are custom-made, however, it may be difficult to find substitutes quickly.

What if some of the employees who were assigned tasks on the assembly line are ill or quit? If the tasks can be done by other employees, the production process may not be disrupted very much. However, the manufacturer can reduce potential problems by having some employees on call in the event that they are needed.

What if the quality control process determines that one specific task needs to be redone? This will disrupt the production process because that task may need to be done properly before the other tasks can be completed. In fact, it is important to catch any production problems when they occur so that the disruption is limited. For example, fixing an incorrectly inserted dashboard is easier before the doors and the windshield are installed.

The integration of tasks is not limited to assembly-line production. Firms such as Motorola, Johnson & Johnson, General Dynamics, and AT&T focus on coordinating all their production tasks in a manner that minimizes production cost while maintaining high quality. In fact, these firms frequently restructure their production process, continually searching for more efficient ways to produce their products.

Integration of Tasks at Service Firms   Even service firms use a production process that is integrated and therefore requires that the tasks described in this chapter are completed in a specific order. For example,

Amazon.com hires employees to produce the service of fulfilling orders made by customers over a website. The production process for Amazon.com involves forecasting the future demand for books, ordering a sufficient number of each book to satisfy demand in a future period, storing books at warehouses, receiving orders, fulfilling orders, and ensuring that customers receive quality service (such as quick delivery). If Amazon.com does not order a sufficient amount of books relative to the amount customers order, it will not be able to accommodate all of the demand. Alternatively, if it has a sufficient inventory of the books but does not have enough employees and computer facilities to fulfill the orders, the production process will be disrupted.

SUMMARY

1 The key resources used for production are human resources, materials, and other resources (such as the plant, machinery, and equipment).

2 The plant site decision is influenced by

▶ cost of workplace space,

▶ cost of labor,

▶ tax incentives,

▶ source of demand for the product produced,

▶ access to transportation, and

▶ supply of labor.

A site evaluation matrix can be used to assign a rating to each relevant factor and derive a total rating for each possible site.

3 The design and layout of a plant are influenced by the

▶ site characteristics,

▶ production process,

▶ product line, and

▶ desired production capacity.

4 Production control involves

▶ purchasing materials, which requires selecting a supplier, negotiating volume discounts, and possibly delegating production to suppliers;

▶ inventory control, which involves managing various inventories at levels that minimize costs;

▶ routing, which determines the sequence of tasks necessary to complete production;

▶ scheduling, which sets time periods for the tasks required within the production process; and

▶ quality control, which can be used to identify improvements (if any) that need to be made in the production process.

5 The key methods used to improve production efficiency are

▶ technology, which increases the speed of the production process;

▶ economies of scale, which reduce the average cost per unit as a result of a higher production volume; and

▶ restructuring, which is a revision of the production process to reduce production expenses.

KEY TERMS

Review & Critical Thinking Questions

1. If you were a plant manager, what primary resources would you use for production?

2. Explain the use of work stations and assembly lines.

3. You are moving your plant from the West Coast to the East Coast. What key location factors should be considered?

4. What general factors influence design and layout decisions?

5. What is e-procurement? How can e-procurement benefit a firm?

6. List the five tasks involved in production control.

7. What is outsourcing? What are the advantages and disadvantages of outsourcing?

8. What is deintegration? How can it benefit a manufacturer?

9. Compare just-in-time (JIT) inventory with materials requirements planning (MRP).

10. What is production scheduling? Why is a production schedule so important for a manager?

11. Define PERT. Explain what steps are involved with PERT. Why is it necessary to identify the critical path when working on a project?

12. Define and explain quality control.

13. What is total quality management (TQM)? Briefly summarize the key guidelines for improving quality under TQM.

14. Briefly summarize the methods used by firms to improve production efficiency.

15. Define downsizing and restructuring. How are the two related?

Discussion Questions

1. Would production management apply to a professional basketball team? How?

2. What is hotelling? Can you think of any disadvantages associated with hotelling?

3. Assume that you are a project manager for a large construction company. You have been given an assignment to develop a schedule for the construction of a skyscraper. Discuss how you would develop and implement a schedule.

4. How could a firm use the Internet to provide information on its production management function? How could it use the Internet to provide information on its production control?

5. Assume that your company plans to relocate its plant to a new region and has assigned you to select the new location. What factors would you consider in making the decision?

6. What type of layout is appropriate for each of the following:

(a) an aircraft manufacturer, such as Boeing; (b) an automotive plant for a firm such as General Motors; (c) a contractor engaged in new housing construction?

7. You are a manager at a software manufacturer. Describe how the different sources of control may apply to your company.

It's Your Decision: **Production Decisions at CHC**

1. The cost of land is much higher in the middle of the city than it is on the outskirts of the city where College Health Club (CHC) is located. How does this affect CHC's expenses?

2. What trade-off is involved in determining the size of the facilities for CHC?

3. CHC can purchase vitamin supplements at a discount if it orders a case of 300 units. It will earn a higher profit per unit when selling the vitamins to its members if it receives that discount. What would be a disadvantage to CHC of buying a large amount of vitamins?

4. Explain why CHC's marketing plan can have an impact on the size of the facilities the club needs.

5. Recall that CHC expects total expenses of $142,000 in the first year. It will set the membership fee at $500 and expects to attract 300 members in its first year. It could rent another unit for an extra $12,000 per year. The extra unit may attract additional members because of the added space. Determine CHC's earnings before taxes in the first year if this extra unit is rented and results in:
   a) A total of 314 memberships in the first year.
   b) A total of 320 memberships in the first year.
   c) If the unit will result in 320 memberships in the first year, would you recommend that CHC rent the unit?

6. How can the quality of the service provided by CHC be measured?

7. How should CHC decide what factors to assess when monitoring the quality of the services that it provides?

8. Assume that CHC's members view five key characteristics as important. Can Sue Kramer monitor quality by monitoring the average rating of those five characteristics? Or should she monitor the rating of each individual characteristic? Explain.

9. CHC uses the marketing function to identify health club services that will generate memberships. It then produces the health club services that it believes are desired by potential members. Explain how CHC's focus on quality is related to production and marketing.

10. Recall that CHC expects total expenses of $142,000 (operating expenses = $138,000 and interest expenses = $4,000) in the first year. It will set its membership fee at $500 and expects to attract 300 members in its first year. Determine the number of memberships at which CHC will break even under the following conditions:
   a) Under prevailing conditions in which the expected total operating expenses are $138,000.
   b) Operating expenses are $146,000 and interest expenses are $4,000.
   c) Operating expenses are $142,000 and interest expenses are $4,000.
   d) Explain the relationship between the total expenses and the break-even level of memberships. How would the break-even level be affected if Sue had rented a smaller facility for her health club? What would be a disadvantage of a smaller facility?

11. A health club differs from manufacturing firms in that it produces a service rather than products. Explain the similarity between the quality control of a service versus a product. Are there any differences between the quality control of a service versus a product?

Investing in a Business

Using the annual report of the firm in which you would like to invest, complete the following:

1 Describe (in general terms) the firm's production process. What products are produced? Where are the production facilities located? Are the facilities concentrated in one location or scattered?

2 Have the firm's operations been restructured in recent years to improve efficiency? If so, how?

3 Does your firm need to consider labor supply issues when selecting a site?

4 Explain how the business uses technology to promote its production management function. For ex-

ample, does it use the Internet to provide information about its production management function? Does it provide information regarding the methods used to control production?

5 Does the firm appear to pay attention to customer satisfaction? Explain.

6 Has the firm improved the quality of its products or services in recent years? If so, how?

7 Go to **http://hoovers.com** and locate the NEWS SEARCH. Type in the name of the firm in the space provided, and review the recent news stories about the firm. Summarize any (at least one) recent news story about the firm that applies to one or more of the key concepts in this chapter.

Case: Selecting the Best Plant Site

Richard Capozzi, an entrepreneur in the high-fashion Italian shoe industry, is planning to relocate his manufacturing operation to the western part of the United States. He is currently considering two different locations. One possible location is outside Los Angeles, and the other is in Oklahoma City.

In analyzing the plant site decision, he is considering several factors. The cost of land is high in Los Angeles. However, local government officials are willing to make tax concessions. This plant location is accessible to transportation; a railroad is adjacent to the plant and an eight-lane interstate is close. Capozzi has identified the West Coast region as his target market for this type of shoe. An artist by trade, he has developed a unique design that should create mass-market appeal in this geographic area.

The Oklahoma City location has several advantages. Land cost is lower than in Los Angeles. Also, a large supply of trained labor is available in this region.

Another key consideration Capozzi must deal with is raw material availability. The raw material is imported

from Italy and is received at the port of entry in Los Angeles. If the operation were located in Oklahoma City, additional ground transportation would be necessary. Transportation costs would, therefore, be lower for the Los Angeles plant, a fact that weighs heavily in Capozzi's decision.

Questions

1 What will influence the plant site decision for Capozzi, and which alternative appears to be optimal?

2 How can each relative factor be rated or evaluated to determine the optimal plant location?

3 How should the decision regarding plant layout and design be determined?

4 What resources will Capozzi need to implement the production plan?

5 Describe the sources to assess quality and how they might apply to a shoe manufacturer.

6 Do you think this particular type of operation could benefit from economies of scale? Explain.

Video Case: Production Management at Vermont Teddy Bear Company

The Vermont Teddy Bear Company produces and delivers hand-crafted teddy bears. Once the demand for teddy bears has been forecasted, the factory purchases enough materials to produce sufficient production volume to satisfy demand. The firm creates a production schedule for cutting and sewing the materials and then monitors the production on a daily basis to ensure that it is on schedule. When the company wants to produce unusually large amounts of teddy bears, it outsources some of the sewing to people who are temporarily hired to do the work at their own residences. At each stage in the pro-

duction process, the teddy bears are checked to make sure that they are not flawed.

Questions

1. How can the firm benefit from outsourcing some of its production during periods of very high demand rather than hiring workers permanently?

2. How does the firm monitor quality control?

3. How is the production volume determined? Would production volume be higher than normal in the months before Christmas? Why?

Internet Applications

1. *http://www.designmgt.org/dmi/html/index.htm*

Describe some of the recent design innovations in manufacturing that are described on this website. Do you think their adoption would benefit manufacturing companies? What research is conducted by Design Management? How is this research useful for a manufacturer that is trying to choose between a fixed-position layout and flexible manufacturing?

2. *http://www.sitelocationassistance.com/free.htm*

How is site selection defined on this website? What factors influence site selection? What steps are described in

the tool kits that a company should follow in selecting a site?

3. *http://www.quality.nist.gov/*

Read the history of the Baldridge National Quality Program and briefly summarize it. What is the program's purpose? How can a firm benefit from the program? How could a firm use total quality management (TQM) to qualify for the Baldridge National Quality Award? List some recent recipients of the award.

The Coca-Cola Company Annual Report Project

Questions for the current year's annual report are available on the text website at **http://madura.swlearning.com.**

The following questions apply concepts presented in this chapter to The Coca-Cola Company. Go to The Coca-Cola Company website (**http://www.cocacola.com**) and find the index for the 2001 annual report.

Questions

1. Download the financial statements and find the "Investments" section. How does The Coca-Cola Company ensure the availability of its products on a global basis?

2. Study the "Selected Market Results" section under "Operations Review." How might a trucking strike

in a particular geographic area affect The Coca-Cola Company's production?

3. Study the "Selected Market Results" section under "Operations Review." In which country do you think The Coca-Cola Company should plan to build new plants over the next five years? What do you think the advantages are of opening a plant in that country versus exporting to that country?

4. Go to **http://hoovers.com** and locate the NEWS CENTER. Key in The Coca-Cola Company in the space provided, click on "Search," and review the recent news stories about the firm. Summarize any (at least one) recent news story about The Coca-Cola Company that applies one or more of the key concepts within this chapter of the text.

In-Text Study Guide

Answers are in an appendix at the back of the book.

True or False

1. A work station is an area in which one or more employees is assigned a specific task. T

2. Design and layout decisions will have an impact on operating expenses. T

3. A fixed-position layout is commonly used for assembly-line production. F

4. Hotelling represents the sequence of tasks necessary to complete the production of a product. F

5. A firm uses outsourcing so that it can hire additional employees. F

6. The term "just-in-time" refers to a schedule that illustrates the expected timing for each task within a project. F

7. Inventories of partially completed products are called work-in-process. T

8. The critical path is the path that takes the shortest time to complete on a PERT diagram. F

9. Quality control can be measured by assessing the various characteristics that enhance customer satisfaction. T

10. Downsizing has enabled firms to reduce the amount of salary expense required. T

Multiple Choice

11. The goal of _____ is to develop an efficient, high-quality process for producing products or services.
    a) conversion management
    b) assembly-line control
    c) flexible manufacturing
    d) production management
    e) routing

12. A _____ represents a series of tasks in which resources are used to produce a product or service.
    a) layout chart
    b) Venn diagram
    c) organization chart

d) production process
e) chain of command

13. A sequence of work stations in which each work station is designed to cover specific phases of the production process is called a(n):
    a) assembly line.
    b) hotelling.
    c) deintegration.
    d) product location.
    e) Gantt chart.

14. The factors that affect a site decision include all of the following except:
    a) cost of workplace space.
    b) tax incentives.
    c) source of demand.
    d) access to transportation.
    e) quality assurance.

15. Once a site for the manufacturing plant is chosen, the next step to be determined is:
    a) design and layout.
    b) production control.
    c) hotelling.
    d) deintegration.
    e) inventory control.

16. All of the following characteristics influence design and layout decisions except the:
    a) production process.
    b) desired production capacity.
    c) product line.
    d) purchasing applications.
    e) site.

17. Which of the following production processes is most commonly used for assembly-line production?
    a) flexible manufacturing
    b) fixed-position layout
    c) product layout
    d) capacity layout
    e) cost-benefit layout

In-Text Study Guide

Answers are in an appendix at the back of the book.

18. A production process where employees go to the position of the product, rather than waiting for the product to come to them, is a(n):
    a) assembly line.
    b) batch process.
    c) fixed-position layout.
    d) unit production process.
    e) mass production process.

19. Firms are forced to search for new sites once demand for their product exceeds their:
    a) quality control.
    b) production capacity.
    c) inspection requirements.
    d) routing schedules.
    e) purchase plans.

20. The development of temporary, shared office space for those employees who normally work at home is called:
    a) flexible manufacturing.
    b) deintegration.
    c) production control.
    d) hotelling.
    e) quality control.

21. All of the following are key tasks in production control except:
    a) layout and design.
    b) inventory control.
    c) routing.
    d) scheduling.
    e) quality control.

22. A company that makes use of a(n) _____ can detect the existing level of supplies and automatically reorder when supplies fall to a specific level.
    a) e-procurement system
    b) e-inventory system
    c) e-outsourcing system
    d) e-purchasing system
    e) e-business system

23. A strategy of delegating some production tasks to suppliers is referred to as:
    a) routing.
    b) dispatching.
    c) deintegration.
    d) quality assurance.
    e) hotelling.

24. A system that attempts to reduce material inventories to a bare minimum by frequently ordering small amounts of materials from suppliers is called:
    a) routing.
    b) just-in-time.
    c) scheduling.
    d) quality control.
    e) deintegration.

25. The process of managing inventory at a level that minimizes costs is called:
    a) scheduling.
    b) routing.
    c) dispatching.
    d) production planning.
    e) inventory control.

26. Firms attempt to minimize the amount of inventory they have in order to reduce their:
    a) purchasing costs.
    b) production costs.
    c) carrying costs.
    d) quality control.
    e) human resources.

27. The sequence of tasks necessary to complete the production of a product is:
    a) dispatching.
    b) quality control.
    c) purchasing.
    d) routing.
    e) deintegration.

In-Text Study Guide

Answers are in an appendix at the back of the book.

28. The act of setting time periods for each task in the production process is called:
    a) routing.
    b) scheduling.
    c) inventory control.
    d) dispatching.
    e) quality control.

29. A method of scheduling tasks that illustrates the expected timing for each task within the production process is a(n):
    a) Venn diagram.
    b) Gantt chart.
    c) MRP system.
    d) just-in-time system.
    e) production plan.

30. To minimize delays the tasks that are part of the _____ are reviewed.
    a) purchasing applications
    b) Gantt chart
    c) critical path
    d) raw material inventory
    e) hotelling

31. Which of the following terms describes the process of monitoring the characteristics of a product to ensure that the firm's standards are met?
    a) expectation downsizing
    b) quality control
    c) critical path management
    d) program evaluation and review technique
    e) work-in-process control

32. A method of evaluating performance by comparison to some specified level, usually a level set by another company, is called:
    a) cost control.
    b) total quality management.
    c) targeting.
    d) benchmarking.
    e) goal setting.

33. Through _____ firms achieve a lower average cost per unit by producing a larger volume
    a) inventory management.
    b) per unit expense control.
    c) economies of scale.
    d) deintegration.
    e) effective marketing.

34. At the break-even point:
    a) the number of units produced equals the number of units sold.
    b) economies of scale fail.
    c) the company begins to lose money.
    d) fixed costs equal variable costs.
    e) total revenue equals total cost.

35. The revision of the production process in an attempt to improve efficiency is called:
    a) restructuring.
    b) realignment.
    c) reintegration.
    d) downsizing.
    e) reengineering.

36. The supply chain is:
    a) the flow of inventory from raw materials to finished goods.
    b) the outsourcing process from supplier to firm.
    c) the marketing process from concept to consumption.
    d) the production process from beginning to consumer purchase.
    e) the conversion of resources to a product or service.

Part III

Summary

Management

The chapters in Part III describe some of the key components of effective management. These components are (1) recognition of the skills necessary to be effective managers (Chapter 7), (2) proper assignments of job responsibilities (Chapter 8), (3) efficient allocation of resources for production (Chapter 9), and (4) proper monitoring and improvement of product quality (Chapter 9). The key skills managers need to be effective are conceptual skills (to understand relationships among tasks of a firm), interpersonal skills, technical skills, and decision-making skills.

In addition to skills, effective management requires that job responsibilities be properly assigned within the organizational structure. Ideally, the organizational structure allows some control over each job assignment so that all types of tasks can be monitored. The organizational structure may also attempt to ensure employee input on various tasks by assigning extra responsibilities to employees. Job tasks and responsibilities can be departmentalized by function, product, location, or type of customer. The method of departmentalizing job tasks and responsibilities is dependent on the characteristics of the business.

Effective management also requires an efficient production process, which involves the selection of a plant site and the design and layout of the production facilities. The plant site decision is influenced by land cost, access to transportation, and other factors that affect the cost of production. Design and layout decisions are influenced by the characteristics of the plant site, production process, product line, and desired production capacity.

Effective management also requires an effort to continuously improve the quality of each product that is produced. Quality management forces employees to specify the desired quality level, to consider how the production process can be revised to achieve that quality level, and to continuously monitor the quality level by using various quality control methods.

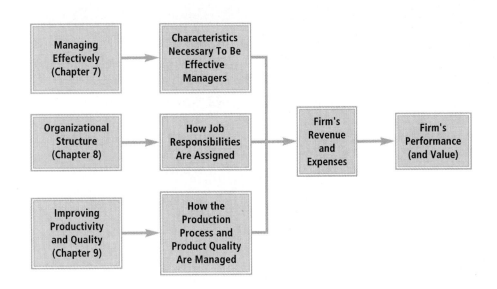

DEVELOPING A MANAGEMENT AND PRODUCTION PLAN FOR CAMPUS.COM

Strategic and Tactical Plans (related to Chapter 7)

Develop a strategic plan for Campus.com, and explain what tactical plans would be consistent with the strategic plan. Insert these plans into your business plan for Campus.com.

Organizational Structure (related to Chapter 8)

Given the nature of Campus.com's business, what job positions are needed? Include these positions in your business plan for Campus.com. You (or your team) are responsible for overseeing Campus.com and therefore are the top management of the firm. Do not focus on which members of your team would take each position. Instead focus on identifying the positions needed.

Productivity and Quality (related to Chapter 9)

In your business plan for Campus.com, describe the production process used to produce its service. Also, describe how the service will change and how Campus.com might create an efficient system for continued revisions of the service it provides.

How can Campus.com maintain the quality of the service it provides? Include an explanation of how the firm will assure quality control in your business plan.

Communication and Teamwork

You (or your team) may be asked by your instructor to hand in and/or present the part of your business plan that is related to this part of the text.

Integrative Video Case: Quality Control (Ping Golf)

Ping Golf is a manufacturer of golf clubs located in Phoenix. The company has about 900 employees. Ping strives to be the leader in everything in its industry, including service. Ping's employees work for the company because of its commitment to greatness, achieving the best, and finding perfection.

Questions

1. Explain how quality control can be used as a marketing tool in Ping's case.

2. Why might quality control affect the amount of financing that is needed?

3. How do the job responsibilities at Ping Golf relate to the company's strive for perfection and quality control?

Integrative Video Case: Managing Human Resources (Gadabout Salon & Spas)

Gadabout Salon & Spas is a day spa with five locations located in Tucson. The company was founded in 1980 and provides a full range of hair, nail, skin care, and spa treatments. Gadabout is like a family of employees, who continuously practice and refine their profession. To ensure a high level of quality, all Gadabout employees are trained and knowledgeable.

Questions

1 What is the role of employees at Gadabout in ensuring customer satisfaction?

2 How does customer satisfaction serve as a marketing tool at Gadabout?

3 How is an effective leader described at Gadabout? Discuss the resulting organizational structure at the company.

THE STOCK MARKET GAME

Go to **http://finance.yahoo.com** and check your portfolio balance, which is updated continuously by Yahoo! Finance.

Check Your Stock Portfolio Performance

1 What is the value of your stock portfolio today?

2 What is your gain on your investment? (The website shows the value of the gain in dollars, and as a percentage of your investment.)

3 How did your return compare to those of other students? (This comparison tells you whether your stock portfolio's performance is relatively high or low.)

Explaining Your Stock Performance

Stock prices are frequently influenced by changes in the firm's management, including changes in the chief executive officer or other high-level managers, the organizational structure, or the production process. A stock's price may rise if such management changes are made and investors expect that the changes will improve the performance of the firm. A stock's price can also decline if the managerial changes are expected to reduce the firm's performance. Review the latest news about some of your stocks on the Yahoo! Finance website.

1 Identify one of your stocks whose price was affected (since you purchased it) as a result of the firm's management (the main topic in this part of the text).

2 Identify the specific type of managerial changes that caused the stock price to change.

3 Did your stock price increase or decrease in response to the announcement of managerial changes?

RUNNING YOUR OWN BUSINESS

1 Describe the strategic plan of your business. In this plan, state the business opportunities that exist and the general direction your business will take to capitalize on those opportunities.

2 Explain in detail how your business will operate to achieve your strategic plan.

3 Describe the organizational structure of your business.

4 Provide an organization chart and describe the responsibilities of any employees whom you plan to hire.

5 How might this structure change as the business grows?

6 Describe the production process of your business. That is, describe the tasks that are required to produce your product or service. Indicate the number of employees required and describe other resources (such as machinery) that are needed for production.

7 Describe the facilities needed for production. Will your business require that you rent space in a shopping mall? Describe in general terms the design and layout of the facilities.

8 Estimate the rent expense during the first year for the facilities needed for your business. Also, estimate (if possible) the annual utility expense (such as electricity) for your business facilities.

9 Describe how your business can ensure (a) customer satisfaction, (b) the quality of the product or service you plan to produce, and (c) that customers are treated properly by any employees that you hire.

10 Describe how technology will enable you to improve the quality of the product or service you plan to produce. Explain how your production or customer service may possibly improve over time as a result of technology.

11 Discuss how economies of scale relate to your business.

12 Explain how your business could use the Internet to give customers an opportunity to provide feedback to management.

Your Career in Business: Pursuing a Major and a Career in Management

If you are very interested in the topics covered in this section, you may want to consider a major in Management. Some of the courses commonly taken by Management majors are summarized here.

Common Courses For Management Majors

▶ *Organizational Behavior*—Provides a broad overview of key managerial functions, such as organizing, motivating employees, planning, controlling, and teamwork.

▶ *Management Environment*—Focuses on the environment in which managers work and the responsibilities of managers to society and to regulators.

▶ *Human Resource Management*—Focuses on the processes of hiring, training, evaluating performance, and compensating employees.

▶ *Labor Relations*—Examines the labor contract relationships among managers, subordinates, and unions; also covers the process of negotiating.

▶ *Management Strategy*—Focuses on the competitive environment faced by a firm and strategies used by a firm's managers to increase its growth or improve its performance.

▶ *Management Systems*—Focuses on the use of computer software and systems to facilitate decision making.

▶ *Entrepreneurship*—Deals with the creation of business ideas, methods of growing a small business, and the challenges of competing with larger firms.

▶ *Operations Management*—Examines the resources used in the production process, the plant site and layout decisions, alternative production processes, and quality control.

Careers in Management

Information about job positions, salaries, and careers for students who major in Management can be found at the following websites:

▶ Job position websites:

http://jobsearch.monster.com   Administrative and Support Services, Consulting Services, Human Resources, Manufacturing, and Production.

http://careers.yahoo.com   Management Consulting, Management Operations, Retail, Restaurant/Food Service, Technology, and Transportation.

▶ Salary website:

http://collegejournal.com// salarydata   Consulting, Hotel and Restaurant Management, Human Resources, Logistics, Manufacturing, and Retailing.

Part IV

Managing Employees

Whereas Part III focused on organizational structure and production, Part IV focuses on human resources (employees), another critical component of management. Part IV contains two chapters that explain how managers can improve the performance of their employees. Chapter 10 describes the methods that can be used to motivate employees. Motivation may be necessary for many employees to perform well. To the extent that managers can effectively motivate employees, they can increase the performance of employees and therefore increase the performance of the firm. Chapter 11 explains the proper methods for hiring, training, and evaluating the performance of employees. If managers can use these methods effectively, they should be able to improve the firm's performance.

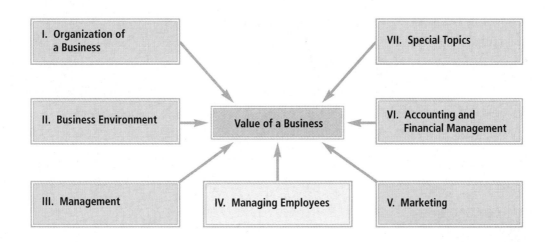

All businesses, including The Gap, need to motivate their employees to get the most out of their employees.

The Learning Goals of this chapter are to:

1 Describe the theories on motivation.

2 Describe how firms can enhance job satisfaction and thereby enhance motivation.

Chapter 10

Motivating Employees

A firm has a strategic plan that identifies opportunities and indicates the future direction of the firm's business. When the firm develops strategies to achieve the strategic plan, it relies on its managers to utilize employees and other resources to make the strategies work. Consider the situation of The Gap, which produces clothing and sells the clothing in retail outlets. Its performance is highly dependent on the efforts of its employees. The Gap must decide:

► How can it motivate its employees?
► How can it ensure that its employees are satisfied with their jobs?

If The Gap can successfully motivate its employees, it benefits in two ways. First, if the employees are motivated to work, they will accomplish more tasks, and The Gap will need fewer employees. Second, if the salespeople are motivated to sell clothes, The Gap's sales volume, and therefore its revenue, will be higher. If The Gap can ensure that its employees are satisfied with their jobs, it will be able to retain employees for a longer period of time and will reduce the expenses associated with training new employees.

The types of decisions described above are necessary for all businesses. This chapter explains how firms can motivate and satisfy employees in a manner that maximizes the firm's value.

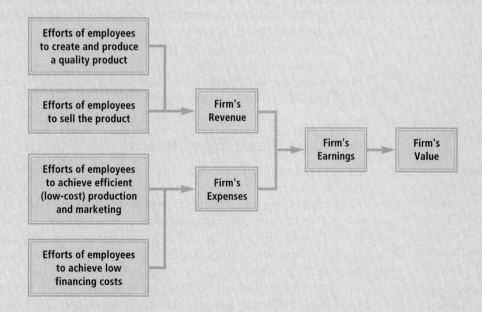

1

Describe the theories
on motivation.

THEORIES ON MOTIVATION

job satisfaction the degree to
which employees are satisfied with
their jobs

The motivation of employees is influenced by **job satisfaction,** or the degree
to which employees are satisfied with their jobs. Firms recognize the need
to satisfy their employees, as illustrated by the following statements from recent annual reports:

*"You will see a greater focus on employee satisfaction . . . which will lead us to
higher quality, better growth, and improved profitability."*

—Kodak

*"Bethlehem's success ultimately depends on the skill, dedication, and support
of our employees."*

—Bethlehem Steel

Since employees who are satisfied with their jobs are more motivated,
managers can motivate employees by ensuring job satisfaction. Some of the
more popular theories on motivation are summarized here, followed by
some general guidelines that can be used to motivate workers.

Hawthorne Studies

In the late 1920s, researchers studied workers in a Western Electric Plant
near Chicago to identify how a variety of conditions affected their level of
production. When the lighting was increased, the production level increased. Yet the production level also increased when the lighting was reduced. These workers were then subjected to various break periods; again,
the production level increased for both shorter breaks and longer breaks.
One interpretation of these results is that workers become more motivated
when they feel that they are allowed to participate. Supervisors may be able
to motivate workers by giving them more attention and by allowing them
to participate. These Hawthorne studies, which ignited further research on
motivation, are summarized in Exhibit 10.1 and suggest that human relations can affect a firm's performance.

Maslow's Hierarchy of Needs

hierarchy of needs needs are
ranked in five general categories.
Once a given category of needs is
achieved, people become motivated to reach the next category.

physiological needs the basic
requirements for survival

safety needs job security and
safe working conditions

social needs the need to be part
of a group

esteem needs respect, prestige,
and recognition

In 1943, Abraham Maslow, a psychologist, developed the **hierarchy of needs**
theory. This theory suggests that people rank their needs into five general
categories. Once they achieve a given category of needs, they become
motivated to reach the next category. The categories are identified in Exhibit 10.2, with the most crucial needs on the bottom. **Physiological needs** are
the basic requirements for survival, such as food and shelter. Most jobs can
help achieve these needs.

Once these needs are fulfilled, **safety needs** (such as job security and safe
working conditions) become the most immediate goal. Some jobs satisfy
these needs. People also strive to achieve **social needs,** or the need to be part
of a group. Some firms attempt to help employees achieve their social
needs, either by grouping workers in teams or by organizing social events
after work hours. People may also become motivated to achieve **esteem
needs,** such as respect, prestige, and recognition. Some workers may achieve
these needs by being promoted within their firms or by receiving special

Exhibit 10.1

Summary of the Hawthorne Studies

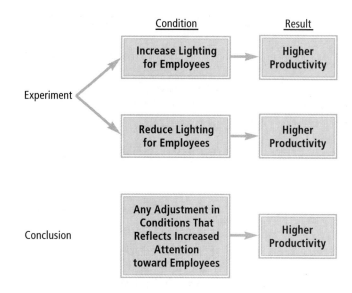

Exhibit 10.1

Summary of the Hawthorne Studies

Exhibit 10.2

Maslow's Hierarchy of Needs

self-actualization the need to fully reach one's potential

recognition for their work. The final category of needs is **self-actualization,** which represents the need to fully reach one's potential. For example, people may achieve self-actualization by starting a specific business that fits their main interests and by successfully running this business.

The hierarchy of needs theory can be useful for motivating employees because it suggests that different employees may be at different places in the hierarchy. Therefore, their most immediate needs may differ. If managers recognize employees' needs, they will be better able to offer rewards that motivate employees.

Herzberg's Job Satisfaction Study

In the late 1950s, Frederick Herzberg surveyed 200 accountants and engineers about job satisfaction. Herzberg attempted to identify the factors that made them feel dissatisfied with their jobs at a given point in time. He also attempted to identify the factors that made them feel satisfied with their jobs. His study found the following:

Common Factors Identified by Dissatisfied Workers	Common Factors Identified by Satisfied Workers
Working conditions	Achievement
Supervision	Responsibility
Salary	Recognition
Job security	Advancement
Status	Growth

hygiene factors work-related factors that can fulfill basic needs and prevent job dissatisfaction

motivational factors work-related factors that can lead to job satisfaction and motivate employees

Employees become dissatisfied when they perceive work-related factors in the left column (called **hygiene factors**) as inadequate. Employees are commonly satisfied when the work-related factors in the right column (called **motivational factors**) are offered.

Herzberg's results suggest that factors such as working conditions and salary must be adequate to prevent workers from being dissatisfied. Yet better-than-adequate working conditions and salary will not necessarily lead to a high degree of satisfaction. Instead, a high degree of worker satisfaction is most easily achieved by offering additional benefits, such as responsibility. Thus, if managers assign workers more responsibility, they may increase worker satisfaction and motivate the workers to be more productive. Exhibit 10.3 summarizes Herzberg's job satisfaction study.

Notice how the results of Herzberg's study correspond with the results of Maslow's hierarchy. Herzberg's hygiene factors generally correspond with Maslow's basic needs (such as job security). This suggests that if hygiene fac-

Exhibit 10.3

Summary of Herzberg's Job Satisfaction Study

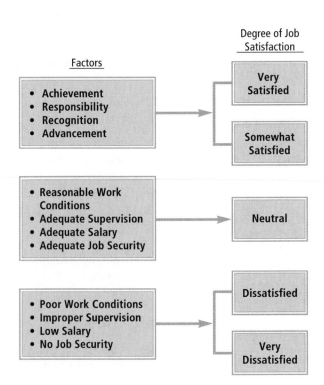

tors are adequate, they fulfill some of workers' more basic needs. Fulfillment of these needs can prevent dissatisfaction as employees become motivated to achieve a higher class of needs. Herzberg's motivational factors (such as recognition) generally correspond with Maslow's more ambitious hierarchy needs.

Several U.S. firms, such as Ford Motor Company and Polaroid Corporation, have implemented workshops to stress teamwork and company loyalty. These workshops build self-esteem by focusing on employees' worth to the company. In this way, the workshops may enable employees to achieve a higher class of needs, thereby increasing job satisfaction.

McGregor's Theory X and Theory Y

Another major contribution to motivation was provided by Douglas McGregor, who developed Theory X and Theory Y. Each of these theories represents supervisors' possible perception of workers. The views of Theories X and Y are summarized as follows:

Theory X	Theory Y
Employees dislike work and job responsibilities and will avoid work if possible.	Employees are willing to work and prefer more responsibility.

The way supervisors view employees can influence the way they treat the employees. Supervisors who believe in Theory X will likely use tight control over workers, with little or no delegation of authority. In addition, employees will be closely monitored to ensure that they perform their tasks. Conversely, supervisors who believe in Theory Y will delegate more authority because they perceive workers as responsible. These supervisors will also allow employees more opportunities to use their creativity. This management approach fulfills employees' needs to be responsible and to achieve respect and recognition. Consequently, these employees are likely to have a higher level of job satisfaction and therefore to be more motivated.

Exhibit 10.4 provides a summary of Theories X and Y. Most employees would prefer that their supervisors follow Theory Y rather than Theory X. Nevertheless, some supervisors may be unable to use Theory Y in specific situations, when they are forced to retain more authority over employees rather than delegate responsibility.

Exhibit 10.4

Summary of McGregor's Theories X and Y

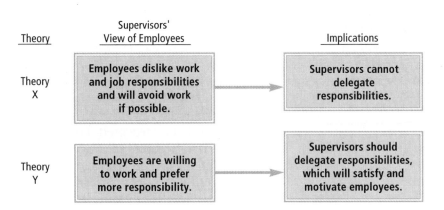

self-scoring exercise

The Frazzle Factor

Read each of the following statements, and rate yourself on a scale of 0 to 3, giving the answer that best describes how you generally feel (3 points for always, 2 points for often, 1 point for sometimes, and 0 points for never). Answer as honestly as you can, and do not spend too much time on any one statement.

Am I Angry?
_____ 1. I feel that people around me make too many irritating mistakes.
_____ 2. I feel annoyed because I do good work or perform well in school, but no one appreciates it.
_____ 3. When people make me angry, I tell them off.
_____ 4. When I am angry, I say things I know will hurt people.
_____ 5. I lose my temper easily.
_____ 6. I feel like striking out at someone who angers me.
_____ 7. When a co-worker or fellow student makes a mistake, I tell him or her about it.
_____ 8. I cannot stand being criticized in public.

Am I Overstressed?
_____ 1. I have to make important snap judgments and decisions.
_____ 2. I am not consulted about what happens on my job or in my classes.
_____ 3. I feel I am underpaid.
_____ 4. I feel that no matter how hard I work, the system will mess it up.
_____ 5. I do not get along with some of my co-workers or fellow students.
_____ 6. I do not trust my superiors at work or my professors at school.
_____ 7. The paperwork burden on my job or at school is getting to me.
_____ 8. I feel people outside the job or the university do not respect what I do.

Scoring

To find your level of anger and potential for aggressive behavior, add your scores from both quiz parts.

40–48: The red flag is waving, and you had better pay attention. You are in the danger zone. You need guidance from a counselor or mental health professional, and you should be getting it now.

30–39: The yellow flag is up. Your stress and anger levels are too high, and you are feeling increasingly hostile. You are still in control, but it would not take much to trigger a violent flare of temper.

10–29: Relax, you are in the broad normal range. Like most people, you get angry occasionally, but usually with some justification. Sometimes you take overt action, but you are not likely to be unreasonably or excessively aggressive.

0–9: Congratulations! You are in great shape. Your stress and anger are well under control, giving you a laid-back personality not prone to violence.

Theory Z

In the 1980s, a new theory on job satisfaction was developed. This theory, called Theory Z, was partially based on the Japanese style of allowing all employees to participate in decision making. Participation can increase job satisfaction because it gives employees responsibility. Job descriptions tend to be less specialized, so employees develop varied skills and have a more flexible career path. To increase job satisfaction, many U.S. firms have begun to allow employees more responsibility.

Expectancy Theory

Expectancy theory suggests that an employee's efforts are influenced by the expected outcome (reward) for those efforts. Therefore, employees will be more motivated to achieve goals if they are achievable and offer some reward.

As an example, consider a firm that offers the salesperson who achieves the highest volume of annual sales a one-week vacation in Paris. This type of reward will motivate employees only if two requirements are fulfilled. First, the reward must be desirable to employees. Second, employees must believe they have a chance to earn the reward. If the firm employs 1,000 salespeople, and only one reward is offered, employees may not be motivated because they may perceive that they have little chance of being the top salesperson. Motivation may be absent even in smaller

expectancy theory holds that an employee's efforts are influenced by the expected outcome (reward) for those efforts

groups if all employees expect that a particular salesperson will generate the highest sales volume.

Motivational rewards are more difficult to offer for jobs where output cannot easily be measured. For example, employees who repair the firm's machinery or respond to customer complaints do not contribute to the firm in a manner that can be easily measured or compared with other employees. Nevertheless, their performance may still be measured by customer satisfaction surveys or by various other performance indicators.

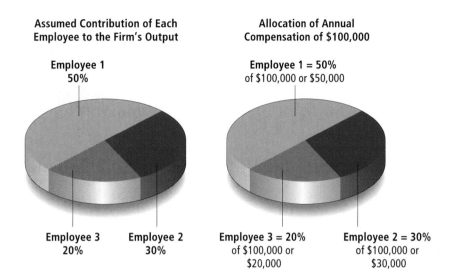

Exhibit 10.5

Example of Equity Theory

Equity Theory

equity theory suggests that compensation should be equitable, or in proportion to each employee's contribution

The **equity theory** of motivation suggests that compensation should be equitable, or in proportion to each employee's contribution. As an example, consider a firm with three employees: Employee 1 contributes 50 percent of the total output, Employee 2 contributes 30 percent, and Employee 3 contributes 20 percent. Assume that the firm plans to allocate $100,000 in bonuses based on the relative contributions of each employee. Using the equity theory, the $100,000 would be allocated as shown in Exhibit 10.5.

If employees believe that they are undercompensated, they may request greater compensation. If their compensation is not increased, employees may reduce their contribution. Equity theory emphasizes that employees can become dissatisfied with their jobs if they believe that they are not equitably compensated.

Supervisors may prevent job dissatisfaction by attempting to provide equitable compensation. A problem, however, is that the supervisor's perception of an employee's contribution may differ from that of the employee. If a firm can define how employee contributions will be measured and compensate accordingly, its employees will be better satisfied and more motivated.

Reinforcement Theory

reinforcement theory suggests that reinforcement can influence behavior

positive reinforcement motivates employees by providing rewards for high performance

Reinforcement theory, summarized in Exhibit 10.6, suggests that reinforcement can influence behavior. **Positive reinforcement** motivates employees by providing rewards for high performance. The rewards can range from an oral compliment to a promotion or large bonus. Employees may react differently to various forms of positive reinforcement. The more they appreciate the form of reinforcement, the more they will be motivated to continue high performance.

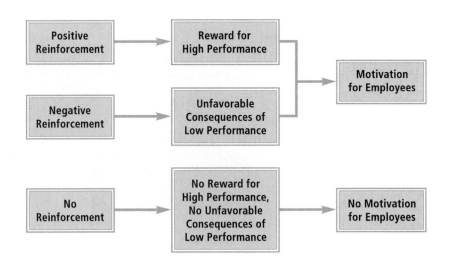

negative reinforcement motivates employees by encouraging them to behave in a manner that avoids unfavorable consequences

Negative reinforcement motivates employees by encouraging them to behave in a manner that avoids unfavorable consequences. For example, employees may be motivated to complete their assignments today to avoid admitting the delay in a group meeting or to avoid negative evaluations by their supervisors.

Various forms of negative reinforcement can be used, ranging from a reprimand to job termination. Some supervisors may prefer to consistently offer positive reinforcement for high performance rather than penalize for poor performance. However, offering positive reinforcement for all tasks that are adequately completed may be difficult. Furthermore, if an employee who has performed poorly is not given negative reinforcement, others may think that employee was given preferential treatment, and their general performance may decline as a result.

To increase job satisfaction, many employees have more responsibility and participate more in decision making.

© Getty Images / PhotoDisc

Motivational Guidelines Offered by Theories

If supervisors can increase employees' job satisfaction, they may motivate employees to be more productive. All of the theories on motivation are briefly summarized in Exhibit 10.7.

Exhibit 10.7

Comparison of Motivation Theories

Theory	Implications
Theory developed from Hawthorne studies	Workers can be motivated by attention.
Maslow's hierarchy of needs	Needs of workers vary, and managers can motivate workers to achieve these needs.
Herzberg's job satisfaction study	Compensation, reasonable working conditions, and other factors do not ensure job satisfaction but only prevent job dissatisfaction. Thus, other factors (such as responsibility) may be necessary to motivate workers.
McGregor's Theory X and Theory Y	Based on Theory X, workers will avoid work if possible and cannot accept responsibility. Based on Theory Y, workers are willing to work and prefer more responsibility. If Theory Y exists, managers can motivate workers by delegating responsibility.
Theory Z	Workers are motivated when they are allowed to participate in decision-making.
Expectancy theory	Workers are motivated if potential rewards for high performance are desirable and achievable.
Equity theory	Workers are motivated if they are being compensated in accordance with their perceived contribution to the firm.
Reinforcement theory	Good behavior should be positively reinforced and poor behavior should be negatively reinforced to motivate workers in the future.

Based on these theories, some general conclusions can be offered on motivating employees and providing job satisfaction:

1 Employees commonly compare their perceived compensation and contribution with others. To prevent job dissatisfaction, supervisors should ensure that employees are compensated for their contributions.

2 Even if employees are offered high compensation, they will not necessarily be very satisfied. They have other needs as well, such as social needs, responsibility, and self-esteem. Jobs that can fulfill these needs may provide satisfaction and therefore provide motivation.

3 Employees may be motivated if they believe that it is possible to achieve a performance level that will result in a desirable reward.

2

Explain how firms can enhance job satisfaction and thereby enhance motivation.

HOW FIRMS CAN ENHANCE JOB SATISFACTION AND MOTIVATION

job enrichment programs programs designed to increase the job satisfaction of employees

Many of the theories on motivation suggest that firms can motivate employees to perform well by ensuring job satisfaction. In general, the key characteristics that affect job satisfaction are money, security, work schedule, and involvement at work. To motivate employees, firms provide **job enrichment programs,** or programs designed to increase the job satisfaction of employees. The following are some of the more popular job enrichment programs:

▶ Adequate compensation program

▶ Job security

▶ Flexible work schedule

▶ Employee involvement programs

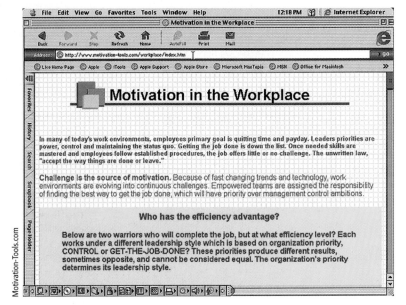

Motivation-Tools.com

business online

Motivation This website provides guidance on motivating employees.

Motivation in the Workplace

In many of today's work environments, employees primary goal is quitting time and payday. Leaders priorities are power, control and maintaining the status quo. Getting the job done is down the list. Once needed skills are mastered and employees follow established procedures, the job offers little or no challenge. The unwritten law, "accept the way things are done or leave."

Challenge is the source of motivation. Because of fast changing trends and technology, work environments are evolving into continuous challenges. Empowered teams are assigned the responsibility of finding the best way to get the job done, which will have priority over management control ambitions.

Who has the efficiency advantage?

Below are two warriors who will complete the job, but at what efficiency level? Each works under a different leadership style which is based on organization priority, CONTROL or GET-THE-JOB-DONE? These priorities produce different results, sometimes opposite, and cannot be considered equal. The organization's priority determines its leadership style.

**http://www.motivation-tools
.com/workplace/Index.htm**

To the extent that firms can offer these job enrichment programs to employees, they may be able to motivate employees. Each program is discussed in turn.

Adequate Compensation Program

Firms can attempt to satisfy employees by offering adequate compensation for the work involved. However, adequate compensation will not necessarily motivate employees to make their best effort. Therefore, firms may attempt to ensure that those employees with the highest performance each year receive the highest percentage raises.

merit system a compensation system that allocates raises according to performance (merit)

A **merit system** allocates raises according to performance (merit). For example, a firm may decide to give its employees an average raise of 5 percent, but poorly performing employees may receive 0 percent while the highest performing employees receive 10 percent. This system provides positive reinforcement for employees who have performed well and punishment for those who have performed poorly. A merit system is normally more effective than the alternative **across-the-board system,** in which all employees receive a similar raise. The across-the-board system provides no motivation because the raise is unrelated to employee performance.

across-the-board system a compensation system that allocates similar raises

incentive plans provide employees with various forms of compensation if they meet specific performance goals

Firms may attempt to reinforce excellent employee performance with other rewards as well as raises. **Incentive plans** provide employees with various forms of compensation if they meet specific performance goals. For example, a firm may offer a weekly or monthly bonus based on the number of components an employee produced or the dollar value of all products an employee sold to customers.

Bonuses can be a very effective way to encourage employees, but this chapter explains that there is a lot more to motivating employees than just compensation.

© Getty Images / EyeWire

Examples of Compensation Programs The compensation at some firms is composed of base pay and "reward" pay that is tied to specific performance goals. The base pay is set lower than the industry norm for a given job, but the additional reward pay (tied to specific goals) can allow the total compensation to exceed the norm. Employees are more motivated to perform well because they benefit directly from high performance.

Some employees of Enterprise Rent-A-Car Company are compensated according to the firm's profits. Steelworkers at Nucor can earn annual bonuses that exceed their annual base salary. Many salespeople earn bonuses based on their own sales volume.

Kodak uses an incentive plan that allows each executive to earn a bonus based on his or her performance. The performance targets are set by the outside board members who are not employees of Kodak. The bonuses are based on performance measures such as revenue and earnings. Procter & Gamble Company provides bonuses to executives based on some nonfinancial measures, such as integrity and leadership.

The bonuses of chief executive officers (CEOs) at General Electric, IBM, and many other firms are tied to the firm's performance. Performance measures may include revenue, earnings, production efficiency, and customer satisfaction. Firms recognize that tying compensation to performance may increase job satisfaction and motivate employees. The following descriptions of policies from recent annual reports confirm this:

"A company lives or dies by results, and at Campbell, executive pay is linked directly to performance . . . and 100 percent of all incentive bonuses are tied to company performance."

— Campbell's Soup Company

"We are working hard to change the culture of the company by emphasizing and rewarding results, not activity."

—IBM

In addition to linking compensation to performance, some firms also grant stock to their employees as partial compensation for their work. The value of this type of compensation depends on the firm's stock price. To the extent that employees can increase the firm's stock price with hard work, they can enhance their own compensation.

Initially, firms used stock as compensation only for CEOs. In recent years, however, other top managers of firms have been granted stock as well to keep them focused on enhancing the value of the stock. Some firms have extended this concept to all or most of their employees. For example, all employees of Avis receive some shares of Avis stock. This may motivate them to perform well because their performance may enhance the value of the stock they own. One limitation of this approach is that some employees who own only a small amount of stock may believe that their work habits will not have much influence on the firm's profits (and therefore on its stock price). Thus, they will not be motivated because they do not expect that their stock's price will increase as a result of their efforts. Stock options can also lead to conflicts of interest, as discussed in the next chapter.

College Health Club: Compensation Program at CHC

One of the decisions that Sue Kramer needs to make as part of her business plan for College Health Club (CHC) is whether to offer an incentive plan to her employees. When prospective customers come to CHC for the first time, an employee shows them the facilities. Sue is considering offering a $20 bonus to be paid each time an employee persuades a prospect to become a member. Recall that Sue initially estimated that CHC would have 300 members by the end of the first year. She thinks that if she uses this incentive plan, the number of members would increase to 310. However, CHC would incur an extra cost of $20 in bonus money for each person who becomes a member.

Sue's analysis of the possible impact of this incentive plan is shown in the following table:

Possible Impact of the Incentive Plan on CHC's First-Year Performance

	Performance if . . .	
	CHC Does Not Use an Incentive Plan	CHC Uses the Incentive Plan
(1) Price per membership	$500	$500
(2) Number of members in first year	300	310
(3) Revenue = (1) × (2)	$150,000	$155,000
(4) Total operating expenses excluding bonuses	$138,000	$138,000
(5) Cost of bonuses = (2) × $20	$0	$6,200
(6) Interest expenses	$4,000	$4,000
(7) Earnings before taxes = (3) − (4) − (5) − (6)	$8,000	$6,800

CHC's revenue would be higher with the incentive plan, but the cost of paying the bonuses would be higher than the increase in revenue. Therefore, CHC's earnings would be reduced as a result of the incentive plan. Sue recognizes that some incentive plans may often potential benefits, but she decides not to implement this plan because it would reduce CHC's performance.

As an illustration of how a firm's performance and value can improve when its employee compensation is linked to performance, consider the case of Paychex. In January 1998, Paychex announced its intent to tie employee compensation to its performance. Over the next year, the firm's performance and its value (as measured by its stock price) increased substantially, as shown in Exhibit 10.8.

Developing a Proper Compensation Plan   Most compensation plans that tie pay to performance are intended to motivate employees to

Exhibit 10.8

Impact of New Employee Compensation
Policy on the Stock Price of Paychex.

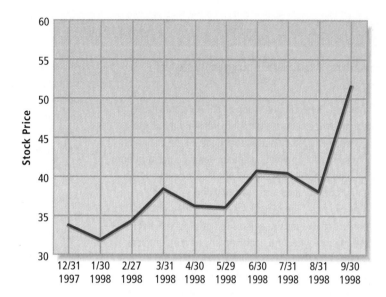

achieve high performance. The following guidelines can help in designing a compensation plan that motivates employees:

1 *Align the Compensation Plan with Business Goals* Compensation formulas for employees should be set only after the goals of the business are established. This ensures that employees are rewarded in line with their ability to satisfy business goals.

2 *Align Compensation with Specific Employee Goals* A compensation plan will motivate employees more successfully if it clearly specifies individual employee goals. Goals for an individual assembly-line employee should focus on specific job responsibilities that the employee can control. Conversely, individual goals that specify high performance for the entire production plant are not under the control of a single employee, and therefore the employee will not be as motivated to perform well.

Some firms compensate employees according to the performance of a group to which they belong within the firm. The groups are small enough that employees believe they have some control over the performance measurement.

3 *Establish Achievable Goals for Employees* The compensation plan will work better if the goals specified for each employee are achievable. By offering numerous achievable bonuses, managers can increase each employee's perception of the chance to earn a reward. Firms with limited budgets for bonuses can offer rewards that are less extravagant but still desirable.

Rewards that are desirable and achievable will motivate employees only if they are aware of the bonuses. Offering rewards at the end of the year is too late to motivate employees for that year. Levels of motivation will be higher if employees know about the potential for bonuses at the beginning of the year.

4 *Allow Employee Input on the Compensation Plan* The compensation plan should be developed only after receiving input from employees on how they should be rewarded. Although some employee requests may be unreasonable, allowing employee input can improve job satisfaction.

cross functional teamwork:

Spreading Motivation across Business Functions

When a firm uses compensation or other incentives to motivate employees, it must attempt to implement this program across all of its business functions. Since business functions interact, motivating employees who perform one type of function will have limited effects if employees performing other functions are not motivated.

For example, suppose that a firm's production employees are given new incentives to perform well, but marketing employees are not given any new incentives. The quality of the product achieved by the production department is somewhat dependent on the feedback it receives from marketing employees who conduct customer satisfaction surveys. Also, the production department's ability to produce an adequate supply of a product is dependent on the sales forecasts provided by the marketing department. If the sales forecast is too low, the production department may produce an insufficient volume, resulting in shortages.

Production tasks can also affect marketing tasks because effective marketing strategies will result in higher sales only if a sufficient volume of products is produced. Employees assigned to a specific function rely on employees assigned to other functions. Thus, employees who are assigned to a given function and are motivated can achieve high performance only if the other employees they rely on are motivated.

Job Security

Employees who have job security may be more motivated to perform well. They are less likely to be distracted at work because of concern about finding a more secure job.

Although firms recognize that job security can motivate their employees, they may not be able to guarantee job security. When a weakened U.S. economy lowers the demand for the goods and services provided by U.S. firms, these firms cannot afford to retain all of their employees. Even when the economy is strong, some firms are pressured to lay off employees to reduce expenses.

Firms can provide more job security by training employees to handle various tasks so that they can be assigned other duties if their usual assignments are no longer needed. Nevertheless, the firm may not have any job openings to which employees can be reassigned. Further, the job openings may be so different that reassignments are not possible. For example, workers on an assembly line normally would not be qualified to perform accounting or financial analysis jobs for an automobile manufacturer.

Flexible Work Schedule

flextime programs programs that allow for a more flexible work schedule

compressed work week compresses the work load into fewer days per week

job sharing two or more persons share a particular work schedule

Another method of increasing job satisfaction is to implement programs that allow for a more flexible work schedule (called **flextime programs**). Some firms have experimented with a **compressed work week,** which compresses the work load into fewer days per week. Most commonly, a five-day, 8-hour-per-day work week is compressed into four 10-hour days. The main purpose of this schedule is to allow employees to have three-day weekends. When employees are on a schedule that they prefer, they are more motivated to perform well.

Another form of a flexible work schedule is **job sharing,** where two or more persons share a particular work schedule. For example, a firm that needs a 40-hour work week for deliveries may hire two people to share that

Pat Raburn, manager at an Intel Corporation factory, speaks with an employee in San Jose, Costa Rica. Intel is a semiconductor chip maker that supplies the computing and communications industries with chips, boards, systems, and software.

© Getty Images North America

position. This allows employees to work part-time and fulfill other obligations such as school or family.

Employee Involvement Programs

As the theories summarized earlier indicate, employees are more motivated when they play a bigger role in the firm, either by being more involved in decisions or by being assigned more responsibility. Firms use various methods to allow more employee involvement and responsibility.

job enlargement a program to expand (enlarge) the jobs assigned to employees

Job Enlargement   One method of increasing employee responsibility is to use **job enlargement,** which is a program to expand (enlarge) the jobs assigned to employees. Job enlargement has been implemented at numerous firms such as Motorola and Xerox Corporation that experienced downsizing in the 1990s. The program was implemented not only to motivate employees but also to reduce operating expenses.

job rotation a program that allows a set of employees to periodically rotate their job assignments

Job Rotation   **Job rotation** allows a set of employees to periodically rotate their job assignments. For example, an assembly-line operation may involve five different types of assignments. Each worker may focus on one assignment per week and switch assignments at the beginning of the next week. In this way, a worker performs five different assignments over each five-week period.

Job rotation not only may reduce boredom but also can prepare employees for other jobs if their primary job position is eliminated. In this way, employees can remain employed by the firm. For example, if the demand for a specific type of car declines, the manufacturer of that car may attempt to reassign the employees who worked on that car to work on other cars or trucks.

empowerment allowing employees the power to make more decisions

Empowerment and Participative Management   In recent years, supervisors of many firms have delegated more authority to their employees. This strategy is referred to as **empowerment,** as it allows employees the

self-scoring exercise

Are You an Empowered Employee?*

Read each of the following statements carefully. Then, indicate which answer best expresses your level of agreement (5 = strongly agree, 4 = agree, 3 = sometimes agree/sometimes disagree, 2 = disagree, 1 = strongly disagree, and 0 = undecided/do not know). Mark only one answer for each item, and be sure to respond to all items.

____ 1.	I feel free to tell my manager what I think.	5	4	3	2	1	0
____ 2.	My manager is willing to listen to my concerns.	5	4	3	2	1	0
____ 3.	My manager asks for my ideas about things affecting our work.	5	4	3	2	1	0
____ 4.	My manager treats me with respect and dignity.	5	4	3	2	1	0
____ 5.	My manager keeps me informed about things I need to know.	5	4	3	2	1	0
____ 6.	My manager lets me do my job without interfering.	5	4	3	2	1	0
____ 7.	My manager's boss gives us the support we need.	5	4	3	2	1	0
____ 8.	Upper management pays attention to ideas and suggestions from people at my level.	5	4	3	2	1	0

Scoring

To determine if you are an empowered employee, add your scores.

32–40: You are empowered! Managers listen when you speak, respect your ideas, and allow you to do your work.

24–31: You have some power! Your ideas are sometimes considered, and you have some freedom of action.

16–23: You must exercise caution. You cannot speak or act too boldly, and your managers appear to exercise close supervision.

8–15: Your wings are clipped! You work in a powerless, restrictive work environment.

*If you are not employed, discuss these questions with a friend who is employed. Is your friend an empowered employee?

power to make more decisions. Empowerment is more specific than job enlargement because it focuses on increased authority, whereas job enlargement may not necessarily result in more authority. Empowerment may motivate those employees who are more satisfied when they have more authority. Also, they may be in a better position to make decisions on the tasks they perform than supervisors who are not directly involved in those tasks.

Empowerment is related to **participative management,** in which employees are allowed to participate in various decisions. For example, DaimlerChrysler has a program in which individual workers are asked for suggestions on cost cutting or improving quality. Managers review these suggestions and respond to the workers within a few days.

Empowerment assigns decision-making responsibilities to employees, whereas participative management simply allows the employees input in decisions. In reality, both terms are used to reflect programs that delegate more responsibilities to employees, whether they have complete or partial influence on decisions. The higher level of involvement by employees is supported by Theory Z, as discussed earlier.

participative management employees are allowed to participate in various decisions made by their supervisors or others

management by objectives (MBO) allows employees to participate in setting their goals and determining the manner in which they complete their tasks

A popular form of participative management is **management by objectives (MBO),** in which employees work with their managers to set their goals and determine the manner in which they will complete their tasks. The employees' participation can be beneficial because they are closer to the production process. In addition, if their tasks can be completed in various ways, they may use their own creativity to accomplish the work.

MBO is commonly applied to salespeople by assigning a monthly sales quota (or goal) that is based on historical sales. The actual sales volume may be dependent on the state of the economy, however. Care must be taken to assign a goal that is achievable.

For production employees, a production volume goal is specified. Some employees may reduce the quality of their work to reach the goal, however, so the objective must specify adequate quality as well as quantity.

teamwork a group of employees with varied job positions have the responsibility to achieve a specific goal

Teamwork Another form of employee involvement is **teamwork,** in which a group of employees with varied job positions have the responsibility to achieve a specific goal. Goodyear Tire and Rubber Company uses nu-

Small Business Survey

Do Employees Want More Influence in Business Decisions?

Employees may desire to be involved in business decision making because it increases their influence on the firm's performance. In recent years, the restructuring of firms has resulted in substantially more responsibilities for many employees. A survey of 4,500 workers of various firms was conducted to determine whether workers still wanted to have more influence in business decisions. The results are shown in the following chart:

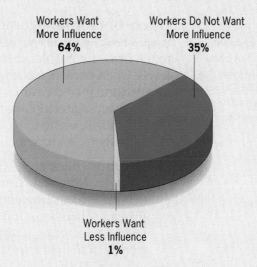

Workers Want
More Influence
64%

Workers Do Not Want
More Influence
35%

Workers Want
Less Influence
1%

The results suggest that even with the recent efforts of firms to give their employees more power and responsibility, employees would generally prefer more responsibility.

merous project teams to achieve its goals. Car manufacturers encourage teamwork to generate new ideas. Employees at Yahoo! are encouraged to share their ideas with others to obtain feedback.

DaimlerChrysler, which was created from Chrysler's merger with Daimler-Benz, designs cars with input from assembly-line workers. Executives establish general guidelines on a type of automobile that will satisfy consumers. The workers are then assembled in teams to work out the design details.

When Jaguar (a subsidiary of Ford Motor Company) desired to improve its customer service, its executives initially attempted to instruct employees on how to provide better service. However, motivating the employees was difficult because they were not satisfied with their jobs. The executives decided to create worker involvement teams to develop a plan for improved customer service. The employees were more willing to deal with the problem once they were allowed to search for the best solution.

A classic example of teamwork that all students can relate to is Belmont University's use of teamwork to resolve course registration hassles experienced by students. Students experienced difficulties when attempting to add a class, drop a class, submit a financial aid form, or any other task requiring service from the university. In addition, each task had to be completed at a different location on campus. Consequently, the university formed a team of administrators to find a solution that would make the process easier for students. The team proposed the creation of Belmont Central, a one-stop shop where students could accomplish all administrative tasks from registering for courses to applying for financial aid. For Belmont

Central to work, its employees would have to be capable of handling all these tasks. Belmont University implemented the plan and trained the employees so that they were capable of handling a wide variety of tasks. As a result, a student now goes to one place and meets with one employee to perform all administrative tasks. The students are much better satisfied with the service than they were in the past, and the university has received an award from *USA Today* for its excellent use of teamwork to resolve its problems.

Open-Book Management　Another form of employee involvement is **open-book management,** which educates employees on their contribution to the firm and enables them to periodically assess their own performance levels. Open-book management educates employees on how they affect the key performance measures that are relevant for the firm's owners. In this way, it encourages employees to make decisions and conduct tasks as if they were the firm's owners.

Open-book management has three distinct characteristics:

1 The firm educates all employees on the key performance measurements that affect the firm's profits and value and ensures that these performance measurements are widely available to employees over time (like an "open book" on the firm's performance). For example, various revenue, expense, and production figures may be displayed daily or weekly in the work area.

2 As employees are given the power to make decisions, they are trained to understand how the results of their decisions will affect the firm's overall performance. Thus, salespeople recognize how their efforts affect the firm's total revenue, while engineers recognize how their efforts reduce the cost of producing a product. Many job positions are not tied directly to revenue or total expenses. Therefore, it is helpful to break performance into pieces that employees can relate to, such as number of customer complaints, proportion of product defects, or percentage of tasks completed on time. Each of these pieces influences the total demand for the firm's product (and therefore the firm's revenue), as well as the expenses incurred.

3 The compensation of employees is typically aligned with their contribution to the firm's overall performance. They may earn some stock so that they are shareholders as well as employees. This reinforces their focus on making decisions that will enhance the firm's value and therefore its stock price. In addition, the firm may provide annual pay raises only to employees who helped improve the firm's performance. Although educating employees on how their work affects the firm's value is useful, a firm may still need to compensate employees for their performance in order to motivate them. Firms may set specific annual performance targets for employees and then continually update the employees on their performance levels throughout the year.

In a recent annual report, Dell Computer's CEO, Michael Dell, stated that it is critical for the company's future success that it recruit, develop, and retain highly skilled people at all levels of the organization. Furthermore, he said that Dell's model of direct customer contact is only as good as the people who apply it to the company's daily business. The CEO also gave credit for the effective implementation of the customer contact model to the 16,000 Dell employees around the world. Thus, Dell used a form of open-book management to motivate the company's employees.

open-book management a form of employee involvement that educates employees on their contribution to the firm and enables them to periodically assess their own performance levels

Exhibit 10.9

Methods Used to Enhance Job Satisfaction

Method	Description
1. Adequate compensation program	▶ Align raises with performance. ▶ Align bonuses with performance. ▶ Provide stock as partial compensation.
2. Job security	▶ Encourage employees to have a long-term commitment to the firm.
3. Flexible work schedule	▶ Allow employees flexibility on the timing of their work schedules.
4. Employee involvement programs	▶ Implement job enlargement. ▶ Implement job rotation. ▶ Implement empowerment and participative management. ▶ Implement teamwork. ▶ Implement open-book management.

Comparison of Methods Used to Enhance Job Satisfaction

The methods that can enhance job satisfaction and therefore motivate employees are compared in Exhibit 10.9. A combination of methods is especially useful for enhancing job satisfaction. When a firm succeeds in increasing employees' job satisfaction, it will be more effective in motivating the employees to achieve high performance. Therefore, putting emphasis on job satisfaction can improve a firm's profits and value.

College Health Club: Motivating Employees at CHC

One of the decisions that Sue Kramer needs to make as part of her business plan for College Health Club (CHC) is how to hire and motivate employees. Sue plans to hire capable employees who are currently exercise science majors at the college. She wants to ensure that the students are satisfied with their jobs and motivated to perform well. First, she plans to determine the typical compensation level for part-time jobs in the area and will offer wages slightly higher than the norm. Second, she plans to accommodate her employees by allowing them to work fewer hours in a week when they have a major exam or class project. Third, she will welcome employee involvement. As manager of CHC, she plans to interact with employees on a daily basis and ask them for suggestions on improving the club's performance. Fourth, if Sue opens an additional health club in the future, she plans to hire a manager to run that club. She will seriously consider hiring someone who has been an employee at CHC as the manager of the new health club after the person earns a college degree.

Firms That Achieve the Highest Job Satisfaction Level

Many firms use a combination of methods to achieve high job satisfaction. Exhibit 10.10 lists some firms that have been frequently cited as the best firms to work for, along with the methods they use to achieve such high job satisfaction. Notice that each firm has its own way of satisfying employees.

Exhibit 10.10

Examples of Firms That Have Achieved
Very High Job Satisfaction

Firm	Methods Used to Achieve High Job Satisfaction
Southwest Airlines	▶ Treats employees with respect.
	▶ Empowers employees to solve problems.
	▶ Gives awards and recognition to employees.
MBNA	▶ Focuses on hiring employees who get along with other people.
	▶ Provides on-site child care.
Microsoft	▶ Casual work environment.
	▶ Empowers employees to solve problems.
Eddie Bauer	▶ Two-week paid sick leave for new parents.
	▶ Flexible work schedules.

Motivating Employees across Countries

The techniques used to motivate employees in the United States may not necessarily be successful in motivating employees in other countries. For example, consider a U.S. firm that has just established a production plant in Eastern Europe. European employees' views on conditions necessary for job satisfaction may differ from those of U.S. production workers. In general, U.S. firms have successfully motivated production workers in the United States by giving them more responsibilities. Assigning additional responsibilities may not motivate production workers in Eastern Europe, however, especially if they have less experience and education. These workers could even be overwhelmed by the extra responsibilities. They might be less capable of striving for efficiency, since their past work experience was in an environment that did not stress efficiency.

In some situations, a U.S. firm may be more capable of motivating foreign workers than U.S. workers. For example, General Motors established a plant in what was then East Germany to produce automobiles. When it trained the workers at this plant, it explained the need for production efficiency to ensure the plant's survival. It asked the workers to provide suggestions on how the plant could increase its production efficiency. These workers offered 10 times as many suggestions as workers at other General Motors plants in Europe. The East German plant could assemble an entire automobile faster than any other General Motors plant. The efficiency of the workers at the East German plant may be attributed to their background. Although these workers did not have many years of experience on automobile assembly lines, they also had not learned any bad habits from working in less efficient assembly systems. Thus, these workers were more capable of learning an efficient production system.

Overall, a firm's ability to motivate workers in a specific country may depend on characteristics that are beyond the firm's control. Workers who will lose their jobs if the firm performs poorly may be more motivated, regardless of the firm's motivation strategies. Workers based in countries with fewer opportunities may be more motivated because they may appreciate their existing jobs more than workers in other countries. Given these differences, a firm may consider using varying motivation strategies for workers in different countries. In general, a firm should attempt to determine what conditions will increase the job satisfaction of workers in a particular country and provide those conditions for workers who perform well.

global business

SUMMARY

1 The main theories on motivation are as follows:

▶ The Hawthorne studies suggest that employees are more motivated when they receive more attention.

▶ Maslow's hierarchy of needs theory suggests that employees are satisfied by different needs, depending on their position within the hierarchy. Firms can satisfy employees at the low end of the hierarchy with job security or safe working conditions. Once basic needs are fulfilled, employees have other needs that must be met. Firms can attempt to satisfy these employees by allowing social interaction or more responsibilities.

▶ Herzberg's job satisfaction study suggests that the factors that prevent job dissatisfaction are different from those that enhance job satisfaction. Adequate salary and working conditions prevent job dissatisfaction, while responsibility and recognition enhance job satisfaction.

▶ McGregor's Theories X and Y suggest that when supervisors believe employees dislike work and responsibilities (Theory X), they do not delegate responsibilities and employees are not motivated; when supervisors believe that employees prefer responsibilities (Theory Y), they delegate more responsibilities, which motivates employees.

▶ Theory Z suggests that employees are more satisfied when they are involved in decision making and therefore may be more motivated.

▶ Expectancy theory suggests that employees are more motivated if compensation is aligned with goals that are achievable and offer some reward.

▶ Equity theory suggests that employees are more motivated if their compensation is aligned with their relative contribution to the firm's total output.

▶ Reinforcement theory suggests that employees are more motivated to perform well if they are rewarded for high performance (positive reinforcement) and penalized for poor performance (negative reinforcement).

2 Firms can enhance job satisfaction and therefore motivate employees by providing

▶ an adequate compensation program, which aligns compensation with performance;

▶ job security;

▶ a flexible work schedule; and

▶ employee involvement programs.

KEY TERMS

across-the-board system 314
compressed work week 318
empowerment 319
equity theory 311
esteem needs 306
expectancy theory 310
flextime programs 318
hierarchy of needs 306
hygiene factors 308
incentive plans 314

job enlargement 319
job enrichment programs 313
job rotation 319
job satisfaction 306
job sharing 318
management by objectives (MBO) 320
merit system 314
motivational factors 308
negative reinforcement 312

open-book management 322
participative management 320
physiological needs 306
positive reinforcement 311
reinforcement theory 311
safety needs 306
self-actualization 307
social needs 306
teamwork 320

Review & Critical Thinking Questions

1. Identify the categories of Maslow's hierarchy of needs theory.

2. Briefly describe Herzberg's job satisfaction study on worker motivation.

3. Distinguish between McGregor's Theory X and Theory Y perceptions of management.

4. Describe how expectancy theory can motivate behavior.

5. Briefly summarize the equity theory of motivation.

6. Describe the reinforcement theories of motivation and explain how a manager could utilize them.

7. Describe some methods that will enhance job satisfaction and motivate employees.

8. Briefly describe the different forms of flexible work schedules firms use.

9. How can managers utilize strategic planning to motivate their employees and maximize the value of the firm?

10. How are empowerment and participative management related?

11. Discuss the methods used to motivate employees in the United States. Should the same methods be used to motivate employees in other countries?

Discussion Questions

1. You are a manager who recognizes that your employees are primarily motivated by money. How could you motivate them at work?

2. Would motivational techniques be more important for the Atlanta Braves than for an organization such as General Motors? Explain your answer.

3. You are a manager of a video store. Which theory of motivation do you think would best apply to your employees?

4. Would you consider using negative reinforcement to improve the performance of lazy employees? Explain your answer.

5. You and your lazy friend work at a car manufacturer. The company just implemented a new compensation plan with a lower base salary but the potential for large bonuses. You are very excited about the plan, but your friend is not. Explain why this may be so.

6. How could a firm use the Internet and technology to motivate its existing and potential employees?

It's Your Decision: **Motivating Employees at CHC**

1. Sue Kramer plans to offer a flexible work schedule, employee involvement, and a free health club membership to employees at College Health Club (CHC). Explain how CHC's performance may increase as a result of these benefits to employees.

2. Which of Maslow's hierarchy of needs are satisfied by employment at CHC? Which of Maslow's hierarchy of needs are not satisfied by employment at CHC?

3. Expectancy theory suggests that employees will perform better if there is a reward for performance. Should CHC have employees compete for an extra reward each year? What is a disadvantage of this strategy?

4. Explain how the job satisfaction of employees at CHC can affect the quality of health club services produced by CHC.

5. A health club differs from manufacturing firms in that it produces a service rather than products. Would a manufacturing firm satisfy Maslow's hierarchy of needs more easily than service firms?

Investing in a Business

Using the annual report of the firm in which you would like to invest, complete the following:

1 Does the firm appear to recognize that its employees are the key to its success?

2 Does the firm empower its workers? Does it encourage teamwork? Provide details.

3 Explain how the business uses technology to motivate its employees. For example, does it use the Internet to provide information about its compensation programs? Does it use the Internet or e-mail to provide feedback to its employees?

4 Go to **http://hoovers.com** and locate the NEWS SEARCH. Type in the name of the firm in the space provided, and review the recent news stories about the firm. Summarize any (at least one) recent news story about the firm that applies to one or more of the key concepts in this chapter.

Case: Using Motivation to Enhance Performance

Tom Fry is a plant manager for Ligonier Steel Corporation, located in Ligonier, Pennsylvania. The plant is small, with 250 employees. Its productivity growth rate has stagnated for the past year and a half.

Tom is concerned and decides to meet with employees in various departments. During the meeting, employees disclose that they do not have a chance to interact with one another while on the job. Furthermore, because they do not receive any recognition for their suggestions, their input of ideas for improvement has stopped.

After a week elapses, Tom calls a meeting to announce a new program. He plans to offer rewards for high performance so that employees will be motivated to surpass their quotas. Bonuses will be awarded to employees who exceed their quotas. Tom believes this program will work because of his perception that "money motivates employees."

A few months later, Tom notices that productivity has increased and that employees are enjoying the bonuses they have earned. Tom decides to provide an additional means of motivation. He wants employees to continue to interact with one another to solve work problems and share information. Supervisors now recognize individual accomplishments. They praise employees who make suggestions and identify an employee of the month in the company newsletter to recognize outstanding performance. Tom strongly supports this feature of the program.

The goal is for employees to grow and develop to their fullest potential. Individuals may be retrained or go back to college to permit job growth within the plant. Employees' ideas and contributions are now perceived as a way to enhance their individual career paths. The results have been overwhelming. Tom Fry, supervisors, and employees are all enjoying the benefits that have made Ligonier Steel a satisfying place to work.

Questions

1 Describe the motivation theory that applies to this case.

2 What needs can employees at Ligonier Steel satisfy in performing their jobs?

3 Describe how bonuses motivated the employees at Ligonier Steel.

4 Describe other rewards besides bonuses that can motivate work behavior in this case.

5 Ligonier does not use any negative reinforcement. Does this case illustrate any disadvantages of providing only positive reinforcement?

Video Case: Motivating Employees at Valassis Communications, Inc.

Valassis Communications, Inc., creates the promotional newspaper inserts for 58 million households. It uses a pay-for-performance system that rewards employees for high performance. The company rewards employees both for individual achievements and for team achievements. The team awards are tied to the performance of the firm overall. In this way, the employees benefit whenever shareholders of the firm benefit.

Questions

1 How is Valassis's reward system related to "expectancy theory"?

2 How does Valassis use positive reinforcement?

3 Is Valassis's success due entirely to monetary rewards, or are there other reasons for employee satisfaction at the firm?

Internet Applications

1. *http://www.nceo.org*

Click on "ESOPs." Briefly describe an employee stock ownership plan (ESOP). How does it work? How do you think an ESOP motivates employees? How do you think ESOPs benefit the companies using them? Discuss how ESOPs relate to the theories of motivation discussed in the chapter.

2. *http://www.motivation-tools.com/*

Click on "Elements of Motivation." What are the three elements of motivation? What are the seven rules of motivation? Do you think motivation results from an individual's own drive, or is it primarily driven by external factors? How do you think following the rules of motivation will benefit a company? How could a company benefit from encouraging its managers to follow the rules of motivation?

3. *http://www.employer-employee.com/*

Read the "Don't Praise Employees . . ." section. How does this section relate to positive and negative reinforcement? Do you agree with the article? What advice does this website provide to employers who are trying to hire self-motivated managers? How do you think hiring self-motivated managers will help a firm achieve its goals?

The Coca-Cola Company Annual Report Project

Questions for the current year's annual report are available on the text website at **http://madura.swlearning.com.**

The following questions apply concepts presented in this chapter to The Coca-Cola Company. Go to The Coca-Cola Company website (**http://www.cocacola.com**) and find the index for the 2001 annual report.

Questions

1 Click on "Letter to Share Owners." Given that The Coca-Cola Company uses its employees to devise new, creative ways to forge bonds with consumers, do you think that a Theory X management style would be appropriate at The Coca-Cola Company?

2 Download the financial statements and find the "Investments" section. Do you think rigid salary scales would be appropriate for The Coca-Cola Company?

3 Study the "Selected Market Results" section and the "Investments" section. How might methods of motivating employees differ across countries within The Coca-Cola Company? Do you think you would be motivated to work at The Coca-Cola Company?

4 Click on "Letter to Share Owners." What does the chairman say in the annual report to motivate The Coca-Cola Company's employees?

5 Go to **http://hoovers.com** and locate the NEWS CENTER. Key in The Coca-Cola Company in the space provided, click on "Search," and review the recent news stories about the firm. Summarize any (at least one) recent news story about The Coca-Cola Company that applies one or more of the key concepts within this chapter of the text.

In-Text Study Guide

Answers are in an appendix at the back of the book.

True or False

1. Maslow's hierarchy of needs identifies superior compensation as the key to employee motivation. F

2. According to Frederick Herzberg, hygiene factors are work-related factors that will motivate and please employees. F

3. The management strategy of empowerment is favored by Theory X managers. F

4. A supervisor who believes in McGregor's Theory Y will likely monitor employees closely to ensure that their work is completed. F

5. Equity theory suggests that an employee's efforts are influenced by the expected outcome of those efforts. F

6. Negative reinforcement motivates employees by encouraging them to behave in a manner that avoids unfavorable consequences. T

7. Most compensation plans that tie pay to performance are intended to motivate employees to achieve high performance. T

8. A merit system allocates raises for all employees according to sales of the firm. F

9. An across-the-board system is appropriate when all employees deserve the same reward for their work. T

10. Open-book management encourages employees to make decisions and conduct tasks as if they were the firm's owners. T

11. The techniques of motivation apply across countries. F

Multiple Choice

12. By _____ employees to properly perform the tasks they are assigned, management can maximize the firm's value.
    a) motivating
    b) threatening
    c) coercing
    d) manipulating
    e) harassing

13. One implication of the Hawthorne studies is that workers can be motivated by receiving:
    a) attention.
    b) money.
    c) stock.
    d) bonuses.
    e) profit sharing.

14. Maslow's hierarchy of needs theory can be useful for motivating employees because it suggests that:
    a) people are motivated to achieve their work-related hygiene factors.
    b) managers respond to the need for corporate profitability.
    c) employee needs are stable.
    d) employees are motivated by unsatisfied needs.
    e) money is the most important motivating factor.

15. Social interaction and acceptance by others are examples of:
    a) physiological needs.
    b) esteem needs.
    c) safety needs.
    d) social needs.
    e) self-actualization needs.

16. Needs that are satisfied with food, clothing, and shelter are called _____ needs.
    a) safety
    b) social
    c) affiliation
    d) self-esteem
    e) physiological

17. Herzberg's hygiene factors most closely correspond with Maslow's:
    a) physiological needs.
    b) psychological needs.
    c) social needs.
    d) esteem needs.
    e) self-actualization needs.

In-Text Study Guide

Answers are in an appendix at the back of the book.

18. According to Herzberg, employees are commonly most satisfied when offered:
    a) adequate supervision.
    b) adequate salary.
    c) recognition.
    d) job security.
    e) safe working conditions.

19. All of the following are methods used to enhance job satisfaction except:
    a) employee involvement programs.
    b) Theory X management.
    c) job security.
    d) adequate compensation programs.
    e) flexible work schedules.

20. Theory Z suggests that employees are more satisfied when:
    a) they receive above-average pay raises.
    b) their compensation is consistent with their efforts.
    c) managers restrict the delegation of authority.
    d) they are involved in decision making.
    e) appropriate hygiene factors are available.

21. Which of the following theories of management suggests that workers will be motivated if they are compensated in accordance with their perceived contributions to the firm?
    a) expectancy theory
    b) equity theory
    c) need theory
    d) Theory Y
    e) reinforcement theory

22. The reinforcement theory that motivates employees by encouraging them to behave in a manner that avoids unfavorable consequences is _____ reinforcement.
    a) positive
    b) neutral
    c) equity
    d) negative
    e) expectancy

23. In an across-the-board system, all employees receive similar:
    a) raises.
    b) job assignments.

    c) offices.
    d) work schedules.
    e) performance appraisals.

24. Which of the following provides employees with various forms of compensation if specific performance goals are met?
    a) flextime programs
    b) job enlargement
    c) participative management
    d) open-book management
    e) incentive plans

25. Which of the following is not a guideline for designing a motivational compensation system?
    a) align the system with business goals
    b) align the system with specific employee goals
    c) establish systems for rewarding employee seniority
    d) set achievable goals for employees
    e) allow employee input on the compensation system

26. Two or more persons sharing a particular work schedule is called:
    a) job enlargement.
    b) job enrichment.
    c) job sharing.
    d) flextime.
    e) job rotation.

27. Even if the company cannot guarantee continuing employment, it can improve employees' sense of job security by:
    a) empowering employees.
    b) granting stock to employees.
    c) using open-book management.
    d) training employees in various tasks.
    e) instituting compressed work weeks.

28. A program to expand the jobs assigned to employees is called:
    a) hygiene theory.
    b) downsizing.
    c) positive reinforcement.
    d) equity theory of motivation.
    e) job enlargement.

In-Text Study Guide

Answers are in an appendix at the back of the book.

29. An employee involvement program that periodically moves individuals from one job assignment to another is:
    a) job enlargement.
    b) job enrichment.
    c) job rotation.
    d) job sharing.
    e) flextime.

30. _____ can reduce boredom and prepare employees for other jobs if their primary job is eliminated.
    a) Job evaluation
    b) Job rotation
    c) Reengineering
    d) Performance appraisal
    e) Reinforcement

31. Which of the following is an employee involvement program where a group of employees with different job positions are given the responsibility of achieving a specific goal?
    a) management by objectives (MBO)
    b) teamwork
    c) job enlargement
    d) job rotation
    e) job sharing

32. When firms delegate more authority to their employees, this strategy is referred to as:
    a) Theory X management.
    b) empowerment.
    c) the merit system.
    d) McGregor's hygiene theory.
    e) the equity system.

33. Which of the following allows employees to set their own goals and determine the manner in which they accomplish their tasks?
    a) equity theory of motivation
    b) expectancy theory of motivation
    c) management by objectives
    d) Theory X management
    e) Theory Y management

34. In open-book management, the compensation of employees is typically aligned with their contribution to the firm's:
    a) hierarchy of needs.
    b) industry demand.
    c) overall performance.
    d) reinforcement theory.
    e) hygiene theory.

35. Which of the following is an employee involvement program that encourages employees to make decisions and conduct tasks as if they were the firm's owners?
    a) Theory X management
    b) open-book management
    c) Theory Y management
    d) Theory Z management
    e) Theory J management

36. In addition to linking compensation with performance, some firms grant employees _____ for good performance.
    a) internal satisfaction
    b) Theory X involvement
    c) Theory Y involvement
    d) corporate bonds
    e) common stock

All businesses, including the White Water Rafting Co., need to properly hire, train, and evaluate their employees in order to be successful.

The Learning Goals of this chapter are to:

Explain human resource planning by firms.

1

Differentiate among the types of compensation that firms offer to employees.

2

Describe the skills of employees that firms develop.

3

Explain how the performance of employees can be evaluated.

4

Chapter 11

Hiring, Training, and Evaluating Employees

A firm's human resources (employees) are crucial to its performance. Therefore, a firm's performance is dependent on how its human resources are managed. The management of human resources involves recruiting employees, developing their skills, and evaluating their performance. The hiring, training, and evaluation of employees are a key to a firm's success. Consider the situation of the White Water Rafting Company, which hires employees to serve as guides to take groups of 8 to 12 tourists on rafting trips. All guides must be experienced at rafting and well acquainted with the area so that they can tell the tourists about the river and its environs during the rafting trip. They must also know the potential dangers of rafting and take the necessary safety precautions to protect the tour groups; they should also be able to apply first aid if necessary. The White Water Rafting Company must decide:

▶ How many employees should it hire?

▶ What criteria should it use when making the hiring decision?

▶ What types of compensation should it provide?

▶ How should the employees be trained to ensure proper safety?

▶ How should the employees be evaluated?

The decision regarding the number of employees is important because it affects the expenses of running the firm. The criteria used to make hiring decisions are also important because they will determine which people are hired. If the firm can hire good employees, it will be more successful. The firm's decisions regarding compensation and training affect its expenses. Its decision about evaluating employees is important because the evaluations will determine which employees are promoted over time and become the key decision makers.

The types of decisions described above are necessary for all businesses. This chapter explains how hiring, training, and evaluating can be conducted by the White Water Rafting Company or any other firm in a manner that maximizes its value.

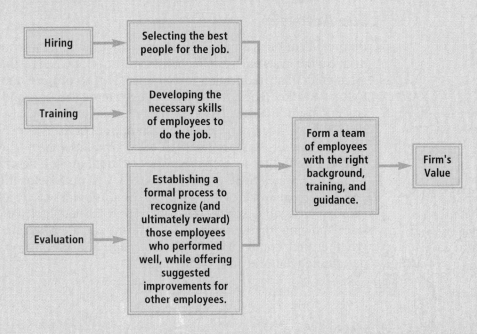

1
Explain human resource planning by firms.

human resource planning
planning to satisfy a firm's needs for employees

HUMAN RESOURCE PLANNING

Human resource planning involves planning to satisfy a firm's needs for employees. It consists of three tasks:

- ▶ Forecasting staffing needs
- ▶ Job analysis
- ▶ Recruiting

Forecasting Staffing Needs

If staffing needs can be anticipated in advance, the firm has more time to satisfy those needs. Some needs for human resources occur as workers retire or take jobs with other firms. Retirement can be forecasted with some degree of accuracy, but forecasting when an employee will take a job with another firm is difficult.

Additional needs for employees result from expansion. These needs may be determined by assessing the firm's growth trends. For example, if the firm is expected to increase production by 10 percent (in response to increased sales), it may prepare for the creation of new positions to achieve the projected production level. Positions that handle accounting and marketing-related tasks may not be affected by the increased production level.

If the firm foresees a temporary need for higher production, it may avoid hiring new workers, since it would soon have to lay them off. Layoffs not only affect the laid-off workers but also scare those workers who are still employed. In addition, firms that become notorious for layoffs will be less capable of recruiting people for new positions.

If firms avoid hiring during a temporary increase in production, they must achieve their objective in some other way. A common method is to offer overtime to existing workers. An alternative method is to hire temporary workers for part-time or seasonal work.

Once new positions are created, they must be filled. This normally involves job analysis and recruiting, which are discussed in turn.

Job Analysis

job analysis the analysis used to determine the tasks and the necessary credentials for a particular position

job specification states the credentials necessary to qualify for a job position

job description states the tasks and responsibilities of a job position

Before a firm hires a new employee to fill an existing job position, it must decide what tasks and responsibilities will be performed by that position and what credentials (education, experience, and so on) are needed to qualify for that position. The analysis used to determine the tasks and the necessary credentials for a particular position is referred to as **job analysis.** This analysis should include input from the position's supervisor as well as from other employees whose tasks are related. The job analysis allows the supervisor of the job position to develop a job specification and job description. The **job specification** states the credentials necessary to qualify for the job position. The **job description** states the tasks and responsibilities of the job position. An example of a job description is provided in Exhibit 11.1. People who consider applying for the job position use the job specification to determine whether they could qualify for the position and use the job description to determine what the position involves.

Exhibit 11.1

Example of a Job Description

Title: Sales Representative
Department: Sales
Location: Southern Division, Atlanta, Georgia

Position Summary
The sales representative meets with prospective customers to sell the firm's products and to ensure that existing customers are satisfied with the products they have purchased.

Relationships
▶ Reports to the regional sales manager for the Southern Division.
▶ Works with five other sales representatives, although each representative has responsibility for his or her own region within the Southern Division.

Main Job Responsibilities
1. Serve existing customers; call on main customers at least once a month to obtain feedback on the performance of products previously sold to them; take any new orders for products.
2. Visit other prospective customers and explain the advantages of each product.
3. Check on customers who are late in paying their bills; provide feedback to the billing department.
4. Meet with the production managers at least once a month to inform them about any product defects cited by customers.
5. Assess the needs of prospective customers; determine whether other related products could be produced to satisfy customers; provide feedback to production managers.
6. Will need to train new sales representatives in the future if growth continues.
7. Overnight travel is necessary for about eight days per month.
8. Sales reports must be completed once a month.

Recruiting

Firms use various forms of recruiting to ensure an adequate supply of qualified candidates. Some firms have a **human resource manager** (sometimes called the "personnel manager") who helps each specific department recruit candidates for its open positions. To identify potential candidates for the position, the human resource manager may check files of recent applicants who applied before the position was even open. These files are usually created as people submit their applications to the firm over time. In addition, the manager may place an ad in local newspapers. This increases the pool of applicants, as some people are unwilling to submit an application unless they know that a firm has an open position.

Most well-known companies receive a large number of qualified applications for each position. Many firms retain applications for only a few months so that the number of applications does not become excessive.

Internal versus External Recruiting Recruiting can occur internally or externally. **Internal recruiting** seeks to fill open positions with persons already employed by the firm. Numerous firms post job openings so that existing employees can be informed. Some employees may desire the open positions more than their existing positions.

Internal recruiting can be beneficial because existing employees have already been proven. Their personalities are known, and their potential capabilities and limitations can be thoroughly assessed. Internal recruiting also allows existing workers to receive a **promotion** (an assignment of a higher-level job with more responsibility and compensation) or to switch to more desirable tasks. This potential for advancement can motivate employees to perform well. Such potential also reduces job turnover and therefore reduces the costs of hiring and training new employees. Many of

human resource manager helps each specific department recruit candidates for its open positions

internal recruiting an effort to fill open positions with persons already employed by the firm

promotion the assignment of an employee to a higher-level job with more responsibility and compensation

increasing value with technology

RECRUITMENT SOFTWARE AND ONLINE RECRUITING

Recruitment software programs and online recruiting are recent innovations. Recruitment software programs eliminate the need for individuals to read and categorize every résumé received. Online recruiting is a low-cost method of accessing potential employees.

Human resource departments typically receive numerous résumés on a continual basis. In the past, human resource employees had to sift through the résumés to find potential matches for open positions. Résumés that were not an appropriate match were thrown out after a specified amount of time. Recruitment software has reduced costs by creating a more efficient system. Résumés are either received electronically or scanned into the computer and keywords are used to sort them. Human resource departments

or the hiring manager can use the software's searching capabilities to identify specific skill or experience requirements. The system also allows for the creation of a database of applicants. This technology allows human resource professionals to spend more time conducting interviews and other important tasks rather than sorting, categorizing, and filing résumés.

Many large firms are using their websites to inform potential applicants about career opportunities and to post open positions. This is particularly useful when the positions are computer related. In the past, positions would be advertised in a newspaper or filled at college recruiting fairs. Online job postings allow more detailed listings at very little cost.

---

the employees that Walt Disney hires for management positions are recruited internally.

Firms can do more internal recruiting if their employees are assigned responsibilities and tasks that train them for advanced positions. This strategy conflicts with job specialization because it exposes employees to more varied tasks. Nevertheless, it is necessary to prepare them for other jobs and to reduce the possibility of boredom. Even when a firm is able to fill a position internally, however, the previous position that the employee held becomes open, and the firm must recruit for that position.

external recruiting an effort to fill positions with applicants from outside the firm

External recruiting is an effort to fill positions with applicants from outside the firm. Some firms may recruit more qualified candidates when using external recruiting, especially for some specialized job positions. Although external recruiting allows the firm to evaluate applicants' potential capabilities and limitations, human resource managers do not have as much information as they do for internal applicants. The applicant's résumé lists previously performed functions and describes the responsibilities of those positions, but it does not indicate how the applicant responds to orders or interacts with other employees. This type of information is more critical for some jobs than others.

Dell Computer uses the Internet extensively in its human resource planning. For example, the company allows potential employees to search for a specific job at its website. Dell also allows applicants to submit their résumés over the Internet. Furthermore, Dell uses its website to provide potential employees with information about benefits and about the areas where its plants and employment sites are located, such as cost-of-living estimates.

Screening Applicants   The recruiting process used to screen job applicants involves several steps. The first step is to assess each application to screen out unqualified applicants. Although the information provided on an application is limited, it is usually sufficient to determine whether the applicant has the minimum background, education, and experience necessary to qualify for the position.

The second step in screening applicants is the interview process. Some firms conduct initial interviews of college students at placement centers on college campuses. Other firms conduct initial interviews at their location. The human resource manager may be able to assess the personality of an applicant from a personal interview, as well as obtain additional information that was not included on the application. Specifically, an interview can indicate an applicant's punctuality, communication skills, and attitude. Furthermore, an interview allows the firm to obtain more detailed information about the applicant's past experience.

If the first two screening steps can substantially reduce the number of candidates, the human resource manager can allocate more time to assess each remaining applicant during the interview process. Even when these steps have effectively reduced the number of candidates, however, the first interview with each remaining candidate will not necessarily lead to a selection. A second and even third interview may be necessary. These interviews may involve other employees of the firm who have some interaction with the position of concern. The input of these employees can often influence the hiring decision. A typical questionnaire for obtaining employee opinions about an applicant is shown in Exhibit 11.2.

A third step for screening applicants is to contact the applicant's references. This screening method offers limited benefits, however, because applicants normally list only those references who are likely to provide strong recommendations. A survey by the Society for Human Resource Management found that more than 50 percent of the human resource managers surveyed sometimes receive inadequate information about a job applicant's personality traits. More than 40 percent of these managers said that they

Exhibit 11.2

Example of Questionnaire to Obtain Employee Opinions about a Job Applicant

Applicant's name _____

Position to be filled _____

	Strongly Agree	Agree	Unsure	Disagree	Strongly Disagree
The applicant possesses the necessary skills to perform the tasks required.					
The applicant would work well with others.					
The applicant would be eager to learn new skills.					
The applicant has good communication skills.					
The applicant would accept responsibility.					

Do you detect any deficiencies in the applicant? (If so, describe them.)

Do you recommend that we hire the applicant? Why, or why not?

Signature of employee who is assessing applicant: _____

Mikki Lam, executive director of Just One Break, Inc., is her own best advertisement that hiring the disabled is good business.

AP Photo/ Marty Lederhandler

sometimes receive inadequate information about the applicant's skills and work habits.

Another possible step in the screening process is an **employment test,** which is a test of the candidate's abilities. Some tests are designed to assess intuition or willingness to work with others. Other tests are designed to assess specific skills, such as computer skills.

Until recently, some firms also requested a physical examination for candidates they plan to hire. However, now firms may request a physical examination only *after* a job offer has been made. This examination can determine whether the individual is physically able to perform

employment test a test of a job candidate's abilities

the tasks that would be assigned. In addition, the examination can document any medical problems that existed before the individual was employed by the firm. This can protect the firm from being blamed for causing a person's medical problems through unsafe working conditions.

Along with physical examinations, some firms ask new hires to take a drug test. Firms are adversely affected in two ways when their employees take illegal drugs. First, the firm may incur costs for health care and counseling for these employees. Second, the performance of these employees will likely be low and may even reduce the performance of their co-workers.

Some firms outsource the task of screening job applicants. For example, Bristol-Myers Squibb Company relies on the company MRI to identify and screen its job applicants. MRI organizes recruiting conferences, where it identifies candidates who may be suitable for the positions that Bristol-Myers Squibb and other firms need to fill.

Make the Hiring Decision   By the time the steps for screening applicants are completed, the application list should have been reduced to a small number of qualified candidates. Some firms take their hiring process very seriously because they recognize that their future performance is highly dependent on the employees that they select, as documented by the following statement:

"The past year's success is the product of a talented, smart, hard-working group, and I take great pride in being a part of this team. Setting the bar high [high standards] in our approach to hiring has been, and will continue to be, the single most important element of Amazon.com's success."

—Amazon.com

Exhibit 11.3

Steps for Screening Job Applicants

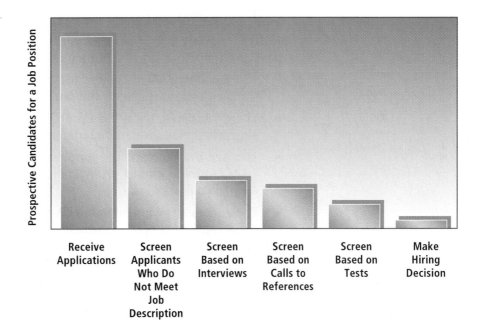

Exhibit 11.4

Summary of Tasks Involved in Human Resource Planning

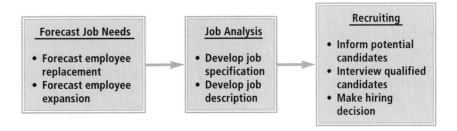

Careful screening enables firms to recruit people who turn out to be excellent employees. Consequently, careful recruiting can result in low turnover.

Once the screening is completed, the top candidate can be selected from this list and offered the job; the remaining qualified applicants can be considered if the top candidate does not accept the job offer. Exhibit 11.3 summarizes the steps used to screen job applicants. Notice that each step reduces the list of applicants who would possibly qualify for the position.

Once hired, the new employee is informed about the firm's health and benefits plans and additional details of the job. A summary of the various tasks necessary to fill a position is provided in Exhibit 11.4.

PROVIDING EQUAL OPPORTUNITY

When recruiting candidates for a job position, managers should not discriminate based on factors that are unrelated to potential job performance. First, such discrimination is illegal. Second, discrimination may reduce the efficiency of the employees in the workplace.

Federal Laws Related to Discrimination

Federal laws prohibit such discrimination. The following are some of the laws enacted to prevent discrimination or improper treatment:

▶ The Equal Pay Act of 1963 states that men and women performing similar work must receive the same pay.

▶ The Civil Rights Act of 1964 prohibits discrimination based on race, gender, religion, or national origin.

▶ The Age Discrimination in Employment Act of 1967, amended in 1978, prohibits employers from discriminating against people who are 40 years old or older.

▶ The Americans with Disabilities Act (ADA) of 1990 prohibits discrimination against people who are disabled.

▶ The Civil Rights Act of 1991 enables women, minorities, and disabled people who believe that they have been subject to discrimination to sue firms. This act protects against discrimination in the hiring process or the employee evaluation process. It also protects against sexual harassment in the workplace.

Overall, the federal laws have helped encourage firms to make hiring decisions without discriminating.

Diversity Incentives

While the federal laws can prevent discrimination, many firms now recognize the potential benefits of a more diverse workplace. These firms strive for diversity not just to abide by the laws, but because it can enhance their value.

Diversity can benefit firms in three ways. First, studies have shown that employees who work in a diverse workplace tend to be more innovative. Second, employees in a diverse workplace are more likely to understand different points of view and be capable of interacting with a diverse set of customers. The proportion of a firm's customer base that consists of minorities will continue to increase. Third, a larger proportion of eligible employees will be from minority groups in the future.

The future growth in the number of minority customers and eligible minority employees is supported by U.S. Census Bureau data. For the period 1990–2000, the white population increased by 3.4 percent; the African American population increased by 16 percent; the Native American population, by 15 percent; and the Hispanic population, by 50 percent. Thus, U.S. population growth is heavily dominated by minority groups. Together, these three minority groups represent 25 percent of the U.S. population now, and by the year 2050, they are expected to represent 38 percent.

By the year 2025, minority groups will in aggregate represent the majority of the population in some states. The total college-age population in the United States is expected to grow by 16 percent by the year 2015, and minorities will account for 80 percent of this growth. Hispanics will account for half of the growth in the minority college-age population, while African Americans and Native Americans will make up the remainder. Thus, firms that create a diverse workplace will be able to match the more diverse customer base that will develop over time and will have better access to the pool of eligible employees.

Exhibit 11.5

Sampling of Firms That Are Known for Establishing a More Diverse Workplace

Name of Firm	Proportion of New Hires Who Are Minorities	Proportion of Workforce Who Are Minorities	Proportion of Managers Who Are Minorities	Number of Board Members Who Are Minorities
McDonald's	37%	55%	38%	2 out of 16
BellSouth	39	31	26	2 out of 13
Lucent Technologies	44	30	23	1 out of 6
PepsiCo	33	27	16	4 out of 15
Colgate-Palmolive	43	29	27	1 out of 8
Procter & Gamble	17	17	17	2 out of 16
Levi Strauss	47	57	33	1 out of 14
United Parcel Service	52	35	28	3 out of 13
American Express	35	27	20	2 out of 12
Coca-Cola	40	32	19	1 out of 12

Firms Recognized for Achieving Diversity   Some of the firms that have made much progress in establishing a more diverse workplace are listed in Exhibit 11.5. These firms not only have recently hired minorities, but also have achieved diversity among their managers, and even among their board members. These firms demonstrate that diversity in the workplace can be accomplished and that firms with diverse sets of employees can be successful. Some of the largest firms in the United States, including Merrill Lynch, American Express, and Symantec, now have minorities serving as chief executive officer (CEO).

A survey of human resource managers conducted by the Society of Human Resource Management in 1999 found that 85 percent of the managers surveyed expect to see more opportunities for women in the future and 79 percent expect to see more opportunities for minorities.

2

Differentiate among the types of compensation that firms offer to employees.

COMPENSATION PACKAGES THAT FIRMS OFFER

Firms attempt to reward their employees by providing adequate compensation. The level of compensation is usually established by determining what employees at other firms with similar job characteristics earn. Information on compensation levels can be obtained by conducting a salary survey or from various publications that report salary levels for different jobs. The wide differences in compensation among job positions are attributed to differences in the supply of people who have a particular skill and the demand for people with that skill. For example, demand for employees who have extensive experience in business financing decisions is high, but the supply of people with such experience is limited. Therefore, firms offer a high level of compensation to attract these people. Conversely, the supply of people who can qualify as a clerk is large, so firms can offer relatively low compensation to hire clerks.

If a firm does not provide adequate compensation and working conditions, it may not be able to retain its employees. Consider the case of Pacific Health Care Systems, which experienced a high level of employee turnover

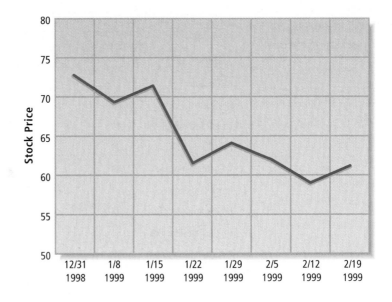

in January 1999. Its value (as measured by its stock price) declined substantially, as shown in Exhibit 11.6.

compensation package the total monetary compensation and benefits offered to employees

A **compensation package** consists of the total monetary compensation and benefits offered to employees. Some employees consider their salary to be their compensation, but the benefits that some firms offer may be more valuable than the salary. The typical elements of a compensation package are salary, stock options, commissions, bonuses, profit sharing, benefits, and perquisites.

Salary

salary (or wages) the dollars paid for a job over a specific period

Salary (or wages) is the dollars paid for a job over a specific period. The salary can be expressed per hour, per pay period, or per year and is fixed over a particular time period.

Stock Options

stock options a form of compensation that allows employees to purchase shares of their employer's stock at a specific price

Stock options allow employees to purchase the firm's stock at a specific price. Consider employees who have been given stock options to buy 100 shares of stock at a price of $20 per share. This means that they can purchase the stock for this price, regardless of the stock's market price. Thus, even if the stock's market price rises to $30 per share, the employees can still buy the stock for $20 per share. They would need $2,000 (computed as 100 shares × $20 per share) to purchase 100 shares. If the firm performs well over time, the stock price will rise, and their 100 shares will be worth even more. Thus, these employees are motivated to perform well because they benefit directly when the firm performs well. As part-owners of the firm, they share in its profits.

Many firms provide stock options to their high-level managers, such as the CEO, vice-presidents, and other managers. Some firms, however, such as Starbucks and Microsoft, provide stock options to all of their employees. This can motivate all employees to perform well. Starbucks grants stock op-

French media giant Vivendi Universal's former chairman Jean-Marie Messier was ousted in part because of an outrage over his 5.1 million euro ($5.2 million) salary and bonus and €835,000 stock options. Messier got the increased pay package after his company suffered a record loss in 2001 and its shares fell more than 50 percent.

AP Photo/ Remy de la Mauviniere

tions to its employees in proportion to their salaries. An employee who received a salary of $20,000 in 1991 would have earned more than $50,000 by the year 2000 from owning the stock options.

Microsoft attributes much of its success to its use of stock options. Because of its strong performance (and therefore substantial increase in its stock price) since 1992, its managers who were hired in 1992 or before are now millionaires because their shares are worth more than $1 million.

Stock options not only motivate employees but can help to retain employees, as documented by the following comment:

"We will continue to focus on hiring and retaining versatile and talented employees, and continue to weight their compensation to stock options rather than cash. We know our success will be largely affected by our ability to attract and retain a motivated employee base, each of whom must think like, and therefore must actually be, an owner."

—Amazon.com

How Options Can Cause a Conflict of Interests Stock options can also lead to problems for a firm's shareholders, however. When the top managers use their stock options to obtain the firm's stock, they want to sell that stock during a period when the stock's price is high. Although owning stock is supposed to encourage managers to improve the firm so that they benefit from a higher stock price, stock ownership may tempt them to manipulate the financial statements to boost the stock price. In some cases, a firm's managers have increased investor demand for the stock by using accounting methods that temporarily boosted the firm's earnings. The high demand caused the stock price to rise, allowing the managers to sell their holdings of stock at a high price. When investors learned that the firm's earnings were exaggerated, they sold their stock, causing the price to decline, but by that time the managers had already sold their shares. During the 2001–2002 period, managers of several firms, including Enron, Global Crossing, and WorldCom, were accused of using accounting to inflate their earnings and mislead investors in this way.

Some firms not only exaggerated their earnings, but failed to disclose financial problems. In several cases, managers knew of problems at a firm but withheld relevant information from the public until after they had sold

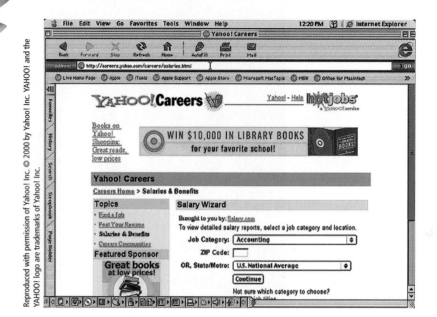

e-business

business online

Employee Compensation This website provides employee compensation information for a wide variety of occupations.

http://careers.yahoo.com/
careers/salaries.html

their holdings of the firm's stock. The managers issued overly optimistic financial reports so that other shareholders would not sell the firm's stock and cause the price to decline until the managers had sold their shares. Thus, the managers were able to benefit at the expense of other investors who purchased the stock from them at a high price without realizing the firm's financial problems.

As an example, Enron manipulated its earnings so that they increased over 20 consecutive quarters leading up to 2001. Enron's stock price rose over time along with the earnings. When investors recognized that Enron was manipulating its earnings, however, they dumped the stock, and the stock price declined abruptly in 2001. In November 2001, Enron filed for bankruptcy. Yet, before Enron's price declined, 29 Enron executives or board members sold their holdings of Enron stock for more than $1 billion. In particular, Enron's CEO sold more than $100 million worth of Enron stock before the financial problems were disclosed. The CEO and other top managers were able to sell their shares at a high price because other shareholders did not know about Enron's problems. Thus, the managers benefited at the expense of the other shareholders. Similar abuses have occurred at other firms, although to a lesser extent.

The lesson of the Enron scandal is that managers who receive stock options as compensation may be tempted to manipulate the firm's stock price so that they can sell their shares at a high price. Although managers cannot control the stock's price directly, they can influence the price indirectly through the information that they release or withhold. Thus, they have an incentive to exaggerate the earnings, issue overly optimistic reports, or withhold bad news; by doing so, they can indirectly push the stock price higher and then sell their stock holdings at a high price.

A firm's board of directors should attempt to prevent such abuses. The board of directors can enact guidelines that allow the managers or board members to sell only a small amount of their stock holdings in any particular quarter or year. In this way, the managers will not have an incentive to create an artificially high stock price in any particular quarter or year because they will not be able to sell all of their stock at that time.

Commissions

commissions compensation for meeting specific sales objectives

Commissions normally represent compensation for meeting specific sales objectives. For example, salespeople at many firms receive a base salary, plus a percentage of their total sales volume as monetary compensation. Commissions are not used for jobs where employee performance cannot be as easily measured.

Bonuses

bonus an extra one-time payment at the end of a period in which performance was measured

A **bonus** is an extra one-time payment at the end of a period in which performance was measured. Bonuses are usually paid less frequently than commissions (such as once a year). A bonus may be paid for efforts to increase revenue, reduce expenses, or improve customer satisfaction. In most cases, the bonus is not set by a formula; thus, supervisors have some flexibility in determining the bonus for each employee. The total amount of bonus funds that are available for employees may be dependent on the firm's profits for the year of concern.

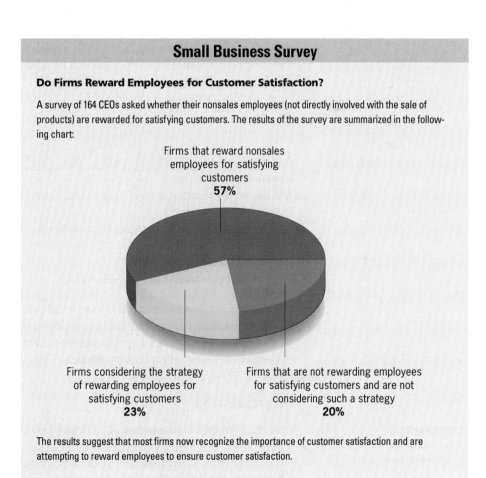

Small Business Survey

Do Firms Reward Employees for Customer Satisfaction?

A survey of 164 CEOs asked whether their nonsales employees (not directly involved with the sale of products) are rewarded for satisfying customers. The results of the survey are summarized in the following chart:

Firms that reward nonsales employees for satisfying customers
57%

Firms considering the strategy of rewarding employees for satisfying customers
23%

Firms that are not rewarding employees for satisfying customers and are not considering such a strategy
20%

The results suggest that most firms now recognize the importance of customer satisfaction and are attempting to reward employees to ensure customer satisfaction.

Profit Sharing

profit sharing a portion of the firm's profits is paid to employees

Some firms, such as Continental Airlines and General Motors, offer employees **profit sharing,** in which a portion of the firm's profits is paid to employees. Boeing, J.P. Morgan Chase, and many other firms also offer profit sharing to some of their employees. This motivates employees to perform in a manner that improves profitability.

Employee Benefits

employee benefits additional privileges beyond compensation payments, such as paid vacation time; health, life, or dental insurance; and pension programs

Employees may also receive **employee benefits,** which are additional privileges beyond compensation payments, such as paid vacation time; health, life, or dental insurance; and pension programs. Typically, these employee benefits are not taxed. Many firms provide substantial employee benefits to their employees. The cost of providing health insurance has soared in recent years. Many firms, such as Johnson & Johnson, have responded by offering preventive health-care programs. Some firms now give employees incentives to stay healthy by reducing the insurance premiums charged to employees who receive favorable scores on cholesterol levels, blood pressure, fitness, and body fat.

College Health Club: **Employee Benefit Decision at CHC**

As Sue Kramer develops her business plan for College Health Club (CHC), she must decide whether to pay an annual bonus to the five part-time employees she will hire. She considers paying each of them a Christmas bonus of $200. Alternatively, she considers offering them the benefit of a free membership to the club. Her analysis of how these alternatives would affect the first-year performance of CHC is shown in the following table:

	Performance if . . .	
	CHC Provides a Christmas Bonus of $200 to Each Part-Time Employee	CHC Provides a Free Membership to Each Part-Time Employee
(1) Price per membership	$500	$500
(2) Number of members in first year	300	300
(3) Revenue = (1) × (2)	$150,000	$150,000
(4) Total operating expenses excluding Christmas bonus	$138,000	$138,000
(5) Payment of Christmas bonus to 5 part-time employees	$1,000	$0
(6) Interest expenses	$4,000	$4,000
(7) Earnings before taxes = (3) − (4) − (5) − (6)	$7,000	$8,000

The Christmas bonus would cost $1,000 and would reduce earnings by $1,000. The free memberships would not have a direct cost. Sue decides that she will give each of her employees a free membership; she thinks the employees are likely to prefer the memberships to a Christmas bonus, and CHC's earnings will not be affected.

Perquisites

perquisites additional privileges beyond compensation payments and employee benefits

Some firms offer **perquisites** (or "perks") to high-level employees, which are additional privileges beyond compensation payments and employee benefits. Common perquisites include free parking, a company car, club memberships, telephone credit cards, and an expense account.

global business

Compensating Employees across Countries The manner in which firms compensate their employees may vary across countries. Salary may be perceived as less important in a country where personal income tax rates are high. If a large portion of the salary is taxed, employees may prefer other forms of compensation. The health benefits that a firm offers may be less important in countries that provide free medical services.

Some U.S. firms, such as Gillette and PepsiCo, offer their employees opportunities to purchase their stock at below-market prices. Most employees in the United States perceive this form of employee compensation as desirable. Employees in other countries, however, perceive it as less desirable. The rules for individuals who purchase stock vary among countries. For example, individuals in Brazil, China, and India are restricted from purchasing or owning stock under some circumstances.

The taxes imposed on the profits earned by individuals on their stocks also vary across countries, which makes stock ownership less desirable for employees based in certain countries. Furthermore, individuals in some countries are more comfortable investing in bank deposits rather than in stocks.

Since employees based in different countries may have varying views about compensation, a firm with employees in several countries should consider tailoring its compensation plans to fit the characteristics of each country. The firm may provide higher salaries in one country and more health benefits in another. Before establishing a compensation plan in a given country, the firm should assess the specific tax laws of that country and survey individuals to determine the types of compensation that are most desirable. When a firm designs a compensation plan to fit the country's characteristics, it can improve employee job satisfaction.

Exhibit 11.7

How Forms of Compensation Can Vary across Job Descriptions

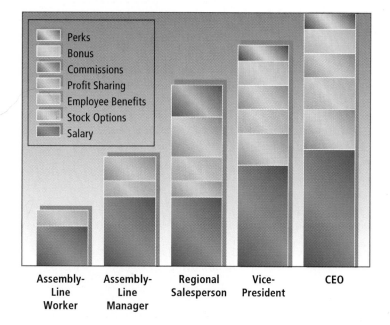

Comparison across Jobs

The forms of compensation allocated to employees vary with their jobs, as shown in Exhibit 11.7. Employees who are directly involved in the production process (such as assembly-line workers) tend to receive most of their compensation in the form of salary. Low-level managers may also receive most of their compensation as salary but may receive a small bonus and profit sharing.

Many salespeople in the computer and technology sectors earn more compensation in the form of commissions than as salary. High-level managers, such as vice-presidents and CEOs, normally have a high salary and the potential for a large bonus. Their employee benefits are also relatively large, and they normally are awarded various perks as well.

DEVELOPING SKILLS OF EMPLOYEES

3

Describe the skills of employees that firms develop.

Firms that hire employees provide training to develop various employee skills. Motorola has established its own university where each employee receives at least one week of training per year. A study by the management consulting firm Ernst & Young found that firms that invest in training programs are more profitable. To illustrate the attention that can be given to training, consider the case of The Home Depot Company. Its employees frequently interact with customers and need to have sufficient expertise to explain how various products can be used. The managers interact with the employees and with customers. The Home Depot Company has established an initiative focused on training, as explained in its recent annual report:

"We believe our greatest competitive advantage is our people. That's why in 2001, we launched human resources initiatives designed to attract, motivate, and retain the best employees in the industry. Through learning programs for associates and leadership development of district and store managers, we will increasingly shift our store management focus from 'operating a box' to 'managing a business.'"

Some of the more common types of training provided to employees are discussed next.

Kelly Bulla, 17, of Lake Geneva, Wisconsin, jumps to the moving mailboat after picking up mail from a pier mailbox. She and five others tried out to be "mailjumpers" for the Lake Geneva Boat Tours company. Hiring the right people for the job is critical to a firm's success. This company has found a creative way to evaluate potential employees prior to hiring them.

AP Photo/ Beloit Dailey News, Casey Riffe

Technical Skills

Employees must be trained to perform the various tasks they engage in daily. Ace Hardware offers courses to train its employees on the use of the products that it sells. As factories owned by firms such as General Motors and Boeing incorporate more advanced technology, employees receive more training. These firms spend millions of dollars every year on training. As computer technology improves, employees of travel agencies, mail-order clothing firms, retail stores, and large corporations must receive more training

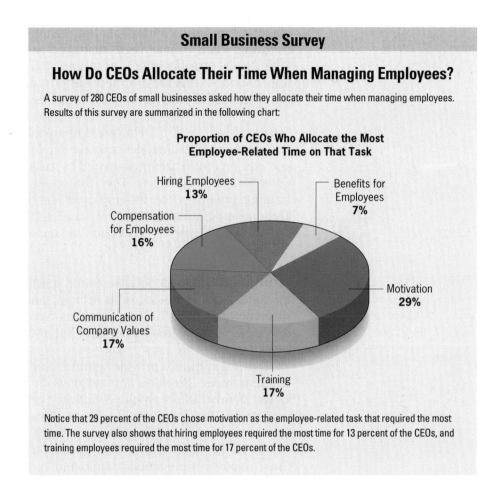

Small Business Survey

How Do CEOs Allocate Their Time When Managing Employees?

A survey of 280 CEOs of small businesses asked how they allocate their time when managing employees. Results of this survey are summarized in the following chart:

**Proportion of CEOs Who Allocate the Most
Employee-Related Time on That Task**

Hiring Employees
13%

Benefits for
Employees
7%

Compensation
for Employees
16%

Motivation
29%

Communication of
Company Values
17%

Training
17%

Notice that 29 percent of the CEOs chose motivation as the employee-related task that required the most time. The survey also shows that hiring employees required the most time for 13 percent of the CEOs, and training employees required the most time for 17 percent of the CEOs.

on using computers. In addition, employees who are assigned to new jobs will require extra training. Firms recognize that expenses may be incurred each year to continually develop each employee's skills.

Decision-Making Skills

Firms can benefit from providing their employees with some guidelines to consider when making decisions and generating ideas. For example, Xerox trains all of its employees to follow a six-step process when generating ideas and making decisions. Kodak employees who recently created new products are asked to share their knowledge with other employees who are attempting to develop new products. Motorola trains its employees to apply new technology to develop new products. Ace Hardware offers courses on management skills for its managers.

Customer Service Skills

Employees who frequently deal with customers need to have customer service skills. Many employees in tourism industries such as airlines and hotels are trained to satisfy customers. The hotel chain Marriott International provides training on serving customers, with refresher sessions after the first and second months. The training is intended not only to ensure customer satisfaction but also to provide employees with an orientation that makes them more comfortable (and increases employee satisfaction). Ace Hardware offers courses for its managers to develop customer service skills. Walt Disney provides extensive training to its newly hired employees. Customer service skills are also necessary for employees hired by firms to sell products or deal with customer complaints.

Safety Skills   Firms educate employees about safety within the work environment. This includes training employees on how to use machinery and equipment in factories owned by large manufacturing firms, such as Caterpillar and Goodyear Tire. United Parcel Service (UPS) implements training programs for its employees on handling hazardous materials. Training programs not only reassure employees but also reduce healthcare and legal expenses that could be incurred as a result of work-related injuries.

Human Relations Skills   Some training seminars may be necessary for supervisors who lack skills in managing other employees. In general, this type of training helps supervisors recognize that their employees not only deserve to be treated properly but also will perform better if they are treated well.

Firms commonly provide seminars on diversity to help employees of different races, genders, and religions become more sensitive to other views. Denny's offers employee training on diversity to prevent racial discrimination. Diversity training may enable a firm to create an environment in which people work together more effectively, thereby improving the firm's performance. It may also prevent friction between employees and thus can possibly prevent discrimination or harassment lawsuits against the firm.

Training seminars are also designed to improve relationships among employees across various divisions so that employees can work together in teams. For example, Motorola and Xerox provide seminars on teamwork for employees. Anheuser-Busch organizes regular meetings between employees and executives.

College Health Club: **Developing Employee Skills at CHC**

One of the decisions that Sue Kramer needs to make as part of her business plan for College Health Club (CHC) is how to train employees. If her employees are trained properly, they will serve the members better, and the members will be more satisfied with the health club.

Sue plans to focus her employee training on three areas. First, when she hires her part-time employees, she will stress the need for safety. She wants to ensure that each employee understands the potential dangers in using the weight and exercise machines. Sue will provide all of her members with a booklet on safety, but she also wants her employees to understand the safety features so that they can help any members who are not using the machines properly.

Second, Sue wants to make sure that her employees understand the importance of customer relations, especially in a service business like a health club. Third, she plans to emphasize human relations skills by explaining the need for the part-time employees to work together.

EVALUATION OF EMPLOYEE PERFORMANCE

4

Explain how the performance of employees can be evaluated.

Employees often perceive performance evaluation as only a method for allocating raises. Yet, if supervisors properly conduct the evaluation, it can also provide feedback and direction to employees. An evaluation should indicate an employee's strengths and weaknesses and may influence an employee's chances of being promoted within the firm in the future.

Segmenting the Evaluation into Different Criteria

The overall performance of most employees is normally based on multiple criteria. Therefore, an evaluation can best be conducted by segmenting the evaluation into the criteria that are relevant for each particular job position. For example, consider employees who have excellent technical skills for their jobs, but are not dependable. Since they rate high on one criterion and low on another, their overall performance might be evaluated as about average. An average rating for overall performance, however, does not specifically pinpoint the employees' favorable or unfavorable work habits.

Segmenting performance evaluation into different criteria can help supervisors pinpoint specific strengths and weaknesses. Evaluating each criterion separately provides more specific information to employees about how they may improve. In our example, the employees who receive a low rating on dependability can focus on improving that behavior. Furthermore, these employees can see from their evaluation that their supervisor recognized their strong technical skills. Without a detailed evaluation, employees may not recognize what tasks they do well (in the opinion of supervisors) and what specific weaknesses need to be improved.

Objective versus Subjective Criteria   Some performance criteria are objective, such as parts produced per week, number of days absent, percentage of deadlines missed, and the proportion of defective parts caused by employee errors. Examples of direct measures of performance are provided for specific job positions in Exhibit 11.8 to illustrate how the measures vary by type of job. Other characteristics not shown in Exhibit 11.8 that are

Exhibit 11.8

Examples of Direct Measures of Performance

Job Position	Direct Measures of Performance
Salesperson	Dollar volume of sales over a specific period Number of new customers Number of delinquent accounts collected Net sales per month in territory
Manager	Number of employee grievances Cost reductions Absenteeism Unit safety record Timeliness in completing appraisals Employee satisfaction with manager Division production Diversity of new hires
Administrative assistant	Number of letters prepared Word processing speed Number of errors in filing Number of tasks returned for reprocessing Number of calls screened

commonly assessed for some job positions include organization, communication, and decision-making skills.

Some criteria are less objective but still important. For example, the quality of work cannot always be measured by part defects, because many jobs do not focus on producing a single product. Therefore, quality of work may be subjectively assessed by a supervisor. Also, the willingness of an employee to help other employees is an important criterion that is subjective.

Using a Performance Evaluation Form

Supervisors are typically required to complete a performance evaluation form at the end of each year. An example of such a form is shown in Exhibit 11.9. When supervisors measure the performance of employees, they normally classify the employee in one of several categories such as the following: (1) outstanding, (2) above average, (3) average, (4) below average, and (5) poor. The set of criteria can be more specific for particular jobs within the firm. For example, assembly-line workers may be rated by the total components produced and production quality. A company salesperson may be evaluated by the number of computers sold and the quality of service provided to customers. It is important that supervisors inform employees of the criteria by which they will be rated. Otherwise, they may allocate too much time to tasks that supervisors view as not important.

Assigning Weights to the Criteria

An employee's ratings on all relevant criteria can be combined to determine the employee's overall performance level. Some firms use systems that weight and rate the criteria used to evaluate the employee. For example, bank tellers may be rated according to their speed in handling customer transactions, their quality (accuracy) in handling money transactions, and their ability to satisfy customers. The speed may be monitored by supervisors over time, while accuracy is measured by balancing the accounts at the end of each day, and customer satisfaction is measured from customer feedback over time.

The different criteria must also be weighted separately because some of the employee's assignments may be considered more important than others. Using our example, assume that the weights are determined as follows:

Speed in handling customer transactions	30%
Accuracy in handling customer transactions	50%
Satisfying customers	20%
	100%

The sum of the weights of all criteria should be 100 percent. The weighting system should be communicated to employees when they begin a job position so that they understand what characteristics are most important within the evaluation.

To demonstrate how an overall performance measure is derived, assume that in our example the supervisor rated the bank teller as shown in Exhibit 11.10. The overall rating is the weighted average of 4.5; this rating is in between "above average" and "outstanding." Other bank tellers could also be periodically rated in this manner. At the end of each year, the

Exhibit 11.9

Example of Performance Appraisal Form

Employee Name _____ Date _____

Position _____

Behavior Ratings: Check the one characteristic that best applies.
Quality of Work (refers to accuracy and margin of error):

_____ 1. Makes errors frequently and repeatedly
_____ 2. Often makes errors
_____ 3. Is accurate; makes occasional errors
_____ 4. Is accurate; rarely makes errors
_____ 5. Is exacting and precise

Quantity of Work (refers to amount of production or results):

_____ 1. Usually does not complete work load as assigned
_____ 2. Often accomplishes part of a task
_____ 3. Handles work load as assigned
_____ 4. Turns out more work than requested
_____ 5. Handles an unusually large volume of work

Timeliness (refers to completion of task, within time allowed):

_____ 1. Does not complete duties on time
_____ 2. Is often late in completing tasks
_____ 3. Completes tasks on time
_____ 4. Usually completes tasks in advance of deadlines
_____ 5. Always completes all tasks in advance of time frames

Attendance and Punctuality (refers to adhering to work schedule assigned):

_____ 1. Is usually tardy or absent
_____ 2. Is often tardy or absent
_____ 3. Normally is not tardy or absent
_____ 4. Makes a point of being on the job and on time
_____ 5. Is extremely conscientious about attendance

Responsibility (refers to completing assignments and projects):

_____ 1. Usually does not assume responsibility for completing assignments
_____ 2. Is at times reluctant to accept delegated responsibility
_____ 3. Accepts and discharges delegated duties willingly
_____ 4. Accepts additional responsibility
_____ 5. Is a self-starter who seeks out more effective ways to achieve results or seeks additional responsibilities

Cooperation with Others (refers to working and communicating with supervisors and co-workers):

_____ 1. Has difficulty working with others and often complains when given assignments
_____ 2. Sometimes has difficulty working with others and often complains when given assignments
_____ 3. Usually is agreeable and obliging; generally helps out when requested
_____ 4. Works well with others; welcomes assignments and is quick to offer assistance
_____ 5. Is an outstanding team worker; always assists others and continually encourages cooperation by setting an excellent example

Performance Summary (include strong areas and areas for future emphasis in improving performance or developing additional job skills):

Employee Comments or Concerns:

Signatures:
Human Resource Manager _____ Date _____
Employee _____ Date _____
Supervisor _____ Date _____

Exhibit 11.10

Developing an Overall Rating

Characteristic	Rating	Weight	Weighted Rating
Speed in handling customer transactions	4 (above average)	30%	$4 \times 30\% = 1.2$
Accuracy in handling customer transactions	5 (outstanding)	50%	$5 \times 50\% = 2.5$
Satisfying customers	4 (above average)	20%	$4 \times 20\% = .80$
			Overall rating = 4.5

ratings may be used to determine the raise for each teller. The ratings may also be reviewed along with other characteristics (such as experience) when the employees are considered for a promotion.

This system of developing an overall rating is more appropriate when a few key criteria can be used to assess an employee throughout a period. When employees have numerous job assignments, however, accounting for all types of assignments within the performance evaluation is more difficult. Nevertheless, some of the assignments may be combined into a single characteristic, such as "customer service" or "ability to complete tasks on time."

Some supervisors may believe that a weighted system is too structured and does not account for some relevant characteristics, such as ability to get along with other employees. However, characteristics like these could be included within the weighting system.

Steps for Proper Performance Evaluation

Firms can follow specific steps to demonstrate fairness to employees and also satisfy legal guidelines in recognizing employee rights.

1 Supervisors should communicate job responsibilities to employees when they are hired. Supervisors should also communicate any changes in employee job responsibilities over time. This communication can be done orally, but it should be backed up with a letter to the employee. The letters are not as personal as oral communication, but they provide documentation in case a disagreement arises in the future about assignments and responsibilities. The letters may not only provide support to defend against employee lawsuits, but they also force supervisors to pinpoint the specific tasks for employees in a particular job position.

2 When supervisors notice that employees have deficiencies, they should inform the employees of those deficiencies. This communication may occur in the form of a standard periodic review. Supervisors may prefer to inform employees of deficiencies immediately, rather than wait for the review period. Employees should be given a chance to respond to the criticism. Supervisors may also allow a short period of time for employees to correct the deficiencies. Supervisors should also communicate with employees who were evaluated favorably so that those employees recognize that their efforts are appreciated.

3 Supervisors should be consistent when conducting performance evaluations. That is, two employees who have a similar deficiency should be treated equally in the evaluation process. Many supervisors find it easier to communicate deficiencies to employees who are more willing to accept criticism, but it is only fair to treat employees with the same deficiencies similarly.

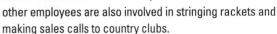

cross functional teamwork:

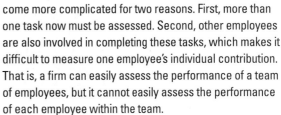

How Job Responsibilities across Business Functions Can Complicate Performance Evaluations

Firms have increasingly encouraged employees to perform a variety of business functions to achieve higher levels of job satisfaction and efficiency. Although this form of job enlargement has been successful, it can complicate the evaluation of an employee's performance. Consider an employee of a sporting goods store whose only responsibility is stringing tennis rackets. The performance of this employee is judged by the number of tennis rackets strung and the quality of the stringing (as measured by customer feedback).

The employee's responsibilities are then enlarged to include visiting country clubs and selling tennis rackets to them. Whereas the employee's initial job focused on assembly of tennis rackets, the enlarged responsibilities involve marketing the tennis rackets. Furthermore, other employees are also involved in stringing rackets and making sales calls to country clubs.

The performance evaluation of the employee has become more complicated for two reasons. First, more than one task now must be assessed. Second, other employees are also involved in completing these tasks, which makes it difficult to measure one employee's individual contribution. That is, a firm can easily assess the performance of a team of employees, but it cannot easily assess the performance of each employee within the team.

Action Due to Performance Evaluations

Some performance evaluations require supervisors to take action. Employees who receive a very favorable evaluation may deserve some type of recognition or even a promotion. If supervisors do not acknowledge such outstanding performance, employees may either lose their enthusiasm and reduce their effort or search for a new job at a firm that will reward them for high performance. Supervisors should acknowledge high performance so that the employee will continue to perform well in the future.

Employees who receive unfavorable evaluations must also be given attention. Supervisors must determine the reasons for poor performance. Some reasons (such as a family illness) may have a temporary adverse impact on performance and can be corrected. Other reasons, such as a bad attitude, may not be temporary. When supervisors give employees an unfavorable evaluation, they must decide whether to take any additional actions. If the employees were unaware of their own deficiencies, the unfavorable evaluation can pinpoint the deficiencies that employees must correct. In this case, the supervisor may simply need to monitor the employees closely and ensure that the deficiencies are corrected.

If the employees were already aware of their deficiencies before the evaluation period, however, they may be unable or unwilling to correct them. This situation is more serious, and the supervisor may need to take action. The action should be consistent with the firm's guidelines and may include reassigning the employees to new jobs, suspending them temporarily, or firing them. A supervisor's action toward a poorly performing worker can affect the attitudes of other employees. If no penalty is imposed on an employee for poor performance, other employees may rebel by reducing their productivity as well.

Firms must follow certain procedures to fire an employee. These procedures are intended to prevent firms from firing employees without reason. Specifically, supervisors should identify deficiencies in employees' evaluations and give them a chance to respond.

Dealing with Lawsuits by Fired Employees

It is not uncommon for employees to sue the firm after being fired. Some lawsuits argue that the fired employee did not receive due process. Others argue that the firing occurred because of discrimination based on race, gender, age, religion, or national origin. Complaints of discrimination are first filed with the Equal Employment Opportunity Commission (EEOC), which is responsible for enforcing the discrimination laws. About 20 percent of complaints filed with the EEOC are judged as having a reasonable cause for the fired employee to take action, while 80 percent of the complaints are judged to have no reasonable basis. Even when the EEOC believes the complaint is not valid, however, the fired employee can still sue the firm.

The surge of employee lawsuits in recent years is partially attributed to the following factors. First, as of 1991, plaintiffs were allowed the right to trial by jury. The common perception is that juries are more sympathetic toward plaintiffs than judges are. Also, juries are perceived as more unpredictable, which concerns firms that are sued by employees. A second reason for the rise in lawsuits is the increase in potential damages that can be awarded to plaintiffs. As a result of the Civil Rights Act of 1991, plaintiffs can be awarded not only compensatory damages (such as back pay) but also punitive damages (to penalize the firm) and legal expenses. Therefore, plaintiffs and their attorneys can now receive much larger amounts of money.

Much media attention has been given to employee lawsuits. Firms recognize that such lawsuits can be very costly. Nevertheless, a firm should not ignore an employee's deficiencies out of fear that the employee will sue. Doing so will reduce the motivation of other employees if they recognize that one employee is receiving special treatment. The court system has generally sided with firms in cases in which supervisors followed proper procedures in firing employees.

In recent years, many employees who were dismissed have charged that the dismissal was based on discrimination because of race, religion, gender, or age. Many firms with numerous employees have been sued for this reason, even when their supervisors have followed all proper procedures. Although the laws that prohibit discrimination have good intentions, the court system has not effectively separated the frivolous cases from the valid ones. Consequently, legal expenses for many firms have risen substantially.

Some firms have attempted to settle lawsuits before trial to reduce their legal expenses and avoid negative publicity. However, settling a lawsuit that has no merit may result in other frivolous lawsuits by employees.

Despite the increase in employee lawsuits, firms must still attempt to ensure that their employees are doing the jobs that they are paid to do. While firms cannot necessarily avoid employee lawsuits, they can attempt to establish training and performance evaluation guidelines that will reduce the chances of lawsuits.

Employee Evaluation of Supervisors

Some firms allow employees to evaluate their supervisors. The evaluations can then be used to measure the managerial abilities of the supervisors. These so-called **upward appraisals** have been used by many firms, including AT&T and Dow Chemical. An upward evaluation is more effective if it is anonymous. Otherwise, workers may automatically offer a very favorable evaluation either in the hope that their supervisor will return the favor or

upward appraisals used to measure the managerial abilities of supervisors

to avoid retaliation. Evaluations of the supervisor may identify deficiencies, which can then be corrected so that the supervisor can more effectively manage employees in the future. The evaluation form should allow each criterion to be evaluated separately so that the supervisor can recognize which characteristics need to be improved.

College Health Club: **Employee Performance Evaluation at CHC**

As Sue Kramer develops her business plan for College Health Club (CHC), she wants to decide on a method for evaluating the performance of the part-time employees that she will hire. She recognizes that a key role of the employees is to satisfy CHC's members. Therefore, she will rate each employee's customer relations skills. The survey forms that request feedback from members ask if they have any comments about the individual employees. In addition, Sue will rate employees according to how well they work with other employees. Now that she has identified the specific criteria to be used to evaluate the employees, she will communicate these criteria to the employees when she hires them so that they know how they will be evaluated.

SUMMARY

1 The main functions involved in human resource planning are

▶ forecasting human resource needs,

▶ job analysis, and

▶ recruiting.

2 Compensation packages offered by firms can include salary, stock options, commissions, bonuses, profit sharing, employee benefits, and perquisites.

3 After firms hire employees, they commonly provide training to enhance technical skills, decision-making skills, customer service skills, safety skills, and human relations skills.

4 The performance of employees can be evaluated by segmenting the evaluation into different criteria, assigning an evaluation rating to each criterion, and weighting each criterion. The overall performance rating is the weighted average of all criteria that were assigned a rating.

Once supervisors evaluate employees, they should discuss the evaluations with the employees and identify any specific strengths, as well as any specific weaknesses that need to be improved.

KEY TERMS

Review & Critical Thinking Questions

1. Describe the tasks involved in developing a human resource plan.

2. What is the purpose of a job analysis? What two documents can be developed from a job analysis?

3. Distinguish internal recruiting from external recruiting.

4. Describe the steps involved in the recruiting process to screen job applicants.

5. Describe the various types of compensation packages that could be offered to employees.

6. Discuss the types of skills that an employee could develop from a firm's training program.

7. How can segmenting an evaluation into different criteria help a supervisor pinpoint specific strengths and weaknesses of an employee's job performance?

8. Why has the number of employee lawsuits that claim discrimination increased in recent years? How should a firm deal with these lawsuits?

9. How can striving for diversity enhance the value of firms?

10. What is the purpose of an upward appraisal? How should such an appraisal be conducted?

11. How can stock options cause a conflict of interest between shareholders and the firm's managers? What can the board of directors do to minimize such conflicts of interest?

12. How can management reduce employees' need for union representation? (See the chapter appendix.)

Discussion Questions

1. You are a human resource manager and have been assigned to develop a compensation policy with supplemental pay benefits for your employees. What benefit do you think employees most desire today?

2. You are a manager and have an employee with three years' work experience who refuses to be retrained. This employee further refuses to discuss his performance appraisal with you. What should your next step be?

3. How could a firm use the Internet to attract new employees? How could it use the Internet to evaluate existing employees?

4. You have just opened a Jeep Cherokee dealership. Which of your employees would be paid salaries? Which would be paid hourly wages? Which would receive commissions and/or perquisites?

5. You know your firm's chief financial officer (CFO). He just told you that he will sell the company's stock as soon as possible and advises you to do the same. What do you think this indicates? What do you think you should do?

6. You are a manager in a company where a group of workers have petitioned for union representation. What factors would cause workers to do this? What can managers do to reduce the possibility that workers will vote in favor of union representation? (See the chapter appendix.)

It's Your Decision: **Hiring and Evaluating Employees at CHC**

1. Should Sue Kramer require job applicants at CHC to take drug tests?

2. What criteria can Sue use to measure the performance of an aerobics instructor that she hires?

3. What steps should Sue take if an employee she hires performs poorly?

4. Employees at CHC have various tasks, such as responding to members' requests for help using exercise machines (this is a production task) and showing prospective members around the club (this is a marketing task). If Sue creates a bonus plan that offers a bonus to any employee who signs up new members, why might the production quality decline?

5. A health club differs from manufacturing firms in that it produces a service rather than products. Explain why a bonus plan for high performance may be more difficult to implement in a service firm such as CHC than for a manufacturing firm.

Investing in a Business

Using the annual report of the firm in which you would like to invest, complete the following:

1 Does the firm periodically provide special training to its employees? If so, provide details.

2 Does the firm offer bonuses to its employees as an incentive? If so, are the bonuses tied to employee performance? Provide details.

3 Does the firm offer any other programs that are designed to achieve employee satisfaction, such as a flexible work schedule? If so, provide details.

4 Explain how the business uses technology to hire, train, and evaluate employees. For example, does it use the Internet to provide information about job openings or its compensation programs?

5 Go to **http://hoovers.com** and locate the NEWS SEARCH. Type in the name of the firm in the space provided, and review the recent news stories about the firm. Summarize any (at least one) recent news story about the firm that applies to one or more of the key concepts in this chapter.

Case: Filling Job Positions

George DeCaro, a human resource manager of Bobcat International, a manufacturer of bobcats, has just received a directive from the president of the company. The directive reads: "We have just completed our strategy for the year. The thrust of this strategy is to increase our market share by 22 percent over the next three years." It continues: "We must be ready for this challenge by increasing production, and the human resource department must staff the organization with 37 new jobs."

George's task is to forecast job requirements each year for the next three years. George recognizes that both internal and external recruiting will have to be undertaken. The firm's philosophy is to promote from within whenever possible. This procedure promotes high morale and contributes to the overall success of the organization. However, most of the 37 jobs will have to be filled externally. He ponders the sources for recruiting potential job candidates for semiskilled plant jobs that pay an hourly rate.

Another consideration for George is diversity. Bobcat is currently not very diversified, and George contemplates whether the externally filled positions should be used to increase Bobcat's diversity.

George works well with the firm's president and wants to request a meeting to demonstrate how the human resource department will perform a vital role in helping the firm meet its objectives.

Questions

1 What is the human resource plan in this case? Discuss its major tasks.

2 What is job analysis in general? How should it be used in this case?

3 Discuss George's sources for recruiting potential employees for the plant jobs.

4 What should be on George's agenda for the meeting with the company's president?

5 How could Bobcat benefit from a more diverse workforce?

Video Case: Recruiting and Training at Valassis Communications

Valassis Communications, Inc., creates promotional inserts for newspapers. It attributes much of its success to its employees. Its human resource department spends much time screening and interviewing applicants for jobs. The department also tests applicants in various ways to determine whether they would fit into the firm's environment. Applicants who can be assigned goals and are motivated to meet goals are more likely to be satisfied working at Valassis. Once hired, employees who perform well are rewarded well so that Valassis can retain the best employees.

Questions

1 Valassis has a close relationship with colleges. How can this relationship help its recruiting?

2 Valassis spends much time and money on its interviews. Why?

3 Valassis mentions employee retention as one of its key tasks. How does this relate to recruiting?

Internet Applications

1. **http://www.filemaker.com**

Click on "Company". What are some of the job opportunities available at Filemaker, Inc.? How do you think the company's website helps Filemaker in the human resource planning process? What benefits does Filemaker offer its employees? What is Filemaker's corporate culture, and how do you think this culture helps the company develop the skills of its employees? Does Filemaker appear to have a diversified workforce?

2. **http://www.monster.com**

How does this website benefit employees seeking jobs? How does it benefit employers in screening potential employees? Click on "Search Jobs." Search for a job category of your choice in your geographic area and list some of the positions available. Would you post your résumé on this website? Why or why not?

3. **http://www.recruit2hire.com/articles.html**

What information is provided on this website for employers seeking to hire and recruit for a sales position? Summarize two articles that you think would be useful for employers in the hiring and recruiting process. Is this website useful for companies that are recruiting internally or externally? Explain.

The Coca-Cola Company Annual Report Project

Questions for the current year's annual report are available on the text website at **http://madura.swlearning.com.**

The following questions apply concepts presented in this chapter to The Coca-Cola Company. Go to The Coca-Cola Company website (**http://www.cocacola.com**) and find the index for the 2001 annual report.

Questions

1 Download the financial statements and find the "Investments" section. What are the most fundamental and enduring attributes of The Coca-Cola Company's business? What kind of corporate culture do these attributes imply the company is trying to maintain and refine?

2 Download the financial statements and find "Note 13: Pension and Other Postretirement Benefits." Does The Coca-Cola Company restrict its employee pension plans to its U.S. employees? What other benefits do employees receive?

3 Study the "Selected Market Results" and the "Operations Reviews" sections. What challenges do you think are unique to multinational firms such as The Coca-Cola Company with respect to hiring, training, and evaluating employees?

4 Study the "Letter to Share Owners." Do you think The Coca-Cola Company has a diverse workforce? Explain. How do you think this workforce benefits The Coca-Cola Company?

In-Text Study Guide

Answers are in an appendix at the back of the book.

True or False

1. Job analysis represents the forecasting of a firm's employee needs. F

2. One task of human resource planning is recruiting. T

3. Firms tend to avoid hiring new full-time workers to meet temporary needs for higher production levels. T

4. A job specification states the credentials necessary to qualify for the position. T

5. Federal laws make it illegal to discriminate on the basis of factors not related to potential job performance. T

6. Employee benefits such as health insurance and dental insurance are taxed. F

7. Firms should offer the same compensation package to their workers in foreign countries that they offer to employees in their home country. F

8. The overall performance evaluation of most employees is based on multiple criteria. T

9. Employees perceive performance evaluation as a method for allocating wage increases. T

10. Each of the performance criteria must be weighted equally to avoid unbalancing the performance appraisal. F

Multiple Choice

11. The document that specifies credentials necessary to qualify for the job position is a:
    a) job specification.
    b) job description.
    c) job analysis.
    d) job evaluation.
    e) performance evaluation.

12. A major responsibility of a human resource manager is to:
    a) help each specific department recruit candidates for its open positions.
    b) conduct the performance evaluations for all employees.
    c) establish the information system and local area network used by the firm's employees.

d) help select the members of top management who will serve on the firm's board of directors.
    e) prevent the formation of labor unions.

13. The tasks and responsibilities of a job position are disclosed in a(n):
    a) job specification.
    b) indenture agreement.
    c) job description.
    d) organization chart.
    e) staffing report.

14. The process used to determine the tasks and the necessary credentials for a particular position is referred to as:
    a) job analysis.
    b) job screening.
    c) human resource planning.
    d) human resource forecasting.
    e) recruiting.

15. Human resource planning includes all of the following tasks except:
    a) designing the appropriate compensation package.
    b) performing job analysis.
    c) forecasting employment needs.
    d) recruiting.

16. If firms wish to avoid hiring during a temporary increase in production, they can offer _____ to existing workers.
    a) overtime
    b) vacations
    c) training programs
    d) affirmative action
    e) orientation programs

17. When a firm attempts to fill job openings with persons it already employs, it is engaging in:
    a) intrapreneurship.
    b) internal recruiting.
    c) entrenchment.
    d) precruiting.
    e) focused recruiting.

In-Text Study Guide

Answers are in an appendix at the back of the book.

18. A(n) _____ is an assignment to a higher-level job with more responsibility and greater pay.
    a) transfer
    b) lateral assignment
    c) perquisite
    d) upward appraisal
    e) promotion

19. A firm's human resource manager can obtain detailed information about the applicant's past work experience through a(n):
    a) employment test.
    b) physical exam.
    c) interview.
    d) orientation program.
    e) job analysis.

20. A step in the recruiting process that involves screening applicants is the:
    a) training procedure.
    b) orientation procedure.
    c) upward appraisal.
    d) interview.
    e) probation period.

21. All of the following are advantages of diversity in the workplace except:
    a) increased innovation.
    b) lesser chance of discrimination lawsuits.
    c) enhanced ability to interact with customers.
    d) better access to the pool of eligible employees.
    e) a change in the production process.

22. A company gives employees the right to purchase its stock at a specified price when it provides them with:
    a) presumptive rights.
    b) an indenture agreement.
    c) stock options.
    d) a stock preference.
    e) a closed-end agreement.

23. The use of stock options as a means of compensation:
    a) legally can be provided only to top executives and members of the board of directors.

    b) is declining in popularity since options reduce the firm's profits.
    c) is opposed by labor unions, since options are available only to nonunion employees.
    d) may tempt managers to manipulate financial statements to boost stock prices.
    e) has allowed workers in many firms to control who serves on the board of directors of their firm.

24. The case of Enron and other corporate scandals shows that managers who receive stock options may be tempted to do all except:
    a. magnify company expenses.
    b. manipulate the stock price.
    c. exaggerate company earnings.
    d. issue overly optimistic reports.
    e. withhold bad news.

25. An extra one-time payment at the end of a period in which performance was measured is a:
    a) salary.
    b) wage.
    c) stock option.
    d) piece rate.
    e) bonus.

26. _____ normally represent compensation for achieving specific sales objectives and often are part of the compensation received by people working in sales positions.
    a) Pensions
    b) Commissions
    c) Perquisites
    d) Stock options
    e) Dividends

27. Additional privileges given to high-level employees, such as a company car or membership in an exclusive club, are known as:
    a) professional privileges.
    b) commissions.
    c) executive options.
    d) perquisites.
    e) golden parachutes.

In-Text Study Guide

Answers are in an appendix at the back of the book.

28. _____ are additional privileges, such as paid vacation time and health and dental insurance, given to most or all employees.
    a) Employee benefits
    b) Perquisites
    c) Commissions
    d) Implicit compensations
    e) Kickbacks

29. Employees who are directly involved in the production process (such as assembly-line workers) tend to receive most of their compensation in the form of a:
    a) bonus.
    b) commission.
    c) salary.
    d) stock option.
    e) perquisite.

30. If a manager is having difficulties managing his or her subordinates, _____ would be recommended.
    a) human relations training
    b) safety skills training
    c) decision making skill training
    d) customer service training
    e) technical training

31. A performance evaluation:
    a) should avoid subjective criteria since they are impossible to measure with any accuracy.
    b) is only useful as a means of determining whether employees qualify for pay raises.
    c) is typically based on multiple criteria, some of which are objective while others are subjective.
    d) is only necessary for workers who are likely candidates for higher-level positions.
    e) should be given only to workers who are experiencing job-related problems.

32. The following are objective criteria in performance evaluation except for:
    a) parts produced per week.
    b) number of days absent.

c) percentage of deadlines missed.
d) defective parts produced by employee errors.
e) willingness of an employee to help other employees.

33. If an employee receives a poor performance appraisal, the first action that should be taken is:
    a) communicating the performance criteria to the employee.
    b) terminating the employee.
    c) determining the reasons for poor performance.
    d) suspending the employee.
    e) reassigning the employee.

34. When firms allow employees to evaluate their supervisors, this process is known as a(n):
    a) management audit.
    b) upward appraisal.
    c) forward appraisal.
    d) peer review.
    e) executive evaluation.

35. When employees evaluate their supervisors, the results are likely to be more meaningful if the appraisal is done:
    a) verbally, with nothing put in writing.
    b) without the supervisor's knowledge.
    c) no more than once every two years.
    d) anonymously.
    e) only by employees who have known the supervisor for more than two years.

36. Lawsuits against firms by fired employees:
    a) have become much less common in recent years.
    b) allow the fired employees to collect compensatory damages, but not punitive damages.
    c) are decided by a judge rather than a jury.
    d) usually should be settled out of court as soon as possible to avoid negative publicity.
    e) are usually settled in favor of the firm if supervisors followed proper procedures when firing the employees.

Appendix: Labor Unions

labor union an association established to represent the views, needs, and concerns of labor

A **labor union** is established to represent the views, needs, and concerns of labor. A union can attempt to determine the needs of its workers and then negotiate with the firm's management to satisfy those needs. The needs may include job security, safer working conditions, and higher salaries. The union may be able to negotiate for the workers better than they can themselves, because the workers do not have the time or the expertise for negotiating with management. Furthermore, management would not have the time to deal with each worker's needs separately. The union serves as the representative for all workers.

BACKGROUND ON UNIONS

craft unions unions organized according to a specific craft (or trade), such as plumbing

industrial unions unions organized for a specific industry

local unions unions composed of members in a specified local area

national unions unions composed of members throughout the country

international unions unions that have members in several countries

Unions can be classified as either craft or industrial. **Craft unions** are organized according to a specific craft (or trade), such as plumbing. **Industrial unions** are organized for a specific industry. Unions can also be classified as either local or national. **Local unions** are composed of members in a specified local area. **National unions** are composed of members throughout the country. Some local unions are part of a national union. **International unions** have members in several countries.

History of Union Activities

The popularity of unions has been affected by various laws, summarized next.

Norris-LaGuardia Act restricted the use of injunctions against unions and allowed unions to publicize a labor dispute

yellow-dog contract a contract requiring employees to refrain from joining a union as a condition of employment

The Norris-LaGuardia Act   Before 1932, the courts commonly accommodated employer requests to issue injunctions against unions. In 1932, Congress passed the **Norris-LaGuardia Act,** which restricted the use of injunctions against unions and allowed unions to publicize a labor dispute. It also prohibited employers from forcing workers to sign a **yellow-dog contract,** which was a contract requiring employees to refrain from joining a union as a condition of employment.

Wagner Act prohibited firms from interfering with workers' efforts to organize or join unions

The Wagner Act   Even with the Norris-LaGuardia Act, firms were able to discourage employees from joining or organizing unions. The **Wagner Act** (also referred to as the National Labor Relations Act) prohibited firms from interfering with workers' efforts to organize or join unions. Employers could not discriminate against employees who participated in union activities. In addition, the act required employers to negotiate with the union representing employees.

Taft-Hartley Act an amendment to the Wagner Act that prohibited unions from pressuring employees to join

right-to-work allows states to prohibit union shops

The Taft-Hartley Act   Although the Wagner Act reduced employer discrimination against union participants, it was unable to reduce strikes. The **Taft-Hartley Act,** an amendment to the Wagner Act, prohibited unions from pressuring employees to join. An exception is the union shop, where new employees are required to join the union. The **right-to-work** section of this act allows states to prohibit union shops (several states have used this power).

Landrum-Griffin Act required labor unions to specify in their bylaws the membership eligibility requirements, dues, and collective bargaining procedures

The Landrum-Griffin Act   In 1959, Congress passed the **Landrum-Griffin Act** (originally called the Labor-Management Reporting and Disclosure Act of 1959). This act required labor unions to specify in their bylaws the membership eligibility requirements, dues, and collective bargaining procedures.

Trends in Union Popularity

Union membership declined slightly in the early 1930s, as firms discouraged workers from participating in labor activities. After the Wagner Act was passed in 1935, union membership increased rapidly. By 1945, more than one-fourth of all workers were union members. During the 1980s and 1990s, however, union membership consistently declined. By 2000, less than 12 percent of all workers were union members. One of the reasons for the decline was the inability of some unionized firms to compete with nonunion firms whose expenses were lower.

NEGOTIATIONS BETWEEN UNIONS AND MANAGEMENT

Contracts between unions and management commonly last for two to three years. An attempt is made to agree to a new contract before the existing contract expires. The union obtains feedback from its members on what working provisions need to be improved. The union also obtains data on existing wages and employee benefits provided for jobs similar to those of members. Management assesses existing conditions and determines the types of provisions it may be willing to make.

Before the actual negotiations begin, the union may offer a proposed revision of the existing contract. This proposal often includes very high demands, which management will surely refuse. Management may also offer a proposed revision of the existing contract that the union will surely refuse. Normally, the original gap between the two sides is very large. This establishes the foundation for negotiations.

When the union and management meet to negotiate a new contract, the more critical issues to be discussed include the following:

▶ Salaries

▶ Job security

▶ Management rights

▶ Grievance procedures

Salaries

A general concern of unions is to improve or at least maintain their members' standard of living. Unions are credited for negotiating high wages for their members. Unionized grocery store employees commonly receive at least double the salaries of nonunionized employees in the same job positions. Airline pilot captains of unionized airlines, such as American and Delta, earn more than $100,000 per year, while pilot captains of nonunionized airlines commonly earn less than $50,000 per year.

Unions attempt to negotiate for salary increases that will at least match expected increases in the cost of living. They also monitor salaries of workers at other firms to determine the salary increases that they will request. For example, the United Auto Workers (UAW) commonly uses the content of its contract with one car manufacturer to negotiate its new contract with another car manufacturer.

If the firm has experienced high profits in recent years, a union may use this as reason to negotiate for large wage increases. Conversely, firms that recently experienced losses will argue that they cannot afford to make pay increases. When pilots at Continental Airlines did not receive a salary increase over several years, poor relations developed between the pilots and management at Continental.

Job Security

Job security is a key issue from the perspective of workers. They want to be assured of a job until retirement. Management may not be willing to guarantee job security but may at least specify the conditions under which workers will be laid off. Workers with less seniority are more likely to be laid off.

Although unions are unable to force management to guarantee lifetime jobs, they are somewhat successful at obtaining supplemental unemployment benefits for workers. Firms that offer these benefits contribute an amount for each hour worked into a fund. The fund is used to compensate workers who are laid off. This compensation is a supplement to the normal unemployment compensation workers receive.

Unions may also attempt to prevent management from replacing workers with machines. Management may agree to such demands if the unions reduce some of their other demands. Unions emphasize this issue in industries such as automobile manufacturing, where some tasks are highly repetitive and therefore workers are more likely to be replaced by machines.

For some workers, job security may be more important than higher wages. Therefore, firms that are willing to provide job security may not have to provide large increases in wages.

Management Rights

Management expects to have various rights as to how it manages its workers. For example, the union–management contract may state a specified number of work hours. Management may also retain the rights to make hiring, promotional, and transferring decisions without influence by unions.

Grievance Procedures

A grievance is a complaint made by an employee or the union. Contracts between a union and management specify procedures for resolving a grievance. The first step normally calls for a meeting between the employee, his or her supervisor, and a union representative. If this meeting does not resolve the grievance, the union normally meets with high-level managers.

CONFLICTS BETWEEN UNIONS AND MANAGEMENT

Unions use various methods to bargain for better working conditions or higher compensation. Employees may attempt to pressure management by **picketing,** or walking around near the employer's building with signs complaining of poor working conditions. Employees can also **boycott** the products and services offered by refusing to purchase them.

picketing walking around near the employer's building with signs complaining of poor working conditions

boycott refusing to purchase products and services

strike a discontinuation of employee services

Labor Strikes

A more dramatic method of bargaining is a **strike,** which is a discontinuation of employee services. Two recent well-publicized strikes were those by employees at UPS and at General Motors. The goal of the UPS strike was to achieve better wages. The objective of the General Motors strike was to ensure that some of GM's plants would not be closed.

The impact of a strike on a firm depends on the firm's ability to carry on operations during the strike. For example, if all machinists of a manufacturing firm strike, the firm's production will be severely reduced unless its other workers can substitute. Most firms carry an inventory of finished products that may be used to accommodate orders during the strike. However, even a large inventory will not be sufficient if the strike lasts long enough.

The publicity of a strike can reduce a firm's perceived credibility. Even though a strike is only temporary, it can create permanent damage. Some firms have long-term arrangements with other companies to provide a specified volume of supplies periodically. If these companies fear that their orders will not be satisfied because of a strike, they will search for a firm that is less likely to experience a strike.

To illustrate how the dissatisfaction of employees can affect a firm's value, consider the case of Caterpillar. About 14,000 of Caterpillar's workers went on strike on June 21, 1994. Exhibit 11.A1 shows the stock price of

Exhibit 11.A1

Example of How a Strike Can Affect a Firm's Value

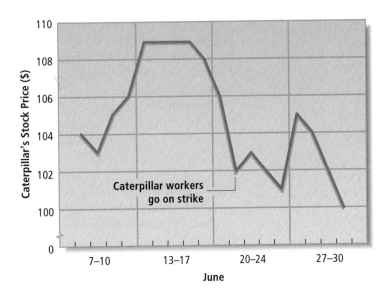

Caterpillar around the time of the strike. Notice how the stock price declined by more than $4 per share in response to the strike. The strike lasted more than 17 months. Caterpillar replaced many of the strikers with temporary workers and experienced record earnings over the strike period. By the end of the strike, about one-third of the strikers returned to work without any compromise by Caterpillar.

Management's Response to Strikes

injunction a court order to prevent a union from a particular activity such as picketing

lockout prevents employees from working until an agreement between management and labor is reached

Management may respond to union pressure by obtaining an **injunction,** which is a court order to prevent the union from a particular activity such as picketing. Alternatively, it could use a **lockout,** which prevents employees from working until an agreement between management and labor is reached.

Another common response by management is to show how large benefits to workers will possibly result in the firm's failure, which would effectively terminate all jobs. The management of Northwest Airlines and US Air (now US Airways) used this approach in the mid-1990s to prevent excessive demands by the union. US Air also offered its pilots partial ownership of the firm in place of salary increases.

The amount of bargaining power a union has is partially dependent on whether the firm can easily replace employees who go on strike. For example, an airline cannot easily replace pilots in a short period of time because of the extensive training needed. Other workers with specialized mechanical skills also have some bargaining power. When 33,000 machinists of Boeing (a producer of aircraft) went on strike in 1995, they forced Boeing to provide a larger salary increase as an incentive to end the strike. However, a strike by workers at Bridgestone/Firestone (a producer of tires) was not as successful, as the firm hired replacement workers.

Management's Criticism of Unions

Unions are criticized by management for several reasons, some of which are discussed here.

Higher Prices or Lower Profits   If unions achieve high wages for employees, firms may pass the increase on to consumers in the form of higher prices. If firms do not pass the increase on, their profits may be reduced and the shareholders of the firm will be adversely affected. In essence, the disadvantages to the consumers or shareholders offset the benefits to employees.

A related criticism is that high wages resulting from the union can reduce the firm's ability to compete internationally. This was a major criticism during the 1980s, when many foreign competitors increased their market share in the United States.

Adverse Impact on Economic Conditions   A decision to strike by some unions can severely damage a given industry. Unions have the power to close large manufacturing plants, shut down an airline's operations, or even halt garbage collection. Some shutdowns can have a severe impact on the local area.

Production Inefficiency Some unions have negotiated for a minimum number of workers to perform a specific task. In some cases, the number of workers has exceeded the number actually needed. A related criticism is that workers are sometimes perceived to be protected from being fired if they are in a union. A firm may be unwilling to fire an unproductive employee if it believes the union will file a grievance. If a firm retains unproductive workers, its efficiency is reduced, and its cost of production increases.

How Firms Reduce Employees' Desire for a Union

The management of some firms has consistently maintained good relations with labor. Consequently, labor has not attempted to organize a union. The following guidelines are some of the more common methods used to maintain good relations with employees:

1 Management should promote employees from within so that employees are satisfied with their career paths.

2 Management should attempt to avoid layoffs so that employees do not feel threatened whenever business slows down. This may be achieved by reassigning job positions to some employees who are no longer needed in their original positions.

3 Management should allow employees responsibility and input into some decisions. Labor contracts between labor and management may require labor-management committees to be created at each plant to develop methods for improving efficiency. This is a classic example of considering input from employees.

4 Management should maintain reasonable working conditions to demonstrate fairness to employees.

5 Management should offer reasonable and competitive wages so that employees feel properly rewarded and are not continually quitting to take other jobs.

The points just listed represent the key provisions for which unions negotiate. If the firm adheres to these guidelines, workers may not need to organize a union.

Part IV

Summary

Managing Employees

The performance of a firm is highly dependent on the performance of its employees. Firms commonly attempt to improve employee performance by increasing job satisfaction. The following methods can be used to improve job satisfaction. First, firms can provide compensation that is linked with employee performance. This strategy rewards employees directly for their efforts. Second, firms may provide job security to their employees, which may reduce work-related stress. Third, firms may allow their employees to have a flexible work schedule, which allows employees to have more input on their daily or weekly work schedule. Fourth, firms may implement more employee involvement programs to give employees more input on most business decisions.

Firms can improve their performance by using proper methods of hiring, training, and evaluating their employees. Proper hiring methods ensure that employees have the right background for the types of jobs that may be assigned. Proper training enables employees to apply their skills to perform specific tasks. Proper evaluation methods ensure that employees are rewarded when they perform well and that they are informed of any deficiencies so that they can correct them in the future.

DEVELOPING THE HUMAN RESOURCE PLAN FOR CAMPUS.COM

Motivating Employees (related to Chapter 10)

In your business plan for Campus.com, describe how you can offer favorable working conditions (do not include compensation here) that will motivate the employees whom you may need to hire over time. That is, explain how you will ensure that employees help you achieve high performance and are willing to continue working at this business for several years. Identify any disadvantages of these methods that may limit their effectiveness.

Evaluating Employees (related to Chapter 11)

In your business plan for Campus.com, describe how you will assess the performance of your employees. How can you compensate the employees in a manner that will ensure that they will try to maximize the performance of the firm?

Communication and Teamwork

You (or your team) may be asked by your instructor to hand in and/or present the part of your business plan that relates to this part of the text.

Integrative Video Case: Effective Management (Café Pilon)

Café Pilon is run by the third generation of the Soto family, who are immigrants from Cuba. The Soto family attributes the success of their company to several factors, including hard work and perseverance. Eventually, the family hopes to penetrate the Cuban coffee market once Cuba is free. Café Pilon also has its own website.

Questions

1 Explain how effective production of products by Pilon is related to marketing.

2 Explain why the reasons for Café Pilon's success may result in improved employee performance.

3 How could Café Pilon use its website to motivate its employees?

Integrative Video Case: Benefits of Diversity (Hudson's Department Stores*)

Dayton Hudson Department Stores, headquartered in Minneapolis, is the fourth largest retailer in the United States. Stores included in the corporation are Target and Marshall Field's, which cater to upscale discount and upscale customers. Hudson is committed to promoting the diversity of its employees both at individual stores and at its headquarters. The company promotes diversity in various ways.

Questions

1 How do you think a firm can benefit from promoting diversity?

2 How does diversity of employees relate to marketing decisions such as reaching a target market at Hudson's?

3 Describe some of the things Hudson's does to promote diversity. How does this relate to the training of employees?

*Note that since the time the video was created that Target Corporation, formerly Dayton Hudson Corporation, is comprised of three operating segments: Target, Mervyn's and Marshall Field's. Marshall Field's, including stores formerly named Dayton's and Hudson's, is a traditional department store located in eight states in the upper Midwest.

THE STOCK MARKET GAME

Go to **http://finance.yahoo.com.** and check your portfolio balance, which is updated continuously by Yahoo! Finance.

Check Your Stock Portfolio Performance

1 What is the value of your stock portfolio today?

2 What is your return on your investment?

3 How did your return compare to those of other students? (This comparison tells you whether your stock portfolio's performance is relatively high or low.)

Explaining Your Stock Performance

Stock prices are frequently influenced by changes in the firm's management policies toward its employees, including new policies for awarding bonuses or other compensation. A stock's price may increase if such management policies are changed and investors expect the changes to improve the firm's performance. A stock's price can also decrease if the policy changes are expected to reduce the firm's performance. Review the latest news about some of your stocks on the Yahoo! Finance website.

1 Identify one of your stocks whose price was affected (since you purchased it) as a result of the firm's motivation and personnel policy changes (the main topic in this part of the text).

2 Identify the specific change in managerial policies related to motivation or personnel decisions that caused the stock price to change.

3 Did the stock price increase or decrease in response to the announcement of new policies related to employee motivation or personnel?

Running Your Own Business

1 How can you empower your employees so that they have an incentive to perform well?

2 Describe how you might encourage your employees to use teamwork.

3 Describe how each of the theories discussed in this part of the text would apply to your employees or yourself.

4 Develop a job description for the employees that you would need to hire for your business. Include the required education and skills within the job description.

5 Describe the training (if any) that you would have to provide to any employees you hire for your business.

6 Describe how you would compensate your employees. Would you offer bonuses as an incentive? If so, describe how you would determine the bonus.

7 Describe the criteria you would use to evaluate the performance of your employees.

8 Describe how you could use the Internet to attract new employees or to motivate existing employees.

Your Career in Business: Pursuing a Major and a Career in Human Resources

If you are very interested in the topics covered in this section, you may want to consider a major in Human Resources (sometimes referred to as "Personnel Management"). Some of the courses commonly taken by Human Resource majors are summarized here.

Common Courses for Human Resource Majors

▶ *Organizational Behavior*   Provides a broad overview of key managerial functions, such as organizing, motivating employees, planning, controlling, and teamwork.

▶ *Management Environment*   Focuses on the environment in which managers work and the responsibilities of managers to society and to regulators.

▶ *Human Resource Management*   Focuses on the processes of hiring, training, evaluating performance, and compensating employees.

▶ *Labor Relations*   Examines the labor contract relationships among managers, subordinates, and unions; also covers the process of negotiating.

▶ *Management Strategy*   Focuses on the competitive environment faced by a firm and strategies used by a firm's managers to increase its growth or improve its performance.

▶ *Management Systems*   Explains the application of computer software and systems to facilitate decision making.

▶ *Psychology*   In particular, courses that attempt to explain human behavior and the human response to penalties, rewards, and incentives.

Careers in Human Resources

Information about job positions, salaries, and careers for students who major in Human Resources can be found at the following websites:

▶   Job position websites:

http://jobsearch.monster.com   Administrative and Support Services, Consulting Services, and Human Resources.

http://careers.yahoo.com   Management Consulting.

▶   Salary website:

http://collegejournal.com/ salarydata   Consulting, Human Resources, and Logistics.

Some of the job positions described at these websites may require work experience or a graduate degree.

Part V

Marketing

Marketing can be broadly defined as the actions of firms to plan and execute the design, pricing, distribution, and promotion of products. A firm's marketing mix is the combination of the product, pricing, distribution, and promotion strategies used to sell products. Examples of marketing decisions include the product decision by Kodak to design a miniature video camera, the pricing decision by Ford to price its new model Mustang, the distribution decision by Nike on how to distribute its running shoes across various outlets around the world, and the promotion decision by American Airlines to use television advertising when promoting its airline services.

To recognize how all four strategies are used by a single firm, consider a computer firm that identifies a software package that consumers need. The firm develops the software (product strategy), sets a price for the software (pricing strategy), decides to sell the software through specific computer stores (distribution strategy), and decides to advertise the software in magazines (promotion strategy). Chapter 12 focuses on the creation and pricing of products, Chapter 13 focuses on distributing products, and Chapter 14 focuses on promoting products.

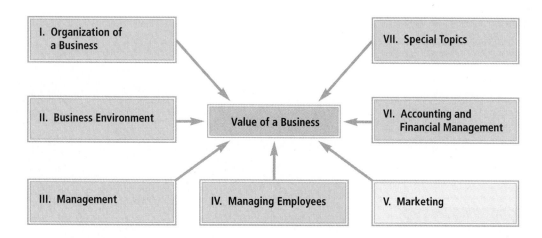

I. Organization of a Business → Value of a Business ← VII. Special Topics

II. Business Environment → Value of a Business ← VI. Accounting and Financial Management

III. Management → Value of a Business ← V. Marketing

IV. Managing Employees → Value of a Business

All businesses, including NightLife Film Co., need to decide on the products to be produced, and the pricing of those products.

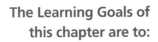

The Learning Goals of this chapter are to:

Identify the main factors that affect a product's target market. **1**

Identify the steps involved in creating a new product. **2**

Explain the common methods used to differentiate a product. **3**

Identify the main phases of a product life cycle. **4**

Identify the factors that influence the pricing decision. **5**

Chapter 12

Creating and Pricing Products

12

Product strategies dictate the types of products that a firm creates to satisfy customers, whereas pricing strategies determine the prices to be charged for those products. Both strategies influence the demand for the products produced by the firm and therefore determine the amount of revenue that the firm will generate over a particular period. Consider the situation of NightLife Film Company, which produces movies that are shown in theaters. When NightLife plans the production of a new film, it must decide:

▶ What types of consumers (target market) will pay to see this film?

▶ How can this film be differentiated from other films that consumers might see instead?

▶ How can the film's popularity be sustained over a long period of time?

▶ What prices should be charged for the film's DVD and videocassette?

If NightLife can successfully determine the target market that will be interested in the film, it can focus its advertising on those customers. NightLife needs to differentiate its business from others to attract customers. If it can sustain the popularity of its product (and therefore the demand) over a long period of time, it will generate more revenue. Its pricing decisions on the film's DVD and videocassette are also important because those prices will affect the amount of revenue generated from selling DVDs and videos.

The types of decisions described here are necessary for all businesses. This chapter explains how the product and pricing decisions by NightLife Film Company or any other firm can be conducted in a manner that maximizes the firm's value.

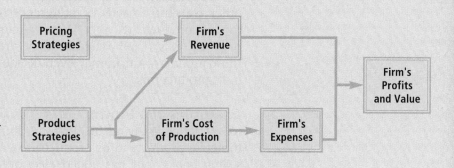

BACKGROUND ON PRODUCTS

product a physical good or service that can satisfy consumer needs

The term **product** can be broadly defined to include both physical goods and services that can satisfy consumer needs. Firms must continually improve existing products and develop new products to satisfy customers over time. In this way, firms generate high sales growth, which normally increases their value.

convenience products products that are widely available to consumers, are purchased frequently, and are easily accessible

Most products produced to serve consumers can be classified as (1) convenience products, (2) shopping products, or (3) specialty products. **Convenience products** are widely available to consumers, are purchased frequently, and are easily accessible. Milk, newspapers, soda, and chewing gum are examples of convenience products.

shopping products products that are not purchased frequently

Shopping products differ from convenience products in that they are not purchased frequently. Before purchasing shopping goods, consumers typically shop around and compare the quality and prices of competing products. Furniture and appliances are examples of shopping products.

specialty products products that specific consumers consider to be special and therefore make a special effort to purchase

Specialty products are products that specific consumers consider to be special and therefore make a special effort to purchase. A Rolex watch and a Jaguar automobile are examples of specialty products. When evaluating specialty products, consumers base their purchasing decision primarily on personal preference, not on comparative pricing.

Product Line

product line a set of related products or services offered by a single firm

A **product line** is a set of related products or services offered by a single firm. For example, Coke, Diet Coke, Caffeine-Free Diet Coke, and Sprite are all part of a single product line at The Coca-Cola Company. Pepsi, Diet Pepsi, Mountain Dew, and All-Sport are all part of a single product line at PepsiCo.

A product line tends to expand over time as a firm identifies other consumer needs. The Coca-Cola Company recognizes that consumers differ with respect to their desire for a specific taste, caffeine versus no caffeine, and diet versus regular. It has expanded its product line of soft drinks to satisfy various needs. Dell Computer has added portable computers to its product line over time, while Taco Bell has added various low-fat food items to its menus.

Product Mix

product mix the assortment of products offered by a firm

The assortment of products offered by a firm is referred to as the **product mix.** Most firms tend to expand their product mix over time as they identify other consumer needs or preferences. Before firms add more products to their product mix, they should determine whether a demand for new products exists and whether they are capable of efficiently providing those products. A firm may even decide to discontinue one of the products in its product mix.

Examples of a Product Mix   Quaker State originally focused on motor oil but added windshield washer fluid, brake fluid, and many other automobile products to its product mix. Amazon.com originally focused on selling books, but has added electronics, toys, music, kitchen products, drugs, and health and beauty products. The product mix of Liz Claiborne, Inc., includes clothing for women, jewelry, fashion accessories, and clothing for men.

IBM's product mix includes software, hardware, and global services, as shown in Exhibit 12.1. The hardware segment generates more sales than either of the other segments, but its proportion of total sales is lower than in previous years. Meanwhile, the proportion of total sales generated by IBM's global services segment (which includes information technology) has increased substantially. This change in the relative proportions reflects IBM's shift away from its hardware product line and into other product lines related to information technology.

Service firms also have a product mix. For example, some commercial banks accept deposits, allow checking services, provide loans, and provide insurance products.

Exhibit 12.1

Product Mix of IBM

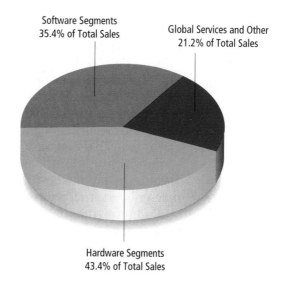

Software Segments
35.4% of Total Sales

Global Services and Other
21.2% of Total Sales

Hardware Segments
43.4% of Total Sales

Diversifying the Product Mix   When their primary product is subject to wide swings in demand, firms tend to diversify their product mix so that they will not be completely dependent on one market. By diversifying, they are not as reliant on a single product whose performance is uncertain. Firms with flexible production facilities that allow for the production of additional goods are more capable of diversifying their product mix.

A common diversification strategy is for a firm to diversify products within its existing production capabilities. For example, hospital supply companies offer a wide variety of supplies that can be sold to each hospital. The Walt Disney Company, which had focused on producing films for children, now offers many gift products. Clothing manufacturers such as Donna Karan offer several types of clothes that can be sold to each retail outlet. A product mix that contains several related products can allow for more efficient use of salespeople.

To understand how firms can benefit from expanding their product mix, consider the case of Amazon.com, which initially focused on filling book orders requested over the Internet. First, it began to offer CDs as well, recognizing that if customers are willing to order books online, they may also order other products. Second, it had already proved that it could provide reliable service, so customers trusted that the additional services would be reliable as well. Third, it could use its existing technology to fill CD orders, which increased efficiency.

In 1999, Amazon.com acquired a stake in Drugstore.com because it believed that it could fill drug orders requested over the Internet. The growth of Amazon.com demonstrates how a firm can expand by using the resources that initially made it successful to offer additional products.

1 IDENTIFYING A TARGET MARKET

Identify the main factors that affect a product's target market.

The consumers who purchase a particular product may have specific traits in common and thus also have similar needs. Firms attempt to identify these traits so that they can target their marketing toward people with those

target market a group of individuals or organizations with similar traits who may purchase a particular product

consumer markets markets for various consumer products and services (such as cameras, clothes, and household items)

industrial markets markets for industrial products that are purchased by firms (such as plastic and steel)

traits. Marketing efforts are usually targeted toward a particular **target market,** which is a group of individuals or organizations with similar traits who may purchase a particular product.

Target markets can be broadly classified as consumer markets or industrial markets. **Consumer markets** exist for various consumer products and services (such as cameras, clothes, and household items), while **industrial markets** exist for industrial products that are purchased by firms (such as plastic and steel). Some products (such as tires) can serve consumer markets or industrial markets (such as car manufacturers). Classifying markets as consumer or industrial provides only a broad description of the types of customers who purchase products, however. Consequently, firms attempt to describe their target markets more narrowly.

Common traits used to describe a target market include the consumer's gender, age, and income bracket. For example, the target market for dirt bikes may be males under 30 years of age, while the target market for three-month cruises may be wealthy males or females over 50 years of age. Eddie Bauer produces a line of casual clothes for a target market of customers between 30 and 50 years of age, while Carters produces clothes for babies.

Factors That Affect the Size of a Target Market

As time passes, the demand for products changes. Firms attempt to be in a position to benefit from a possible increase in demand for particular products. For example, some hotels in Los Angeles and New York have anticipated an increase in Japanese guests and have offered new conveniences to capture that portion of the market. Common conveniences offered are Japanese translators, rooms with bamboo screens, and a Japanese-language newspaper for these guests.

As consumer preferences change, the size of a particular target market can change. Firms monitor consumer preferences over time to anticipate how the size of their target market may be affected. The following are key factors that affect consumer preferences and therefore affect the size of the target market:

▶ Demographics

▶ Geography

▶ Economic factors

▶ Social values

demographics characteristics of the human population or specific segments of the population

Demographics   The total demand for particular products or services is dependent on the **demographics,** or characteristics of the human population or specific segments of the population. As demographic conditions change, so does the demand. For example, demographic statistics show an increase in women who work outside the home. Firms have adjusted their product lines to capitalize on this change. Clothing stores have created more lines of business clothing for women. Food manufacturers have created easy-to-fix frozen foods to accommodate the busy schedules of wage-earning women. The tendency for people to have less free time and more income has resulted in increased demand for more convenience services, such as quick oil changes and tire replacement services.

One of the most relevant demographic characteristics is age because target markets are sometimes defined by age levels. Demographic statistics

business online

e-business

Marketing Plans   This website provides a tutorial about developing marketing strategies.

http://smallbusiness.yahoo
.com/resources/business_
plans/marketing_planning_
guide.html

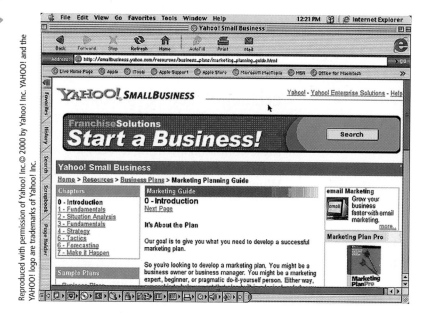

show that the population has grown older. Consequently, the popularity of sports cars has declined as customers look for cars that are dependable and safe. Automobile manufacturers have adjusted to this demographic change by supplying fewer sports cars. Home Depot created an installation service business to capitalize on the growing number of mature customers who prefer not to do repair or installation work themselves.

Although the population has generally grown older, the number of children in the United States has recently increased. Many of these recently born children have two parents who work outside the home and spend large sums of money on their children. Firms such as OshKosh B' Gosh and The Gap have capitalized on this trend by producing high-quality (and high-priced) children's clothing.

To illustrate how characteristics of the population can change over time, consider the changes over the 20-year period 1982–2002, shown in Exhibit 12.2. In general, the population has grown larger, while both the number of people age 65 or older and the number of households earning more than $60,000 annually have increased. Such information is relevant to firms because it suggests that the size of specific target markets may be changing over time.

Geography   The total demand for a product is also influenced by geography. Firms target snow tires to the northern states and surfboards to the east and west coasts of the United States. Tastes are also influenced by geography. The demand for spicy foods is higher in the southwestern states than in other states.

Exhibit 12.2

Changes in Consumer Characteristics in
Last 20 Years (from 1982 to 2002)

1. U.S. population has increased
2. Higher proportion of people age 65 or older
3. Higher proportion of households with income over $60,000
4. Higher proportion of minority households with income over $60,000
5. Higher proportion of high school students who enter college
6. Higher proportion of minority high school students who enter college

Economic Factors As economic conditions change, so do consumer preferences. During a recessionary period, the demand for most types of goods declines. Specialty and shopping products are especially sensitive to these conditions. During a recession, firms may promote necessities rather than specialty products. In addition, their pricing may be more competitive. When the economy becomes stronger, firms have more flexibility to raise prices and may also promote specialty products more than necessities.

Interest rates can also have a major impact on consumer demand. When interest rates are low, consumers are more willing to purchase goods with borrowed money. The demand for products such as automobiles, boats, and homes is especially sensitive to interest rate movements because these products are often purchased with borrowed funds.

Social Values As the social values of consumers change, so do their preferences. For example, the demand for cigarettes and whiskey has declined as consumers have become more aware of the health dangers of using these products. If a firm producing either of these products anticipates a change in preferences, it can begin to shift its marketing mix. Alternatively, it could modify its product to capitalize on the trend. For example, it could reduce the alcohol content of the whiskey or the tar and nicotine content of the cigarettes. It may also revise its promotion strategy to inform the public of these changes.

College Health Club: CHC's Target Market

College Health Club (CHC) provides a product mix of aerobics classes, weight machines, and exercise machines for its customers. Sue Kramer, the president of CHC, intends to target the students enrolled at Texas College who want to join a health club. However, Sue also wants to retain the students as members after they graduate if they continue to live in the local area. Since the health club is not on campus but in a shopping mall across the street from the campus, she believes she can also attract local people who are not affiliated with the college.

The Use of E-Marketing to Expand the Target Market

The term *e-marketing* refers to the use of the Internet to execute the design, pricing, distribution, and promotion of products. E-marketing is part of *e-commerce*, which is the use of electronic technology to conduct business transactions, such as selling products and acquiring information about consumers, more efficiently. In a recent survey of 109 executives, 62 percent said that marketing is the most important component of their e-commerce. Amazon.com's use of e-marketing to differentiate itself from other book retailers demonstrates the importance of e-marketing. Amazon uses its website to accept orders and payment online from customers anywhere in the United States and delivers the products directly to the customers. By using the Internet, it offers customers convenience because they can purchase books without going to a store. Thus, Amazon has created a means by which it can reach a much broader target market than if it had simply opened bookstores in various locations, and it is able to offer lower prices by selling direct, without the need for retail outlets. Amazon has also personalized the website for each customer depending on what books the customer recently ordered. Thus, its "store" is structured to highlight the books that will fit the particular customer's interests.

Other retailers have noticed the popularity of ordering books online and have developed their own online systems to complement their "bricks and mortar" stores. In this way, they have also extended their target markets. Many firms that sell clothing, office supplies, travel services, electronic equipment, and many other products are using e-marketing to reach a larger target market. Marriott International has an efficient website that helps match its hotels with travelers' interests. Southwest Airlines has an effective website that accepts online orders. It receives about 30 percent of its revenue from online orders. UPS has developed a very efficient website that allows customers to track packages. The brokerage firm Charles Schwab has set up a website to receive orders to buy or sell stocks or other securities. More than 80 percent of its orders are conducted online.

The Internet also enables firms to target foreign markets. By establishing a foreign-language website that can accept orders and allow customers

---

global business

Targeting Foreign Countries

When firms sell their product mix in foreign countries, they must recognize that consumer characteristics vary across countries. Consider the case of Bestfoods International. This former U.S. firm was acquired by the Dutch firm Unilever in 2000, but it provides an excellent example of international marketing. Bestfoods produced numerous food products, including Skippy peanut butter, Mazola corn oil, and Hellmann's mayonnaise. Its global marketing strategy was to penetrate any foreign markets where there was sufficient demand. It recognized that some of its products would be more successful than others in particular foreign markets. Thus, it considered the characteristics of the foreign country before it decided which products to market in that country.

The following brief summary of just a few of Bestfoods' products illustrates how it targeted its products to specific countries:

1 Bestfoods sold mayonnaise in Argentina, Brazil, and Chile and introduced it in Panama and Venezuela in the late 1990s. It experienced high sales of mayonnaise in the Czech Republic and Slovakia and also marketed mayonnaise in Spain.

2 Bestfoods sold ready-to-eat desserts and dessert mixes in Europe, including Yabon cakes in France and Ambrosia rice puddings in the United Kingdom. It also sold dessert mixes in Latin America under the Kremel, Maizena, and Maravilla brands.

3 Bestfoods sold pasta in Europe under the Napolina and Knorr brands and in Asia under the Royal and Bestfoods brands.

In general, the product mix marketed by Bestfoods in any given country was dependent on the characteristics of the people in that country. It periodically changed the product mix that it marketed in a particular country in response to changes in that country's characteristics.

Rapper Nelly is the new spokesperson for SongPro, Inc. They have a new product capable of converting the Nintendo Game Boy into a digital music player.

© Getty Images

to pay by credit card, a firm can sell its products in foreign countries. It does not need to establish an office or hire employees in a foreign country to conduct this type of business. It can rely on its existing facilities to produce the products, use its website to market the product and accept payment, and deliver its product to the foreign customers via mail services.

In addition to allowing firms to receive orders at lower costs and to expand their target markets, e-marketing can enhance a firm's distribution (as described in Chapter 13) and its promotion of products (as described in Chapter 14).

CREATING NEW PRODUCTS

2
Identify the steps involved in creating a new product.

In a given year, firms may offer more than 20,000 new products. The vast majority of these products will be discontinued within six months. These statistics suggest how difficult it is to create new products that are successful. Nevertheless, the profits from a single successful product may offset the losses resulting from several failed products.

A new product does not have to represent a famous invention. Most new products are simply improvements of existing products. Existing products become **obsolete,** or less useful than in the past, for two reasons. They may experience **fashion obsolescence** and no longer be in fashion. For example, the demand for some types of clothes declines over time because of fashion obsolescence.

Alternatively, products may experience **technological obsolescence** and be inferior to new products that are technologically more advanced. For example, when Hewlett-Packard creates faster printers, the old models are subject to technological obsolescence.

obsolete less useful than in the past

fashion obsolescence no longer in fashion

technological obsolescence inferior to new products

Use of Marketing Research to Create New Products

When firms develop products, they assess the market to monitor the marketing strategies of their competitors. However, merely monitoring competitors may cause the firm to be a follower rather than a leader. Many firms prefer to make product decisions that are more innovative than those of their competitors. To obtain more insight on what consumers want, firms use **marketing research,** which is the accumulation and analysis of data in order to make a particular marketing decision.

marketing research the accumulation and analysis of data in order to make a particular marketing decision

Marketing research is useful for making product decisions. A marketing survey may find that many consumers desire a specific product that is not available. It may also identify deficiencies in the firm's existing products; this information can then be used to correct these deficiencies. The design and quality of a product may be revised to accommodate consumer preferences. For example, computer firms build computers and automobile manufacturers design their new cars to accommodate their perception of what consumers want. Firms' perceptions of consumer preferences are more accurate when backed by marketing research.

Both new and revised products may be tested with marketing research. The products are given to prospective customers who are asked to assess various features of the products. This type of research allows firms to make further revisions that will satisfy customers.

To enable a firm to have confidence in the data obtained from marketing research, sample groups of consumers who represent the target market are studied. Many marketing research studies result in a marketing decision that will cost millions of dollars. If the marketing research leads to incorrect conclusions, the decision could result in a large loss to the firm.

One limitation of using marketing research to identify consumer preferences is that tastes change rapidly. Products, such as clothing, that were popular when the marketing research was conducted may be out of style by the time they are designed and distributed to the market.

How E-Marketing Complements Marketing Research A key to developing or improving new products is to receive feedback on existing or experimental products. Many firms rely on e-marketing to support their product development. The Internet is particularly useful for marketing research because of its speed: companies and customers get the information they want much faster.

Firms can use the Internet for marketing research in several ways. First, by having a customer service e-mail system, a firm can obtain comments from customers about its existing products. Customers are more likely to provide feedback if they can simply send an e-mail than if they must send a letter. Second, because the firm has its customers' e-mail addresses, it can easily contact the customers to request feedback about a particular product or about their preferences. An online survey is a fast way of gathering information. Third, a firm may even send out samples of an experimental product to customers who are willing to e-mail their assessment of the product to the firm. Samples have been so popular with many customers that some retailers have begun to offer online order services as well.

Procter & Gamble is well known for its extensive market research. In 2002, about 50 percent of its huge market research budget was used for online market research. It can usually complete an online survey within 10 days, versus three or four weeks for a personal survey. In addition, an online survey costs substantially less than a personal survey. Another advantage is that some consumers are more open with their opinions online than when they are asked to respond to a survey conducted by a person.

Use of Research and Development to Create Products

Firms invest funds in research and development (R&D) to design new products or to improve the products they already produce. Manufacturing firms tend to invest more money in R&D than service firms because technology can improve manufactured products more easily than services.

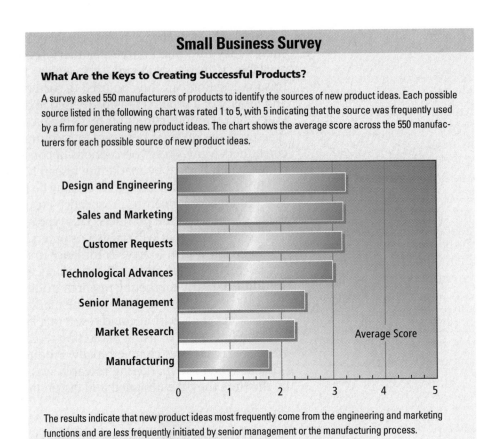

Small Business Survey

What Are the Keys to Creating Successful Products?

A survey asked 550 manufacturers of products to identify the sources of new product ideas. Each possible source listed in the following chart was rated 1 to 5, with 5 indicating that the source was frequently used by a firm for generating new product ideas. The chart shows the average score across the 550 manufacturers for each possible source of new product ideas.

The results indicate that new product ideas most frequently come from the engineering and marketing functions and are less frequently initiated by senior management or the manufacturing process.

Firms that spend money on R&D expect the benefits to exceed the expenses. Procter & Gamble's R&D resulted in its two-in-one shampoo and conditioner technology. It attributes the success of its Pantene Pro-V to its product technology. This product is now the leading shampoo in several countries. Procter & Gamble has improved the technology of Tide detergent more than 70 times. Technological development can also enable a firm to gain an advantage over its competitors. Many large firms typically spend more than $1 billion on R&D per year.

Because R&D can be so expensive, some firms have created alliances to conduct R&D. They share the costs and their technology in attempting to develop products. An alliance not only combines expertise from two or more firms, but it may also reduce the costs to each individual firm.

To expand their product line, many firms have recently increased their investment in R&D. For example, Abbott Laboratories has consistently increased its investment in R&D. Since Abbott Laboratories produces various medical drugs, its future performance is heavily dependent on its ability to create new drugs.

Using Patents to Protect Research and Development   One potential limitation of R&D is that a firm that creates a new product may not always be able to prevent its competitors from copying the idea. The potential to recover all the expenses incurred from R&D may depend on whether the ideas can be protected from competitors. To protect their ideas, firms apply for **patents,** which allow exclusive rights to the production and sale of a

patents allow exclusive rights to the production and sale of a specific product

specific product. The U.S. Patent Office grants about 3,500 patents per week. Patents are pursued for a wide variety of products, ranging from medical drugs to special sunglasses and microwave popcorn.

Patents can enable firms that engage in extensive R&D, such as IBM and 3M, to benefit from their inventions because the patents prevent competitors from copying the ideas. The 3M Company, which created Post-it notes, commonly obtains at least 400 patents per year. As an example of the importance of patents, consider the following comments from a recent annual report of Hewlett-Packard:

"HP's R&D budgets and activity continue to ensure our leadership as one of the most productive product development and research institutes in the world. . . . In 2001, HP was awarded nearly 1,000 patents in the United States and filed 5,000 patent applications worldwide. This essentially translates into protecting 20 new inventions every working day."

Patents also have some disadvantages that should be recognized. Patent applications are quite tedious and may require a 20- to 40-page description of the product. Some technical patent applications are even more detailed and may contain more than 100 pages of description. Because of the large backlog of patent applications, the approval process can take several months. Many applications are not approved because the patent office decides that the ideas do not represent a new product. Even when a patent application is approved, it is difficult for the inventor to prevent other businesses from copying the idea in some form. Obtaining patents can also be expensive. To obtain a patent internationally, the cost is typically at least $100,000.

Steps Necessary to Create a New Product

The following steps are typically necessary to create a new product:

▶ Develop a product idea.

▶ Assess the feasibility of a product idea.

▶ Design and test the product.

▶ Distribute and promote the product.

▶ Post-audit the product.

Develop a Product Idea   The first step in creating a new product is to develop an idea. When the focus is on improving an existing product, the idea already exists, and the firm simply attempts to make it better. When developing an entirely new product, a common method is to identify consumer needs or preferences that are not being satisfied by existing products. The ultimate goal is to develop a product that is superior to existing products in satisfying the consumer.

As firms attempt to improve existing products or create new products, they must determine what will satisfy customers. The commitment of some firms to customer satisfaction is confirmed by the following statements in recent annual reports:

"Kodak's future is in total customer satisfaction."

—Eastman Kodak

"I [the CEO] want everyone in IBM to be obsessed with satisfying our customers."

—IBM

"We aim to redouble our efforts . . . toward one simple goal: meeting the needs of our customers."

—Apple Computer

Identifying consumer preferences so as to improve a product or create a new product may involve monitoring consumer behavior. For example, an airline may monitor flights to determine the most disturbing inconveniences, such as cramped seating. This leads to ideas for an improved product, such as wider seats. To satisfy consumer preferences, rental car companies at airports now allow their key customers to go straight from the airplane to their cars (rather than stand in line at the counter).

Technology can be used to monitor consumer behavior. When Amazon.com fills orders, it requests information about the customers. Thus, when Amazon considers expanding its product line, it knows the characteristics of the consumers who are buying its existing products. Based on this information about consumer preferences, it can attempt to identify other products that will sell over the Internet.

An alternative to monitoring consumer behavior is surveying people about their behavior. Surveys may be conducted by employees or consulting firms. Again, the goal is to identify consumer preferences that have not been fulfilled. In recent years, recognition of heightened consumer concern about health has led to many ideas for new products and revisions of existing products. For example, food manufacturers responded by creating cereals and frozen dinners that are more nutritious.

Each consumer preference that deserves attention results from a lack of or a deficiency in an existing product. The firm must determine how this lack or deficiency can be corrected by creating a new product or improving an existing product. In the mid-1990s, IBM decided that it needed to increase the processing speed of its computers. IBM incurred substantial expenses as a result of this decision to improve its products. However, the demand for these improved products increased, resulting in higher revenue.

Assess the Feasibility of a Product Idea   Any idea for a new or improved product should be assessed by estimating the costs and benefits. The idea should be undertaken only if the benefits outweigh the costs. For example, American Airlines recently removed some seats to better satisfy customers by providing more leg room. The most obvious cost was the expense of removing the seats, but other costs were incurred as well. The strategy reduced the airline's seating capacity. The cost of this reduction was forgone revenue on those flights that were at full capacity. In addition, an airplane could not be used while the work was being performed. Any forgone revenue during that period also represented a cost of improving the product. Nevertheless, American hoped that the benefit of more leg room would lead to greater consumer satisfaction and thus to greater demand for its service, resulting in more revenue.

Design and Test the Product   If the firm believes the new (or revised) product is feasible, it must determine the design and other characteristics of the product. The new product may be tested before being fully implemented. For example, an airline such as American Airlines may first

cross functional teamwork:

Interaction among Product Decisions and Other Business Decisions

When marketing managers create a new product, they must design it in a manner that will attract customers. They must also decide the price at which the product will be sold. These marketing decisions require communication between the marketing managers and the managers who oversee production. Marketing managers explain to the production managers how they would like the product to be designed. The production managers may offer revisions that can improve the design. They also provide estimates on the costs of production. The cost per unit is typically dependent on the volume of products to be produced; therefore, the cost per unit can be estimated only after the marketing managers determine the volume that will need to be produced to satisfy the demand. Since the pricing decision is influenced by the cost of producing the product, the price cannot be determined by the marketing managers until they receive cost estimates from the production managers.

Once the marketing managers have received the necessary input from the production managers and have developed plans for the design and pricing of the product, a financial analysis by the financial managers is necessary to ensure that the proposal is feasible. The financial analysis involves estimating the revenue the firm will generate as a result of creating this product. It also involves estimating production expenses. Using these estimates, the financial managers can determine whether the new product will provide an adequate return to make the firm's investment in the development of this product worthwhile. The marketing managers should attempt to develop the product only if the financial analysis suggests that it will provide an adequate return to the firm. If the marketing managers decide to develop this product, they will inform the production managers, who may need to hire additional production employees. In addition, the financial managers must be informed because they may need to obtain funds to finance production.

Although the marketing managers may be responsible for the creation of new products, they rely on input from the production and financial managers when deciding whether each product is worthwhile and when determining the design and price of the new product.

revise its seating structure in a few planes to determine consumer reaction. If the actual costs exceed the benefits, the proposed changes will not be made on other airplanes. If the change has a favorable impact, however, it may be made throughout the entire fleet.

Distribute and Promote the Product   When firms introduce new products or improve existing products, they typically attempt to inform consumers. New or improved products are introduced to consumers through various marketing techniques. As an example, an airline that widens its seats may advertise this feature in the media. Additional expenses required to promote the revised design should be accounted for when determining whether it is worthwhile to create a new design.

Post-Audit the Product   After the new product has been introduced into the market, the actual costs and benefits should be measured and compared with the costs and benefits that were forecasted earlier. This comparison determines whether the cost-benefit analysis was reasonably accurate. If costs were severely underestimated or benefits were severely overestimated, the firm may need to adjust its method of analysis for evaluating other new products in the future. In addition, the post-audit of costs and benefits can be used for future development of the same product. For example, if the actual costs of improving the airplanes outweigh the benefits, the airline may revert to its original product design when new airplanes are needed.

Exhibit 12.3

Steps Involved in Creating or Revising a
Product

Summary of Steps Used to Create or Revise a Product   A summary of the steps involved in creating or revising a product is shown in Exhibit 12.3. Notice that the whole process is initiated by attempting to satisfy consumer preferences.

3
Explain the common methods
used to differentiate
a product.

product differentiation a
firm's effort to distinguish its product from competitive products in a
manner that makes the product
more desirable

PRODUCT DIFFERENTIATION

Product differentiation is the effort of a firm to distinguish its product from competitive products in a manner that makes the product more desirable. Some products are differentiated from competitive products by their quality. For example, Starbucks has become a popular coffee shop around the country because of its special coffee, even though its prices are high. Kay-Bee Toys used a marketing strategy of specializing in a small selection of high-quality toys, rather than competing with Wal-Mart for the entire line of toys.

All firms look for some type of competitive advantage that will distinguish their product from the rest. The following are some of the more common methods used to differentiate the product:

▶ Unique product design

▶ Unique packaging

▶ Unique branding

Unique Product Design

Some products are differentiated by their design. Consider a homebuilder who builds homes and sells them once they are completed. The builder can attempt to build homes that will satisfy buyers by considering the following questions:

1 Would consumers in this neighborhood prefer one- or two-story homes?

2 Is a basement desirable?

3 Is a fireplace desirable?

4 What is a popular size for homes in this neighborhood?

5 What type of architecture is popular in this neighborhood?

Once these and other issues are resolved, the builder can build homes with specifications that will attract buyers.

Various characteristics can make one product better than others, including safety, reliability, and ease of use. Firms such as AT&T, Kodak, and Audi have a reputation for reliability, which helps create a demand for their products. Producers attempt to improve reliability by using high-quality materials, providing service, and offering warranties. However, attempts to improve reliability usually result in higher costs.

Differentiating the Design of a Service   Just as firms that produce products attempt to create unique designs for their products, service firms attempt to develop unique services. For example, Southwest Airlines designed a differentiated service by focusing on many short routes that previously were not available to customers. Some grocery stores allow customers to purchase groceries online and provide a delivery service so that the customers do not have to shop at the store.

Unique Packaging

A packaging strategy can determine the success or failure of a product, especially for products whose quality levels are quite similar. In an attempt to differentiate themselves from the competition, some firms have repackaged various grocery products in unbreakable or easily disposable containers.

Many packaging strategies focus on convenience. Motor oil is now packaged in containers with convenient twist-off caps, and many canned foods have pull-tabs. Tide detergent is packaged in both powder and liquid so that consumers can choose their preferred form.

Packaging can also provide advertising. For example, many food products such as microwave dinners are packaged with the preparation instructions on the outside. These instructions also demonstrate how simple the preparation is. Packaging also informs consumers about the nutrition of foods or the effectiveness of health-care products. The advertising on the package may be the key factor that encourages consumers to purchase one product instead of others.

Unique Branding

branding a method of identifying products and differentiating them from competing products

trademark a brand's form of identification that is legally protected from use by other firms

Branding is a method of identifying products and differentiating them from competing products. Brands are typically represented by a name and a symbol. A **trademark** is a brand's form of identification that is legally protected from use by other firms. Some trademarks have become so common that they represent the product itself. For example, "Coke" is often used to refer to any cola drink, and "Kleenex" is frequently used to refer to any facial tissue. Some symbols are more recognizable than the brand name. Levi's jeans, Nike, Pepsi, and Mercedes all have easily recognized symbols.

family branding branding of all or most products produced by a company

Family versus Individual Branding   Companies that produce goods assign either a family or an individual brand to their products. **Family branding** is the branding of all or most products produced by a company. The Coca-Cola Company sells Coca-Cola, Diet Coke, Cherry Coke, and other soft drinks. Ford, RCA, IBM, and Intel use family branding to distinguish their products from the competition.

individual branding the assignment of a unique brand name to different products or groups of products

Companies that use **individual branding** assign a unique brand name to different products or groups of products. For example, Procter & Gamble produces Tide, Bold, and Era. General Mills produces numerous brands of cereal. Many clothing manufacturers use different brand names. One product line may be marketed to prestigious clothing shops. A second line may be marketed to retail stores. To preserve the prestige, the top quality brand may not be sold in retail stores.

Producer versus Store Brands

Most products can be classified as either a producer brand, a store brand, or a generic brand. **Producer brands** reflect the manufacturer of the products. Examples of producer brands include Black & Decker, Frito-Lay, and Fisher Price. These brands are usually well known because they are sold to retail stores nationwide. **Store brands** reflect the retail store where the products are sold. For example, Sears and J. C. Penney offer some products with their own label. Even if store brands are produced by firms other than the retailer, the names of the producers are not identified. Store brand products do not have as much prestige as popular producer brands; however, they often have a lower price.

producer brands brands that reflect the manufacturer of the products

store brands brands that reflect the retail store where the products are sold

Some products are not branded by either the producer or the store. These products have a so-called **generic brand.** The label on generic products simply describes the product. Generic brands have become increasingly popular over the last decade because their prices are relatively low. They are most popular for products that are likely to be similar among brands, such as napkins and paper plates. Customers are comfortable purchasing generic brands of these products because there is not much risk in buying a cheaper product.

generic brands products that are not branded by the producer or the store

Benefits of Branding

Branding continually exposes a company's name to the public. If the company is respected, its new products may be trusted because they carry the company brand name. If they carried a different name, new products introduced by the firm would likely not sell as well.

Many firms with a brand name use their name to enter new markets. The Coca-Cola Company uses its name to promote new soft drinks that it creates. Nabisco can more easily penetrate the market for various specialty foods because of its reputation for quality food products. These firms not only are able to offer new products but also may enter new geographic markets (such as foreign countries) because of their brand name.

A brand is especially useful for differentiating a product when there are only a few major competitors. For example, many consumers select among only two or three brands of some products, such as toothpaste or computers. The importance of branding is emphasized in a recent annual report of Procter & Gamble:

"Consumers have to trust that a brand will meet all their needs all the time. That requires superior product technology. And it also requires sufficient breadth of product choices. We should never give consumers a . . . reason to switch away from one of our brands."

Having an established brand name is also often crucial to obtaining space in a store. For example, Coca-Cola and Pepsi often receive the majority of a store's soft drink shelf space. The same is true for some cereals, detergents, and even dog food. Retail stores normally allocate more space for products with popular brand names.

Exhibit 12.4

Methods Used to Differentiate Products

Method	Achieve Superiority by:
Unique design	Higher level of product safety, reliability, or ease of use.
Unique packaging	Packaging to get consumers' attention or to improve convenience.
Unique branding	Using the firm's image to gain credibility, or using a unique brand name to imply prestige.

Branding also applies to services. When Southwest Airlines begins to serve a new route, it uses its brand (reliability, good service, low prices) to attract customers.

A recent trend in branding is **co-branding,** in which firms agree to offer a combination of two noncompeting products at a discounted price. For example, Blockbuster Entertainment Group issues VISA cards. Blockbuster Video customers can get discounts on video rentals by using their VISA cards.

co-branding firms agree to offer a combination of two noncompeting products at a discounted price

Summary of Methods Used to Differentiate Products

Exhibit 12.4 summarizes the methods used to achieve product differentiation. Firms sometimes combine several methods to differentiate their products. For example, if Kodak creates a product that is technologically superior to others, it may also differentiate the product by packaging it in a special manner and by using the Kodak family brand name.

To understand how some firms use all three methods to differentiate their products, consider the following comment from an annual report:

"Liz Claiborne, Inc., must work more diligently than ever to truly differentiate its brands, . . . applying product innovation [such as a unique design], canny brand marketing, . . . superb customer service and exceptional instore presentation [unique packaging] to win over a consumer who has abundant choices."

—Liz Claiborne, Inc.

College Health Club: **CHC's Product Differentiation**

Services such as aerobics classes, weight machines, and exercise machines are somewhat similar among health clubs. Nevertheless, Sue Kramer, the president of College Health Club (CHC), thinks that she can differentiate CHC from other health clubs. For college students, CHC offers several advantages. Perhaps the most important advantage is its location. It is located across from the college campus, so students can walk to the club. Since many students do not have cars, this location is a major advantage over other health clubs for the students who live on campus. In addition, CHC's membership fee is lower than that of other health clubs in the area, which is important to college students.

Identify the main phases of a product life cycle.

PRODUCT LIFE CYCLE

Most products experience a **product life cycle,** or a typical set of phases over their lifetime. The marketing decisions made about a particular product may be influenced by the prevailing phase of the cycle. The typical product life cycle has four specific phases:

product life cycle the typical set of phases that a product experiences over its lifetime

▶ Introduction

▶ Growth

▶ Maturity
▶ Decline

Introduction

introduction phase the initial period in which consumers are informed about a product

The **introduction phase** is the initial period in which consumers are informed about a new product. The promotion of the product is intended to introduce the product and make consumers aware of it. In some cases, the product is first tested in particular areas to determine consumer reaction. For example, the concept of direct satellite television was tested in various locations. The initial cost of producing and advertising the product may exceed the revenue received during this phase. The price of the product may initially be set high if no other competing products are in the market yet. This strategy is referred to as **price skimming.**

price skimming the strategy of initially setting a high price for a product if no other competing products are in the market yet

Growth

growth phase the period in which sales of a product increase rapidly

The **growth phase** is the period in which sales of the product increase rapidly. The marketing of the product is typically intended to reinforce its features. Cellular telephones and direct satellite TVs are in the growth phase. Other firms that are aware of the product's success may attempt to create a similar or superior product. The price of the product may be lowered once competing products enter the market.

Maturity

maturity phase the period in which additional competing products have entered the market, and sales of a product level off because of competition

The **maturity phase** is the period in which additional competing products have entered the market, and sales of the product level off because of the increased competition. At this point, most marketing strategies are used to ensure that customers are still aware that the product exists. Some marketing strategies may offer special discounts to maintain market share. The firm may also revise the design of the existing product (product differentiation) to maintain market share. Standard cable television service is an example of a product at the maturity phase.

Decline

decline phase the period in which sales of a product decline, either because of reduced consumer demand for that type of product or because competitors are gaining market share

The **decline phase** is the period in which sales of the product decline, either because of reduced consumer demand for that type of product or because competitors are gaining market share. If firms do not prepare for a decline phase on some products, they may experience an abrupt decline in business. Some firms begin to prepare two or more years before the anticipated decline phase by planning revisions in their existing products or services.

The product life cycle is illustrated in Exhibit 12.5. The length of a cycle tends to vary among types of products. It also varies among the firms that sell a particular type of product because some firms lengthen the cycle by continually differentiating their product to maintain market share.

Identify the factors that influence the pricing decision.

PRICING STRATEGIES

Whether a firm produces industrial steel, textbooks, or haircuts, it needs to determine a price for its product. Managers typically attempt to set a price that will maximize the firm's value. The price charged for a product affects

Exhibit 12.5

Product Life Cycle Phases

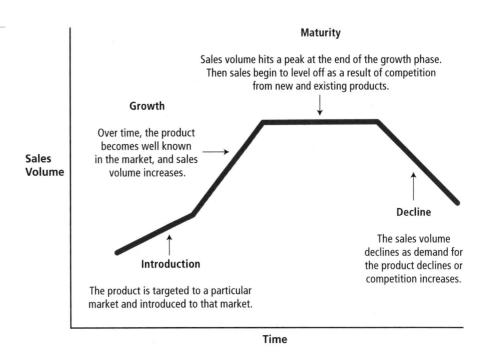

the firm's revenue and therefore its earnings. Recall that the revenue from selling a product is equal to its price times the quantity sold. Although a lower price reduces the revenue received per unit, it typically results in a higher quantity of units sold. A higher price increases the revenue received per unit but results in a lower quantity of units sold. Thus, an obvious trade-off is involved when determining the price for a product.

Firms set the prices of their products by considering the following:

▶ Cost of production

▶ Supply of inventory

▶ Competitors' prices

Pricing According to the Cost of Production

cost-based pricing estimating the per-unit cost of producing a product and then adding a markup

Some firms set a price for a product by estimating the per-unit cost of producing the product and then adding a markup. This method of pricing products is commonly referred to as **cost-based pricing.** If this method is used, the firm must also account for all production costs that are attributable to the production of that product. Pricing according to cost attempts to ensure that production costs are covered. Virtually all firms consider production costs when setting a price. The difference in price between a Cadillac and a Saturn is partially attributed to the difference in production costs. However, other factors may also influence the pricing decision.

Economies of Scale   The per-unit cost of production may be dependent on production volume. For products subject to economies of scale, the average per-unit cost of production decreases as production volume increases. This is especially true for products or services that have high fixed costs (costs that remain unchanged regardless of the quantity produced), such as automobiles. A pricing strategy must account for economies of scale. If a high price is charged, not only does sales volume decrease, but also the average cost of producing a small amount increases. For those products or services that are subject to economies of scale, the price should be sufficiently low to achieve a high sales volume (and therefore lower production costs).

Pricing According to the Supply of Inventory

Some pricing decisions are directly related to the supply of inventory. For example, computer firms such as Apple typically reduce prices on existing personal computers to make room for new models that will soon be marketed. Automobile dealerships frequently use this strategy as well. Most manufacturers and retailers tend to reduce prices if they need to reduce their inventory.

Pricing According to Competitors' Prices

Firms commonly consider the prices of competitors when determining the prices of their products. They can use various pricing strategies to compete against other products, as explained next.

penetration pricing the strategy of setting a lower price than those of competing products to penetrate a market

Penetration Pricing   If a firm wants to be sure that it can sell its product, it may set a lower price than those of competing products to penetrate the market. This pricing strategy is called **penetration pricing** and has been used in various ways by numerous firms, including airlines, automobile manufacturers, and food companies.

price-elastic the demand for a product is highly responsive to price changes

The success of penetration pricing depends on the product's price elasticity, on the responsiveness of consumers to a reduced price. When demand for a product is **price-elastic,** the demand is highly responsive to price changes. Some grocery products such as napkins and paper plates are price-elastic, as price may be the most important criterion that consumers use when deciding which brand to purchase. Many firms, such as Ameritrade, IBM, and Taco Bell have been able to increase their revenue by lowering prices.

When Southwest Airlines entered the airline industry, its average fare was substantially lower than the average fare charged by other airlines for the same routes. Southwest not only pulled customers away from competitors but also created some new customer demand for airline services because of its low prices. Penetration pricing is not always successful, however. Allstate Insurance increased its market share by lowering its insurance prices (premiums), but its profits declined because it lowered its prices too much.

price-inelastic the demand for a product is not very responsive to price changes

When demand for a product is **price-inelastic,** the demand is not very responsive to price changes. A firm should not use penetration pricing if its product is price-inelastic because most consumers would not switch to the product to take advantage of the lower price. For some products, such as deli products and high-quality automobiles, personalized service and perceived quality may be more important than price. The demand for many services is not responsive to price reductions because consumers may prefer one firm over others. For example, some consumers may be unwilling to switch dentists, hair stylists, or stockbrokers even if a competitor reduces its price.

Pricing gasoline is a continuous decision-making activity for oil companies.

© Getty Images

Defensive Pricing

Some pricing decisions are defensive rather than offensive. If a firm recognizes that the price of a competing product has been reduced, it may use **defensive pricing,** in which a product's price is reduced to defend (retain) market share. For example, airlines commonly reduce their airfares in response when a competitor lowers its airfares. This response tends to allow all airlines to retain their market share, but their revenue decreases (because of the lower price). Computer firms such as IBM and Dell commonly reduce their prices in response to price reductions by their competitors.

Some firms lower their price to drive out new competitors that have entered the market. This strategy is called **predatory pricing.**

Prestige Pricing   Firms may use a higher price if their product is intended to have a top-of-the-line image. This pricing strategy is called **prestige pricing.** For example, GapKids sells baby clothing at relatively high prices to create a high-quality image for customers who are not as concerned about price. Microbreweries use prestige pricing in an attempt to create a high-quality image for their beers.

Firms with a diversified product mix may use a penetration pricing strategy for some products and a prestige pricing strategy for others. For example, car manufacturers price some cars as low as possible to increase market share, but use prestige pricing on other models that have a top-of-the-line image.

EXAMPLE OF SETTING A PRODUCT'S PRICE

To show how a firm may set a product's price, assume that you move to New Orleans and start your own business as a hot dog vendor on the streets of the French Quarter (a tourist district). Assume that you plan to run this business for one year and that a hot dog cooker can be rented for $4,000 annually. This cost is referred to as a **fixed cost** because the cost of production remains unchanged regardless of how many units are produced. Also assume that your costs for hot dogs, buns, ketchup, and so on are about $.60 per hot dog. These costs are called **variable costs** because they vary with the quantity of hot dogs produced.

Other vendors in the area charge $2.00 per hot dog. After talking with several other vendors, you forecast that you can sell 20,000 hot dogs in one year as long as your price is competitive.

defensive pricing the strategy of reducing a product's price to defend (retain) market share

predatory pricing the strategy of lowering a product's price to drive out new competitors

prestige pricing the strategy of using a higher price for a product that is intended to have a top-of-the-line image

fixed cost the cost of production that remains unchanged regardless of how many units are produced

variable costs costs that vary with the quantity produced

increasing value with technology

PRICING INFORMATION-BASED PRODUCTS

As information technology (IT) is increasingly incorporated into products, manufacturers are having to rethink their traditional pricing strategies. Traditionally, most product costs have come from labor and raw materials. This meant that the variable cost of each unit produced (the costs directly associated with a given unit) was a critical factor in the pricing decision. The IT components of products have a markedly different cost structure, however. Although it may cost tens or hundreds of millions of dollars to design and test a single chip, once chips are in production, the variable cost of producing additional chips is very small (such as a few dollars or even pennies). The same is true for producing software. As a result, although incorporating IT into a product may dramatically improve product quality, it can have little impact on the variable cost of that product. Therefore, variable cost is less useful in deciding on price.

How can manufacturers recoup the investment they make in incorporating IT into their products? One way is to raise product prices to reflect the higher value of the re-designed products to consumers. However, other opportunities are available to gain revenue from the technology. Licensing the product to other manufacturers, as Adobe did with its PostScript printer language, is one way of deriving revenue. Another is to market the specialized test equipment needed to service the new technology. Some companies even use technology as a source of ongoing revenue from prior customers, periodically offering upgrades to the on-board information systems in their products.

Whether or not a product contains IT, it is ultimately the market that determines if the "price is right." As such technologies become increasingly important to product performance, however, companies will have to be more creative in their product and pricing strategies.

To determine an appropriate price, begin with the cost information and determine the total cost of production over the first year. The total cost is calculated as follows:

$$
\begin{aligned}
\text{Total Cost} &= (\text{Fixed Cost}) + [(\text{Quantity}) \times (\text{Variable Cost per Unit})] \\
&= \$4{,}000 + [(20{,}000) \times (\$.60)] \\
&= \$4{,}000 + \$12{,}000 \\
&= \$16{,}000
\end{aligned}
$$

Assume that you price the hot dogs at $1.80 so that your price is slightly lower than those of competitors. Since the total revenue is equal to price times the quantity sold, your total revenue is estimated to be:

$$
\begin{aligned}
\text{Total Revenue} &= (\text{Quantity}) \times (\text{Price per Unit}) \\
&= (20{,}000) \times (\$1.80) \\
&= \$36{,}000
\end{aligned}
$$

Thus, your profits would be:

$$
\begin{aligned}
\text{Profits} &= \text{Total Revenue} - \text{Total Cost} \\
&= \$36{,}000 - \$16{,}000
\end{aligned}
$$

Your actual revenue over a future period is subject to uncertainty, however. For example, if you sell only 10,000 hot dogs, your revenue would be:

$$
\begin{aligned}
\text{Total Revenue} &= (\text{Quantity}) \times (\text{Price}) \\
&= (10{,}000) \times (\$1.80) \\
&= \$18{,}000
\end{aligned}
$$

Your profits would be as follows:

$$\text{Profits} = \text{Total Revenue} - \text{Total Cost}$$
$$= \$18,000 - \$16,000$$
$$= \$2,000$$

Thus, your profits (revenue minus costs) would be only $2,000. You could attempt to increase your price to make up for the possibility of low sales, but this strategy may conflict with your goal of setting a price that is no higher than the competition. The quantity of hot dogs you sell may decline if you use a higher price.

The total cost and total revenue are depicted in Exhibit 12.6 for various quantities of hot dogs produced. Notice that the fixed cost remains

Exhibit 12.6

Estimation of Costs and Revenue at Various Quantities Produced

Quantity (Q)	Fixed Cost	Variable Cost (Q × $.60)	Total Cost	Total Revenue (Q × $1.80)	Profits
1,000	$4,000	$600	$4,600	$1,800	−$2,800
3,000	4,000	1,800	5,800	5,400	−400
4,000	4,000	2,400	6,400	7,200	800
7,000	4,000	4,200	8,200	12,600	4,400
10,000	4,000	6,000	10,000	18,000	8,000
15,000	4,000	9,000	13,000	27,000	14,000
20,000	4,000	12,000	16,000	36,000	20,000
25,000	4,000	15,000	19,000	45,000	26,000
30,000	4,000	18,000	22,000	54,000	32,000

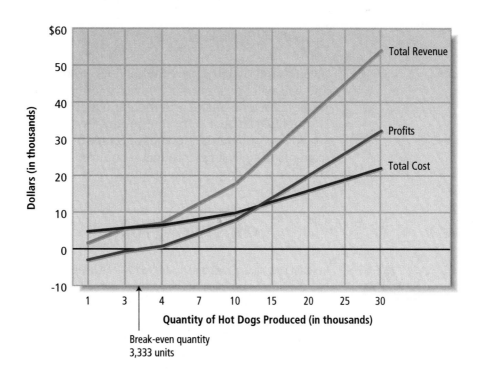

unchanged for any quantity produced. The variable cost is equal to the quantity times $.60 per hot dog produced. The total cost is equal to the fixed cost plus the variable cost. The total revenue is equal to the price of $1.80 per hot dog times the quantity of hot dogs produced.

Break-Even Point

break-even point the quantity of units at which total revenue equals total cost

contribution margin the difference between price and variable cost per unit

The **break-even point** is the quantity of units at which total revenue equals total cost. At any quantity less than the break-even point, total costs exceed total revenue. For any quantity above the break-even point, total revenue exceeds total cost.

The break-even point can be determined by first estimating the **contribution margin**, which is the difference between price and variable cost per unit. In our example, the difference is as follows:

$$\text{Price} - \text{Variable Cost per Unit} = \$1.80 - \$.60 = \$1.20$$

For every unit sold, the price received exceeds the variable cost by $1.20. Given that each unit is priced above the variable cost, the break-even quantity of units that must be produced and sold to cover the fixed cost is as follows:

$$\text{Break-Even Quantity} = \frac{\text{Fixed Cost}}{\text{Price} - \text{Variable Cost per Unit}}$$

In our example, the break-even quantity is as follows:

$$\text{Break-Even Quantity} = \frac{\$4,000}{\$1.80 - \$.60}$$

$$= 3,333$$

If you charge a higher price for hot dogs, your contribution margin is higher, and you will break even at a lower quantity. However, a higher price may result in lower demand and therefore may be less profitable. This example is simplified in that only one product was produced. A hot dog vendor would likely offer other food or beverage products as well. Nevertheless, the example using a single product is sufficient to illustrate the factors that are considered when pricing a product.

College Health Club: **CHC's Pricing Policy**

In setting the annual membership fee for College Health Club (CHC), Sue Kramer considers both the cost of production and competitors' prices. First, she has determined that her rent, salaries, interest, and other expenses will be about $142,000. Sue also recognizes that she must offer competitive pricing for students who are on a very limited budget. She estimates that if CHC charges $400 per membership, it will attract 350 members. If CHC charges $500 per membership, it will attract about 300 members. If CHC charges a membership fee of $600, it will attract about 200 members.

Sue's analysis of how the pricing will affect CHC's earnings is shown in the following table:

	CHC's Performance In the First Year If . . .		
	Annual Membership Price Is $400	Annual Membership Price Is $500	Annual Membership Price Is $600
(1) Price per membership	$400	$500	$600
(2) Number of members in first year	350	300	200
(3) Revenue = (1) × (2)	$140,000	$150,000	$120,000
(4) Total operating expenses	$138,000	$138,000	$138,000
(5) Interest expenses	$4,000	$4,000	$4,000
(6) Earnings before taxes = (3) − (4) − (5)	− $2,000	$8,000	− $22,000

The membership price of $500 results in the best performance for CHC. It not only will cover her cost of production, but is competitive.

ADDITIONAL PRICING DECISIONS

In addition to setting the price of a product, firms must decide whether to offer special discounts, periodic sales prices, and credit terms for specific customers. Each of these decisions is discussed separately.

Discounting

Since some consumers are willing to pay more for a product than others, a firm may attempt to charge different prices to different customers. For example, restaurants and hotels often offer discounts for senior citizens. Magazines offer student discounts on subscriptions. Airlines tend to charge business travelers at least twice the fares of customers who are paying for the flight themselves. Discounting can enable a firm to attract consumers who are more price conscious, while charging higher prices to other consumers who are less price conscious.

Some firms offer discounted prices to customers who submit orders via the Internet. In this way, the firms encourage more online orders, an

The number of people age 65 or older have increased. Such information is relevant to companies that may choose to target specific markets with strategies like senior discounts.

Photo/ Winona Daily News, Kevin E. Schmidt

advantage because a salesperson is not needed to take these orders. Some airlines and hotels offer special discounts when reservations are made through their websites.

Sales Prices

Many firms use sales prices as a means of discounting for those consumers who will make purchases only if the price is reduced. For example, retail stores tend to put some of their products on sale in any given week. This strategy not only attracts customers who may have been unwilling to purchase those products at the full price, but it also encourages them to buy other products while they are at the store.

Stores normally put high prices on many products, such as televisions and shoes, to allow for a major reduction in the prices when the products are on sale. Since most consumers recognize that these products may soon be priced at a 20 to 40 percent discount, they tend to purchase these products only when they are on sale.

Credit Terms

Regardless of the price charged for a product, firms must determine whether they will allow the product to be purchased on credit. Supplier firms commonly allow manufacturing firms to purchase supplies on credit. They would obviously prefer cash sales, since a cash payment avoids the possibility of bad debt and also provides an immediate source of funds. Nevertheless, they may still offer credit to attract some manufacturing firms that do not have cash available. Firms can encourage their customers to pay off their credit by offering a discount. For example, the terms "2/10 net 30" indicate that a 2 percent discount can be taken if the bill is paid within 10 days and that the bill must be paid in full within 30 days.

A change in credit terms can affect a firm's sales. Thus, firms may revise their credit terms as a marketing tool. If a firm desires to increase demand, it may offer an extended period to pay off the credit, such as 2/10 net 60. A disadvantage of this strategy is that many credit balances will be paid off at a slower rate. In addition, the level of bad debt tends to be higher for firms that offer such loose credit terms.

Many retail stores offer credit to customers through MasterCard and VISA credit cards. Retailers pay a percentage of their credit sales (usually around 4 percent) to the sponsor of the card. The advantage of these cards is that the credit balance is paid by a bank, which in turn is responsible for collecting on customer credit.

Many companies, such as Sears, issue their own credit cards to consumers. These companies frequently use the Internet to make customers aware of the benefits associated with owning a credit card issued by the company. Advertising the card on the company's website allows customers to assess the potential benefits of owning the credit card.

College Health Club: **CHC's Discounting and Credit Decision**

Sue Kramer has considered various types of discounting strategies to increase membership at College Health Club (CHC). First, she considered offering a 10 percent discount to any students who signed up in the first week of the fall semester. She decided against that strategy, however, because she was afraid that existing members might become upset that they were not offered the discount.

She also considered increasing the annual membership fee to $525 and offering a student discount so that students could still become members for $500. Nonstudents could more easily afford to pay a slightly higher membership fee. She decided against this policy, however, because she wants to attract more nonstudent members.

Sue also considered offering credit terms to members as a way of increasing memberships. For example, she could allow them to sign up for a membership and then pay three or six months later. She decided against this strategy because some members who receive credit might not ever pay their bill.

SUMMARY

1 The main factors affecting the size of a product's target market are

▶ demographic trends, such as age and income levels;

▶ geography;

▶ economic factors, such as economic growth; and

▶ changes in social values, such as a decline in demand for products perceived to be unhealthy.

2 The main steps involved in creating a new product are

▶ develop a product idea, which may be in response to changes in consumer needs or preferences;

▶ assess the feasibility of the product idea, which requires comparing the expected benefits with the costs of the product;

▶ design the product and test it with some consumers in the target market;

▶ distribute the product so that it is accessible to the target market, and promote the product to ensure that consumers are aware of it; and

▶ post-audit the product to determine whether the product needs to be revised in any way.

3 Some common methods used to differentiate a product are

▶ unique design, in which the product produced is safer, more reliable, easier to use, or has some other advantages;

▶ unique packaging, which can enhance convenience or contain advertising; and

▶ unique branding, which may enhance consumers' perception of the product's quality.

4 The phases of the product life cycle are

▶ introduction phase, in which consumers are informed about the product;

▶ growth phase, in which the product becomes more popular and increases its share of the market;

▶ maturity phase, in which the sales volume levels off as a result of competition; and

▶ decline phase, in which the sales volume is reduced as a result of competition or reduced consumer demand.

5 The key factors that influence the pricing decision are

▶ cost of production, so the price charged can recover costs incurred;

▶ inventory supply, so the price can be lowered to remove excess inventory; and

▶ prices of competitors, so the price may be set below those of competitors to gain an advantage (penetration pricing) or above those of competitors to create an image of high quality (prestige pricing).

Key Terms

Review & Critical Thinking Questions

1. What is a product mix? Is it in the best interest of management to expand or contract the firm's product mix over time?

2. Briefly describe the general factors influencing the size of a product's target market. Identify the target market for the following organizations: (a) Dallas Cowboys, (b) Wal-Mart stores, (c) Midas Muffler, (d) Jeep Cherokee, and (e) Jenny Craig.

3. Discuss the key factors that affect consumer preferences and therefore affect the size of the target market.

4. Discuss the following statement: "We are emphatically global in our strategy of building a few core businesses worldwide." Are most large corporations going in this direction today?

5. What is e-marketing? How can a firm use e-marketing to expand the target market?

6. Define marketing research. How could a firm attempting to create new products use marketing research?

7. How can e-marketing complement marketing research?

8. Assume that you are an inventor who has just created a new product. Will a patent protect your invention in a domestic market? Are there any disadvantages of patents?

9. Describe the steps you should follow in developing a new product.

10. Discuss the product life cycle phases. Identify the current phase for the following products: (a) snowboards, (b) electric typewriters, (c) Harley-Davidson "full-dresser," and (d) 2003 Ford automobile.

11. Briefly describe the different types of pricing strategies. How do you think the type of strategy used by Calvin Klein jeans differs from that used by community colleges?

12. Assume that you are a manager of a retail outlet that markets T-shirts. You must determine a price. What factors should you consider in setting a pricing strategy?

Discussion Questions

1. Assume that you are a marketing manager for a nationally known pizza chain. You have just read a marketing research article describing the tastes and preferences of consumers throughout the country. You are planning to discuss this subject with your employees at a meeting. Identify the topics that you would discuss with this group.

2. How can a firm use the Internet to differentiate its products from the products of competitors? How can it use the Internet to identify its target market?

3. You are the marketing manager of a car manufacturer. How could you use e-marketing to expand your target market?

4. What general advice would you give to a retailer when you are very dissatisfied with a service that you have purchased?

5. You are a marketing manager for a restaurant chain. You are aware that the aging population in this country has become health conscious. What impact do you think these developments will have on the restaurant industry? How could marketing research help in this situation?

6. Although Harley-Davidson "full-dressers" are popular with consumers over 35 years of age, younger motorcycle buyers perceive this vehicle as staid and not sporty enough to suit their tastes. These younger motorcycle buyers are more likely to buy foreign-made sport motorcycles like the Kawasaki Ninja. Product managers at Harley-Davidson may want to reposition their top-of-the-line "full-dressers" in order to appeal to younger consumers as well. You are the product manager in charge of developing a plan to achieve this goal. What strategy do you think would be most effective for reaching this market segment?

It's Your Decision: **Pricing Decisions at CHC**

1. Would prestige pricing be an effective strategy for CHC based on its primary target market?

2. If Sue Kramer, the president of CHC, is considering a pricing strategy of reducing the membership fee, why must she first consider the size of the facilities?

3. Recall that Sue expects total expenses of $142,000 in CHC's first year. Sue will price a membership at $500 and expects to attract 300 members in the first year. Assume that Sue considers lower membership prices than she originally planned. Determine CHC's estimated earnings before taxes based on the following possible pricing scenarios:

If CHC's Membership Price Is:	The Expected Number of Members in the First Year Would Be:	CHC's Earnings before Taxes in the First Year Would Be:
$500 (original plan)	300	_____
$480	310	_____
$460	320	_____
$440	335	_____

Which price should Sue charge? Explain.

4. A health club differs from manufacturing firms in that it produces a service rather than products. Explain how the process of targeting by a service-oriented firm is different than the process of targeting by a manufacturing-oriented firm.

Investing in a Business

Using the annual report of the firm in which you would like to invest, complete the following:

1 Describe the firm's product line or product mix. Does the firm benefit from its brand name?

2 Has the firm developed any new products recently? If so, are these products extensions of the firm's existing product line?

3 Has the firm established any new pricing policies? If so, provide details.

4 Explain how the business uses technology or the Internet to price its products. Explain how the business uses technology or the Internet to identify its target market and to differentiate its product from the products of competitors.

Case: Marketing T-Shirts

Richard Schilo is the owner-operator of Richard's T-Shirts, a manufacturing business. The business has been in operation for two years. Richard has discovered through marketing research that teenagers desire his T-shirts. As a result of this research, Richard introduced a sports line of T-shirts with the endorsements of professional franchises. Richard has had tremendous success with this product line. His business has become highly profitable, having grown 100 percent from the first year's operation of $150,000 in sales to a current level of $300,000 in sales.

Additional marketing research has indicated that the collegiate market offers high growth potential. In the fall, Richard plans to introduce a line of collegiate sweaters at a retail price of $29.95. These sweaters will be sold in college bookstores around the country and will be priced competitively with other comparable sweater lines. The sweaters will be unique in appearance, with embroidered college insignias in school colors and the school mascot on the sweater sleeve. Each sweater will be packaged in a gym bag highlighting the athletic program of the student's choice. An exclusive brand name will be selected for each college and university. The plan is that the brand name will feature that school's athlete of the year.

In the future, Richard plans to introduce his product line to a nationwide network of retail establishments. His pricing strategy will continue during this expansion. His projections show that he will continue to build volume, especially in the retail discount sector, where much growth has taken place in recent years.

Questions

1 Describe the target market for Richard's T-Shirts.

2 Identify and explain some common methods Richard is planning to use to differentiate his sweaters from other competing products.

3 What is the current stage of the product life cycle for these T-shirts?

4 Discuss the pricing strategy that Richard plans to use when he introduces the sweaters.

5 Explain how Richard could use e-marketing to expand his target market.

Video Case: Product Development by Second Chance

Second Chance is a company that produces concealable body armor (bullet-proof vests) for police officers. The vests were initially relatively heavy and were used only in specific situations. Now many police officers wish to wear concealable body armor all the time that they are on duty. In fact, they may even be required to wear concealable body armor while they are on duty as a means of continual protection. Because police officers now use concealable body armor more than in the past, Second Chance recognized the need to make the armor as lightweight and comfortable as possible. However, it was concerned that the lightweight armor would be more expensive and therefore would not be purchased by police departments. Second Chance then created an expanded product line of body armor, with each product differing in terms of its weight and comfort. Now the company provides relatively heavy (and low-cost) armor for police departments that can afford only this type of armor. It also provides relatively lightweight (and more expensive) concealable body armor for police departments that can afford this type of armor.

The incentive to provide a more advanced product comes from the customers (police officers) who want to be comfortable if they are going to wear the armor all day. When Second Chance uses the latest technology to develop body armor, it first attempts to design the new armor. Then it allows the employees who manufacture the armor to offer their input because they understand the potential manufacturing problems that may result from a particular design. Thus, several employees participate in the development of the new product.

Questions

1 Why does Second Chance provide a variety of armor types rather than simply selling its most technologically advanced type of armor?

2 How do you think Second Chance determined its target market?

3 The initial body armor that was created more than 20 years ago has become obsolete. Do you think this reflects fashion obsolescence or technological obsolescence?

4 How would Second Chance use marketing research to help it improve its concealable body armor?

Internet Applications

1. *http://www.autoworld.com/*

Find the price of a new car of your choice; then find the price of a used car of your choice. How do you think Autoworld makes its pricing decisions? Do you think the company prices cars according to the cost of production, the supply of inventory, or competitors' prices? How do you think Autoworld differentiates its products from those of other car dealers, if at all? Do you think Autoworld has a high break-even point? Why or why not?

2. *http://www.bottomdollar.com/*

Search this website for a computer of your choice and list the retailers that offer that computer and the various prices they charge. Why do you think the price for the same computer varies across different retailers? Do you think a website like this is useful for retailers and consumers? Why or why not? What do you think will happen to the price of this computer as it moves through the product life cycle?

3. *http://ecommerce.internet.com*

Browse through the articles and news provided on this website. Summarize some ways in which retailers are using e-commerce and e-marketing. Do you think these strategies are effective? Why or why not?

The Coca-Cola Company Annual Report Project

 Questions for the current year's annual report are available on the text website at **http:// madura.swlearning.com.**

The following questions apply concepts presented in this chapter to The Coca-Cola Company. Go to The Coca-Cola Company website (**http://www.cocacola.com**) and find the index for the 2001 annual report.

Questions

1 Study the online annual report. Is Coca-Cola a convenience product, a shopping product, or a specialty product?

2 Download the financial statements and find "Investments." How do you think marketing relates to brand strength at The Coca-Cola Company?

3 Download the financial statements and find "Investments." Also consult the "Operations Review" section.

a. The first product of The Coca-Cola Company was Coke. Has The Coca-Cola Company's product line expanded over time? What are some of the additional products manufactured by the company now?

b. How do you think the expanded product line benefits The Coca-Cola Company?

4 Click on "Letter to Share Owners." Which stage of the product life cycle do you think Coca-Cola is in?

5 Go to **http://hoovers.com** and locate the NEWS CENTER. Key in The Coca-Cola Company in the space provided, click on "Search," and review the recent news stories about the firm. Summarize any (at least one) recent news story about The Coca-Cola Company that applies one or more of the key concepts within this chapter of the text.

In-Text Study Guide

Answers are in an appendix at the back of the book.

True or False

1. Consumers purchasing convenience goods will shop around and compare quality and price of similar products. F

2. As new consumer needs are identified, firms tend to expand both their product lines and product mix. T

3. Demographics can be used to identify a target market. T

4. During a recession, the demand for specialty goods tends to increase. F

5. Price skimming is a strategy commonly used in highly competitive markets. F

6. A change in interest rates can have a major impact on consumer demand. T

7. E-marketing is highly successful in domestic (U.S.) markets, but the high cost of shipping has prevented U.S. companies from using it successfully in foreign markets. F

8. A change in credit terms can affect a firm's sales. T

9. Warranties can be used to achieve product differentiation. T

10. Firms should use penetration pricing if their products are price-inelastic. F

Multiple Choice

11. A Rolex watch and a Jaguar automobile are considered:
    a) convenience products.
    b) shopping goods.
    c) industrial products.
    d) specialty products.
    e) priority products.

12. When a hospital supply company offers a wide variety of products to its customers, the firm is:
    a) offering quantity price discounts in order to attract price-conscious customers.
    b) encouraging customers to pay their outstanding debts in order to take advantage of discounts.
    c) practicing product differentiation.

    d) diversifying its product mix.
    e) responding to the needs of a diverse labor force.

13. All of the following are key factors that influence consum preferences and the size of a target market except:
    a) social values.
    b) anthropology.
    c) economic factors.
    d) geography.
    e) demographics.

14. Cameras, clothes, and household items are examples of products that exist in:
    a) industrial markets.
    b) business markets.
    c) consumer markets.
    d) government markets.
    e) foreign industrial markets.

15. The size of a particular target market is most likely to change in response to a change in:
    a) inflation.
    b) consumer preferences.
    c) interest rates.
    d) the number of competitors.
    e) the size of the largest competitor.

16. When firms develop products, they assess the markets of their competitors to determine their:
    a) financial plans.
    b) marketing strategies.
    c) industrial strategies.
    d) geographic segmentation.
    e) business segmentation.

17. Personal computers are subject to _____ because of the rapid changes in the development of computer hardware components.
    a) product feasibility
    b) penetration pricing
    c) planned obsolescence
    d) the development of generic brands
    e) technological obsolescence

In-Text Study Guide

Answers are in an appendix at the back of the book.

E-marketing supports marketing research in all the following ways except:
- a) low cost of personal surveys
- b) speed of receiving marketing information
- c) customer openness with opinions
- d) access to customers of varied income levels
- e) customer service e-mail

19. To develop new ideas for expanding their product line, many firms have recently increased their investment in:
- a) research and development.
- b) production facilities.
- c) distribution facilities.
- d) overseas production and assembly operations.
- e) inventory control.

20. Which of the following can be used by a firm to protect its investments in research and product development?
- a) marketing research
- b) patents
- c) demographics
- d) target market selection
- e) product mix

21. The first step in creating a new product is to:
- a) assess the feasibility of the product.
- b) develop a product idea.
- c) design the product.
- d) test the product.
- e) distribute and promote the product.

22. New and revised products may be tested through:
- a) commercialization.
- b) geographic sales.
- c) product life cycle.
- d) family brands.
- e) marketing research.

23. All of the following are methods commonly used to differentiate products from those of competitors except:
- a) quality.
- b) design.
- c) tax policies.

- d) packaging.
- e) branding.

24. The Coca-Cola Company sells Coca-Cola, Diet Coke, Cherry Coke, and other soft drinks, which is an example of a(n):
- a) family brand.
- b) individual brand.
- c) corporate brand.
- d) trademark.
- e) copyright.

25. Many _____ strategies are focused on convenience.
- a) packaging
- b) economic
- c) partnership
- d) obsolescence
- e) finance

26. Products that are not branded by the producer or retail store are called:
- a) manufacturer brands.
- b) national brands.
- c) store brands.
- d) obsolete brands.
- e) generic brands.

27. All of the following are benefits of product branding except:
- a) greater company name recognition.
- b) lower prices.
- c) easier to introduce new products.
- d) easier to enter new geographic markets.
- e) easier to obtain retail store shelf space.

28. The process of combining two noncompeting products at a discounted price is called:
- a) complementary advertising.
- b) multiple discounts.
- c) co-branding.
- d) sales promotion double.
- e) quantity pricing.

In-Text Study Guide

Answers are in an appendix at the back of the book.

29. Sales of the product increase rapidly during the _____ phase of the product life cycle.
    a) maturity
    b) introduction
    c) saturation
    d) growth
    e) declining

30. Which of the following pricing strategies would likely be used in a market where no other competitive products are available?
    a) cost-based pricing
    b) penetration pricing
    c) predatory pricing
    d) price skimming
    e) defensive pricing

31. Managers typically attempt to set a price that will maximize a firm's:
    a) value.
    b) cost.
    c) production.
    d) advertising.
    e) promotion.

32. When a firm lowers its price and total revenue increases, it tells us that:
    a) the demand for the product is price-inelastic.
    b) a penetration pricing strategy is being followed.
    c) consumers are not very responsive to price changes.
    d) the demand for the product is price-elastic.
    e) the firm is using a price-skimming strategy.

33. Some pricing decisions are directly related to the supply of:
    a) social values.
    b) social norms.
    c) maintenance operations.
    d) creditors in the marketplace.
    e) inventory.

34. Which of the following pricing strategies adds a profit markup to the per-unit cost of production?
    a) prestige pricing
    b) cost-based pricing
    c) defensive pricing
    d) profit pricing
    e) penetration pricing

35. When a cost of production remains unchanged regardless of how many units are produced, it is referred to as:
    a) variable.
    b) semifinished.
    c) fixed.
    d) in process.
    e) terminal.

36. (Fixed Cost) + (Quantity × Variable Cost per Unit) describes:
    a) Total Cost
    b) Total Revenue
    c) Break-Even Point
    d) Profits
    e) Average Cost Per Unit

37. The break-even point occurs when:
    a) profits are maximized.
    b) sales are at a minimum.
    c) total revenue equals total cost.
    d) contribution margin is highest.
    e) sales discounts are minimized.

38. Discounts:
    a) are considered predatory pricing.
    b) work best in price-inelastic situations.
    c) tend to erode profits.
    d) attract consumers who are price conscious.
    e) are an inefficient means of segmenting the market.

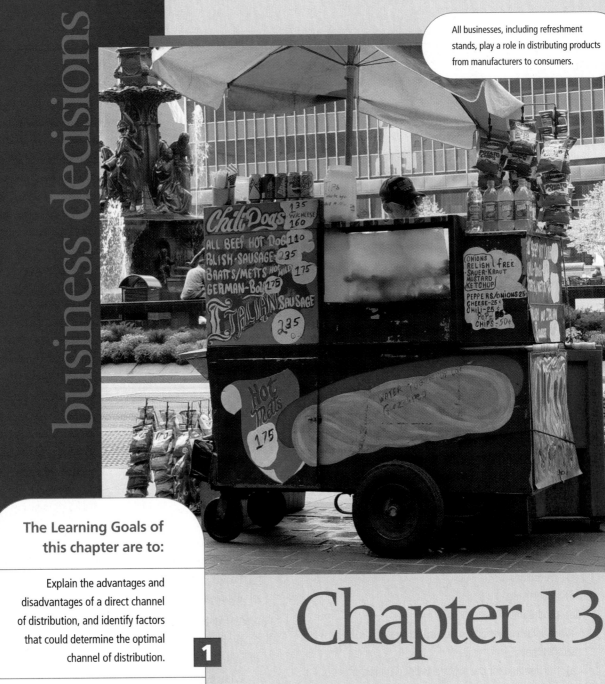

All businesses, including refreshment stands, play a role in distributing products from manufacturers to consumers.

Chapter 13

business decisions

The Learning Goals of this chapter are to:

1 Explain the advantages and disadvantages of a direct channel of distribution, and identify factors that could determine the optimal channel of distribution.

2 Differentiate between types of market coverage.

3 Explain how the distribution process can be accelerated.

4 Explain how retailers serve customers.

5 Explain how wholesalers can serve manufacturers and retailers.

6 Explain the strategy and potential benefits of vertical channel integration.

Distributing Products

A distribution channel represents the path of a product from the producer to the consumer. The channel often includes marketing intermediaries, or firms that participate in moving the product toward the customer. Consider the situation of Rick Walsh, who owns a refreshment stand. Rick serves as a marketing intermediary by selling refreshment products produced by other manufacturers to customers.

Rick must make the following decisions about his business.

▶ Given the limited space that he has, what products should he focus on distributing in order to generate a high level of earnings?

▶ In what part of the city should he set up his business to ensure a strong demand for the products he distributes?

▶ Should he produce his own products to distribute, or should he continue to serve as the marketing intermediary for products he obtains from manufacturers?

These types of decisions are necessary for all businesses. This chapter explains how various distribution decisions can be conducted in a manner that maximizes the firm's value.

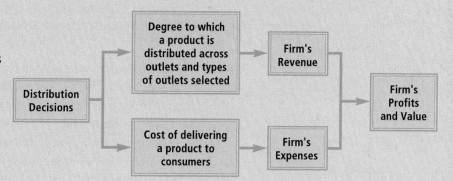

CHANNELS OF DISTRIBUTION

1 Explain the advantages and disadvantages of a direct channel of distribution, and identify factors that could determine the optimal channel of distribution.

A firm's distribution decision determines the manner by which its products are made accessible to its customers. Firms must develop a strategy to ensure that products are distributed to customers at a place convenient to them. Black & Decker distributes its power tools at various retail stores where customers shop for power tools. Liz Claiborne distributes its clothing at upscale clothing stores where customers shop for quality clothing. Ralston Purina distributes its dog food to grocery stores where customers shop for dog food.

Direct Channel

When a producer of a product deals directly with customers, marketing intermediaries are not involved; this situation is called a **direct channel.** An example of a direct channel is a firm such as Land's End that produces clothing and sells some clothing directly to customers. Land's End distributes catalogs in the mail to customers, who can call in their orders. It also has a website where consumers can place orders online.

Advantages of a Direct Channel The advantage of a direct channel is that the full difference between the manufacturer's cost and the price paid by the consumer goes to the producer. When manufacturers sell directly to customers, they have full control over the price to be charged to the consumer. Conversely, when they sell their products to **marketing intermediaries,** they do not control the prices charged to consumers. Manufacturers also prefer to avoid intermediaries because the prices of their products are increased at each level of the distribution channel, and the manufacturers do not receive any of the markup.

Another advantage of a direct channel is that the producer can easily obtain firsthand feedback on the product. This allows the producer to respond quickly to any customer complaints. Customer feedback also informs the producer about potential problems in the product design and therefore allows for improvement.

Dell Computer Corporation uses a direct channel and justifies this form of distribution in a recent annual report:

"The direct model eliminates the need to support an extensive network of wholesale and retail dealers, thereby avoiding dealer mark-ups; avoids the higher inventory costs associated with the wholesale/retail channel and the competition for retail shelf space. . . . In addition, the direct model allows the Company to maintain, monitor, and update a customer data base that can be used to shape the future product offerings. . . . This direct approach allows the Company to rapidly and efficiently deliver relevant technology to its customers."

When Dell sells its computers online, there is no additional markup by intermediaries, so customers get what they want at a lower price, and Dell can still be very profitable. Dell relies heavily on the Internet to facilitate its direct channel of distribution and to receive customer questions. About half of the technical support communication between customers and Dell occurs online. Recently, Dell established some small kiosks where consumers can view and test the computers, but the consumers must still place orders online.

Dell continues the direct relationship with its customers after they purchase their computers. If the customers have complaints, they contact Dell directly. Consequently, Dell can identify any deficiencies and correct them when it designs the next generation of computers. For example, assume that Dell sells a computer model that is popular but would be even more desirable with a redesigned keyboard. Because Dell deals directly with its customers, it will receive frequent feedback from the customers about the keyboard. If instead Dell sold computers to marketing intermediaries, it would not have direct access to customer opinions because the intermediaries would be dealing with the customers.

Disadvantages of a Direct Channel A direct channel also has some disadvantages. First, manufacturers that use a direct channel need more employees. If a company that produces lumber wants to avoid intermediaries, it has to hire sales and delivery people to sell the lumber directly to consumers. By using intermediaries, the company can specialize in the production of lumber rather than be concerned with selling the lumber directly to consumers. In addition, producers that use a direct channel may have to incur more expenses to promote the product. Intermediaries can promote products through advertisements or even by placing the product in a visible place for consumers.

Another disadvantage of a direct channel is that the manufacturer may have to sell its products on credit when selling to customers directly. By selling to intermediaries, it may not have to provide credit.

One-Level Channel

one-level channel one marketing intermediary is between the producer and the customer

merchants marketing intermediaries that become owners of products and then resell them

In a **one-level channel,** one marketing intermediary is between the producer and the customer, as illustrated in Exhibit 13.1. Some marketing intermediaries (called **merchants**) become owners of the products and then resell them. For example, wholesalers act as merchants by purchasing products in bulk and reselling them to other firms. In addition, retail stores (or "retailers") such as Wal-Mart and Sears act as merchants by purchasing products in bulk and selling them to consumers. GNC (General Nutrition Centers) uses its chain of more than 4,200 retail stores to distribute its vitamins and related products. Foot Locker has more than 2,700 retail outlets that sell athletic shoes produced by Nike, Reebok, and other shoe producers. Other marketing intermediaries, called **agents,** match buyers and sellers of products without becoming owners.

agents marketing intermediaries that match buyers and sellers of products without becoming owners

AOL Time Warner commonly uses a one-level channel of distribution for its films and records, tapes, and CDs. Its film company distributes films to movie theaters (the retailer), while its record companies distribute records, tapes, and CDs to retail music shops.

Exhibit 13.1

Example of a One-Level Channel of Distribution

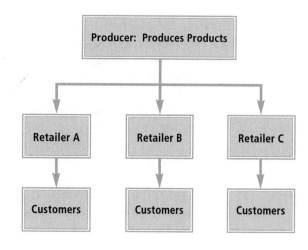

Exhibit 13.2

Example of a Two-Level Channel of Distribution

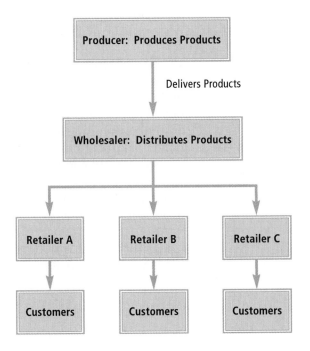

Two-Level Channel

two-level channel two marketing intermediaries are between the producer and the customer

Some products go through a **two-level channel** of distribution, in which two marketing intermediaries are between the producer and the customer. This type of distribution channel is illustrated in Exhibit 13.2. As an example, consider a company that produces lumber and sells it to a wholesaler, who in turn sells the lumber to various retailers. Each piece of lumber goes through two merchants before it reaches the customer.

As an alternative, an agent could take lumber orders from retail stores; then, the agent would contact the lumber company and arrange to have the lumber delivered to the retailers. In this case, the merchant wholesaler is replaced with an agent, but there are still two intermediaries.

Anheuser-Busch typically uses a two-level channel to distribute Budweiser and its other brands of beer. It relies on 900 beer wholesalers to distribute its beer to retail outlets such as grocery and convenience stores.

Benefits for Small Producers Small businesses that produce one or a few products commonly use a two-level channel of distribution. Because these businesses are not well known, they may not receive orders from retail outlets. Therefore, they rely on agents to sell the products to retailers. Consider all the products that a retailer like Home Depot sells. If an entrepreneur creates a new paint product or other home improvement product, it may use an agent to meet with a representative (called a buyer) of Home Depot who will decide whether Home Depot should carry this product in its stores. A small business that creates only a few products may have a much better chance of succeeding if it can convince a large retailer to carry its products. Thus, an agent can be critical to the success of such a firm.

Exhibit 13.3

Comparison of Common Distribution Systems

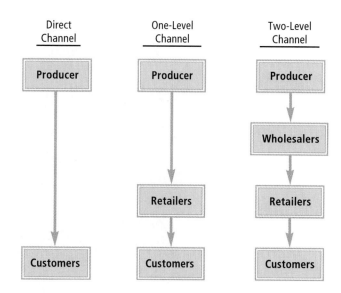

Summary of Distribution Systems

The most common distribution systems are compared in Exhibit 13.3. Firms can use more than one distribution system. Many firms sell products directly to customers through their websites but also sell their products through intermediaries. When firms can avoid a marketing intermediary, they may be able to earn a higher profit per unit on their products, but they will likely sell a smaller quantity unless they use other marketing strategies.

A firm may change its distribution system as circumstances change. For example, Dell Computer will soon open an integrated customer center and production facility in Xiamen, China. The facility will give Dell its first major presence in the world's most populous country, where it has marketed computers through distributors for several years. Thus, in China Dell will be moving from a two-level distribution channel to a direct distribution channel, which is perfect for a product that may be damaged during transport and is not standardized.

Factors That Determine the Optimal Channel of Distribution

The optimal channel of distribution depends on the product's characteristics, such as its ease of transporting and degree of standardization. The firm's ability to fulfill Internet orders is also a factor. The effects of these characteristics are described next.

Ease of Transporting If a product can be easily transported, the distribution channel is more likely to involve intermediaries. If the product cannot be transported, the producer may attempt to sell directly to consumers. For example, a manufacturer of built-in swimming pools must deal directly with the consumer, since the product cannot be channeled to the consumer. Conversely, above-ground pools are transportable and are more likely to involve intermediaries.

A Peapod delivery driver delivers groceries to customers' doorsteps. Even after eight straight years of doubling its annual revenues, the longest-established U.S. cybergrocer has yet to turn a profit.

AP Photo/ Brian Kersey

Degree of Standardization Products that are standardized are more likely to involve intermediaries. When specifications are unique for each consumer, the producer must deal directly with consumers. For example, specialized office furniture for firms may vary with each firm's preferences. Specialized products cannot be standardized and offered at retail shops.

Internet Orders Firms that fill orders over the Internet tend to use a direct channel because their website serves as a substitute for a retail store. For example, Amazon.com provides a menu of books and other products that it can deliver to customers so that customers do not need to go to a retail store to purchase these products. Amazon fills orders by having products delivered directly from its warehouses to customers. In fact, Amazon has recently built new warehouses in additional locations so that it can ensure quick delivery to customers throughout the United States and in many foreign countries.

Gateway sells its computers directly to customers. It states in its annual report that "the direct channel—delivering goods and services directly from manufacturing to customer—is simply the most efficient channel for business." The Gap uses the Internet to sell clothes directly to customers, but it still maintains its retail stores for customers who wish to shop at the mall rather than online.

2

Differentiate between types of market coverage.

market coverage the degree of product distribution among outlets

SELECTING THE DEGREE OF MARKET COVERAGE

Any firm that uses a marketing intermediary must determine a plan for **market coverage,** or the degree of product distribution among outlets. Firms attempt to select the degree of market coverage that can provide consumers with easy access to their products, but they may also need to ensure that the outlets are capable of selling their products. Market coverage can be classified as intensive distribution, selective distribution, or exclusive distribution.

Intensive Distribution

intensive distribution the distribution of a product across most or all possible outlets

To achieve a high degree of market coverage for all types of consumers, **intensive distribution** is used to distribute a product across most or all possible outlets. Firms that use intensive distribution ensure that consumers will have easy access to the product. Intensive distribution is used for products such as chewing gum and cigarettes that do not take up much space in outlets and do not require any expertise for employees of outlets to sell.

For example, PepsiCo uses intensive distribution to distribute its soft drinks and snacks. PepsiCo's products are sold through retail outlets that focus on food and drinks. The company distributes its soft drinks and snack foods to virtually every supermarket, convenience store, and warehouse club in the United States and in some foreign countries.

Selective Distribution

selective distribution the distribution of a product through selected outlets

Selective distribution is used to distribute a product through selected outlets. Some outlets are intentionally avoided. For example, some specialized computer equipment is sold only at outlets that emphasize computer sales because some expertise may be necessary. Some college textbooks are sold only at college bookstores and not at retail bookstores. Liz Claiborne distributes its clothing only to upscale clothing stores.

Exclusive Distribution

exclusive distribution the distribution of a product through only one or a few outlets

With **exclusive distribution,** only one or a few outlets are used. This is an extreme form of selective distribution. For example, some luxury items are distributed exclusively to a few outlets that cater to very wealthy consumers. By limiting the distribution, the firm can create or maintain the prestige of the product. Some Nike brands are sold exclusively to Foot Locker's retail stores.

Some products that have exclusive distribution require specialized service. A firm producing high-quality jewelry may prefer to distribute exclusively to one particular jewelry store in an area where the employees receive extensive training.

Selecting the Optimal Type of Market Coverage

Exhibit 13.4 compares the degrees of market coverage achieved by different distribution systems. The optimal degree of coverage depends on the characteristics of the product.

Marketing research can determine the optimal type of coverage by identifying where consumers desire to purchase products or services. For example, a marketing survey could determine whether a firm should distribute its DVDs and videocassettes for sale through video stores only or through grocery stores as well. If the survey leads to a decision to distribute through grocery stores, the firm can then use additional marketing research to compare the level of sales at its various outlets. This research will help determine whether the firm should continue distributing DVDs and videocassettes through grocery stores. Marketing research shows that Foot Locker retail stores attract teenagers who are willing to spend $80 or more for athletic shoes. Nike distributes its shoes to Foot Locker because it views these teenagers as its target market.

Exhibit 13.4

Alternative Degrees of Market Coverage

	Advantage	Disadvantage
Intensive distribution	Gives consumers easy access.	Many outlets will not accept some products if consumers are unlikely to purchase those products there.
Selective distribution	The distribution is focused on outlets where there will be demand for the products and/or where employees have expertise to sell the products.	Since the distribution is selective, the products are not as accessible as they would be if intensive distribution were used.
Exclusive distribution	Since the distribution is focused on a few outlets, the products are perceived as prestigious. Also the producer can ensure that the outlets where the products are distributed are able to service the product properly.	The product's access to customers is limited.

SELECTING THE TRANSPORTATION USED TO DISTRIBUTE PRODUCTS

Any distribution of products from producers to wholesalers or from wholesalers to retailers requires transportation. The cost of transporting some products can exceed the cost of producing them. An inefficient form of transportation can result in higher costs and lower profits for the firm. For each form of transportation, firms should estimate timing, cost, and availability. This assessment allows the firm to choose an optimal method of transportation. The most common forms of transportation used to distribute products are described next.

Truck

Trucks are commonly used for transport because they can reach any destination on land. They can usually transport quickly and can make several stops. For example, The Coca-Cola Company uses trucks to distribute its soft drinks to retailers in a city.

Rail

Railroads are useful for heavy products, especially when the sender and receiver are located close to railroad stations. For example, railroads are commonly used to transport coal to electricity-generating plants. If a firm is not adjacent to a station, however, it must reload the product onto a truck. Because the road system allows much more accessibility than railroad tracks, railroads are not useful for short distances. For long distances, however, rail can be a cheaper form of transportation than trucks.

Air

Transportation by air can be quick and relatively inexpensive for light items such as computer chips and jewelry. For a large amount of heavy products such as steel or wood, truck or rail is a better alternative. Even when air is used, trucks are still needed for door-to-door service (to and from the airport).

Trucks are a common mode of transportation, because they can reach any destination on land fairly quickly.

AP Photo/ Topeka Capital-Journal, David Eulitt

Water

For some coastal or port locations, transportation by water deserves to be considered. Shipping is necessary for the international trade of some goods such as automobiles. Water transportation is often used for transporting bulk products.

Pipeline

For products such as oil and gas, pipelines can be an effective method of transportation. However, the use of pipelines is limited to only a few types of products.

Additional Transportation Decisions

The selection of the proper form of transportation (such as truck, rail, and so on) is only the first step in developing a proper system for transporting products. To illustrate how complex the transporting of products can be, consider the case of PepsiCo, which may receive orders for its snack foods and soft drinks from 100 stores in a single city every week. It must determine an efficient way to load the products and then create a route to distribute those products among stores. It must decide the best route and the number of trucks needed to cover the 100 stores. It must also decide whether to distribute snack foods and soft drinks simultaneously or have some trucks distribute snack foods and others distribute soft drinks.

In reality, no formulas are available to determine the ideal distribution system. Most firms attempt to estimate all the expenses associated with each possible way of delivering products that are ordered. Firms compare the total estimated expenses of each method and select the one that is most efficient.

3
Explain how the distribution process can be accelerated.

How to Accelerate the Distribution Process

The structure of a firm's distribution system affects its performance. A lengthy distribution process has an adverse effect. First, products will take longer to reach customers, which may allow competitors to supply products to the market sooner. As a result, retail stores or customers may order their products from other firms.

A slow distribution process will also result in a lengthy period from the time the firm invests funds to produce the product until it receives revenue from the sale of the product. In most cases, firms will not receive payment until after customers receive the products. Consequently, firms are forced to invest their funds in the production process for a longer period of time.

To illustrate the importance of speed in the distribution process, consider that the actual time required to distribute a typical cereal box from the producer to the retailer (the grocery store) is about 100 days. Now consider a cereal firm that receives $100 million per year in revenue from the sale of cereal and finds a way to reduce its distribution time from 100 days to 60 days on average. In a typical year, this firm will receive its $100 million of revenue 40 days earlier than before, meaning that it will have 40 extra days to reinvest those funds in other projects. Thus, a reduction in distribution time can enhance a firm's value.

Streamline the Channels of Distribution

Many firms are attempting to streamline the channels of distribution so that the final product reaches customers more quickly. For example, by eliminating some of its six regional warehouses, National Semiconductor reduced its typical delivery time by 47 percent and its cost of distribution by 2.5 percent. It now sends its microchips directly to customers around the world from its distribution center. This restructuring has removed one level of the distribution process, as shown in Exhibit 13.5.

Exhibit 13.5

Example of a Restructured Distribution Process

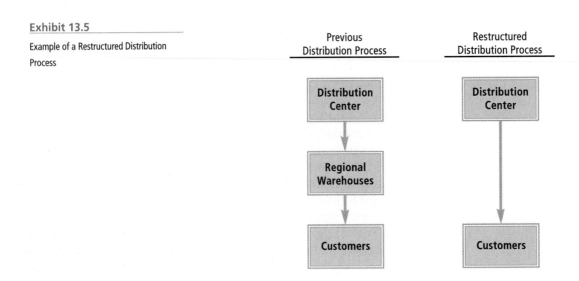

Exhibit 13.6

Relationship between Production and Distribution

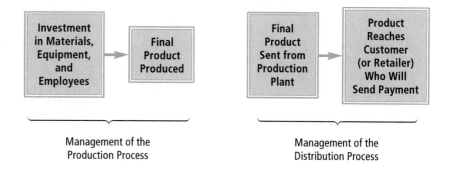

Restructuring a distribution process commonly results in the elimination of warehouses. When products are light (such as microchips) and can be easily delivered by mail to customers, warehouses may not be needed. Heavy products (such as beverages), however, cannot be easily delivered by mail, so warehouses are necessary.

Integrate the Production and Distribution Processes

The distribution process can also be accelerated by improving its interaction with the production process. Notice in Exhibit 13.6 how the production process interacts with the distribution process. As an example, if a firm produces automobiles but does not distribute them quickly, it may have to halt the production process until it has room to store the newly produced automobiles. Alternatively, if an insufficient quantity of automobiles is produced, the manufacturer will not be able to distribute as many automobiles as dealers desire, no matter how efficient its distribution process is.

Saturn ensures that its production and distribution processes interact. Its factories must always have the supplies and parts needed to produce a large volume of automobiles. Then, the automobiles are distributed to numerous dealerships around the country. Local or economic conditions can cause the amount of new automobiles that dealerships periodically need to change abruptly. Thus, Saturn's production and distribution processes must be able to respond quickly to abrupt changes in the demand by dealerships. Since Saturn allows interaction between its production process and its distribution process, it can adjust to satisfy demand.

Compaq Computer also used interaction between production and distribution to accelerate its process of distributing computers to more than 30,000 wholesalers and retail stores. It significantly reduced the time from when a final product was produced until it left the production plant. Computer technology was used to indicate which products should be loaded onto specific trucks for delivery purposes.

Exhibit 13.7 provides another perspective on the tasks involved from the time supplies and materials used to produce a product are ordered until the product is delivered to retailers. This exhibit shows how the distribution of products relies on production. If any step in the production process breaks down and lengthens the production period, products will not be distributed on a timely basis.

Assuming that the production process is properly conducted, the firm still needs an efficient distribution system to ensure that products are consistently available for customers. One of the keys to an efficient

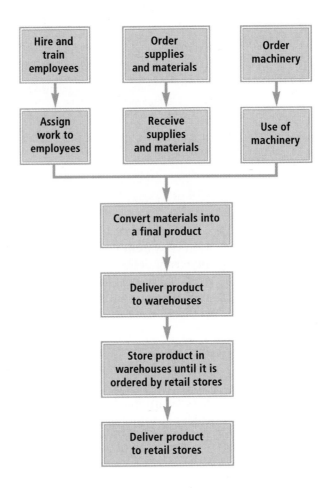

distribution system is to ensure that any intermediaries used to transfer products from producers to consumers maintain an adequate inventory. The producer must maintain sufficient inventory in anticipation of orders from wholesalers, retailers, or customers. If it does not, it will experience shortages. This task is especially challenging when the firm produces a wide variety of products and sells them to several different intermediaries or customers.

Role of E-Marketing   E-marketing can facilitate the integration between a firm's production and distribution processes. The firm's volume of orders should be updated online and be accessible to both the intermediaries and the production facilities. Consider a manufacturer of video games that has a sales force assigned to sell its games to retail stores. Each salesperson can use the same online ordering service to transmit new orders. The online service continuously updates the total orders received by the entire sales force. The firm fills these orders from its existing inventory. Thus, by checking the orders, the firm can determine where future inventory shortages may occur and can increase its production of whatever video games have a low inventory.

cross functional teamwork:

Interaction between Distribution Decisions and Other Business Decisions

When marketing managers decide how to distribute a product, they must consider the existing production facilities. Firms that have production facilities scattered around the United States can more easily distribute their products directly from those facilities to the retailer or to the customer. Conversely, firms that use a single manufacturing plant may rely on intermediaries to distribute the product. When a large production facility is needed to achieve production efficiency (as in automobile manufacturing), intermediaries are used to distribute the product.

When a firm creates a new product that will be demanded by customers throughout the United States, it must decide where to produce and how to distribute the product. The two decisions are related. Financial managers of the firm use input provided by production managers on estimated production costs and from marketing managers on estimated distribution costs. If the product is to be produced at a single manufacturing plant, the production cost can be minimized, but the distribution costs are higher. Conversely, if the product is produced at several small manufacturing plants, the production costs are

higher, but the distribution costs are relatively low. The financial analysis conducted by financial managers can determine the combination of production and distribution that is most efficient.

Many firms use a single manufacturing plant in the United States and distribute their products throughout the country. If they experience some demand from foreign customers, they may initially attempt to export the products. The cost of distributing products to foreign countries can be very high, however, so U.S. firms often establish a foreign production facility to accommodate the foreign demand. For example, Apple Computer now has three manufacturing plants. Its original plant in California is used to accommodate the demand by U.S. customers. Its plant in Europe produces computer products that are distributed to sales offices throughout Europe. Its plant in Singapore produces computer products that are distributed to sales offices throughout Asia. Apple Computer maintains relatively low distribution expenses by having a manufacturing plant in each region of the world where there is a large demand for its products.

---

4 Explain how retailers serve customers.

BACKGROUND ON RETAILERS

Retailers serve as valuable intermediaries by distributing products directly to customers. Most retailers can be described by the following characteristics:

▶ Number of outlets
▶ Quality of service
▶ Variety of products offered
▶ Store versus nonstore

Number of Outlets

independent retail store a retailer that has only one outlet

chain a retailer that has more than one outlet

An **independent retail store** has only one outlet, whereas a **chain** has more than one outlet. Although there are more independent stores than chain stores, the chain stores are larger on average. Chain stores such as Home Depot, Ace Hardware, and Wal-Mart can usually obtain products at a lower cost because they can buy in bulk from the producer (or its intermediaries). Wal-Mart typically deals with the manufacturer so that it can avoid any markup by marketing intermediaries. Chain stores often have a nationwide reputation, which usually provides credibility. This is a major advantage over independent stores.

A capacity crowd of shoppers pack the cash registers at a Best Buy store on the Friday after Thanksgiving. Retailers serve as intermediaries for manufacturers by distributing products directly to customers.

Quality of Service

full-service retail store a retailer that generally offers much sales assistance to customers and provides servicing if needed

self-service retail store a retailer that does not provide sales assistance or service and sells products that do not require much expertise

A **full-service retail store** generally offers much sales assistance to customers and provides servicing if needed. Some products are more appropriate for full service than others. For example, a men's formal wear store offers advice on style and alters the fit for consumers. An electronics store such as Radio Shack provides advice on the use of its products. A **self-service retail store** does not provide sales assistance or service and sells products that do not require much expertise. Examples of self-service stores are Publix Supermarkets and Seven-Eleven.

Some retail stores are adapting to the varied preferences of their customers. For example, stores such as Sears and Circuit City offer personalized sales service for customers who need that service. At the same time, they also allow other customers who do not want personalized service to place orders online and pick up the merchandise from the stores. By placing their orders online, the customers avoid time in the store; by picking up the merchandise, they avoid a delivery fee. In addition, they receive the products quicker by picking them up than if they waited for delivery.

Variety of Products Offered

specialty retail store a retailer that specializes in a particular type of product

variety retail store a retailer that offers numerous types of goods

A **specialty retail store** specializes in a particular type of product, such as sporting goods, furniture, or automobile parts. Kinney's Shoes, which specializes in shoes, is an example of a specialty store. These stores tend to focus on only one or a few types of products but have a wide selection of brands available. A **variety retail store** offers numerous types of goods. For example, KMart, J. C. Penney, and Sears are classified as variety stores because they offer a wide variety of products, including clothes, household appliances, and even furniture.

The advantage of a specialty store is that it may carry a certain degree of prestige. If an upscale clothing store begins to offer other types of products, it may lose its prestige. The disadvantage of a specialty store is that it is not as convenient for consumers who need to purchase a variety of goods. Some consumers may prefer to shop at a store that sells everything they need.

Specialty shops in a shopping mall can retain their specialization and prestige while offering consumers more convenience. Because the mall contains various specialty shops, consumers may perceive it as one large outlet with a variety of products.

Several of these characteristics can be used to describe a single retailer. For example, consider Blockbuster Video. It is a chain, a self-service store, and a specialty store. The Athlete's Foot is a chain, a full-service store, and a specialty store.

Store versus Nonstore

Although most retailers use a store to offer their service, others do not. The three most common types of nonstore retailers are mail-order retailers, websites, and vending machines.

Mail-Order Retailers   A mail-order retailer receives orders through the mail or over the phone. It then sends the products through the mail. Mail-order retailers have become very popular in recent years because many consumers have less leisure time than before and desire shopping convenience. In particular, mail-order clothing retailers have been extremely successful, as consumers find it more convenient to order by phone than to shop in stores. Mail order is more likely to work for products that are light, are somewhat standardized, and do not need to be serviced.

Home shopping networks are a form of mail-order retailing. They have become very popular for specialized items such as jewelry.

Websites   Many firms have created websites where their products can be ordered. One of the main advantages of this method over mail order is that the firm does not have to send out catalogs. In addition, changes can be made easily and frequently.

A giant vending machine in Washington, D.C., is the only one of its kind in the United States. It works like an automatic convenience store that can carry up to 200 items and accepts both cash and credit cards.

© Getty Images / EyeWire

Vending Machines   Vending machines have also become popular as a result of consumer preferences for convenience. They are often accessible at all hours. Although they were initially used mainly for cigarettes, candy, and soft drinks, some machines are now being used for products such as aspirin, razors, and travel insurance.

5

Explain how wholesalers can
serve manufacturers
and retailers.

BACKGROUND ON WHOLESALERS

Wholesalers are intermediaries that purchase products from manufacturers and sell them to retailers. They are useful to both manufacturers and retailers, as explained next.

How Wholesalers Serve Manufacturers

Wholesalers offer five key services to manufacturers:

► Warehousing

► Sales expertise

► Delivery to retailers

► Assumption of credit risk

► Information

Warehousing   Wholesalers purchase products from the manufacturer in bulk and maintain these products at their own warehouses. Thus, manufacturers do not need to use their own space to store the products. In addition, manufacturers can maintain a smaller inventory and therefore do not have to invest as much funds in inventory.

To illustrate how manufacturers can benefit from this warehousing, consider Jandy Industries, which produces equipment for swimming pools. Jandy sells its products in bulk to wholesalers that are willing to maintain an inventory of parts. Jandy focuses on maintaining its own inventory of uncommon parts that are not carried by wholesalers.

Sales Expertise   Wholesalers use their sales expertise when selling products to retailers. The retailer's decision to purchase particular products may be primarily due to the wholesaler's persuasion. Once a wholesaler persuades retailers to purchase a product, it will periodically contact the retailers to determine whether they need to purchase more of that product.

Delivery to Retailers   Wholesalers are responsible for delivering products to various retailers. Therefore, manufacturers do not need to be concerned with numerous deliveries. Instead, they can deliver in bulk to wholesalers.

Assumption of Credit Risk   When the wholesaler purchases the products from the manufacturer and sells them to retailers on credit, it normally assumes the credit risk (risk that the bill will not be paid). In this case, the manufacturer does not need to worry about the credit risk of the retailers.

Information   Wholesalers often receive feedback from retailers and can provide valuable information to manufacturers. For example, they can explain to the manufacturer why sales of the product are lower than expected and can inform the manufacturer about new competing products that are being sold in retail stores.

How Wholesalers Serve Retailers

Wholesalers offer five key services to retailers:

▶ Warehousing

▶ Promotion

▶ Displays

▶ Credit

▶ Information

Warehousing   Wholesalers may maintain sufficient inventory so that retailers can order small amounts frequently. Thus, the retailers do not have to maintain a large inventory because the wholesalers have enough inventory to accommodate orders quickly.

Promotion   Wholesalers sometimes promote their products, and these efforts may increase the sales of those products by retail stores. The promotional help comes in various forms, including posters or brochures to be displayed in retail stores.

Displays   Some wholesalers set up a display of the products for the retailers. The displays are often designed to attract customers' attention but take up little space. This is important to retailers because they have a limited amount of space.

Credit   Wholesalers sometimes offer products to retailers on credit. This provides a form of financing for retailers, who may have to borrow funds if they are required to make payment when receiving the products.

Information   Wholesalers can inform retailers about policies implemented by other retailers regarding the pricing of products, special sales, or changes in the hours their stores are open. A retailer can use this type of information when it establishes its own related policies.

6

Explain the strategy and potential benefits of vertical channel integration.

vertical channel integration
two or more levels of distribution are managed by a single firm

VERTICAL CHANNEL INTEGRATION

Some firms use **vertical channel integration,** in which two or more levels of distribution are managed by a single firm. This strategy can be used by manufacturers or retailers, as explained next.

Vertical Channel Integration by Manufacturers

Manufacturers may decide to vertically integrate their operations by establishing retail stores. Consider a producer of clothing that has historically sold its clothes to various retailers. It notices that the retailers' prices are typically

increasing value with technology

DISTRIBUTION THROUGH THE INTERNET

Electronic business has increased the power of the buyer and reduced the importance of sales relationships. Customers have traditionally faced time and distance obstacles when trying to obtain lower prices and quality products. The Internet has eliminated many of those obstacles. Companies and websites now exist that compare prices and quality of products for the consumer.

For example, Autobytel.com provides information about new car purchases, offers suggestions about leasing, gives access to dealer invoices, and enables the consumer to find a low-cost car dealer in the area. Paperexchange.com acts as a broker for paper products and equipment. The way consumers make their purchases is gradually changing. The result is more competition among firms and less brand loyalty.

Companies must adapt to this changing business model. Perhaps the most significant change will be the disruption of traditional distribution channels. As the Internet eliminates the distance between producers and consumers, it also eliminates the need for wholesalers, distributors, and retailers. Amazon.com and Dell Computer are examples of companies that have prospered without traditional retail outlets.

When firms sell their products directly to customers without using retail stores, they can improve their efficiency. They may be able to sell their product at a lower price as a result. Another significant change occurs in firms' relationships with suppliers and freight haulers. A web of communication allows for increased collaboration and the creation of a partnership in the production chain. The ultimate result of electronic business will be increased price competition.

---

about 90 percent above what they paid for the clothes. Consequently, the clothing manufacturer may consider opening its own retail shops if it can achieve higher sales by selling its clothes through these shops.

L. L. Bean has established its own outlet stores that sell the clothing it produces. In this way, the firm serves as the producer and as an intermediary. The intermediaries (outlets) allow the product to be widely distributed. Meanwhile, all earnings generated by the producer or the outlets are beneficial to the owners of L. L. Bean.

When a producer or wholesaler considers expanding into retailing operations, it must address the following questions:

▶ Can it absorb the cost of leasing store space and employing workers? These costs can be substantial.

▶ Can the firm offer enough product lines to make full use of a store? If the firm specializes in producing pullover shirts, it will not have a sufficient variety to attract consumers.

▶ Will the additional revenue to be earned cover all additional costs incurred?

▶ Will the firm lose the business that it had developed with other retail firms, once it begins to compete with those firms on a retail level?

The idea of expansion may become less appealing when the wholesaler addresses these questions.

The trade-off involved in a vertically integrated channel is shown in Exhibit 13.8. The left side of Exhibit 13.8 reflects a strategy in which Zuma Company produces tennis shoes and distributes them to a wholesaler that it owns. Zuma's wholesaler sells the tennis shoes to retailers for $65. The alternative distribution strategy, shown on the right side of Exhibit 13.8, is for

Exhibit 13.8

Trade-off from Using Vertical Integration.

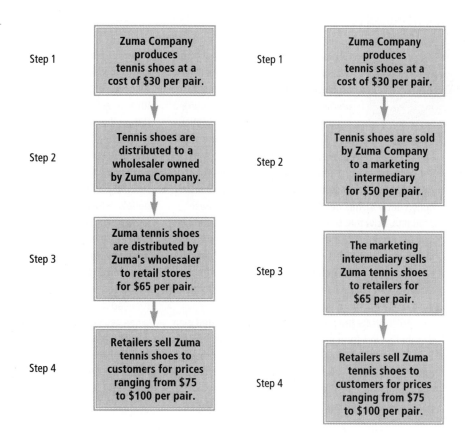

Zuma Company to sell its tennis shoes to a marketing intermediary for $50. In this case, it receives $15 less per pair than if it establishes its own wholesaler that sells to retailers. However, it also incurs lower costs if it does not set up a wholesale operation.

Vertical Channel Integration by Retailers

Just as a producer may consider establishing retail outlets, a retailer may consider producing its own products. Consider a clothing retailer that has historically purchased its clothes from several different producers. It believes that the producer's cost is about 50 percent less than the price charged to retailers. Consequently, it begins to consider producing the clothes itself. This is the reverse of the previous example. Yet it also involves a firm that is considering vertical integration.

When a retailer considers expanding into production of products, it must address the following questions:

▶ Can it absorb the expenses resulting from production, including the cost of a production plant and new employees?

▶ Does it have the expertise to adjust the production process as consumer tastes change over time? If a clothing manufacturer cannot adjust, it may be stuck with a large inventory of out-of-date clothing.

In general, the firm must decide whether the benefits from producing the clothes itself are greater than the additional costs.

Global Distribution In the United States, the distribution network is well organized. Manufacturers of most products are able to find distributors that have the knowledge and relationships with retailers to distribute the products. In many foreign countries, however, distribution networks are not well organized. Many products have simply not been marketed in some less-developed countries, so a distribution network has never been established for these products. Now that U.S. firms have begun to market numerous products to these countries, they recognize that they cannot necessarily rely on intermediaries to distribute the products. Therefore, the firms may need to distribute their products directly to retail outlets or to the customers who purchase the products.

To illustrate the potential problems associated with distribution in a foreign country, consider the dilemma of Ben & Jerry's Homemade, which has begun to produce and sell ice cream in Russia. In Russia and in some other countries, the distribution of some products is controlled by organized crime. Consequently, distributing products through the existing distribution network may necessitate extra payoffs to the intermediaries. Also, the intermediaries may decide to focus their efforts on selling other products that offer higher payoffs. Rather than search for an intermediary to distribute its ice cream, Ben & Jerry's decided to distribute the ice cream to outlets itself. It identified a reputable firm in Russia to establish a distribution network.

As Ben & Jerry's was distributing ice cream to outlets, it found that they had limited capacity in their freezers to store ice cream. So it provided the outlets with freezers. This allows Ben & Jerry's to distribute more ice cream to each outlet.

Ben & Jerry's also needed to train the outlets' employees about the different flavors of ice cream, which resulted in another type of expense that is not incurred when selling ice cream in the United States. Ben & Jerry's experience in distributing ice cream to outlets in Russia illustrates how the strategy used for distributing a specific product may vary with the country where the product is being sold.

College Health Club: CHC's Distribution

As Sue Kramer develops her business plan for College Health Club (CHC), she must determine her method of distribution. Her business will provide health club services. Like most services, health club services will be distributed directly to the customer.

Sue also plans to use CHC as a retailer for vitamin supplements. CHC will purchase jars of supplements from a vitamin wholesaler and then sell them to its members. In addition, she considers serving as a retailer of exercise clothing for CHC's members. She met with a wholesaler of exercise clothing to learn what types of clothing she could purchase and at what prices. The retail price charged at CHC would be higher than the wholesale price, resulting in a profit for CHC.

SUMMARY

1 The advantages of a direct channel of distribution are

- the full difference between the producer's cost and the price paid by the consumer goes to the producer; and

- the producer can easily obtain firsthand feedback on the product, allowing for quick response to customer complaints and the opportunity to quickly correct any deficiencies.

The disadvantages of a direct channel of distribution are

- the producer must employ more salespeople;

- the producer must provide all product promotions (some intermediaries might be willing to promote the products for producers); and

- the producer may have to provide credit to customers and incur the risk of bad debt (some intermediaries might be willing to incur this risk).

The optimal channel of distribution is dependent on ease of transportation: the greater the ease, the more likely that intermediaries could be used. It is also dependent on the degree of standardization: the more standardized the product, the more likely that intermediaries could be used.

2 The three types of market coverage are

- intensive distribution, which is used to distribute the product across most or all outlets;

- selective distribution, which is used to intentionally avoid some outlets; and

- exclusive distribution, which uses only one or a few outlets.

3 A quick distribution process not only satisfies customers but also reduces the amount of funds that must be used to support this process. Firms may accelerate their distribution process by reducing the channels of distribution. Alternatively, they may improve the interaction between the distribution and production processes. The distribution process relies on the production process to have products ready when needed.

4 Retailers serve as intermediaries for manufacturers by distributing products directly to customers. Each retailer is distinguished by its characteristics, such as number of outlets (independent versus chain), quality of service (self-service versus full-service), variety of products offered (specialty versus variety), and whether it is a store or a nonstore retailer.

5 Wholesalers serve manufacturers by

- maintaining the products purchased at their own warehouse, which allows manufacturers to maintain smaller inventories;

- using their sales expertise to sell products to retailers;

- delivering the products to retailers;

- assuming credit risk in the event that the retailer does not pay its bills; and

- providing information to manufacturers about competing products being sold in retail stores.

Wholesalers serve retailers by

- maintaining sufficient inventory so that retailers can order small amounts frequently;

- sometimes promoting the products they sell to the retailers;

- setting up product displays for retailers;

- offering products on credit to retailers; and

- informing retailers about policies implemented by other retailers regarding the pricing of products, allocation of space, and so on.

6 Vertical channel integration is the managing of more than one level of the distribution system by a single firm. For example, a manufacturer of a product may create an intermediary such as a retail store to distribute the product. Alternatively, an intermediary may decide to produce the product instead of ordering it from manufacturers. In either example, a single firm serves as a manufacturer and an intermediary and would no longer rely on another firm to manufacture or distribute its product.

KEY TERMS

agents 417
chain 427
direct channel 416
exclusive distribution 421
full-service retail store 428
independent retail store 427

intensive distribution 421
market coverage 420
marketing intermediaries 416
merchants 417
one-level channel 417
selective distribution 421

self-service retail store 428
specialty retail store 428
two-level channel 418
variety retail store 428
vertical channel integration 431

Review & Critical Thinking Questions

1. Discuss the advantages and disadvantages of direct channel distribution.

2. Compare and contrast one-level and two-level channels of distribution.

3. Briefly summarize the factors that determine an optimal channel of distribution.

4. What type of distribution system would a manufacturer use for the following products:
   (a) Calvin Klein jeans,
   (b) hometown newspapers,
   (c) Kenmore automatic washers?

5. Explain why Liz Claiborne distributes its clothing at upscale clothing stores as opposed to discount chain stores.

6. How can marketing research determine the optimal type of distribution coverage for a firm?

7. List the various modes of transportation that can be used to distribute a product.

8. What mode of transportation should be considered by an orchid grower in Hawaii who sends orchids to retail stores in other states? Why?

9. A manufacturer who sells staple products to mini-mart service stations would utilize wholesalers and retailers to reach the final customer. Why?

10. What is the relationship between production and distribution in reaching the ultimate consumer.

11. In the United States, the distribution network is well organized. However, in foreign countries, especially developing countries, distribution networks are not well organized. Why is this so?

12. Briefly summarize the characteristics of retailers.

13. List the five key services provided by wholesalers to manufacturers.

Discussion Questions

1. Discuss the likely events resulting from the elimination of intermediaries for the following products: (a) Rolling Rock beer, (b) Levi's jeans, (c) Jeep Grand Cherokee.

2. How can a firm use the Internet to enhance its degree of market coverage? How can it use the Internet to accelerate the distribution process?

3. Recently, community colleges have started to realize that they must give thought to their distribution systems. What distribution decisions might community colleges have to make?

4. Describe an appropriate channel of distribution for (a) a loaf of bread sold in a local grocery store, (b) a Buick Regal, (c) a door-to-door salesperson.

5. Select the appropriate distribution (intensive, selective, or exclusive) for the following products: (a) Ethan Allen furniture, (b) Marlboro cigarettes, (c) Starter jackets, (d) Reebok shoes, (e) *USA Today*.

It's Your Decision: **Distribution Decisions at CHC**

1. A manufacturer of exercise clothing has asked Sue Kramer, the president of CHC, if she wants CHC to serve as a retailer by selling clothes to its members. If Sue agrees to sell exercise clothing produced by the manufacturer, will the distribution system be a direct channel, a one-level channel, or a two-level channel?

2. Sue has considered producing her own line of exercise clothing and selling it at CHC. Would this type of distribution be a direct channel, a one-level channel, or a two-level channel?

3. If Sue decides to produce her own line of clothing to be sold at CHC, does this strategy reflect intensive distribution, selective distribution, or exclusive distribution?

4. A health club differs from manufacturing firms in that it produces a service rather than products. Explain why the distribution strategy of a service firm (such as CHC) is more limited than that of a manufacturing firm.

Investing in a Business

Using the annual report of the firm in which you would like to invest, complete the following:

1 How does the firm distribute its products to consumers? Does it rely on wholesalers? Does it rely on retail stores?

2 Has the firm revised its distribution methods in recent years? If so, provide details.

3 Explain how the business displays its products and prices over the Internet. Does it distribute products directly to customers who order over the Internet? Does it advertise on the Internet?

4 Go to **http://hoovers.com** and locate the NEWS SEARCH. Type in the name of the firm in the space provided, and review the recent news stories about the firm. Summarize any (at least one) recent news story about the firm that applies to one or more of the key concepts in this chapter.

Case: Distribution Decisions by Novak, Inc.

Novak, Inc., is a wholesaler in business to sell engine parts for cars. It recently installed a website order system. The system allows a customer (such as a car repair shop) to order inventory parts from anywhere in the United States. Novak can ship directly to the customer.

Larry Novak, president of Novak, Inc., decided to sell more than car engine parts. His plan was to sell technical expertise to provide his customers who own repair shops with information pertaining to car engine parts. With recent technological changes and an increased number of imports entering the United States, repair shops must now handle many different car engine parts. Larry placed his company in a position to be more competitive in the industry by emphasizing information rather than price. His website offers numerous product catalogs and handbooks that provide extensive, detailed descriptions and diagrams of every transmission, as well as specific parts needed to complete the repairs.

With the staggering selection of transmissions in use today, shops cannot begin to keep all the essential parts. To help alleviate this problem, Novak has organized a national computer network linking its regional offices around the country. It provides information on the status of in-stock inventory, orders expected to come in, and shipping schedules for parts expected to go out. With this information, salespeople can access data on the availability of a product anywhere in the United States and have it shipped to them directly.

Questions

1 Is Novak a wholesaler or a retailer?

2 What is the advantage that Novak is now providing to its customers?

3 Is Novak considered an intermediary? How many levels do Novak's channels of distribution include?

4 Does Novak have a quick distribution process? If so, how?

Video Case: Distribution Strategies at Burton Snowboards

Burton Snowboards is the leading manufacturer of snowboards and snowboard apparel. Retail stores place orders with manufacturer representatives (reps) before the snowboard season (winter). Burton does not maintain a large inventory, as it attempts to produce its snowboards upon demand. It works closely with retail stores to ensure that the store employees have some knowledge about the snowboards. Burton listens to the feedback that stores receive from customers so that it knows what customers want. Burton also provides advertising signs and promotional brochures to the stores to promote its image. It also offers support over the phone if store employees have specific questions about the products it offers. In addition, Burton has a website that provides much information to customers and answers their specific online questions.

Questions

1. How is feedback from retail stores within the distribution network related to Burton's production?

2. Why is it important for Burton to screen the potential retail stores that sell its snowboards?

3. How can Burton's website improve the efficiency of its distribution system?

Internet Applications

1. *http://www.mapquest.com*

Obtain driving information from your home to a location of your choice. How could a business use a website such as MapQuest to direct its customers to appropriate retailers and service locations? How could a company use this website to expand its degree of market coverage?

2. *http://www.mapnp.org/library/prod_mng/dist.htm*

What are the direct distribution methods mentioned on this website? What indirect methods of distribution are mentioned? Summarize the steps necessary to select distribution and sales force representation under "Choosing Distribution Methods." How can a company use this website to refine its distribution methods?

3. *http://www.franklynn.com/inprint/distribution_strategies.html*

Click on "Selecting the Right Channels to Market Your Product." Summarize the eight steps of the channel selection process. Do you think the importance of each step varies with the type of business involved? Consider a car manufacturer and a software company and discuss how the eight steps would apply to each.

The Coca-Cola Company Annual Report Project

Questions for the current year's annual report are available on the text website at **http://madura.swlearning.com.**

The following questions apply concepts presented in this chapter to The Coca-Cola Company. Go to The Coca-Cola Company website (**http://www.cocacola.com**) and find the index for the 2001 annual report.

Questions

1. Download the financial statements and find "Investments." How does The Coca-Cola Company understand consumers' tastes?

2. Download the financial statements and find "Investments." Why is it advantageous for The Coca-Cola Company to acquire a controlling interest in a bottling operation?

3. Download the financial statements and find "Investments." Do you think The Coca-Cola Company utilizes intensive distribution, selective distribution, or exclusive distribution?

4. Download the financial statements and find "Volume." Do you think The Coca-Cola Company utilizes one-level or two-level distribution channels?

5. Click on "Our Building Blocks" and study the "Africa" section. How did The Coca-Cola Company strengthen its distribution system in Africa?

6. Go to **http://hoovers.com** and locate the NEWS CENTER. Key in The Coca-Cola Company in the space provided, click on "Search," and review the recent news stories about the firm. Summarize any (at least one) recent news story about The Coca-Cola Company that applies one or more of the key concepts within this chapter of the text.

In-Text Study Guide

Answers are in an appendix at the back of the book.

True or False

1. Retailers sell primarily to wholesalers. F

2. Manufacturers that use a direct distribution channel need fewer employees than they would need if they used a one-level or two-level channel. F

3. Small business firms that produce only a few products typically use a two-level channel of distribution. T

4. Products that are standardized are more likely to involve intermediaries. T

5. One reason firms may choose an exclusive distribution strategy is to create or maintain prestige for their product. T

6. Distribution decisions do not affect the cost of delivering a product. F

7. Mathematical formulas are available that determine the ideal distribution system. F

8. A lengthy distribution process adversely affects a firm's performance. T

9. Wholesalers commonly offer manufacturers sales expertise. T

10. Manufacturers can vertically integrate their operations by establishing retail stores. T

Multiple Choice

11. The manner by which a firm's products are made accessible to its customers is determined by its:
    a) advertising strategies.
    b) product decisions.
    c) pricing strategies.
    d) distribution decisions.
    e) package designs.

12. A distribution channel represents the path of a product from producer to:
    a) retailer.
    b) wholesaler.
    c) consumer.
    d) manufacturer.
    e) industrial distributor.

13. With a direct channel of distribution, the full difference between the manufacturer's cost and the price paid by the consumer goes to the:
    a) manufacturer.
    b) wholesaler.
    c) retailer.
    d) intermediary.
    e) merchant.

14. Wholesalers are marketing intermediaries who purchase products from manufacturers and sell them to:
    a) final users.
    b) retailers.
    c) other manufacturers.
    d) primary customers.
    e) secondary customers.

15. Marketing intermediaries that match buyers and sellers of products without becoming the owners of the products themselves are known as:
    a) single-service marketers.
    b) agents.
    c) commission-based wholesalers.
    d) stockers.
    e) mediators.

16. Products that are standardized and easily transported are likely to:
    a) be sold at a high markup.
    b) have limited market areas.
    c) use intermediaries in their distribution channels.
    d) be sold at steep discounts.
    e) use a direct channel of distribution.

17. _____ refers to the degree of product distribution among outlets.
    a) The marketing mix
    b) Demographic distribution
    c) Market coverage
    d) Channelization
    e) The retail ratio

In-Text Study Guide

Answers are in an appendix at the back of the book.

18. Firms that fill orders over the Internet tend to use a(n) _____ channel of distribution.
    a) one-level
    b) unidirectional
    c) multimodal
    d) direct
    e) intrinsic

19. _____ distribution is used when a producer distributes its products through certain chosen outlets while intentionally avoiding other possible outlets.
    a) Restrictive
    b) Exclusive
    c) Intensive
    d) Narrow
    e) Selective

20. An advantage of exclusive distribution is that it:
    a) makes the product widely available to consumers at a variety of outlets.
    b) eliminates all market intermediaries.
    c) allows the firm to avoid charging a sales tax on the goods.
    d) may allow the firm to create and maintain an image of prestige.
    e) provides the goods to consumers at the lowest possible cost.

21. Newspaper publishers have their papers available in grocery stores, convenience stores, and vending machines and at many other locations throughout a city. This is an example of a(n) _____ distribution of a product.
    a) nonspecific
    b) specialized
    c) geographically dispersed
    d) intensive
    e) decentralized

22. Exclusive distribution can be viewed as an extreme form of:
    a) intensive distribution.
    b) the one-channel approach.
    c) selective distribution.

    d) price discrimination.
    e) mass merchandising.

23. A(n) _____ is a retailer with only one outlet.
    a) exclusive retailer
    b) independent retail store
    c) wholesaler
    d) franchise retailer
    e) sole proprietorship

24. _____ are usually the best way to ship goods when the goods must be delivered quickly to several different locations in a local area.
    a) Trucks
    b) Barges
    c) The railroads
    d) Pipelines
    e) Containerized modules

25. One way to accelerate the distribution process is to make sure that it is integrated with the _____ process.
    a) marketing
    b) financing
    c) credit approval
    d) advertising
    e) production

26. Restructuring a distribution process commonly results in the elimination of:
    a) production.
    b) warehouses.
    c) manufacturers.
    d) product lines.
    e) product mixes.

27. A method by which the firm can check orders, determine where future inventory shortages may occur and can increase its production accordingly is:
    a) e-marketing.
    b) integrated production.
    c) source-to-source coordination.
    d) marketing logistics.
    e) inventory management.

In-Text Study Guide

Answers are in an appendix at the back of the book.

28. Specialty stores in a shopping mall can offer the customer convenience while retaining their:
    a) selectivity.
    b) prestige.
    c) price advantage.
    d) wide customer appeal.
    e) product variety.

29. A camera shop that has knowledgeable salespeople who can provide advice to purchasers and also offers to service and repair the cameras it sells is an example of a(n):
    a) mass merchandiser.
    b) agent-seller.
    c) one-stop shopping outlet.
    d) distribution chain.
    e) full-service retailer.

30. Stores that tend to focus on only one or a few types of products are:
    a) specialty retailers.
    b) variety department stores.
    c) retail outlets.
    d) discount stores.
    e) cash-and-carry retailers.

31. When the wholesaler purchases the products from the manufacturer and sells them to retailers on credit, it normally assumes the:
    a) package design.
    b) credit risk.
    c) promotional expenses of the manufacturer.
    d) manufacturer's guarantee.
    e) producer's risk.

32. A wholesaler provides all of the following services to manufacturers except:
    a) production.
    b) warehousing.
    c) delivery to retailers.
    d) sales expertise.
    e) feedback from retailers.

33. A situation in which two or more levels of distribution are managed by a single firm is called:
    a) vertical channel integration.
    b) horizontal channel integration.
    c) multilevel marketing.
    d) wheel of retailing.
    e) conglomeration.

34. When a _____ considers vertical integration, it must be concerned whether it will lose its established business with retail firms.
    a) retailer
    b) producer
    c) service provider
    d) retailer
    e) chain store

35. All of the following are distribution difficulties that firms may encounter when operating internationally except:
    a) poorly organized distribution networks.
    b) organized crime.
    c) payoffs.
    d) inability to use direct distribution.
    e) lack of intermediaries.

business decisions

Chapter 14

The Learning Goals of this chapter are to:

1 Explain how promotion can benefit firms.

2 Describe how advertising is used.

3 Describe the steps involved in personal selling.

4 Describe the sales promotion methods that are used.

5 Describe how firms can use public relations to promote products.

6 Explain how firms select the optimal mix of promotions to use.

Promoting Products

Firms regularly engage in promotion, which is the act of informing or reminding consumers about a specific product or brand. They can use promotion to increase the demand for the product and thereby increase the value of the firm. Consider the situation of car manufacturers, which use many forms of advertising (such as a billboard or television ads) to promote their vehicles. They may promote a new vehicle that was just created this year, or may use promotions to remind consumers about existing vehicles. Some of the more common promotion decisions made by car manufacturers are:

▶ what type of advertising should it use?

▶ what other promotion methods should it use?

▶ how it can use public relations to promote its vehicles?

▶ what is the optimal mix of promotions to use?

The decision about the type of advertising is important because it affects the demand by customers. The use of other promotion methods can also affect the demand by customers, and therefore affects the revenue of the car manufacturer. The decision about public rela-

tions can also affect the customer demand, and therefore the revenue. If a car manufacturer can determine the optimal mix of promotions, it will be able to increase the demand for its vehicles and therefore increase its revenue.

The types of decisions described above are necessary for all businesses. This chapter explains how promotion decisions by a car manufacturer or any other firm can be made in a manner that maximizes its value.

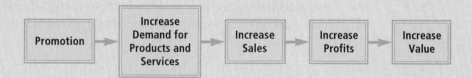

Promotion → Increase Demand for Products and Services → Increase Sales → Increase Profits → Increase Value

BACKGROUND ON PROMOTION

1
Explain how promotion
can benefit firms.

promotion the act of informing
or reminding consumers about a
specific product or brand

Even if a firm's product is properly produced, priced, and distributed, it still needs to be promoted. Firms commonly use **promotion** to supplement the other marketing strategies (product, pricing, and distribution strategies) described in the previous two chapters. For example, an automaker supplements its strategy of improving product quality with promotions that inform consumers about the strategy. An airline typically supplements its strategy to lower prices with promotions that inform consumers about the pricing strategy. A quality product that is reasonably priced may not sell unless it is promoted to make customers aware of it.

To make consumers aware of a new product, promotion can be used when the product is introduced. Promotion can also remind consumers that the product exists. Furthermore, promotion reminds consumers about the product's qualities and the advantages it offers over competing products. Promotion may also include special incentives to induce consumers to purchase a specific product. Promotion may also be used on a long-term basis to protect a product's image and retain its market share.

Effective promotion should increase demand for the product and generate a higher level of sales. To recognize how promotions can enhance product sales, consider the following statement in a recent annual report by Procter & Gamble:

"Our leading brands begin with world-class product technology, but it's advertising that gets consumers' attention and persuades them to use our products again and again. 'Advertising is the lifeblood of our brands.' . . . [A]dvertising is the key driver in all our businesses, but it's especially important for health care products—because consumers want a brand they know and trust. Advertising helps establish the trust."

As an illustration of how promotion can affect a firm's value, consider the case of Abercrombie & Fitch. It implemented a major promotion to boost awareness of its clothing. Its sales increased substantially just after the promotion, and so did its value (as measured by its stock price), as shown in Exhibit 14.1.

PROMOTION MIX

promotion mix the combination
of promotion methods that a firm
uses to increase acceptance of its
products

The **promotion mix** is the combination of promotion methods that a firm uses to increase acceptance of its products. The four methods of promotion are:

▶ Advertising

▶ Personal selling

▶ Sales promotion

▶ Public relations

Some firms use one of these promotion methods to promote their products, while other firms use two or more. The optimal promotion mix for promoting the product depends on the characteristics of the target market. Each of the four promotion methods is discussed in detail next.

Exhibit 14.1

Impact of a Major Promotion on Abercrombie & Fitch's Stock Price

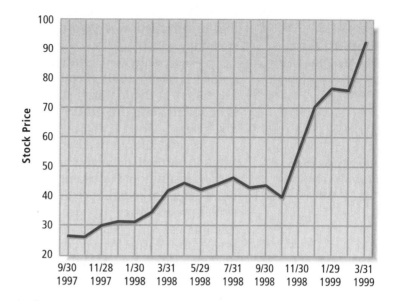

ADVERTISING

2
Describe how advertising is used.

advertising a nonpersonal sales presentation communicated through media or nonmedia forms to influence a large number of consumers

Advertising is a nonpersonal sales presentation communicated through media or nonmedia forms to influence a large number of consumers. It is a common method for promoting products and services. Although advertising is generally more expensive than other methods, it can reach many consumers. Large firms commonly use advertising agencies to develop their promotion strategies for them. Many firms such as Anheuser-Busch, General Motors, and Exxon spend more than $100 million per year on advertising. Procter & Gamble spends more than $3 billion a year in advertising.

Although advertising can be expensive, it can increase a product's market share. One reason for Frito-Lay's increase in market share over time is its heavy use of advertising. Frito-Lay typically spends more than $50 million a year on advertising.

Reasons for Advertising

Advertising is normally intended to enhance the image of a specific brand, institution, or industry. The most common reason is to enhance the image of a specific brand. **Brand advertising** is a nonpersonal sales presentation about a specific brand. Some brands are advertised to inform consumers about changes in the product. GNC (General Nutrition Centers) spends more than $80 million per year on brand advertising. The Gap and The Coca-Cola Company also spend heavily on brand advertising. Amazon.com uses extensive brand advertising on its own website.

brand advertising a nonpersonal sales presentation about a specific brand

comparative advertising intended to persuade customers to purchase a specific product by demonstrating a brand's superiority by comparison with other competing brands

Common strategies used to advertise a specific brand are comparative advertising and reminder advertising. **Comparative advertising** is intended to persuade customers to purchase a specific product by demonstrating a brand's superiority by comparison with other competing brands. Some soft drink makers use taste tests to prove the superiority of their respective soft drinks. Volvo advertises its superior safety features, while Saturn advertises that its price is lower than that of its competitors and that its quality is superior.

reminder advertising intended to remind consumers of a product's existence

Reminder advertising is intended to remind consumers of a product's existence. It is commonly used for products that have already proved successful and are at the maturity stage of their life cycle. This type of advertising is frequently used for grocery products such as cereal, peanut butter, and dog food.

A second reason for advertising is to enhance the image of a specific institution. **Institutional advertising** is a nonpersonal sales presentation about a specific institution. For example, firms such as IBM and ExxonMobil sometimes advertise to enhance their overall image, without focusing on a particular product they produce. Utility companies also advertise to enhance their image.

institutional advertising a nonpersonal sales presentation about a specific institution's product

A third reason for advertising is to enhance the image of a specific industry. **Industry advertising** is a nonpersonal sales presentation about a specific industry. Industry associations advertise their respective products (such as orange juice, milk, or beef) to increase demand for these products.

industry advertising a nonpersonal sales presentation about a specific industry's product

Forms of Advertising

Firms can advertise their products through various means. The most effective advertising varies with the product and target market of concern. Most types of advertising can be classified as follows:

- ▶ Newspapers
- ▶ Magazines
- ▶ Radio
- ▶ Television
- ▶ Internet
- ▶ E-mail
- ▶ Direct mail
- ▶ Telemarketing
- ▶ Outdoor ads
- ▶ Transportation ads
- ▶ Specialty ads

Newspapers   Many small and large businesses use newspaper advertising. It is a convenient way to reach a particular geographic market. Because many stores generate most of their sales from consumers within a 10-mile radius, they use a local newspaper for most of their ads. Newspaper ads can be inserted quickly, allowing firms to advertise only a few days after the idea was created. Best Buy, Publix, and other stores frequently use newspapers as a means of advertising.

Magazines   Because most magazines are distributed nationwide, magazine advertising is generally used for products that are distributed nationwide. Some magazines such as *Business Week* have the flexibility to offer regional ads that are inserted only in magazines distributed to a certain area.

Radio   An advantage of radio advertising is that, unlike magazines and newspapers, it talks to the audience. However, it lacks any visual effect. Because most radio stations serve a local audience, radio ads tend to focus on a particular local area. Furthermore, the particular type of music or other content on each radio station attracts consumers with similar characteristics. Therefore, each station may be perceived to reach a particular target market.

Television   Television ads combine the advantages of print media (such as newspapers and magazines) and radio. They can talk to the audience and provide a visual effect. Ads can be televised locally or nationwide. McDonald's, Sears, Duracell, and AT&T commonly run a commercial more than 20 times in a given week. Although television ads are expensive, they reach a large audience and can be highly effective. Some large firms, such as McDonald's and AT&T, run more than 1,000 television ads per year.

Firms attempt to use television advertising during shows that attract their target market. For example, lipstick and fashion firms may focus on the annual Academy Awards because more than 40 million women are watching. Beer and snack food producers focus on football games, which attract mostly men. A one-minute ad during the Super Bowl costs more than $3 million. The rates are much cheaper for ads that are only televised locally or are run on less-popular shows.

In recent years, many firms (including Procter & Gamble) have created **infomercials,** or commercials that are televised separately rather than within a show. Infomercials typically run for 30 minutes or longer and provide detailed information about a specific product promoted by the firm.

Together, television, radio, magazines, and newspapers account for more than 50 percent of total advertising expenditures. The allocation is shown in Exhibit 14.2.

Internet   The Internet has become a popular way for firms to advertise their products and services. It is a form of nonpersonal communication that can create awareness and persuade the customer. Some firms use their own website to advertise all of their products. Other firms promote their products on other websites that are commonly viewed by people who may purchase their products.

infomercials commercials that are televised separately rather than within a show

Exhibit 14.2
Allocation of Advertising Expenditures

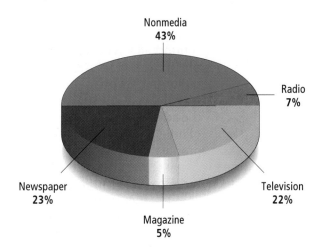

Nonmedia
43%

Radio
7%

Newspaper
23%

Magazine
5%

Television
22%

This office worker is excited about her upcoming vacation. She is reading an advertisement about a resort where she might stay complete with descriptions and photos.

© CORBIS / David Raymer

Initially, firms questioned whether people surfing the Internet would pay attention to ads. There is now much evidence that the Internet can be an effective way to advertise. Consider the case of Bristol-Myers Squibb Company, which experimented with an ad on some financial websites offering a free sample of Excedrin (one of its products) to all viewers who typed in their name and address next to the ad on the website. Bristol-Myers Squibb expected that it would receive 10,000 responses at the very most over a one-month period. Yet, in one month, 30,000 people responded. Thus, the Internet ad experiment was a success. Furthermore, the Internet ads cost less than traditional methods of advertising. Other firms experienced similar results with ads on the Internet.

Firms such as Microsoft and IBM spend more than $10 million per year on technology-based Internet ads. The total amount spent on Internet advertising is now well over $1 billion per year. One of the most popular types of Internet ads is a "banner ad," which is usually rectangular and placed at the top of a web page. Toyota, which frequently uses banner ads, found that more than 150,000 Internet users typed in their name and address next to the ad to get more information in a 12-month period. More than 5 percent of those users purchased a Toyota. An alternative type of Internet ad is the "button ad," which takes the viewer to the website of the firm advertised there if the viewer clicks on the ad. When a firm advertises on a website other than its own, it may pay a set fee to the firm that owns the website. Alternatively, the fee may be based on the number of clicks (by viewers) on the ad itself (to learn more about the advertised product) or on the number of orders of the product by viewers (if the ad results in viewers ordering the product).

A recent Internet advertising success story involves the promotion of the movie *X-Men*. Its production company, Twentieth Century Fox, spent about $50 million to create a website for the movie. The website featured online games and chat room discussions with the stars. The company considered the advertising successful because 28 percent of the survey respon-

business online

Using Technology for Promotions   This website provides valuable information about using e-commerce and technology for promotion purposes.

e-business

http://www.internet.com/
sections/marketing.html

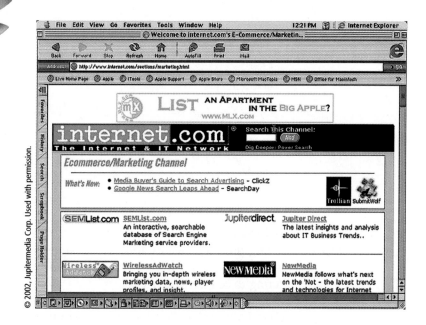

© 2002, Jupitermedia Corp. Used with permission.

dents who saw the movie had previously visited the *X-Men* website. Almost 5 million people logged on to the *X-Men* website during the six months before the film opened in theaters. The movie generated more than $150 million in sales.

E-Mail   Many firms send e-mail messages to their customers to promote products. Some e-mail promotions are general and apply to all customers on the e-mail list. Other e-mail promotions are personalized to fit the customer's interests. For example, Amazon.com sends promotions about specific books to customers who have previously expressed an interest on that topic. Marriott International sends promotions about hotels in specific locations to customers who have previously expressed an interest in those locations.

Direct Mail   Direct-mail advertising is frequently used by local service firms, such as realtors, home repair firms, and lawn service firms. It is also used by cosmetic firms (including Avon Products), as well as numerous clothing firms that send catalogs directly to homes.

If a firm plans to advertise through the mail, it should first obtain a mailing list that fits its target market. For example, Ford Motor Company sends ads to previous Ford customers. Talbots (a clothing firm) sends ads to a mailing list of its previous customers. Another common approach is for a firm to purchase the subscriber list of a magazine that is read by its targeted consumers. Many mailing lists can be separated by state or even zip code. As the price of paper and postage has increased, advertising by direct mail has become more expensive.

Exhibit 14.3

Forms of Advertising

Forms of Advertising	Typical Area Targeted
Newspaper	Local
Magazine	National
Radio	Local
Television	National or local
Internet	National
E-mail	National
Direct mail	National or local
Telemarketing	Local
Outdoor	Local
Transportation	Local
Specialty	National or local

telemarketing the use of the telephone for promoting and selling products

Telemarketing   **Telemarketing** uses the telephone for promoting and selling products. Many local newspaper firms use telemarketing to attract new subscribers. Phone companies and cable companies also use telemarketing to sell their services.

Outdoor Ads   Outdoor ads are shown on billboards and signs. Such ads are normally quite large because consumers are not likely to stop and look at them closely. Vacation-related products and services use outdoor advertising. For example, Disney World ads and Holiday Inn Hotel ads appear on billboards along many highways.

Transportation Ads   Advertisements are often displayed on forms of transportation, such as buses and the roofs of taxi cabs. These ads differ from the outdoor ads just described because they are moving rather than stationary. The ads generally attempt to provide a strong visual effect that can be recognized by consumers while the vehicle is moving.

Specialty Ads   Other forms of nonmedia advertising are also possible, such as T-shirts, hats, and bumper stickers. T-shirts advertise a wide variety of products, from shoes such as Adidas and Nike to soft drinks such as Coca-Cola and Pepsi.

Summary of Forms of Advertising

Exhibit 14.3 summarizes the forms of advertising. It also indicates whether each form targets the national market (nationwide advertising) or a local market.

College Health Club: **Advertising at CHC**

One of the decisions that Sue Kramer needs to make as part of her business plan for College Health Club (CHC) is how to advertise her health club services. She wants to use advertising, but must ensure that the funds used for advertising are well spent. She needs to reach a large number of potential members without spending too much money. CHC's target market is the set of students enrolled at Texas College. Sue rules out magazines, local television, radio, and the Internet because they are too expensive. She does not think that telemarketing, outdoor ads, transportation ads, or specialty ads would attract many members. Sue decides that the easiest way to reach her target market is to advertise in the college's school newspaper. This weekly newspaper is free to students, and most students read it or at least skim it. Sue decides on an ad that takes up one-quarter of a page and plans to run it for the next 10 weeks. Then she will determine the impact the ad has had on memberships and decide whether to continue running it.

3 PERSONAL SELLING

Describe the steps involved in personal selling.

personal selling a personal sales presentation used to influence one or more consumers

Personal selling is a personal sales presentation used to influence one or more consumers. It requires a personal effort to influence a consumer's demand for a product. Salespeople conduct personal selling on a retail basis, on an industrial basis, and on an individual basis. The sales effort on a retail basis is usually less challenging because it is addressed mostly to consumers who have already entered the store with plans to purchase. Many salespeople in retail stores do not earn a commission and thus may be less motivated to make a sale than other salespeople.

Selling on an industrial basis involves selling supplies or products to companies. Salespeople in this capacity are normally paid a salary plus commission. The volume of industrial sales achieved by a salesperson is highly influenced by that person's promotional efforts.

Selling on an individual basis involves selling directly to individual consumers. Some insurance salespeople and financial planners fit this description. Their task is especially challenging if they do not represent a well-known firm, because they must prove their credibility.

Salespeople who sell on an industrial or individual basis generally perform the following steps:

▶ Identify the target market.

▶ Contact potential customers.

▶ Make the sales presentation.

▶ Answer questions.

▶ Close the sale.

▶ Follow up.

Identify the Target Market

An efficient salesperson first determines the type of consumers interested in the product. In this way, less time is wasted on consumers who will not purchase the product, regardless of the sales effort. If previous sales have been made, the previous customers may be an obvious starting point.

Industrial salespeople can identify their target market by using library references and the Yellow Pages of a phone book. If they sell safety equipment, they will call almost any manufacturer in their area. If they sell printing presses, their market will be much more limited.

Individual salespeople have more difficulty identifying their market because they are unable to obtain information on each household. Thus, they may send a brochure to the "resident" at each address, asking the recipient to call if interested. The target market initially includes all households but is then reduced to those consumers who call back. Specific subdivisions of households that fit the income profile of typical consumers may be targeted.

Contact Potential Customers

Once potential customers are identified, they should be contacted by phone, e-mail, direct mail, or in person and provided with a brief summary of what the firm can offer them. Interested customers will make an appointment to meet with salespeople. Ideally, the salespeople should schedule appointments so that their time is used efficiently. For example, an industrial salesperson working the state of Florida should not make appointments in Jacksonville (northeast Florida), Miami (southeast), and Pensacola (northwest) within the same week. Half the week would be devoted to travel alone. The most logical approach is to fill the appointment schedule within a specific area. Individual salespeople should also attempt to schedule appointments on a specific day when they are near the same area.

Small Business Survey

What Skills Are Needed to Be Successful in Sales?

A survey asked 1,500 sales managers and sales representatives to rank 14 different skills in order of importance for their success. The following table shows the percentage of respondents who ranked each skill as being one of the top four skills in importance:

Skill	Percentage of Respondents
Planning before the sales call	54
Sales approach	48
Assessing the potential customer's needs	47
Managing time	45
Overcoming concerns about the product	42
Closing the sale	36
Initiating sales calls (cold calling)	30
Making presentations	26
Handling problems with the product	20
Negotiating	19
Following up after sales calls	16
Using the telephone to make sales calls	15
Managing paperwork	7
Demonstrating the product	4

Notice that the four activities that were perceived to be most important are conducted before the sales call. This confirms the need for salespeople to plan and organize if they are to be successful.

Make the Sales Presentation

A sales presentation can range from demonstrating how a printing press is used to explaining the benefits of an insurance policy. Industrial salespeople usually bring equipment with them. They also provide free samples of some products to companies. The sales presentation generally describes the use of each product, the price, and the advantages over competing products. The presentation should focus on how a particular product satisfies customer needs.

Answer Questions

Potential customers normally raise questions during the course of the sales presentation. Salespeople should anticipate common questions and prepare responses to them.

Close the Sale

Most salespeople prefer to make (or "close") a sale right after the sales presentation, while the product's advantages are still in the minds of potential customers. For this reason, they may offer some incentive to purchase immediately, such as a discounted price.

Follow Up

A key to long-term selling success is the attention given to purchasers after the sale is made. This effort increases the credibility of salespeople and encourages existing customers to call again when they need additional products. Salespeople should also follow up on potential customers who did not purchase the product after a sales presentation. These potential customers may experience budget changes and become more interested in purchasing the product over time. E-mail facilitates the follow-up communication between the purchasers and the salespeople. Exhibit 14.4 summarizes the steps in personal selling.

Exhibit 14.4

Summary of Tasks Involved in Personal Selling

Task	Description
Identify target market	Focus on types of customers most likely to purchase the product; contact these potential customers by phone or mail.
Contact potential customers	Schedule appointments with potential customers who are located in the same area on the same days.
Make sales presentation	Demonstrate the use and benefits of the product.
Answer questions	Prepare for typical questions and allow potential customers to ask questions.
Close the sale	Close the sale after the presentation, perhaps by offering a discount if a purchase is made immediately.
Follow up	Call customers who recently purchased the product to ensure their satisfaction. Call other potential customers who decided not to purchase the product to determine whether they would like to reconsider.

College Health Club: **Personal Selling at CHC**

Sue Kramer has found a way to use personal selling to promote College Health Club (CHC). Since the students at Texas College are her target market, she meets with college administrators, who agree to let her make a presentation to students about exercise and health at the auditorium on one Friday afternoon each month. Although she cannot directly advertise CHC during the presentation, it will provide some name recognition for her health club.

4

Describe the sales promotion methods that are used.

sales promotion the set of activities that is intended to influence consumers

rebate a potential refund by the manufacturer to the consumer

coupons a promotional device used in newspapers, magazines, and ads to encourage the purchase of a product

SALES PROMOTION

Sales promotion is the set of activities that is intended to influence consumers. It can be an effective means of encouraging consumers to purchase a specific product. The following are the most common sales promotion strategies:

▶ Rebates

▶ Coupons

▶ Sampling

▶ Displays

▶ Premiums

Rebates

A **rebate** is a potential refund by the manufacturer to the consumer. When manufacturers desire to increase product demand, they may offer rebates rather than lowering the price charged to the retail store. Lowering the price to the retail store does not guarantee that the store will pass on the discount. Thus, this strategy could result in lower profit per unit without increasing demand. A rebate ensures that consumers receive the manufacturer's discount. Automobile manufacturers frequently offer rebates of $500 or more.

Coupons

Coupons are used in newspapers, magazines, and ads to encourage the purchase of a product. They are also commonly packaged with a product so that consumers can use the coupon only if they purchase this same product again. Coupons used in this way can encourage consumers to repeatedly purchase the same brand. Consequently, consumers may become loyal to that brand.

Some coupons are not available until consumers make repeated purchases. For example, airlines offer free flights to frequent fliers, and some hotels offer a free night's stay to frequent customers.

Promoting with coupons may be inefficient for some firms. General Mills had historically used coupons to promote its cereals. However, after learning from marketing research that 98 percent of all cereal coupons are not used, it decided to cut back on this promotion strategy. It reduced annual spending on some promotions by $175 million and focused on improving its product.

Exhibit 14.5

Impact of AOL's Sampling Strategy on Its Stock Price

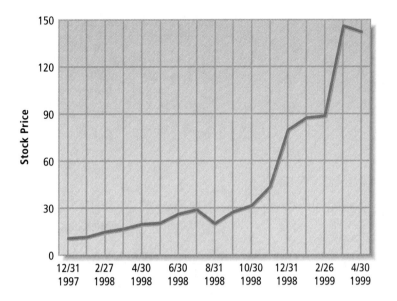

Sampling

sampling offering free samples to encourage consumers to try a new brand or product

Sampling involves offering free samples to encourage consumers to try a new brand or product. The intent is to lure customers away from competing products. For example, Clinique samples are available in cosmetics departments of retail stores. Food samples are offered in grocery stores. Manufacturing firms also provide samples so that consumers can try out equipment. Samples are even sent through direct mail.

Samples are most commonly used to introduce new products. Firms recognize that once customers become accustomed to a particular brand, they tend to stick with that brand. Thus, the free sample is intended to achieve **brand loyalty,** or the loyalty of consumers to a specific brand over time.

brand loyalty the loyalty of consumers to a specific brand over time

Sampling of Services
Sampling is used for services as well as products. For example, in 1999 America Online (AOL) provided a limited amount of free online time to potential customers. This strategy allowed customers to experience the service that AOL provides and resulted in a large number of subscriptions to AOL's online service. Consequently, AOL's value (as measured by its stock price) increased substantially, as shown in Exhibit 14.5. Subsequently, AOL merged with media giant Time Warner.

Displays

Many stores create special displays to promote particular products. The displays are used to attract consumers who are in the store for other reasons. Products are more likely to get attention if they are located at a point of purchase, such as by the cash registers where consumers are waiting in line. Because there is limited room for displays, companies that want retail stores to display their products are typically willing to set up the display themselves. They may even offer a reduced price to retail stores that allow a display.

Exhibit 14.6

Comparison of Sales Promotion Strategies

Strategy	Description
Rebates	Firm sends refund directly to consumers after product is purchased.
Coupons	Product is sold at a discounted price to consumers with coupons.
Sampling	Free samples of products are distributed to consumers.
Displays	Products are placed in a prominent area in stores.
Premiums	Gifts or prizes are provided free to consumers who purchase a specific product.

NSYNC join with Famous Fixins, Inc. to launch a new product line featuring their names and images.

premium a gift or prize provided free to consumers who purchase a specific product

Premiums

A **premium** is a gift or prize provided free to consumers who purchase a specific product. For example, *Sports Illustrated* magazine may offer a free sports video to new subscribers. A boat manufacturer may offer a free fishing rod to anyone who purchases its boats. Premiums offer an extra incentive to purchase products.

Summary of Sales Promotion Strategies

Exhibit 14.6 provides a summary of sales promotion methods. The ideal strategy is dependent on the features of the product. Sampling and displays are intended to make the consumer aware of the product's qualities, while other sales promotion strategies are intended to make the price of the product appear more reasonable.

5 Describe how firms can use public relations to promote products.

public relations actions taken with the goal of creating or maintaining a favorable public image

PUBLIC RELATIONS

The term **public relations** refers to actions taken with the goal of creating or maintaining a favorable public image. Firms attempt to develop good public relations by communicating to the general public, including prospective customers. Public relations can be used to enhance the image of a product or of the firm itself. It may also be used to clarify information in response to adverse publicity. Many firms have a public relations department that provides information about the firm and its products to the public. Public rela-

global business

Promoting Products across Countries When firms promote products, they tend to emphasize the features that give those products an advantage over all others. Yet consumers in different countries may base their purchase decisions on different features. A product may be popular in the United States because it is durable, but it may be popular in another country because of its low price. Therefore, a firm may need to revise its promotional strategy according to the country. In addition, the manner in which a feature is promoted may vary with the country. Television commercials may not reach a large audience in some less-developed countries, where they may be seen by only the relatively wealthy consumers. Some television commercials may still be effective in these countries if the product is being promoted to the type of people who would likely purchase the product. U.S. firms must recognize that the typical profile of the people in foreign countries who watch television or read specific newspapers may vary from the profile in the United States.

Furthermore, firms that hire celebrities to promote products must consider the perceptions of the consumers in each country. Cindy Crawford, Mark McGuire, and Sammy Sosa may be more effective for promotions of products in the United States than in other countries. Arnold Schwarzenegger is very popular in Asia because of the distribution of his action films. Another reason promotions of a particular product vary across countries is that each country's government has its own rules and restrictions. A commercial that is acceptable in one country may be restricted in another country. The United Kingdom prohibits commercials from directly comparing one product with a competing product. Therefore, commercials that compared Pepsi with Coca-Cola had to be revised to compare Pepsi against Brand X.

Given the different perceptions of products by consumers across countries and different government regulations, a firm may have to create a different promotion for a particular product in each country where the product is sold. Just as firms create products that are tailored to the unique characteristics of consumers in a specific country, they should also promote products in a manner that appeals to specific consumers.

tions departments typically use the media to relay their information to the public.

Firms commonly attempt to be very accessible to the media because they may receive media coverage at no charge. When employees of a firm are quoted by the media, the firm's name is mentioned across a large audience. Some banks assign employees to provide economic forecasts because the media will mention the bank's name when reporting the forecast. Some public relations is not planned but results from a response to circumstances. For example, during the tragedy of September 11, Home Depot offered its support and was recognized by the media for its efforts.

The following are the most common types of public relations strategies:

▶ Special events

▶ News releases

▶ Press conferences

Special Events

Some firms sponsor a special event such as a race. Anheuser-Busch (producer of Budweiser) supports many marathons and festivals where it promotes its name. 7 UP promotes local marathons and has even printed the marathon logo and running figures on 7 UP cans, which may attract consumers who run or exercise.

Advertising signs are proliferating at ballparks everywhere.

AP Photo / Adam Nadell

News Releases

news release a brief written announcement about a firm provided by that firm to the media

A **news release** is a brief written announcement about a firm provided by that firm to the media. It enables the firm to update the public about its products or operations. It may also be used to clarify information in response to false rumors that could adversely affect the firm's reputation. The news release may include the name and phone number of an employee who can provide more details if desired by the media. There is no charge for providing a news release, but the firm incurs an indirect cost for hiring employees to promote news releases. Also, there is no guarantee that a news release will be announced by the media.

Press Conferences

press conference an oral announcement about a firm provided by that firm to the media

A **press conference** is an oral announcement about a firm provided by that firm to the media. Like a news release, a press conference may be intended to enhance the firm's image or to eliminate any adverse effects caused by false rumors. A press conference is more personal than a news release because an employee of the firm makes the announcement directly to the media and may even be willing to answer questions from the media. There is no charge for organizing a press conference, but there is an indirect cost of hiring employees to perform the necessary tasks.

6

Explain how firms select the optimal mix of promotions to use.

DETERMINING THE OPTIMAL PROMOTION MIX

Exhibit 14.7 provides a brief summary of the various promotion methods. Each method offers its own advantages and disadvantages, so no single method is ideal for all products. Firms must decide whether to use adver-

Exhibit 14.7

Summary of Methods That Make Up the Promotion Mix

Promotion Method	Advantages	Disadvantages
Advertising	Reaches a large number of customers.	Can be expensive; is not personalized.
Personal selling	Provides personalized attention.	Difficult to reach a large number of customers.
Sales promotion	Offers various incentives for consumers to purchase products.	May not reach as many consumers as advertising.
Public relations	Inexpensive method of enhancing the image of the firm or its products.	Provides only a limited amount of promotion because news releases and press conferences may not always be covered by the media.

tising, personal selling, sales promotion, publicity, or some mix of these promotion methods to promote their products. Firms must consider the characteristics of their target market and their promotion budget when determining the optimal promotion mix, as explained next.

Target Market

If a firm's target market is made up of a wide variety of customers throughout a specific region, it may use advertising to promote its product. If a firm produces a surgical device for a target market of hospital surgeons, it may consider using some advertising to make surgeons aware of the device, along with personal selling to explain how the device is used. If the target market is made up of consumers on tight budgets (such as retired people), the firm may use sales promotion methods such as coupons or rebates.

Any of these promotion methods may be complemented with public relations such as sponsoring a special event for consumers who are in the target market for the product. For example, to promote its female athletic shoes, Reebok sponsored a Sports Training Challenge for high school female athletes.

Firms typically attempt to direct their promotion to the target market. Miller Brewing, Anheuser-Busch, and other beer producers run commercials during sports events and direct the ads at a target market of men. Women's clothing ads are placed in fashion magazines and directed at a target market of women. Procter & Gamble promotes its household products on television shows watched by women, since women generally make most of the household purchases.

When firms direct their promotion directly at the target market, they provide information to the consumers who would most likely purchase the products. Consumers become aware of the product without hearing about it from a retailer. They may then request the product from retailers, who in turn request it from wholesalers or producers. This strategy is called a **pull strategy,** because the product was pulled through the distribution channel as a result of consumer demand. For example, suppose that a firm develops a new type of DVD player and advertises it to consumers. As consumers become aware of the product, their demand at retail outlets pulls the product through the distribution channel.

Some producers direct their promotion at wholesalers or retailers instead of their target market. When producers promote their products to wholesalers or retailers, their promotion effort is called a **push strategy.** Wholesalers promote the product to retailers, who in turn promote it to consumers. Thus, the product is pushed through the distribution channel.

pull strategy firms direct their promotion directly at the target market, and consumers in turn request the product from wholesalers or producers

push strategy producers direct their promotion of a product at wholesalers or retailers, who in turn promote it to consumers

Exhibit 14.8

Comparison of Pull and Push Strategies

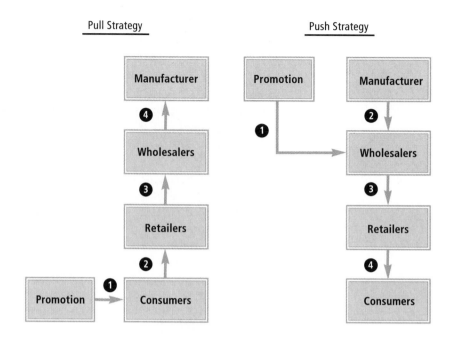

For example, assume that a manufacturer of a new DVD player has representatives demonstrate its advantages to all wholesalers. The wholesalers then promote the DVD player to retailers so that they can inform consumers. The difference between a push strategy and a pull strategy is illustrated in Exhibit 14.8. Personal selling is commonly used to apply a push strategy.

Surveying the Target Market   Marketing research can enhance a firm's promotion decisions by determining the types of promotions that are favorably received by the target market of concern. For example, a firm that sells clothing to teenagers may survey a sample of teenagers for feedback on various promotions that it may offer. The firm will implement the promotion strategy that is likely to result in the highest level of sales (assuming each promotion strategy has the same cost), based on the feedback from the teenagers surveyed.

Promotion Budget

promotion budget the amount of funds that have been set aside to pay for all promotion methods over a specified period

A **promotion budget** is the amount of funds that have been set aside to pay for all promotion methods over a specified period. Firms may establish a promotion budget for each product that they produce. The budget may be large if the firm believes that promotion will have a major effect on sales or is necessary to prevent a substantial decline in sales. If the promotion budget for a specific product is small, advertising on television or in widely distributed magazines may not be possible. The firm may have to rely on inexpensive advertising (such as local newspapers) and inexpensive sales promotion methods (such as displays). Perhaps no single type of promotion will be as effective by itself.

The promotion budget varies substantially across firms and may even vary for each firm's product line over time. The promotion budget for a specific product is influenced by the following characteristics:

▶ Phase of the product life cycle

▶ Competition

▶ Economic conditions

Phase of the Product Life Cycle
Products that are just being introduced to the market will require more promotions to inform customers about the products. Products that are in the growth phase are promoted to inform and remind customers. Products in the maturity or decline phases of the life cycle may not require as much promotion. Nevertheless, they may still need some promotion to remind customers and retain their market share. The amount of promotion used for different phases of the life cycle is shown in Exhibit 14.9. Firms that revise their products in an effort to extend the life cycle may use a large amount of promotion even in the maturity phase.

Competition
A firm may feel compelled to match competitors that frequently advertise with its own promotional campaign. This is a defensive strategy. It indicates that advertising is used not only as an aggressive strategy to increase market share but also to retain existing market share.

Economic Conditions
Firms respond in different ways to favorable economic conditions. Some firms may increase their promotion because they can better afford it. Others will cut back, expecting the strong economy to carry their products. In a stagnant economy, firms may attempt to heavily promote their products in an attempt to maintain demand.

College Health Club: Promotion Mix at CHC

As Sue Kramer develops her business plan for College Health Club (CHC), she must decide on the mix of different strategies that she will use to promote CHC. Based on the promotion decisions described so far, she will use a promotion mix consisting of (1) advertising through the Texas College newspaper, (2) coupons for vitamin supplements and a free day pass inserted in the Texas College newspaper, and (3) personal selling through monthly presentations about exercise and health to students on campus. All three parts of her promotion mix are focused on the students at the college.

Exhibit 14.9

Amount of Promotion Used throughout the Product's Life Cycle

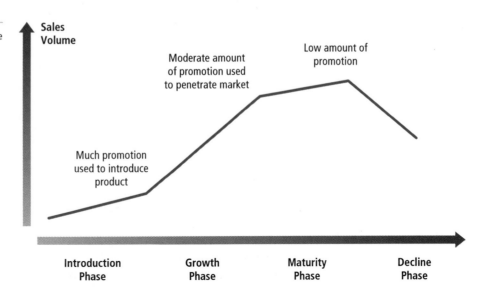

Interaction between Promotion Decisions and Other Business Decisions

When marketing managers make promotion decisions, they must interact with other managers of the firm. The amount of promotion that is used for a particular product will influence demand for that product. If marketing managers anticipate a larger demand for the product in response to new promotion strategies, they must inform the production department. The production managers must be aware of the anticipated demand so that they can produce a sufficient volume of products. Promotions that increase demand will increase sales only if the firm produces a larger volume in anticipation of the larger demand. Otherwise, the firm will experience shortages, and customers who are unable to purchase the product may purchase it from a competitor. In some cases, production may already be at full capacity, which means that the promotion may not be worthwhile until the manufacturing process can be revised to increase capacity.

Marketing managers also interact with financial managers about promotion decisions for the following reasons. First, when marketing managers estimate the costs of a specific promotion and the extra revenue that will be generated over time as a result of that promotion, they may rely on financial managers to assess whether the promotion will provide an adequate return to make it worthwhile to the firm. Second, when marketing managers decide to implement large promotions, they may need a substantial amount of funds; they can inform the financial managers, who may determine the best method to obtain those funds. This discussion illustrates how marketing managers rely on input from the production managers and financial managers when making their promotion decisions.

MANAGING SALESPEOPLE

sales manager an individual who manages a group of sales representatives

A common goal of many sales representatives is to become a **sales manager** and manage a group of sales representatives. For example, a company with 40 sales representatives around the country may split the geographic markets into four regions. Each region would have 10 sales representatives who are monitored by a sales manager.

Sales managers require some of the same skills as sales representatives. They need to have knowledge of the product and the competition. In addition, they must be able to motivate their representatives to sell. They must also be able to resolve customer complaints on the service provided by representatives and reprimand representatives when necessary. Some people are better suited to selling than managing salespeople. There is a distinct difference between motivating consumers to purchase a product and motivating employees to sell a product.

Since sales managers do not perform the daily tasks of selling the product, they can concentrate on special projects, such as servicing a major customer's massive order of products. They should evaluate the long-term prospects of the product and consider possible plans for expanding the geographic market. Information from their sales representatives may help their assessments.

EVALUATING THE EFFECTS OF PROMOTION

Although the costs of a proposed promotion can be accurately estimated, the benefits of the promotion are uncertain. After firms promote products, however, they can determine whether the promotion strategy was successful. If they establish measurable objectives at the time of the promotion, they can assess whether the objectives were achieved. For example, consider a marketing plan that is intended to increase revenue by 10 percent over the next year. Once the year is over, the actual revenue can be compared with the revenue goal to determine whether the goal was achieved. This type of comparison can be useful for determining whether various promotion strategies are successful over time.

If the objectives of the promotion strategy are not accomplished, the firm may revise its strategy. Sometimes a marketing plan fails because the objectives were overly optimistic. In this situation, the firm may need to revise its objectives rather than its strategies. Firms must also recognize that changes in other conditions may affect revenue. For example, poor economic conditions may cause a firm's revenue to be less than the goal established even if the promotion strategy was effective.

College Health Club: **Evaluating the Effects of Promotion at CHC**

One of the decisions that Sue Kramer needs to make as part of her business plan for College Health Club (CHC) is how to evaluate the effects of promotion. Sue needs a method to determine whether her promotion mix is effective. She plans to monitor how the number of memberships changes after implementing her promotion mix. She realizes, however, that memberships may increase for reasons other than the promotion strategies. Therefore, she has included a question on the membership application asking what caused the applicant to purchase a membership. The choices are (1) referral from a friend, (2) advertising in the student newspaper, (3) coupons in the student newspaper, (4) the exercise and health presentations on campus, or (5) other. She can determine from the membership applications which promotion strategies are attracting the most members. This information can help her decide how to use her promotion budget in the future.

Summary

1 Promotional efforts can increase sales or at least prevent a decrease in sales because the brand name stays in the consumer's mind, consumers are informed about the product's advantages, and the product's perceived credibility may be enhanced.

2 The key forms of advertising are newspapers, magazines, radio, television, the Internet, e-mail, direct mail, telemarketing, outdoor ads, transportation ads, and specialty ads.

3 The main steps involved in personal selling are to

▶ identify the target market,

▶ contact potential customers,

▶ make the sales presentation,

▶ answer questions,

▶ close the sale, and

▶ follow up.

4 The most common sales promotion methods include

▶ rebates, in which firms give refunds directly to consumers after the product is purchased;

▶ coupons, which allow products to be sold to specific consumers at discounted prices;

▶ sampling, in which consumers receive free samples of products;

▶ displays, in which products are placed in prominent areas of stores; and

▶ premiums, in which gifts or prizes are provided free to consumers who purchase a specific product.

5 Firms can use public relations to enhance a product's or a firm's image. The most common types of public relations strategies are

▶ special events, which can be sponsored by a firm to promote a specific product;

- news releases, which are brief written announcements about a firm provided by the firm to the media; and

- press conferences, which are oral announcements about a firm provided by that firm to the media.

6 When a firm selects the optimal promotion mix to use for promoting a product, it considers the

- target market, so that it can use a promotion method that properly reaches that target market; and

- promotion budget, since only those promotion methods that are affordable can be considered.

Key Terms

advertising   445
brand advertising   445
brand loyalty   455
comparative advertising   445
coupons   454
industry advertising   446
infomercials   447
institutional advertising   446

news release   458
personal selling   451
premium   456
press conference   458
promotion   444
promotion budget   460
promotion mix   444
public relations   456

pull strategy   459
push strategy   459
rebate   454
reminder advertising   446
sales manager   462
sales promotion   454
sampling   455
telemarketing   450

Review & Critical Thinking Questions

1. How can promotion be used when introducing a new product?

2. What is the promotion mix? List and briefly describe the four methods of promotion.

3. You are planning to start a florist business in your hometown. Would you use media advertising, nonmedia advertising, or both? Why?

4. Why do you think newspaper publishers use telemarketing to develop a customer base?

5. Briefly summarize the steps involved in personal selling.

6. Discuss the types of sales promotion strategies that a donut shop would most likely utilize.

7. Define public relations and explain the role it would play in the law enforcement department of a major city.

8. Compare the pull strategy with the push strategy associated with promotion.

9. Discuss the different types of promotion that would be utilized throughout the product life cycle for a product or service.

10. How do economic conditions affect a firm's promotion budget?

11. What are the skills a good sales manager should possess?

Discussion Questions

1. As a sales manager in a new automobile dealership, what role would you play in the company, and what would your responsibilities be?

2. You are the owner of a mini-mart convenience store. What processes could you utilize to identify your target market?

3. You are a salesperson in an office supply business. Why is it important to be persistent and utilize follow-up visits with your customers?

4. Identify and explain the different types of promotion methods in the following examples:

   a. Tiger Woods plays golf wearing Nike apparel.

   b. A local supermarket introduces a scratch-and-win ticket.

   c. Assume that you are a college graduate. Your local college telephones, asking you to make a donation for its capital funding program.

5. How can a firm use the Internet to identify its target market? How can it use the Internet to promote its products?

6. Discuss the promotion strategies that would be utilized by a manufacturer in promoting the following brands. Indicate whether the strategy focuses on product positioning or image building.

   a. Corvette convertible

   b. Dove facial soap

   c. Craftsman tools

   d. Mountain Dew soft drink

It's Your Decision: **Promotion Decisions at CHC**

1. How could Sue Kramer, the president of CHC, use direct-mail advertising to focus specifically on CHC's target market?

2. How could Sue use personal selling to promote CHC?

3. How could Sue use premiums to promote CHC?

4. If Sue is planning a major promotion strategy that will attract additional members, why must she first consider the size of CHC's facilities?

5. Recall that Sue expects total expenses of $142,000 in CHC's first year. She will set the membership fee at $500 and expects to attract 300 members in the first year. Sue is considering a promotion involving coupons inserted in the school newspaper. Determine CHC's earnings based on the following coupon strategies over the first year:

If CHC Provides a Discount Coupon of:	The Expected Number of Memberships Would Be:	CHC's Earnings before Taxes in the First Year Would Be:
$5	302	_____
10	303	_____
20	310	_____
30	320	_____

Which discount coupon strategy would you use? Explain.

6. A health club differs from manufacturing firms in that it produces a service rather than products. Explain why the promotion policy of a service firm (such as CHC) is different from that of a manufacturing firm.

Investing in a Business

Using the annual report of the firm in which you would like to invest, complete the following:

1 How does the firm promote its products? Does it use the media to promote its products? Provide details.

2 Does the firm rely heavily on promotion to sell its products? How much money has it allocated toward its promotion budget this year?

3 In reviewing the key terms in this chapter, which do you think could apply to promoting your company's products?

4 Explain how the business uses technology to promote its products over the Internet. Does it provide rebates to customers using the website to purchase products? What do you find most appealing about the firm's website? What do you find least appealing?

5 Go to **http://hoovers.com** and locate the NEWS SEARCH. Type in the name of the firm in the space provided, and review the recent news stories about the firm. Summarize any (at least one) recent news story about the firm that applies to one or more of the key concepts in this chapter.

Case: Promoting Products on the Internet

Ken Brabec has created a video, "How to Improve Your Tennis Game," by compiling tips on specific aspects of the game from several tennis pros around the country. He would like to sell the video to video stores, but he realizes that video stores normally deal with large broadcasting and movie companies instead of individuals.

Ken decides that he will try to market the videos to people directly. He can easily mail a video to anyone who orders one, but he needs to decide how to promote the video. Since he can easily mail videos to customers, he wants to promote his video throughout the United States. He first considers advertising in various tennis magazines, but he cannot afford the fee they charge for even a single ad. Ken's funds are limited, and he is not willing to risk all of his money on a few advertisements. Consequently, he decides to advertise his video on various websites, where the advertising fees are relatively low. He still needs to decide the best way to advertise over the Internet, however.

Questions

1 What types of websites should Ken use to advertise his tennis video?

2 Ken plans to advertise initially on five different websites. He may continue ads on the websites that generate the most sales of his videos. How can Ken determine which of his ads on the Internet are receiving the most attention?

3 Ken is trying to decide whether the promotion on the website should provide an order form for customers to send in. This method would be relatively inexpensive. Alternatively, he could allow customers to order the video over the Internet. This method is more expensive. Is there any benefit to allowing customers to order the video over the Internet using a credit card?

Video Case: Promotion Strategies for Red Roof Inn

Red Roof Inn provides economy lodging. Its performance declined in 1986, and its slogan "sleep cheap" did not seem to be attracting customers. Consequently, Red Roof Inn hired W. B. Doner & Company to create a new promotional strategy. The strategy focused on the theme that Red Roof Inn was a smart choice for travelers. Doner had access to bills of American Express credit card holders who used economy hotels and targeted those customers with promotional material. Doner also helped establish a website so that customers can make reservations online and learn where Red Roof Inns are located. The perception of Red Roof Inns has improved over time as a result of this promotion strategy.

Questions

1 Explain why a new promotion strategy could help Red Roof Inn.

2 One of Red Roof Inn's advertisements suggested that customers can save money by staying at the inn because it does not buy hair nets, shampoo, or mints for its customers as some of its competitors do, but it still offers a comfortable room at a low price. Is this brand advertising, comparative advertising, or reminder advertising?

3 Who is the target market for Red Roof Inn?

Internet Applications

1. *http://auctions.amazon.com*

Click on a category of your choice and view some of the items currently for sale in that category. What types of sales promotion methods does Amazon.com use to auction off other people's products? How do you think Amazon.com generates revenue by selling products for other parties? Do you think Amazon.com advertises its products in other media outlets (other than the Internet)? Why or why not?

2. *http://www.admedia.org/index.html*

Define the word *media*. What is the difference between "mass" and "niche" media? How is the Internet different from conventional media? How do the steps involved in personal selling apply to the Internet as a medium? How could a firm use information released by Nielsen Media Research?

3. *http://www.promotionbase.com*

Summarize two articles from this website. What are some current topics in promotion? As a manager, would you use a site like this to increase your promotion using the Internet? Why or why not? Do you think individuals surfing the Internet pay attention to ads?

The Coca-Cola Company Annual Report Project

Questions for the current year's annual report are available on the text website at **http://madura.swlearning.com.**

The following questions apply concepts presented in this chapter to The Coca-Cola Company. Go to The Coca-Cola Company website (**http://www.cocacola.com**) and find the index for the 2001 annual report.

Questions

1 Click on "Operations Review" and study the "North America Group." What are some promotional campaigns that The Coca-Cola Company has used recently?

2 Click on "Our Building Blocks" and study the "Qoo" section. Describe the promotional campaign surrounding Qoo in Japan. What were the results of this campaign?

3 Study the "Selected Market Results" and the "Operations Review" sections. If The Coca-Cola Company reduced its advertising, do you think sales and profits would fall?

4 Study the "France" section under "Our Building Blocks." Describe the "Hot and Cool" campaign The Coca-Cola Company initiated in France.

5 Go to **http://hoovers.com** and locate the NEWS CENTER. Key in The Coca-Cola Company in the space provided, click on "Search," and review the recent news stories about the firm. Summarize any (at least one) recent news story about The Coca-Cola Company that applies one or more of the key concepts within this chapter of the text.

In-Text Study Guide

Answers are in an appendix at the back of the book.

True or False

1. Comparative advertising is intended to enhance the image of a firm without focusing on a particular product. F

2. The promotion mix is the combination of promotion methods that a firm uses to increase the acceptance of its products. T

3. The Internet, magazines, direct mail, and television are all forms of advertising. T

4. A key to successful selling is the follow-up service to customers provided by salespeople. T

5. Television advertising is the most widely used form of personal selling for medium and large businesses. F

6. Rebates and coupons are used to offer a price discount from retailers to their customers. F

7. A firm using a push strategy will aim its promotional message directly at the target market customers. F

8. Public relations is one of the most expensive forms of sales promotion. F

9. One factor that will influence the size of the promotion budget for a product is the phase of the product in the product life cycle. T

10. Sales managers perform the daily tasks of selling the product. F

Multiple Choice

11. Even if a firm's product is properly produced, priced, and distributed, it still needs to be:
    a) manufactured.
    b) inspected.
    c) graded.
    d) promoted.
    e) market tested.

12. All of the following are methods of promotion except:
    a) target marketing.
    b) personal selling.
    c) advertising.

    d) sales promotion.
    e) public relations.

13. The act of informing or reminding consumers about a specific product or brand is referred to as:
    a) personal selling.
    b) production.
    c) finance.
    d) promotion.
    e) research and development.

14. Which of the following promotion strategies is a nonpersonal sales promotion aimed at a large number of consumers?
    a) advertising
    b) public relations
    c) telemarketing
    d) retail selling
    e) mega-marketing

15. A nonpersonal sales presentation about a specific brand is:
    a) institutional advertising.
    b) personal selling.
    c) brand advertising.
    d) comparative advertising.
    e) reminder advertising.

16. The type of advertising that is used for grocery products such as cereal, peanut butter, and dog food is:
    a) institutional advertising.
    b) reminder advertising.
    c) the push strategy.
    d) industry advertising.
    e) public relations advertising.

17. The popular "Louie the Lizard" Budweiser commercials are examples of _____ advertising.
    a) comparative
    b) institutional
    c) industry
    d) reminder
    e) generic

In-Text Study Guide

18. All of the following are forms of advertising except:
    a) direct mail.
    b) outdoor ads.
    c) personal selling.
    d) online banner ads.
    e) transportation ads.

19. Ads that are televised separately rather than within a show are called:
    a) commercials.
    b) specialty ads.
    c) infomercials.
    d) institutional ads.
    e) direct-mail ads.

20. All of the following are advantages of internet advertising except:
    a) direct, personal contact with the potential consumer.
    b) low cost.
    c) fees can be based on the number of customer orders.
    d) generates high levels of response.
    e) can create product awareness.

21. The use of the telephone for promoting and selling products is known as:
    a) terepromotion.
    b) telemarketing.
    c) online sales promotion.
    d) telecommunication mix.
    e) annoying phone calls.

22. Salespeople generally perform all of the following steps except:
    a) identify the target market.
    b) follow up.
    c) contact potential customers.
    d) make the sales presentation.
    e) advertising.

23. A salesperson who has just completed an effective sales presentation should attempt to:
    a) analyze the market.
    b) win at all costs.
    c) close the sale.

    d) exploit the customer.
    e) maximize sales returns and allowances.

24. A visual method that retail stores use in promoting particular products is a:
    a) display.
    b) rebate.
    c) coupon.
    d) premium.
    e) market.

25. The promotion strategy of sampling is most often used to:
    a) provide customers with a premium as an incentive to purchase more of the product.
    b) introduce new products.
    c) give customers a discount if a larger quantity is purchased.
    d) serve as a reminder for former customers to buy the product again.
    e) unload surplus inventory.

26. The main, immediate goal of public relations is to:
    a) remind customers of the firm's existence.
    b) compare the firm's brand to a competitor's brand.
    c) identify the firm's target market.
    d) enhance the image of the firm.
    e) increase sales.

27. Which of the following sales promotion strategies provides a gift or prize to consumers who purchase a specific product?
    a) pull
    b) push
    c) sampling
    d) rebates
    e) premiums

28. When firms promote products, they highlight the advantages over all other products. They emphasize the product's:
    a) publicity.
    b) features.
    c) sales promotion.
    d) labeling.
    e) life cycle.

In-Text Study Guide

Answers are in an appendix at the back of the book.

29. Firms that hire _____ to promote products must consider the perceptions of the consumers in each country.
    a) accountants
    b) economists
    c) suppliers
    d) clients
    e) celebrities

30. Which of the following is a public relations strategy in which an organization provides the media with a written announcement?
    a) special events
    b) press conference
    c) concert sponsorship
    d) direct mail
    e) news release

31. If a firm's target market is made up of a wide variety of customers throughout a specific region, it would likely use _____ to promote its product.
    a) personal selling
    b) advertising
    c) door-to-door sales
    d) one-on-one communication
    e) target marketing

32. When producers promote their products to wholesalers or retailers, their promotion effort is called a:
    a) push strategy.
    b) premium price strategy.
    c) sales promotion.
    d) market segmentation.
    e) pull strategy.

33. Which of the following is a strategy where firms focus their promotional messages on the target market customers, who in turn request the product from wholesalers or producers?
    a) push
    b) co-branding
    c) product life cycle
    d) sponsorship
    e) pull

34. The promotion budget varies substantially across firms and may even vary for each firm's product line over time. Its characteristics are influenced by all of the following except:
    a) size of human resource department.
    b) competition.
    c) phase of the product life cycle.
    d) economic conditions.

35. If marketing managers anticipate a larger demand for a product in response to new promotion strategies, they must inform their:
    a) labor union.
    b) stockholders.
    c) creditors.
    d) production department.
    e) appropriate government agency.

Part V

Summary

Marketing

The key marketing strategies described in Chapters 12 through 14 can be summarized as follows. First, a firm uses market research to define a consumer need. Once a product is developed to satisfy this need, a pricing decision is made. The pricing policy affects the demand for the product and therefore affects the firm's revenue. Then, a method of distributing the product to consumers must be selected. The use of intermediaries tends to make the product more accessible to customers but also results in higher prices. Finally, a promotion strategy must be designed to make consumers aware of the product or to convince them that this product is superior to others.

The marketing strategies just described are continually used even after a product follows the typical life cycle. For example, marketing research may be conducted to determine whether an existing product should be revised or targeted toward a different market. The pricing policy could change if the target market is revised or if the production costs change. The decision regarding the channel of distribution should be periodically reviewed to determine whether some alternative channel is more feasible. The promotion strategy may be revised in response to changes in the target market, pricing, phase of the life cycle, or the channel of distribution.

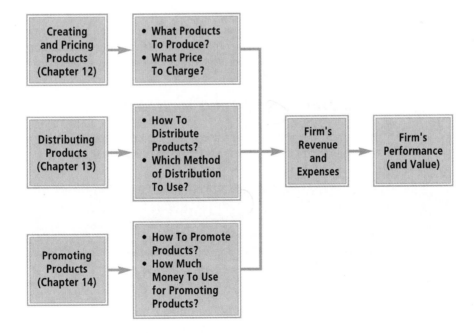

DEVELOPING THE MARKETING PLAN FOR CAMPUS.COM

Product Line and Target Market (related to Chapter 12)

In your business plan for Campus.com, suggest how the firm could expand its product line. That is, what other services could it offer to its customers while still continuing its main type of business? How could it expand its target market?

Pricing (related to Chapter 12)

Campus.com will charge a price per standard service offered (information on one college). What factors should be considered when determining the price to be charged? The initial idea was to charge $1 per request (for information about one college provided to one customer). In your business plan for Campus.com, state your plans for pricing the service. You do not need to use the pricing of $1 per request if you think you have a better pricing policy. If you plan to offer some type of quantity discount, specify that within your business plan.

Distribution (related to Chapter 13)

In your business plan, explain how Campus.com distributes its service. If some customers cannot obtain a hard copy of the information (if their printer is not working), how will Campus.com distribute its services to them?

Promotion (related to Chapter 14)

In your business plan for Campus.com, explain how the firm should advertise its services. Should it focus on high school students, on the parents of the high school students, or on both target markets? Explain. Where should Campus.com advertise its services, assuming it wants to limit its advertising expenditures?

Communication and Teamwork

You (or your team) may be asked by your instructor to hand in and/or present the part of your business plan that relates to this part of the text.

Integrative Video Case: Target Marketing (Zubi Advertising)

Founded in 1973 by a Cuban immigrant, Zubi Advertising is located in Miami, with satellite offices, Los Angeles, Chicago, Huston, Detroit, and New York. The company has 70 employees who are focusing almost entirely on the Hispanic target market. With about $80 million in billings, Zubi's clientele includes blue chip firms like American Airlines and Ford. Zubi views its focus on the Hispanic target market as "erasing stereotypes."

Questions

1 Explain how the focus on a target market can affect the production process.

2 What do you think is Zubi's key marketing decision? Is it about the creation of a product, the distribution of a product, the promotion of a product, or all of the above? Explain.

3 How do you think Zubi prices its ads? How do you think that relates to its promotional strategy of targeting Hispanics?

Integrative Video Case: Product and Distribution Strategies (NoUVIR)

NoUVIR is a small company located in Delaware. With nine employees and $1 million in sales, the company has redefined the standard of lighting. Specifically, using fiberoptic technology, NoUVIR takes ultraviolet and infrared light out of light, which results in light that is gentler on artwork and fabrics. The company's owners recognize the importance of patents to protect their technology. Also, in order to solicit sales, NoUVIR conducts frequent seminars across the country.

Questions

1 Explain how NoUVIR's number of patents can affect its production decisions.

2 What do you think is NoUVIR's key marketing decision? Is it about the creation of a product, the distribution of a product, the promotion of a product, or all of the above? Explain.

3 Discuss the patents NoUVIR has. Why does it have multiple patents? How do you think these patents affect the company's profitability?

THE STOCK MARKET GAME

Go to **http://finance.yahoo.com.** and check your portfolio balance, which is updated continuously by Yahoo! Finance.

Check Your Stock Portfolio Performance

1 What is the value of your stock portfolio today?

2 What is your return on your investment?

3 How did your return compare to those of other students? (This comparison tells you whether your stock portfolio's performance is relatively high or low.)

Explaining Your Stock Performance

Stock prices are frequently influenced by changes in the firm's marketing strategies, including new products, pricing, or promotion strategies. A stock's price may increase if such marketing strategies are instituted and investors expect the changes to improve the performance of the firm. A stock's price can also decline if the marketing strategies are expected to reduce the firm's performance. Review the latest news about some of your stocks on the Yahoo! Finance website.

1 Identify one of your stocks whose price was affected (since you purchased it) as a result of changes in the firm's marketing strategies (the main topic in this part of the text).

2 Identify the specific type of marketing policies that caused the stock price to change.

3 Did the stock price increase or decrease in response to the announcement of new marketing policies?

RUNNING YOUR OWN BUSINESS

1 Describe in detail how the product you plan to produce is different from those offered by competitors. Identify any advantages of your product over those of the competition.

2 Explain how the pricing of your product will be determined. Explain how your product's price will compare with prices of competing products.

3 Can the unique features of your product be protected from competitors?

4 Describe how your business will distribute the product to customers.

5 Explain whether the cost of distributing your product will be affected substantially if there is a large increase in the price of gasoline or in postal rates.

6 Describe how your business will promote its product. Will it use the Internet? Will it use media to advertise? If so, how?

7 Estimate the amount of money that will be allocated for promotion during the first year.

8 Would coupons or rebates be an effective promotion method for your product? Why or why not?

9 How could your firm use public relations to promote your company or product?

10 How could your firm use the Internet (or other technology) to promote your company or product?

YOUR CAREER IN BUSINESS: PURSUING A MAJOR AND A CAREER IN MARKETING

If you are very interested in the topics covered in this section, you may want to consider a major in marketing. Some of the more common courses taken by marketing majors are summarized here.

Common Courses for Marketing Majors

▶ *Advertising*—Focuses on methods of promoting products, alternative types of advertising, the use of the media for advertising, and the role of advertising agencies.

▶ *Marketing Environment*—Discusses the impact of social, technological, and other environmental conditions on marketing decisions and looks at how marketing decisions have changed in response to changes in the marketing environment.

▶ *Distribution Systems*—Examines the role of inventory maintenance for distribution, channels of distribution, and transportation methods used for distribution.

▶ *Promotional Management*—Examines how consumers make purchasing decisions, what factors drive their decisions, and how firms can capitalize on this information.

▶ *Marketing Research*—Focuses on methods of assessing consumer purchases and the effects of marketing strategies; discusses gathering data, analysis, and deriving implications from the analysis.

▶ *Marketing Strategy*—Explains how marketing concepts can be applied to solve marketing problems and make marketing decisions.

▶ *Services Marketing*—Describes the application of marketing strategy to services.

▶ *Marketing Planning*—Focuses on the process of developing a marketing plan, including the creation of a product, the identification of a target market, and the creation of a structure for distribution and promotion.

▶ *Psychology courses*—Specifically, those courses that explain human behavior as related to consumption, preferences, and needs.

Careers in Marketing

Information about job positions, salaries, and careers for students who major in marketing can be found at the following websites:

▶ Job position websites:

http://jobsearch.monster.com	Advertising, marketing, public relations, retail, wholesale, sales, transportation, warehousing
http://careers.yahoo.com	Advertising, public relations, marketing, retail, transportation, logistics

▶ Salary website:

http://collegejournal.com/ salarydata	Advertising, marketing, public relations, food processing, retailing, sales

Part VI

Financial Management

F inancial management involves the analysis of financial data, as well as the determination of how to obtain and use funds. Chapter 15 explains how a financial analysis of a firm can be conducted to determine how it is performing, and why. This type of analysis is used to detect a firm's deficiencies so that they can be corrected.

Finance is the means by which firms obtain funds (financing) and invest funds in business projects. Firms may obtain funds to build a new factory, purchase new machinery, purchase more supplies, or even purchase an existing business owned by another company.

Chapter 16 describes the common financing methods that firms use and also identifies the types of financial institutions that provide financing. It also explains the factors that influence the ideal type of financing. Chapter 17 describes the tasks that are necessary when a firm determines whether to invest in a particular business project. In addition, it explains why firms sometimes use their funds to acquire other firms. The chapters on financing and business investment are closely related because financing supports the firm's investment in new business projects.

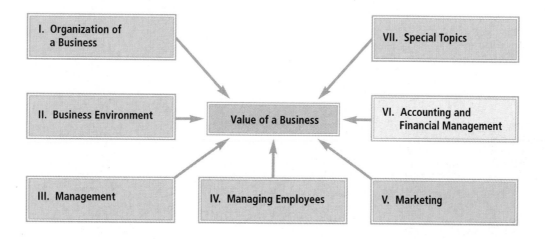

All businesses, including Showcase Cinemas, can use accounting and financial statements to assess their recent performance and present financial condition.

The Learning Goals of this chapter are to:

1 Explain how firms use accounting.

2 Explain how to interpret financial statements.

3 Explain how to evaluate a firm's financial condition.

Chapter 15

Accounting and Financial Analysis

Accounting is the summary and analysis of a firm's financial condition. The accounting process generates financial statements, which provide detailed information about a firm's recent performance and its financial condition. Managers of all types of firms use financial statements to assess their performance and to make business decisions. Consider the situation of Showcase Cinemas, which operates a number of movie theaters and is considering opening a new theater. Showcase needs to know how its existing theaters are performing and whether its financial condition is adequate to support the cost of building a new theater in the near future. In this case, Showcase Cinemas must decide:

▶ How can it measure its recent performance?

▶ How can it measure its present financial condition?

Showcase Cinemas can assess its financial statements to determine how its revenue, expenses, and earnings changed in response to specific strategies that it used in the past. Its financial statements allow Showcase to monitor the recent performance of its theaters so that it can detect any weakness in time to revise its strategies. Showcase can also ensure that its present financial condition is strong enough to allow for expansion.

The types of decisions described above are necessary for all businesses. This chapter explains how the accounting and financial analysis functions described here can be used by Showcase Cinemas or by any other firm in a manner that maximizes its value.

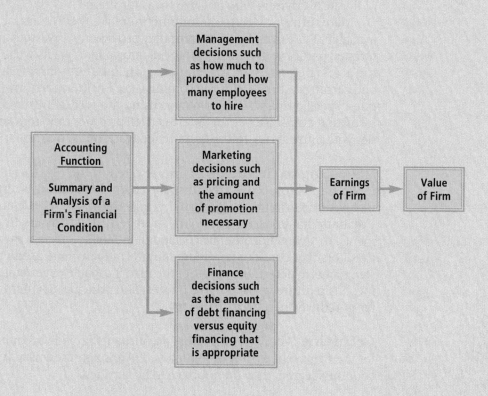

1
Explain how firms use
accounting.

accounting the summary and analysis of a firm's financial condition

bookkeeping the recording of a firm's financial transactions

financial accounting accounting performed for reporting purposes

How Firms Use Accounting

Firms use **accounting** to report their financial condition, support decisions, and control business operations, as explained in this order next.

Reporting

One accounting task is to report accurate financial data. **Bookkeeping** is the recording of a firm's financial transactions. For example, the recording of daily or weekly revenue and expenses is part of the bookkeeping process.

Firms are required to periodically report their revenue, expenses, and earnings to the Internal Revenue Service (IRS) so that their taxes can be determined. The type of accounting performed for reporting purposes is called **financial accounting.**

Financial accounting must be conducted in accordance with generally accepted accounting principles (GAAP) that explain how financial information should be reported. The Financial Accounting Standards Board (FASB), Securities and Exchange Commission (SEC), and IRS establish the accounting guidelines. The use of a common set of guidelines allows for more consistency in reporting practices among firms. Consequently, a comparison of financial statements between two or more different firms may be more meaningful.

Reporting to Shareholders   Publicly owned firms are required to periodically report their financial condition for existing or potential shareholders. Shareholders assess financial statements to evaluate the performance of firms in which they invested. If the analysis indicates that the firm has performed poorly, existing shareholders may attempt to replace the board of directors or sell their stock. Some shareholders do not take the time to analyze the firms in which they invest. Instead, they rely on the advice of financial advisers who analyze firms for them.

Many firms are using the Internet to make their financial information available. For example, Dell Computer provides its investors and other interested parties with detailed financial information via its website. Investors can access Dell's most recent annual report, quarterly "financial fact sheets," and earnings estimates for the coming year. Furthermore, investors can request specific financial information using the website. By making this information available over the Internet, Dell provides investors and other parties with current, up-to-the-minute feedback on its financial performance.

Reporting to Creditors   Firms also report their financial condition to existing and prospective creditors. The creditors assess firms' financial statements to determine the probability that the firms will default on loans. Creditors that consider providing short-term loans assess financial statements to determine the firm's liquidity (ability to sell existing assets). Creditors that consider providing long-term loans may assess the financial statements to determine whether the firm is capable of generating sufficient income in future years to make interest and principal payments on the loan far into the future.

Certifying Accuracy   Private accountants provide accounting services for the firms where they are employed. Although they usually have an accounting degree, they do not have to be certified.

A financial analysis of a firm is conducted to determine how it is performing.

© Getty Images / EyeWire

public accountants accountants who provide accounting services for a variety of firms for a fee

certified public accountants (CPAs) accountants who meet specific educational requirements and pass a national examination

Public accountants provide accounting services for a variety of firms for a fee. A license is required to practice public accounting. Accountants who meet specific educational requirements and pass a national examination are referred to as **certified public accountants (CPAs).**

A common job for a public accountant is auditing to ensure that the firm's financial statements are accurate. All publicly owned firms must have their financial statements audited by an independent accounting firm. When public accountants audit a firm, they examine its financial statements for accuracy. A public accountant's stamp of approval does not imply anything about a firm's performance, only that the information contained within the financial statements is accurate.

College Health Club: Reporting Performance at CHC

As Sue Kramer develops her business plan for College Health Club (CHC), she considers how she can monitor the club's performance. She will use accounting to report CHC's revenue, expenses, and earnings to the IRS. She will also give this information to Diane Burke (who has loaned funds to Sue) to show her how CHC is performing. If Sue decides to obtain a bank loan in the future, she knows that the bank will ask to see CHC's financial statements. In addition, Sue will use the statements to assess how CHC's revenue, expenses, and earnings are changing over time. Such a review will allow her to determine why CHC's performance is changing.

Decision Support

Firms use financial information developed by accountants to support decisions. For example, a firm's financial managers may use historical revenue and cost information for budgeting decisions. The marketing managers use sales information to evaluate the impact of a particular promotion strategy. The production managers use seasonal sales information to determine the necessary production level in the future. The type of accounting performed to provide information to help managers make decisions is referred to as

e-business

Financial Disclosure   This website illustrates the types of financial information that businesses disclose and explains how to retrieve the information.

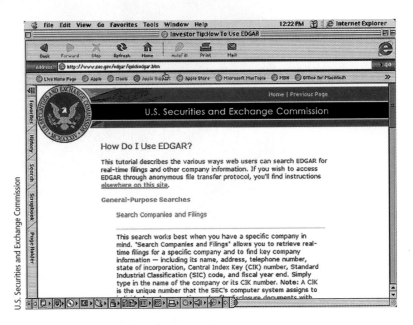

U.S. Securities and Exchange Commission

http://www.sec.gov/edgar/
quickedgar.htm

managerial accounting accounting performed to provide information to help managers of the firm make decisions

managerial accounting. Financial accounting also reports information, but to shareholders and the IRS (outside the firm). To provide a complete set of information, the information generated by managerial accounting can be included with other information (such as industry characteristics).

Control

In addition to providing information to support decisions, managerial accounting helps managers maintain control. By reviewing financial information, managers monitor the performance of individuals, divisions, and products. Accounting information on sales is used to monitor the performance of various products and the salespeople who sell them. Information on operating expenses is used to monitor production efficiency.

Managers evaluate their firm's financial statements to monitor operations and to identify the firm's strengths and weaknesses. Financial statements can be generated and analyzed as frequently as necessary to identify problems and resolve them quickly before they become serious.

Another accounting task used for control is **auditing,** which is an assessment of the records that were used to prepare the firm's financial statements. **Internal auditors** specialize in evaluating various divisions within a firm to ensure that they are operating efficiently.

auditing an assessment of the records that were used to prepare a firm's financial statements

internal auditors specialize in evaluating various divisions of a business to ensure that they are operating efficiently

2

Explain how to interpret financial statements.

INTERPRETING FINANCIAL STATEMENTS

The purpose of financial statements is to inform interested parties about the operations and financial condition of a firm. The most important financial statements are the income statement and the balance sheet. The

Vermont State Auditor of Accounts, Elizabeth Read, meets with analysts in her office. Financial management involves the analysis of financial data, as well as the determination of how to obtain and use funds.

income statement indicates the revenue, costs, and earnings of a firm over a period of time

balance sheet reports the book value of all assets, liabilities, and owner's equity of a firm at a given point in time

income statement indicates the firm's revenue, costs, and earnings over a period of time (such as a quarter or year), and the **balance sheet** reports the book value of all the firm's assets, liabilities, and owner's equity at a given point in time.

It is possible for a firm to show high earnings on its income statement while being financially weak according to its balance sheet. It is also possible for a firm to show low earnings or even losses on its income statement while being financially strong according to its balance sheet. Because the two statements reveal different financial characteristics, both financial statements must be analyzed along with other information to perform a complete evaluation.

Understanding the information reported on income statements and balance sheets is a necessary part of financial analysis. These financial statements are explained briefly next.

Income Statement

net sales total sales adjusted for any discounts

cost of goods sold the cost of materials used to produce the goods that were sold

gross profit net sales minus the cost of goods sold

operating expenses composed of selling expenses and general and administrative expenses

earnings before interest and taxes (EBIT) gross profit minus operating expenses

earnings before taxes earnings before interest and taxes minus interest expenses

net income (earnings after taxes) earnings before taxes minus taxes

The annual income statement for Taylor, Inc., a manufacturing firm, is presented in Exhibit 15.1. The income statement items shown in Exhibit 15.1 are disclosed in the income statements of most manufacturing firms. **Net sales** reflect the total sales adjusted for any discounts. **Cost of goods sold** is the cost of the materials used to produce the goods that were sold. For example, the cost of steel used to produce automobiles is part of the cost of goods sold for Ford Motor Company. **Gross profit** is equal to net sales minus the cost of goods sold. Thus, gross profit measures the degree to which the revenue from selling products exceeded the cost of the materials used to produce them.

Operating expenses are composed of selling expenses and general and administrative expenses. For example, the cost of labor and utilities and advertising expenses at Ford Motor Company are part of operating expenses. Gross profit minus a firm's operating expenses equals **earnings before interest and taxes (EBIT).** Earnings before interest and taxes minus interest expenses equals **earnings before taxes.** Finally, earnings before taxes minus taxes equals **net income** (sometimes referred to as **earnings after taxes**).

Net Sales		$20,000,000
Cost of Goods Sold		16,000,000
Gross Profit		$4,000,000
Selling Expense	$1,500,000	
General & Administrative Expenses	1,000,000	
Total Operating Expenses		2,500,000
Earnings before Interest and Taxes (EBIT)		$1,500,000
Interest Expense		500,000
Earnings before Taxes		$1,000,000
Income Taxes (at 30%)		300,000
Net Income		$700,000

Net Sales		100.0%
Cost of Goods Sold		80.0%
Gross Profit		20.0%
Selling Expense	7.5%	
General & Administrative Expenses	5.0%	
Total Operating Expenses		12.5%
Earnings before Interest and Taxes (EBIT)		7.5%
Interest Expense		2.5%
Earnings before Taxes		5.0%
Income Taxes (at 30%)		1.5%
Net Income		3.5%

Firms commonly measure each income statement item as a percentage of total sales, as illustrated in Exhibit 15.2 for Taylor, Inc. The exhibit shows how each dollar of sales is used to cover various expenses that were incurred to generate the sales. Notice that 80 cents of every dollar of sales is used to cover the cost of the goods sold, while 12.5 cents of every dollar of sales is needed to cover operating expenses; 2.5 cents of every dollar of sales is needed to cover interest expense, and 1.5 cents of every dollar of sales is needed to pay taxes. That leaves 3.5 cents of every dollar of sales as net income. This breakdown for a firm can be compared with other firms in the industry. Based on this information, the firm may notice that it is using too much of its revenue to cover the cost of goods sold (relative to other firms in the industry). Therefore, it may search for ways to reduce the cost of producing its goods.

Balance Sheet

asset anything owned by a firm

liability anything owed by a firm

Anything owned by a firm is an **asset**. Anything owed by a firm is a **liability.** Firms normally support a portion of their assets with funds of the owners, called "owner's equity" (also called "stockholder's equity"). The remaining portion is supported with borrowed funds, which creates a liability. This relationship is described by the following **basic accounting equation:**

$$\text{Assets} = \text{Liabilities} + \text{Owner's Equity}$$

For example, consider a person who purchases a car repair shop for $200,000. Assume that the person uses $40,000 of savings for the purchase and borrows the remaining $160,000 from a local bank. The accounting statement for this business will show assets of $200,000, liabilities of $160,000, and owner's equity of $40,000. As the business acquires equipment and machinery, its total asset value will increase. The funds used to purchase more assets will be obtained through either additional borrowing or additional support from the owner. Any increase in assets will therefore be matched by an equal increase in liabilities and owner's equity.

The balance sheet for Taylor, Inc., as of the end of the year, is shown in Exhibit 15.3. The assets listed on a balance sheet are separated into current assets and fixed assets. **Current assets** are assets that will be converted into cash within one year. They include cash, marketable securities, accounts receivable, and inventories. Cash typically represents checking account

Exhibit 15.3

Example of Balance Sheet for Taylor, Inc.

Taylor, Inc.	
Assets	
Current Assets:	
Cash	$200,000
Marketable Securities	300,000
Accounts Receivable	500,000
Inventory	1,000,000
Total Current Assets	$2,000,000
Fixed Assets:	
Plant and Equipment	$10,000,000
Less: Accumulated Depreciation	2,000,000
Net Fixed Assets	$8,000,000
Total Assets	$10,000,000
Liabilities & Owner's Equity	
Current Liabilities:	
Accounts Payable	$600,000
Notes Payable	400,000
Total Current Liabilities	$1,000,000
Long-Term Debt	$5,000,000
Owner's Equity:	
Common Stock ($5 par value, 200,000 shares)	$1,000,000
Additional Paid-In Capital	2,000,000
Retained Earnings	1,000,000
Total Owner's Equity	$4,000,000
Total Liabilities and Owner's Equity	$10,000,000

balances. Marketable securities are short-term securities that can easily be sold and quickly converted to cash if additional funds are needed. Marketable securities earn interest for the firm until they are sold or redeemed at maturity. Accounts receivable reflect sales that have been made for which payment has not yet been received. Inventories are composed of raw materials, partially completed products, and finished products that have not yet been sold.

fixed assets assets that will be used by a firm for more than one year

Fixed assets are assets that the firm will use for more than one year. They include the firm's plant and equipment. In Exhibit 15.3, depreciation is subtracted from plant and equipment to arrive at net fixed assets. **Depreciation** represents a reduction in the value of fixed assets to reflect deterioration in the assets over time. Specific accounting rules are used to measure the depreciation of fixed assets.

depreciation a reduction in the value of fixed assets to reflect deterioration in the assets over time

accounts payable money owed by a firm for the purchase of materials

Liabilities and owner's equity are also shown in Exhibit 15.3. Current (short-term) liabilities include accounts payable and notes payable. **Accounts payable** represent money owed by the firm for the purchase of materials. **Notes payable** represent short-term loans to the firm made by creditors such as banks. Long-term liabilities (debt) are liabilities that will not be repaid within one year. These liabilities commonly include long-term loans provided by banks and the issuance of bonds.

notes payable short-term loans to a firm made by creditors such as banks

owner's equity includes the par (or stated) value of all common stock issued, additional paid-in capital, and retained earnings

Owner's equity includes the par (or stated) value of all common stock issued, additional paid-in capital, and retained earnings. Additional paid-in capital represents the dollar amount received from issuing common stock that exceeds par value. Retained earnings represent the accumulation of the firm's earnings that are reinvested in the firm's assets rather than distributed as dividends to shareholders.

A firm can use its balance sheet to determine the percentage of its investment in each type of asset. An example is provided in Exhibit 15.4. Notice that 80 percent of the firm's assets are allocated to net fixed assets. Most manufacturing firms allocate a large portion of their funds to net fixed assets because these are the assets used in the production process.

Exhibit 15.4

Breakdown of Balance Sheet for Taylor, Inc.

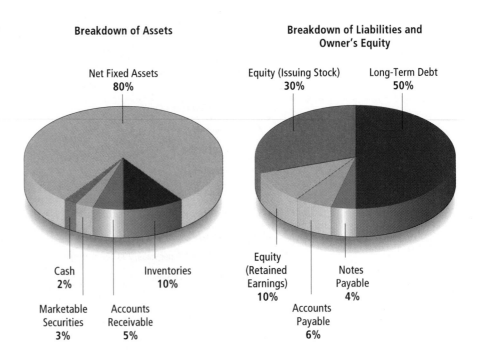

Breakdown of Assets

Net Fixed Assets 80%

Cash 2%

Marketable Securities 3%

Accounts Receivable 5%

Inventories 10%

Breakdown of Liabilities and Owner's Equity

Equity (Issuing Stock) 30%

Long-Term Debt 50%

Equity (Retained Earnings) 10%

Accounts Payable 6%

Notes Payable 4%

The liabilities and owner's equity can also be broken down to determine where the firm is obtaining most of its financial support. Notice that the firm obtained 50 percent of its funds by issuing long-term debt and another 30 percent from issuing stock. Retained earnings made up 10 percent of the firm's funds.

RESPONSIBLE FINANCIAL REPORTING

Firms have some flexibility when accounting for their financial condition. Some firms tend to use whatever method of accounting will inflate their earnings because they know that their stockholders will be better satisfied if earnings are high. Moreover, some of a firm's top managers who hold stock of the firm may want a favorable financial report to ensure that the stock value stays high until they sell their stock holdings. Enron, Inc., used accounting gimmicks to inflate its revenue and its earnings until 2001 when investors finally realized that the financial statements were distorted. Enron filed for bankruptcy in November 2001. WorldCom used accounting gimmicks to reduce its expenses. In June 2002, it admitted that its expenses over the previous five quarters were underestimated by $3.9 billion. In July 2002, it went bankrupt.

A firm should use whatever method of accounting provides the most accurate indication of its financial condition. By doing so, the firm may benefit in two ways. First, it may gain some credibility with existing and prospective stockholders by providing clear and consistent reports that are easily understood. Second, using an understandable and logical accounting method makes it easier for the firm's managers to detect and correct deficiencies.

The Role of Auditors in Ensuring Proper Reporting

Publicly traded firms are required to have their annual financial reports audited by an independent auditor. The auditor's role is to certify that the financial reports are accurate and within the generally accepted reporting guidelines. Nevertheless, some auditors have certified financial reports that were misleading. Perhaps the best-known example was the audit of Enron by the accounting firm Arthur Andersen in the year 2000. Andersen certified some of Enron's financial reports that were very questionable. Auditors are sometimes tempted to certify financial reports because they want to be hired by the firm again in the future. In 2000, Arthur Andersen earned more than $50 million in fees for its auditing and other work provided to Enron. The auditors knew that if they did not certify the financial reports, Enron would hire another accounting firm instead. This ethical dilemma does not absolve Arthur Andersen from blame, but it does explain why auditors sometimes certify financial reports that should not be certified. Arthur Andersen was also the auditor of WorldCom during the period when WorldCom's expenses were underestimated.

Given the conflict of interest that may arise, auditors cannot always be trusted to ensure that a firm properly reports financial information to its stockholders. The publicity surrounding the demise of Enron and WorldCom has caused investors to be more cautious when interpreting financial statements. Some firms have responded by disclosing more details about their financial condition to demonstrate that they have nothing to hide.

The Role of the Board of Directors in Ensuring Proper Reporting

Since a firm's board of directors represents the shareholders, it can try to prevent the firm from providing misleading financial reports. However, some boards do not effectively represent the stockholders. For example, a problem may arise when board members are compensated with the firm's stock, just like the firm's top managers. Thus, they too might benefit from misleading financial reporting that artificially inflates the stock's price because they could sell their shares while the stock is priced artificially high. The board members may be more willing to enforce proper disclosure if they cannot sell any of their stock holdings while serving on the board. If forced to hold on to their shares for a long-term period, directors may be more likely to make decisions that benefit the long-term performance of the firm.

3

Explain how to evaluate a firm's financial condition.

ratio analysis an evaluation of the relationships between financial statement variables

RATIO ANALYSIS

A firm's financial managers can use the financial statements to assess the financial condition of the firm. An important part of this assessment is **ratio analysis,** an evaluation of the relationships between financial statement variables. Firms can assess their financial characteristics by comparing their financial ratios with those of other firms in the same industry. In this way, they can determine how their financial condition differs from that of other firms that conduct the same type of business.

Firms can also assess the ratios over time to determine whether financial characteristics are improving or deteriorating. The industry average serves as a benchmark for what would be considered normal for the firm. Differences from the norm can be favorable or unfavorable, depending upon the size and direction of the difference.

Financial ratios are commonly classified according to the characteristics they measure. These include the following:

▶ Measures of liquidity
▶ Measures of efficiency
▶ Measures of financial leverage
▶ Measures of profitability

The ratios that are used to assess each of these characteristics are defined and discussed next. Each ratio is computed for Taylor, Inc., based on its financial statements in Exhibits 15.1 and 15.3.

Chairman of ExxonMobil, Lee Raymond, speaks to reporters and analysts at the company's headquarters. He declared the company's financial reports to be free and clear of obscure dealings that caused energy trader Enron to collapse.

AP Photo/Michael Stravato

increasing value with technology

HOW SOFTWARE HAS EASED ACCOUNTING FUNCTIONS

Large companies have used complex computer systems to handle their accounting transactions for many years. Now smaller companies have begun to use computer-based accounting as well. These systems ease the process of gathering and summarizing data for financial reporting and tax purposes.

Accounting software designed for small businesses offers online banking, bill paying, time-billing, integration with other popular software packages, and other cost-saving incentives. Another reason to upgrade an accounting system is to accommodate customers who prefer e-bills (bills sent via e-mail). Finally, accounting software ensures that financial practices are kept in line with government regulations. All of the accounting programs follow generally accepted accounting principles (GAAP).

The accounting programs all contain a general ledger, accounts payable, accounts receivable, inventory, and pay-roll. Repetitive actions are greatly reduced by creating organized databases of business contacts and products. This allows information to be accessed quickly when transactions are entered. For example, once a sale has been completed, an invoice can be created by selecting the customer and product sold from a list. The customer information, payment terms, appropriate sales tax, and product cost are immediately included on the invoice. These software programs also have the ability to produce business reports. They can sift through large quantities of data to produce customized reports about almost anything in the business. Cost breakdowns, inventory carrying time and costs, delinquent payments, and outstanding payables are among the reports that can be produced. Such reports would be much more costly to create without software programs.

Measures of Liquidity

liquidity a firm's ability to meet short-term obligations

Liquidity refers to a firm's ability to meet short-term obligations. Since short-term assets are commonly used to pay short-term obligations (which are current liabilities), most liquidity measures compare current assets with current liabilities. The greater the level of current assets available relative to current liabilities, the greater the firm's liquidity.

A high degree of liquidity can enhance the firm's safety, but an excessive degree of liquidity can reduce the firm's return. For example, holding an excessive amount of cash is a waste and can reduce a firm's returns. Firms that have excessive cash, marketable securities, accounts receivable, and inventories could have invested more funds in assets such as machinery or buildings (fixed assets) that are used for production. Firms attempt to maintain sufficient liquidity to be safe, but not excessive liquidity. Two common liquidity measures are identified next.

Current Ratio   The current ratio compares current assets with current liabilities in ratio form. It is defined as:

$$\text{Current Ratio} = \frac{\text{Current Assets}}{\text{Current Liabilities}}$$

For Taylor:

$$\text{Current Ratio} = \frac{\$2,000,000}{\$1,000,000}$$

$$= 2.00$$

For most manufacturing firms, the current ratio is between 1.0 and 1.5. For Taylor, current assets are twice the amount of its current liabilities. A more detailed comparison of Taylor's liquidity and other financial ratios to the industry norms is conducted later in this chapter after all financial ratios have been discussed.

Quick Ratio The quick ratio requires a slight adjustment in the current ratio. Inventory may not be easily converted into cash and therefore may be excluded when assessing liquidity. To get a more conservative indication of a firm's liquidity, the quick ratio does not include inventory in the numerator:

$$\text{Quick Ratio} = \frac{\text{Cash} + \text{Marketable Securities} + \text{Accounts Receivable}}{\text{Current Liabilities}}$$

For Taylor:

$$\text{Quick Ratio} = \frac{\$1,000,000}{\$1,000,000}$$

$$= 1.00$$

Since the quick ratio does not include inventory in the numerator, it is smaller than the current ratio for any firm that has some inventory. The larger the firm's quick ratio, the greater its liquidity.

Measures of Efficiency

Efficiency ratios measure how efficiently a firm manages its assets. Two of the more popular efficiency ratios are described next.

Inventory Turnover Firms prefer to generate a high level of sales with a low investment in inventory because fewer funds are tied up. However, very low levels of inventory can also be unfavorable because they can result in shortages, which can reduce sales. To assess the relationship between a firm's inventory level and sales, the inventory turnover ratio can be used:

$$\text{Inventory Turnover} = \frac{\text{Cost of Goods Sold}}{\text{Inventory}}$$

For Taylor:

$$\text{Inventory Turnover} = \frac{\$16,000,000}{\$1,000,000}$$

$$= 16.00$$

This ratio suggests that Taylor turns its inventory over 16 times during the year. The cost of goods sold is used instead of sales in the numerator to exclude the markup that is reflected in sales.

The average inventory over the period of concern should be used in the denominator when it is available, since inventory can change substantially during that period. When the average inventory is not available, the year-end inventory is used.

Asset Turnover   Firms prefer to support a high level of sales with a relatively small amount of assets so that they efficiently utilize the assets they invest in. Firms that maintain excess assets are not investing their funds wisely. To measure the efficiency with which firms use their assets, the asset turnover ratio can be calculated. It is defined and computed for Taylor as follows:

$$\text{Asset Turnover} = \frac{\text{Net Sales}}{\text{Total Assets}}$$

$$= \frac{\$20,000,000}{\$10,000,000}$$

$$= 2.00$$

Taylor's sales during the year were two times the level of its total assets. Like all other financial ratios, the asset turnover should be evaluated over time and in comparison with the industry norm.

Measures of Financial Leverage

Financial leverage represents the degree to which a firm uses borrowed funds to finance its assets. Firms that borrow a large proportion of their funds have a high degree of financial leverage. This can favorably affect the firm's owners when the firm performs well, because the earnings generated by the firm can be spread among a relatively small group of owners. When the firm experiences poor performance, however, a high degree of financial leverage is dangerous. Firms with a high degree of financial leverage incur higher fixed financial costs (interest expenses) that must be paid regardless of their levels of sales. These firms are more likely to experience debt repayment problems and therefore are perceived as having more risk. Conversely, firms that obtain a larger proportion of funds from equity financing incur smaller debt payments and therefore have less risk.

Although a high proportion of equity financing reduces risk, it may also force earnings to be widely distributed among many shareholders. Firms that rely heavily on equity typically have a large number of shareholders who share the firm's earnings. This may dilute the earnings that are distributed to each shareholder as dividends.

debt-to-equity ratio a measure of the amount of long-term financing provided by debt relative to equity

Debt-to-Equity Ratio   A measure of the amount of long-term financing provided by debt relative to equity is called the **debt-to-equity ratio.** This ratio is defined and computed for Taylor as follows:

$$\text{Debt-to-Equity Ratio} = \frac{\text{Long-Term Debt}}{\text{Owner's Equity}}$$

$$= \frac{\$5,000,000}{\$4,000,000}$$

$$= 1.25$$

For Taylor, long-term debt is 1.25 times the amount of owner's equity.

times interest earned ratio measures the ability of a firm to cover its interest payments

Times Interest Earned   The **times interest earned ratio** measures a firm's ability to cover its interest payments. If a firm has a low level of earnings before interest and taxes (EBIT) relative to the size of its interest expense, a small decrease in EBIT in the future could force the firm to default on the loan. Conversely, a high level of EBIT relative to the annual interest expense suggests that even if next year's EBIT declines substantially, the firm will still be able to cover the interest expense. The times interest earned ratio is defined and computed for Taylor as follows:

$$\text{Times Interest Earned} = \frac{\text{Earnings before Interest and Taxes (EBIT)}}{\text{Annual Interest Expense}}$$

$$= \frac{\$1,500,000}{\$500,000}$$

$$= 3.0$$

A times interest earned ratio of 3.0 indicates that Taylor's earnings before interest and taxes were three times its interest expense.

Measures of Profitability

Profitability measures indicate the performance of a firm's operations during a given period. The dollar amount of profit generated by the firm can be measured relative to the firm's level of sales, assets, or equity. The ratios that measure these relationships are discussed next.

net profit margin a measure of net income as a percentage of sales

Net Profit Margin   The **net profit margin** is a measure of net income as a percentage of sales. This ratio measures the proportion of every dollar of sales that ultimately becomes net income. The net profit margin is computed for Taylor as follows:

$$\text{Net Profit Margin} = \frac{\text{Net Income}}{\text{Net Sales}}$$

$$= \frac{\$700,000}{\$20,000,000}$$

$$= 3.50\%$$

Even with a low profit margin, firms with a high volume of sales can generate a reasonable return for their shareholders. However, firms with a low volume of sales may need a higher profit margin to generate a reasonable return for their shareholders.

return on assets (ROA) measures a firm's net income as a percentage of the total amount of assets utilized by the firm

Return on Assets   A firm's **return on assets (ROA)** measures the return (net income) of the firm as a percentage of the total amount of assets utilized by the firm. It is defined and computed for Taylor as follows:

$$\text{Return on Assets} = \frac{\text{Net Income}}{\text{Total Assets}}$$

$$= \frac{\$700,000}{\$10,000,000}$$

$$= 7.00\%$$

The ROA provides a broad measure of a firm's performance. The higher the ROA, the more efficiently the firm utilized its assets to generate net income.

Return on Equity

The **return on equity (ROE)** measures the return to the common stockholders as a percentage of their investment in the firm. Existing and potential investors monitor this ratio closely because it indicates the recent return on the investment of the existing shareholders. The ROE measures the firm's performance from using the equity provided. The return on equity is defined and computed for Taylor as follows:

$$\text{Return on Equity} = \frac{\text{Net Income}}{\text{Owner's Equity}}$$

$$= \frac{\$700,000}{\$4,000,000}$$

$$= 17.50\%$$

Stockholders prefer ROE to be very high because a high ROE indicates a high return relative to the size of their investment. Using high levels of financial leverage can increase ROE (because less equity is used) so that the net income is distributed among fewer shareholders, but high levels of financial leverage increase the firm's exposure to risk.

Comparison of Ratios with Those of Other Firms

Exhibit 15.5 provides the common interpretations for ratios that deviate substantially from what is normal in the industry. Note, however, that there may be a perfectly acceptable reason why a ratio deviates from the norm. For example, consider a firm that has an abnormally large amount of cash according to a comparison with the industry average. Common stockholders may interpret this as evidence of inefficient use of assets. However,

Exhibit 15.5

Interpretation of Financial Ratios That Differ from the Industry Norm

Ratios	Common Interpretation If Ratio Is Significantly Lower than Normal	Common Interpretation If Ratio Is Significantly Higher than Normal
Liquidity Ratios		
Current ratio	Insufficient liquidity	Excessive liquidity
Quick ratio	Insufficient liquidity	Excessive liquidity
Efficiency Ratios		
Inventory turnover	Excessive inventory	Insufficient inventory
Asset turnover	Excessive level of assets relative to sales	Insufficient assets based on existing sales
Leverage Ratios		
Debt-to-equity ratio	Low level of long-term debt	Excessive long-term debt
Times interest earned	Potential cash flow problems because required interest payments are high relative to the earnings available to pay interest	The firm can easily make its debt payments.
Profitability Ratios		
Net profit margin	Expenses are high relative to sales.	Expenses are low relative to sales.
Return on assets	Net income is low relative to the amount of assets maintained by the firm.	Net income is high relative to the amount of assets maintained by the firm.
Return on equity	Net income is low relative to the amount of equity invested in the firm.	Net income is high relative to the amount of equity invested in the firm.

Exhibit 15.6

Evaluation of Taylor, Inc., Based on Ratio Analysis

Ratio	Calculation	Ratio for Taylor	Average for Industry	Evaluation of Taylor Based on the Ratio
Liquidity				
Current	$\dfrac{\text{Current Assets}}{\text{Current Liabilities}}$	2.00	1.60	Too high
Quick	$\dfrac{\text{Cash + Marketable Securities + Accts. Receivable}}{\text{Current Liabilities}}$	1.00	0.90	Too high
Efficiency				
Inventory Turnover	$\dfrac{\text{Cost of Goods Sold}}{\text{Inventory}}$	16.00	16.22	OK, unless shortages are occurring
Asset Turnover	$\dfrac{\text{Net Sales}}{\text{Total Assets}}$	2.00	4.11	Too low
Financial Leverage				
Debt-to-Equity Ratio	$\dfrac{\text{Long-Term Debt}}{\text{Owner's Equity}}$	1.25	0.60	Too high
Times Interest Earned	$\dfrac{\text{Earnings before Interest and Taxes}}{\text{Annual Interest Expense}}$	3.0	7.4	Too low
Profitability				
Net Profit Margin	$\dfrac{\text{Net Income}}{\text{Net Sales}}$	3.5%	4.00%	Too low
Return on Assets	$\dfrac{\text{Net Income}}{\text{Total Assets}}$	7.00%	16.44%	Too low
Return on Equity	$\dfrac{\text{Net Income}}{\text{Owner's Equity}}$	17.50%	26.30%	Too low

further investigation may reveal that the firm has built up its cash because it plans to purchase machinery in the near future. Financial analysis based on an assessment of financial ratios does not necessarily lead to immediate conclusions, but it does lead to questions about a firm that deserve further investigation.

Exhibit 15.6 provides a general summary of the financial ratios commonly used for ratio analysis. Comparing a firm's ratios with an industry average can help identify the firm's strengths and weaknesses. Columns 1 and 2 of Exhibit 15.6 identify and define the financial ratios presented in this chapter. Column 3 lists Taylor's ratios, and the industry averages are provided in column 4. Column 5 uses the information in columns 3 and 4 to provide an evaluation of Taylor's ratios relative to those of the industry average.

In terms of liquidity, Taylor's current and quick ratios are above the industry average. This suggests that although Taylor probably has sufficient liquidity, it may have an excessive amount of current assets.

Taylor's inventory turnover ratio is similar to the industry average. This suggests that Taylor maintains the normal amount of inventory.

Taylor's asset turnover ratio is below the industry average. This suggests that Taylor is not using all of its assets efficiently. That is, it has an excessive investment in assets, given the level of sales. Taylor might consider either taking steps to increase sales (which would force more production from its assets) or selling some of its assets.

Exhibit 15.7

Example of How Management, Marketing, and Finance Deficiencies Can Be Detected with Ratio Analysis

Management Decisions

One of a firm's relevant management decisions is the production process used to produce products. An efficient production process can result in a relatively higher amount of production and sales with a given level of assets. The asset turnover ratio is an indicator of the efficiency of production because it measures the level of sales generated with a given level of assets. Taylor has a low asset turnover ratio, implying an inefficient use of assets.

Marketing Decisions

Since Taylor's asset turnover ratio is low, it should either eliminate those assets that are not efficiently utilized or maintain its assets but produce and sell a higher volume of products. If it decides to maintain its assets and increase production, it will need effective marketing strategies to sell the extra amount of products produced. Thus, proper marketing strategies may help Taylor to improve its asset turnover ratio.

Finance Decisions

Taylor's debt-to-equity ratio is higher than the norm, which reflects its high degree of financial leverage. Its high proportion of debt financing may make it difficult for Taylor to cover its interest payments. Taylor may use more equity financing in the future, but this will reduce its return on equity. Given its poor utilization of assets, Taylor might consider selling some of its assets and using the proceeds to reduce its debt level. This would allow for a more acceptable degree of financial leverage.

With regard to financial leverage, the debt-to-equity ratio is higher than the industry average. This suggests that Taylor has a relatively high proportion of long-term financing provided by debt relative to equity. The times interest earned ratio for Taylor is lower than the industry norm. Other firms of the same size and in the same industry have lower interest expenses (because they use a lower proportion of debt financing). Since Taylor already has a relatively high proportion of debt, it may be less able to borrow additional funds.

Regarding profitability, Taylor's net profit margin is lower than the industry norm, which suggests that Taylor is not generating adequate net income based on its level of sales. Also, its return on assets is too low, which is partially attributed to its inefficient use of assets. Since Taylor is not using its assets efficiently to generate sufficient sales, they cannot generate a sufficient amount of net income.

Taylor's ROE is too low, which means that it is not generating an adequate net income, given the size of the equity investment in the firm. If Taylor could more efficiently utilize its assets, it could increase its net income and therefore increase its ROE.

Exhibit 15.7 illustrates how the financial analysis identifies different business functions that may need improvement. Taylor's management, marketing, and finance functions may need to be reassessed to improve its performance. In general, management strategies may be revised to improve production efficiency, marketing strategies may be revised to increase sales, and financing strategies may be revised to establish a more appropriate degree of financial leverage.

Limitations of Ratio Analysis

Ratio analysis is useful for detecting a firm's strengths and weaknesses. Nevertheless, it has some limitations, which can result in misleading conclusions. The major limitations of ratio analysis are as follows:

1 Comparing some firms with an industry average can be difficult because the firms operate in more than one industry. Consider a firm that produces gas grills, machinery, and aluminum panels. The firm's ratios may deviate from a specific industry norm as a result of the characteristics of the other industries in which the firm operates. Also, the industry used as a benchmark for comparison may include firms that are involved in a variety of other businesses. This distorts the average ratios for the industry.

2 Accounting practices vary among firms. A firm's financial ratios can deviate from the norm because of differences in accounting methods rather than differences in operations. For example, one firm may have used an accounting method that inflates its revenue or defers the reporting of some expenses until the following quarter. Consequently, this quarter's earnings will be inflated, and ratios such as ROA or ROE will be inflated. The firm's performance is essentially exaggerated in the quarter because of the accounting method used. Investors may overvalue a firm when its reported earnings are inflated.

3 Firms with seasonal swings in sales may show large deviations from the norm at certain times but not at others. Normally, however, the seasonal swings should not distort annual financial statements.

Sources of Information for Ratio Analysis

To help perform ratio analysis, industry data can be obtained from a variety of sources. The following are two of the more common sources:

▶ *Robert Morris Associates* The booklet *Annual Statement Studies,* published by Robert Morris Associates, provides financial ratios for many different industries. Ratios for firms of various sizes are included so that a firm's ratios can be compared with those of similar-sized firms in the same industry.

▶ *Dun and Bradstreet* Dun and Bradstreet provides financial ratios for industries and for groups of firms within industries classified by size.

College Health Club: Financial Condition of CHC

Sue Kramer is conducting a financial analysis of College Health Club (CHC), which she will open soon. Her analysis raises two concerns. First, her expenses may exceed her income for several months, which will result in a loss (negative profits) over that period. Sue realizes, however, that as CHC's memberships increase, its revenue will increase. In addition, many of CHC's expenses are fixed and should not change significantly. Thus, CHC's revenue should exceed its expenses once the memberships increase.

Sue is also concerned that CHC's financial leverage (based on the debt-to-equity ratio) is high. Since Sue is investing $20,000 of her own money (equity) and is borrowing an additional $40,000 (debt), CHC's initial debt-to-equity ratio is 2.0, indicating that its debt is twice its equity. Since Sue plans to reinvest any profits back into the business, CHC's equity will increase over time as profits accumulate. By increasing the equity over time without borrowing additional funds, she will be able to reduce CHC's degree of financial leverage.

Overall, Sue's financial analysis helps her realize that her concerns about CHC's profitability and its financial leverage should be alleviated over time. If CHC's memberships increase as expected, its profitability and financial leverage ratios will improve.

Effect of Exchange Rate Movements on Earnings A U.S. firm that has subsidiaries (including offices and factories) in foreign countries typically generates earnings in the local currencies of the countries where those subsidiaries are located. Any firm with foreign subsidiaries must consolidate the financial data from all subsidiaries when preparing its financial statements. Because of the consolidation process, changes in exchange rates can have an impact on the firm's reported earnings, as illustrated next.

Consider a U.S. firm that has a subsidiary in the United Kingdom that generated £10 million in earnings last year. Also assume that the firm's U.S. operations generated $12 million in earnings. The firm must consolidate the £10 million with the $12 million when preparing its income statement. The £10 million cannot simply be added to the $12 million because the British and U.S. currencies have different values. Therefore, the British earnings must be "translated" by determining the dollar amount of those earnings. The average exchange rate of the currency of concern over the period in which income was generated is used to translate the foreign earnings. For example, if the average exchange rate of the British pound during the last year was $2.00, the British earnings would be converted into $20 million (computed as £10 million × $2.00 per pound). In this case, the firm would report total earnings of $32 million (computed as $20 million translated from the British subsidiary plus the $12 million of earnings generated in the United States).

To recognize how the firm's reported earnings are affected by the exchange rate, assume that the average exchange rate during the last year was $1.70 per pound instead of $2.00 per pound. Based on this assumption, the British earnings are translated into $17 million (£10 million × $1.70 per pound). Thus, the British earnings are translated into a smaller amount of dollar earnings. The firm's consolidated earnings in this example are $29 million (computed as $17 million from the British operations plus $12 million from the U.S. operations), which is $3 million less than in the first example. This illustrates how the reported amount of earnings is affected by the average exchange rate over the period of concern.

If the foreign currency has a high value over the period of concern, the foreign earnings will be translated into a higher amount of dollar earnings reported on the income statement. Many U.S. firms with foreign subsidiaries may report unusually high earnings when the values of foreign currencies are high in that period (when the dollar is weak). Under these conditions, the foreign earnings are translated into a large amount of dollar earnings on the income statement. If the values of foreign currencies decline over a particular year (when the dollar strengthens), the foreign earnings will translate into a smaller amount of dollar earnings, which will reduce the level of consolidated earnings reported on the firm's income statement.

SUMMARY

1 A firm's financial condition is important to financial managers as well as to the creditors and stockholders of the firm. Financial managers evaluate the firm to detect weaknesses that can be corrected and strengths that can be exploited. Creditors evaluate the firm with a view toward determining creditworthiness, and stockholders evaluate the firm's performance to determine whether they should buy or sell the firm's stock.

2 The key financial statements necessary to perform a thorough evaluation are the income statement and balance sheet. The income statement reports costs, revenue, and earnings over a specified period. The balance sheet reports the book value of assets, liabilities, and owner's equity at a given point in time.

3 Most financial ratios help evaluate one of four characteristics: liquidity, efficiency, financial leverage, and profitability. The liquidity ratios measure a firm's ability to meet its short-term obligations. Efficiency ratios measure how efficiently a firm utilizes its assets. Financial leverage ratios measure the firm's relative use of debt financing versus equity financing and indicate the firm's ability to repay its debt. Profitability ratios measure the firm's net income relative to various size levels. In evaluating a firm's financial ratios, it is useful to compare them with an industry norm. This approach can help detect any deficiencies that exist so that corrective action can be taken. Furthermore, it provides useful input for implementing new policies.

KEY TERMS

accounting 482
accounts payable 488
asset 486
auditing 484
balance sheet 485
basic accounting equation 487
bookkeeping 482
certified public accountants
  (CPAs) 483
cost of goods sold 485
current assets 487
debt-to-equity ratio 493

depreciation 488
earnings before interest and taxes
  (EBIT) 485
earnings before taxes 485
financial accounting 482
fixed assets 488
gross profit 485
income statement 485
internal auditors 484
liability 486
liquidity 491
managerial accounting 484

net income 485
net profit margin 494
net sales 485
notes payable 488
operating expenses 485
owner's equity 488
public accountants 483
ratio analysis 490
return on assets (ROA) 494
return on equity (ROE) 495
times interest earned ratio 493

Review & Critical Thinking Questions

1. What is accounting? Why is accounting important for a firm?

2. List the parties that would be interested in a firm's financial condition. How would each use financial information about the firm?

3. What is a public accountant? What is his most common job?

4. What is the difference between a balance sheet and an income statement?

5. What is the difference between current assets and fixed assets?

Provide examples of each type of asset.

6. Discuss how assets can be financed by a firm.

7. Why is responsible financial reporting important?

8. What is the role of the board of directors of a firm to ensure proper financial reporting? If board members are being compensated with shares of the firm's stock, how could they be forced to act in the long-term interests of the company?

9. Discuss the pros and cons of financial leverage for a firm.

10. Why is profitability relevant for a firm? How can profitability be measured?

11. What are the limitations of ratio analysis?

12. Discuss the effect of exchange rates on the earnings of a foreign subsidiary whose parent corporation is located in the United States.

Discussion Questions

1. Discuss the concept of short-term financing for short-term assets and long-term financing for long-term assets.

2. How can a firm use the Internet to provide information about its financial performance?

3. Indicate the ratio that measures each of the following and classify it as a measure of liquidity, efficiency, financial leverage, or profitability: (a) the return of profits to owners, (b) the amount of debt financing rela-

tive to the owner's investment, and (c) the ratio of the firm's short-term assets to its short-term liabilities.

4. Discuss the difference between gross profit and earnings before interest and taxes.

5. Assume that you are planning to invest in a corporation. Before you do this, however, you would like to examine its financial statements. Which statements would you want to review and why?

6. You are ready to invest in a company, primarily because the financial statements of the firm have recently been audited by a reputable accounting firm. Those statements show that the company had a very strong financial performance recently. Why might you conduct some additional research before investing in this firm?

It's Your Decision: **Financial Management at CHC**

1. Explain why the current ratio is important to CHC.
2. Explain how CHC's financial leverage can be measured. If the leverage is too high, what is the danger to CHC?
3. Explain how Sue Kramer can monitor CHC's performance by comparing its net income to the amount of equity invested in CHC.
4. If Sue decides to expand CHC's existing facilities, explain why its earnings may be lower initially.
5. A health club differs from manufacturing firms in that it produces a service rather than products. Manufacturing firms tend to require more machinery than service firms. Explain why manufacturing firms may need more financing than service firms.

Investing in a Business

Using the annual report of the firm in which you would like to invest, complete the following:

1 Review the income statement and balance sheet in the firm's annual report. Determine the return on equity that the firm generated last year for its investors. Do you believe that this return is satisfactory? What was the firm's return on equity in the previous year? Did the firm's performance improve last year?

2 Use the balance sheet to determine the firm's liquidity ratio as of the end of last year. Interpret that ratio.

3 Use the balance sheet to determine the firm's debt-to-equity ratio. Interpret that ratio.

4 Explain how the business uses technology to publicize its financial performance. For example, does it use the Internet to provide information about its financial performance? Does it provide information regarding the methods used to assess its financial performance and to improve it in the future?

5 Go to **http://hoovers.com** and locate the NEWS SEARCH. Type in the name of the firm in the space provided, and review the recent news stories about the firm. Summarize any (at least one) recent news story about the firm that applies to one or more of the key concepts in this chapter.

Case: Using an Accounting System

Sue Williams is an artist who creates drawings that are purchased by individuals. She displays her drawings at various art fairs, where she has obtained many orders. She has also received many referrals from her previous customers, and her business continues to grow. Sue maintains her own financial records, which include a separate checking account for the business and two notebooks.

In one notebook, Sue records her sales. When she sells a drawing to a customer, Sue records the date, amount, customer name, and a brief description of the drawing.

In the second notebook, Sue enters similar information for each purchase of art supplies that she makes. She is planning to meet with her accountant and is not

sure if she has all the accounting data regarding the transactions of her business.

Questions

1 If Sue wants to assess her firm's performance, what type of firms should she use for purposes of comparison?

2 Explain how the two notebooks that Sue uses could be used to develop an income statement.

3 Sue notices that her asset turnover is low. Interpret this situation.

4 How will a low asset turnover ratio affect the profits at Sue's firm?

5 Considering this is a sole proprietorship without shareholders, do you think responsible financial reporting still applies to Sue's business? Why or why not?

Video Case: Accounting Information System at Weathervane

Weathervane Terrace Inn and Suites owns a condominium complex. The owners of the units in the complex rent them out part of the year. Weathervane manages the rentals of these units. The owners receive a portion of the rental fee. Given numerous units and a large number of owners who rent out their units over time, Weathervane must keep organized records so that it can report how much rental income was received and whether any expenses were incurred in repairing the units. It has created a computerized accounting system that accumulates all the information for each unit separately. Thus, Weathervane has a clear record of income and expenses for each unit and sends the owner of each unit a

summary statement at the end of each month. The system provides organized financial information not only to the owners of the units, but also to the owners of Weathervane.

Questions

1 How does Weathervane's accounting information system serve the task of reporting?

2 How does Weathervane's accounting information system serve the task of control?

3 Explain how Weathervane's accounting information system coud be used to determine whether Weathervane should expand by building an additional complex of condominium units.

Internet Applications

1. **http://www.marriott.com/corporateinfo**

Look at Marriott's most recent annual report and briefly summarize its financial performance this year.

    a. Compute some ratios as part of this process. Has Marriott's financial performance improved or deteriorated?

    b. Look at the financial performance of another hotel franchise. How has Marriott performed relative to other firms in the industry?

    c. What other financial highlights on a website such as this would be useful for analyzing a company?

2. **http://finance.yahoo.com**

Click on "Financials" under "Stock Research." What financial statements are available on this website? Could this information be used to conduct ratio analysis? In what other ways does this website benefit investors? For example, could investors use this website to determine whether a firm is using responsible financial reporting practices?

3. **http://www.finweb.com/finweb.html**

What is the purpose of FINWeb? Click on "FreeEdgar" and obtain financial information for a company that recently filed financial statements with the SEC. How has this company performed? Assess the liquidity, efficiency, financial leverage, and profitability of this firm.

The Coca-Cola Company Annual Report Project

Questions for the current year's annual report are available on the text website at **http://madura.swlearning.com.**

The following questions apply concepts presented in this chapter to The Coca-Cola Company. Go to The Coca-Cola Company website (**http://www.cocacola.com**) and find the index for the 2001 annual report.

Questions

1 Click on "Financial Highlights." Examine the dividends paid by The Coca-Cola Company to shareholders during the last year. What was the total amount of dividends paid last year? Did the amount of dividend payments grow during the year?

2 Download the financial statements and find "Financial Strategies." What was The Coca-Cola Company's most recent dividend payout ratio? Why does the company plan on reducing the dividend payout ratio over time?

3 Click on "Financial Highlights." What was The Coca-Cola Company's return on common equity in 2000 and 2001?

4 Download the financial statements and find "Liquidity and Capital Resources." What is The Coca-Cola Company's primary source of short-term financing?

5 Study the "Financials Section." Compute the asset turnover for 2000 and 2001. What was the percentage change in this ratio from 2000 to 2001?

In-Text Study Guide

Answers are in an appendix at the back of the book.

True or False

1. Accounting is the summary and analysis of a firm's financial condition. T

2. Financial accounting is primarily used to help managers make decisions. F

3. Bookkeeping is the recording of a firm's financial transactions. T

4. An accountant working for Microsoft, a publicly owned corporation, is an example of a public accountant. F

5. The two primary financial statements for a firm are the balance sheet and the bookkeeping statement. F

6. Inventory and accounts receivables are shown as fixed assets on a firm's financial statements. F

7. A balance sheet reports the book value of a firm's assets, liabilities, and owner's equity. T

8. Firms are encouraged to design their financial accounting reports to best satisfy their managers' need for information. F

9. Independent auditors are sometimes tempted to certify questionable financial reports because the auditors usually sit on the board of directors of the firm. F

10. The debt-to-asset ratio measures the liquidity of a firm. F

11. Financial leverage represents the degree to which a firm uses borrowed funds to finance its assets. T

Multiple Choice

12. Publicly owned firms are required to periodically report their financial condition for existing or potential:
    a) suppliers.
    b) customers.
    c) employees.
    d) shareholders.
    e) unions.

13. The type of accounting performed for reporting purposes is referred to as:
    a) ratio analysis.
    b) financial accounting.
    c) managerial accounting.
    d) cost accounting.
    e) payroll accounting.

14. Which of the following groups are primarily concerned with the risk of default on a loan?
    a) owners
    b) certified public accountants
    c) creditors
    d) auditors
    e) stockholders

15. Firms use financial information developed by accountants to:
    a) support financial data.
    b) analyze job descriptions.
    c) support decisions.
    d) prepare job specifications.
    e) analyze working conditions.

16. Individuals who provide accounting services to a variety of firms for a fee are:
    a) master accountants.
    b) managerial accountants.
    c) internal auditors.
    d) corporate controllers.
    e) public accountants.

17. The type of accounting performed to provide information to help managers of the firm make decisions is referred to as:
    a) certified public accounting.
    b) external auditing.
    c) public accounting.
    d) government accounting.
    e) managerial accounting.

18. Which of the following financial statements summarizes a firm's revenues, costs, and earnings for a specific period of time?
    a) balance sheet
    b) income statement
    c) cash budget
    d) retained earnings statement
    e) sources and uses of funds statement

In-Text Study Guide

19. The statement that reports the book value of all assets, liabilities, and owner's equity of firms at a given point in time is the:
    a) income statement.
    b) cash budget.
    c) profit and loss statement.
    d) revenue statement.
    e) balance sheet.

20. A firm's operating expenses are subtracted from gross profit to determine its:
    a) net sales.
    b) cost of goods sold.
    c) profit or loss.
    d) balance sheet.
    e) earnings before interest and taxes (EBIT).

21. The value of materials used in the production of goods that are then sold is called:
    a) net sales.
    b) cost of goods sold.
    c) sales return and allowances.
    d) gross profit.
    e) net income.

22. Which of the following represents funds provided by the owners of a business?
    a) revenue
    b) cost of goods sold
    c) gross profit
    d) net income
    e) owner's equity

23. The firm's assets are financed with its:
    a) cost of goods sold.
    b) earnings before interest and taxes.
    c) liabilities and owner's equity.
    d) plant and equipment.
    e) net sales.

24. If a firm has $1,000 in assets and $300 in liabilities, the owner's equity must be:
    a) $700.
    b) $333.

    c) $1,300.
    d) $3,000.
    e) $0.30.

25. Assets that will be converted into cash within one year are:
    a) fixed assets.
    b) current assets.
    c) plant and equipment.
    d) owner's equity.
    e) liabilities.

26. A reduction in the value of the assets to reflect deterioration in assets over time is:
    a) cost of goods sold.
    b) gross profit.
    c) sales revenue.
    d) depreciation.
    e) owner's equity.

27. In order to encourage board members to enforce proper financial disclosures:
    a) all board members should be certified public accountants or financial analysts.
    b) all board members should be outside members.
    c) board members should not be allowed to own the firm's stock.
    d) all board members should be officers of the corporation.
    e) board members should not be able to sell the firm's stock while serving on the board.

28. An evaluation of the relationship between financial statement variables is called:
    a) ratio analysis.
    b) asset turnover.
    c) cost of goods sold.
    d) operating expenses.
    e) gross profit.

29. All of the following are characteristics commonly used to classify financial ratios except for:
    a) revenue.
    b) liquidity.
    c) efficiency.
    d) leverage.
    e) profitability.

All businesses, including Cincinnati Tattoo Company, must decide how they are going to obtain sufficient funds to support their expansion.

business decisions

The Learning Goals of this chapter are to:

1 Identify the common methods of debt financing for firms.

2 Identify the common methods of equity financing for firms.

3 Explain how firms issue securities to obtain funds.

4 Describe how firms determine the composition of their financing.

Chapter 16

In-Text Study Guide

Answers are in an appendix at the back of the book.

30. Which of the following categories of financial ratios measures how well management uses its assets to generate sales?
    a) liquidity
    b) profitability
    c) efficiency
    d) financial leverage
    e) sales leverage

31. Long-term borrowing undertaken by a firm can be assessed through:
    a) liquidity ratios.
    b) profitability ratios.
    c) current ratios.
    d) efficiency ratios.
    e) leverage ratios.

32. A ratio that measures net income as a percentage of sales is the:
    a) net profit margin.
    b) leverage ratio.
    c) liquidity ratio.
    d) activity ratio.
    e) asset turnover.

    $$\frac{net\ income}{OE} = ROE$$

    $$\frac{net\ income}{assets}$$

33. A ratio that measures the firm's dollar amount of profit relative to sales, assets, or equity is a(n):
    a) current ratio.
    b) liquidity ratio.
    c) profitability ratio.
    d) activity ratio.
    e) leverage ratio.

34. All of the following are limitations of ratio analysis except:
    a) the identification of a comparable firm.
    b) the firm operates in more than one industry.
    c) accounting practices may vary between firms.
    d) firms are too much alike.
    e) firms may have large seasonal swings in sales.

35. Any firm with foreign subsidiaries must consolidate the financial data from all subsidiaries when preparing its:
    a) mission statement.
    b) foreign exchange.
    c) balance of payment.
    d) financial statements.
    e) domestic policy.

36. A U.S. firm will report the earnings of its foreign subsidiaries in:
    a) the currencies of the countries where the subsidiaries exist.
    b) U.S. dollars.
    c) units of the product sold.
    d) the consolidated balance sheet of the firm.
    e) the annual liquidity report.

Financing

16

Firms obtain capital (long-term funds) in the form of debt or equity. With debt financing, the firm borrows funds. With equity financing, the firm receives investment from owners (by issuing stock or retaining earnings). The manner in which a firm decides to finance its business can affect its financing costs and thus can affect its value. Consider the situation of the Cincinnati Tattoo Company, which is planning to expand. Before undertaking the expansion, Cincinnati Tattoo will address the following questions:

▶ What are some common methods of debt financing that it could use to finance its expansion?

▶ What are some common methods of equity financing that it could use to finance its expansion?

▶ How could it issue securities to obtain funds?

▶ What is the optimal composition of the financing for its expansion?

The debt-financing decisions made by Cincinnati Tattoo or by any other business are relevant because they affect the firm's interest expenses. Equity financing decisions determine the number of owners and therefore determine how the earnings will be spread among owners. The decision to issue securities will affect the amount of funds that a business can attract and therefore the degree to which it can grow. The decision about the composition of financing will affect the firm's financing costs and its degree of risk.

The types of decisions described here are necessary for all businesses. This chapter explains how Cincinnati Tattoo Company or any other firm can make financing decisions in a manner that maximizes its value.

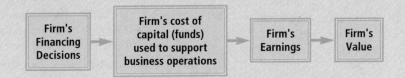

METHODS OF DEBT FINANCING

1 Identify the common methods of debt financing for firms.

capital long-term funds

debt financing the act of borrowing funds

Firms borrow funds to invest in assets such as buildings, machinery, and equipment. Those firms that invest in more assets typically need to borrow more funds. Service firms spend more money on employees and less on machinery and factories. Thus, they may not need to borrow as much because they do not have to purchase machinery for production purposes. In contrast, industrial firms tend to have large investments in assets such as buildings and machinery and therefore need to obtain more **capital.** The common methods of **debt financing** are described next.

Metsing Malebo sits on the pavement outside his London Pie Co. shop in Johannesburg, South Africa. Malebo and his two partners struggled for a year to find start-up funds. In the end, they turned to a franchiser who helped them get a loan and find rental space for their fast food business.

AP Photo/ Adil Bradlow

Borrowing from Financial Institutions

As a common method of debt financing, firms obtain loans from financial institutions. When a firm applies for a loan, it must present a detailed financial plan that includes specific projections of future revenue and expenses. The plan should demonstrate how the firm will generate sufficient revenue over time to repay the loan.

Many loans are for three years or longer. Lenders assess the credit-worthiness of a firm according to several factors, including (1) the firm's planned use of the borrowed funds, (2) the financial condition of the firm's business, (3) the outlook for the industry or environment surrounding the firm's business, and (4) available collateral of the business that can be used to back the loan. Because the lender must assess the financial condition of any business to which it lends, it requires financial statements. The lender will assess the financial statements to determine whether the firm will be able to repay its loan on schedule.

If the lender determines that the firm is creditworthy, it will attempt to establish terms of the loan that are acceptable to the firm. The terms of the loan specify the amount to be borrowed, the maturity, the collateral, and the rate of interest on the loan.

Pledging Collateral   Firms that need to borrow may be asked to pledge a portion of their assets as collateral to back the loan. Lenders are more comfortable providing loans when the loans are backed by collateral. A common form of collateral is the asset for which the borrowed funds will be used. For example, a firm that is borrowing funds to purchase a machine may offer that machine as collateral. If the lender expects that it could sell the machine for 70 percent of its existing value, the lender may finance 70 percent of the purchase and require the machine to be used as collateral. If the firm defaults on the loan, the lender can sell the machine for an amount that covers the loan.

A firm may also pledge its accounts receivable (payments owed to the firm for previous sales of products) as collateral. If the firm defaults on the loan, the lender takes control of the accounts receivable. To ensure that the accounts receivable collateral sufficiently covers the loan balance, the lender will provide a loan amount that is just a fraction (say, 65 percent) of the required collateral. Thus, even if some customers never pay off

business online

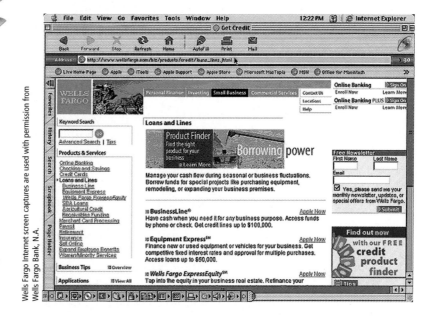

Business Financing This website provides guidance for pursuing a business loan.

e-business

http://www.wellsfargo.com/
biz/products/credit/
loans_lines.html

Wells Fargo Internet screen captures are used with permission from Wells Fargo Bank, N.A.

their accounts receivable, the collateral may still cover the full amount of the loan.

Setting the Loan Rate   When setting the loan rate, banks determine the average rate of interest that they pay on their deposits (which represents their cost of funds) and add on a premium. Since deposit rates change over time in response to general interest rate movements, loan rates change as well.

The premium is dependent on the credit risk of the loan or the probability of default. If the firm appears to be in good financial condition and the collateral covers the loan amount, the premium may be about 4 percentage points. For example, if the lender's cost of funds is 6 percent, the loan rate may be 10 percent. If the borrowing firm is perceived to have more credit risk, however, the premium may be more than 4 percentage points. The rate of interest typically charged on loans to the most creditworthy firms that borrow is called the **prime rate.**

prime rate the rate of interest typically charged on loans to the most creditworthy firms that borrow

Fixed-Rate versus Floating-Rate Loans   When firms need funds, they must choose between a fixed-rate loan and a floating-rate loan. Most commercial loans charge floating interest rates that move in tandem with market interest rates. Consider a firm that can obtain a five-year floating-rate loan with an interest rate that is adjusted by the bank once a year according to changes in the prime rate. Assume that the initial loan rate of interest is 8 percent (based on the prevailing prime rate) and will be adjusted once a year. Alternatively, the firm can obtain a fixed-rate loan of 10 percent. Which loan is preferable? The answer depends on future interest rate movements, which are uncertain. Firms that expect interest rates to

Exhibit 16.1

Interest Rate Charged on Loans under
Three Different Scenarios

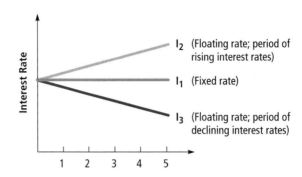

rise consistently over the five-year period will prefer a fixed-rate loan so that they can avoid the upward adjustments on a floating-rate loan. Firms that expect interest rates to decline or remain stable over the five-year period will prefer a floating-rate loan.

Exhibit 16.1 shows the interest rates that would be charged under three different scenarios. If the firm has a fixed-rate loan, the interest rate charged on its loan is I_1, regardless of how market interest rates move over time. If the firm has a floating-rate loan, the interest rate charged on its loan will be I_2 if market interest rates increase over time, or I_3 if market interest rates decrease over time. Rising interest rates adversely affect firms that obtain floating-rate loans because the interest rate on their loans will increase.

The interest rate charged on a new loan is based on the general level of interest rates at that time. The top part of Exhibit 16.2 shows how the prime rate has changed over time. The lower part of the exhibit shows the interest expense that a firm would have incurred if it was charged the prime rate on a $1 million loan at that time.

Issuing Bonds

bonds long-term debt securities (IOUs) purchased by investors

Large firms may obtain funds by issuing **bonds,** which are long-term debt securities (IOUs) purchased by investors. Some large firms prefer to issue bonds rather than obtain loans from financial institutions because the interest rate may be lower. Bondholders are creditors, not owners, of the firm that issued the bonds.

Small firms that are not well known are unable to issue bonds. Even if they could issue their own bonds, a bond issuance typically raises more funds than a small firm would need.

par value the amount that bond-holders receive at maturity

The **par value** of a bond is the amount that the bondholders receive at maturity. Most bonds have a maturity of between 10 and 30 years. The coupon (interest) payments paid per year are determined by applying the so-called coupon rate to the par value. If the coupon rate is 10 percent, the coupon payments paid per year will be $100 for every $1,000 of par value. The coupon payments are normally paid semiannually and are fixed over the life of the bond. The coupon rate of bonds is influenced by the general level of interest rates at the time the bonds are issued. Firms typically prefer to issue bonds at a time when interest rates are relatively low. By doing so, they can lock in a relatively low coupon rate over the life of the bond. Forecasting interest rates is difficult, however, so firms cannot easily time a bond issue to take place when interest rates have hit their bottom. Also, firms that need funds immediately cannot wait until interest rates are at a more desirable level.

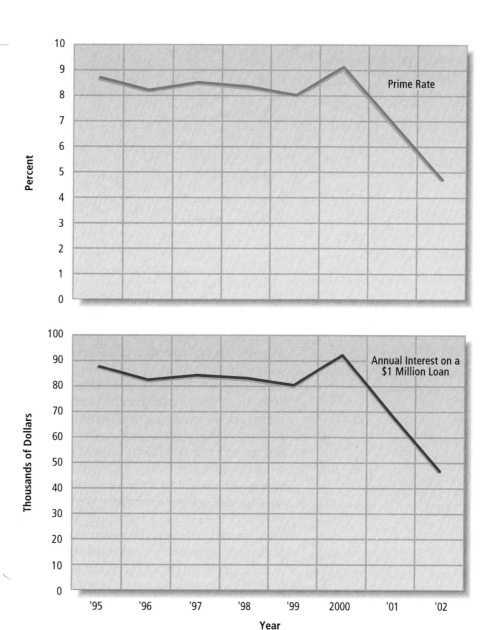

Exhibit 16.2

Effect of Interest Rates on Interest
Expenses Incurred by Firms

indenture a legal document that
explains the firm's obligations to
bondholders

secured bonds bonds backed by
collateral

unsecured bonds bonds that are
not backed by collateral

call feature provides the right for
the issuing firm to repurchase its
bonds before maturity

When a firm plans to issue bonds, it creates an **indenture,** which is a legal
document that explains its obligations to bondholders. For example, the indenture will state what collateral (if any) is backing the bonds. **Secured bonds**
are backed by collateral, whereas **unsecured bonds** are not backed by collateral. The indenture also states whether the bonds have a **call feature,** which
provides the right for the issuing firm to repurchase the bonds before maturity. To recognize the benefits of a call feature, consider a firm that issued
bonds when interest rates were very high. If interest rates decline a few years
later, the firm could issue new bonds at the lower interest rate and use the
proceeds to repay the old bonds. Thus, the call feature gives the firm the flexibility to replace old bonds with new bonds that have a lower interest rate.
Bonds that have a call feature typically need to pay a higher rate of interest.

Default Risk of Bonds The interest rate paid on bonds is influenced
not only by prevailing interest rates but also by the issuing firm's risk level.
Firms that have more risk of default must provide higher interest to bondholders to compensate for the risk involved. Rating agencies such as

Exhibit 16.3

Summary of Risk Ratings Assigned by
Bond Rating Agencies

	Rating Assigned by:	
	Moody's	Standard & Poor's
Highest quality	Aaa	AAA
High quality	Aa	AA
High-medium quality	A	A
Medium quality	Baa	BBB
Medium-low quality	Ba	BB
Low quality (speculative)	B	B
Poor quality	Caa	CCC
Very poor quality	Ca	CC
Lowest quality (in default)	C	DDD,D

Moody's Investor Service and Standard & Poor's Corporation rate the bonds according to their quality (safety). The rating agencies assign ratings after evaluating the financial condition of each firm. They closely assess the amount of debt that a firm has and the firm's ability to cover interest payments on its existing debt. Firms are periodically reevaluated since their ability to repay debt can change in response to economic or industry conditions, or even conditions unique to the firm.

Exhibit 16.3 provides a summary of the different ratings that can be assigned. Although each rating agency uses its own criteria for rating bonds, most bonds are rated within a similar risk level by the agencies. Investors may prefer to rely on the rating agencies rather than develop their own evaluations of the firms that issue bonds. At a given point in time, firms with higher ratings will be able to issue bonds with lower interest rates.

If a firm's financial condition weakens, the rating agencies may lower their ratings on the bonds it has issued. As a firm's bond ratings decline, it is less able to issue new bonds because investors will be concerned about the lower rating (higher risk).

protective covenants restrictions imposed on specific financial policies of a firm

Bondholders may attempt to limit the risk of default by enforcing **protective covenants,** which are restrictions imposed on specific financial policies of the firm. The purpose of these covenants is to ensure that managers do not make decisions that could increase the firm's risk and therefore increase the probability of default. For example, some protective covenants may restrict the firm from borrowing beyond some specified debt limit until the existing bonds are paid off.

Issuing Commercial Paper

commercial paper a short-term debt security normally issued by firms in good financial condition

Many firms also issue **commercial paper,** which is a short-term debt security normally issued by firms in good financial condition. Its normal maturity is between three and six months. Thus, the issuance of commercial paper is an alternative to obtaining loans directly from financial institutions. The minimum denomination of commercial paper is usually $100,000. Typically, denominations are in multiples of $1 million. Various financial institutions commonly purchase commercial paper. The interest rate on commercial paper is influenced by the general market interest rates at the time of issuance.

Impact of the Debt Financing Level on Interest Expenses

To illustrate how the level of debt financing (whether by borrowing from financial institutions or by issuing IOUs) affects interest expenses, consider a firm that borrows $1 million for a five-year period at an interest rate of 9 percent. This firm will pay $90,000 in interest in each of the next five years (computed as $1,000,000 × 9%). Thus, the firm will need sufficient revenue to cover not only its operating expenses (such as salaries) but also its interest expenses. If the firm had borrowed $2 million, it would have to pay $180,000 in annual interest (computed as $2,000,000 × 9%). When firms borrow money excessively, they have large annual interest payments that are difficult to cover. For this reason, the firms have a higher probability of defaulting on the loans than they would if they had borrowed less funds.

Common Creditors That Provide Debt Financing

Various types of creditors can provide debt financing to firms. **Commercial banks** obtain deposits from individuals and use the funds primarily to provide business loans. **Savings institutions** (also called "thrift institutions") also obtain deposits from individuals and use some of the deposited funds to provide business loans. Although savings institutions lend most of their funds to individuals who need mortgage loans, they have increased their amount of business loans in recent years.

Finance companies typically obtain funds by issuing debt securities (IOUs) and lend most of their funds to firms. In general, finance companies tend to focus on loans to less established firms that have a higher risk of loan default. The finance companies charge a higher rate of interest on these loans to compensate for the higher degree of risk.

Pension funds receive employee and firm contributions toward pensions and invest the proceeds for the employees until the funds are needed. They commonly invest part of their funds in bonds issued by firms.

Insurance companies receive insurance premiums from selling insurance to customers and invest the proceeds until the funds are needed to pay insurance claims. They also commonly invest part of their funds in bonds issued by firms.

Mutual funds are investment companies that receive funds from individual investors; the mutual funds pool the amounts and invest them in securities. Mutual funds can be classified by the type of investments that they make. Some mutual funds (called **bond mutual funds**) invest the funds received from investors in bonds that are issued by firms.

commercial banks financial institutions that obtain deposits from individuals and use the funds primarily to provide business loans

savings institutions financial institutions that obtain deposits from individuals and use the deposited funds primarily to provide mortgage loans

finance companies financial institutions that typically obtain funds by issuing debt securities (IOUs) and lend most of their funds to firms

pension funds receive employee and firm contributions toward pensions and invest the proceeds for the employees until the funds are needed

insurance companies receive insurance premiums from selling insurance to customers and invest the proceeds until the funds are needed to pay insurance claims

mutual funds investment companies that receive funds from individual investors and then pool and invest those funds in securities

bond mutual funds investment companies that invest the funds received from investors in bonds

College Health Club: **Debt Financing at CHC**

One of the decisions that Sue Kramer needs to make as part of her business plan for College Health Club (CHC) is how to finance the business. Sue has obtained a loan for $40,000 to finance CHC. One advantage of using debt rather than obtaining additional equity is that the interest payments are tax-deductible. A second advantage is that since Sue has not accepted an equity investment from another person, she has full control over the business. The disadvantage of using debt rather than equity financing is that CHC will incur an interest expense each month as long as the loan exists. Sue expects that the annual interest expense will be $4,000, which means that CHC's earnings before taxes will be $4,000 less than if it had no debt. Sue decided to use debt financing rather than additional equity financing because she prefers to be the sole owner and feels confident that CHC can afford the $4,000 interest payment.

METHODS OF EQUITY FINANCING

The common methods of **equity financing** are retaining earnings and issuing stock, as explained next.

equity financing the act of receiving investment from owners (by issuing stock or retaining earnings)

Retaining Earnings

A firm can obtain equity financing by retaining earnings rather than by distributing the earnings to its owners. Managers may retain earnings to provide financial support for the firm's expansion. For example, if a firm needs $10 million for expansion and has just received $6 million in earnings (after paying taxes), it may retain the $6 million as equity financing and borrow the remaining $4 million.

Many small firms retain most of their earnings to support expansion. Larger corporations tend to pay out a portion of their earnings as dividends and retain only part of what they earned. Large firms can more easily obtain debt financing, so they can afford to pay out a portion of their earnings as dividends.

Issuing Stock

common stock a security that represents partial ownership of a particular firm

A firm can also obtain equity financing by issuing stock. **Common stock** is a security that represents partial ownership of a particular firm. Only the owners of common stock are permitted to vote on certain key matters concerning the firm, such as the election of the board of directors, whether to issue new shares of common stock, and whether to accept a merger proposal. Firms can issue common stock to obtain funds. When new shares of stock are issued, the number of shareholders who own the firm increases.

preferred stock a security that represents partial ownership of a particular firm and offers specific priorities over common stock

Preferred stock is a security that represents partial ownership of a particular firm and offers specific priorities over common stock. If a firm does not pay dividends over a period, it must pay preferred stockholders all dividends that were omitted before paying any dividends to common stockholders.

Equity financing is the act of receiving investment from owners.

© Getty Images/ EyeWire

Also, if the firm goes bankrupt, the preferred stockholders have priority claim to the firm's assets over common stockholders. If a firm goes bankrupt, however, there may not be any assets left for preferred stockholders, since creditors (such as lenders or bondholders) have first claim. Preferred stockholders normally do not have voting rights. Firms issue common stock more frequently than preferred stock.

Issuing Stock to Venture Capital Firms   Firms can issue stock privately to a **venture capital firm,** which is a firm composed of individuals who invest in small businesses. These individuals act as investors in firms rather than as creditors. They expect a share of the businesses in which they invest. Their investments typically support projects that have potential for high returns but also have high risk.

venture capital firm a firm composed of individuals who invest in small businesses

Entrepreneurs who need equity financing can attend venture capital forums, where they are allowed a short time (15 minutes or so) to convince the venture capital firms to provide them with equity financing. If an entrepreneur's presentation is impressive, venture capital firms may arrange for a longer meeting with the entrepreneur to learn more about the business that needs financing.

Providers of venture capital recognize that some of the businesses they invest in may generate little or no return. They hope that the successful businesses will more than make up for any unsuccessful ones. Venture capital firms commonly assess businesses that require an equity investment of between $200,000 and $2 million. Small projects are not popular because their potential return is not worth the time required to assess their feasibility.

Going Public   If a small privately held business desires to obtain additional funds, it may consider an **initial public offering (IPO)** of stock (also called "going public"), which is the first issue of stock to the public. Firms such as Yahoo! and Amazon.com went public so that they would have sufficient funds to support their expansion.

initial public offering (IPO) the first issue of stock to the public

Betsy Holden, president and CEO of Kraft Foods, carries a large Velveeta Cheese box. On June 13, 2001, Kraft Foods division spun off an 8.7 billion initial public offering that was the second largest ever in the United States.

© Getty Images/ Steve Kagan

increasing value with technology

DIRECT PUBLIC OFFERINGS

Smaller firms in need of capital now have a new alternative—the Internet. The Internet is allowing firms to go public without the expenses of a traditional IPO.

The usual process for a small and growing firm is to seek financing from a venture capitalist or a venture capital fund. After the firm has grown, the venture capitalist assists the firm in a public stock offering. The underwriting, legal, and filing fees are substantial. Now, however, a firm can avoid venture capital funding and the fees associated with traditional public offerings by taking the firm public over the Internet.

The communication power of the Internet and a relaxation in the exemption standard by the Securities and Exchange Commission (SEC) have given rise to direct public offerings (DPOs). The SEC allows firms to raise up to $5 million and is supportive of Internet use to distribute offering memoranda and to sell shares.

The issuer usually performs the underwriting, filing, and selling of the offer with an underwriter. Firms such as Wit Capital are available to assist firms interested in DPOs. They charge much less for their services than investment banks charge for underwriting traditional IPOs.

A DPO also offers an opportunity for investors who are left out of the traditional IPO market. Investment banks underwriting IPOs offer the shares to institutional investors and their other large clients. The individual investor must buy after the firm's shares have begun trading, which is frequently after a large increase in price. A DPO gives individuals the opportunity to invest in a newly public firm at the offer price.

For example, W. R. Hambrecht & Co.'s OpenIPO system allows equal access to institutional and individual investors. All investors are allowed to bid on shares and receive a fair allocation based on their bid. The system makes it easier for individual investors to participate and also decreases the likelihood of an improperly priced IPO.

---

stock mutual funds investment companies that invest funds received from individual investors in stocks

Insurance companies and pension funds commonly purchase large amounts of stocks issued by firms. In addition, **stock mutual funds** (investment companies that invest pooled funds received from individual investors in stocks) purchase large amounts of stocks issued by firms. An IPO allows a firm to obtain additional funds without boosting its existing debt level and without relying on retained earnings. Firms can obtain a large amount of funds by going public without increasing future interest payments to creditors.

Along with the advantages, IPOs have some disadvantages. First, firms that go public are responsible for informing shareholders of their financial condition. All firms that issue stock to the public must file periodic financial reports with the Securities and Exchange Commission, and preparing these reports can be expensive. Furthermore, the financial information then is accessible to investors. Some firms may prefer not to disclose information that would reveal the success (and perhaps the wealth) of the owners.

A second disadvantage is that when a small business attempts to obtain funding from the public, it may have difficulty convincing investors that its business plans are feasible. This limits the amount of funding that can be obtained from an IPO. It also forces the firm to sell part of the ownership at a relatively low cost. If a firm goes public and cannot obtain funding at a reasonable price, its original owners may feel that they gave away part of the firm for nothing.

A third disadvantage of an IPO is that the firm's ownership structure is diluted. Once shares are sold to the public, the proportion of the firm owned by the original owners is reduced. Thus, the original owners have less control of the firm, and other investors have more influence on the firm's board of directors and therefore on major decisions. Also, the profits earned by the firm that are distributed among owners as dividends must be allocated among more owners.

A fourth disadvantage of an IPO is that investment banks charge high fees for advising and placing the stock with investors. The firm also incurs legal fees, accounting fees, and printing fees. The fees may be about 10 percent of the total amount of funds received from the IPO. Thus, an IPO of $20 million may result in fees of $2 million.

IPOs are generally more popular when most stock prices are high, as firms may receive a higher price for their newly issued stock under these conditions. For example, stock prices were very high in the late 1990s, and there were numerous IPOs in that period.

Listing the Stock   Once a firm has issued stock to the public, it lists its stock on a stock exchange. This allows the investors to sell the stock they purchased from the firm to other investors over time. The stock exchange serves as a **secondary market,** or a market where existing securities can be traded among investors. Thus, investors have the flexibility to sell stocks that they no longer wish to hold.

secondary market a market where existing securities can be traded among investors

The most popular stock exchanges in the United States are the New York Stock Exchange (NYSE), the American Stock Exchange (AMEX), and the over-the-counter (OTC) market. Stocks in the OTC market trade via an electronic network known as the National Association of Securities Dealers Automated Quotations (Nasdaq). Each exchange has a set of listing requirements that firms must satisfy to have their stocks listed on that exchange.

College Health Club: Equity Financing at CHC

As part of her business plan for College Health Club (CHC), Sue Kramer decided to invest $20,000 of her own money and borrow $40,000. Sue also needs to consider how she can obtain additional equity investment to support the possible expansion of CHC over time. She wants to avoid borrowing additional funds because she knows that CHC's interest expenses will increase if more funds are borrowed. One way to build her equity investment in the firm is to reinvest any earnings in the business. Another way for a small business like CHC to obtain funds is by accepting an equity investment from a venture capital firm. By doing this, however, Sue would give up part of her ownership of CHC. Thus, when she sells the business someday, she would have to share the proceeds of the sale with the venture capital firm. In addition, she might lose some of her power to make decisions since the venture capital firm may insist on having input in all key decisions. Given these trade-offs, Sue decides that the ideal way to obtain additional financing is to reinvest any earnings in CHC. She feels this form of equity financing is preferable to additional debt financing because it will not result in additional interest expenses.

Comparison of Equity Financing with Debt Financing

Equity financing and debt financing are compared in Exhibit 16.4. Notice from the exhibit that the forms of debt financing (loans and bonds) require the firm to make interest and principal payments. Conversely, the forms of equity financing (retained earnings and stock) do not require any payments. Financing with stock may result in dividend payments, but only if the firm cannot afford them. Also, there are no principal payments to the stockholders, as the stock has no maturity.

Exhibit 16.4

Summary of Firm's Debt and Equity Financing Methods

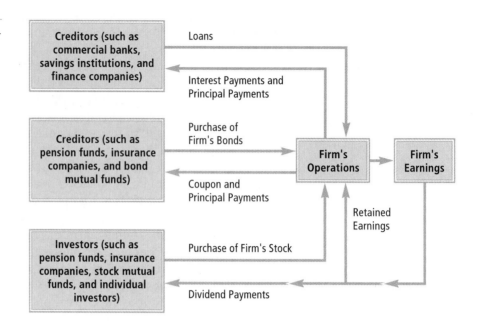

Firms typically use a variety of financing methods to obtain funds. General Motors, Ford Motor Company, Motorola, and many other firms frequently obtain funds by borrowing from banks, issuing bonds, and issuing new stock.

HOW FIRMS ISSUE SECURITIES

3

Explain how firms issue securities to obtain funds.

A **public offering** of securities (such as bonds or stocks) represents the selling of securities to the public. A firm that plans a public offering of securities can receive help from investment banks, which originate, underwrite, and distribute the securities.

public offering the selling of securities to the public

Origination

Investment banks advise firms on the amount of stocks or bonds they can issue. The issuance of an excessive amount of securities can cause a decline in the market price because the supply of securities issued may exceed the demand. Also, the issuance of bonds requires the determination of a maturity date, a coupon rate, and collateral.

Underwriting

underwritten the investment bank guarantees a price to the issuing firm, no matter what price the securities are sold for

best-efforts basis the investment bank does not guarantee a price to the firm issuing securities

underwriting syndicate a group of investment banks that share the obligations of underwriting securities

When securities offerings are **underwritten,** the investment bank guarantees a price to the issuing firm, no matter what price the securities are sold for. In this way, the investment bank bears the risk that the securities may be sold only at low prices. Alternatively, the investment bank may attempt to sell the securities on a **best-efforts basis;** in this case, it does not guarantee a price to the issuing firm.

For large issues of securities, the investment bank may create an **underwriting syndicate,** which is a group of investment banks that share the obligations of underwriting the securities. Each investment bank in the syndicate is allocated a portion of the securities and is responsible for selling that portion.

Distribution

prospectus a document that discloses relevant financial information about securities and about the firm issuing them

The issuing firm must register the issue with the Securities and Exchange Commission (SEC). It provides the SEC with a **prospectus,** which is a document that discloses relevant financial information about the securities (such as the amount) and about the firm.

Once the SEC approves the registration, the prospectus is distributed to investors who may purchase the securities. Some of the more likely investors are pension funds and insurance companies that have large amounts of funds to invest. Some issues are completely sold within hours. When an issue does not sell well, the investment bank may lower the price of the securities to increase demand.

private placement the selling of securities to one or a few investors

Some firms may prefer to use a **private placement,** in which the securities are sold to one or a few investors. An investment bank may still be used for advisory purposes and for help in identifying a financial institution (such as an insurance company) that may purchase the entire issue. The selling costs are lower with a private placement because there is only one or a few investors. A disadvantage, however, is that many investors cannot afford to purchase an entire issue. Consequently, privately placing the securities may be difficult.

flotation costs costs of issuing securities; include fees paid to investment banks for their advice and efforts to sell the securities, printing expenses, and registration fees

Firms that issue securities incur **flotation costs,** which include fees paid to investment banks for advice and for selling the securities, printing expenses, and registration fees.

OTHER METHODS OF OBTAINING FUNDS

In addition to debt financing and equity financing, firms may obtain funds in other ways, as discussed next.

Financing from Suppliers

When a firm obtains supplies, it may be given a specific period to pay its bill. The supplier is essentially financing the firm's investment over that period. If the firm is able to generate adequate revenue over that time to pay the bill, it will not need any more financing. Even if it needs more financing, the supplier's willingness to wait for payment saves the firm some financing costs.

Exhibit 16.5 shows the benefits of supplier financing. In the top diagram, the firm receives supplies on March 1, but does not have to pay its bill until August 1. By August 1, the firm will have sold the product that required the use of the supplies. Thus, it can use a portion of the revenue received from selling the product to pay the supplier.

The lower diagram shows that with no supplier financing, the firm must obtain funds from another source. For example, it may borrow funds from a commercial bank on March 1 to pay the supplier at that time. When the firm receives its payment for the product on August 1, it can use a portion of the revenue received to pay off the debt. In this case, the firm had to borrow funds for five months and incurred interest expenses over that period. The difference between these two scenarios is that the firm incurs only the

Exhibit 16.5

How Firms Can Benefit from Supplier Financing

Supplier Financing

Firm receives supplies from supplier

Supplies are used by firm to produce product

Firm sells product and pays supplier for the supplies

March 1 — April 1 — May 1 — June 1 — July 1 — August 1

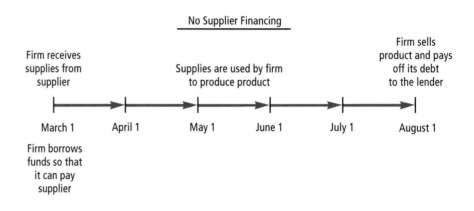

No Supplier Financing

Firm receives supplies from supplier

Supplies are used by firm to produce product

Firm sells product and pays off its debt to the lender

March 1 — April 1 — May 1 — June 1 — July 1 — August 1

Firm borrows funds so that it can pay supplier

expense of the supplies when it obtains supplier financing, but it incurs the expense of supplies plus interest expenses if supplier financing is not available.

Leasing

leasing renting assets for a specified period of time

Some firms prefer to finance the use of assets by **leasing,** or renting the assets for a specified period of time. These firms rent the assets and have full control over them over a particular period. They return the assets at the time specified in the lease contract. Many firms that lease assets cannot afford to purchase them. By leasing, they must make periodic lease payments but do not need to make a large initial outlay.

Some firms prefer to lease rather than purchase when they may need the assets for only a short period of time. For example, consider a new firm that does not know how much factory space it will need until it can assess the demand for its product. This firm may initially lease factory space so that it can switch factories without having to sell its existing factory if it needs more space.

College Health Club: **Leasing Decision at College Health Club**

One of the decisions that Sue Kramer had to make as part of her business plan for College Health Club (CHC) was whether to lease or buy equipment. She also had to decide whether to purchase the land and facilities for the health club or lease the space. The advantage of owning assets such as the weight and exercise machines and the facilities is that they would be hers to keep, unless she sold them. In addition, she would not have to make lease payments. The disadvantage, however, is the expense associated with purchasing the equipment and facilities. To purchase them, she would need a very large loan. Creditors might not be willing to extend such a large amount. Even if they did, her interest payments would be much higher because of the large loan. Also, leasing gives her flexibility. If Sue decides to discontinue the business, for example, she will not need to find a buyer for the equipment or facilities. Given the advantages of leasing, Sue has decided to lease the equipment and the facilities. If she accumulates substantial funds in the future, she will reconsider whether to purchase these assets.

4

Describe how firms determine the composition of their financing.

capital structure the amount of debt versus equity financing

DECIDING THE CAPITAL STRUCTURE

All firms must decide on a **capital structure,** or the amount of debt versus equity financing. No particular capital structure is perfect for all firms. However, some characteristics should be considered when determining the appropriate capital structure. The use of debt (such as bank loans or bonds) as a source of funds is desirable because the interest payments made by the firm on its debt are tax-deductible. Firms can claim their interest payments during the year as an expense, thereby reducing their reported earnings and their taxes. When firms use equity as a source of funds, they do not benefit in this way.

Although debt offers the advantage of tax deductibility, too much debt can increase the firm's risk of default on its debt. A higher level of debt results in a higher level of interest payments each year, which can make it difficult for a firm to cover all its debt payments. When creditors are concerned about the firm's ability to make future interest payments, they are less willing to provide additional credit. A firm's ability to increase its debt level is also constrained by the amount of collateral available.

Firms tend to retain some earnings as an easy and continual form of equity financing. When they need additional funds to support their operations, they typically use debt financing if they have the flexibility to do so. When they approach their debt capacity, however, they may have to retain more earnings or issue stock to obtain additional capital.

Revising the Capital Structure

Many firms revise their capital structure in response to changes in economic conditions, such as economic growth and interest rates. If economic growth declines and their earnings decline, they may reduce their debt because it is more difficult to cover interest payments. When interest rates decline, firms may increase their debt because the interest payments will be relatively low.

To reduce the strain of meeting high interest payments in the 1990s, many firms reduced their debt levels by hundreds of millions of dollars. Conversely, other firms such as IBM increased their debt because they anticipated that they could easily cover future interest payments resulting from the additional debt.

Sometimes firms revise their capital structure by changing the amount of stock they have outstanding. As described earlier, a firm can obtain equity financing by issuing additional shares of stock. Firms may also decrease the amount of stock outstanding by repurchasing shares issued previously. This strategy may have a favorable impact on the firm's stock price. To illustrate how the repurchasing of stock can improve a firm's value (and therefore its stock price), consider the following statements from a recent annual report of Wal-Mart:

"In a move to improve shareholder value, the Board of Directors authorized a $2 billion share repurchase program. . . . We started buying [when the stock price was] in the low 20s, and the stock ended up rising 73 percent in the last calendar year."

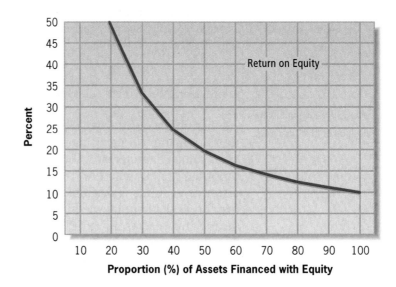

How the Capital Structure Affects the Return on Equity

A firm's earnings performance (as measured by its return on equity) can be significantly influenced by the capital structure decision. Consider a firm that had earnings of $1 million last year and has $10 million in assets. The firm's return on equity (measured as earnings divided by owner's equity) depends on the amount of the firm's assets that were financed with equity versus debt. Exhibit 16.6 shows how the firm's return on equity is dependent on its financial leverage. If the firm used all equity to finance its $10 million in assets, its return on equity (ROE) would be:

$$\text{ROE} = \frac{\$1,000,000}{\$10,000,000}$$

$$= 10\%$$

At the other extreme, if the firm used only 20 percent equity ($2 million) to finance its assets, its ROE would be:

$$\text{ROE} = \frac{\$1,000,000}{\$2,000,000}$$

$$= 50\%$$

Although using little equity (mostly debt) can achieve a higher return on equity, it exposes a firm to the risk of being unable to cover its interest payments. To illustrate the risk, Exhibit 16.7 shows how the annual interest expense incurred by a firm (with $10 million in assets) is dependent on the firm's degree of financial leverage. This exhibit assumes a 10 percent interest rate. For example, if the firm uses all equity, it does not incur any interest expenses. At the other extreme, if it uses only 20 percent ($2 million) of equity financing and relies on 80 percent ($8 million) of debt financing, it will incur an interest expense of $800,000 per year.

Exhibit 16.7

How a Firm's Interest Expense Is Dependent on Financial Leverage
Note: Assume that the firm has $10 million in assets; also assume a 10 percent interest rate on debt.

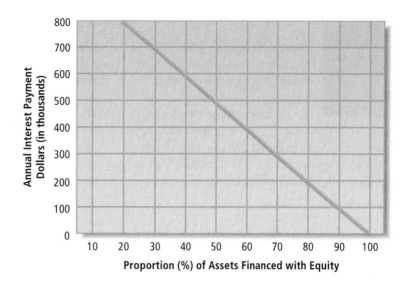

The relationship shown in Exhibit 16.7 is intended simply to illustrate how a high degree of financial leverage can result in high interest expenses. In reality, the impact of high financial leverage may be even more pronounced than in Exhibit 16.7, because lenders may charge a higher interest rate to firms that wish to borrow an excessive amount. The extra premium on the interest rate compensates the lenders for the risk that the firm may be unable to repay its debt.

Firms weigh the potential higher return on equity that results from using mostly debt financing against the risk resulting from high interest

Small Business Survey

Financing Choices of Small Firms

A recent survey asked small firms how they are financing their businesses, with the results as shown:

	Proportion of Firms That Recently Used This Type of Financing
Commercial bank loans	36%
Credit cards	27
Retained earnings	24
Private loans	18
Personal bank loans	17
Supplier credit	14
Leasing	10
Other	13

The results of this survey show that small firms use a wide variety of methods to obtain funds. The commercial bank loans, credit cards, and private loans reflect debt financing, while the use of retained earnings reflects equity financing.

global business

Global Financing When U.S. firms establish businesses in foreign countries (called "foreign subsidiaries"), they must obtain sufficient funds to support them. Foreign subsidiaries must decide not only whether to use debt or equity but also what currency to use. A common method is for the subsidiary to borrow funds locally. This financing strategy allows the interest expense to be in the same currency as the revenue. Consequently, the subsidiary does not need to exchange its local currency into another currency to pay off the debt.

payments. Many firms compromise by balancing their amounts of equity and debt financing. For example, a firm might finance its $10 million in assets by using $5 million of equity and the remaining $5 million of debt. Assuming an interest rate of 10 percent on debt, the interest expense would be $500,000 (computed as $10\% \times \$5,000,000$), as shown in Exhibit 16.7.

DIVIDEND POLICY

dividend policy the decision regarding how much of the firm's quarterly earnings should be retained (reinvested in the firm) versus distributed as dividends to owners

The board of directors of each firm decides how much of the firm's quarterly earnings should be retained (reinvested in the firm) versus distributed as dividends to owners. This decision, referred to as the firm's **dividend policy,** is important because it influences the amount of additional financing the firm must obtain. For example, consider a firm that earned $30 million after taxes. Assume that it will need $40 million for various expenses in the near future. If it retains all of the earnings, it will need an additional $10 million. At the other extreme, if it pays out the entire $30 million as dividends, it will need to obtain an additional $40 million.

Some firms establish their dividend payment as a percentage of future earnings. For example, General Mills sets a dividend target of 50 percent of earnings, while Goodyear Tire sets a dividend target of between 20 and 25 percent of earnings.

Factors That Affect a Firm's Dividend Policy

There is no optimal dividend policy to be used by all firms. Each firm's unique characteristics may influence its dividend policy. Two characteristics that can influence the dividend policy are shareholder expectations and the firm's financing needs.

Shareholder Expectations   A firm's shareholders may expect to receive dividends if they have historically been receiving them. If the firm discontinues or reduces the dividend payment, shareholders could become dissatisfied. Thus, many firms such as ConAgra and Campbell's Soup make an effort to either maintain or increase dividends from year to year.

Firm's Financing Needs   A firm that has no need for additional funds may distribute most of its earnings as dividends. However, it may be concerned that if it pays high dividends, shareholders will come to expect them. Thus, instead of trying to maintain its high dividend payment, the firm may decide to use a portion of the earnings for another purpose. For example, it may consider replacing old assets or expanding part of its business.

cross functional teamwork:

Interaction between Financing Decisions and Other Business Decisions

When financial managers make financing decisions, they rely on input from other managers. The amount of financing is dependent on the difference between the amount of cash outflows resulting from the payment of expenses and the cash inflows resulting from sales. The larger the difference, the more financing will be needed. Financial managers can ask production managers to estimate the salaries and other production expenses that will be incurred by the firm in the future. They can ask marketing managers to estimate the marketing expenses to be incurred by the firm. They can also ask marketing managers to estimate the future demand for each of the firm's products; this information can be used to estimate the firm's future revenue.

When financial managers decide whether to finance with debt or equity, they rely on input from marketing managers. If the future revenue to be received by the firm is somewhat stable over time, the firm may be willing to finance with debt because cash inflows each month will be sufficient to cover its interest payments on debt. If the monthly revenue is expected to be erratic, however, cash inflows each month may not be sufficient to make interest payments. In this case, the firm may use equity financing instead of debt financing. The marketing managers can offer useful input on this topic because they should know whether the demand for the product will be somewhat stable over time.

A firm's dividend policy will also benefit from the input of its marketing and production managers. If the marketing managers anticipate that the sales will be stable over time, the firm may consistently receive cash each quarter to pay its owners a dividend. However, if it generates erratic sales over time, it may not have a sufficient amount of cash each quarter to make its dividend payment. If the production managers anticipate large expenses in upcoming quarters because of the establishment of new production facilities, they can warn financial managers to retain any earnings rather than distribute them as dividends. Although the financial managers are responsible for decisions such as the amount and type of financing needed, they can make better decisions when considering input from the marketing and production managers.

SUMMARY

1 The common sources of debt financing are obtaining bank loans, issuing bonds, or issuing commercial paper.

The financial institutions that provide loans to firms are commercial banks, savings institutions, and finance companies. The financial institutions that commonly purchase the corporate bonds issued by firms are insurance companies, pension funds, and bond mutual funds.

2 The common sources of equity financing are retaining earnings and issuing stock. The financial institutions that purchase stocks issued by firms are insurance companies, pension funds, and stock mutual funds.

3 When firms issue debt securities or stocks, they normally hire an investment bank. The investment bank may provide advice on the amount of securities the firm should issue, (origination), underwrite the securities, and find buyers of the securities that the firm issues (distribution).

4 Firms may prefer to use debt financing over equity financing because the interest payments are tax-deductible. This can allow debt to be a relatively cheap form of financing. However, a high level of debt financing results in a high level of interest payments, which could make it difficult for the firm to make those payments. Therefore, firms may prefer to avoid such a risk by using some equity financing as well. With equity financing, the firm does not have to make periodic payments.

KEY TERMS

best-efforts basis   518
bond mutual funds   513
bonds   510
call feature   511
capital   507
capital structure   521
commercial banks   513
commercial paper   512
common stock   514
debt financing   507
dividend policy   524
equilibrium interest rate
   (chap. appendix)   533

equity financing   514
finance companies   513
flotation costs   519
indenture   511
initial public offering (IPO)   515
insurance companies   513
leasing   520
mutual funds   513
par value   510
pension funds   513
preferred stock   514
prime rate   509
private placement   519

prospectus   519
protective covenants   512
public offering   518
savings institutions   513
secondary market   517
secured bonds   511
stock mutual funds   516
underwriting syndicate   518
underwritten   518
unsecured bonds   511
venture capital firm   515

Review & Critical Thinking Questions

1. Compare the use of funds required by a service firm with the use of funds required by an industrial firm.

2. What factors do lenders use to assess the creditworthiness of firms?

3. What determines the loan rate a business could obtain?

4. When would a firm obtain a floating-rate loan rather than a fixed-rate loan?

5. When a firm plans to issue bonds, what legal document is created by the firm, and what is included in this document?

6. What is the call feature associated with bonds? Do callable bonds have higher or lower interest rates than noncallable bonds?

7. List the common types of creditors that can provide debt financing to firms.

8. Briefly describe the common methods of equity financing for a firm.

9. What are the advantages and disadvantages of IPOs (initial public offerings)?

10. What is the difference between debt financing and equity financing?

11. Identify and explain other methods of obtaining funds that a firm can use in addition to debt financing and equity financing.

12. What factors influence a firm's choice of financing?

13. List and briefly describe the factors that affect a firm's dividend policy.

Discussion Questions

1. You are a financial manager. Why would you want to use a very high degree of financial leverage for your firm?

2. You are a business entrepreneur who is starting a business that requires a $50,000 investment. You have very little cash; however, you own your own home that is appraised at $120,000, and you own a car valued at

   $10,000. Both of these assets are free and clear from any indebtedness. Offer opinions on how you might negotiate a loan with the bank.

3. How can a firm use the Internet and technology to research financing alternatives?

4. You are a vice-president of finance for a large privately held

   corporation and you must raise $20 million for a project. Discuss why you might consider an IPO.

5. Why do you think stockholders of a firm that is performing very well would prefer that the firm pay only a low percentage of its earnings as dividends?

It's Your Decision: Financing Decisions at CHC

1. If CHC expands by creating three new health clubs, should Sue Kramer (CHC's president) finance the expansion with an initial public offering?
2. How can CHC obtain additional funds if Sue does not want to borrow any more funds?
3. What is a disadvantage of CHC obtaining additional financing with borrowed funds?
4. If Sue decides to expand CHC's existing facilities, why must she first consider its financial situation?
5. Recall that Sue expects total expenses of $142,000 in CHC's first year. She will price memberships at $500 and expects to attract 300 members in the first year. She can reduce CHC's debt by $3,600 if she does not spend any money on marketing this year. However, the expected membership in the first year would be only 280 rather than 300 if no marketing is conducted.
   a. What is the expected level of earnings in the first year if Sue decides to reduce CHC's debt as described here?
   b. Should CHC's debt level be reduced in the manner described here? Explain.
6. A health club differs from manufacturing firms in that it produces a service rather than products. Why are manufacturing firms more likely to go public than service firms? When service firms go public, how do you think they expand? By expanding one or a few facilities? Or by creating a large number of smaller facilities around the United States?

Investing in a Business

Using the annual report of the firm in which you would like to invest, complete the following:

1 Has the firm obtained new funding over the last year? If so, how?

2 When the firm borrows funds, does it rely mostly on loans from commercial banks, or does it issue bonds?

3 Has the firm's degree of financial leverage changed in the last year because of new financing? If so, has the degree of financial leverage increased or decreased?

4 Explain how the business uses technology to provide information on its financing alternatives and decisions. For example, does it use the Internet to provide information on interest rates on debt instruments that it issues? Does it provide information on the stock price received when issuing stock?

5 Go to **http://hoovers.com** and locate the NEWS SEARCH. Type in the name of the firm in the space provided, and review the recent news stories about the firm. Summarize any (at least one) recent news story about the firm that applies to one or more of the key concepts in this chapter.

Case: The IPO Decision

Lauderdale Clothing manufactures shirts and pants with the Lauderdale logo. It is attempting to engage in an initial public offering (IPO). Three years ago, the firm planned an IPO, but because market conditions and earnings for the year came in below expectations, the full value of the firm would not have been realized. Therefore, the plan was scrapped.

In the last three years, sales have increased by 20 percent and are currently over $250 million. Furthermore, profits have increased to more than $60 million, up from last year's profits of $32 million.

The investment banker that will issue the stock for Lauderdale Clothing believes that Lauderdale is in much better financial shape today and better prepared to un-

dertake an IPO of stock. The company has developed stronger management and has aggressively pursued international business.

Questions

1 Explain why the IPO is expected to be more successful now than it would have been three years ago.

2 What is the role of the investment banker in this IPO?

3 Explain what types of debt and equity financing Lauderdale Clothing could undertake now and in the future.

4 Assume that Lauderdale Clothing prefers debt over equity financing. Why might this strategy change in the future?

Video Case: Business Planning by Yahoo!

Scotsman Industries sells refrigeration products around the world. It recently acquired several companies and had to decide whether to use equity or debt financing. Scotsman recognizes the benefits from using leverage in which it borrows money rather than issuing stock. Yet, excessive debt could create extreme cash flow pressure to cover interest payment obligations. In addition, the interest rate on some debt varies over time and may rise if market rates rise. Scotsman generally attempts to balance its debt and equity, targeting a 50–50 ratio. In this way, it achieves some benefits from leverage, while minimizing risk by limiting the amount of debt used.

Questions

1 If Scotsman uses debt rather than equity to finance a profitable project, will its earnings per share be affected more favorably than if it used equity? Explain.

2 How will Scotsman's potential profitability and its risk change if it uses a higher proportion of debt in the future?

3 Why might Scotsman's recent willingness to use more debt than its target debt ratio be related to prevailing interest rates?

Internet Applications

1. *http://www2.ipo.com/ipoinfo/default.asp?p=IPO*

Briefly summarize the information for a future IPO of your choice. How many shares is this firm planning to offer? What will its ticker symbol be? What is the estimated price the firm's stock will sell for? How do you think this price is determined? Also, comment on the firm's recent financial performance, if any. Would you invest in this firm? Why or why not?

2. *http://bonds.yahoo.com/*

   a. Find information on the most recent corporate bond rates. Why do you think bond rates are at their current level? Also, summarize some recent news items about the bond market. How do you think these developments affect a firm's decision to finance with bonds instead of equity?

   b. Click on "Bond Screener." Obtain information on a Treasury bond of your choice. Then, obtain information on a corporate bond with a similar maturity. Why do the two bonds have different rates? Explain.

3. *http://www.sba.gov/financing/*

Describe loan programs offered by the Small Business Administration (SBA). Why do you think these programs are offered especially for small businesses? Assume you own a small sole proprietorship in consulting. Which loan program would you most likely use? Why?

The Coca-Cola Company Annual Report Project

Questions for the current year's annual report are available on the text website at **http://madura.swlearning.com.**

The following questions apply concepts presented in this chapter to The Coca-Cola Company. Go to The Coca-Cola Company website (**http://www.cocacola.com**) and find the index for the 2001 annual report.

Questions

1 Download the financial statements and find "Financial Strategies." Why does The Coca-Cola Company's management say it uses debt financing?

2 Download the financial statements and find "Financial Strategies." The annual report states that The Coca-Cola Company has continued to buy back its own shares of stock. Explain how this affects the company's financial leverage.

3 Click on "Financial Highlights." In 2001, The Coca-Cola Company's total return on its shareholders' equity was 38.5 percent. What was the average compound annual growth rate in the market value of the Company's common stock over the last 10 years?

4 Click on "Financial Highlights." What dollar amount of shares did The Coca-Cola Company repurchase in 2000 and in 2001?

5 Go to **http://hoovers.com** and locate the NEWS CENTER. Key in The Coca-Cola Company in the space provided, click on "Search," and review the recent news stories about the firm. Summarize any (at least one) recent news story about The Coca-Cola Company that applies one or more of the key concepts within this chapter of the text.

In-Text Study Guide

Answers are in an appendix at the back of the book.

True or False

1. Debt financing is the act of issuing stock or retaining earnings. F

2. A common form of collateral is the asset purchased with the borrowed funds. T

3. Both bonds and commercial paper represent debt financing sources for a firm. T

4. The higher a firm's probability of default, the lower the interest rate charged for a loan. F

5. A call feature on a bond allows the issuing firm to repurchase the bond before maturity. T

6. Par value represents the rate of interest charged on loans to the most creditworthy firms. F

7. Preferred stock is a security that represents partial ownership of a particular firm and offers specific priorities over common stock. T

8. When firms obtain all new financing by going public, they do not increase future interest payments to creditors. T

9. The issuance of an excessive amount of securities can cause a decline in market prices, because the supply of securities issued may exceed the demand. T

10. A firm can increase its financial leverage by increasing the proportion of equity financing in its capital structure. F

Multiple Choice

11. Firms obtain capital (funds) in the form of:
    a) inventory and accounts receivable.
    b) revenues and expenses.
    c) equity and assets.
    d) working capital and cost of goods sold.
    e) debt and equity.

12. When comparing manufacturing firms to service businesses, we find that manufacturing firms:
    a) borrow more funds.
    b) have fewer dollars invested in assets.

    c) pay larger dividends than other businesses.
    d) use less financial leverage.
    e) accumulate less retained earnings.

13. When assessing the creditworthiness of a business, a lender will consider all of the following factors except:
    a) planned use of the borrowed funds.
    b) financial condition of the firm.
    c) industry outlook.
    d) voting rights of preferred stockholders.
    e) availability of collateral.

14. When firms apply for loans, they must organize and project their future revenue and expenses in a detailed:
    a) marketing mix.
    b) production plan.
    c) accounting plan.
    d) financial plan.
    e) production schedule.

15. Long-term debt securities purchased by investors are called:
    a) corporate bonds.
    b) common stock.
    c) preferred stock.
    d) accounts payable.
    e) notes payable.

16. Firms that expect interest rates to fall will likely:
    a) pay dividends to their stockholders.
    b) borrow funds at double the prime rate.
    c) borrow funds with a fixed-rate loan.
    d) borrow funds with a floating-rate loan.
    e) default on their existing bonds.

17. When a firm plans to issue bonds, it explains its obligations to bondholders in a legal document known as a(n):
    a) equity ownership.
    b) asset acquisition.
    c) sales revenue.
    d) indenture.
    e) note payable.

In-Text Study Guide

Answers are in an appendix at the back of the book.

18. The interest rate paid on bonds issued by firms is influenced not only by prevailing interest rates but also by the firm's:
    a) retained earnings.
    b) risk level.
    c) dividend policy.
    d) earnings per share.
    e) return on equity.

19. Moody's and Standard and Poor's:
    a) rate the firm's ability to cover interest payments on its existing debt.
    b) organize investor syndicates.
    c) issue initial public offerings.
    d) evaluate the credibility of the firm's financial statements.
    e) predict the amount of dividends the firm will pay in the future.

20. All of the following are creditors that can provide debt financing to firms except:
    a) commercial banks.
    b) insurance companies.
    c) management consultants.
    d) pension funds.
    e) mutual funds.

21. Investment companies that invest pooled funds from individual investors are:
    a) mutual funds.
    b) bond indentures.
    c) new primary issues.
    d) retained earnings.
    e) cash dividends.

22. _____ represent earnings of the firm that are reinvested into the business.
    a) Dividends
    b) Collateral
    c) Retained earnings
    d) Working capital
    e) Capital structure

23. If a privately held firm desires to obtain additional funds and "go public," it will:
    a) borrow funds from a commercial bank.
    b) sell bonds in the primary market.
    c) merge with a multinational corporation.
    d) engage in a public commercial paper offering.
    e) engage in an initial public offering.

24. A group of investment banks that share the obligations of underwriting the securities is a(n):
    a) bond indenture.
    b) corporate charter.
    c) savings and loan institution.
    d) mutual savings bank.
    e) underwriting syndicate.

25. Fees charged by investment banks for their efforts in selling a firm's securities are called:
    a) coupon payments.
    b) best-effort fees.
    c) cost of capital.
    d) interest fees.
    e) flotation costs.

26. Corporate stock and bond issues must be registered with the:
    a) Federal Trade Commission.
    b) Securities and Exchange Commission.
    c) Internal Revenue Service.
    d) Department of Commerce.
    e) Bureau of Labor.

27. Some firms prefer to finance the use of assets by renting the assets for a specified period of time. This is referred to as:
    a) capital structure.
    b) leasing.
    c) retained earnings.
    d) sales revenue.
    e) notes payable.

In-Text Study Guide

Answers are in an appendix at the back of the book.

28. The composition of debt versus equity financing is known as:
    a) retained earnings.
    b) revenue.
    c) asset composition.
    d) working capital.
    e) capital structure.

29. Which of the following describes the best response for a firm anticipating a long-term decline in sales?
    a) The firm should increase the proportion of debt in its capital structure.
    b) The firm should increase the proportion of bonds in its capital structure.
    c) The firm should decrease the proportion of preferred stock in its capital structure.
    d) The firm should decrease the proportion of debt in its capital structure.
    e) The firm should increase dividends to its stockholders.

30. Firm A and Firm B have identical earnings. Firm A has a higher proportion of debt in its capital structure than does Firm B. Firm A will likely:
    a) achieve a lower return on equity than Firm B.
    b) achieve a higher return on equity than Firm B.
    c) have a lower degree of financial leverage than Firm B.
    d) have a lower degree of financial risk than Firm B.
    e) have a greater proportion of equity in its capital structure.

31. A firm with mostly debt in its capital structure will likely have:
    a) low inventory turnover.
    b) high accounts receivable.
    c) high retained earnings.
    d) a large amount of preferred stock.
    e) high interest payments.

32. Some firms target their dividend payment as a percentage of their:
    a) present debt level.
    b) past debt level.
    c) future earnings.
    d) revenue.
    e) capital structure.

33. Shareholder expectations and the firm's financing needs are two characteristics that can influence the firm's:
    a) exchange rates.
    b) governmental relationships.
    c) dividend policy.
    d) foreign exchange.
    e) counter trade.

34. Which of the following forms of financing does not require a fixed payment?
    a) bonds
    b) stocks
    c) bank loans
    d) leases
    e) commercial paper

35. U.S. firms doing business overseas typically:
    a) borrow funds locally and repay in local currency.
    b) borrow funds in the U.S. and repay in the local currency.
    c) borrow funds in the U.S. and repay in dollars.
    d) borrow funds locally and repay in dollars.
    e) avoid debt financing entirely because of currency fluctuations.

Appendix: How Interest Rates Are Determined

Firms closely monitor interest rates because they affect the cost of borrowing money. The interest rate is the price charged for borrowing money. Managers of firms should understand how interest rates change and should recognize the factors that can cause interest rates to change, as explained by this appendix.

HOW INTEREST RATES CHANGE

The interest rate on funds to be borrowed is influenced by the supply of loanable funds (provided by depositors) and the demand for those loanable funds by borrowers. The interaction between demand and supply causes interest rates to change, as explained next.

Demand for Loanable Funds

To illustrate the effects of demand on interest rates, assume that the United States has only one commercial bank. The bank receives all deposits from depositors and uses all the funds to make loans to borrowers. Demand for loans by borrowers will vary with the interest rate the bank charges on loans. The higher the interest rate it charges, the lower the amount of loanable funds demanded (requested for loans). This is because some firms (and other borrowers) are unwilling to pay a high interest rate. If the interest rate is too high, firms may simply not borrow the funds they were hoping to use for expansion. Consider the demand schedule for loanable funds shown in the second column of Exhibit 16A.1. The demand schedule for loanable funds is also shown on the graph in Exhibit 16A.1 and is labeled D_1. This schedule shows the inverse relationship between the interest rate and the quantity of loanable funds demanded.

Supply of Loanable Funds

The quantity of funds supplied (by depositors) to the bank is also related to possible interest rate levels, but in a different manner. The higher the interest rate offered on deposits, the higher the quantity of loanable funds (in the form of deposits) that will be supplied by depositors to banks. The supply schedule for loanable funds to be supplied by depositors is shown in the third column of Exhibit 16A.1. It is also shown on the accompanying graph and is labeled S_1. This schedule shows the positive relationship between the interest rate and the quantity of funds supplied.

Combining Demand and Supply

Interest rates are determined by the interaction of the demand and supply schedules for loanable funds. Notice in Exhibit 16A.1 that at relatively high interest rates (such as 12 percent), the quantity of loanable funds supplied exceeds the quantity of loanable funds demanded, resulting in a surplus of

Exhibit 16A.1

How the Demand and Supply of Loanable
Funds Affect Interest Rates

At an Interest Rate of:	The Quantity of Loanable Funds Demanded by Borrowers Would Be:	The Quantity of Loanable Funds Supplied by Savers Would Be:
12%	$300 billion	$500 billion
10%	350 billion	450 billion
8%	400 billion	400 billion
6%	450 billion	350 billion

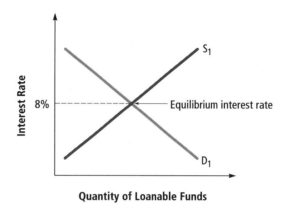

Quantity of Loanable Funds

loanable funds. When the interest rate is relatively low (such as 6 percent), the quantity of loanable funds supplied is less than the quantity of loanable funds demanded, resulting in a shortage of funds.

Notice from Exhibit 16A.1 that at the interest rate of 8 percent, the quantity of loanable funds supplied by depositors is $400 billion, which is equal to the quantity of loanable funds demanded by borrowers. At this interest rate, there is no surplus or shortage of loanable funds. The interest rate at which the quantity of loanable funds supplied is equal to the quantity of loanable funds demanded is called the **equilibrium interest rate.**

equilibrium interest rate the interest rate at which the quantity of loanable funds supplied is equal to the quantity of loanable funds demanded

Effect of a Change in the Demand Schedule

As time passes, conditions may change, causing the demand schedule of loanable funds to change. Consequently, a change will occur in the equilibrium interest rate. Reconsider the previous example and assume that most firms suddenly decide to expand their business operations. This decision may result from optimistic news about the economy. Those firms that decide to expand will need to borrow additional funds from the bank. Assume that the demand schedule for loanable funds changes, as shown in Exhibit 16A.2. The graph in the exhibit shows that the demand curve shifts outward from D_1 to D_2.

Now consider the effect of this change in the demand for loanable funds on the equilibrium interest rate, as shown in Exhibit 16A.2. Assuming that the supply schedule of loanable funds remains unchanged, there is now a shortage of loanable funds at the equilibrium interest rate. However, at an interest rate of 10 percent, the quantity of loanable funds supplied by savers will once again equal the quantity of loanable funds demanded by borrowers. Therefore, the new equilibrium interest rate is 10 percent. The graph in Exhibit 16A.2 confirms that the new equilibrium interest rate is 10 percent.

Exhibit 16A.2

Effect of a Change in the Demand for
Loanable Funds on Interest Rates

At an Interest Rate of:	The Quantity of Loanable Funds Demanded Was:	But the Quantity of Loanable Funds Demanded Would Now Be:
12%	$300 billion	$400 billion
10%	350 billion	450 billion
8%	400 billion	500 billion
6%	450 billion	550 billion

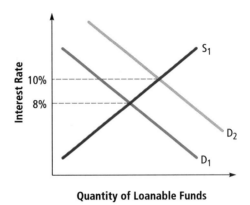

Quantity of Loanable Funds

Effect of a Change in the Supply Schedule

Just as the demand schedule for loanable funds may change, so may the supply schedule. To illustrate how a change in the supply schedule can affect the interest rate, reconsider the original example in which the equilibrium interest was 8 percent. Now assume that savers decide to save more funds than they did before, which results in a new supply schedule of loanable funds, as shown in Exhibit 16A.3. At any given interest rate, the quantity of loanable funds supplied is now higher than it was before. The graph in Exhibit 16A.3 shows how the supply curve shifts out from S_1 to S_2.

Now consider the effect of the shift in the supply schedule on the equilibrium interest rate. Assuming that the demand schedule remains unchanged, the supply of loanable funds will exceed the demand for loanable funds at the previous equilibrium interest rate of 8 percent. However, at an equilibrium interest rate of 6 percent, the quantity of loanable funds supplied by savers will equal the quantity of loanable funds demanded by borrowers. The graph in Exhibit 16A.3 confirms that the shift in the supply schedule from S_1 to S_2 causes a new equilibrium interest rate of 6 percent.

This discussion of interest rates has assumed just one single commercial bank that receives all deposits from savers and provides those funds as loans to borrowers. In reality, many commercial banks and other financial institutions provide this service. Nevertheless, this does not affect the general discussion of interest rates. The equilibrium interest rate in the United States is determined by the interaction of the total demand for loanable funds by all U.S. borrowers and the total supply of loanable funds provided by all U.S. savers.

Exhibit 16A.3

Effect of a Change in the Supply of Loanable Funds on Interest Rates

At an Interest Rate of:	The Quantity of Loanable Funds Supplied by Savers Was:	But the Quantity of Loanable Funds Supplied by Savers Would Now Be:
12%	$500 billion	$600 billion
10%	450 billion	550 billion
8%	400 billion	500 billion
6%	350 billion	450 billion

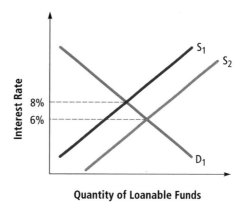

Quantity of Loanable Funds

FACTORS THAT CAN AFFECT INTEREST RATES

Several factors can cause shifts in the demand schedule or supply schedule of loanable funds and therefore can cause shifts in equilibrium interest rates. Firms monitor these factors so that they can anticipate how interest rates may change in the future. In this way, firms can anticipate how their interest owed on borrowed funds may change.

Monetary Policy

Recall that the Federal Reserve System can affect interest rates by implementing monetary policy. As the money supply is adjusted, so is the supply of funds that can be lent out by financial institutions. When the Fed increases the supply of funds, interest rates decrease (assuming no change in demand for funds). Conversely, when the Fed reduces the supply of funds, interest rates increase.

Economic Growth

When economic conditions become more favorable, firms tend to make more plans for expansion. They borrow more money, which reflects an increase in their demand for loanable funds. Assuming that the supply of loanable funds remains unchanged, the increased demand for loanable funds will result in a higher equilibrium interest rate.

The *Wall Street Journal, Business Week,* and other business publications frequently monitor the indicators of economic growth and suggest how interest rates may be affected. A common headline might be something like this: "Economic Growth Increases; Higher Interest Rates Expected." When firms read this headline, they may interpret it as both good news and bad. The good news is higher economic growth, which may increase the demand for the firm's products, thereby increasing the firm's revenue. The bad news is that if the higher economic growth causes higher interest rates, it may also increase the annual interest expenses owed by the firm on its borrowed funds.

Conversely, a decline in economic growth can cause firms to reduce their plans for expansion. These firms may see no reason to expand if they expect poor economic conditions, because the demand for their products may decline. If firms demand (borrow) less loanable funds, and the supply of loanable funds remains unchanged, the equilibrium interest rate will decline.

To confirm the relationship just described, consider the effects of a weak economy during 2001 and 2002. In that period, firms lowered their demand for loans because of pessimism about the future, and interest rates decreased substantially.

Expected Inflation

When consumers and firms expect a high rate of inflation, they tend to borrow more money. To understand why, assume you plan to purchase a Ford Mustang in two years, once you have saved enough money to pay for it with cash. However, if you believe that the price of the Mustang you wish to purchase will rise substantially by then, you may decide to use borrowed funds to buy it now before the price rises. So when the rate of inflation in the United States is high (or is expected to be high in the near future), many consumers attempt to purchase automobiles, homes, or other products before the prices rise. Firms may also purchase machinery or buildings before the prices rise. These conditions cause an increase in the demand for loanable funds by consumers and firms, which results in higher interest rates. This explains why U.S. interest rates tend to be high when U.S. inflation is high.

Expectations of lower inflation can have the opposite effect. Consumers and firms may be more willing to defer making some purchases if they cannot afford them. They may wait until they are in a better financial situation. When planned purchases are put off until the future, consumers and firms do not need to borrow as much money. Given a lower demand for loanable funds, the interest rate should decline.

Changes in expected inflation could also affect the supply of loanable funds. However, the demand for loanable funds tends to be much more sensitive than the supply of loanable funds to changes in expected inflation.

Savings Behavior

As the savings behavior of people changes, so does the supply schedule of loanable funds, and so does the interest rate. For example, if people become more willing to save money, this increases the amount of money that will be deposited in banks at any possible interest rate. Since the amount of funds that can be loaned out by banks to borrowers has increased, a surplus of funds is available at the previous equilibrium interest rate. Therefore, the new equilibrium interest rate will decline to the level at which the quantity of funds supplied equals the quantity of funds demanded.

Exhibit 16A.4

Summary of Key Factors That Affect Interest Rates

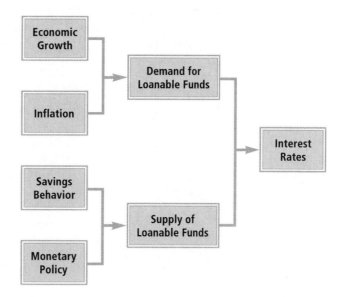

Summary of Factors That Affect Interest Rates

Four factors that influence interest rates have been identified and are illustrated in Exhibit 16A.4. The main effects of economic growth and inflation on interest rates occur as a result of influencing the demand for loanable funds. The main effects of savings behavior and monetary policy on interest rates occur as a result of influencing the supply of loanable funds.

The factors that affect interest rates can all change at the same time. One factor may be pushing interest rates up while the others are pushing interest rates down. The final effect on interest rates may depend on which factor has the biggest impact.

All businesses, including Zombie Internet Café, must be able to assess the feasibility of investing additional funds in machinery, equipment, or the acquisition of another company.

business decisions

The Learning Goals of this chapter are to:

1 Describe the tasks necessary to make business investment decisions.

2 Explain how a firm can use capital budgeting to determine whether it should invest in a project.

3 Describe the factors that motivate investment in other firms (acquisitions).

4 Explain how firms make decisions for investing in short-term assets.

Chapter 17

538

Expanding the Business

17

Whereas the previous chapter focused on how firms obtain funds (financing), this chapter focuses on how firms utilize funds (business investment). A firm makes short-term investment decisions when it considers investing in accounts receivable and inventory. It makes long-term investment decisions when it considers investing in long-term assets. Consider the situation of Zombie Internet Café, which serves drinks and allows customers online computer access for a fee. It wants to expand by acquiring existing Internet cafés in nearby cities. Zombie Internet Café must decide:

▶ What tasks are necessary to make business investment decisions?

▶ How can it assess the feasibility of investing in additional cafés?

▶ How should it make decisions to invest in short-term assets?

If Zombie can make investment decisions properly, it will use its funds in a manner that is beneficial to its owners. That is, the benefits from expansion will exceed the costs. Its decisions on investing in short-term assets are also intended to enhance its business per-formance by using funds in an efficient manner.

The types of decisions described above are necessary for all businesses. This chapter explains how Zombie Internet Café or any other firm can make investment decisions in a manner that maximizes the firm's value.

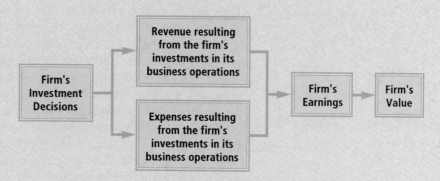

INVESTMENT DECISIONS

1

Describe the tasks necessary to make business investment decisions.

Firms continually evaluate potential projects in which they may invest, such as the construction of a new building or the purchase of a machine. Many firms plan for growth every year. DuPont, IBM, and 3M Company expand by continually creating new products. Retailers such as The Gap and The Children's Place expand by establishing new stores. Exhibit 17.1 shows how The Children's Place (a clothing store for children)has increased its investment in assets over time so that it can support the growth in its business. In the last five years, it has more than tripled the amount of its assets. To decide whether proposed projects should be implemented, firms such as The Children's Place conduct **capital budgeting,** which is a comparison of the costs and benefits of a proposed project to determine whether it

capital budgeting a comparison of the costs and benefits of a proposed project to determine whether it is feasible

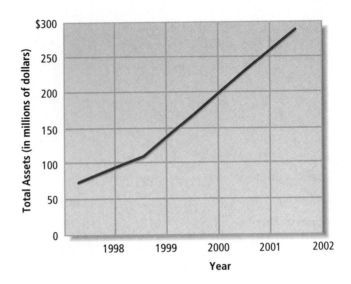

is feasible. The costs of a project include the initial outlay (payment) for the project, along with the periodic costs of maintaining the project. The benefits of a project are the revenue it generates.

For example, when McDonald's establishes a new restaurant, the initial outlay includes the construction of the building, the furniture needed, utensils, and cooking facilities. It also includes costs of food as well as labor. The benefits of this project are the revenue that the restaurant will generate over time. In most cases, the precise amounts of a project's costs and benefits are not known in advance and can only be estimated.

Many decisions that result from capital budgeting are irreversible. That is, if the project does not generate the benefits expected, it is too late to reverse the decision. For example, if a restaurant is unsuccessful, its selling price will likely be much lower than the cost of establishing it.

To illustrate how an inaccurate budgeting analysis can affect the firm, consider the case of Converse, which invested in a company called Apex One. Unfortunately, Converse underestimated the expenses involved in this project and overestimated the revenue. Consequently, just three months after the initial outlay, Converse terminated the project and incurred a $41.6 million loss. As an illustration of how firms focus on each project's return versus its cost, consider the following statements from recent annual reports:

"Our goal is to achieve a return on invested capital over the course of each business cycle that exceeds the company's cost of capital."

—Boise Cascade

"With a return on capital roughly three times our cost of capital, this strategy [of borrowing more funds to expand] makes even more sense now than before."

—The Coca-Cola Company

"All of our divisions use the measurement of return on invested capital relative to the cost of capital as their standard."

—Textron

How Interest Rates Affect Investment Decisions

Interest rates determine the cost of borrowed funds. A change in interest rates can affect the cost of borrowing as well as the project's feasibility. Firms require a return on projects that exceeds their cost of funds. If they use borrowed funds to finance a project and pay 15 percent on those funds, they would require a return of at least 15 percent on that project. If interest rates decrease, the cost of financing decreases, and the firm's required rate of return decreases. Thus, a project once perceived by the firm as unfeasible may be feasible once the firm's required rate of return is lowered.

Capital Budget

capital budget a targeted amount of funds to be used for purchasing assets such as buildings, machinery, and equipment that are needed for long-term projects

Firms plan a **capital budget,** or a targeted amount of funds to be used for purchasing assets such as buildings, machinery, and equipment that are needed for long-term projects. The annual capital budget for firms such as PepsiCo, The Coca-Cola Company, IBM, and ExxonMobil commonly exceeds $1 billion. The size of a firm's capital budget is influenced by the amount and size of feasible business projects.

A firm's capital budget can be allocated across its various businesses. PepsiCo distributes its capital budget across snack foods and beverages.

A capital budget can also be segmented by geographic markets. PepsiCo allocates its capital budget for projects in the United States and for projects in foreign countries.

Classification of Capital Expenditures

The types of potential capital expenditures considered by a firm can be broadly classified into the following three categories.

Expansion of Current Business If the demand for a firm's products increases, a firm invests in additional assets (such as machinery or equipment) to produce a large enough volume of products to accommodate

Maker's Mark, a family-run distillery has undergone a 13.5 million expansion that will double its annual 34,000-barrel capacity. The distillery, which was designated a national historic landmark in 1980, will show off the results of the expansion during an upcoming ceremony.

AP Photo/ Patti Longmire

FedEx Ground is currently expanding their daily package volume capacity from 2.5 million in 2002 to 4.8 million by the end of fiscal year 2009.

© Getty Images/ Tim Boyle

the increased demand. For example, many health-care firms have increased their capital budgets as they anticipate an increase in demand for their products.

Development of New Business When firms expand the line of products that they produce and sell, they need new facilities for production. They may also need to hire employees to produce and sell the new products. The car manufacturers frequently invest millions of dollars every year to expand their product line and to improve their exporting capabilities.

Investment in Assets That Will Reduce Expenses Machines and equipment wear out or become technologically obsolete over time. Firms replace old machines and equipment to capitalize on new technology, which may allow for lower expenses over time. For example, a new computer may be able to generate a firm's financial reports more economically than an older computer. The benefits of lower expenses may outweigh the initial outlay needed to purchase the new computer.

Firms also purchase machines that can perform the work of employees. For example, machines rather than employees could be used on an assembly line to package a product. The benefits of these machines are the cost savings that result from employing fewer workers. To determine whether the machines are feasible for this purpose, the cost savings must be compared with the price of the machines.

College Health Club: **Investment Decisions at CHC**

One of the decisions that Sue Kramer needs to make as part of her business plan for College Health Club (CHC) is how to invest funds in the business. Since she has decided to lease the equipment and facilities rather than purchase them, she does not need funds to make such purchases. Nevertheless, she needs to have sufficient funds on hand to cover the monthly lease payments and other operating expenses such as salaries, utility expenses, insurance, and marketing expenses. Though she ultimately hopes to use funds generated from memberships to cover these expenses, it will be several months before the revenue from memberships is large enough to cover expenses. She will also need some funds to improve the facilities for the members. For example, she may install a computer that is accessible to members who want online access or want to maintain a record of their exercise performance for the day.

CAPITAL BUDGETING TASKS

2

Explain how a firm can use capital budgeting to determine whether it should invest in a project.

The process of capital budgeting involves five tasks:

▶ Proposing new projects

▶ Estimating cash flows of projects

▶ Determining whether projects are feasible

▶ Implementing feasible projects

▶ Monitoring projects that were implemented

Proposing New Projects

New projects are continually proposed within the firm as various departments or divisions offer input on new projects to consider.

Estimating Cash Flows of Projects

Each potential project affects the cash flows of the firm. Estimating the cash flows that will result from the project is a critical part of the capital budgeting process. Revenue received from the project represents cash inflows, while payments to cover the project's expenses represent cash outflows. The decision whether to make a capital expenditure is based on the size of the periodic cash flows (defined as cash inflows minus cash outflows per period) that are expected to occur as a result of the project.

Determining Whether Projects Are Feasible

Once potential projects are proposed and their cash flows estimated, the projects must be evaluated to determine whether they are feasible. Specific techniques are available to assess the feasibility of projects. One popular method is the net present value technique, which compares the expected periodic cash flows resulting from the project with the initial outlay needed to finance the project. This process is discussed in more detail later in this chapter. If the present value of the project's expected cash flows is above or equal to the initial outlay, the project is feasible. Conversely, if the present value of the project's expected cash flows is below the initial outlay, the project is not feasible.

In some cases, the evaluation involves deciding between two projects designed for the same purpose. When only one of the projects can be accepted, such projects are referred to as **mutually exclusive.** For example, a firm may be considering two machines that perform the same task. The two alternative machines are mutually exclusive because the purchase of one machine precludes the purchase of the other.

When the decision of whether to adopt one project has no bearing on the adoption of other projects, the project is said to be **independent.** For example, the purchase of a truck to enhance delivery capabilities and the

mutually exclusive the situation in which only one of two projects designed for the same purpose can be accepted

independent project project whose feasibility can be assessed without consideration of any others

purchase of a large computer system to handle payroll processing are independent projects. That is, the acceptance (or rejection) of one project does not influence the acceptance (or rejection) of the other project.

The authority to evaluate the feasibility of projects may be dependent on the types of projects evaluated. Larger capital expenditures normally are reviewed by high-level managers. Smaller capital expenditures may be made by other managers.

Implementing Feasible Projects

Once the firm has determined which projects are feasible, it must focus on implementing those projects. All feasible projects should be given a priority status so that those projects that fulfill immediate needs can be implemented first. As part of the implementation process, the firm must obtain the necessary funds to finance the projects.

Monitoring Projects That Were Implemented

After a project has been implemented, it should be monitored over time. The project's actual costs and benefits should be compared with the estimates made before the project was implemented. The monitoring process may detect errors in the previous estimation of the project's cash flows. If any errors are detected, the employees who were responsible for project evaluation should be informed of the problem so that future projects can be evaluated more accurately.

A second purpose of monitoring is to detect and correct inefficiencies in the current operation of the project. Furthermore, monitoring can help determine if and when a project should be abandoned (liquidated) by the firm.

Summary of Capital Budgeting Tasks

The five tasks necessary to conduct capital budgeting are summarized in Exhibit 17.2. The most challenging task is the estimation of cash flows, because it is difficult to accurately measure the revenue and expenses that will result from a particular project.

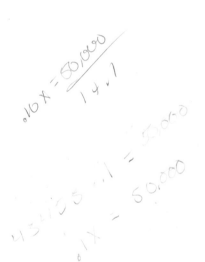

Exhibit 17.2

Summary of Capital Budgeting Tasks

Task	Description
Propose new projects.	Propose new projects that require expenditures necessary to support expansion of existing businesses, development of new businesses, or replacement of old assets.
Estimate cash flows of projects.	Cash flows in each period can be estimated as the cash inflows (such as revenue) resulting from the project minus cash outflows (expenses) resulting from the project.
Determine whether projects are feasible.	A project is feasible if the present value of its future cash flows exceeds the initial outlay needed to purchase the project.
Implement feasible projects.	Feasible projects should be implemented, with priority given to those projects that fulfill immediate needs.
Monitor projects that were implemented.	Projects that have been implemented need to be monitored to determine whether their cash flows were estimated properly. Monitoring may also detect inefficiencies in the project and can help determine when a project should be abandoned.

CAPITAL BUDGETING ANALYSIS

A firm performs a capital budgeting analysis of each project by comparing the project's initial outlay with the project's expected benefits. The benefits represent the cash flows generated by the project. Before providing an example of a firm's capital budgeting analysis, the procedure for estimating the present value of future cash flows is described.

Background on Present Value

Because money has a time value, a payment received by a firm at a future point in time has less value than the same payment received today. For this reason, future payments are commonly discounted to determine their present value. For example, if a payment of $50,000 is received in one year, it can be discounted to determine its present value. Assume that the firm can achieve a return of 10 percent over the next year on funds available today. It will use this interest rate to discount the $50,000 payment to be received in one year.

$$\text{Present Value } (PV) \text{ of } \$50,000 \text{ Payment} = \frac{\$50,000}{(1 + .10)}$$

$$= \$45,455$$

This means that the $50,000 payment to be received in one year has a present value of $45,455. If the firm received $45,455 today (instead of $50,000 in one year) and invested the funds at 10 percent, the funds would accumulate to $50,000 at the end of the year.

Capital budgeting analysis compares future cash flows resulting from the project with the initial outlay needed to purchase the project. The initial outlay is made immediately (if the project is implemented), but the cash flows resulting from the project may be received over several years. Since the timing of the cash flows differs from that of the initial outlay, the cash flows must be converted to a present value so that they can be compared with the initial outlay.

The present value of a project's future cash flows is determined by discounting the cash flows at the rate of return that the firm could have earned on the funds if it had used them for an alternative project with similar risk. That is, the discount rate reflects the return that the firm would require to make the investment. The firm must earn at least that return, or it would simply invest the funds in the alternative project.

For example, assume a firm can invest in a project today that would generate a lump-sum cash flow (CF) of $10,000 from the investment in one year. If the firm has a required return (r) on this investment of 12 percent, the present value (PV) of the cash flow is as follows:

$$PV = \frac{CF \text{ at End of Year 1}}{(1 + r)}$$

$$= \frac{\$10,000}{(1 + .12)^1}$$

$$= \$8,929$$

This indicates that if the firm had the cash amount of $8,929 available today and could invest it at 12 percent, the investment would be worth $10,000 in one year. Therefore, if the initial outlay is more than $8,929, the firm should not invest in the project, because the initial outlay would exceed the present value of the cash flow generated by the investment.

Now adjust the example to determine the present value of the $10,000 cash flow if it is received at the end of the second year instead of the first year. The present value of this project based on a required return of 12 percent is as follows:

$$PV = \frac{CF \text{ at End of Year 2}}{(1 + r)^2}$$

$$= \frac{\$10,000}{(1 + .12)^2}$$

$$= \$7,972$$

The exponent of the denominator is adjusted to discount the amount based on a period of two years instead of one year. Notice that the present value of cash flows in Year 2 is less than the present value of cash flows in Year 1. The further out the time when a given amount is received, the lower the present value.

The present value of a cash amount in any year can be estimated by adjusting the exponent to reflect the number of years in the future. As one final example, the present value of a $10,000 cash flow to be received three years from now is estimated as follows (assuming the required return is 12 percent):

$$PV = \frac{CF \text{ at End of Year 3}}{(1 + r)^3}$$

$$= \frac{\$10,000}{(1 + .12)^3}$$

$$= \$7,118$$

$$PV = \frac{FV}{(1+r)^n}$$

Now consider a project that generates a cash flow of $10,000 for the firm in Years 1, 2, and 3. Each cash flow can be discounted separately to derive its present value; then, the discounted cash flows are added to determine the present value of the investment. The present value of these cash flows is estimated as follows:

$$PV = \frac{CF \text{ at End of Year 1}}{(1 + r)^1} + \frac{CF \text{ at End of Year 2}}{(1 + r)^2} + \frac{CF \text{ at End of Year 3}}{(1 + r)^3}$$

$$= \frac{\$10,000}{(1 + .12)^1} + \frac{\$10,000}{(1 + .12)^2} + \frac{\$10,000}{(1 + .12)^3}$$

$$= \$8,929 + \$7,972 + \$7,118$$

$$= \$24,019$$

This example is illustrated in Exhibit 17.3. It shows how the present value of cash flows is determined by discounting the cash flows in each year at the firm's required rate of return. Then, those discounted cash flows are added together to determine the present value of the cash flows. If the initial outlay necessary to purchase this project is less than $24,019, the project is feasible and should be implemented. If the initial outlay necessary to purchase the project is more than $24,019, the project is not feasible and should not be implemented.

Exhibit 17.3

Example of Discounting Cash Flows

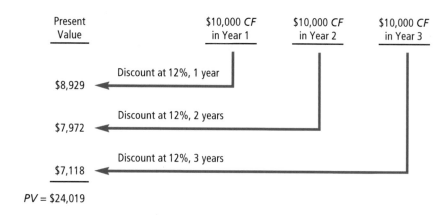

$PV = \$24,019$

Estimating the Net Present Value   To reinforce the use of capital budgeting analysis, consider a firm that decides to purchase a used delivery truck for $15,000 that will be used to make extra deliveries and will last only two years. By having this truck, the firm estimates that it will generate an extra $8,000 in cash flow at the end of next year and an extra $12,000 at the end of the following year. Assume that the firm requires a return of 15 percent on this project. The present value of these cash flows is estimated as follows:

$$PV = \frac{\$8,000}{(1 + .15)^1} + \frac{\$12,000}{(1 + .15)^2}$$
$$= \$6,957 + \$9,074$$
$$= \$16,031$$

net present value equal to the present value of cash flows minus the initial outlay

The **net present value** of a project is equal to the present value (*PV*) of cash flows minus the initial outlay (*I*). In our example, the net present value (*NPV*) is as follows:

$$NPV = PV - I$$
$$= \$16,031 - \$15,000$$
$$= \$1,031$$

When the net present value is positive, the present value exceeds the initial outlay, and the project is feasible. When the net present value is negative, the present value of cash flows is less than the initial outlay, and the project is not feasible. Projects are undertaken only when they are expected to generate benefits (present value of cash flows) that exceed the cost (initial outlay).

Now let's progress to larger-scale decisions by firms. Assume that a firm considers opening up a new store, which would require an initial outlay of $2 million. The firm has estimated its revenue and expenses as shown in the first three columns of Exhibit 17.4 over a four-year period. To simplify the example, assume that the firm conducts all transactions on a cash basis (no accounts payable or receivable). At the end of four years, the firm expects to sell the store for $1 million (after paying taxes on the proceeds of the sale). The amount of money that a firm can receive from selling a project is referred to as the **salvage value**. Assume that the firm requires a 20 percent rate of return on this project. Assume a tax rate of 30 percent charged on earnings generated by the project.

salvage value the amount of money that a firm can receive from selling a project

Exhibit 17.4

Capital Budgeting Example

(1) End of Year	(2) Revenue	(3) Expenses	(4) Earnings	(5) Tax (30%)	(6) After-Tax Cash Flow	(7) Discounted Value of Cash Flow
1	$4,000,000	$4,000,000	0	0	0	0
2	5,000,000	4,000,000	$1,000,000	$300,000	$ 700,000	$ 486,111
3	6,000,000	5,000,000	1,000,000	300,000	700,000	405,093
4	7,000,000	5,000,000	2,000,000	600,000	1,400,000	675,154
Salvage Value					1,000,000	482,253
					$PV =$	$2,048,611
					$I =$	2,000,000
					$NPV = $$	48,611

Steps

1. Subtract expenses (in column 3) from revenue (in column 2) to derive earnings (shown in column 4) each year.

2. Apply the 30 percent tax rate on earnings to determine the tax on earnings each year (as shown in column 5).

3. Subtract the taxes from earnings to determine the after-tax cash flow each year (as shown in column 6).

4. Discount the after-tax cash flow each year, as shown in column 7.

cross functional teamwork:

Cross Functional Relationships Involved in Business Investment Decisions

When financial managers make capital budgeting decisions, they rely on information from the production and marketing departments, as shown in the diagram below. The expected cash inflows resulting from a project are dependent on the expected sales to be generated by the project, which are normally forecasted by the marketing department. The expected cash outflows resulting from a project are dependent on the expected expenses incurred by the project. The marketing department can forecast the expenses that would be incurred by marketing (such as promotion expenses). The production department can forecast the expenses that would be incurred by production (such as labor expenses). The financial manager's ability to estimate a project's net present value is dependent on the input provided by marketing and production managers.

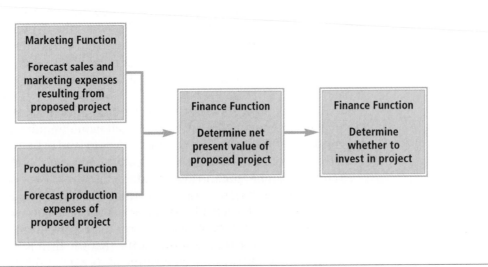

Global Investing U.S. firms frequently consider investing funds in foreign projects. The Coca-Cola Company commonly invests more than $1 billion per year to expand its worldwide business. The Coca-Cola Company typically invests the bulk of its capital budget overseas, because international markets offer more opportunities for the company.

When U.S. firms such as Coca-Cola consider the purchase of a foreign company, they conduct a capital budgeting analysis to determine whether this type of project is feasible. The capital budgeting analysis required to assess a foreign project is more complex than the analysis for a domestic project because of the need to assess specific characteristics of the foreign country. First, the initial outlay required to purchase the foreign firm will depend on the exchange rate at that time. The lower the value of the foreign currency needed, the lower the initial outlay needed by the U.S. firm to invest in the foreign country. Firms prefer to invest in foreign companies (or any other foreign projects) under these conditions.

Firms that consider foreign projects must also determine the required rate of return for the foreign project to be feasible. Many foreign projects are considered to be more risky than domestic projects, so U.S. firms require higher rates of return on foreign projects than on domestic projects. Foreign projects in developing countries are especially risky, because the probability is high that these projects could be terminated by the governments of those countries. When a U.S. firm requires a higher return, it uses a higher discount rate to derive the present value of the project's future cash flows. This point is especially important in light of recent trends by U.S. firms to invest in large projects based in developing countries. General Motors typically invests more than $100 million per year in developing countries. The large amount of investment by General Motors in these countries suggests that it expects the projects to generate very high returns, making them worthwhile even though they are riskier than projects in the United States.

To determine whether this project is feasible, the firm takes the following steps:

1 The earnings are derived by subtracting expenses from revenue, as shown in column 4 of Exhibit 17.4.

2 The tax on the earnings is estimated as 30 percent of each year's earnings, as shown in column 5.

3 The taxes are subtracted from earnings to derive the cash flows shown in column 6.

4 The firm discounts the cash flows received (including the salvage value) using its required rate of return (20 percent) as the discount rate.

5 The discounted cash flows for each year (shown in column 7) are then added at the bottom of column 7 to determine the present value (*PV*) of future cash flows.

The process of discounting the project's cash flows to derive its present value is illustrated in Exhibit 17.5. In this example, the cash flows had to be determined before they could be discounted. Notice that because of the time value of money, the $700,000 cash flow in Year 3 has a much lower present value than the $700,000 cash flow in Year 2.

The present value is equal to $2,048,611 in our example. To derive the project's net present value (*NPV*), the project's initial outlay (*I*) of $2,000,000 is subtracted from the present value. In our example, the *NPV* = $48,611. This means that the present value of future cash flows resulting from the project is expected to exceed the project's initial outlay (*I*) by $48,611. Since the *NPV* is positive, the proposed project should be undertaken. When the present value of the project's cash flows exceeds the

Exhibit 17.5

Deriving a Project's Net Present Value

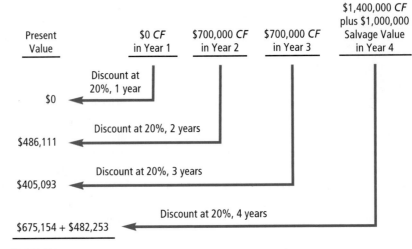

Present Value	$0 *CF* in Year 1	$700,000 *CF* in Year 2	$700,000 *CF* in Year 3	$1,400,000 *CF* plus $1,000,000 Salvage Value in Year 4

Discount at
20%, 1 year

$0

Discount at 20%, 2 years

$486,111

Discount at 20%, 3 years

$405,093

Discount at 20%, 4 years

$675,154 + $482,253

$PV = \$2,048,611$

initial outlay (cost) of the project, the return of the project is expected to exceed the cost of capital used to support the project.

College Health Club: **CHC's Investment Decision**

Sue Kramer, president of College Health Club (CHC), learns that the Silver Health Club in a nearby town is for sale for $100,000 and that its owners would be willing to help finance its purchase. Like CHC, Silver is close to a college campus, but it has not made much of an effort to attract that college's students. This club's largest expense is the rent. Sue believes that she could improve Silver's performance if she purchased it. Sue decides to conduct a capital budgeting analysis of Silver Health Club. She estimates her cash inflows each year and subtracts the estimated cash outflows to derive annual cash flows. Her cash outflows include the cost of hiring a manager to oversee the club's business, since Sue would still devote most of her time to CHC. She estimates that her cash flows would be $5,000 in each of the first two years and $20,000 over each of the following three years. All cash flows are expected to occur at the end of each year. Sue also estimates that she would be able to sell the Silver Health Club in five years for $120,000 (after taxes). Based on the possible financing that Sue would have to obtain and the risk of this venture, Sue decides that she would need to generate a rate of return of at least 20 percent from Silver to make it worth purchasing.

Sue's capital budgeting analysis of Silver Health Club is shown in the following table:

Capital Budgeting Analysis of Silver Health Club

(1) End of Year	(2) Estimated Cash Flow	(3) Discounted Cash Flow (at 20%)
1	$ 5,000	$ 4,167
2	5,000	3,472
3	20,000	11,574
4	20,000	9,645
5	20,000	8,038
	+ $120,000 (Salvage Value)	48,225
	Present Value =	$85,121
	− Initial Outlay =	$100,000
	Net Present Value =	−$14,879

The cash flows shown in column 2 are discounted at a rate of 20 percent (Sue's required rate of return) to derive their present value in column 3. Notice that the salvage value of $120,000 (the expected sales price of the firm) is also included in the estimated cash flows for Year 5. The discounted annual cash flows are summed at the bottom of Column 3 to derive the present value of future cash flows.

Sue estimates the present value of the Silver Health Club's future cash flows to be $85,121, which is less than the initial outlay (purchase price) of $100,000. Therefore, the net present value from acquiring the Silver Health Club is negative, causing Sue to reject this project. The present value of future cash flows does not cover the amount she would have to pay for the club. Sue decides to monitor the status of the Silver Health Club over time, however. If its price is lowered, she will reassess whether to acquire it by conducting a new capital budgeting analysis.

MERGERS

3 Describe the factors that motivate investment in other firms (acquisitions).

merger two firms are merged (or combined) to become a single firm owned by the same owners (shareholders)

horizontal merger the combination of firms that engage in the same types of business

vertical merger the combination of a firm with a potential supplier or customer

conglomerate merger the combination of two firms in unrelated businesses

A firm may invest in another company by purchasing all the stock of that company. This results in a **merger,** in which two firms are merged (or combined) to become a single firm owned by the same owners (shareholders). A merger may be feasible if it can increase a firm's value either by increasing the return to the firm's owners or by reducing the firm's risk without a reduction in return.

Mergers can be classified as one of three general types. A **horizontal merger** is the combination of firms that engage in the same types of business. For example, the merger between First Union Corporation and Wachovia Corporation was a horizontal merger, as it combined two large commercial banks. A **vertical merger** is the combination of a firm with a potential supplier or customer, such as General Motors' acquisition of a battery manufacturer that could produce the batteries for many of its automobiles. A **conglomerate merger** is the combination of two firms in unrelated businesses. For example, a merger between a book publisher and a steel manufacturer

Two employees walk toward Intel Corporation's plant in Rio Rancho, N.M. Despite the recent high-tech slump, Semiconductor giant Intel opened a $2 billion expansion of the chip-making plant to meet demand when the economy rebounds.

AP Photo/Vasquez-Cunningham

would be a conglomerate merger. The term *conglomerate* is sometimes used to describe a firm that is engaged in a variety of unrelated businesses.

Corporate Motives for Mergers

Mergers are normally initiated as a result of one or more of the following motives.

Immediate Growth A firm that plans for growth may prefer to achieve its objective immediately through a merger. Consider a firm whose production capacity cannot fully satisfy demand for its product. The firm would need two years to build additional production facilities. To achieve an immediate increase in production, the firm may search for a company that owns the appropriate facilities. By acquiring either part or all of such a company, the firm can achieve immediate growth in its production capacity, thereby allowing for growth in its sales. When Walt Disney Company purchased Capital Cities/ABC, it created more growth potential than if it had simply attempted to expand its existing businesses.

Economies of Scale Growth may also be desirable to reduce the production cost per unit. Products that exhibit economies of scale can be produced at a much lower cost per unit if a large amount is produced. A merger may allow a firm to combine two production facilities and thereby achieve a lower production cost per unit.

For example, assume that Firm A and Firm B produce a similar product. Also assume that each firm uses an assembly-line operation for about eight hours per day and sells its product to its own set of customers. Firm A sells 500 units per month, while Firm B sells 400 units per month. The variable cost per unit is $10 for each firm. Each firm pays $6,000 per month to rent its own factory. This rent is a fixed cost because it is not affected by the amount of the product produced. If Firm A acquires Firm B, it will be able to serve both sets of customers, which will result in a higher production level. The factory can be used for 16 hours a day by running a second shift for the assembly line.

Based on the initial assumptions, the average cost per unit for each firm is shown in Exhibit 17.6. Notice that when Firm A acquires Firm B, the average cost per unit is lower than it was for either individual firm. This occurs because only one factory is needed when the firms are merged. Thus, the average cost per unit declines when Firm A makes more efficient use of the factory.

There may be additional ways for the combination of firms to reduce costs, beyond the savings resulting from renting only one factory. For ex-

Exhibit 17.6

Illustration of How an Acquisition Can Generate Economies of Scale

Firm	Total Output Produced	Variable Cost per Unit	Variable Cost	Fixed Cost (Rent)	Total Cost	Average Cost per Unit
A	500 units	$10	$5,000	$6,000	$11,000	($11,000/500) = $22.00
B	400 units	$10	$4,000	$6,000	$10,000	($10,000/400) = $25.00
A & B Combined	900 units	$10	$9,000	$6,000	$15,000	($15,000/900) = $16.67

increasing value with technology

INTEGRATING TECHNOLOGY AFTER MERGERS

The integration of information technology (IT) is a difficult process for firms involved in mergers and acquisitions. Data centers must be consolidated, data access methods standardized, and data integrity problems solved. Cost reductions from the economies of scale that motivate many merg- ers do not occur for IT. In fact, most companies experience an increase in expenses immediately following the merger. The cost reductions will happen after the integration process is complete and redundant IT operations and positions are eliminated.

ample, assume each firm has its own accountant. Each firm pays a salary for this position, which reflects a fixed cost. However, Firm A's accountant may be able to cover all the accounting duties for the combined firm, which means that it need not incur the cost of Firm B's accountant. Therefore, it can further reduce costs by removing any job positions in Firm B that can be handled by Firm A's existing employees.

Horizontal mergers are more likely to achieve economies of scale than vertical or conglomerate mergers, because they involve firms that produce similar products. Firms with similar operations can allow for the elimination of similar positions once the firms are combined.

Managerial Expertise   The performance of a firm is highly dependent on the managers who make the decisions for the firm. Since the firm's value is influenced by its performance, its value is influenced by its managers. To illustrate this point, consider a firm called "Weakfirm" that has had weak performance recently because of its managers. This firm's value should be low if its performance has been weak and is not expected to improve.

Also assume, however, that another firm in the same industry, called "Strongfirm," has more competent managers. If the managers of Strong- firm had been managing the operations of Weakfirm, the performance of Weakfirm might have been much higher. Given this information, Strong- firm may consider purchasing Weakfirm. The price for Weakfirm should be relatively low because of its recent performance. Yet, once Strongfirm pur- chases Weakfirm, it can improve Weakfirm's performance. The owners (shareholders) of Strongfirm will benefit because their firm is able to ac- quire another firm at a relatively low price and turn it into something more valuable. In other words, the additional earnings generated by Strongfirm following the acquisition may exceed the cost of the acquisition.

The example just described occurs frequently. Some firms that have had relatively weak performance (compared with other firms in the industry) become targets. Consequently, weak firms are always in danger of being acquired.

Some mergers can be beneficial when each firm relies on the other firm for specific managerial expertise. For example, consider Disney's acquisition of the ABC television network. Disney produced movies that were sold to television networks. When television networks began to produce their own movies, Disney could have had difficulty selling its movies to various net- works. By acquiring the ABC network, Disney could rely on the network to show some of its movies, while the ABC network was assured that it would be supplied with various popular Disney movies. Disney had expertise as the producer of the product (movies), and ABC had expertise as the distributor of that product. Both firms benefited as a result of the acquisition.

Tax Benefits   Firms that incur negative earnings (losses) are sometimes attractive candidates for mergers because of potential tax advantages. The previous losses incurred by the company prior to the merger can be carried forward to offset positive earnings of the acquiring firm. Although the losses of the acquired firm have occurred prior to the acquisition, they reduce the taxable earnings of the newly merged corporation. To illustrate the potential tax benefits, consider an acquisition in which the acquiring firm applies a $1 million loss of the acquired firm to partially offset its earnings. If the acquiring firm is subject to a 30 percent tax rate, it can reduce its taxes by $300,000 (computed as 30 percent times the $1 million in earnings that is no longer subject to tax because of applying the $1 million loss).

LEVERAGED BUYOUTS

leveraged buyout (LBO) the purchase of a company (or a subsidiary of a company) by a group of investors with borrowed funds

In a **leveraged buyout,** or **LBO,** a group of investors purchase a company (or a subsidiary of a company) with borrowed funds. In many cases, the investors are the previous managers of the business. For example, consider a diversified firm that plans to sell off its financial services division to obtain cash. The management of this division may attempt to borrow the necessary funds to purchase the division themselves and become the owners. The newly owned business would be supported with mostly borrowed funds.

A well-known LBO was the acquisition of RJR Nabisco by Kohlberg Kravis Roberts for about $25 billion. About 94 percent of the funds used to purchase RJR Nabisco were borrowed.

Any business with characteristics that enable it to operate adequately with a large amount of borrowed funds is a potential candidate for an LBO. Such characteristics include established product lines, stable cash flow, and no need for additional fixed assets. These characteristics increase the probability that a sufficient amount of cash flows will consistently be forthcoming to cover periodic interest payments on the debt. Growth normally is not a primary goal, since the firm does not have excess cash to expand and may have already borrowed up to its capacity.

Although an LBO can place a strain on cash, it does offer an advantage. The ownership of the business is restricted to a small group of people. All earnings can be allocated to this group, which allows the potential for high returns to the owners (although most earnings will likely be reinvested in the business in the early years). However, since businesses that experience LBOs have a debt-intensive capital structure (high degree of financial leverage), they are risky.

DIVESTITURES

divestiture the sale of an existing business by a firm

A **divestiture** is the sale of an existing business by a firm. Firms may have several motives for divestitures. First, a firm may divest (sell) businesses that are not part of its core operations so that it can focus on what it does best. For example, Eastman Kodak, Ford Motor Company, and many other firms have sold various businesses that were not closely related to their core business. A second motive for divestitures is to obtain funds. Divestitures generate funds for the firm, because one of the firm's businesses is sold in exchange for cash. For example, CSX Corporation made divestitures to focus on its core railroad business and also to obtain funds so that it could pay off some of its existing debt.

A third motive for divesting is that a firm's "break-up" value is sometimes believed to be worth more than the firm as a whole. In other words, the sum of a firm's individual asset liquidation values exceeds the market value of the firm's combined assets. This encourages firms to sell off what would be worth more when liquidated than when retained.

SHORT-TERM INVESTMENT DECISIONS

4

Explain how firms make decisions for investing in short-term assets.

working capital management the management of a firm's short-term assets and liabilities

Working capital management involves the management of a firm's short-term assets and liabilities. A firm's short-term assets include cash, short-term securities, accounts receivable, and inventory. Its short-term liabilities include accounts payable and short-term loans. Working capital management is typically focused on the proper amount of investment in a firm's cash, short-term securities, accounts receivable, and inventory. All of these strategies can be classified as a firm's investment strategies. Working capital management can be segmented into liquidity management, accounts receivable management, and inventory management.

Liquidity Management

liquid having access to funds to pay bills when they come due

liquidity management the management of short-term assets and liabilities to ensure adequate liquidity

Treasury bills short-term debt securities issued by the U.S. Treasury

Firms that are **liquid** have adequate access to funds to pay bills when they come due. **Liquidity management** involves the management of short-term assets and liabilities to ensure adequate liquidity. To remain liquid, firms may maintain cash and short-term securities. For example, they may invest in **Treasury bills,** which are short-term debt securities issued by the U.S. Treasury. Treasury bills have maturities of 13 weeks, 26 weeks, and one year. Treasury bills offer a relatively low return. They provide a firm with easy access to funds because they can easily be sold to other investors. When firms need funds to pay bills, they sell the Treasury bills and use the proceeds to pay the bills. Firms such as DuPont and The Coca-Cola Company hold hundreds of millions of dollars worth of short-term securities to maintain liquidity.

line of credit an agreement with a bank that allows a firm access to borrowed funds upon demand over some specified period

Firms normally attempt to limit their holdings of cash and short-term securities so that they can use their funds for other purposes that generate higher returns. They can be liquid without holding cash and short-term securities if they have easy access to borrowed funds. Most firms have a **line of credit** with one or more banks, which is an agreement that allows access to borrowed funds upon demand over some specified period (usually one year). If a firm experiences a temporary shortage of funds, it can use its line of credit to obtain a short-term loan immediately. The interest charged by the banks on the loan is normally tied to some specified market-determined interest rate. Thus, the interest rate will be consistent with existing market rates at the time of the loan. Firms with a line of credit do not need to go through the loan application process. They can normally reapply for a new line of credit each year.

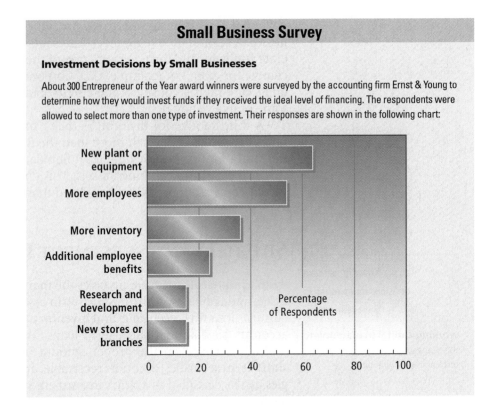

Small Business Survey

Investment Decisions by Small Businesses

About 300 Entrepreneur of the Year award winners were surveyed by the accounting firm Ernst & Young to determine how they would invest funds if they received the ideal level of financing. The respondents were allowed to select more than one type of investment. Their responses are shown in the following chart:

Because of its line of credit, its cash, and its short-term securities, The Coca-Cola Company always has access to a sufficient amount of funds to pay its bills.

When firms build up an excessive amount of cash, they search for ways to use the excess. For example, they commonly use excess cash to repurchase some of their existing stock. Alternatively, they may use excess cash to pay off some of their existing debt.

Accounts Receivable Management

Firms have accounts receivable when they grant credit to customers. By granting credit, firms may generate more sales than if they required an immediate cash payment. Allowing credit has two potential disadvantages, however. The first is that the customers may not pay the credit balance for a long time. Thus, the firm does not have use of the cash until several months after the sale was made. Consequently, the firm may have to borrow funds until the cash is received and will have to pay interest on those funds.

The second potential disadvantage of extending credit to customers is that the customers may default on the credit provided. In this case, the firm never receives payment for the products it sold to customers.

accounts receivable management sets the limits on credit available to customers and the length of the period in which payment is due

Accounts receivable management sets the limits on credit available to customers and the length of the period in which payment is due. The goal is to be flexible enough so that sales increase as a result of credit granted but strict enough to avoid customers who would pay their bills late (beyond the period specified) or not at all.

Given the possibilities of late payments or no payments (default) on the credit, firms need to closely assess the creditworthiness of any customers who wish to pay their bills with credit.

College Health Club: Accounts Receivable Management at CHC

One of the decisions that Sue Kramer needs to make as part of her business plan for College Health Club (CHC) is whether to implement a credit policy for her members. Recall that she expects that CHC will attract 300 members in its first year. Sue knows that some students who may want to become members cannot afford CHC's annual membership fee. She thinks that by implementing a credit policy that would allow members to pay later in the year, she could increase the membership to 330 members in the first year. However, Sue also thinks that 40 of those members would never pay their membership fee if they were not required to pay when they first joined the club. Her analysis of the impact of a credit policy on CHC's first-year performance is shown in the following table:

	CHC's Performance If . . .	
	Credit Is Not Offered	Credit Is Offered
(1) Price per membership	$500	$500
(2) Number of members in first year	300	330
(3) Number of members who pay their fees	300	290
(4) Revenue = (1) × (3)	$150,000	$145,000
(5) Total operating expenses	$138,000	$138,000
(6) Interest expenses	$4,000	$4,000
(7) Earnings before Taxes = (4) − (5) − (6)	$8,000	$3,000

Although the number of members would be higher if Sue allows credit, fewer members would pay their fees. Based on this analysis, Sue decides not to allow credit. However, she will consider an alternative plan that would allow a student to purchase a four-month membership for $110. This price is slightly higher (on a monthly basis) than the annual membership fee. This plan would attract students who could not afford the annual membership. In addition, it does not allow an extension of credit, as these students will not be allowed to continue receiving health club services unless they renew their membership.

Inventory Management

When firms maintain large amounts of inventory, they can avoid stockouts (shortages). By holding so much inventory, however, they invest a large amount of funds that they could have used for other purposes. Consider the case of Wal-Mart, which continuously attempts to order enough of each product to satisfy customers. Yet, it does not want to order an excessive amount of any product so that it can use its funds more efficiently.

Inventory management determines the amount of inventory that is held. Managers attempt to hold just enough inventory to avoid stockouts, without tying up funds in excess inventories. This task is complicated because it requires forecasts of future sales levels, which can be erratic. If sales are more than expected, stockouts may occur unless the firm has excess inventory.

inventory management determines the amount of inventory that is held

Best Buy store manager Danny Wong checks inventory of Compaq computers.

© Getty Images / Justin Sullivan

SUMMARY

1 Capital budgeting analysis is normally applied to determine whether proposed projects are feasible. If the present value of the project's expected cash flows exceeds the project's initial outlay, the project has a positive net present value and should be implemented. If the present value of the project's expected cash flows is less than the project's initial outlay, the project has a negative net present value and should not be implemented.

2 The process of capital budgeting involves five tasks:

▶ Proposing new projects that deserve to be assessed.

▶ Estimating cash flows of projects, which represent the cash inflows (derived from revenue) minus the cash outflows (derived from expenses) per period.

▶ Determining which projects are feasible, which can be accomplished by comparing the present value of the project's cash flows with the project's initial outlay.

▶ Implementing feasible projects based on a priority status.

▶ Monitoring projects that were implemented, so that any errors from estimating project cash flows are recognized and may be avoided when assessing projects in the future.

3 Firms consider investing funds to acquire other companies as a result of one or more of the following motives:

▶ A firm can achieve immediate growth by acquiring another firm, whereas growth without a merger will be slower.

▶ Mergers can create a higher volume of sales for a firm, which allows it to spread its fixed cost across more units, thereby reducing costs (economies of scale).

▶ Mergers can allow firms to combine resources and contribute those resources in which they have the most managerial expertise.

▶ Mergers can allow the acquiring firm to reduce its taxable earnings when it acquires a company that recently incurred a loss.

4 Firms invest in short-term assets such as cash, short-term securities, accounts receivable, and inventory. They invest in a sufficient amount of cash and short-term securities to maintain adequate liquidity. However, excessive investment in cash and short-term securities represents an inefficient use of funds.

Firms desire to invest in sufficient accounts receivable so that they can increase revenue over time. They must impose adequate credit standards, however, so that they can avoid excessive defaults on credit they have provided.

Firms desire to invest in a sufficient amount of inventory so that they can avoid stockouts. However, excessive investment in inventory represents an inefficient use of funds.

KEY TERMS

Review & Critical Thinking Questions

1. What investment decisions should financial managers consider in achieving the firm's objectives?

2. How do interest rates affect the capital budgeting analysis?

3. List the classifications of capital expenditures.

4. Distinguish between mutually exclusive and independent projects.

5. Briefly summarize the major tasks involved in the capital budgeting process.

6. Discuss the process of capital budgeting analysis when a firm assesses a foreign project.

7. Briefly describe the different types of mergers that can take place between firms.

8. Explain how cross functional teamwork is involved in business investment decisions.

9. Briefly describe some corporate motives for mergers.

10. What is a divestiture? Why would a firm's management consider a divestiture?

11. What is working capital management? Briefly describe the short-term investment decisions undertaken by a firm.

12. Discuss the pros and cons of carrying a small versus a large inventory for a retailer.

Discussion Questions

1. How can a firm use the Internet to research investment opportunities?

2. Explain why a horizontal merger could reduce competition in the automobile industry.

3. Assume that you are a financial manager. How would you work with production and marketing managers in making capital budgeting decisions to introduce a new product? What must the product generate to make it economically feasible?

4. Jason Boone has just opened a go-cart track. He has timed the opening of the go-cart track to coincide with the annual county fair. Because his business has grown rapidly, cash flow remains a problem. Analyze Jason's financial problems. Could this be a good business?

5. Why might a horizontal merger achieve economies of scale?

6. Over lunch, you are listening to your firm's chief financial officer. He is telling you that he just undertook a capital budgeting project because it "looked good and attractive." What steps should the officer have followed to assess the feasibility of this project?

It's Your Decision: **Investment Decisions at CHC**

1. Recall from the chapter that Sue Kramer considered the purchase of Silver Health Club. If Sue was willing to accept a lower rate of return on her investment in the Silver Health Club, how would this affect the present value of the club's future cash flows?

2. What is the key information that Sue used to estimate the future cash flows of the Silver Health Club? Could this information be wrong?

3. Recall that Sue expects total expenses of $142,000 in CHC's first year. She will price a membership at $500 and expects to attract 300 members in the first year. Sue is considering ways to boost CHC's potential membership. She thinks that if she allows members to pay their membership fees later in the year, the number of members will increase to 320. The expected number of paid memberships is equal to the total number of memberships minus the expected number of memberships that are never paid. Determine the expected earnings of CHC based on the following possible scenarios if Sue implements a credit policy.

Number of Members who Never Pay Their Fee	CHC's Earnings before Taxes in the First Year
10	
20	
30	
40	

   a. Explain the relationship between the number of members who do not pay their fee and CHC's earnings.
   b. Describe the trade-off between offering credit for members versus not offering credit. Would you recommend that Sue allow credit for her members?

4. A health club differs from manufacturing firms in that it produces a service rather than products. When a service firm such as a health club considers the creation of a new facility, it must forecast demand for services there. When a manufacturing firm considers the creation of a new facility to produce more of its product, it must forecast its demand. Is it generally easier for a service or a manufacturing firm to forecast demand?

Investing in a Business

Using the annual report of the firm in which you would like to invest, complete the following:

1 What is the firm's capital budget for this year? Is this budget higher or lower than last year's?

2 What types of new projects has the firm invested in recently?

3 Has the firm divested any of its operations? If so, did it divest to focus more on its core business?

4 Has the firm been involved in any recent merger activity? If so, what is its justification for this action?

5 Explain how the business uses technology to promote its capital budgeting activities. For example, does it use the Internet to provide information about recent investment projects? Does it use the Internet to provide information on planned future capital budgeting activities?

6 Go to **http://hoovers.com** and locate the NEWS SEARCH. Type in the name of the firm in the space provided, and review the recent news stories about the firm. Summarize any (at least one) recent news story about the firm that applies to one or more of the key concepts in this chapter.

Case: Deciding Whether to Acquire a Business

Benson, Inc., is a publisher of books that it sells to retail bookstores in the United States. Judith Benson, the owner of Benson, Inc., is concerned because its suppliers continue to increase the price of paper and other materials that Benson purchases from them weekly. One supplier to Benson, Inc., is Hill Company, which provides high-quality supplies but has experienced financial problems recently because of inefficient management.

Judith believes that Benson could benefit from merging with Hill Company. She believes that she could acquire (purchase) Hill at a low price because it has performed poorly in the past. She also believes that she could improve Hill's performance by reorganizing its

business. In addition, the merger with Hill would give Benson, Inc., more control over the cost of its supplies. It could obtain supplies from Hill, which would now be part of Benson, Inc. Therefore, it would not be subjected to increased prices by other suppliers. Meanwhile, Hill would not only produce supplies for Benson, Inc., but would also sell them to other customers, as it did in the past.

Questions

1 What type of merger is Judith considering?

2 Explain how Judith might decide on a purchase price for Hill Company.

3 How could the purchase of Hill Company backfire?

Video Case: Investment Decisions at Maksood's, Inc.

Maksood's, Inc., is a retailer of leisure products such as swimming pools and lawn furniture. It is a member of the Delta Marketing Group, an organization of 15 retailers in the Midwest that makes purchases as a group so that they can buy in bulk. Maksood's can maintain a lower inventory because it can turn to the other retailers if it suddenly needs more of a particular item (such as a swimming pool, a pool table, or a gas grill). Thus, Maksood's can obtain the item from another retailer in the group that has excess inventory rather than having to wait for more to be delivered from the manufacturer.

Another advantage of participating in the organization is that the group can buy products in bulk from manufacturers at lower prices. This reduces their costs. In addition, Maksood's and the other retailers in the group are allowed to pay their bills between 60 and 90 days after receiving the products from the manufacturer. Maksood's is allowed a relatively long time to pay

its bills because it is a member of the organization, and the manufacturer is more willing to give favorable credit terms to a group of 15 retailers than to just a single retailer.

Maksood's invests its excess cash in marketable securities. If it needs funding, it can sell some of its marketable securities, or it can draw upon a line of credit that it has with a bank.

Questions

1 How does Maksood's participation in the organization of retailers help it minimize its inventory? How can this increase its value?

2 How does Maksood's participation in the organization of retailers help it lengthen its credit terms? How can this increase its value?

3 Identify two sources of funds that Maksood's uses when it needs short-term funds. Which source of funds would it most likely use first? Why?

Internet Applications

1. *http://biz.yahoo.com/n/group/latest.z00.html*

Scroll down and type the word "mergers" next to "Search News." Find two articles related to recent merger activity. What types of mergers do the articles discuss (i.e., horizontal, vertical, or conglomerate)? Do you think these mergers will result in future growth or economies of scale? How do you think these mergers will affect the stock prices of the firms involved? Why?

2. *http://www.investbio.com/wealthy/top_200.asp*

   a. Summarize two recent news articles about biotech sector investing. Do you think the infor-

mation in these articles could help another biotech company make investment decisions? How?

   b. Obtain quotes for two of the top biotech companies. Look at their annual reports and determine what recent capital budgeting projects these firms have undertaken. What steps were likely involved in the capital budgeting analyses for these projects?

The Coca-Cola Company Annual Report Project

 Questions for the current year's annual report are available on the text website at **http://madura.swlearning.com.**

The following questions apply concepts presented in this chapter to The Coca-Cola Company. Go to The Coca-Cola Company website (**http://www.cocacola.com**) and find the index for the 2001 annual report.

Questions

1. Download the financial statements and find "Investments." What are The Coca-Cola Company's criteria for investment? Is the focus of its investments different in developed versus emerging markets? Explain.

2. Download the financial statements and find the balance sheet. Describe the trend in capital expenditures of The Coca-Cola Company from 2000 to 2001.

3. Study the "Selected Market Results" under "Operations Review." What type of investments do you think The Coca-Cola Company undertakes in emerging markets? Do you think these investments are different from its investments in developed markets? Why?

4. Download the financial statements and find "Investments." Study the table in the "Our Bottling Partners" section. What does the difference between fair values and carrying values illustrate?

5. Go to **http://hoovers.com** and locate the NEWS CENTER. Key in The Coca-Cola Company in the space provided, click on "Search," and review the recent news stories about the firm. Summarize any (at least one) recent news story about The Coca-Cola Company that applies one or more of the key concepts within this chapter of the text.

In-Text Study Guide

Answers are in an appendix at the back of the book.

True or False

1. Capital budgeting involves the comparison of assets and revenue. F

2. Many decisions that result from capital budgeting decisions are irreversible. T

3. One of the most popular methods available to assess the feasibility of projects is the net present value (NPV) technique. T

4. A payment received by a firm at a future point in time has more value than the exact payment received today. F

5. A payment of $1,000 received two years from today has a higher present value than a payment of $1,000 received one year from today. F

6. A firm should invest in a project only if its net present value is less than zero. F

7. The amount of money that a firm can receive from selling a project is referred to as the net present value. F

8. Capital budgeting analysis for investment projects in foreign countries tends to be more complex than analysis for domestic projects. T

9. Firms can merge only if they are producing similar products. F

10. Firms can be liquid even if they are not holding large amounts of cash and short-term securities. T

Multiple Choice

11. A capital budgeting project is considered to be feasible if:
    a) the sum of future cash flows from the project is greater than the initial outlay.
    b) the sum of the present values of all future cash flows from the project is greater than the initial outlay.
    c) no other projects have a higher initial outlay.
    d) the initial outlay is greater than the sum of all discounted future cash flows that result from the project.
    e) the discount rate used to compute present values is less than the rate of inflation.

12. When interest rates rise, a firm will:
    a) require a higher discount rate when it evaluates capital budgeting proposals.
    b) find that more of its capital budgeting proposals are feasible.
    c) find that present values of future cash flows are unaffected.
    d) want to borrow more funds.
    e) find that cash flows in the early years of a project will be discounted more heavily than cash flows that occur during later years.

13. A firm's _____ is a targeted amount of funds to be used for purchasing assets such as buildings, machinery, and equipment that are needed for long-term projects.
    a) master budget
    b) capital budget
    c) working capital projection
    d) escrow account
    e) sinking fund

14. All of the following are motives for capital budgeting expenditures except:
    a) expansion of current business.
    b) development of new business.
    c) acquisition of assets that will reduce expenses.
    d) acquisition of liabilities.

15. If the adoption of investment A has no bearing on whether other investments should be adopted, investment A is said to be:
    a) redundant.
    b) irrelevant.
    c) independent.
    d) expedient.
    e) unrestricted.

16. All of the following are tasks involved in capital budgeting except:
    a) estimating cash flows from the investment.
    b) determining which projects are feasible.
    c) monitoring projects that are implemented.

d) determining the appropriate size of the line of credit.

e) implementing feasible projects.

17. The discount rate used to compute the present values of future cash flows from an investment should be equal to the:

a) rate of inflation expected to exist over the life of the investment.

b) tax rate applied to the earnings from the investment.

c) rate of return the firm could have earned on an alternative project of similar risk.

d) rate at which the assets purchased to make the investment will depreciate.

e) rate of interest the government pays on Treasury bills of the same duration as the investment project.

18. If the discount rate is 12 percent, the present value of a $20,000 payment received three years from today would be found by:

a) dividing $20,000 by 3 and dividing the result by .12.

b) multiplying $20,000 by .12 and dividing the result by 3.

c) dividing $20,000 by $(1 + .12)^3$.

d) multiplying $20,000 by $(1 + .12)^3$.

e) multiplying $20,000 by 3 and dividing the result by $(1 + .12)$.

19. The _____ of an investment is computed by subtracting the initial outlay for the investment from the present value of all future cash flows that result from the investment.

a) net present value

b) capitalization factor

c) discount value

d) investment premium

e) gross cash position

20. A merger between a tire manufacturer and a firm that produces clocks and watches is:

a) illegal.

b) a horizontal merger.

c) a diagonal merger.

d) a vertical merger.

e) a conglomerate merger.

21. The three general types of mergers are horizontal, conglomerate, and:

a) cooperative.

b) vertical.

c) divestiture.

d) bureaucratic.

e) parallel.

22. Which of the following is the best example of a vertical merger?

a) A chain of fast-food restaurants merges with a firm that produces electronic components for computers.

b) A small book publisher that specializes in travel and history books merges with a larger book publisher that specializes in biographies and popular fiction.

c) A golf club manufacturer merges with a firm that helps people prepare their income taxes.

d) A firm that publishes a newspaper in the St. Louis area merges with a firm that publishes a newspaper in the Chicago area.

e) A firm that sells flour, sugar, and spices merges with a firm that bakes pies and cakes.

23. The result of a firm investing in another company by purchasing all the stock of that company is a(n):

a) divestiture.

b) net present value.

c) economies of scale.

d) line of credit.

e) merger.

24. If the per unit cost of producing a good decreases as a greater quantity is produced, the production process exhibits:

a) economies of scale.

b) diminishing returns.

c) higher fixed costs than variable costs.

d) an exception to the law of supply.

e) a very high break-even point.

In-Text Study Guide

Answers are in an appendix at the back of the book.

25. Economies of scale are more likely to be achieved by:
    a) vertical mergers.
    b) horizontal mergers.
    c) conglomerate mergers.
    d) divestitures.
    e) accounts receivable management.

26. Firms that incur negative earnings are sometimes attractive candidates for mergers because of potential:
    a) tax advantages.
    b) cash advantages.
    c) profit exploitation.
    d) retained earnings.
    e) divestitures.

27. A purchase of a company (or the subsidiary of the company) by a group of investors with borrowed funds is a(n):
    a) common stock purchase.
    b) purchase from retained earnings.
    c) equity purchase.
    d) preferred stock purchase.
    e) leveraged buyout.

28. When a firm sells off one of its existing businesses, the process is known as a:
    a) reverse merger.
    b) leveraged buyout.
    c) corporate downsizing.
    d) conglomeration strategy.
    e) divestiture.

29. A firm's short-term assets include all of the following except:
    a) cash.
    b) accounts receivable.
    c) short-term loans.
    d) inventory.
    e) short-term securities.

30. Firms are said to be _____ if they have adequate access to funds so that they can pay their bills as they come due.
    a) leveraged
    b) fully endowed
    c) vested
    d) bonded
    e) liquid

31. _____ are short-term debt securities offered by the U.S. Treasury that provide firms with easy access to funds since they can be sold to other investors.
    a) Federal warrants
    b) Treasury trust certificates
    c) Treasury stock
    d) Treasury bills
    e) Federal Reserve notes

32. The management of a firm's short-term assets and liabilities is:
    a) accounts receivable management.
    b) working capital management.
    c) sales management.
    d) plant and equipment management.
    e) fixed asset management.

33. An agreement that allows a firm access to borrowed funds upon demand over some specified period of time is a:
    a) bond indenture.
    b) stock flotation.
    c) note receivable.
    d) line of credit.
    e) note payable.

34. The goal of _____ management is to be flexible enough to increase sales to credit customers while being strict enough to limit losses due to customers who pay their bills late or not at all.
    a) leverage
    b) accounts receivable
    c) trade credit
    d) accounts payable
    e) invoice

35. Firms try to maintain a large enough inventory to avoid:
    a) stockouts.
    b) the need for trade credit.
    c) leveraged financing.
    d) default on bonds.
    e) undiversified portfolios.

Appendix: Merger Analysis

When a firm plans to engage in a merger, it must conduct the following tasks:

▶ Identify potential merger prospects.

▶ Evaluate potential merger prospects.

▶ Make the merger decision.

IDENTIFY POTENTIAL MERGER PROSPECTS

Firms attempt to identify potential merger prospects that may help them achieve their strategic plan. If the firm plans for growth in its current line of products, it will consider purchasing (or "acquiring") companies in the same business. If it needs to restructure its production process, it may attempt to acquire a supplier. If it desires a more diversified product line, it may attempt to acquire companies in unrelated businesses. The firm's long-run objectives influence the selection of merger prospects that are worthy of evaluation.

The size of the firm is also a relevant criterion, as some firms may be too small to achieve the desired objectives while others may be too large to acquire. The location is another possible criterion, since a firm's product demand and production costs are dependent on its location.

EVALUATE POTENTIAL MERGER PROSPECTS

Once merger prospects have been identified, they must be analyzed thoroughly, using publicly available financial statements. The financial analysis may detect problems that will eliminate some prospects from further consideration. Prospects with deficiencies that can be corrected should still be considered, however. Along with the firm's financial condition, additional characteristics of each prospect must be assessed, including its reputation and labor-management relations. From this assessment, potential problems that may not be disclosed on financial statements can be detected.

The firm planning the acquisition needs to evaluate the prospect's specific characteristics, such as its facilities, its dependence on suppliers, and pending lawsuits. Unfortunately, a full evaluation of such specific characteristics may not be possible unless the prospect provides the information. The firm planning the acquisition may contact the prospect to request more detailed information. The prospect may comply if it is willing to consider the possibility of a merger.

MAKE THE MERGER DECISION

Once the firm has identified a specific prospect it wishes to acquire, it can assess the feasibility of acquiring that prospect by using capital budgeting analysis. Thus, the acquisition prospect can be evaluated just like any other project. The cost of this project is the outlay necessary to purchase the firm.

The benefits are the extra cash flows that will be generated over time as a result of the acquisition. If the present value of the future cash flows to be received by the acquiring firm exceeds the initial outlay, the acquisition is feasible.

MERGER PROCEDURES

If an attempt is made to acquire a prospect, that prospect becomes the "target." It is set apart from all the other prospects that were considered. To enact the acquisition, firms will normally hire an investment bank (such as Morgan Stanley or Goldman Sachs) for guidance. Some firms that continuously acquire or sell businesses may employ their own investment banking department to handle many of the necessary tasks. Most tasks can be classified into one of the following:

▶ Financing the merger

▶ Tender offer

▶ Integrating the businesses

▶ Postmerger evaluation

Financing the Merger

A merger normally requires a substantial amount of long-term funds, as one firm may purchase the existing stock of another firm. One common method for a firm to finance a merger is by issuing more of its own stock to the public. As new stock is sold to the public, the proceeds are used to purchase the target's stock. Alternatively, the acquiring firm may trade its new stock to the shareholders of the target firm in exchange for their stock. Instead of issuing new stock, the acquiring firm may also borrow the necessary funds to purchase the target's stock from its shareholders.

Tender Offer

The acquiring firm first contacts the management of the target firm to negotiate a merger. The acquiring firm normally pays a premium on the target firm's stock to make the deal worthwhile to the target firm's stockholders.

tender offer a direct bid by an acquiring firm for the shares of a target firm

When two firms cannot come to terms, the acquiring firm may attempt a **tender offer.** This is a direct bid by the acquiring firm for the shares of the target firm. It does not require prior approval of the target firm's management. Thus, a tender offer could accomplish a merger even if the management of the target firm disapproves.

The acquiring firm must decide the price at which it is willing to purchase the target firm's shares and then officially extend this tender offer to the shareholders. The tender offer normally represents a premium of 20 percent or more above the prevailing market price, which may be necessary to encourage the shareholders of the target firm to sell their shares. The acquiring firm can achieve control of the target firm only if enough of the target firm's shareholders are willing to sell.

Integrating the Businesses

If a merger is achieved, various departments within the two companies may need to be restructured. The key to successfully integrating the management of two companies is to clearly communicate the strategic plan of the firm. In addition, the organizational structure should be communicated to clarify the roles of each department and position. This includes identifying to whom each position will report and who is accountable for various tasks. If the roles are not clearly defined up front, the newly integrated management will not function properly. Tensions are especially high in the beginning stages of a merger, since the employees of the acquired firm are not fully aware of the acquiring firm's plans. Once the merger has occurred, the personnel involved in the initial evaluation of the target firm should guide the integration of the two firms. For example, if the primary reason for a horizontal merger was to reduce the duplication of some managerial functions (to increase production efficiency), management of the newly formed firm should make sure that these reasons for initiating the merger are realized.

A newly formed merger typically requires a period in which the production, financing, inventory management, capital structure, and dividend policies must be reevaluated. Policies are commonly revised to conform to the newly formed firm's characteristics. For example, to deal with the larger volume of sales, inventory of the combined firm may need to be larger than for either original business (although perhaps not as large as the sum of both businesses).

Although identifying ways by which a merger could be beneficial is often easy, it may not be as easy to achieve those benefits without creating any new problems. As a final point, the process of creating the merger can also be much more expensive than originally anticipated and can often place a financial strain on the acquiring company (especially when the target fights the takeover effort). Therefore, firms that are considering acquisitions should attempt to anticipate all types of expenses that may be incurred as a result of the acquisitions.

Postmerger Evaluation

After the merger, the firm should periodically assess the merger's costs and benefits. Were the benefits as high as expected? Did the merger involve unanticipated costs? Was the analysis of the target firm too optimistic? Once the merger takes place, it cannot easily be reversed. Thus, any errors detected from the analysis that led to the merger cannot be washed away. However, lessons can be learned from any errors so that future merger prospects will be more accurately evaluated.

DEFENSE AGAINST TAKEOVER ATTEMPTS

In some cases, managers of a target firm may not approve of the takeover attempt by the acquiring firm. They may believe that the price offered for their firm is less than it is worth or that their firm has higher potential if it is not acquired. They may view the potential acquiring firm as a shark approaching for the kill (takeover). Under such conditions where the takeover attempt is hostile, management of the target firm can choose from a variety of "shark repellents" to defend itself.

A common defensive tactic against a takeover attempt is an attempt to convince shareholders to retain their shares. Another tactic to avoid a merger is a private placement of stock. By selling shares directly (privately) to specific institutions, the target firm can reduce the acquiring firm's chances of obtaining enough shares to gain a controlling interest. The more shares outstanding, the larger the amount of shares that must be purchased by the acquiring firm to gain a controlling interest.

A third defensive tactic is for the target firm to find a more suitable company (called a **white knight**) that is willing to acquire the firm and rescue it from the hostile takeover efforts of some other firm. The white knight rescues the target firm by acquiring the target firm itself. Although the target firm no longer retains its independence, it may prefer being acquired by the white knight firm.

white knight a more suitable company that is willing to acquire a firm and rescue it from the hostile takeover efforts of some other firm

Part VI

Summary

Financial Management

The performance of a firm can be assessed by conducting a financial analysis, as discussed in Chapter 15. A financial analysis is also used to identify the reasons for poor performance, such as excessive (or deficient) investment in long-term or short-term assets, or an excessive amount of debt used to finance its investment.

The key financial management decisions made by a firm can be classified as either financing (explained in Chapter 16) or investing funds in business projects (Chapter 17). Firms use either debt financing or equity financing to obtain funds. The common methods of debt financing are obtaining bank loans, issuing bonds, and issuing commercial paper. The common methods of equity financing are retaining earnings or issuing stock. The ideal type of financing is dependent on the firm's characteristics. If the firm does not have a large amount of debt, it may consider debt financing to capitalize on the tax advantage of using debt. If the firm already has a large amount of debt financing, however, it may use equity financing instead.

When firms consider using funds to invest in business projects, they must determine whether the return on the investment is sufficient to make the investment feasible. Capital budgeting analysis is used to determine whether the project is feasible. This analysis determines whether the present value of cash flows exceeds the initial outlay of the project.

In addition to business projects, firms also invest in short-term assets such as accounts receivable and inventory. An investment in accounts receivable is necessary to attract some customers who prefer to purchase products on credit. An investment in inventory is necessary to avoid stockouts. Nevertheless, excessive investment in accounts receivable or in inventory is an inefficient use of funds because the funds could have been used for other purposes.

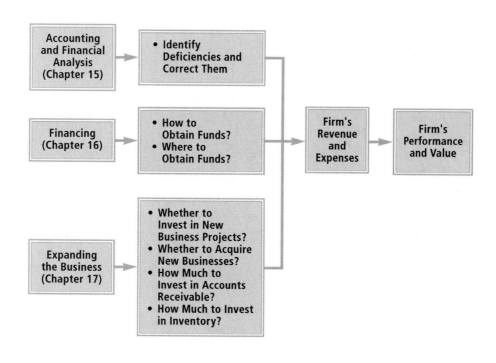

DEVELOPING THE FINANCIAL PLAN FOR CAMPUS.COM

Monitoring Performance (related to Chapter 15)

In your business plan for Campus.com, explain how the firm will monitor its performance over time. That is, describe the specific financial ratios that it can monitor to measure its performance and its efficiency.

Financing Business Expansion (related to Chapter 16)

In your business plan for Campus.com, identify the alternative choices you have to obtain funds to support additional expansion. Which alternative is the best choice for you? Does the financing method that you selected have any disadvantages?

Business Investment (related to Chapter 17)

In your business plan for Campus.com, briefly explain how Campus.com will determine whether future expansion is feasible. That is, describe how it will decide whether to pursue a specific project.

Communication and Teamwork

You (or your team) may be asked by your instructor to hand in and/or present the part of your business plan that is related to this part of the text.

Integrative Video Case: Finding Sources of Financing

Venture capitalists provide funds, contacts, help, and support to start-up companies. Firms in the venture capitalist industry obtain these funds from large institutions like insurance companies who seek a high return on their investment. The normal way to approach a venture capitalist with a new idea is to submit a business plan. An alternative way for companies to obtain financing is to go public, which is especially appropriate for firms that are in need of large amounts of money.

Questions

1 Explain the importance of the business plan to obtain financing from a venture capitalist.

2 Explain how proper financial reporting is a corporate responsibility when attempting to obtain financing.

3 How important is the management function when a firm attempts to obtain funds from a bank or a venture capitalist?

Integrative Video Case: Financing Decisions (Cerner Corporation)

Cerner Corporation designs and develops clinical information systems for health care providers. Recently, the company has had 1,000 associates and revenues of over $150 million. Furthermore, Cerner Corporation has doubled in size every two years for the last twelve years. Cerner CEO Neal Patterson discusses how the company obtained some of its financing and how it used equity to reward its employees.

Questions

1 How can the financing decision to share equity among employees affect the firm's management effectiveness and motivation?

2 How does Cerner Corporation obtain most of its financing today? How does this relate to business investments Cerner undertakes?

3 Explain how Cerner's internal equity financing relates to the company's capital structure.

THE STOCK MARKET GAME

Go to **http://finance.yahoo.com.** and check your portfolio balance, which is updated continuously by Yahoo! Finance.

Check Your Stock Portfolio Performance

1 What is the value of your stock portfolio today?

2 What is your return on your investment?

3 How did your return compare to those of other students? (This comparison tells you whether your stock portfolio's performance is relatively high or low.)

Explaining Your Stock Performance

Stock prices are frequently influenced by changes in a firm's financial strategies, including new financing policies and new investment strategies (such as acquisitions). A stock's price may increase if investors expect the new financial strategies to improve the performance of the firm. A stock's price can also decrease if the financial strategies are expected to reduce the firm's performance. Review the latest news about some of your stocks on the Yahoo! Finance website.

1 Identify one of your stocks whose price was affected (since you purchased it) by changes in the firm's financial strategies (the main topic in this part of the text).

2 Identify the specific type of financial policies that caused the stock price to change.

3 Did the stock price increase or decrease in response to the announcement of new financial policies?

RUNNING YOUR OWN BUSINESS

1 Forecast the revenue of your business in the first year. (Multiply the amount you expect to sell over the year times the price charged.)

2 Forecast the expenses of your business in the first year. Include the cost of materials and supplies, administrative (management) expenses, marketing expenses, rent expenses, and interest expenses.

3 Forecast the earnings (before taxes) of your business. (This is the difference between the forecasted revenue and the forecasted expenses.)

4 Assuming a tax rate of 20 percent, forecast your taxes. (You can apply a different tax rate if you know what your tax rate would be.)

5 Forecast your earnings after taxes. (This is the difference between your earnings before taxes and the amount of taxes you expect to pay.)

6 State how much of your own money you will invest as a form of equity investment in the business.

7 Indicate whether you will have any co-owners in this business and how much money they will have to invest.

8 State how much money you will need to start your business. (To determine this amount, compare expected expenses with expected revenue. Having a cushion is helpful in case the expenses turn out to be higher than expected or revenue turns out to be less than expected.)

9 State how much money you will need to borrow. (You can estimate this amount by comparing the amount of money you will need to start your business with the amount of equity that will be invested in your business.)

10 Indicate where you plan to obtain borrowed funds. For example, do you plan to obtain a loan from a regular commercial bank or from an Internet bank?

11 State the interest rate that you expect to pay on the borrowed funds.

12 Describe how long you expect to need the borrowed funds before you can pay back the loan.

13 Forecast your return on equity over the first year based on your forecast of earnings after taxes and the amount of equity invested in your business.

14 Describe any big purchases (such as a computer or a machine) that you may need to make for your business someday. What factors would be a part of a cost-benefit analysis of this purchase?

15 Explain how much inventory you would have to maintain to avoid shortages.

16 Would your business generate accounts receivable? If so, how would you manage this asset?

Your Career in Business: Pursuing a Major and a Career in Accounting and Finance

If you are very interested in the topics covered in this section, you may want to consider a major in Accounting or Finance. Some of the more common courses taken by Accounting and Finance majors are summarized here.

Common Courses for Accounting Majors

▶ *Principles of Accounting*—Focuses on the creation and interpretation of the income statement and the balance sheet.

▶ *Intermediate Accounting*—Deals with the accounting for inventory, fixed assets, and operating expenses.

▶ *Cost Accounting*—Focuses on internal accounting related to management decisions.

▶ *Accounting Information Systems*—Deals with the design and application of information systems used to facilitate accounting.

▶ *Auditing*—Provides an overview of the concepts and methods used to ensure the accuracy of accounting reports and financial statements.

▶ *Internal Auditing*—Focuses on the evaluation of internal tasks, procedures, and guidelines.

Common Courses for Finance Majors

▶ *Financial Management*—Emphasizes managerial decisions about financing and investing.

▶ *Personal Finance*—Focuses on individuals' financial decisions about budgeting, the use of credit, insurance, investments, and retirement planning.

▶ *Financial Institutions*—Examines the sources and uses of funds of financial institutions; also covers the management, performance, and regulation of financial institutions.

▶ *Financial Management of Institutions*—Discusses decision making by financial institutions, exposure of institutions to risk, and how the risk can be managed.

▶ *Financial Markets*—Provides an overview of securities that are traded in financial markets, with emphasis on how financial markets facilitate security transactions.

▶ *Advanced Financial Management*—Provides an in-depth analysis of decisions by financial managers, including dividend policy, capital structure, and capital budgeting.

▶ *Investment Analysis*—Focuses on valuation of securities, investment strategies, and managing the risk of investment portfolios.

▶ *International Financial Management*—Discusses financial management from the perspective of a firm in an international environment, with emphasis on how financial decisions account for exchange rate movements.

▶ *Real Estate*—Provides a survey of real estate investments, the valuation of real estate, and the risk of real estate investments.

Careers in Accounting and Finance

The following websites provide information about job positions, salaries, and careers for students who major in Accounting or Finance:

▶ Job position websites:

http://jobsearch.monster.com   Accounting/Auditing, Banking, Finance, Insurance, and Real Estate

http://careers.yahoo.com   Accounting/Finance, Banking/Mortgage, Insurance, and Real Estate

▶ Salary website:

http://collegejournal.com/ salarydata   Accounting, Banking, Consulting, Insurance, and Real Estate

Part VII

Special Topics

Part VII further explores topics that were introduced in previous chapters and provides a synthesis of the text. Chapter 18 explains how firms use computer information systems to facilitate their operations. Chapter 19 describes the types of risk to which firms are exposed and the methods of managing that exposure. Chapter 20 provides a synthesis of all the key business functions that have been emphasized throughout the text. These functions can be properly conducted only by recognizing how they interact with one another.

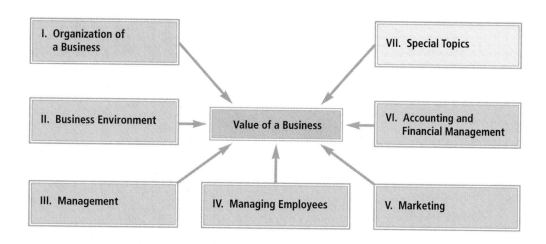

All businesses, including MTV, rely on the use of management information systems to improve their efficiency and to be successful. MTV uses a variety of information systems to organize, schedule, and televise their music videos.

The Learning Goals of this chapter are to:

1 Describe the key components of a computer and explain their purpose.

2 Discuss the different ways computers and related technologies contribute to today's businesses.

3 Describe some of the key challenges of managing today's information technologies.

4 Identify emerging technologies and their implications.

Chapter 18

Using Information Technology

Management information systems (MIS) adopt, use, and manage information technologies, including both computers and telecommunications. These systems have enabled firms to access much more information and have also facilitated communication within a firm. Consequently, these systems have enabled firms to increase their revenue and reduce their expenses. They have also enabled new firms to compete in various product markets, which has forced firms to be very efficient in order to survive. Virtually all firms use some type of MIS to access and analyze information, improve communication with customers, improve communication among employees, and assess recent performance.

Consider the case of MTV, which produces music videos and broadcasts them on television. It generates revenue by selling time slots on its network to firms that want to advertise their products. The more popular the videos are, the more viewers will watch MTV, and the higher the price it can charge when selling the time slots. MTV wants to produce high-quality videos at the lowest possible cost. MTV must decide:

▶ How can it use information technology to monitor its production costs and improve its efficiency?

▶ How can it use the Internet and information technology to attract more viewers and sell additional services?

▶ Does investing in the technology present any challenges or risks?

If MTV determines how to use information technology to improve its efficiency, it can reduce its expenses and increase its earnings. If it can use information technology to attract more viewers or sell additional services, it can increase revenue and increase its earnings. MTV should also recognize the danger of investing an excessive amount of funds in some types of technology that will be useless or obsolete in the near future.

The types of decisions described above are necessary for all businesses. This chapter explains how MTV or any other firm can make information technology decisions in a manner that maximizes its value.

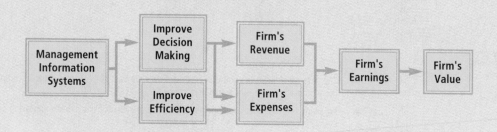

WHAT IS A COMPUTER?

1

Describe the key components of a computer and explain their purpose.

An electronic computer is a device capable of processing and storing vast quantities of information. Today's computers more closely resemble the microcomputer in Exhibit 18.1, comfortably fitting on a desktop and using less power than a light bulb. Today's mainframes—large computers used primarily to service entire organizations—have been so miniaturized that their key circuitry often fits into a casing the size of a pizza box. These physical changes in computers have been accompanied by even more dramatic changes in performance, as illustrated in Exhibit 18.2.

Exhibit 18.1

A Typical Microcomputer

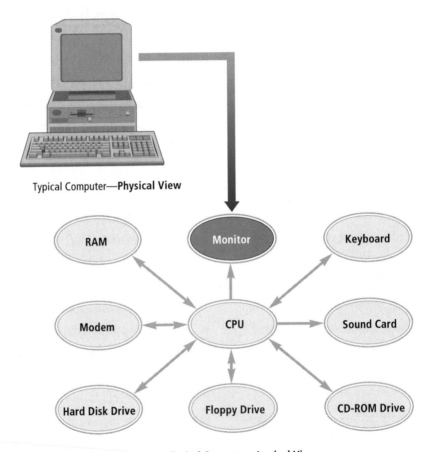

Typical Computer—**Physical View**

Typical Computer—**Logical View**

Exhibit 18.2

How Much Have Computers Improved?

▶ The physical changes in computer hardware over the past 50 years have been accompanied by even more dramatic changes in actual performance.

▶ For many key computer components, price-performance ratios have been improving by a factor of 10 every five years.

▶ To put such improvements in perspective, had automobiles experienced the same rate of price-performance improvement, the luxury car that cost $10,000 in the mid-1960s would now sell for under a nickel (including a liberal allowance for inflation).

Computer information systems greatly facilitate a company's operations. The physical components of a computer are collectively called hardware.

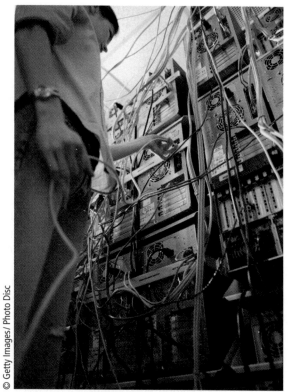

© Getty Images / Photo Disc

hardware the physical components of a computer

system architecture the basic logical organization of a computer

megahertz (MHz) one million cycles per second

gigahertz (GHz) one billion cycles per second

random access memory (RAM) space in which information is temporarily stored in a computer

megabytes millions of characters

hard drive sealed magnetic disks that provide secondary storage in a computer

gigabytes billions of bytes

Computer Hardware

The physical components of a computer are collectively called **hardware.** Although computer hardware is constantly changing, the basic logical organization of computers, often referred to as **system architecture,** has been relatively stable since the mid-1950s. Specifically, nearly all computers are built around four key components:

1 *Central processing unit (CPU)* The heart of the computer, the CPU (commonly referred to as the processor or microprocessor), performs all calculations and moves information between the computer's other components. More than any other single component, the CPU (such as Intel's Pentium processor or Advanced Micro Devices' Athlon processor) determines the basic behavior and capabilities of a particular computer. Generally, the faster the processor (as measured in millions of cycles per second, or **megahertz [MHz];** or billions of cycles per second, or **gigahertz [GHz]**), the faster the computer.

2 *Primary storage* For a computer to function, its processor must have scratch space in which to temporarily store information. In today's computers, such storage typically takes the form of **random access memory (RAM)** chips. RAM is the memory where programs and data in current use are kept and accessed by the CPU. The amount of RAM installed on a particular system is measured in millions of characters (or **megabytes**). Many applications will not run unless a certain amount of RAM is available, and most applications run faster when more RAM is installed.

3 *Secondary storage* Because RAM stores data only as long as the computer is running, computers also have secondary storage available. Today, most secondary storage is in the form of sealed magnetic disks, commonly referred to as a **hard drive.** Hard drives typically contain several billion bytes (**gigabytes**) of storage space.

There are also many forms of removable secondary storage that can be transported from machine to machine. These devices have grown in popularity due to their declining cost, improved performance, and versatility. Some of the more popular secondary storage devices include:

▶ Large capacity disk drives: Different manufacturers offer disk drives with capacity ranging from 100 MB to 1.0 GB per disk. Iomega's ZIP drive is a popular large capacity disk drive with a capacity of 250MB.

▶ CD-Recordable (CD-R): These drives allow users to write data onto a compact disc (CD) once and read many times. Most CDs have a capacity of 650 MB and are an inexpensive method to back up files.

▶ CD-Rewriteable (CD-RW): These drives are similar to CD-Rs except data can be written onto a CD more than once. They can also be used to create CDs that play in audio CD players.

▶ Digital Video Disk (DVD): A better version of the CD-ROM. The increased capacity allows simultaneous audio and video storage. DVDs are often associated with multimedia presentations.

4 *Peripherals* The devices attached to the CPU that are neither primary nor secondary storage are peripherals. Thousands of different types of general-purpose and special-purpose peripherals are available. Those most often found on desktop computers include a keyboard, mouse, monitor, printer, modem, and sound card. On business machines, peripherals often include scanners and network connectors.

Computer Software

The CPU can perform many tasks but needs specific direction. To provide that direction, a collection of step-by-step instructions to the processor, referred to as a **computer program,** is loaded into primary storage (RAM), then run by the CPU. By changing the program that is loaded into RAM, the user can dramatically change how the computer behaves.

computer program a collection of step-by-step instructions to the processor

Just as the actual machinery of the computer is referred to as hardware, the programs that determine the specific tasks a computer will perform at any given time are called **software.** Software can be divided into a few different categories:

software programs that determine the specific tasks a computer will perform at any given time

▶ *System software* Programs that manage the other software programs in a system. The system software (or operating system) handles input and output to peripherals, manages the internal memory, and informs the user of the status of application tasks. Windows 2000, Linux, and O/S 2 are examples of system software.

▶ *Application software* Programs that perform specific functions for the user. One program is intended to create documents (a word processor), while another program is intended to perform financial analysis (a spreadsheet), and yet another program is intended to generate reports from a firm's client list (a database). Computer programmers can develop applications from scratch. They can also be purchased off the shelf as software packages. Such packages are typically sold on removable secondary storage media, such as floppy disks or CD-ROMs.

▶ *Middleware* Programs that allow other application programs to cooperate with each other. Frequently, middleware is designed to give applications access to a variety of databases. It is particularly useful in organizations that operate more than one system or network.

▶ *Utility software* Programs that perform specific functions generally for the system. Antivirus and hard drive recovery programs are examples of utility software.

2 USES OF COMPUTERS

Discuss the different ways computers and related technologies contribute to today's businesses.

The potential uses for computers are limited only by the imagination of programmers and users. In today's businesses, however, three general types of use have become particularly common:

▶ Computational models

▶ Data processing systems

▶ Interorganizational systems

Each of these is considered in turn.

Computational Models

Ever since their invention, computers have held a tremendous advantage over humans in their ability to perform computations. Today's desktop computers, for example, can perform several million multiplications in a second. A human would take roughly 12 years to perform the same number of computations, assuming the individual was willing to work 55 hours a week without vacations and could multiply two 14-digit numbers together in an average time of about a minute. Simply stated, when problems require many computations, the use of computers is necessary.

statistical analysis a computer model that applies statistical principles to understanding relationships between data and certain outcomes

optimization models computer models that are used to represent situations that have many possible combinations of inputs and outputs

"what-if" analysis a computer model that generates different potential business scenarios to answer questions

decision support systems (DSS) computer models that are used to improve managerial decision making

Computer models may take many forms. **Statistical analysis** of data, which is common in finance and operations management, applies statistical principles to understanding relationships between data and certain outcomes. Such analysis often entails billions of computations. **Optimization models** are frequently used to help businesses choose their mix of products or design their distribution systems. **"What-if" analysis** involves generating different potential business scenarios to answer questions such as "What if our sales were 10 percent higher?" or "What if interest rates rise by two points?" Managers typically use "what-if" analysis to determine the sensitivity of a business situation to changes in many factors, such as inflation, economic growth, market share, and costs. Computers are necessary for such analysis, as hundreds of scenarios are often considered.

Computer models that are used to improve managerial decision making are called **decision support systems (DSS)**. DSS applications come in two forms. Some are complete applications designed to help managers make specific decisions. For example, plant location software can help managers decide where to establish a new facility. DSS applications are also available in tool form, such as the spreadsheet software that managers use to make financial projections. Rather than focusing on a specific problem, such tools are designed to help managers create their own models in a given situation.

Data Processing Systems

Computers have replaced paper-based record-keeping systems. Among the advantages of these computer-based systems are the following:

▶ *Accuracy* Paper-based systems are subject to arithmetic and transcription errors. Computer-based systems can be designed to greatly reduce these problems.

▶ *Speed* Using computer-based systems, the time required to sort, look up, and format information is a fraction of that required in paper-based systems. Further, the speed of routine tasks, such as closing a company's books at year-end, is similarly improved.

▶ *Space* The physical space required for record keeping can often be significantly reduced by using a computer-based system. For example, a manager at the United Services Automobile Association (USAA) predicted that the online correspondence system the USAA was implementing would ultimately save 17 acres of storage compared with the company's paper-based system.

▶ *Flexibility* Storing information on computers makes it possible to rapidly create summaries of information that would have taken days or months to prepare manually. Today's information systems often include report-writing tools that enable managers to create their own customized output without the need for programmers.

One area where data processing systems did not initially produce the expected benefits was in labor costs. Although firms often achieved some savings from eliminating the clerical personnel at the heart of the manual system, these savings were nearly always more than offset by the need to add higher-priced computer programmers and operators. Thus, while early efforts to automate often led to huge increases in capacity and accuracy, they rarely led to a reduction in actual labor costs.

Interorganizational Systems

interorganizational systems (IOS) employ computers and telecommunications technology to move information across the boundaries of a firm

remote job entry systems interorganizational systems that allow the user to interact directly with a company's internal systems

electronic data interchange (EDI) an interorganizational system that allows the computers of two or more companies to communicate directly with each other

commercial information service an interorganizational system that provides a packaged assortment of information services to customers (subscribers)

Interorganizational systems (IOS) employ computers and telecommunications technology to move information across the boundaries of a firm. Such IOS represent the logical extension of a company's internal information systems to its customers, its suppliers, and other interested parties.

IOS come in many forms. Systems such as automated teller machines (ATMs) and airline reservation systems that allow the user to interact directly with a company's internal systems are referred to as **remote job entry systems.** These systems not only make transactions easier for the customer but also save the company clerical costs.

Another form of IOS, **electronic data interchange (EDI),** allows the computers of two or more companies to communicate directly with each other, without human intervention. EDI systems can produce significant savings in ordering costs, while improving order processing time and accuracy. Even managers skeptical of the benefits of EDI systems may find they have no choice but to install them because a growing number of companies, such as Wal-Mart, refuse to do business with vendors who will not hook up electronically. This form of IOS has improved the efficiency of transactions and has promoted better relationships between suppliers and customers. It also led to the development of entirely new distribution channels.

A third type of IOS is a **commercial information service,** which provides a packaged assortment of information services to customers, referred to as subscribers. These services, two of the better known of which are CompuServe and America Online, bundle together many different IOS applications, such as Sabre (airline reservations), technical support forums for hardware and software vendors, and electronic shopping malls. They also provide numerous additional services, such as electronic mail, news, and games, to attract subscribers. Most recently, they have provided subscribers with direct connections to the Internet, the global network connecting academic, government, and business institutions. Users subscribe to these services by paying a small monthly fee, usually starting at around $20 per month. They may pay extra for using special services, such as research databases that contain detailed information on public and private companies.

Chairman and CEO, David Steward, and president and COO, Jim Kavanaugh, of Worldwide Technology, Inc., a provider of hardware, software, and computer solutions, are pictured holding their award from *Black Enterprise* magazine after being selected company of the year.

AP Photo/James A. Finley

3

Describe some of the key challenges of managing today's information technologies.

MANAGING TODAY'S INFORMATION TECHNOLOGIES

The growing importance of information technology to today's businesses means that every manager, not just MIS managers, must become familiar with issues relating to the management of information technology. The following five areas are particularly important:

▶ Managing the firm's information system architecture

▶ Acquiring software

▶ Managing the development of information systems

▶ Managing the implementation of information systems

▶ Managing the security of information systems

Managing the Firm's Information System Architecture

The concept of the system architecture of an individual computer can be generalized to the organization as a whole. With today's technologies, many different system architectures are possible. The choice of architecture can play a critical role in determining the capabilities of the firm. For example, the architecture can determine the ability of employees to share information and work together, affect how quickly a company can respond to customer requests, and even alter the ways in which a company offers its goods and services. Several common architectures are considered next.

stand-alone system system architecture consisting of one or more computers that function independently

Stand-Alone System   The **stand-alone system** architecture, illustrated in Exhibit 18.3, consists of one or more computers that function independently.

Exhibit 18.3

Stand-Alone System Architecture

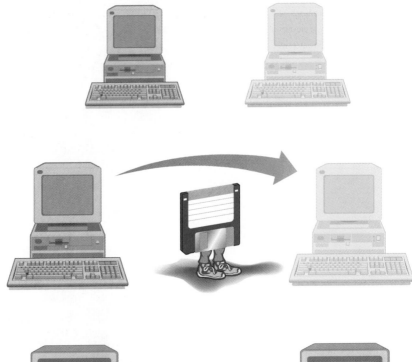

Exhibit 18.4

Mainframe (Multiuser) System Architecture

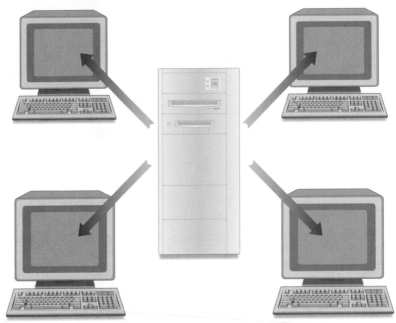

Each system has its own software and its own data and typically services the needs of a single user. Stand-alone architecture, sometimes referred to as a "sneaker network" because users must carry disks between computers to transfer data, is most common in small businesses. Its primary advantages are its low cost and technological simplicity. Its weaknesses are the difficulty of moving information between users and the inability to share resources such as printers. For this reason, stand-alone architectures are generally impractical for firms that use shared information extensively.

mainframe (multiuser) system system architecture that uses a single central computer that performs data processing for all users in the organization

Mainframe (Multiuser) System   The **mainframe (multiuser) system** architecture, illustrated in Exhibit 18.4, uses a single central computer, usually referred to as a mainframe, that performs data processing for all users

terminals devices that combine the functions of a monitor and a keyboard

in the organization. Users typically interact with the mainframe through **terminals,** devices that combine the functions of a monitor and a keyboard. Under the mainframe architecture, all data storage and computer hardware are centralized, usually under the control of an MIS department within the organization. Although other computers may be present in the organization, such as those used by engineering groups for scientific purposes, such systems are usually kept entirely separate from the company's business systems.

The primary advantage of the multiuser system, which was most popular from the late 1960s to the early 1980s, is that all programs and data are centrally located. The ability to share data led to the development of applications such as online reservation systems. It also made possible sophisticated production management systems capable of sharing data across the entire scope of a business, from raw materials to sales of finished products. The main drawback of the multiuser system is that it tends to prevent users from taking advantage of the sophisticated applications and tools that are now available for personal computer (PCs) but not mainframe computers.

network system system architecture that connects individual microcomputers together in ways that allow them to share information

file servers in a network system, one or more machines that store and provide access to centralized data

workstations in a network system, individual computers that access the software and data on the file server

Network System

In the past 10 years, new system architectures have emerged that provide the benefits of both stand-alone and multiuser architectures. **Network system** architecture connects individual computers together in ways that allow them to share information.

The typical network architecture, illustrated in Exhibit 18.5, consists of one or more machines, known as **file servers,** that store and provide access to centralized data. Connected to these file servers are many individual computers, referred to as **workstations.** Workstations can run their own software but can also access the software and data on the file server, duplicating the benefits of the multiuser system.

Networks are classified according to how the individual workstations are connected. When all are directly connected by network cabling to the

Exhibit 18.5

Network System Architecture

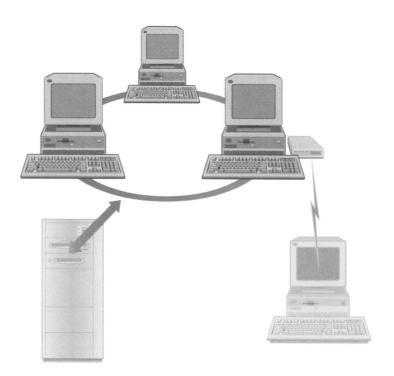

local area network (LAN) a system in which individual workstations are directly connected by network cabling to the file server

wide area network (WAN) a system in which telecommunications technologies are employed to connect pieces of the network

modems devices that permit the digital signals inside computers to be transmitted over lines designed primarily for voice communication

network operating system software that handles the communications between machines in a network

workgroup software network software that provides a broad array of user-friendly features, such as electronic mail, document management systems, and work-sharing systems

file server, as is often the case in a building or headquarters complex, the architecture is called a **local area network (LAN).** When telecommunications technologies are employed to connect pieces of the network, the architecture is called a **wide area network (WAN).** Such telecommunications technologies can be as simple as the use of conventional phone lines and **modems,** devices that permit the digital signals inside computers to be transmitted over lines designed primarily for voice communication. They can also be far more exotic, including the use of leased phone lines, satellites, microwave linkages, and cellular connections.

To construct a network, both hardware and software must be acquired. Network hardware costs include the costs of running network cables throughout an office complex, purchasing network adapters for each workstation, and purchasing hubs necessary to connect clusters of workstations. In addition, networks require their own specialized software. At a minimum, that software will include a **network operating system,** such as Novell's Netware or Microsoft's Windows NT, which handles the communications between machines. Recently, many companies have also installed **workgroup software,** such as Lotus Notes, which provides a broad array of user-friendly features, such as electronic mail, document management systems, and work-sharing systems. Together, the hardware and software costs can easily amount to several thousand dollars per workstation.

In many respects, network architectures combine the benefits of the stand-alone and mainframe architectures. The connectivity aspect of a network provides easy access to and sharing of information. Since users access the network with PC-based workstations, the full range of PC software can be run. The main drawbacks of networks over previous architectures are the added costs. In addition, administering and maintaining a network can be far more complex than keeping stand-alone PCs up and running. Thus, the cost of hiring specially trained network engineers and administrators must be considered when establishing a network.

Acquiring Software

Much of the software used in any business is packaged software, which can be purchased off the shelf and used with no actual programming. The decision as to which software to purchase should not be made lightly. Issues that a manager should consider include the following:

1 *Compatibility* Any new software must be compatible with a firm's existing hardware and software. Questions the manager should ask include:

▶ Will the company's existing hardware handle the new software?

▶ Can the new software convert the information created by the old software?

▶ Can the new software exchange information with other applications that the firm uses?

2 *Upgradeability* Because computer hardware advances so quickly, businesses should anticipate that they will need to upgrade their software regularly, usually every two to three years. The package's upgrade policy and history are therefore important over the long run. Questions the manager should ask include:

▶ How often are upgrades introduced?

▶ What do upgrades typically cost?

An alternative upgrade method is to pay an annual fee to have new versions of software automatically installed. Microsoft has recently offered businesses the option of having new versions of software automatically loaded on to their computers. The businesses pay an annual fee for this service.

3 *Support* The cost of a software package is often far less than the costs of learning to use it. These costs include required training, productivity declines during the period when employees are learning the application, and the use of technical support. Such costs must be factored into the software acquisition decision. Questions the manager should ask include:

▶ How difficult is it to learn the new software?

▶ What training resources are available?

▶ What are the vendor's technical support policies?

In addition, managers should consider the long-term implications of every software decision. Compatibility issues and the need to retrain users mean that all software acquisition decisions ultimately interrelate. Thus, a company should reevaluate its entire software policy every four to five years. At such times, software decisions with long-term implications, such as changing PC and network operating systems, should be made and a plan for future acquisitions established.

Customized Software Although packaged software can provide an inexpensive solution for many needs, on occasion a firm needs software to accomplish a task that is not directly supported by an existing package. In such a situation, the firm frequently faces three alternatives:

▶ *Modify the company's business processes to fit an existing software package* Although many managers may balk at having to change the way they do business to accommodate the needs of a $100 software tool, sometimes this approach makes sense. Packaged software, such as accounting applications and project management tools, is usually designed around sound business practices. As a result, adopting a software package can sometimes provide the means for improving the firm's administrative processes.

▶ *Customize an existing application* Particularly in the accounting area, custom development often starts with a basic package that is modified to meet the firm's specific needs. Much less programming is needed than when an entire system is written from scratch. A problem, however, is that modifications to the basic package may make it difficult and expensive to upgrade when new versions of the basic package are introduced. If the required modifications are extensive, this alternative may turn out to be as expensive as programming the entire application from scratch.

▶ *Build an entirely new application* Particularly for complex, specialized applications, creating an application from scratch is often necessary. The chief advantage of this approach is that it allows the firm to design an application specifically to meet its needs. The costs of custom development can be high, however. Custom development also carries two significant risks: the risk of major cost overruns and the risk that the application will not be completed. These risks increase with the size of the application, its complexity, and the firm's lack of experience with the technologies involved.

Andrew Covey, manager of General Information Systems Lab, holds a CD ROM of a high school classroom. The software will allow emergency workers to take virtual tours and hasten a response to potential violence.

AP Photo/ James A. Finley

Even after choosing one of the three alternatives, managers must decide whether the firm should employ a staff of programmers to build and maintain its computer applications or hire outside consultants to develop them. In today's rapidly changing technology environment, applications commonly must be updated every two to five years, or they become obsolete. In choosing a development strategy, the firm must map out a path that ensures ongoing maintenance.

Managing the Development of Information Systems

The evolution of computer systems, software, and architecture through the years has left many companies with a lack of uniformity in their overall system. To create **connectivity** throughout the entire firm, most large companies and many smaller companies have implemented **enterprise resource planning (ERP) systems** that support the flow of information across all of an organization's departments, including accounting, sales, and manufacturing.

ERP is an elaborate software program that automates all of a firm's business procedures. Customer orders, inventory control, staffing levels, and other functions are linked together through ERP software. The system records every transaction and continually updates all of the connected departments.

This software allows all users to be more informed about their company's resources and commitments. A salesperson who records an order into a laptop begins a transaction that will adjust inventory, notify manufacturing, and create an invoice in accounting. Companies that originally used expensive mainframe computing systems have changed to networks of PCs. These systems work well with ERP software and provide more flexibility.

ERP software has a number of drawbacks, however. The software often costs in excess of $50,000 per user. It is not unusual for large companies to spend more than $100 million and many years to implement ERP systems. A firm must convert data, modify existing systems, overhaul the network infrastructure, and train employees on the new system to create the data

connectivity the ability of a firm's computer systems to work together to permit the flow of information throughout the firm

enterprise resource planning (ERP) systems software programs that automate all of a firm's business procedures and support the flow of information across departments

warehouse the ERP systems allow. Once completed, ERP allows users to easily generate data on transactions, reports on supplier performance, inventory levels, supply prices, performance reports, and demand forecasts.

Monitoring Information Systems Development   The traditional approach to managing systems development, sometimes referred to as the **systems development life cycle (SDLC),** involves decomposing a system into its functional components. For example, an accounting application would be broken down into modules and submodules, each representing a distinct function in the overall accounting process. Project management techniques, such as PERT charts or critical path analysis, are then employed to organize and monitor the development of the system as a whole. Using such techniques, managers are able to assess how the project is proceeding compared with the original plan.

Unfortunately, the accuracy of project management techniques is not guaranteed. Errors in the code, commonly referred to as **bugs,** can lead to major problems. For example, a module or submodule may appear to be complete on paper. When that module is connected to other modules, however, previously undiscovered problems may indicate a need for substantial additional work.

Incremental Development Techniques   In recent years, incremental development techniques, which distribute testing more uniformly throughout the development cycle, have gained in popularity. Such techniques usually involve the rapid creation of a working system with limited functionality, know as a **prototype.** Once the initial prototype has been created, additional features are added, with testing being performed at each stage of development. This ongoing testing reduces the number of bugs uncovered at the end of the development process. As the application approaches full functionality, it is often made available to a carefully selected subset of sophisticated users, a process known as **alpha testing.** These users run the software, reporting problems to the developers and making suggestions for additional functionality. Once a fully functional version of the application has been created, a wider group of users is given the software—a process called **beta testing.** These users, who more closely resemble "average" users in their level of experience, generally focus on detecting bugs. The size and scope of alpha and beta testing programs vary widely, but they can be huge. Before introducing Windows 95, for example, Microsoft had literally hundreds of thousands of beta test sites; most of the testers had paid for the privilege in order to acquire the software before its general release.

Managing the Implementation of Information Systems

Managers often assume that the actual development of a system or the acquisition of appropriate software is the major obstacle to creating a successful information system. Managing system implementation—the process of transferring a system to its intended users—often proves far more difficult than technical development. For some categories of software, when systems are abandoned, it is usually because of unsuccessful implementation, rather than technical or economic issues.

The heart of the implementation challenge is overcoming user resistance to a new system or technology. Users uncomfortable with a new system may resort to **passive resistance.** They may overstate the difficulties associated with learning the technology, in effect claiming that they are not

---

systems development life cycle (SDLC) an approach to system development that involves decomposing a system into its functional components

bugs errors in software code

prototype a working system with limited functionality

alpha testing during systems development, the process of making the new application available to a carefully selected subset of sophisticated users; done when the application approaches full functionality

beta testing during systems development, the process of testing a fully functional version of the new application with a wider group of users than was used for alpha testing

passive resistance occurs when users uncomfortable with a new system overstate difficulties associated with learning the technology

using it because they cannot figure out how it works. Users may also indirectly express their displeasure by overstating the impact of any bugs they discover or by dwelling on situations in which the system creates unnecessary work. Users have also been known to engage in **active resistance.** They may, for example, intentionally type in bad data or repeatedly crash the system to make it unusable. To reduce the chances of passive or active resistance, managers can employ a number of techniques. Among the most important are the following:

active resistance occurs when users type in bad data or repeatedly crash a new system to make it unusable

▶ *Ensure that the system has top management support* In study after study, top management support has been reported as a factor that contributed to successful implementation. When such support is lacking, users are more likely to resist the system.

▶ *Ensure that a need for the system has been established and communicated to users* Users must be aware that a bona fide need for the system exists. The more visible the need, the better. For example, a system that keeps inferior products from getting to the customer has obvious appeal.

▶ *Allow potential users to participate in the system design and development process* Such participation can lead to an increased sense of involvement for users, giving them a sense of system ownership. That sense of ownership, in turn, can cause users to see themselves as partners in trying to ensure the system's success.

▶ *Design systems that are intrinsically motivating for users* When a system (1) provides users with a greater sense of control over their jobs, (2) makes their jobs more interesting, and (3) improves the quality of their job performance in visible ways, potential users are unlikely to resist the system. They may even gravitate toward using it.

Managing the Security of Information Systems

The widespread use of information technology in organizations has significant security implications for management. Information technology increases a firm's vulnerability to both espionage and sabotage.

espionage the process of illegally gathering information

Espionage Information technology has increased the potential for **espionage,** or the process of illegally gathering information. Prior to the widespread adoption of information systems, the physical nature of paper records such as customer lists made them both hard to steal and hard to analyze. When such information is stored in computers, however, sensitive data, such as a company's entire customer list and sales history, may be secretly copied onto a single data tape. To make matters worse, once such information has been transferred, its electronic form makes it much easier to analyze.

Although achieving fail-safe protection against espionage is impossible, some protection may be achieved by limiting access to information. Most applications, for example, allow passwords to be established so that users can access only data relevant to their assigned duties. Keeping such systems current, however, requires significant management commitment and oversight. Particularly critical is ensuring that a user's access rights are terminated when the individual quits or is fired.

Managers can also reduce the espionage threat by ensuring that users are properly trained in security procedures. Stolen passwords represent a particularly serious threat to security. But that threat can also be signifi-

Exhibit 18.6

Protecting Passwords

▶ Avoid writing a password down. Never leave a written password anywhere near the system on which it is used, and never write it down next to the user ID for the system.

▶ Never type a password when someone is looking. The easiest way to get someone's password is to watch it being typed.

▶ Never use the same password on two systems. On many systems, the system operator can read users' passwords. An unscrupulous system operator could use that information to access other user accounts with the same password.

▶ Never use meaningful personal information for a password. Using information such as birthdays, children's names, or your brand of car may make it possible for a persistent co-worker to get into your account.

▶ Never use an actual word for a password. On many systems, passwords are stored in such a way that hackers, using a dictionary, can determine the password of any user who uses an actual word.

cantly reduced through user education (see Exhibit 18.6). Managers can also reduce the threat of compromised passwords by ensuring that users and system administrators periodically change passwords.

sabotage the malicious destruction of information by a perpetrator

Sabotage Even more chilling to a manager than espionage is **sabotage,** or the destruction of information by a perpetrator. Information technology has increased our vulnerability to this threat by making information easier to destroy and by making it possible to destroy records without having physical access to them. For example, a saboteur may be able to destroy data over the phone, without taking the risk of being physically present.

Although sabotage can come from many sources, revenge (by disgruntled employees, for example), commercial gain (by competitors), and vandalism (by hackers who destroy systems for fun) are three of the most common motives. The nature of the sabotage itself can also vary. In some cases, it may consist of the simple erasure of data. In other cases, data may be substituted, as occurred when students in a California school electronically altered their transcripts to get better grades. The best protection against such threats is to employ the same security precautions used against espionage and to back up the system on a regular basis. Such backups, which involve saving all the information on the system's hard disk to tapes or other removable storage media, ensure that lost or damaged data can be restored. In addition, regular backups offer a measure of protection against environmental threats, such as earthquakes, tornadoes, hurricanes, and fires.

computer virus a program that attaches itself to other programs or computer disks

In recent years, a particularly common form of sabotage has been the **computer virus.** A virus is a program that attaches itself to other programs or computer disks, whenever the opportunity presents itself. Because of this replication, users who move programs or disks between machines can inadvertently cause a virus to spread. Viruses can also spread over networks if they are not properly protected.

Viruses differ widely in the damage they cause. Some are relatively benign (for example, drawing peace signs, then disappearing). Others specifically attack the hard disk, erasing data and ultimately rendering the system worthless. Complicating detection, most viruses lie dormant on their host system for a significant period of time so that careless users will give them opportunities to spread to other systems. In other words, a virus may be active on a system for months before actually making its presence known. Some confine their activities to specific days, such as the Michelangelo virus,

increasing value with technology

TECHNOLOGY VOCABULARY

Learn the vocabulary:

▶ *Bandwidth* The amount of data that can be sent through a connection in a certain amount of time. It is usually measured in bits-per-second (bps) for digital devices. A full page of text may have around 16,000 bits. A modem that operates at 57,600 bps has twice the bandwidth of a modem that operates at 28,800 bps.

▶ *Client/server* A network relationship between two computer programs. Clients are PCs that run applications that request information from another program, the server. The server is a computer or program that manages disk drives, printers, databases, or network traffic.

▶ *Ethernet* A widely used local area network (LAN).

▶ *Firewall* A set of programs that protect a private network from outside users. The firewall uses a router program to filter all incoming network transmissions to determine whether to forward them toward their destination.

▶ *HTML (HyperText Markup Language)* The language used to create documents on the World Wide Web.

▶ *Intranet* A network that belongs to an organization and is used to share information. It is a secure network accessible by the organization's employees and others with authorization.

▶ *Java* A programming language designed for network environments. It is a simplified version of the C++ language.

▶ *LAN (local area network)* A network of computers sharing the resources of a single server, usually within a single building. It allows users to share data and peripheral devices.

▶ *Router* A device that connects LANs. It maintains a table of available routes to determine the best route for an information packet.

▶ *Standard* A format that has been recognized by a standards organization or accepted by the industry. Standards exist for programming languages, operating systems, data formats, and communication protocols. Standards are particularly important for relationships between businesses.

▶ *Streaming* A method of transferring data that are processed continuously. The user does not have to wait to download the entire file before viewing.

which destroys hard disks only on the artist's birthday (March 6). Some current viruses include:

▶ *Code Red,* which uses Microsoft Outlook to disguise itself as a response to an e-mail message sent earlier. Once it is received, it copies itself to the Windows directory and begins to destroy files with certain extensions such as .doc and .xls. It will also search your e-mail inbox for unread messages and respond with a message and the virus attached.

▶ *Melissa,* which spreads itself through Microsoft Outlook. Once opened, it attempts to send e-mail messages to 50 individuals listed in the user's address book. It does little damage to individual hard drives but will quickly overload mail systems by the sheer number of messages that are sent.

▶ *Chernobyl,* which is known as the CIH virus and has been around since 1998. The virus is triggered by the April 26 date of the Chernobyl disaster. It destroys data and completely disables the computer.

Although routine backups can protect a firm against other forms of sabotage, they are not effective against viruses. The problem is that in backing up the system, the virus is saved as well. Thus, restoring the system will also restore the virus. As a result, other forms of protection are usually required. The best is to follow the rules of proper virus hygiene, which include the following:

▶ Avoid all software that has not been acquired from known vendors.

▶ Keep floppy disks from unknown sources out of machines.

antivirus applications programs that detect and remove viruses

▶ Use **antivirus applications,** which are programs that detect and remove viruses. These programs are widely available and can be very effective against known viruses. Such programs are often marketed in subscription form, with regular updates that protect against new viruses.

By establishing and enforcing procedures that clearly state what software can and cannot be installed on company systems and by ensuring that antivirus software is used routinely and kept up-to-date, managers play an important role in protecting their companies against computer viruses.

4

Identify emerging technologies and their implications.

EMERGING TECHNOLOGIES AND THEIR IMPLICATIONS

Just as information technologies were transformed over the past few decades, new technologies and new uses for existing technologies will emerge in the next decades. With these new technologies and new uses will come new challenges for managers. Two of the most important developments in technology are the evolution of the worldwide network and the emergence of truly intelligent systems.

The Worldwide Network

Hardly a day goes by when the local newspaper does not carry an article on the Internet. As discussed at the end of the chapter, however, the Internet has a number of weaknesses when it comes to commercial uses. But what about the global networks of the future? At the present time, new communications infrastructures are being put in place. These infrastructures will ultimately change the ways in which we communicate and work.

Computers have changed the way companies do business on every level. Here an order is entered into an Internet site where customers can purchase their John Deere equipment and collectibles online.

AP Photo/ Morning Sun, Katherine Johnson

E-Commerce The Internet has already changed the practices of many businesses. It promises to have a tremendous impact on nearly every industry. The benefits of the Internet to consumers have been obvious and numerous. Researching products and comparing prices have become dramatically easier. Consumers can simply spend a few minutes at the computer rather than going to assorted retail outlets to get product and price information. Alternatively, consumers can go to retail outlets to find the product they want to purchase and then go online to find the best price. Businesses and consumers used the Internet to purchase products valued at more than $100 billion in 2002.

Companies also stand to benefit from increased online retailing. Although profit margins are being squeezed, some retailers are able to compensate through increased sales because they can reach a larger market without a significant investment in traditional outlets. Additionally, online retailers are able to generate revenues through means other than sales of products. Online retailers can profit from advertisement sales, referral fees, and the sale of customer databases.

Companies that produce homogeneous products and do not require individual service will be greatly influenced by the rising popularity of the Internet. The following are some of the industries that are already changing:

▶ *Books* The popularity of Amazon.com has forced traditional retailers to enter the online arena and to compete based on price. Discounts on best-sellers, historically around 10 percent, have reached 50 percent. Amazon.com's costs are very low because it has low overhead and no retail outlets. Other technological advances allow bookstores to electronically access rare and out-of-print books. This allows traditional booksellers to carry a limited inventory while offering customers a large selection.

▶ *Music* A number of online retailers (including Amazon.com) have focused on selling CDs at deep discounts. Like online booksellers, online music retailers benefit from much lower fixed costs than their traditional retail counterparts. New technology allows consumers to download music almost instantly, giving rise to the possibility that artists may be able to bypass traditional retail outlets and music labels.

▶ *Travel* Airline tickets may be purchased at significant discounts through some online retailers. Additionally, travelers can review resort destinations, reserve hotel rooms, and rent cars, all in a few minutes on the computer.

▶ *Computers and accessories* Consumers are most comfortable with online purchases associated with the technology. Computer packages, peripheral devices, and software can all be purchased online.

▶ *Automobiles* Currently, consumers interested in purchasing automobiles can find referrals online. A consumer can go to a variety of websites to research the autos of interest and their prices. Then the consumer can go to the traditional auto dealer and purchase the car at the agreed-upon price. This essentially forces local dealers to bid for sales. Automakers could offer the public the ability to order cars online and specify the particular features desired.

▶ *Toys and other children's products* Online retailers are offering all the toys available at the local stores. Additionally, a few websites offer all the products needed to plan a child's party. Instead of spending an evening driving from store to store, a parent can order decorations, games, toys, and everything else needed from the comfort of home or office.

▶ *Pet supplies* A few retailers have been able to achieve significant sales of pet supplies through their websites. They are able to offer better prices and a larger selection than local pet stores.

▶ *Groceries* A number of ventures have entered the online grocery market. The consumer can select the products desired and have them delivered later in the day. The problem of preserving perishable products and the difficulty of satisfying impulse purchases create obstacles to this idea, however.

Many other industries will also be affected by the growth of the Internet. Almost every industry could be changed through an online retail strategy. Firms typically benefit from significantly lower costs achieved by circumventing traditional distribution channels and selling directly to the consumer.

Infrastructure The amount of information a network can carry is called its **bandwidth,** which is determined by the physical components that make up the system. Today, a worldwide effort is being made to replace existing wiring with fiber-optic cable. A single optical fiber, the diameter of a human hair, can carry as much information as a cable the diameter of a rolling pin containing thousands of wires. As a result, the potential bandwidth available for telecommunications will increase greatly. In practical terms, that means that information transfers that used to take hours will be possible in under a second.

bandwidth the amount of information a network can carry

Implications For businesses, the impact of this change in infrastructure, which will not be fully realized for several decades, will be astounding. As local phone systems are upgraded or replaced, consumers will be able to connect directly into a global network that operates many times faster than today's Internet. The increased bandwidth is making it possible to offer far more goods and services electronically. For example, consumers who wish to purchase clothing online may view three-dimensional photorealistic images of clothing. **Virtual reality** display techniques, which combine computerized sights, sounds, and sensations to create a sense of actually "being there," make it possible to simulate driving a new car and allow the potential home buyer to simulate walking through a new home. As new services are offered over the network, business will have opportunities to develop additional sources of revenue.

virtual reality display techniques that combine computerized sights, sounds, and sensations to create a sense of actually "being there"

The high-speed connections between home and office will also have dramatic implications for how we work, manage, and are managed. Global "distances," already reduced by the telephone and air transportation, will shrink further as people from any part of the globe can meet face-to-face through their computers. **Video conferencing,** holding meetings between remote sites using sound and pictures transmitted over telecommunications links, today is limited mainly by the low bandwidth of existing telephone lines, which makes images grainy and jerky. Over the worldwide network, however, image quality will improve dramatically. The distinction between talking to images and talking face-to-face will blur. With such capabilities in place, the traditional workplace will be transformed.

video conferencing holding meetings between remote sites using sound and pictures transmitted over telecommunications links

The effects of the worldwide network will be sweeping, and the managers who recognize its potential early will be the big winners. To recognize that potential, managers need to be willing to experiment with new technologies as they become available. Today's Internet, for all its weaknesses, affords managers precisely such an opportunity for experimentation, which is perhaps the single best justification for establishing a commercial Internet presence.

Truly Intelligent Systems

artificial intelligence (AI) a field that focuses on developing computers that can perform tasks traditionally associated with biological intelligence, such as logical reasoning, language, vision, and motor skills

Artificial intelligence (AI) is the use of computers to perform tasks traditionally associated with biological intelligence, such as logical reasoning, language, vision, and motor skills. Since its founding nearly 40 years ago, the field has made some impressive strides (see Exhibit 18.7). The field has also

Exhibit 18.7

Artificial Intelligence Examples

> ▶ *Robotics* Today, some of the most productive factories in the world make extensive use of adaptive robots that originated from AI research.
>
> ▶ *Expert systems* These systems use sophisticated reasoning techniques, developed by AI, to accomplish difficult tasks, such as medical diagnosis. Companies such as American Express save millions of dollars a year by using expert systems.
>
> ▶ *Natural language applications* Computers with built-in voice recognition have become commonplace over the past five years, as have voice-driven phone systems. Both owe their existence to speech recognition research done in AI. Grammar checkers and translators depend heavily on natural language interpretation techniques pioneered in AI.
>
> ▶ *Object-oriented programming (OOP)* The OOP style, frequently employed in today's advanced systems, owes its existence to years of AI knowledge representation research.

made another important discovery: tasks that are easy for humans are often extremely difficult for computers.

Researchers are now concluding that many of the problems that AI has faced stem from the fact that human brains and computers are organized very differently. A typical commercial computer has a single processor through which all information passes in a serial fashion, one piece of information at a time. The brain, however, is organized around hundreds of millions of neurons that operate in parallel. Although a single neuron is much slower than a computer CPU, the brain can still process information more than a million times faster than any computer. In pure information processing terms, today's supercomputers are probably less powerful than the brain of a housefly.

massively parallel machines
experimental computers with many CPUs that operate simultaneously

That situation will change, however. Experimental computers with many CPUs that operate simultaneously, known as **massively parallel machines,** are already being constructed. If current trends in technology improvement continue (and they are expected to, at least for the next few decades), computers may well reach parity with the human brain around the middle of this century. What will be the implications of these massively parallel machines for the workforce?

THE FUTURE OF THE INTERNET

The global euphoria that has surrounded the Internet has, in some cases, caused managers to lose perspective on the actual strengths and weaknesses of the system. While the Internet seems to offer unparalleled opportunities for research, public relations, and communications, some serious concerns remain.

▶ *Lack of central authority* Unlike other entities a manager deals with, the Internet is more of a community than an organization. Moreover, it is a community with no leader. As a result, managers who find themselves overly dependent on the Internet may find they have nowhere to go when parts of the system go down, as they routinely do.

▶ *Lack of underlying organization* Although tremendous amounts of information are present on the Internet, there is no obvious way to find any particular piece of information. Further, even when a piece of information is found, there is no way to ensure its accuracy.

▶ *Network performance* Most managers find it disconcerting to have their business depend on a system whose performance changes from minute to minute and that could go down at any time. Yet such performance variation is characteristic of the Internet and is largely unavoidable. A substantial fraction of the computers that make up the heart of the Internet, such as the university computers that route communications and messages, are also used for other purposes. Thus, keeping the local Internet connection functioning smoothly is not always the provider's top priority.

▶ *Individual performance* Although universities and corporations generally have networks directly connected to the Internet, individuals usually access "the Net" using dial-up modems. Many of the most expressive features of the Net, including graphics, sound, and full-motion video, can take minutes or more to download. Such delays are a major obstacle to companies wishing to promote their products.

These weaknesses are being addressed as the Internet evolves. Two examples of the Internet's progress are:

▶ High-speed connections to private homes, using cable TV wiring.

▶ An increasing amount of Internet network traffic handled by private providers, such as MCI and AT&T.

As these changes continue, the possible uses for the Internet will expand dramatically. The Internet will ultimately become a "necessity" for most firms, much as the phone system is today.

College Health Club: **Technology Needs**

One of the decisions that Sue Kramer must make as part of her business plan for College Health Club (CHC) is what technology she will need. She will use a computer to keep track of her expenses and revenue over time so that she can monitor CHC's performance. She also wants to keep track of some marketing information, such as the profiles of her members and how each member heard about CHC. She will also have a computer that is accessible to the members who want to record information about their weekly progress (weight loss, endurance, strength tests, and the like).

Sue is currently creating a website for CHC that will offer a virtual (online) tour of CHC's facilities and provide all the information that prospective members need. She will also establish an e-mail address for CHC in case prospective members have questions.

If Sue opens an additional health club in the future, she will ask the manager of the new club to maintain a website that will provide information on the club's performance, such as updates on new memberships, a summary of feedback from existing customers, a summary of expenses, and so on. Sue could then go online to monitor the club's performance. The information would not be publicly disclosed, as Sue would use a special identification code to access this information on the website.

SUMMARY

1 An electronic computer is a device capable of processing and storing vast quantities of information. The physical components of a computer are called hardware. Most computers are organized around four components: (a) central processing unit (CPU), (b) primary storage, (c) secondary storage, and (d) peripherals.

2 Although firms use computers in many ways, the most common uses are as (a) computational models, (b) data processing systems, and (c) interorganizational systems.

3 Some of the key challenges associated with managing today's information technologies are (a) managing the firm's information system architecture, (b) acquiring software, (c) managing the development of information systems, (d) managing the implementation of information systems, and (e) managing the security of information systems.

4 Two of the key developments in technology are the evolution of the worldwide network and the emergence of truly intelligent systems. The worldwide network has already allowed for high-speed connections between home and office and between firms and customers. Meanwhile, efforts are being applied to develop truly intelligent computer systems that can think and carry out tasks like humans.

KEY TERMS

active resistance 592
alpha testing 591
antivirus applications 595
artificial intelligence (AI) 597
bandwidth 597
beta testing 591
bugs 591
commercial information
    service 584
computer program 582
computer virus 593
connectivity 590
decision support systems
    (DSS) 583
electronic data interchange
    (EDI) 584
enterprise resource planning
    (ERP) systems 590

espionage 592
file servers 587
gigabytes 581
gigahertz (GHz) 581
hard drive 581
hardware 581
interorganizational systems
    (IOS) 584
local area network (LAN) 588
mainframe (multiuser) system 586
massively parallel machines 598
megabytes 581
megahertz (MHz) 581
modems 588
network operating system 588
network system 587
optimization models 583
passive resistance 591

prototype 591
random access memory
    (RAM) 581
remote job entry systems 584
sabotage 593
software 582
stand-alone system 585
statistical analysis 583
system architecture 581
systems development life
    cycle (SDLC) 591
terminals 587
video conferencing 597
virtual reality 597
"what-if" analysis 583
wide area network (WAN) 588
workgroup software 588
workstations 587

Review & Critical Thinking Questions

1. What are decision support systems? Explain how decision support systems can be used to enhance decision making.

2. Define a computer and distinguish between hardware and software.

3. What are the advantages of computer-based systems?

4. Describe the different forms of interorganizational systems (IOS).

5. What are the issues managers must become familiar with regarding the management of information technology.

6. Distinguish between a local area network (LAN) and a wide area network (WAN).

7. Why is the choice of application software confronting a critical issue?

8. Explain the issues that should concern a manager in making a software application decision.

9. Identify the techniques for managing the implementation of an information system.

10. Discuss the security threat to a firm with respect to information technology.

11. What is the goal of artificial intelligence? What is the main obstacle in achieving this goal?

Discussion Questions

1. How do computers influence your everyday life?

2. What is a computer virus? How can you reduce the possibility that the computers you use at home, school, and work will become infected with a virus?

3. How could a firm using the Internet to provide confidential information to certain parties prevent espionage on the Internet? Do you think the Internet has made espionage more or less difficult?

4. How has the introduction of computers changed the way work is done in business offices? Do the benefits of computers outweigh the costs?

5. Discuss the uses of computerized information systems implemented at your college.

6. Your firm needs software to accomplish a task that is not directly supported by an existing software package. What are your options?

It's Your Decision: **Managing Information at CHC**

1. Sue Kramer is considering compiling a computer database to keep track of the profiles of her members. What is the potential benefit of this strategy?
2. How do you think Sue uses her computer for business at CHC?
3. Explain how Sue could improve CHC's production of health club services and its marketing by using a computer database to keep track of customer satisfaction levels.
4. A health club differs from manufacturing firms in that it produces a service rather than products. Explain how the use of technology by service firms may differ from that of manufacturing firms.

Investing in a Business

Using the annual report of the firm in which you would like to invest, complete the following:

1 Does the annual report discuss how the firm uses information systems to monitor its operations?

2 Does the firm use information systems for internal distribution of information or to provide information to external stakeholders (customers, suppliers, stockholders, distributors, and so on)? In what ways could these groups benefit from information systems?

3 Does the firm have its own website on the Internet? Is the address listed in the annual report? If possible, visit this website and describe the information that can be found there.

4 Explain how the business uses technology to promote its information technology management function. For example, does it use the Internet to provide information about its information technology function? Does it provide information about the types of hardware and software it uses to improve production efficiency?

5 Go to **http://hoovers.com** and locate the NEWS SEARCH. Type in the name of the firm in the space provided, and review the recent news stories about the firm. Summarize any (at least one) recent news story about the firm that applies to one or more of the key concepts in this chapter.

Case: Using Management Information Systems

Three years ago, Marianne Hudson started a business in Indiana selling clothes and books out of her van to students at local colleges. She purchased the clothes at a very low price from a factory and added logos that the local students preferred. By pricing her products lower than the campus bookstores, she was able to attract a strong demand for her goods. Recently, she decided to hire her son Zach to set up a similar business in California. She periodically sends Zach clothing to sell on college campuses in California. However, she needs to know what types of clothing Zach is selling so that she can have more of that style in the proper size produced and sent to him.

Marianne also needs to monitor her own sales frequently so that she can replenish her inventory of clothes purchased in Indiana. She establishes a management information system (MIS) on her laptop computer that records each sale. She uses the laptop to record each order and print a receipt for the customer. Whenever an item of clothing is sold, the computer automati-

cally deducts one from its inventory. Thus, Marianne always knows how many items of each style and size she has in inventory. Zach also uses a laptop computer to keep track of his inventory.

Zach maintains a website and posts information regarding recent sales and inventory levels there; Marianne reviews the website daily to make decisions about what she needs to order from the factory. Her MIS allows her not only to monitor her own inventory in Indiana, but also to monitor Zach's inventory in California.

Questions

1 Explain how Marianne's MIS may possibly increase her revenue.

2 Explain how the MIS may possibly reduce Marianne's costs.

3 Could the MIS be replaced by phone calls (Zach calling Marianne each day to update her on his inventory)?

Video Case: Information Technology at Elderly Instruments

Elderly Instruments sells musical instruments, cassettes, and CDs. Elderly has previously used mail-order catalogs to sell its products, but making changes in the catalogs is expensive and time consuming. Now the company has listed its products on its website so that customers can order products online. Customers can e-mail orders, which are filled immediately. The website can be adjusted daily to change product offerings. The website is set up so that it provides information quickly because customers who use online services do not tolerate slow websites. The web servers provide reports to Elderly about which products are receiving the most attention (which products receive the most hits). Thus, Elderly is accumulating information about customer profiles and what customers like.

Questions

1 Explain how technology has improved Elderly's ability to communicate its product offerings.

2 Explain how technology has increased the number of potential customers who may purchase products from Elderly.

3 Explain how technology has increased Elderly's ability to learn what its customers want.

Internet Applications

1. *http://www.symantec.com/us.index.html*

Identify some products Symantec is offering for sale on the Internet. Describe the products and explain how a corporation could use them in managing its information technology. What type of resources does Symantec offer on its website, and how do these resources help corporate managers manage their information systems?

2. *http://www.sysmod.com/*

What services does Systems Modelling provide, and how could a corporation use these services in managing its information systems? What consulting services does Systems Modelling provide?

3. *http://lab-robotics.org/hotlinks.htm*

a. Click on "Careers." What are some possible technology-focused careers? Browse through some of the résumés posted on this website. Would you post your résumé here? Why or why not?

b. Click on "Discussion." What resources are available to enable interested parties to exchange ideas via this website? Do you think a company trying to improve its information systems in robotics could benefit from the resources available here? Why or why not?

The Coca-Cola Company Annual Report Project

Questions for the current year's annual report are available on the text website at **http://madura.swlearning.com.**

The following questions apply concepts presented in this chapter to The Coca-Cola Company. Go to The Coca-Cola Company website (**http://www.cocacola.com**) and find the index for the 2001 annual report.

Questions

1 Download the financial statements and study the "Management's Discussion and Analysis" section. In general, explain how accounting software would be beneficial for consolidating information at The Coca-Cola Company.

2 Download the financial statements and find "Forward-Looking Statement." Suggest one or more ways in which The Coca-Cola Company could use information systems to monitor its inventories.

3 In general, why would The Coca-Cola Company want to have a website on the Internet?

4 Download the financial statements and find "Forward-Looking Statement." Which emerging technology mentioned in the chapter text do you think would be most beneficial for The Coca-Cola Company?

In-Text Study Guide

Answers are in an appendix at the back of the book.

True or False

1. The physical components of a computer are collectively called hardware.

2. Spreadsheets and databases are examples of computer hardware.

3. Automated teller machines (ATMs) and airline reservation systems that allow customers to link directly with an airline's internal systems are both examples of remote job entry systems.

4. A disadvantage of a stand-alone computer system is that users must carry disks from one computer to another to transfer data.

5. Computer viruses are programs that attach themselves to other programs or computer disks and then replicate themselves on other programs and disks whenever the opportunity presents itself.

6. The increasing reliance on information technology in recent years has greatly reduced the risk that information will be sabotaged.

7. Although consumers stand to benefit greatly from online retailing, any benefits of online retailing to companies are hard to identify.

8. Any task that is easy for the human brain to perform will be even easier for a computer to perform.

9. Today's commercial computers are organized to process information in the same way the human brain processes information.

10. The strong centralized authority controlling the Internet hinders its operation.

Multiple Choice

11. The primary storage of a computer is known as its:
    a) hard drive.
    b) central processing unit (CPU).
    c) motherboard.
    d) database.
    e) random access memory (RAM).

12. The heart of a computer is its:
    a) power unit.
    b) universal translator.
    c) central processing unit (CPU).
    d) random access memory (RAM).
    e) hard drive.

13. The amount of random access memory (RAM) installed on a particular computer is measured in:
    a) millibytes.
    b) megahertz.
    c) kilowatts.
    d) megabytes.
    e) processing units.

14. Modems, printers, keyboards, monitors, and scanners are all common examples of computer:
    a) core components.
    b) CPUs.
    c) externalities.
    d) peripherals
    e) serial interfaces.

15. _____ is software that allows other application programs to cooperate with each other.
    a) Middleware
    b) Shareware
    c) Public domain software
    d) Background software
    e) Mediaware

16. Spreadsheets, database, and word processing software are all types of:
    a) operating systems.
    b) utility programs.
    c) application software.
    d) middleware.
    e) simulation software.

17. _____ is software that handles input and output to peripherals, manages internal memory, and informs users of the status of application tasks.
    a) Middleware
    b) System software

In-Text Study Guide

Answers are in an appendix at the back of the book.

c) Application software

d) Shareware

e) Sequencing software

18. All of the following are advantages that computerized data processing systems have over traditional paper-based record keeping except:
    a) they are more accurate.
    b) they save space.
    c) they are more flexible.
    d) they are much faster at performing routine tasks.
    e) they prevent espionage.

19. A system that uses computers and telecommunications technology to share information across organizational boundaries is known as a(n) _____ system.
    a) gate-keeping
    b) broadband
    c) interorganizational
    d) internal information
    e) parallel information

20. _____ allows the computers of two or more companies to communicate with each other without human intervention.
    a) Remote job entry
    b) Decision support system software
    c) Electronic data interchange
    d) A dual boot system
    e) Cryptograhic software

21. _____, such as America Online and CompuServe, provide a packaged assortment of information services such as e-mail, games, electronic shopping malls, and technical support forums to users who subscribe to their services.
    a) Commercial information services
    b) Shareware services
    c) Management information systems
    d) Professional news services
    e) Public domain providers

22. In a mainframe system, individual users typically interact with the computer using a _____ that combines the functions of a keyboard and monitor.
    a) file server
    b) terminal
    c) workstation
    d) personal digital assistant (PDA)
    e) portable input device (PID)

23. A large computer used to service an entire organization's data processing needs is called a:
    a) mainframe.
    b) central processing unit (CPU).
    c) smart terminal.
    d) supercomputer.
    e) megaprocessor.

24. The system architecture where all the networks are directly connected by cabling to the file server is called a:
    a) program network.
    b) wide area network (WAN).
    c) global network.
    d) local area network (LAN).
    e) computer terminal.

25. In typical network architecture, workstations are connected to a _____, which is a machine that stores and provides access to centralized data.
    a) central processing unit
    b) mainframe
    c) stand-alone computer
    d) file server
    e) motherboard

26. _____ software provides a broad array of user-friendly features, such as e-mail, document management systems, and work-sharing systems, to people who are connected to a network.
    a) Shareware
    b) System

c) Routing

d) Database

e) Workgroup

27. When incremental techniques are used to develop software, _____ is the stage in which a fully functional version of the software is made available to a large group of testers who are similar to "average" users in terms of their level of experience.
    a) alpha testing
    b) dispersed testing
    c) intermediate testing
    d) fine-tuning
    e) beta testing

28. Incremental software development techniques typically involve the rapid creation of a working system with limited functionality known as a(n):
    a) alpha version.
    b) mock up.
    c) simulation program.
    d) prototype.
    e) virtual program.

29. In software applications, errors in code are referred to as:
    a) bugs.
    b) quirks.
    c) grinches.
    d) redundancies.
    e) discrepancies.

30. When users who are uncomfortable with a new information system overstate difficulties in learning to use the system and exaggerate problems they encounter when trying to use it, they are engaging in:
    a) active resistance.
    b) passive resistance.
    c) sabotage.
    d) espionage.
    e) organized resistance.

31. _____ is the process of illegally gathering information from an information system.
    a) Sabotage
    b) Mediation
    c) Linear programming
    d) Decrypting
    e) Espionage

32. All of the following are rules of virus hygiene except:
    a) avoid all software acquired from unknown sources
    b) don't use floppy discs from unknown sources
    c) back up the system frequently
    d) use antivirus applications
    e) establish procedures controlling what software can be installed

33. Online retailers can profit from all the following except:
    a) increased sales through reaching a larger market.
    b) revenue from advertising sales.
    c) referral fees.
    d) price markups on online merchandise.
    e) sale of customer databases.

34. _____ is a display technique that combines sight, sounds, and sensations to create a sense of actually "being there."
    a) Sensory management
    b) Virtual reality
    c) "What-if" analysis
    d) Multiple array technology
    e) Video/audio integration optimization

35. The amount of information a network can carry is called its:
    a) information ratings quotient.
    b) load factor.
    c) megahertz rating.
    d) random access capacity.
    e) bandwidth.

In-Text Study Guide

Answers are in an appendix at the back of the book.

36. The goal of _____ is to get computers to perform logical tasks traditionally associated with biological intelligence, such as logical reasoning and language, vision, and motor skills.
    a) artificial intelligence
    b) optical computing
    c) data processing
    d) multidimensional computer design
    e) evolutionary engineering

37. Experimental computers with many central processing units that operate simultaneously are known as:
    a) ultra-redundant arrays (UDAs).
    b) multiple binary processors.
    c) information management systems.
    d) massively parallel machines.
    e) broadband processors (BBPs).

All businesses, including Big Sling Company, should assess their exposure to different types of risk and consider how they can reduce their exposure.

business decisions

Chapter 19

The Learning Goals of this chapter are to:

1 Provide an overview of the tasks involved in risk management.

2 Identify the ways in which firms are exposed to the economic environment.

3 Identify a firm's exposure to firm-specific characteristics.

4 Explain a firm's exposure to potential lawsuits.

5 Explain the alternative remedies for firms that are failing.

Managing Risk

19

Business risk is the possibility that a firm's performance will be lower than expected because of its exposure to specific conditions. Risk can be related to a specific product or to the entire firm. It results from uncertainty about the future, as firms rarely forecast future revenue or costs with perfect accuracy. Firms can use risk management techniques that will reduce their risk and thereby stabilize their performance. Consequently, risk management allows firms to obtain funds at a lower cost and can therefore increase their value.

Consider the situation of Big Sling Company, which sells bungee jumps. Like most businesses, Big Sling is sub-ject to the possibility of lawsuits by customers. Big Sling can use effective risk management to reduce its exposure to risk. Some of the questions Big Sling faces include the following:

▶ What tasks are involved in its risk management?

▶ Why might it be exposed to the risk of lawsuits?

▶ How can it reduce its risk?

If Big Sling conducts its risk management properly, it can insulate itself from some events that could be very costly. By recognizing the ways it is exposed, it can use risk management to reduce or avoid that exposure. Therefore, it can reduce its risk, which should please its owners, creditors, and employees.

The types of decisions described above are necessary for all businesses. This chapter explains how Big Sling Company or any other firm can make risk management decisions in a manner that maximizes its value.

TASKS INVOLVED IN MANAGING RISK

1
Provide an overview of the tasks involved in risk management.

Risk management involves identifying a firm's exposure to risk and protecting against that exposure.

Identifying Exposure to Risk

A firm can identify its risk by reviewing its normal business operations. Firms that use a large amount of machinery will likely be concerned with injuries that could result from the machinery. Firms that produce toys should be concerned about potential injuries to children who use the toys. Since the tragedy of September 11, 2001, firms have been assessing their exposure to terrorist attacks.

Protecting against Risk

Once the exposure to risk is identified, firms must assess the alternative methods that can be used to protect against the risk and decide which method is most appropriate. Common ways to protect against risk are to eliminate the risk, shift the risk, or assume the risk.

Eliminating Risk

Firms can eliminate risk by discontinuing the operations that cause it. For example, firms could eliminate the risk of injury from machinery by discontinuing the use of the machinery. They could avoid the risk of product defects in their toys by eliminating toy production. Although eliminating the operations that caused risk effectively removes particular risks, firms that prefer to continue their existing businesses need an alternative solution.

Shifting Risk

Firms can shift some types of risk to insurance companies by purchasing insurance. **Property insurance** protects a firm against the risk associated with the ownership of property, such as buildings and other assets. Thus, it can provide insurance against property damage by fire or against theft. **Casualty insurance** protects a firm against potential liability for harm to others as a result of product failure or accidents.

Property and casualty insurance companies provide insurance for firms. Firms pay a periodic insurance premium for this type of insurance; the amount of the premium is partially dependent on the types of assets insured. The higher the market value of the insured assets, the higher the insurance premium paid, other things being equal. But not all assets are insured at the same rate. Because a building located in a high-crime area is more vulnerable to theft, the insurance fee will be higher. In addition, the manufacturing operations of some firms are more likely to result in personal injuries than those of other firms. The casualty insurance premium paid is affected by the likelihood of personal injuries.

property insurance protects a firm against the risk associated with the ownership of property, such as buildings and other assets

casualty insurance protects a firm against potential liability for harm to others as a result of product failure or accidents

Insurance is now more difficult to obtain for farm supply cooperatives and grain elevators in the Midwest.

AP Photo/ Larry Smith

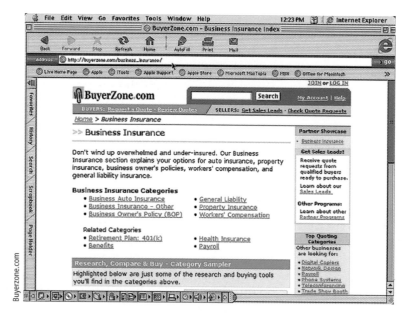

business online

Business Insurance   This website provides information on various forms of business insurance.

e-business

http://buyerzone.com/ business insurance/

Buyerzone.com

actuaries persons employed by insurance companies to forecast the percentage of customers that will experience the particular event that is being insured

Insurance companies recognize that the probability of some events occurring can change over time. Consequently, they adjust their premiums to reflect the change in probability. For example, firms have experienced an increase in liability lawsuits in recent years. Anticipating a higher level of payouts on liability lawsuits, insurance companies have increased their premiums.

Insurance companies employ **actuaries** to forecast the percentage of customers that will experience the particular event that is being insured. This enables the insurance companies to set the premium properly on that type of insurance.

The federal and state governments also offer business-related insurance. Two popular types are summarized in Exhibit 19.1. Old-age, survivors, disability, and health insurance (OASDHI) is funded by the Social Security taxes paid by employers and employees. Unemployment insurance is funded by unemployment taxes, which are usually paid by employers (although employees also incur an unemployment tax in some states). In general, the two types of insurance summarized in Exhibit 19.1 replace part of

Exhibit 19.1

Insurance Offered by the Government

Old-age, survivors, disability, and health insurance (OASDHI)	Workers who are disabled for at least 12 months can receive income payments. People aged 65 years or older receive income payments and hospital benefits. Spouses of workers who die receive income payments.
Unemployment insurance	Workers who are laid off can receive a portion of their previous earnings until they find a new job. They may also receive assistance in finding a new job. The length of time in which they can receive these benefits varies among states; the maximum period is usually around six months.

Exhibit 19.2

Illustration of How to Protect against Risk

Firm's operations	The firm produces ladders and other home repair equipment.
Exposure to risk	Injuries to employees who produce ladders or to customers who purchase ladders.
Protecting against Risk: Possible Solutions	
1. *Eliminating risk*	Discontinue the production and sale of ladders; focus on the production and sale of other home repair equipment that is less risky.
2. *Shifting risk*	Purchase insurance to protect against possible injuries to employees who produce the ladders or customers who use the ladders.
3. *Assuming risk*	Create a fund that can be used to self-insure against possible injuries to employees who produce the ladders or customers who use the ladders.

the income that is lost because of death, retirement, a layoff, or disability. Although other forms of public insurance are available, they are directed more specifically toward particular types of businesses.

Assuming Risk   Some firms are willing to assume their business risk with **self-insurance**, in which a firm creates a fund to cover any future claims. Rather than pay insurance premiums, firms that self-insure contribute to their own insurance fund. Firms consider self-insurance when they believe the insurance premiums charged by insurance companies are higher than would be needed to cover any claims. However, firms that self-insure may be unable to create a fund large enough to cover some awards granted by the court system. Such firms may be forced into bankruptcy if they are judged to be responsible for damages to an employee or customer, especially when the damages granted are in millions of dollars.

> **self-insurance** a firm insures itself by creating a fund to cover any future claims

Comparison of Methods of Protecting against Risk   The three methods used to protect against risk are compared for a firm that produces ladders in Exhibit 19.2. Trade-offs are involved when selecting the proper method. A firm is unlikely to eliminate the production of a product if it specializes in that product. Therefore, it would probably purchase insurance or self-insure. If the firm generates only a small amount of its total earnings from a product that creates substantial exposure to risk, it may eliminate the production of that product. The proper method for protecting against risk can be determined by estimating the costs of each method.

College Health Club: **Insurance Planning at CHC**

One of the decisions that Sue Kramer needs to make as part of her business plan for College Health Club (CHC) is what type of insurance to purchase for her business. CHC is exposed to the possibility of lawsuits if a member is injured while exercising at the facilities. Sue will purchase casualty (liability) insurance to protect the business in the event of injuries. She is also preparing a booklet on how to use the exercise and weight machines safely. She will distribute the booklet to all employees and members in an effort to reduce the likelihood of injuries.

> **business risk** the possibility that a firm's performance will be lower than expected because of its exposure to specific conditions

2 | Identify the ways in which firms are exposed to the economic environment.

EXPOSURE TO THE ECONOMIC ENVIRONMENT

A firm's **business risk** is dependent on its exposure to the economic environment, including industry conditions, the national economy, and global economies.

Exposure to Industry Conditions

The performance of a firm is influenced by industry conditions, such as the degree of competition and industry regulations. A firm in a highly competitive industry is subject to a higher degree of business risk because its market share may be reduced. For example, many video stores went bankrupt after the industry became more competitive. A reduction in industry regulations may lead to more competition in the industry. When the banking industry was deregulated in the 1980s, many banks failed because they could not compete effectively.

Exposure to Economic Conditions

The performance of a firm is also influenced by the national economy. The sensitivity of a firm's performance to economic conditions is dependent on the products or services it sells. If the demand for the firm's products or services is very sensitive to the national economy, the firm has a high degree of business risk.

The performance levels of some firms are exposed to interest rate movements. In particular, firms whose products are purchased with borrowed funds may be affected by changes in interest rates. When interest rates rise, the demand for homes and automobiles may decline because the interest payments that would be incurred by consumers purchasing on credit may be higher than they could afford. Therefore, firms such as homebuilders and automobile manufacturers can be affected by interest rate movements. Furthermore, any related firms such as suppliers of homebuilding materials or automobile parts are also affected.

Firms that diversify their product mix may reduce their sensitivity to economic conditions (including interest rate movements), because some of the products may still be in demand even when economic conditions are poor.

Exposure to Global Conditions

The sensitivity of a firm's performance to global economies is dependent on the firm's target markets and its competition. If the firm exports products to Europe, the demand for its products is influenced by the European economies. A firm that generates a large proportion of its sales in foreign countries can reduce its exposure to its national economy, but it increases its exposure to specific foreign economies.

When firms conduct international business, their performance typically becomes more exposed to exchange rate movements. U.S. firms that rely heavily on exports may be severely affected by the depreciation of foreign currencies because foreign demand for U.S. products declines when the values of foreign currencies decline. U.S. firms that rely heavily on imported materials for their production process may be severely affected by the appreciation of foreign currencies because the cost of the imported materials increases when the values of foreign currencies increase. Firms that conduct international business may reduce their exposure to exchange rate movements by hedging with special exchange rate contracts.

Firms that conduct international business are also exposed to political events that could adversely affect their performance. For example, a foreign government may impose trade barriers or new tax rules that could reduce the earnings of U.S. firms that conduct business in that country. Such forms

Risk of Conducting Business in Less-Developed Countries

Although less-developed countries offer numerous business opportunities, they also present various types of risk for U.S. firms. Consider the following examples:

1 Some U.S. firms made business agreements with Chinese government officials on conducting business in China. They later learned that those officials had no authority to make such agreements.

2 Some U.S. firms that established businesses in Russia have been exposed to massive corruption by suppliers and government officials.

Although various types of insurance can reduce exposure to risks involved in international business, insurance cannot cover every possible type of risk in a foreign country. Firms can follow some general guidelines to reduce their exposure to risk. First, firms need to fully understand the country's rules regarding the taxes on earnings generated in that country. Second, they must determine whether there are any restrictions on sending funds back to the United States and whether any taxes will be imposed as a result. Third, firms should obtain approval for their business from the proper government officials. These may include city officials as well as central government officials. Fourth, firms should attempt to determine the characteristics of the industry in which they would compete in that foreign country. For example, some industries in foreign countries are controlled by organized crime. These general guidelines can help firms avoid specific countries that may present excessive risk. Alternatively, the guidelines may enable firms to properly prepare for the types of risk that exist in some foreign countries.

of so-called political risk can increase the firm's business risk. U.S. firms that conduct business in less-developed countries are more exposed to political risk than U.S. firms doing business in industrialized countries.

Summary of Exposure to the Economic Environment

Exhibit 19.3 summarizes the exposure to the economic environment that firms face. The primary reason for the exposure is that the demand for a firm's product is affected by industry, economic, and global conditions. In addition, the firm's expenses may also be affected by these conditions.

Exhibit 19.3

Firm's Exposure to the Economic Environment

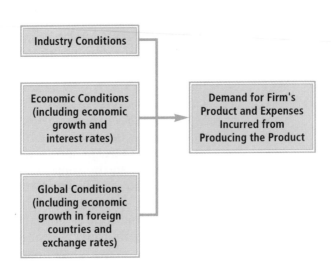

HEDGING RISK FROM ECONOMIC CONDITIONS

derivative instruments instruments whose values are derived from values of other securities, indexes, or interest rates

One way that firms may reduce their exposure to risk from economic conditions is by using derivative instruments. **Derivative instruments** are financial instruments whose values are derived from values of other securities, indexes, or interest rates. Firms use many types of derivative instruments to hedge their risk.

To illustrate how a firm could use derivative instruments to reduce its risk, consider the following example. Assume that the firm recognizes that it will be adversely affected by rising interest rates. It desires to take a position in a derivative instrument that will generate a gain if interest rates rise, which can offset the adverse effect on the firm. A popular derivative instrument known as an **interest rate swap** allows a firm to swap fixed interest payments for payments that adjust to movements in interest rates. Assume that the firm owes $100 million and that it can negotiate an interest rate swap agreement in which it provides a fixed annual interest payment of $7 million per year over the next five years. In exchange, it will receive a payment based on the existing Treasury bill rate, as applied to $100 million. If interest rates are high at the end of each year, the firm will generate a gain on the interest rate swap. If the Treasury bill rate is 8 percent, the firm will receive 8 percent of $100 million, or $8 million ($1 million more than it pays out per year on the swap). If the Treasury bill rate is 9 percent, the firm will receive 9 percent of $100 million, or $9 million ($2 million more than it pays out per year on the swap). The higher the interest rates, the larger the gain, which can partially offset any adverse effects of the high interest rates on the firm's performance. Many banks and other financial service firms commonly use derivative instruments such as interest rate swaps to reduce potential adverse effects of interest rate movements.

interest rate swap a derivative instrument that allows a firm to swap fixed interest payments for payments that adjust to movements in interest rates

Some firms, including Procter & Gamble, experienced losses as a result of improperly using derivative instruments. Consequently, firms began to take steps to ensure that they used derivative instruments properly. Shortly after Procter & Gamble incurred a loss of about $100 million due to derivative instruments, it made a special effort to monitor its derivative positions more closely, as explained in its annual report:

"Our policy on derivatives is not to engage in speculative leveraged transactions."

"The Company has taken steps to substantially increase the oversight of the Company's financial activities, including the formation of a Risk Management Council."

"The Council's role is to insure that the policies and procedures approved by the Board of Directors are being followed within approved limits."

Derivative instruments can reduce risk when used properly. Numerous firms, including PepsiCo and DuPont, use derivative instruments to reduce risk.

EXPOSURE TO FIRM-SPECIFIC CHARACTERISTICS

A firm's business risk is also influenced by any unique characteristics of the firm that affect its ability to cover its expenses. In general, any characteristics that could cause the firm to experience a sudden large loss tend to increase the firm's degree of business risk. Some of the more obvious firm-specific characteristics that influence business risk are identified next.

Limited Funding

Small firms tend to have less access to funding and therefore have less flexibility to cover their expenses. Limited funding results in more business risk. As firms grow, they expand their debt capacity and have more financial flexibility.

Reliance on One Product

Firms that rely on a single product to generate most of their revenue are susceptible to abrupt shifts in their performance and therefore have a high degree of business risk. If the demand for the product declines for any reason, the firm's performance will be adversely affected. Firms that offer a diversified product mix are affected less by a reduction in the demand for a single product.

Reliance on One Customer

Firms that rely on a single customer for most of their business have a high degree of business risk, because their performance will decline substantially if the customer switches to a competitor. There are numerous examples of firms that rely heavily on one customer. For example, firms such as Boeing and Lockheed rely on federal government orders for some of the products they produce. When the federal government reduces its spending, it orders fewer products from these firms. Whirlpool Corporation historically relied on Sears for much of its appliance sales. When Sears experienced a decline in appliance sales, it reduced its orders from Whirlpool.

Firms can reduce their reliance on a single customer by spreading sales of the product across markets. For example, in a recent year, less than 15 percent of Dell Computer's $26 billion in sales came from consumers. The bulk of Dell's business came from corporate and government customers. By focusing on more orders from individuals over the Internet, Dell Computer was able to reduce its reliance on corporate and government customers and stay a step ahead of its competition.

Reliance on One Supplier

Firms that rely on a single supplier for most of their supplies may be severely affected if that supplier does not fulfill its obligations. If that supplier suddenly goes out of business, the firm may experience a major shortage of supplies. Firms that use several suppliers are less exposed to the possibility of a single supplier going out of business, because they will still receive their supply orders from the other suppliers.

Reliance on a Key Employee

When a firm relies on a key employee for its business decisions, the death of that employee could have a severe impact on the firm's performance. Consider a computer repair business that has only one employee who can perform the repairs. If the employee dies, other employees may not be able to perform this job. Until the employee can be replaced, business performance may decline. Since a business cannot be managed as well following the death of a key employee, it may be less capable of covering its expenses.

Hedging against Losses Resulting from a Key Employee's Death   Firms can hedge against losses resulting from a key employee's death by purchasing life insurance for their key employees. The policy identifies the firm as the beneficiary in the event that a key employee dies. Thus, when a key employee dies, this type of insurance provides the firm with compensation, which the firm can use to offset the possible losses or reduced performance. The firm is cushioned from the loss of a key employee and may be able to survive while attempting to hire a person to fulfill the key employee's responsibilities. Consider an individual who runs a small business and applies for a business loan at a local bank. If the individual is killed in an accident, the business may deteriorate and the loan would not be paid off. A life insurance policy could designate creditors (such as a bank) as the beneficiaries to protect them against such a risk. Using this strategy, the business is more likely to be approved for a loan.

To illustrate the use of key employee insurance, consider the case of PRP, a research and development company located in Massachusetts. While PRP was developing a product to be used by cancer patients, its chief executive officer died. Consequently, investors were unwilling to invest in further development of the product because they were concerned that PRP would not survive without its chief executive officer. However, PRP had a $2.5 million life insurance policy on its chief executive officer, which provided sufficient funding when investors were unwilling to invest more funds in the firm.

Several types of life insurance are available. From the perspective of the insured policyholder, **whole-life insurance** is life insurance that exists until death or as long as premiums are promptly paid. In addition to providing insurance, whole-life policies provide a form of savings to the policyholder. These policies build a cash value that the policyholder is entitled to even if the policy is canceled.

Term insurance provides insurance for a policyholder only over a specified term and does not build a cash value for the policyholder. The premiums paid by policyholders represent only insurance and not savings. Although term insurance is only temporary and does not build a cash value, it is significantly less expensive than whole-life insurance. Policyholders must compare the cash value of whole-life insurance with its additional costs to determine whether it is preferable to term insurance.

To accommodate firms that need more insurance now than later, **decreasing term insurance** provides insurance benefits to a beneficiary that decrease over time. A firm might use this form of insurance to cover a key employee. As time passes and the firm is more capable of surviving without the employee, less insurance would be needed.

Universal life insurance combines the features of term and whole-life insurance. It specifies a period of time over which the policy will exist but

whole-life insurance life insurance that exists until death or as long as premiums are promptly paid and has a cash value to which the policyholder is entitled

term insurance provides life insurance for a policyholder only over a specified term and does not build a cash value for the policyholder

decreasing term insurance provides life insurance benefits to a beneficiary that decrease over time

universal life insurance combines the features of term and whole-life insurance; specifies a period of time over which the policy will exist, but builds a cash value for the policyholder over time

builds a cash value for the policyholder over time. Interest is accumulated from the cash value until the policyholder uses those funds. Universal life insurance allows flexibility in the size and timing of the premium. The growth in a policy's cash value is dependent on the premium payment, which is divided into two portions. The first portion is used to pay the death benefit identified in the policy and to cover any administrative expenses. The second portion is used for investments and reflects savings for the policyholder. Under Internal Revenue Service rules, the value of these savings cannot exceed the policy's death benefits.

Hedging against the Illness of a Key Employee   The illness of one or more key employees may adversely affect the performance of a firm. Many firms offer a program that enables their employees to obtain health insurance from health insurance companies. The insurance is generally cheaper when purchased through the firm. Even if a firm provides a health insurance plan for its employees, it may still be affected by the temporary absence of an employee. Firms can reduce the potential adverse effect of an employee's illness by ensuring that more than one employee can perform each task.

College Health Club: **Reducing Risk at CHC**

Sue Kramer wants to assess other types of risk to which College Health Club (CHC) is exposed besides liability risk. CHC has limited funding, so if the number of memberships ever declines substantially, it will be difficult for the business to survive. CHC relies heavily on one product— the provision of health club services. Yet this is the one service in which Sue has expertise, and she does not believe that diversification into other businesses would be appropriate.

Most of CHC's members are from the nearby college. If Texas College ever experiences a decline in enrollment, CHC's membership could decline. Sue hopes to increase the number of nonstudent members over time so that CHC will not be so dependent on the college students.

Sue is CHC's key employee. If she is unable to work, she will have to rely on her part-time employees to manage the health club temporarily. She will train her employees to cover all day-to-day tasks, so they will be capable of managing CHC temporarily.

Exposure to Property Losses

property losses financial losses resulting from damage to property

Property losses are financial losses resulting from damage to property. The damage may be caused by fire, theft, or weather conditions. The financial losses to the firm can result from payments that must be made to repair the damage or from the interruption of the firm's operations. For example, if a fire forces a firm to close a factory for one month, the financial loss is not just the cost of repairs but also the forgone earnings resulting from closing the factory.

Hedging against Property Losses   Property losses may be avoided if the firm enforces policies that can prevent fire or theft. For example, firms that use flammable chemicals may attempt to ensure that all chemicals are kept far away from smoking areas. Firms can also use alarm systems to detect fire or theft. Furthermore, they can design their facilities in a way that protects against burglaries and poor weather conditions.

Although firms can take many precautions to prevent property damage, they do not have complete control. Firms cannot completely safeguard

Flames roll out of a Los Angeles bank. Damage and losses to businesses as a result of accidents and natural disasters can be devastating, even with insurance coverage.

AP Photo/ Mike Meadows

against damage caused by fire, theft, or poor weather conditions. Therefore, they normally purchase insurance for protection. Insurance policies vary in what they cover. Some firms may purchase insurance that covers the property in the event of a fire. Other firms may purchase insurance that covers the property under any conditions (including burglary and poor weather).

The annual premium paid for property insurance is dependent on the value of the assets that are to be insured. The annual premium charged to insure the property of a small factory is less than the premium charged for insuring a production plant of General Motors. Insurance companies assess the potential insurance claims that could occur, and set the insurance premiums accordingly.

The annual premium paid for property insurance is also dependent on the probability of damage. The higher the probability, the higher the insurance premium. For example, the insurance premium for a factory that uses flammable chemicals will be higher than one of similar size that does not use flammable chemicals.

Exposure to Liability Losses

liability losses financial losses due to a firm's actions that cause damage to others or to their property

Liability losses are financial losses due to a firm's actions that cause damage to others or to their property. For example, a firm may be held responsible for an employee who is hurt on the job or for a customer who is hurt because of a defective product produced by the firm.

Hedging against Liability Losses   Firms can hedge against liability losses by enforcing policies that ensure safety on the job and quality control of products produced. Nevertheless, they cannot completely safeguard against liability losses with these policies. Consequently, most firms purchase insurance to cover liability damages. Some insurance policies cover damages resulting from injuries to employees, while other policies cover damages resulting from product defects. Because of the large awards

---

RISK MANAGEMENT OF INFORMATION TECHNOLOGY

Information technology has created new risks and increased the complexity of risk management. Risk associated with electronic business is referred to as e-risk, and a number of programs have been developed to minimize it.

Online banking and securities trading have created large exposures to risk. These services are vulnerable to potential losses from security breaches through network hacking, viruses, and electronic thefts. Zurich Financial Services Group offers a risk management program that includes evaluation of current systems by IBM consultants.

The program begins with remote scans of the client's websites, an examination of current security, and a review of previous incidents to determine what is needed to bring the company up to widely accepted security benchmarks. The program also offers insurance coverage against loss of business income, damage to reputation, loss of intellectual property, interruption of service liability, and liabilities incurred as a result of electronically published information. This and similar programs allow firms to aggressively pursue electronic business while protecting against the risk and exposures associated with it.

---

granted by the court system for various claims in recent years, liability insurance has become very expensive.

The annual premium paid for liability insurance is dependent on the probability of a liability claim and the size of the claim. Firms in the healthcare industry are charged very high liability insurance premiums because their potential liability is so high. Also, firms that produce toys pay high liability insurance premiums because many liability claims result from injuries experienced by children playing with toys.

Exposure to Employee Compensation Claims

Firms must pay compensation (including all medical bills and lost wages) to employees who are injured at work. As part of proper risk management, a firm should assess its existing business operations to ensure that all machinery and equipment are safe and that tasks are conducted in ways that will not cause injuries.

The Occupational Safety and Health Administration (OSHA) monitors firms to make sure that they use tools, machinery, and office facilities that are considered safe. In recent years, OSHA has focused on reducing the possibility of cumulative trauma disorder (CTD) that can affect a worker's wrists or hands. The use of computers, word processors, and other equipment that places pressure on the wrists has caused a major increase in compensation claims due to CTDs in recent years.

Hedging against Compensation Claims Firms can use effective risk management techniques to reduce their exposure to employee compensation claims. As an example, consider OshKosh B'gosh, a manufacturer of children's clothing that experienced a large number of compensation claims because of CTDs. An investigation found that many workers were affected by repetitious tasks that required force with the hands. Consequently, OshKosh B'gosh revised its operations so that employees could

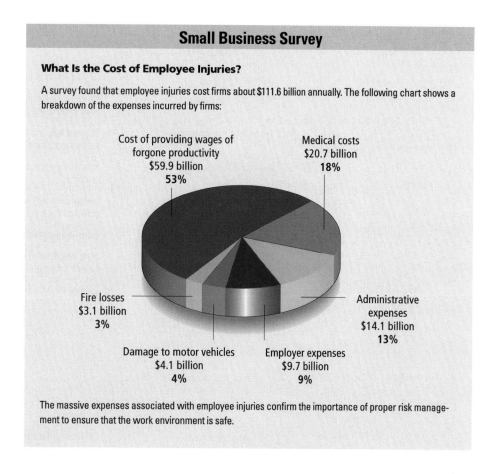

Small Business Survey

What Is the Cost of Employee Injuries?

A survey found that employee injuries cost firms about $111.6 billion annually. The following chart shows a breakdown of the expenses incurred by firms:

Cost of providing wages of forgone productivity
$59.9 billion
53%

Medical costs
$20.7 billion
18%

Fire losses
$3.1 billion
3%

Administrative expenses
$14.1 billion
13%

Damage to motor vehicles
$4.1 billion
4%

Employer expenses
$9.7 billion
9%

The massive expenses associated with employee injuries confirm the importance of proper risk management to ensure that the work environment is safe.

avoid motions that could cause CTDs. It also rotated jobs among employees to alleviate stress over time on any particular part of the body. Finally, it provided job safety training to educate employees on how to perform tasks to avoid injuries. When firms use risk management techniques like these, they can improve employee morale and lower the expenses associated with workers' compensation.

Some firms self-insure to establish a fund for covering employee compensation. Other firms purchase employee compensation insurance. The insurance premiums are dependent on the potential employee compensation that a firm may pay for on-the-job injuries.

Summary of Exposure to Firm-Specific Characteristics

Exhibit 19.4 summarizes the firm-specific characteristics to which a firm is exposed. The funding can be increased if the firm experiences strong performance. The risk of relying on a single product, customer, or supplier can be reduced by diversifying the firm's product line across many customers and by diversifying among suppliers. The risk of relying on a single employee can be reduced by diversifying job responsibilities or by purchasing insurance. The risk of property, casualty, or employee compensation losses can be covered by purchasing insurance or by self-insuring.

Other firm-specific characteristics may also expose a firm to risk. Insurance may be purchased to cover these types of risk. A brief summary of other types of insurance that can be obtained is provided in Exhibit 19.5.

Exhibit 19.4

Exposure to Firm-Specific Characteristics

Characteristic	How Firm Is Exposed
Limited funding	Limited ability to cover expenses.
Reliance on one product	Revenue will be reduced substantially if there is a large decline in the demand for a single product.
Reliance on one customer	Revenue will decline substantially if the customer no longer purchases the firm's product.
Reliance on one supplier	Potential shortages of supplies if supplier experiences problems.
Reliance on a key employee	Performance will decline if the employee dies, becomes ill, or leaves the firm.
Property losses	Expenses incurred from covering damage to property.
Liability losses	Expenses incurred from covering liability for damage to others or their property.
Employee compensation claims	Expenses incurred from covering compensation claims.

Exhibit 19.5

Other Types of Insurance

Type of Insurance	Coverage Provided
Business interruption insurance	Covers against losses due to a temporary closing of the business.
Credit line insurance	Covers debt payments owed to a creditor if a borrower dies.
Fidelity bond	Covers against losses due to dishonesty by employees.
Marine insurance	Covers against losses due to damage during transport.
Malpractice insurance	Covers professionals from losses due to lawsuits by dissatisfied customers.
Surety bond	Covers losses due to a contract not being fulfilled.
Umbrella liability insurance	Provides additional coverage beyond that provided by other existing insurance policies.
Employment liability insurance	Covers claims against wrongful termination and sexual harassment.

4 Explain a firm's exposure to potential lawsuits.

EXPOSURE TO LAWSUITS

In recent years, firms have been bombarded by lawsuits. To illustrate, consider the following statements from annual reports:

"The company is a defendant in various suits, including environmental ones, and is subject to various claims which arise in the normal course of business."

—Motorola

"The Corporation is involved in various lawsuits in the ordinary course of business. These lawsuits primarily involve claims for damages arising out of the use of the Corporation's products and allegations of patent and trademark infringement."

—Black & Decker

"PepsiCo is subject to various claims and contingencies related to lawsuits, taxes, environmental and other matters arising out of the normal course of business."

—PepsiCo

These examples are not the exception but are typical for most large firms. It is not unusual for firms such as retailers or wholesalers to be sued for a product defect, even when they had nothing to do with the design or production of the product.

Assume that you are a firm's risk manager who is responsible for ensuring that the firm's customers and employees are treated properly. Answer the following questions about whether the firm is subject to a possible lawsuit:

1 Your firm's product is tested by a government agency and found to be completely safe. Can your firm be sued by a customer for product defects?

2 Your firm has an employee who is consistently performing poorly at work and has consistently been given clear evaluations citing poor performance. If this employee is fired, can your firm be sued by that employee?

3 Your firm has an employee who not only performs poorly at work but also has begun to take illegal drugs at work. If this employee is fired, can your firm be sued?

4 Your firm recently promoted an employee who was selected as the most qualified for a new position. Can your firm be sued by other employees who are less qualified?

5 An employee recently walked into the firm's offices with a loaded gun. If this employee is fired, can your firm be sued by that fired employee? If this employee is not fired, can your firm be sued by other employees?

Pictured here is a truck stopping device designed to halt a runaway or hijacked truck by being bumped from behind by another car. This device can protect a firm from specific damages caused by an accident. This is one of many devices used to avoid a lawsuit or business failure due to an accident.

© Getty Images

The answer to every one of these questions is a definite yes. Furthermore, you may be sued personally along with the firm. That is, the plaintiff may attempt to obtain a court judgment on your individual assets as well as the firm's assets. The court system may ultimately prevent a plaintiff from suing other employees personally, but there is nothing to prevent the plaintiff from trying, regardless of the actual circumstances.

The court system may also ultimately rule in favor of a firm that has attempted to treat customers and employees properly. Nevertheless, the firm still incurs the large cost of defending against lawsuits. It may also experience a decline in business when the public is informed by the media about lawsuits. Plaintiffs' attorneys often spread the news of a lawsuit to the media in the hope that public pressure will force the firm to settle the lawsuit before the news does damage to its business. Furthermore, attorneys receive free advertising from the media when their names are mentioned. Many frivolous lawsuits have been settled because firms do not wish to use time or resources to defend against so-called nuisance lawsuits. Even when a firm is willing to defend against a frivolous lawsuit and wins, it may take several years before a court judgment occurs.

In summary, risk managers may have some ability to prevent specific exposure to risk that can result in lawsuits and therefore in major expenses incurred by the firm. However, risk managers cannot prevent frivolous lawsuits that will be filed against the firm. They must simply recognize that such lawsuits may occur and should establish a budget that can be used to defend against them.

How the Threat of Lawsuits Can Affect Business Strategies

The size of the damages for compensating injured persons can vary among states. Consequently, managers must consider state laws when establishing or expanding a firm in a specific location. In California, large damages imposed by the court system have forced many firms into bankruptcy. Several other firms have moved out of California to reduce their exposure to the risk that a court will impose such damages.

Some products are more likely to result in lawsuits than others. A recent survey found that 47 percent of firms had eliminated at least one of their product lines because of the threat of lawsuits, and 39 percent of firms had withheld new products from the market because of the possible threat of lawsuits.

Concern about Arbitrary Judgments

Since laws cannot be explicitly written to cover every possible aspect of business, there will always be court cases where the judgments are dependent on the specific judges or juries involved. Consequently, attorneys attempt to position the court case so that it will involve judges or jurors who have a favorable bias. Plaintiffs tend to choose a court location where the jury may be biased in favor of the plaintiff. Defendants will likely prefer that the case be conducted in a different court.

To illustrate how positioning can determine the outcome of court cases, consider that in federal court cases, plaintiffs win a larger percentage of their cases when the case is heard in the court where the lawsuit was originally filed than when it is transferred to another court.

The preceding discussion suggests that positioning may be more relevant than the law itself. Because some laws are arbitrary, firms may be subject to major damages even if they make every effort to follow the law.

Conclusion for Risk Managers

A firm can use effective risk management to prevent exposure to various types of risk that can injure customers or employees. In this way, risk management can also enhance the firm's value by enabling it to avoid the expenses of compensating injured customers or employees or the legal expenses that result from lawsuits. In reality, risk managers must recognize that their firm may incur major legal expenses even if they conduct risk management properly. Thus, the managers can more accurately estimate their future expenses by anticipating that some lawsuits will be filed against the firm, regardless of their efforts to conduct business properly.

Although a firm cannot prevent arbitrary judgments through risk management, it may be able to avoid unfavorable judgments by attempting to use procedures that are well documented and clearly demonstrate the firm's efforts to treat customers and employees properly.

College Health Club: Protecting Against Lawsuits at CHC

Sue Kramer recognizes that College Health Club (CHC) is exposed to lawsuits by either employees or members. Beyond creating a booklet on how to use the exercise and weight machines safely, she is going to require that all employees and members sign a waiver form. By signing this form, they will acknowledge that they have read the safety booklet, that they are in good health, and that they understand that they should stop exercising and see their doctor if they feel any discomfort.

REMEDIES FOR BUSINESS FAILURES

5 Explain the alternative remedies for firms that are failing.

The extreme consequence of business risk is business failure, in which the firm's assets are sold to pay creditors part of what they are owed. In this case, a formal bankruptcy process is necessary. First, however, the firm should consider alternative informal remedies, which could avoid some legal expenses. Common remedies include the following:

▶ Extension

▶ Composition

▶ Private liquidation

▶ Formal remedies

Extension

extension provides additional time for a firm to generate the necessary cash to cover its payments

If a firm is having difficulty covering the payments it owes, its creditors may allow for an **extension,** which provides additional time for the firm to generate the necessary cash to cover its payments. An extension is feasible only if the creditors believe that the firm's financial problems are temporary. If formal bankruptcy is inevitable, an extension may only delay the liquidation process and possibly reduce the liquidation value of the firm's assets.

If creditors allow an extension, they may require that the firm abide by various provisions. For example, they may prohibit the firm from making dividend payments until the firm retains enough funds to repay its loans. The firm will likely agree to any reasonable provisions because the extension gives the firm a chance to survive.

A creditor cannot be forced to go along with an extension. Creditors who prefer some alternative action must be paid off in full if an extension is to be allowed. If too many creditors disapprove, an extension will not be feasible, as the firm would first have to pay all disapproving creditors what they are owed.

Composition

composition specifies that a firm will provide its creditors with a portion of what they are owed

If the failing firm and its creditors do not agree on an extension, they may attempt to negotiate a **composition** agreement, which specifies that the firm will provide its creditors with a portion of what they are owed. For example, the agreement may call for creditors to receive 40 cents on every dollar owed to them. This partial repayment may be as much as or more than the creditors would receive from formal bankruptcy proceedings. In addition, the firm may be able to survive, since its future interest payments will be eliminated after paying off the creditors. As with an extension, creditors cannot be forced to go along with a composition agreement. Any dissenting creditors must be paid in full.

Private Liquidation

private liquidation creditors may informally request that a failing firm liquidate (sell) its assets and distribute the funds received from liquidation to them

If an extension or composition is not possible, the creditors may informally request that the failing firm liquidate (sell) its assets and distribute the funds received from liquidation to them. Although this can be achieved through formal bankruptcy proceedings, it can also be accomplished informally outside the court system. An informal agreement will typically be accomplished more quickly than formal bankruptcy proceedings and is less expensive as it avoids excessive legal fees. All creditors must agree to this so-called **private liquidation,** or an alternative remedy will be necessary.

To carry out a private liquidation, a law firm with expertise in liquidation will normally be hired to liquidate the debtor firm's assets. Once the assets are liquidated, the remaining funds are distributed to the creditors on a pro rata basis.

Formal Remedies

If creditors cannot agree to any of the informal remedies, the solution to the firm's financial problems will be worked out formally in the court system. The formal remedies are either reorganization or liquidation under bankruptcy. Whether a firm should reorganize or liquidate depends on its estimated value under each alternative.

liquidation value the amount of funds that would be received as a result of the liquidation of a firm.

Reorganization
Reorganization of a firm can include the termination of some of its businesses, an increased focus on its other businesses, revisions of the organizational structure, and downsizing. Consider a firm whose value as a "going concern" (a continuing business) would be $20 million after it reorganizes. Now consider the **liquidation value** of that firm, which is the amount of funds that would be received from liquidating all of the firm's assets. If the firm's liquidation value exceeds $20 million, it should

Kmart closed 283 stores, cutting about 22,000 jobs, an expected move following Kmart's Chapter 11 filing in January 2002.

© Getty Images

be liquidated. The creditors would receive more funds from liquidation than they would expect to receive if the firm were reorganized. Conversely, if its liquidation value is less than $20 million, the firm should be reorganized.

In the case of reorganization, the firm or the creditors must file a petition. The bankruptcy court then appoints a committee of creditors to work with the firm in restructuring its operations. The firm is protected against any legal action that would interrupt its operations. The firm may revise its capital structure by using less debt, so that it can reduce its periodic interest payments owed to creditors. Once the restructuring plan is completed, it is submitted to the court and must be approved by the creditors.

Liquidation under Bankruptcy   If the firm and its creditors cannot agree on some informal agreement, and if reorganization is not feasible, the firm will file for bankruptcy. A petition for bankruptcy must be filed by either the failing firm or the creditors.

The failing firm is obligated to file a list of creditors along with up-to-date financial statements. A law firm is appointed to sell off the existing assets and allocate the funds received to the creditors. Secured creditors are paid with the proceeds from selling off any assets serving as their collateral.

Summary

1 Business risk is the possibility that the firm's performance will be lower than expected because of its exposure to specific conditions. Risk management involves identifying the risk to which a business is exposed and protecting against that risk. The common ways to protect against risk are to

▶ eliminate the risk (by eliminating the business operations that caused the risk),

▶ shift the risk (by purchasing insurance), or

▶ assume the risk (by creating self-insurance).

2 Firms are exposed to economic conditions, such as the national and global economies and interest rate movements. Firms can reduce their exposure to the economic environment by producing a variety of products that have different sensitivities to economic conditions.

3 Firms are exposed to risk because of limited funding; reliance on one product, customer, supplier, or key employee; and exposure to property, liability, and employee compensation losses. Firms that are exposed to risk because of reliance on a single supplier, customer, or key employee can reduce their risk by diversifying among suppliers and customers and by diversifying the key managerial responsibilities among employees. Firms can protect against the risk of property or liability losses by purchasing insurance.

4 Firms are exposed to potential lawsuits by customers or employees. They can reduce this risk by ensuring that their products are safe and that working conditions are safe.

5 If a firm is unable to make its payments to creditors, it may consider three informal remedies. First, it can ask its creditors to allow an extension, which provides additional time for the firm to cover its payments. Second, it could negotiate a composition agreement, in which it pays its creditors a portion of what they are owed. Third, it could liquidate its assets and distribute the proceeds to its creditors.

In addition to these informal remedies, the firm may also consider formal remedies such as liquidation or reorganization through the court

KEY TERMS

actuaries 611
business risk 612
casualty insurance 610
composition 626
decreasing term insurance 617
derivative instruments 615

extension 625
interest rate swap 615
liability losses 619
liquidation value 626
private liquidation 626
property insurance 610

property losses 618
self-insurance 612
term insurance 617
universal life insurance 617
whole-life insurance 617

Review & Critical Thinking Questions

1. Compare the methods a firm could use to protect itself against risk.

2. Why would a firm eliminate a product from its product line due to risk considerations?

3. Discuss a derivative instrument a firm could utilize when it is adversely affected by rising interest rates.

4. Identify specific characteristics of a firm's operations that could expose it to risk.

5. Briefly describe the different types of life insurance a business can purchase for its key employees.

6. What are liability losses? How can a firm hedge against liability losses?

7. Define product liability. Can a firm hedge against product liability?

8. How is a firm exposed to employee compensation claims? What should the firm do to reduce this exposure?

9. How can risk managers prevent "nuisance lawsuits" from being filed against their firms?

10. Discuss alternative informal remedies a business should consider before selling its assets in order to pay creditors and claiming formal bankruptcy.

11. Discuss the advantages of an informal bankruptcy proceeding versus a formal proceeding.

12. What are some typical forms of a reorganization? Who works with the firm in a reorganization to restructure the operations of the firm?

Discussion Questions

1. You are a financial manager and your firm is faced with possible bankruptcy. You are in charge of negotiating credit arrangements with your suppliers. Discuss some possible arrangements.

2. Why would anyone consider life insurance for a business partner? After all, it is simply an expense. Defend your answer.

3. How can a firm use the Internet and technology to manage its risk?

4. Assume you are an entrepreneur and that your business has only one customer, the federal government. What are the various types of business risks to which your firm is exposed?

5. Assume that you are a business entrepreneur of a rollerblade manufacturing company. To what extent could you use risk elimination, risk shifting, and risk assumption in your risk management program?

It's Your Decision: **Risk Management at CHC**

1. What steps can Sue Kramer take to try to prevent injuries that would result in liability claims against CHC?
2. Some firms are viewed as risky because they rely on sales of one product that could be affected by declining demand by consumers. Is CHC too reliant on one service?
3. Explain how production decisions such as the decision about the layout at CHC are related to managing risk of an injury at CHC.
4. A health club differs from manufacturing firms in that it produces a service rather than products. Explain how the liability risk of service firms like CHC is similar to that of manufacturing firms.

Investing in a Business

Using the annual report of the firm in which you would like to invest, complete the following:

1 Is the firm highly exposed to economic or industry conditions? Has it used any strategies to reduce its exposure to that risk?

2 Is the firm highly exposed to the liability risk that customers or employees may sue the firm? Has it used any strategies to reduce its exposure to that risk? Is it currently being sued by customers, employees, or the government? (Review the notes in the section called "Litigation" or "Contingent Liabilities" near the firm's financial statements.)

3 Explain how the business uses technology to manage risk. For example, does it use the Internet to research the types of risk it is exposed to? Does it use the Internet to obtain insurance quotations?

4 Go to **http://hoovers.com** and locate the NEWS SEARCH. Type in the name of the firm in the space provided, and review the recent news stories about the firm. Summarize any (at least one) recent news story about the firm that applies to one or more of the key concepts in this chapter.

Case: The Decision to Insure a Business

Bruce Leonard and David Mikan own and operate Master Lawncare, located in Cleveland, Ohio. The business has grown significantly over the years. An insurance agent has called on the partners to recommend an insurance plan. The partners want to protect their investment in case anything happens to either of them. They currently have no insurance on either partner or on the business operations. The partners have viewed insurance as a cost of operations with very little benefit to the business. Also, until recently, they have not had adequate funds to purchase insurance.

Master Lawncare concentrates on one major commercial account that keeps the crew busy all summer long landscaping flower gardens, pruning shrubs and trees, and mowing grass. The operation has had few customer-related problems; however, some customers have complained recently about the quality of the mowing and trimming services provided by employees.

The partners are also concerned about their employees. Several accidents have occurred in the handling of equipment, especially when mowing grass. David states, "We are going to get sued some day by our own employees, and the employees will own this company."

Questions

1 Is Master Lawncare subject to risk? If so, how can the risk be eliminated?

2 What are the business risks to which this partnership is exposed?

3 Recommend an insurance plan to Bruce and David. Be specific on the types of insurance you would recommend.

4 Should the partnership consider self-insuring its business, even if it needs its funds to support its growth? Why or why not?

Video Case: Risk Management by JIAN

JIAN created the BizPlan Builder and other software that is used by entrepreneurs to run their businesses. It has focused on creating software that can be used to help manage a business. JIAN attempts to control its risk when creating new products. First, it determines whether there is a niche for the product that it is considering. Second, it tries to focus on creating products that will have no competition. Third, it attempts to determine the potential benefits (cash inflows) and expenses (cash outflows) associated with a new product. JIAN's accounting department plays an important role in providing data that can be used to estimate cash inflows and cash outflows. The company attempts to forecast potential sales of the new product and then determines whether the forecasted sales volume is sufficient to recover the expenses that would be incurred. As with any new product created by any firm, JIAN faces the risk that a new product will not sell enough units to recover the expenses incurred.

Questions

1 How is JIAN exposed to industry conditions?

2 Some firms are exposed to a high level of risk because they rely solely on one product or on one large customer. Is JIAN highly exposed to this type of risk?

3 Some firms are exposed to a high level of risk because of their exposure to economic conditions. Is JIAN highly exposed to this type of risk?

Internet Applications

1. *http://www.insurance-online-texas.com/index.htm*

Locate insurance quotations for two types of insurance policies. Do you think these quotes as competitive? Why or why not? Discuss some of the other services provided on this website. Do you find these services useful? Overall, how do you think this website could be improved? Be specific.

2. *http://finance.yahoo.com*

Click on "Options." View some of the most active options currently available. How do you think a firm might use options to hedge the risk from economic conditions? Be specific. Why do you think most firms use derivative instruments such as options only to reduce risk and not to speculate?

3. *http://www.statefarm.com/insurance/life/life.htm*

a. Describe some of the different life insurance policies available. Which type of policy do you think would be best for you?

b. Click on "What type of life insurance policy is right for me?" What factors should you consider in choosing a life insurance policy?

c. How might corporations use insurance companies such as State Farm to hedge against the death or illness of a key employee?

The Coca-Cola Company Annual Report Project

Questions for the current year's annual report are available on the text website at **http://madura.swlearning.com.**

The following questions apply concepts presented in this chapter to The Coca-Cola Company. Go to The Coca-Cola Company website (**http://www.cocacola.com**) and find the index for the 2001 annual report.

Questions

1 What type of insurance do you think The Coca-Cola Company would purchase to protect its manufacturing facilities? What other types of insurance might The Coca-Cola Company purchase to reduce its exposure to various types of risk?

2 Download the financial statements and find "Financial Risk Management." Why does The Coca-Cola Company use derivative financial instruments? Does the company ever use derivative financial instruments for speculative purposes?

3 Study the "Selected Market Results" section under "Operations Review." What type of risk might The Coca-Cola Company expose itself to when it builds plants outside the United States? How might it reduce this risk?

4 In recent years, foreign economies have experienced some turmoil. Do you think The Coca-Cola Company's global presence will help the company reduce the negative impact from these countries' economies? Why?

In-Text Study Guide

Answers are in an appendix at the back of the book.

True or False

1. The only effective way to deal with risk is to completely eliminate the factors that contribute to the risk.

2. Self-insurance represents life insurance for one individual.

3. Firms in highly competitive industries are subject to a higher degree of risk than firms in less competitive industries.

4. Firms that produce only one type of product are subject to less risk than firms that produce a diversified mix of products.

5. From the perspective of the insured policyholder, term life insurance is in effect until death or as long as premiums are promptly paid.

6. Under Internal Revenue Service rules, the value of the savings reflected on a universal life insurance policy cannot exceed the policy's death benefits.

7. Firms can usually eliminate their exposure to liability losses by simply following federal and state regulations dealing with product safety and worker safety.

8. Effective risk management techniques can reduce a firm's exposure to employee compensation claims.

9. Creditors are most likely to grant an extension if they believe a firm's financial problems are permanent.

10. Reorganization is a formal remedy for business failure.

Multiple Choice

11. _____ involves identifying a firm's exposure to risk and protecting against that exposure.
    a) Risk management
    b) Accounting
    c) Marketing
    d) Human resource management
    e) Capital budgeting

12. The common ways a firm can protect against risk are to eliminate the risk, assume the risk, or:
    a) acquire more risk.
    b) redefine the risk.

c) hide the risk from shareholders.
    d) ignore the risk.
    e) shift the risk by purchasing insurance.

13. The two types of insurance offered by the government are:
    a) OASDHI and unemployment insurance.
    b) life and health insurance.
    c) property and casualty insurance.
    d) product and performance insurance.
    e) term and group insurance.

14. _____ are employed by insurance companies to forecast the percentage of customers that will experience a particular outcome that is being insured against.
    a) Sales agents
    b) Actuaries
    c) Accountants
    d) Brokers
    e) Assayers

15. When firms believe the casualty insurance premiums charged by insurance companies are higher than the losses they are likely to suffer from casualty claims, they may decide to deal with this type of risk by:
    a) using an interest rate swap.
    b) creating a fund for self-insurance against future losses.
    c) relying more on equity financing.
    d) setting up an indenture agreement to avoid responsibility for casualty losses.
    e) incurring the legal expenses needed to file a loss exemption form with the local government.

16. Which of the following firms is most likely to face the greatest risk from a rise in interest rates?
    a) an automobile manufacturer
    b) a newspaper publisher
    c) the owner of a small shoe repair shop
    d) the operator of a barber shop
    e) a sole proprietor who operates an income tax preparation service

17. A firm's business risk is dependent on its exposure to the economic environment, which includes industry conditions, the national economy, and:
    a) actuaries.

In-Text Study Guide

Answers are in an appendix at the back of the book.

b) insurance agents.

c) global economies.

d) casualty insurance agents.

e) universal insurance agents.

18. All of the following are examples of firm-specific characteristics that contribute to business risk except:
    a) changes in interest rates.
    b) reliance on one product.
    c) reliance on one supplier.
    d) property losses.
    e) liability losses.

19. The value of _____ is based on the values of other securities, indexes, or interest rates.
    a) derivative instruments
    b) spot market assets
    c) term insurance
    d) flood insurance
    e) risk-free funds

20. Derivative instruments are useful to firms that want to:
    a) hedge against risk resulting from economic conditions.
    b) liquidate their assets in the event of business failure.
    c) reorganize their business to take advantage of new market opportunities.
    d) insure against liability losses.
    e) sell more shares of stock.

21. A(n) _____ is a derivative instrument in which firms substitute fixed interest payments for payments that adjust to movements in interest rates.
    a) fixed exchange agreement
    b) composition agreement
    c) bond indenture
    d) interest rate swap
    e) whole-life policy

22. One way for a firm to reduce its sensitivity to economic conditions is to:
    a) concentrate authority in the hands of experienced managers.
    b) buy liability insurance.

c) avoid the use of any derivative instruments.

d) diversify its product mix.

e) focus most of its efforts on one or two key global markets rather than on the domestic market for its products.

23. _____ insurance is a type of life insurance that remains in effect until death as long as the premiums are promptly paid.
    a) Term-life
    b) Decreasing term-life
    c) Permanent-life
    d) Whole-life
    e) Mutual-term life

24. _____ life insurance has lower premiums than other forms of life insurance, but it does not build up a cash value.
    a) Whole-life
    b) Universal life
    c) Term
    d) General purpose
    e) Pure coverage

25. Universal life insurance is similar to whole-life in that both:
    a) are cheaper than term life insurance.
    b) cover employees only for periods of 10 years or less.
    c) build up a cash value.
    d) pay the beneficiary only a fraction of the stated coverage if the insured dies less than five years after taking out the policy.
    e) invest any premiums received into a "sinking fund."

26. A firm may be subject to _____ losses if its actions cause damage to others or their property.
    a) coincidental
    b) liability
    c) incidental
    d) second party
    e) spillover

27. In recent years, the Occupational Safety and Health Administration has focused on:
    a) reducing air pollution in the workplace.
    b) making sure that firms carry adequate liability insurance.

In-Text Study Guide

Answers are in an appendix at the back of the book.

c) encouraging firms to give their employees better medical care.

d) reducing the possibility of cumulative trauma disorders (CTDs).

e) revising workers' compensation laws to make sure each state has the same coverage.

28. Exposure to lawsuits by customers and employees:

a) has never been a serious problem for most firms, though excessive media attention sometimes makes it seem as though it is.

b) can be eliminated almost completely if a firm simply treats its employees and customers properly.

c) is a problem faced by many large firms.

d) is a serious problem for firms that operate in global markets but not much of a problem for firms operating only in the United States.

e) tends to be very similar regardless of where a firm operates.

29. All of the following are potential outcomes of a frivolous lawsuit against a company except:

a) decline in business.

b) public pressure.

c) negative media coverage.

d) high risk management budgets.

e) lower fees for plaintiff's attorneys.

30. All of the following are true about lawsuits except:

a) damages for injury vary across states

b) judges may be biased for plaintiffs

c) some laws are arbitrary

d) transferring the case to another court may improve the firm's chance of winning

e) California has a anti-plaintiff bias in its laws regarding damages

31. A(n) _____ specifies that a firm that is unable to meet all its financial obligations will provide its creditors with a portion of what they are owed.

a) indemnity agreement

b) surety bond

c) composition agreement

d) indenture agreement

e) consolidation bond

32. Under a(n) _____ agreement, creditors agree to give a firm more time to generate the necessary cash to cover its debts.

a) no-fault

b) extension

c) composition

d) formal bankruptcy

e) Chapter 11 bankruptcy

33. _____ would be classified as a formal remedy for business failure.

a) An extension agreement

b) Liquidation under bankruptcy

c) A composition agreement

d) Purchase of liability insurance

e) Private liquidation

34. The amount of funds that would be received if all of a firm's assets were sold off is called its:

a) equity position.

b) net worth.

c) marginal revenue.

d) break-even value.

e) liquidation value.

35. When creditors informally request that a firm that is unable to meet its obligations sell off its assets without going through formal bankruptcy proceedings, they are asking the failing firm to:

a) violate the law.

b) enter into a composition agreement.

c) become a limited liability company.

d) become a subsidiary firm.

e) go through a private liquidation.

All businesses, including vitamin stores, should periodically estimate their value, and consider how changes in various production, marketing, or financing decisions could affect the value.

The Learning Goals of this chapter are to:

1 Explain how a firm's value is determined.

2 Summarize the key business decisions and explain how they affect the firm's value.

3 Illustrate how one particular firm (IBM) recently made several key business decisions to increase its value.

Chapter 20

Synthesis of Business Functions

Managers of a firm commonly make management, marketing, and finance decisions. These managers must recognize how their decisions may affect the firm's revenue or expenses and therefore its value.

To illustrate how management, marketing, and finance decisions can affect the value of a firm, consider the case of Natural Remedies, which sells vitamins to customers. It must make business decisions, including site selection, inventory of vitamins, recruiting employees, and marketing. It must also use financial management to determine how it should obtain the funds needed to support its business. The amount of financing needed by Natural Remedies is dependent on its cost of doing business. Like any firm, Natural Remedies must consider whether the different functions of its business are properly integrated. That is, it must decide:

▶ How can the value of its business be estimated?

▶ How have its site selection and inventory decisions affected the value of the business?

▶ How have its marketing decisions affected the value of the business?

▶ How have its financing decisions affected the value of the business?

By recognizing how a business is valued by potential investors, as well as how production, marketing, and finance decisions affect its value, Natural Remedies can make decisions in a manner that will increase its value over time.

The types of decisions described above are necessary for all businesses. This chapter summarizes the ways that the key types of decisions made by Natural Remedies or by any other firm can affect its value.

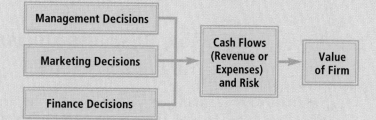

VALUATION OF A BUSINESS

1 Explain how a firm's value is determined.

Recall that the value of a project is determined by estimating the present value of its expected future cash flows. A firm that assesses a new project is willing to invest in it if the present value of future cash flows exceeds the initial outlay that is needed to invest in the project. When investors consider investing in a firm, they can use the same logic. A firm's value is equal to the present value of its future cash flows. The firm's cash flow in any particular period is equal to its cash inflows minus the cash outflows.

Most of the firm's cash inflows result from its sales. Most of its cash outflows typically result from payment of expenses or taxes. If the payments a firm receives from sales and uses to cover expenses are made with cash, its cash flows normally reflect its earnings (after taxes). Thus, the

business online

e-business

Accessing Business Information This website provides access to information on all aspects of business.

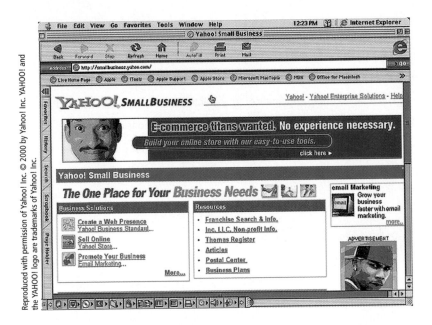

Reproduced with permission of Yahoo! Inc. © 2000 by Yahoo! Inc. YAHOO! and the YAHOO! logo are trademarks of Yahoo! Inc.

http://smallbusiness.yahoo.com

firm's value is highly influenced by its expected future earnings. The cash flows of a firm may also be affected by some other factors, but earnings are typically the driving force.

2

Summarize the key business decisions and explain how they affect the firm's value.

HOW BUSINESS DECISIONS AFFECT THE FIRM'S VALUE

Managers should manage the firm with the objective of maximizing its value. This objective is in the best interests of the owners who have invested their funds in the firm. Since the value of a firm is the present value of its future cash flows, managers should make decisions that increase these future cash flows.

Most business decisions that are intended to increase the firm's value can be classified as management, marketing, and finance functions. The main types of these decisions have been described throughout the text. When these decisions result in higher cash flows, they enhance the value of the firm. A summary of those decisions is provided next, with an emphasis on how each decision can enhance the firm's value.

Management Decisions

Management is the means by which the firm uses employees and other resources (such as machinery). Some of the key management decisions focus on strategic planning, determining the organizational structure, determining the production process, and motivating employees.

Strategic Planning   Many decisions are based on the firm's strategic plan, which identifies the opportunities and direction of the firm's business. Thus, the way a firm utilizes its employees and other resources is dependent on the opportunities available and the types of business projects that the firm implements. Proper planning can capitalize on opportunities that will lead to higher revenue or lower production costs for the firm. Either result can improve earnings, which should increase the present value of the firm's future cash flows.

A firm that develops a more effective strategic plan has more potential to enhance its value. Consider two computer firms that were successful in the United States during the early 1990s but have given up market share to new competitors in recent years. One of these firms may maintain its old strategic plan of simply trying to provide a specific type of computer to U.S. customers. The other firm may revise its strategic plan to change the product it offers and the geographic market that it serves. It may offer a variety of computers to accommodate customers' various needs. It may also develop software packages to complement its computers. Furthermore, it may attempt to serve foreign markets as well. This revised strategic plan gives the firm more ways to maintain or increase its market share.

Organizational Structure   An important management decision is the organizational structure, which identifies job descriptions for each job position and the relationships among those positions. The organizational structure determines the manner in which human resources are allocated to various tasks. Organizational structure is not a onetime decision, as the structure must be revised when the firm's strategic plan changes. A properly developed organizational structure can result in a low level of operating expenses.

In recent years, many firms have revised their organizational structures to make more efficient use of human resources. Specifically, firms have downsized their workforces and delegated more responsibilities to employees whose job positions were not eliminated. The downsizing was commonly intended to achieve the same level of production at a lower cost. Consequently, firms have been able to reduce their salary expenses, which resulted in higher cash flows and enhanced their values.

Production Process   A firm develops a production process to produce its products or services. The process defines how human resources are combined with other resources (such as the firm's plant and machinery) to produce the products or services.

Plant Site Decision   An important production decision is the selection of the plant site. This decision will determine the land cost. It will also determine the costs of hiring human resources and of transporting products.

Although managers want to select a plant site in an area where costs are low, they must also consider how revenue might be affected. If products can easily be transported, the optimal site may be in a low-cost location because the products could be sent to other locations where demand is strong. However, some locations that have a low land cost may not have an adequate supply of human resources.

Since the plant site decision can have a major impact on the firm's costs and possibly even its revenue, the decision can affect the firm's value. A large plant site can achieve a high production volume, but it also results in high expenses. The plant site is not a onetime decision, but is reassessed whenever the firm experiences substantial growth or plans to produce new products.

Design and Layout Decisions The design and layout decisions have a significant impact on production costs. The design determines the size and structure of the plant, while the layout is the arrangement of the machinery and equipment within the plant. In recent years, many firms have begun to use flexible manufacturing in which the layout can be easily adjusted to accommodate a revision in the production process. Ideally, the layout can also be easily adjusted to accommodate a revision in the types of products produced. This allows the firm to revise its product line without incurring the costs of moving to a new site.

Another recent strategy used by firms is to reduce their layout space as they downsize their workforce. Consequently, these firms reduce not only their salary expenses but also their expenses resulting from renting or owning work space. This further reduction in expenses can result in larger cash flows and therefore higher firm values.

Quality Decisions The quality of the product that a firm produces is dependent on the production process used and the commitment of employees to quality. The higher the quality, the higher the level of customer satisfaction, and the better the product's reputation. Thus, the demand for a product is dependent on its quality and on the production process used. In an effort to increase referrals and repeat buyers, firms have begun to pay more attention to quality and customer satisfaction.

The emphasis on ensuring quality throughout the entire production process is referred to as total quality management (TQM). Although TQM is used in various ways, it typically involves defining a desired quality level, developing a production process that can achieve that quality level, and controlling the quality level over time. TQM has been especially successful when employees have been allowed to help develop the production process intended to achieve the desired quality level. It has also been successful when employee teams have been assigned to monitor and control quality. Since higher quality can lead to higher customer satisfaction, it results in higher sales and therefore in higher cash flows to the firm.

Other Decisions Related to the Production Process Firms may also improve the production process through the use of technology. They have automated many parts of the production process so that tasks are performed by machines without the help of human resources.

A final method of improving the production process is to produce in large volume so that economies of scale can be realized. Products that have a relatively high level of fixed costs can benefit from economies of scale.

Motivating Employees Employees tend to be more satisfied with their jobs if they are provided (1) compensation that is aligned with their performance, (2) job security, (3) a flexible work schedule, and (4) employee involvement programs. Firms have been unable to offer job security, as they continually attempt to reduce their operating expenses by downsizing their workforce. However, they have begun to offer compensation that is tied to employee performance, more flexible work schedules, and more employee involvement programs. To the extent that job satisfaction can motivate employees to improve their performance, firms may be able to achieve a higher production level by creating greater job satisfaction. Therefore, they may be able to increase cash flows (lower production costs per

Communication among managers of different departments is critical to ensure that any decision in one department considers the potential impact on other departments.

© Getty Images / Photo Disc

employee) and increase their value as a result of motivating human resources.

Managing Employees Beyond motivation, firms have some control over how well their employees perform. First, they have control at the hiring stage. Proper recruiting and screening can result in the selection of well-qualified employees. Firms can also control how well their employees perform by developing their skills. Specifically, firms focus on developing employees' technical, decision-making, customer service, safety, and human relations skills. Firms can also control employee performance by establishing proper procedures for evaluation. Employees should be informed about the criteria that are used to evaluate their performance and the weight assigned to each criterion. Proper management of human resources can help firms achieve a high level of production, which may enhance their value.

Marketing Decisions

Each firm uses a marketing mix, which is the combination of its product, pricing, distribution, and promotion strategies used to sell its products or services.

Product Strategies The success of a firm is highly influenced by the product that it is attempting to sell. Once a firm determines the product (or product line) that it will offer, it must identify its target market so that it can

Small Business Survey

What Are the Major Concerns of Small Businesses?

A survey of small businesses was conducted to determine their major concerns. The businesses were segmented into two groups: those with annual sales of less than $3 million and those with annual sales of more than $3 million. The following table shows the percentage of firms in each group that identified various problems as a serious concern:

Problem	Firms with Less Than $3 Million in Sales	Firms with More Than $3 Million in Sales
Inadequate planning	58%	33%
Inadequate financing	48%	21%
Inadequate managerial skills of some employees in key positions	46%	23%
Not prepared for economic downturns	37%	26%
Inability to respond to market changes	30%	31%
Environmental regulations	29%	38%
Nonenvironmental regulations	18%	22%
Litigation (such as defending against lawsuits)	15%	21%
Employee theft or fraud	13%	11%
Foreign competition	11%	24%

Many of the major concerns detected by this survey have been discussed in this text. Some of the concerns reflect exposure to economic conditions (economic downturns), industry conditions (regulations), and global conditions (foreign competition). Other concerns focus on the firm's management (planning), marketing (response to market changes), and financing.

determine the profile of the customers that it must attract. As time passes, firms may attempt to revise their existing products so that they can differentiate their products from those of competitors. To create new products, they may also invest in research and development. In general, strategies to create or improve products can enhance the firm's revenue, which can result in higher cash flows and therefore in a higher firm value.

Pricing Strategies   The revenue that a firm generates is directly related to the price charged for its product. The pricing decision can be influenced by the production cost and by competitors' prices. Pricing a product too high can limit the quantity that consumers demand, but pricing a product too low may not allow for sufficient profits. Proper pricing decisions can increase future cash flows (higher revenue) and can therefore increase the firm's value.

Distribution Strategies   The distribution channel determines the path of a product from the producer to the consumer. It determines the different locations where the product will be available. The firm's distribution strategies will influence the number of customers that the product reaches. It may also affect the costs of delivering the product from the point of production to the consumer. Therefore, proper distribution strategies can enhance the firm's future cash flows.

Promotion Strategies   Firms use promotion strategies to increase the acceptance of products through special deals, advertising, and publicity. They commonly use promotions to supplement their product, pricing, and distribution strategies. New products are promoted to introduce them to potential customers. In addition, many popular products are promoted to protect their image and retain their market share. Effective promotion strategies enhance cash flows (by increasing revenue) and can therefore enhance the firm's value.

Financial Management Decisions

The finance function determines how the firm obtains and invests funds, as summarized next.

Financing Strategies   Firms use financing strategies to obtain the amount and type of financing desired. They may borrow from various financial institutions, such as commercial banks, finance companies, or savings institutions. Alternatively, if they have a national reputation and need a large amount of funds, they may issue bonds.

  If firms prefer to obtain equity financing instead of debt financing, they may attempt to obtain funds from a venture capital firm. Alternatively, if they need a large amount of funds, they may issue stock. Proper financing strategies can enable the firm to obtain funds at a low cost and can therefore increase the firm's value.

Business Expansion Strategies   Firms use investing strategies to allocate their funds across their business operations. They use capital budgeting to determine whether potential projects are feasible and should be implemented. For a project to be feasible, the present value of its cash flows

When Kellogg's uses a Spiderman promotion strategy to sell its Rice Krispies, it needs to ensure that the production is large enough to accommodate the large demand that could result from the promotion.

Getty Images/ Mario Tama

Exhibit 20.1

Summary of Key Business Functions

	Primary Impact of Strategy Decision Is on:	
	Cash Inflows	Cash Outflows
Type of Management Strategy		
Planning	✓	✓
Organizational structure		✓
Plant site		✓
Production design		✓
Production layout		✓
Production quality	✓	✓
Motivating employees		✓
Managing employees		✓
Type of Marketing Strategy		
Product strategies	✓	
Pricing strategies	✓	
Distribution strategies	✓	
Promotion strategies	✓	
Type of Finance Strategy		
Financing strategies		✓
Investment strategies	✓	

must exceed its initial outlay. The discount rate used to discount future cash flows is based on the firm's cost of funds used to support the project. If the firm can obtain funds for the project at a relatively low cost, the project has a better chance of being considered feasible. Since many projects require substantial funding and are irreversible, capital budgeting decisions can have a major impact on the value of the firm.

Summary of Business Strategies

The most common types of business strategies are summarized in Exhibit 20.1. Notice from this exhibit that the primary impact of most management strategies is on the firm's cash outflows because these strategies determine the cost of utilizing human resources and other resources. Conversely, the primary impact of most marketing strategies is on the firm's cash inflows because these strategies determine the amount of revenue generated.

RELATIONSHIPS AMONG BUSINESS STRATEGIES

Although the management, marketing, and finance decisions are distinctly different, they are all related. Thus, the management decisions can be determined only after considering marketing information, and marketing decisions can be determined only after considering management information. Finance decisions are dependent on management and marketing information.

Relationship between Organizational Structure and Production

To illustrate how the management, marketing, and finance decisions are related, consider a firm that produces office desks and distributes them to various retail office furniture outlets. The organizational structure will be partially dependent on the product mix (a marketing decision). If the firm diversifies its product line to include office lamps, file cabinets, and bookcases, its organizational structure will have to specify who is assigned to produce and manage these other products. The plant site selected must be large enough, and the firm's design and layout must be flexible enough, to allow for the production of these other products.

Relationship between Pricing and Production Strategies

The firm's plant site, design, and layout decisions are also influenced by the pricing of the office furniture (another marketing decision). If the pricing strategy is to price the furniture high, the sales volume will be smaller. The firm's plant site, design, and layout should allow for sufficient (but not excessive) work space to achieve the relatively low production level needed to accommodate the expected sales volume.

If the firm prices its office furniture more competitively, it will anticipate a much larger sales volume. In this case, it would use a plant site, design, and layout to achieve a much larger level of production. Most firms determine the type of target market they wish to pursue and then implement a pricing strategy before deciding on the plant's site, design, and layout. Thus, the pricing strategy dictates the level of production needed, which influences the plant site, design, and layout.

Relationship between Pricing and Distribution Strategies

The firm's pricing strategy also influences its distribution strategy. If the pricing strategy is intended to focus only on wealthy customers, the office furniture may be distributed exclusively to upscale outlets. If the prices are set lower to attract a wide variety of customers, however, the furniture will be distributed across many outlets to achieve broad coverage.

Just as pricing can influence distribution, distribution can influence pricing. When firms began to offer products directly to consumers over the Internet instead of through retail stores, the firms were able to reduce the prices charged because they avoided any intermediaries.

Relationship between Pricing and Promotion Strategies

The firm's promotion strategies will also be affected by the pricing strategy. If the pricing strategy is intended to focus only on wealthy customers, the promotions will be targeted exclusively toward those customers. If the prices are set lower to attract a wide variety of customers, however, the promotions will be targeted to cover a much broader group of potential customers.

Integrating Business Functions on a Global Basis U.S. firms that conduct international business must apply their business strategies in a global environment. As explained in many chapters, when U.S. firms apply a particular business function (such as managing resources, marketing, or financing) to international business, they must consider the unique characteristics of the foreign country. The business functions that are applied to a particular foreign country are integrated. That is, the international management of resources is integrated with the international marketing strategies and financing strategies.

To recognize how these functions are integrated, consider the case of IBM, which generates more than 50 percent of its sales in foreign countries. IBM produces and sells a variety of computer products in numerous foreign countries. Its production decision of how much to produce in a particular country is influenced by input from the marketing function on the expected demand for each product in that area. The number of employees to be hired for production in a specific country is also dependent on the expected demand for IBM's products in that country. The demand for IBM's products within a particular country is affected by the degree to which the products are promoted there. The marketing function can consider this information when forecasting the demand for various products in a country. Because of the large demand for its products in Europe, IBM's European production facilities are massive. IBM's Latin American facilities are not as large because there is less demand for its products in Latin America than in Europe.

IBM's decisions regarding the design of its various products are influenced by the marketing research that obtains feedback from customers who have purchased IBM's products or from surveys of prospective customers. The design of a product may be revised in a particular country if the marketing research determines that prospective customers in that country would prefer a revised design.

IBM's financing decisions for a particular country are based on the production and marketing decisions, which dictate the amount of funds that are needed to support the planned production volume and the marketing efforts. The larger IBM's anticipated production and marketing expenses in a particular country, the more funds will be needed to cover these expenses. IBM obtains substantial financing for its operations in Europe because it needs a large amount of funds to support its substantial European operations. It requires less funds in Latin America because its operations are not as large there.

Overall, this brief description of IBM illustrates how its resources, marketing, and financing decisions for any particular country are integrated, just as they are when managing its operations in the United States.

The amount of funds spent on promotion will influence the firm's sales volume and therefore the production level. Consequently, the plant site, design, and layout decisions must consider the amount of promotion planned by the firm.

Relationship between Pricing and Financing Strategies

The firm's finance decisions will be dependent on its pricing decisions. If the firm is using a pricing strategy that will result in a relatively low level of sales (and therefore a low level of production), it will need a small amount of funds to support that production level. If the firm uses a pricing strategy that will result in a high level of sales (and therefore a high level of production), however, it will need a much larger amount of funds to support that production level. If the firm needs a relatively small amount of funds, it may decide to borrow from a commercial bank. If it needs a large amount of funds, it may issue bonds. It may also need to consider using some equity financing if the amount of funds needed will exceed its debt capacity.

Summary of Relationships among Business Strategies

Exhibit 20.2 shows the typical sequence of business functions. Many functions can be considered only after deciding on the type of product that will be produced and sold. The management and marketing decisions can be made after identifying the product (or product line). Once all management and marketing decisions are made, the amount of funds needed to support the business can be determined. The financing decision of how to finance the firm is dependent on how much funding is needed. All of these key business decisions must be reassessed periodically as the firm's business grows and its product line expands.

Exhibit 20.2

Common Sequence of Business Functions

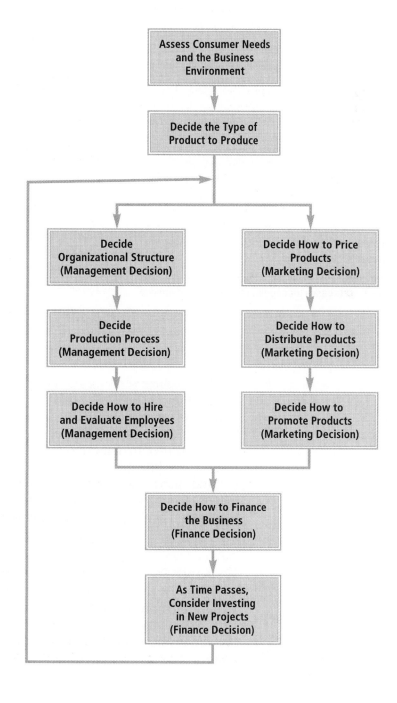

increasing value with technology

SOFTWARE THAT INTEGRATES BUSINESS ACTIVITIES

Ten years ago, an important software category for today's businesses didn't even exist. Workgroup software packages are designed to help coordinate the various functions of a business, offering new means of communication and new methods of sharing work and information. In the mid-1990s, their popularity skyrocketed in the business world. Because Lotus Development Corporation held the premier position in this software category with its Lotus Notes package, it was acquired by IBM in 1995.

A workgroup software package typically runs on a computer network. Rather than having a single, well-defined function, workgroup packages offer a collection of features that help users share work. Among these features are the following:

▶ *Electronic mail* Workgroup packages offer sophisticated electronic mail capabilities, allowing users to exchange messages and files across the network. Advanced packages also offer gateways to other mail systems, such as the Internet. As a result, users throughout the world can communicate.

▶ *Time management and scheduling* Packages provide the ability to create centralized company schedules and individual calendars, accessible by all who have the proper security.

▶ *Document sharing systems* Packages allow users to create databases that contain or point to documents

they are working on. Using these systems allows remote users to collaborate on the same document.

▶ *External linkages* Most packages provide users with the ability to call into the system and conduct activities remotely (for example, from a hotel room). Some packages also incorporate fax handling capability, allowing faxes to be sent, received, and routed automatically by the package.

▶ *Discussions and conferencing* Packages provide online discussion capability, allowing users to conduct conferences between remote sites and keep a record of the proceedings.

▶ *Work flow processing* Packages can be programmed to allow specific work flows, such as the process of creating and sending a bill, to be completely automated. Once a user initiates a specific job, the software keeps track of each step in the process and, once a given step has been completed, automatically routes it to the next step.

▶ *Security* Packages allow users to designate security for documents, preventing unauthorized reading or editing.

Many managers believe that the real benefit of workgroup software is its use as a platform for further development. It is designed to be customized with add-on products, such as fax servers, video conferencing, project management software, and a host of industry-specific applications.

Although accounting and information systems are not included in this exhibit, they are needed to make proper business decisions. The accounting function is used to monitor the firm's financial condition and assess the performance of previous management, marketing, and finance decisions. It can also be used to detect inefficient business operations so that they can be revised to reduce expenses.

Information systems are used to continually compile and analyze information about the firm's operations. The information can be used to help managers make proper management, marketing, and finance decisions.

3

Illustrate how one particular firm (IBM) recently made several key business decisions to increase its value.

BUSINESS STRATEGIES IMPLEMENTED BY IBM

To illustrate how a single firm must consider all the business strategies described throughout the text, recent strategies by IBM are summarized next. The various statements by IBM that follow appeared in IBM's recent annual reports.

IBM's Value

Each annual report includes a letter to shareholders from IBM's chief executive officer (CEO). The letter documents IBM's focus on maximizing the value of its stock for its shareholders:

"The strength of our performance relative to our mainstream competitors was reflected in a 42 percent increase in our stock price."

IBM's Mission and Strategic Plan

The primary mission of IBM is as follows:

"We strive to lead in the creation, development, and manufacture of the industry's most advanced information technologies, including computer systems, software, networking systems, storage devices, and microelectronics."

Most firms do not change their mission very often, but they periodically revise their strategic plan in response to new business opportunities. IBM describes its strategic plan as follows:

"Consistent with the fundamental strategy that it put in place several years ago, the company is well positioned to build integrated e-business solutions. Services software and OEM technology that are required for this business will drive the growth in IBM's revenue and earnings."

IBM's Social Responsibilities

IBM meets its social responsibilities by focusing on education and the environment, as explained next:

"Through a $40 million grant program called Reinventing Education, we apply advanced information technologies . . . to improve learning . . . consumers identified IBM as the company that best exemplifies corporate citizenship."

IBM's expenditures not only demonstrate its social responsibility but may also enable IBM to sell more computers to school systems.

IBM's Assessment of Its Industry

Since IBM is in the information technology industry, it closely monitors this industry and sets its plans in accordance with industry trends:

"We realized that the future of the computer industry wasn't in computers. In 1991, we were a $64.8 billion company that got less than $6 billion from nonmaintenance services. Ten short years later, the business of information technology services generated more than 40 percent of our $86 billion in sales and became the single largest source of revenue in our portfolio."

Managers at IBM's headquarters must make decisions about a particular part of the business only after considering the potential impact on other parts of the business, as explained in this chapter.

© Getty Images/ Joe Raedle

IBM's Penetration in Foreign Markets

IBM has penetrated numerous foreign markets where competition in the information technology industry is not as intense as in the United States:

"IBM Global Services has grown in just eight years from a $4 billion to a $24 billion business, with better than 20 percent annual growth."

IBM's Management Strategies

IBM's key management strategies include its organizational structure, the design and layout of its facilities, its production process, its total quality management, and its training and motivation of employees. Each of these strategies is discussed next.

IBM's Organizational Structure   IBM recently revised its organizational structure in two ways. First, it has downsized its workforce. It has also reorganized to focus more on Internet business opportunities.

IBM's Design and Layout   Since IBM downsized its workforce, it also revised its work space. It has consolidated work done by data centers and reduced office space worldwide.

IBM's Production Process   IBM produces products in large volume to capitalize on economies of scale. Once it develops new technology, it produces and sells its new products and services in bulk. In this way, it spreads the cost over a large volume of units.

A key task in planning the production process is to forecast demand for products so that the volume of products produced is adequate to accommodate the demand. IBM attempts to use flexible production processes so that it can shift production to accommodate the demand.

IBM's Total Quality Management (TQM)   Like most successful firms, IBM has increased its efforts to satisfy customers. Specifically, it has developed a variety of methods to enhance customer service. Customers can now offer feedback and request assistance both over the phone and online.

Training and Motivation of Employees   IBM devotes substantial resources to training employees and to rewarding those who achieve high performance.

IBM's Marketing Strategies

IBM's key marketing strategies include its products, pricing, and distribution. Each of these strategies is discussed next.

IBM's Product Strategies   IBM and other firms in the information technology industry continually assess their product strategies. Improvements in technology have resulted in numerous new products and revisions of existing products. In 2001, IBM obtained more than 3,000 patents. For nine straight years, it has received more patents than any other firm.

IBM's Pricing Strategies   A review of IBM's main product lines suggests that it has lowered its prices in response to intense competition. Given the intense competition throughout the industry, IBM's strategy to reduce prices may have been intended simply to maintain market share. To increase market share, it attempts to capitalize on its technological advantages.

IBM's Distribution Strategies   IBM delivers some products directly to the customer. Some of its customers are individuals, while others are businesses that need computer systems.

IBM's Finance Strategies

IBM's key finance strategies include obtaining funds (financing) and investing funds in its businesses, as discussed next.

IBM's Financing Strategies   IBM obtains financing in the countries where it conducts its business:

"The company issued debt to a diverse set of investors, including significant funding in the United States, Japan, and Europe. The funding has a wide range of maturities."

In the mid-1990s, IBM increased its use of equity financing while relying less on debt financing. As a result, Moody's Rating Service upgraded its credit rating on some of IBM's debt. In the late 1990s, IBM increased its use of debt to capitalize on the low interest rates.

IBM's Business Investment Strategies   IBM, like most firms, frequently invests in long-term projects as well as in short-term assets. Although IBM has reduced its work space as it has downsized its workforce, it still uses large amounts of funds for capital expenditures such as new plants and offices. It also uses funds to repurchase some of its stock:

"The company . . . [made] investments of approximately $20 billion in capital expenditures, research and development, strategic acquisitions, and the repurchase of stock."

Conclusion about IBM's Strategies

Even though all its management, marketing, and finance decisions are made to enhance shareholder wealth, IBM recognizes that it must strive for continual improvement. Every year, IBM attempts to capitalize on new opportunities that result from new technology and also continually focuses on improving efficiency.

"My colleagues are preoccupied not with our achievements of the recent past but with the vast prospects opening before us."

To assess how IBM's strategies have affected its performance, look at Exhibit 20.3, which shows some of the key income statement items from 1992 (before many new strategies were implemented) and from 2001 (after these strategies were implemented). In 2001, the revenue was much higher than in 1992. At the same time, operating expenses were lower than in 1992, due to the reorganization of the workforce and the facilities. Consequently, IBM's earnings before interest and taxes were much better in 2001.

Recall that ratio analysis is commonly used to assess a firm's liquidity, efficiency, and financial leverage. Exhibit 20.4 compares IBM's liquidity and efficiency over time to show how the company improved its financial condition as a result of implementing its strategies. The exhibit shows that IBM was able to increase its liquidity and its efficiency.

Exhibit 20.3

Change in IBM's Revenue, Expenses, and Earnings
Note: Figures are in millions of dollars.

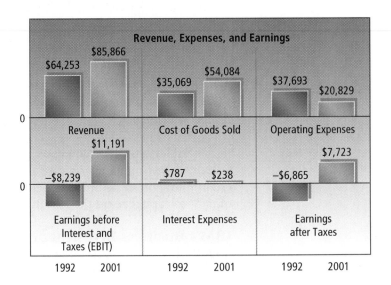

Exhibit 20.4

Change in IBM's Liquidity and Efficiency
Note: Figures other than ratios are in
millions of dollars.

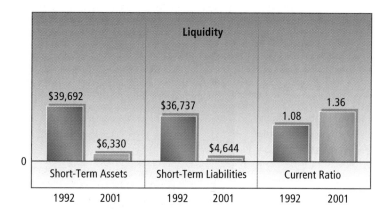

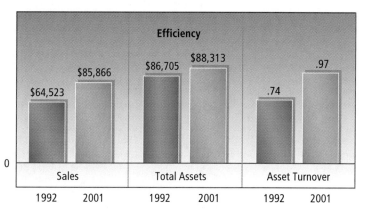

CONSOLIDATING ALL MAJOR STRATEGIES IN THE BUSINESS PLAN

Each chapter of the text has explained specific strategies, each of which represents a portion of the business plan. A complete business plan consolidates all of the firm's major strategies. Exhibit 20.5 shows the complete business plan for College Health Club (CHC), which consolidates the various business plan segments that were discussed in each chapter. Notice that every major business function is covered, in the order that it was discussed in the text. As time passes, Sue Kramer may change various strategies in CHC's business plan, and each change could affect other parts of the business plan. If Sue decides on an investment plan of expanding the club, she will have to revise the financial plan to finance the additional investment. If CHC needs additional financing, Sue will have a better chance of obtaining funds from a creditor if she can present a revised business plan showing how CHC will efficiently use those funds.

Every business, including College Health Club, needs to understand how its management, marketing, and finance decisions are related. CHC's decision about its site and facilities determines the amount of memberships that can be sold, which affects the amount of marketing that is necessary. The decision about its site and facilities also affects its expenses and the amount of financing needed.

© Getty Images / Photo Disc

Exhibit 20.5

Example of a Business Plan

Business Plan for College Health Club (CHC)

Part I. Organization of the Business

1. *Business Idea*
The business is a health club called College Health Club (CHC) that will be located in a shopping mall just across from the Texas College campus. The health club should appeal to the students, because it is convenient and will be affordable to them.

2. *Business Ownership*
CHC is structured as a proprietorship, with Sue Kramer as the sole proprietor. She will invest $20,000 in the business. An additional $40,000 is needed and will be obtained in the form of a loan.
  The business is expected to incur a small level of earnings in the first year, but earnings should increase over the years as the number of memberships increases. The main source of risk of the firm is uncertainty regarding the number of future memberships, which is the key to the success of the business. However, given the strong interest by the local students in joining a health club, the membership level is expected to increase rapidly over time.

3. *Business Responsibilities*
CHC has a responsibility to its customers, its employees, its owners, its creditors, and the environment. It intends to offer its customers excellent service at reasonable prices. It will encourage feedback from customers and attempt to continually improve its services to satisfy customers. It intends to offer its employees a safe working environment and equal opportunities without bias. The firm will be managed in a manner that will maximize the value of the business for any owners who are invited to invest in the firm over time. CHC recognizes its responsibility to make timely payments on debt owed to creditors. It also pledges to conduct its business in a manner that will not harm the environment. By satisfying customers, employees, and creditors, CHC should establish a good reputation and attract more customers in the future.

Part II. Business Environment

4. *Exposure to Economic Conditions*
CHC's membership is exposed to local economic conditions. If a weaker economy causes some students to lose their part-time jobs in the local area, the number of memberships will likely decline. Consequently, CHC's revenue and its earnings will also decline. A stronger economy will allow for more part-time jobs and will result in more memberships at CHC. Consequently, CHC's revenue and earnings will increase.

5. *Exposure to Industry Conditions*
Currently, no other health clubs are convenient to the Texas College campus. New health clubs may be established over time and could pull some of CHC's customers away. Nevertheless, because most of CHC's business is expected to come from students at the college, CHC should not be significantly affected by other health clubs that focus on customers who have full-time jobs and are not currently enrolled at the college. CHC needs to develop a strategy for retaining its members over time. The overall demand for health club services is expected to remain strong because of the desire by people to stay in shape.

6. *Exposure to Global Conditions*

CHC serves the local community and is not directly affected by global conditions. It will sell vitamin supplements (which are imported from Mexico), and the cost of the supplements will rise when the dollar weakens against the Mexican peso. Since vitamins are not expected to be a primary source of revenue, CHC's exposure to global conditions is negligible.

Part III. Management

7. *Strategic Plan*

CHC must attract a large number of members to fully utilize the health club space and achieve high performance. As memberships increase, CHC's earnings will increase.

A longer-term objective is to expand over time by capitalizing on the same business concept by establishing other health clubs near college campuses. CHC will assess other college campuses to determine whether there is sufficient demand for health club services. If students appear to want these services and no health club is located nearby, CHC will conduct a more thorough analysis of the expenses and potential revenue associated with establishing a new health club near that campus. CHC will open additional health clubs near other college campuses only if and when it is feasible to do so.

8. *Organizational Structure*

CHC uses a wide span of control, as all employees report directly to Sue Kramer. Tasks at CHC are departmentalized: some employees conduct aerobics classes in one part of the club while others assist members with the exercise and weight machines. Sue Kramer sets up a weekly aerobics schedule and assigns a specific employee (or herself) to lead each class. When employees are not leading an aerobics class, they are assigned to help members use the exercise and weight machines.

If CHC expands by opening new health clubs over the long term, it will departmentalize by location. A manager will be hired for each new health club and will be responsible for managing all of its operations. The manager of each new health club will be trained by Sue Kramer, so that she can ensure that the manager is trained in the procedures that have made CHC successful.

9. *Production*

Resources Used at CHC

CHC's resources are combined to produce health club services. First, human resources are used to lead aerobics classes and interact with customers. Second, equipment such as exercise and weight machines is provided for customers' use. A health club facility is available to the customers. The main expenses of providing these resources are salaries to the human resources and the rental cost of equipment and the facilities.

Site

CHC is located in a shopping mall across the street from the Texas College campus. Since the goal of the business is to target students at this college who want to join a health club, the site selection serves those students. The rent at this facility is reasonable. The health club has easy access to labor because it hires exercise science majors on internships to work part-time.

Design and Layout

The production of health club services is organized by type of service. Aerobics classes are offered in one part of the health club, and exercise and weight machines are available in another part. While Sue Kramer leads aerobics classes, another employee is responsible for overseeing the machines in case the members need any assistance. The facilities are large enough to allow for some expansion. The layout of the facilities allows flexibility so that the exercise and weight machines can be rearranged.

Production Control

CHC engages in production control to ensure that its services are provided in a timely manner and achieve the desired level of quality. CHC purchases vitamin supplements from its supplier every month and attempts to have a sufficient number of jars of each type of supplement available for its customers. Since the jars are inexpensive and do not take up much space, CHC maintains a large inventory of all of its supplements.

Routing for CHC involves the sequence of tasks necessary to complete the production of health club services. Sue Kramer has a daily schedule of aerobics classes that she teaches. She also posts a weekly schedule of aerobics classes so that members know when they are offered. The main preparation is to ensure that equipment (e.g., a step for step aerobics) and towels are available for the participants. The exercise and weight machines are always available to members.

Production Quality and Efficiency

Total quality management is needed to ensure customer satisfaction. Survey cards will be periodically distributed to members to obtain their feedback about the services. In particular, members will be asked to rate the aerobics classes they take at CHC and the quality of the exercise and weight machines. They will also be asked for suggestions on any other services that they would like CHC to provide.

Production efficiency is needed for CHC to achieve a high level of earnings. Many of its expenses are fixed. Therefore, CHC needs a large number of members to achieve production efficiency. To the extent that CHC offers a membership at an attractive price and provides the types of health club services that students desire, it should attract a large number of members. With a large number of members, CHC's revenue will be high, and since many of its expenses are fixed, they will not be affected by the high membership level.

Part IV. Managing Employees

10. *Motivating Employees*
Part-time employees tend to like working in a health club. CHC can easily find qualified part-time employees by recruiting students who are majoring in exercise science at Texas college. CHC offers compensation that is slightly higher than other local employers of part-time college students. It allows flexible work schedules so that students can work fewer hours in a particular week if they have a major exam or class project. CHC welcomes employee involvement.

11. *Human Resource Planning*
CHC's part-time staffing needs are filled by hiring students who are currently majoring in exercise science at the Texas College. Ads are posted in that department to recruit new applicants. The typical tasks of part-time employees include leading aerobics classes, helping members use the weight and exercise machines, washing towels, and responding to phone inquiries. Students submit applications online.

Developing Employee Skills
When part-time employees are hired at CHC, they are told that the focus is on safety in using the weight and exercise machines. Although all members are given a booklet on safety, employees should understand the safety features in case they see a member who is not using the machines properly. Second, employees are trained on the importance of customer relations. Third, employees are trained to work together.

Employee Evaluation
Part-time employees are evaluated according to their customer relations and their employee relations. The survey forms that request feedback from members ask if they have any comments about the individual part-time employees.

Part V. Marketing

12. *Product and Pricing*

Product Mix
CHC's product mix includes the provision of aerobics classes, weight machines, and exercise machines. All of these services are provided at no charge to customers who pay an annual membership fee. In addition, CHC sells vitamin supplements to members. It may expand its product mix over time by selling workout clothing.

Target Market
The target market is the set of students enrolled at Texas College who want to join a health club. CHC also wants to retain the students as members after they graduate if they continue to live in the local area. Since the health club is not on the campus but in a shopping mall across the street from the campus, CHC should also be able to attract local people who are not affiliated with the college.

Product Differentiation
The main appeal of CHC to the students at Texas College is its location. It is located across from the college campus, so students can walk to the club. Since many of them do not have a car, this location is ideal and separates CHC from all other health clubs.

Pricing Policy
The membership fee is influenced by the cost of production and by competitors' prices. CHC's annual expenses are expected to be about $142,000. Assuming that CHC can attract 300 members, an annual membership fee of $500 will be sufficient to cover the cost of production and will also be competitive. The number of members is expected to grow over time.

13. *Distribution*
Since CHC provides its services directly to members, channels of distribution are not needed. However, CHC does serve as a retailer for vitamin supplements and may serve as a retailer for a limited amount of exercise clothing. CHC purchases its vitamin supplements from a vitamin wholesaler and may purchase exercise clothing from a clothing wholesaler.

14. *Promotion*

Advertising
CHC reaches its target market by advertising in the college's school newspaper. This weekly newspaper is free to students, and most students read it or at least skim it.

Personal Selling
CHC offers presentations about exercise and health to students at the auditorium on one Friday afternoon each month. The presentations do not directly advertise CHC's services, but they provide some name recognition for CHC.

Sales Promotion Strategy

CHC distributes coupons for the vitamin supplements in the Texas College newspaper. The intent is to attract nonmember students who will come to CHC to buy the vitamin supplements at a discounted price (with the coupon) and will look at the health club facilities while they are there. CHC also distributes coupons in the student newspaper that allow a free pass for a day to try out an aerobics class or the weight machines. These coupons may entice some students who will try out the facilities and later become members. A display of the vitamin supplements is set up near the door of CHC so that they are visible to anyone who walks into the health club.

Promotion Mix

CHC uses a promotion mix consisting of (1) advertising in the Texas College newspaper, (2) a sales promotion of coupons for vitamin supplements and a free day pass in the Texas College newspaper, and (3) personal selling through monthly presentations about exercise and health to students on campus. All three parts of the promotion mix are focused on the students.

Evaluating the Effects of Promotion

The membership application requests information about what caused the person to purchase a membership. The choices are (1) referral from a friend, (2) advertising in the student newspaper, (3) coupons in the student newspaper, (4) the exercise and health presentations on campus, or (5) other. A review of the information provided by applicants indicates what promotion strategy was effective. This information will be considered when deciding what sales promotion strategies should be used in the future.

Part VI. Financial Plan

15. *Financial Plan at CHC*

Revenue from annual memberships, sales of vitamin supplements, and sales of exercise clothing is expected to be about $150,000 at the end of the first year. CHC's expenses in the first year are expected to be $142,000, as shown below. Its main expenses are the rent for the facilities ($60,000 per year), salaries ($48,000), rental expenses for the weight and exercise machines ($7,200), and marketing expenses ($3,600). Other expenses are expected to be $23,200 over the first year.

Operating Expenses	Monthly Expenses	Total Expenses in First Year
Rent of facilities	$5,000	$60,000
Salaries	4,000	48,000
Utilities	700	8,400
Rent of exercise and weight machines	600	7,200
Marketing expenses	300	3,600
Liability insurance	800	9,600
Miscellaneous	100	1,200
Total operating expenses		$138,000
Interest expenses		4,000
Total Expenses		**$142,000**

Given the estimated revenue of $150,000 and total expenses of $142,000, CHC's estimated earnings before taxes are $8,000 in the first year. In the following years, the expenses are expected to be about the same, but memberships are expected to increase, so revenue should be higher. In addition, sales of vitamin supplements and exercise clothing are expected to increase.

16. *Financing*

Equity Financing

Sue Kramer, president of CHC, invests $20,000 of her own money as an equity investment in CHC. She will reinvest any earnings in the business over time. Sue has no plans to rely on additional equity funding from venture capital firms.

Debt Financing

CHC needs a loan for $40,000 to finance this business. The prevailing interest rate for small business loans is about 10 percent. The desired loan maturity is seven years. At the end of seven years, CHC will repay the loan. Given a 10 percent interest rate on the loan amount of $40,000, CHC's annual interest expense is $4,000.

Leasing

The exercise and weight machines will be leased. The facilities for the health club will also be leased. Thus, in the event that the business is discontinued, there will be no need to find a buyer for the machines or the facilities. This flexibility makes CHC a more favorable opportunity for lenders because they are less exposed to the possibility of failure by the business. If CHC has substantial funds in the future, it will reconsider whether to purchase these assets.

Dividend Policy
Once CHC begins to generate positive earnings, it will retain the earnings and reinvest them rather than pay dividends to the owner. This will allow for more expansion.

17. Business Investment and Expansion

Investment of Funds
CHC will lease its equipment and facilities rather than purchase them, so it does not need funds to make such purchases. However, CHC needs to have sufficient funds on hand to cover the monthly lease payments. It will initially use its funds to cover operating expenses such as salaries, utility expenses, insurance, and marketing expenses. As time passes, CHC should generate sufficient revenue to cover these operating expenses.

If CHC accumulates substantial funds over time, it may purchase the exercise and weight machines that it leases. Second, it may purchase the facilities that it currently leases. Third, it may acquire an existing health club as a means of expanding its business. It would likely need some additional financing if it purchases its present facilities or acquires another health club.

Credit Policy
CHC will not extend credit to its members. To make its membership more affordable to students who want credit, it will offer shorter-term memberships, such as a three-month membership for $110.

Part VII. Technology and Insurance

18. Technology Needs
CHC will use a computer to store its information about memberships, its monthly expenses, and feedback from members. In the near future, CHC will install a portable computer near the exercise machines so that members can record their performance on their own individual files each day.

If CHC establishes new health clubs, each health club will provide information about its memberships, monthly expenses, and feedback from members. The information will be monitored by Sue Kramer so that she can determine if there are any deficiencies that need to be corrected.

19. Protecting against Risk
CHC is exposed to liability risk. It attempts to reduce its risk as follows. First, it provides its employees and members with a booklet on how to use the exercise and weight machines safely. Second, it requires that employees and members sign a waiver form, acknowledging that they have read the safety booklet, that they are in good health, and that they understand that they should stop exercising and see their doctor if they feel any discomfort from exercising. Third, CHC has liability insurance, which is expensive but necessary. If CHC expands by establishing any additional health clubs over time, those clubs will use these same methods to protect against liability risk.

SUMMARY

1 A firm's value is equal to the present value of its expected future cash flows. The cash flows in any period are the difference between cash inflows (revenue) and cash outflows (expenses or taxes).

2 When management, marketing, and finance decisions are implemented in a manner that will increase cash flows, these decisions can enhance the firm's value. Management decisions focus on using human and other resources to produce products or services. Thus, these decisions typically affect cash outflows (expenses). Marketing decisions tend to focus on increasing revenue and therefore affect cash inflows. Finance decisions can affect interest expenses due to financing and future cash flows due to the firm's business investments.

3 IBM applied several key business decisions to increase its value. Specifically, IBM used

▶ management decisions such as downsizing to reduce cash outflows,

▶ product and pricing decisions to increase (or at least maintain) cash inflows, and

▶ finance decisions to fund new investments intended to capitalize on new opportunities.

Review & Critical Thinking Questions

1. How can a manager determine the value of a project?

2. How does total quality management (TQM) relate to production?

3. How can a firm motivate employees and improve job satisfaction?

4. Explain how firms can exert some control over employee performance.

5. How does a firm's promotion strategy relate to its pricing strategy?

6. Why is it important for a business to obtain funds at a low cost?

7. Explain the relationship between the organizational structure and production.

8. Discuss the relationship among business strategies in general.

9. Explain why IBM obtains more financing for its European operations than for its Latin American operations.

10. Discuss how IBM has revised its organizational structure.

11. Discuss IBM's marketing strategy.

Discussion Questions

1. You are a production manager. Why is total quality management (TQM) important for your firm to be competitive in your industry environment?

2. You are the promotions manager of a well-known consumer products firm. You have been given the assignment of developing a promotion strategy for a new soap powder that is about to be introduced. Discuss.

3. Why should a firm select a target market before determining a pricing strategy or production capacity (or both)?

4. How could a firm use the Internet to maximize shareholder wealth (i.e., the firm's value)?

5. You are a strategic planner for a computer manufacturer. Your mission is to develop a production strategy for your organization. Discuss.

It's Your Decision: **Future Decisions at CHC**

1. If Sue Kramer decides to establish another health club, can she use CHC's business plan without changes for the new club, or will she have to revise the plan to fit the new club's characteristics?

2. Why might the expenses of a new health club be different from CHC's expenses?

3. Why might the revenue of a new health club be different from CHC's revenue?

4. In general, larger production facilities are needed when a firm does more marketing, and more financial support is needed when a firm has larger production facilities. Which decision should come first for CHC? That is, should Sue decide to obtain more financing first and then decide how to spend the funds? Or should she decide to expand the facilities first and then decide how to fill that space and obtain the financial support? Or should she decide on a marketing plan that will increase membership and then decide how to expand and finance the production to satisfy the increase in membership?

5. A health club differs from manufacturing firms in that it produces a service rather than products. The functions of a service-oriented firm such as CHC are integrated, as was illustrated in this text. For example, the marketing decisions of CHC affect the layout and facilities it needs. Do you think the functions of manufacturing firms are integrated? Explain.

Investing in a Business

Using the annual report of the firm in which you would like to invest, complete the following:

1 Provide a brief summary of the firm's management strategies.

2 Provide a brief summary of the firm's marketing strategies.

3 Provide a brief summary of the firm's financing strategies.

4 Now that you have briefly summarized the firm's management, marketing, and finance strategies, explain how these strategies are related. For example, suggest how this firm's marketing decisions will affect its production decisions. Also, explain how the amount of financing is dependent on the firm's marketing and production decisions.

5 Explain how the business uses technology to maximize shareholder wealth. For example, does it use the Internet to research or promote any of its business functions?

6 Go to **http://hoovers.com** and locate the NEWS SEARCH. Type in the name of the firm in the space provided, and review the recent news stories about the firm. Summarize any (at least one) recent news story about the firm that applies to one or more of the key concepts in this chapter.

Case: Integrated Business Decisions

Recall from the case in Chapter 1 that Mike Cieplak recently created an idea for a business. He wants to provide lessons on how to use the Internet and e-mail. He believes that this idea will work because many people (especially older people) do not know how to use the Internet. He will provide hands-on experience and show his customers how to conduct searches for information, buy products online, and use other features that are available. He will also show people how to create a website. Mike produces a service, and he will try to produce this service by himself. If the demand for the service is more than he can handle, he will hire employees to produce more of the service for his customers.

Mike has decided that he will initially travel to the customer's home instead of renting a place of business. Consequently, he can provide the lessons on the customer's own computer.

Mike has also decided that he will advertise his service under "Services" in the classified ads of the local newspaper.

Questions

1 Mike initially plans to offer hands-on lessons to each customer individually. If he increases his marketing efforts, how might that decision affect the demand for his services? How would an increase in demand affect his decision to hire employees?

2 If Mike increases his marketing efforts, how might that affect his financing needs for the business?

3 Assume that Mike considers renting some space so that he can provide his services to a combined group of customers. He considers renting a large office where he can provide lessons for groups of 40 customers at one time. The rent would be expensive but could be worthwhile if the demand for his service is high. He would incur the rental cost of his office regardless of the demand for his service. How is this production facility decision related to Mike's marketing decision? Do you think he might use a different marketing approach if he decides to rent the office space? Will this affect his financing decision?

Video Case: Synthesis of Business Strategies at Vermont Teddy Bear

Recall that Vermont Teddy Bear Company is a manufacturer of teddy bears. It is one of the fastest growing firms in the United States. It developed a management strategy, a marketing strategy, and a finance strategy that were designed to increase cash flows and therefore increase the value of the firm. It developed a marketing strategy that focused on bear grams, which worked like candy grams that are sent through the mail. Its marketing department decided that this direct selling to the customer was preferable to selling teddy bears through retail stores. It accepts orders directly from customers. It advertises directly to customers using well-known radio personalities. Its marketing department forecasts demand for its teddy bears, and its forecast influences the production decision. When advertising bear grams, it attempts to ensure that there will be sufficient production to satisfy the orders by customers. Thus, its production is tied to the amount of orders expected. If it produces an excessive amount, it is forced to finance the excessive inventory, which increases financing costs. If it does not produce enough teddy bears, it experiences a shortage, which results in forgone sales. Thus, an accurate forecast can lead to a proper decision on the amount of teddy bears to produce, which increases the firm's value.

Questions

1 Explain how Vermont Teddy Bear's marketing strategy can affect its decision regarding how much to produce.

2 Explain how Vermont Teddy Bear's marketing and production decisions could affect its financing costs.

3 Explain how Vermont Teddy Bear's marketing and production decisions affect its value.

4 Explain how Vermont Teddy Bear's financing decisions may be affected by its marketing and production decisions.

Internet Applications

1. *http://finance.yahoo.com*

   a. Identify some recent initial public offerings (IPOs). Summarize the financial performance of each firm since the offering.

   b. Summarize the recent market activity. Have firms in the aggregate been performing well recently? Substantiate your answer. Do you think this performance is due to general economic activity or to a lack of integration between firms' management, marketing, and finance decisions in the aggregate?

   c. What companies recently had earnings surprises? Why do you think these surprises occurred?

2. *http://www.businessbookpress.com/*

   a. Select "Business Valuation Software" from the pull-down menu. What software is available on this website to value your business? What factors must this software incorporate to be accurate? Be specific.

   b. Select "How to Buy or Sell A Business" from the pull-down menu. Summarize two books that are currently for sale that might aid you in buying or selling a business.

The Coca-Cola Company Annual Report Project

Questions for the current year's annual report are available on the text website at **http://madura.swlearning.com.**

The following questions apply concepts presented in this chapter to The Coca-Cola Company. Go to The Coca-Cola Company website (**http://www.cocacola.com**) and find the index for the 2001 annual report.

Questions

1 Click on "North America Group" under "Operations Review." Considering that Coke is promoted heavily in the United States, how do you think The Coca-Cola Company's marketing and manufacturing functions of Coke soft drink are related?

2 Download the financial statements and find "Financial Strategies." How do you think The Coca-Cola Company's plans for future manufacturing are related to its financing decisions?

3 Download the financial statements and find "Financial Strategies." How do you think The Coca-Cola Company's marketing and financing tasks are related?

4 Based on what you have learned throughout this annual report project, discuss how The Coca-Cola Company integrates marketing, finance, and production to achieve the company's ultimate goal—maximizing shareholder value over time.

5 Go to **http://hoovers.com** and locate the NEWS CENTER. Key in The Coca-Cola Company in the space provided, click on "Search," and review the recent news stories about the firm. Summarize any (at least one) recent news story about The Coca-Cola Company that applies one or more of the key concepts within this chapter of the text.

In-Text Study Guide

Answers are in an appendix at the back of the book.

True or False

1. The value of a firm is determined by estimating the market value of the firm's assets.

2. The firm's cash flow in any particular period is equal to its cash inflows minus the cash outflows.

3. The overall objective of a firm's management is to maximize the firm's revenue.

4. The selection of the site for a plant or office affects the firm's costs and revenues.

5. The recent downsizing in business organizational structures is intended to achieve lower production costs.

6. Firms with a high level of fixed costs will benefit from large production levels.

7. In an attempt to provide greater job satisfaction, most U.S. firms guarantee the job security of their employees.

8. The goal of financing strategies is to lower the cost of funds and increase the value of the firm.

9. Marketing and management decisions are best made independently, although they must both be integrated with financial decisions.

10. The decision of how to finance the business is one of the first decisions to be made in forming a company.

11. A company is more likely to change its business plan than its mission.

Multiple Choice

12. Which of the following is the most important determinant of a firm's value?
    a) earnings
    b) debt
    c) liabilities
    d) liquidity
    e) asset turnover

13. Most business decisions that are intended to increase the firm's value can be classified as management, marketing, and _____ functions.
    a) job sharing
    b) competitive
    c) union
    d) finance
    e) steering committee

14. The selection of a plant site will determine the land cost, the cost of hiring human resources, and:
    a) production layout.
    b) the cost of transporting products.
    c) process layout.
    d) production control.
    e) dispatching.

15. A firm's direction and opportunities are identified by the firm's:
    a) production schedule.
    b) advertising plan.
    c) strategic plan.
    d) channels of distribution.
    e) pricing strategy.

16. The process that defines how human resources are combined with other resources to produce products or services is the:
    a) financial process.
    b) marketing process.
    c) distribution channel.
    d) net present value.
    e) production process.

17. Which of the following describes each job position and the relationships between those positions?
    a) leadership structure
    b) organizational structure
    c) control process
    d) mission statement
    e) job planning process

In-Text Study Guide

Answers are in an appendix at the back of the book.

18. Which of the following is a production process that emphasizes quality?
    a) total quality management (TQM)
    b) management by objective (MBO)
    c) certified production and assembly (CPA)
    d) production design and quality (PDQ)
    e) just-in-time management (JTM)

19. Firms that have a high level of fixed costs can benefit from:
    a) economies of scale.
    b) higher-priced strategies.
    c) curtailing promotion strategies.
    d) eliminating distribution channels.
    e) more government regulations.

20. All of the following provide employees with job satisfaction except:
    a) employee involvement programs.
    b) job security.
    c) maximum corporate profitability.
    d) flexible work schedules.
    e) compensation aligned with performance.

21. Downsizing is intended to:
    a) increase the firm's commitment to quality.
    b) better serve foreign markets.
    c) motivate employees.
    d) enhance the public image of the firm.
    e) decrease the cost of production.

22. The combination of a firm's product, pricing, distribution, and promotion strategies used to sell products and services is a:
    a) production schedule.
    b) PERT diagram.
    c) marketing mix.
    d) GANTT chart.
    e) promotion strategy.

23. All of the following are job skills that can be developed in employees to improve their performance except:
    a) technical skills.
    b) decision-making skills.

c) customer service skills.
d) estate planning skills.
e) human relations skills.

24. The path of a product from the producer to the consumer is determined by the:
    a) GANTT chart.
    b) PERT diagram.
    c) production schedule.
    d) distribution channel.
    e) advertising campaign.

25. The pricing decision is influenced mostly by the production cost and by:
    a) the size of the firm.
    b) competitors' prices.
    c) social responsibility.
    d) business ethics.
    e) public relations.

26. Small firms can attempt to obtain equity financing from:
    a) the Small Business Administration.
    b) a venture capital firm.
    c) a commercial bank.
    d) an insurance company.
    e) a commercial finance company.

27. Capital budgeting is used to determine:
    a) the critical path of a firm's production process.
    b) the feasibility of a potential project.
    c) the optimum capital structure for the firm.
    d) the relationship between the firm's pricing and promotion strategies.
    e) the strategic approach to the firm's target market.

28. Firms use _____ strategies to increase the acceptance of products through special deals, advertising, and publicity.
    a) pricing
    b) product
    c) promotion
    d) distribution
    e) strategic planning

In-Text Study Guide

29. How funds are obtained and invested by the firm is determined by the:
    a) finance function.
    b) marketing function.
    c) organizing function.
    d) human resource plan.
    e) advertising strategy.

30. The primary impact of most management strategies is on the firm's:
    a) cash outflows.
    b) cash budgets.
    c) social responsibilities.
    d) working capital.
    e) debt level.

31. Effective marketing strategies are intended to affect the firm's:
    a) financial leverage.
    b) social responsibilities.
    c) GANTT chart.
    d) strategic plan.
    e) cash inflows.

32. U.S. firms that conduct international business must apply their business strategies in a:
    a) global environment.
    b) cartel arrangement.
    c) noncompetitive spirit.
    d) tariff country.
    e) quota country.

33. The first decision a company must make is:
    a) the amount of financing required.
    b) the type of product to be produced and sold.
    c) the elements of the marketing mix to be used.
    d) the location of the firm's office and plant facilities.
    e) the minimum qualifications of the employees to be hired.

34. The _____ function is used to evaluate a firm's past business decisions and monitor its current financial condition.
    a) marketing
    b) accounting
    c) finance
    d) human resource management
    e) production

35. _____ are used to continually compile and analyze information about the firm's operations.
    a) Leadership functions
    b) Organizing functions
    c) Information systems
    d) Planning processes
    e) Motivating functions

36. _____ allow(s) a company to shift production so that it can accommodate demand.
    a) Flexible production processes
    b) Total quality management
    c) Downsizing
    d) Restructuring
    e) Reengineering

37. A _____ consolidates all the firm's major strategies.
    a) company overview
    b) strategic forecast
    c) production plan
    d) marketing mix
    e business plan

Part VII

Summary

Special Topics

Completing the Business Plan for Campus.com

Technology (related to Chapter 18)

In your business plan for Campus.com, explain how the firm could use technology to ensure continuous communication with the survey respondents (who provide information about the colleges). Also, explain how Campus.com can use technology to ensure continuous feedback from its customers.

Business Risk and Insurance (related to Chapter 19)

In your business plan for Campus.com, explain the potential risk to the business related to its reliance on key managers. That is, if you (or your team) were suddenly unable to oversee its operations due to illness or other reasons, would Campus.com survive? In your business plan, describe the protection you would use (if any) to ensure that Campus.com would still perform well even if you could not oversee the operations. Do you think Campus.com is exposed to any potential lawsuits? If so, describe the conditions under which Campus.com could be sued. Describe how Campus.com could reduce its exposure to lawsuits.

Synthesis (related to Chapter 20)

At this point in the school term, you (or your team) have developed a production plan, a plan for human resources, a marketing plan, and a financial plan. Reassess the plans, and determine whether they fit together. In particular, consider the implications of your plan to run Campus.com's business. Is the production plan consistent with the marketing plan? That is, can more services be accomplished if the marketing plan is very successful?

Are the production and marketing plans consistent with the financial plan? That is, will there be sufficient funds to support any growth that occurs due to the marketing efforts? Does the financial plan allow sufficient funding to support the planned production?

Communication and Teamwork

Your business plan should now be complete. You (or your team) may be asked by your instructor to hand in your business plan and/or to present your plan to the class.

Integrative Video Case: Information and Profitability (World Gym)

World Gym is about eight years old and has a membership in excess of 8,000 members. Its clientele is very diverse, ranging from overweight individuals to body builders. World Gym offers its members a variety of programs and activities, like aerobics classes. At the heart of World Gym's operation is its information system, which helps the company plan and manage all aspects of the business.

Questions

1 Explain how the management information system used by World Gym can affect its various types of business decisions.

2 What factors do you think World Gym would consider before deciding to open another gym in a different part of the country? How do you think the activities and programs offered by a new gym relate to World Gym's organizational structure?

3 What does World Gym do to stay on top of industry trends? How do you think this relates to its pricing decision?

Integrative Video Case: Integrated Decisions (Le Travel Store)

In the 1970s, Le Travel Store started with a college student who sold trip to Europe out of his suitcase. Today, the company has twelve employees and thousands of customers. Le Travel Store is very committed to diversity, resulting in a staff with different types of energy. Furthermore, Le Travel Store views its competitive edge as its focus on independent international travelers.

Questions

1 Explain how the marketing at TLS may affect the amount of hiring and financing that is needed.

2 What did the owners of Le Travel Store do to avoid high lease payments? How does this relate to financing decisions at Le Travel Store?

3 How does the diversity of Le Travel Store's employees relate to its competitive edge? How do you think this affects the company's profitability and need for financing?

The Stock Market Game

Go to **http://finance.yahoo.com**, and check your portfolio balance, which is updated continuously by Yahoo! Finance.

Check Your Stock Portfolio Performance

It is time to determine the performance of your stock portfolio over the school term.

1 What is the value of your stock portfolio today?

2 What is your return on your investment over the school term?

3 How did your return compare to those of other students? (This comparison tells you whether your stock portfolio's performance is relatively high or low.)

Explaining Your Stock Performance

As you learned throughout the school term, stock prices can be influenced by changes in the firm's:

▶ Business environment (economic, industry, and global conditions), covered in Part II

▶ Managerial policies (such as organizational structure and production), covered in Part III

▶ Human resource policies, covered in Part IV

▶ Marketing strategies, covered in Part V

▶ Financial strategies, covered in Part VI

Review the latest news about some of your stocks on the Yahoo! Finance website.

1 Based on the news about the firms whose stocks you purchased, what business concept covered in this text seems to be most influential on stock prices?

2 Identify a stock in your portfolio that performed relatively well. What caused that stock to perform well (according to related news)?

3 Identify a stock in your portfolio that performed relatively poorly. What caused that stock to perform poorly (according to related news)?

RUNNING YOUR OWN BUSINESS

1 Explain how you would use information systems to monitor the operations within your business.

2 Explain how you might use the Internet to enhance the performance of your business.

3 What would you do to protect your system from sabotage, espionage, and computer viruses?

4 Describe how your business will reduce the risk of a loss due to a catastrophe such as a flood or fire.

5 Describe how your business will reduce the risk of a loss due to liability.

6 Your business plan to make your business successful contains a set of management strategies (which includes production), marketing strategies, and finance strategies. If you have completed the "Running Your Own Business" exercises in the previous parts, you have already addressed many important decisions on management, marketing, and finance. Provide a brief, general summary of the management (including production) plan for your business idea.

7 Provide a brief, general summary of the marketing plan for your business idea.

8 Provide a brief, general summary of the finance plan for your business idea.

9 Now that you have briefly summarized the management, marketing, and finance plans for your business idea, explain how the different plans are related. That is, explain how your plan for the facilities (in the management plan) is related to the type of product you plan to produce and the price you plan to charge (marketing plan). Also, explain how the financing decisions, such as the amount of financing needed, are dependent on your management and marketing plans.

YOUR CAREER IN BUSINESS: PURSUING A MAJOR AND A CAREER IN INFORMATION TECHNOLOGY OR RISK MANAGEMENT

If you are very interested in the topics covered in this section, you may want to consider taking courses in Information Technology or Risk Management. Some of the related courses are summarized here.

Common Information Technology Courses

▶ *Information Technology courses*—Cover a wide range of topics, including computer programming, data storage, networks, website development, and information analysis; normally offered by the Information Technology Department.

Common Risk Management Courses

▶ *Risk Management*—Focuses on the types of risk to which a firm is exposed and the methods used to reduce that exposure; normally offered by the Finance Department.

> ▶ *Insurance*—Focuses on the types of insurance that can be obtained to protect against risk, including homeowners insurance, life insurance, health insurance, and business insurance; normally offered by the Finance Department.

Careers in Information Technology

The following websites provide information about job positions, salaries, and careers for students who major in Information Technology:

▶ Job position websites:

http://jobsearch.monster.com	Computer Hardware, Computer Software, Consulting Services, Information Technology, and Internet/e-Commerce
http://careers.yahoo.com	Management Consulting, Manufacturing/Operations, Technology, and Telecommunications

▶ Salary website:

http://collegejournal.com/ salarydata	Consulting, Engineering, and Telecommunications

Careers in Risk Management

The following websites provide information about job positions, salaries, and careers for students who major in Risk Management:

▶ Job position websites:

http://jobsearch.monster.com	Insurance
http://careers.yahoo.com	Insurance and Risk Management

▶ Salary website:

http://collegejournal.com/ salarydata	Insurance

Appendix A: How to Invest in Stocks

As a firm's business performance changes, so does its stock price. Since performance levels vary among firms, so do stock price movements. Investors who select high-performing firms will typically earn higher returns on their investments. From March 20, 1999, to March 20, 2000, the stock price of Qualcomm, Inc., increased by 1,500 percent. Thus, an investor who invested $10,000 in Qualcomm stock at the beginning of this period and sold the stock one year later would have received $150,000. Meanwhile, the stock prices of some other firms declined by 100 percent over that same period. Thus, investors who invested $10,000 in these stocks at the beginning of the period would have lost their entire investment. Investors who understand how stock prices are affected by various factors may be better able to select stocks that will generate high returns.

HOW A FIRM'S STOCK PRICE AND VALUE ARE RELATED

A stock's price should represent the value of the firm on a per-share basis. For example, if a firm is valued at $600 million and has 20 million shares, its stock price is:

$$\text{Stock Price} = \frac{\text{Value of Firm}}{\text{Number of Shares}}$$

$$= \frac{\$600,000,000}{20,000,000 \text{ Shares}}$$

$$= \$30 \text{ per Share}$$

As the performance of the firm improves, investors' demand for the stock will increase. Consequently, the stock price will rise.

A stock price by itself does not clearly indicate the firm's value. Consider Firms A and B, each with stock priced at $40 per share. Assume, however, that Firm A has 10 million shares outstanding and Firm B has 20 million shares. Thus, the value of Firm A is $400 million, while the value of Firm B is $800 million.

UNDERSTANDING STOCK QUOTATIONS

Financial newspapers such as *The Wall Street Journal, Barrons,* and *Investors Business Daily* publish stock quotations, as do *USA Today* and local newspapers. Although the format of stock quotations varies among newspapers, most quotations provide similar information. Stock prices are always quoted on a per-share basis. Some of the more relevant characteristics that are quoted are summarized next. Use the stock quotations for IBM shown in Exhibit A.1 to supplement the following discussion.

Exhibit A.1

Example of a Stock Quotation for IBM

| 52-Week | | | | | | | | | | | |
Hi	Lo	Stock	Symbol	DIV	YLD	PE	Vol. in 100s	Hi	Lo	Close	Change
126	55	IBM	IBM	$0.60	.75%	28	76,520	82	79	81	+1

(handwritten note: don't buy at its high)

52-Week Price Range

The stock's highest price and lowest price over the last 52 weeks are commonly quoted just to the left of the stock's name. The high and low prices indicate the range for the stock's price over the last year. Some investors use this range as an indicator of how much the stock fluctuates. Other investors compare this range with the prevailing stock price, as they purchase a stock only when its prevailing price is not at its 52-week high.

Notice that IBM's 52-week high price was $126 and its low price was $55 per share. The low price is about 56 percent below the high price, which suggests a wide difference over the last year. At the time IBM's stock price hit its 52-week low price, IBM's market value was about 56 percent less than its market value at the time its stock price reached its 52-week high.

Symbol

Each stock has a specific symbol that is used to identify the firm. This symbol may be used to communicate trade orders to brokers. Ticker tapes displayed in brokerage firms or on financial news television shows use the symbol to identify each firm. The symbol is normally placed just to the right of the firm's name if it is shown in the stock quotations. The symbol is usually composed of two to four letters for each firm. For example, IBM's symbol is IBM, Home Depot's is HD, Motorola's is MOT, and Yahoo!'s is YHOO.

Dividend

The annual dividend (DIV) is commonly listed just to the right of the firm's name and symbol. It indicates the dividends distributed to stockholders over the last year on a per-share basis. For example, a dividend quotation of $4 indicates that annual dividends of $4 per share were distributed, or an average of $1 per share for each quarter. The annual dollar amount of dividends paid can be determined by multiplying the dividends per share times the number of shares outstanding. If the firm that paid dividends of $4 per share had 100 million shares of stock outstanding during the last year, it paid out annual dividends of $400 million.

Some stock quotation tables also show a dividend yield (YLD) next to the annual dividend, which represents the annual dividend per share as a percentage of the stock's prevailing price. For example, if the annual dividend is $4 per share and the stock's prevailing price is $80 per share, the stock's dividend yield is:

$$\text{Dividend Yield} = \frac{\text{Dividends Paid per Share}}{\text{Prevailing Stock Price}}$$

$$= \frac{\$4}{\$80}$$

$$= 5\%$$

Some firms (such as General Electric) attempt to provide a somewhat stable dividend yield over time, while other firms do not. For other firms (such as Nike), the dividend yield varies substantially over time. Some other firms (such as Yahoo!) reinvest all of their earnings rather than pay dividends.

Price-Earnings Ratio

Most stock quotations include the stock's price-earnings (PE) ratio, which represents the firm's prevailing stock price per share divided by the firm's earnings per share (earnings divided by number of existing shares of stock) generated over the last year. For example, if a stock is currently priced at $80 per share, and its earnings over the last year were $8 per share, the stock's price-earnings ratio is:

$$\text{Price-Earnings Ratio} = \frac{\text{Stock Price per Share}}{\text{Earnings per Share}}$$

$$= \frac{\$80}{\$8}$$

$$= 10$$

The price-earnings ratio is closely monitored by some investors who believe that a low PE ratio (relative to other firms in the same industry) signals that the prevailing price is too low based on the firm's earnings. That is, they perceive the stock as undervalued.

Volume

The volume (referred to as "Vol" or "Sales") of shares traded on the previous day is commonly included in stock quotations. The volume is normally quoted in hundreds of shares. It is not unusual for 1 million shares of a large firm's stock to be traded on a single day. Some newspapers also show the percentage change in the volume of trading from the day before.

Previous Day's Price Quotations

The high price (Hi) and low price (Lo) for the previous trading day are normally included in stock quotations, along with the closing price (Close) at the end of the day. In addition, the change in the price is also typically provided and indicates the increase or decrease in the stock price from the closing price on the previous trading day.

Stock Index Quotations

Most financial news reports on the general performance of the stock market over a given day mention how particular stock indexes changed. Each stock index represents a particular set of stocks. For example, the following indexes are commonly quoted:

Index	Description
Standard & Poor's (S&P) 500 Index	500 large firms
Dow Jones Industrial Average (DJIA)	30 large industrial firms
Standard & Poor's (S&P) 600 Small Cap	600 small publicly traded firms
Nasdaq 100	100 firms traded on the Nasdaq

The two most commonly cited indexes are the S&P 500 Index and the Dow Jones Industrial Average, which are monitored to assess general market performance for the previous day or a previous period. The firms that make up the Dow Jones Industrial Index are identified in Exhibit A.2. The S&P 500 and Dow Jones Industrial Average indexes are not proper indicators for specific industries or for smaller stocks, however.

Exhibit A.2

Firms That Make Up the Dow Jones Industrial Average Index

Firm	Recent Stock Price
Aluminum Co. of America	23.52
American Express	37.53
AT&T	27.66
Boeing	34.18
Caterpillar	47.43
Citigroup	36.11
Coca-Cola	44.74
Dupont	43.45
Eastman Kodak	37.43
ExxonMobil	35.50
General Electric	25.40
General Motors	38.54
Hewlett-Packard	18.57
Home Depot	21.38
Honeywell	24.75
IBM	81.65
Intel	16.54
International Paper	35.22
Johnson & Johnson	56.81
JP Morgan Chase	25.94
McDonald's	16.12
Merck	58.99
Microsoft	53.79
Philip Morris	39.80
Procter & Gamble	86.85
SBC Communications	28.88
3M	126.27
United Technologies	64.41
Wal-Mart	50.00
Walt Disney	17.36

MEASURING THE RETURN ON STOCKS

Stockholders can earn a return from a particular stock through a dividend or an increase in the stock's price. Over a given period, the return to stockholders who invest in the stock can be measured as:

$$\text{Return} = \frac{(\text{Selling Price} - \text{Purchase Price}) + \text{Dividend}}{\text{Purchase Price}}$$

Notice that the numerator reflects a dollar amount composed of the difference between the sales price and purchase price, plus the dividend. This dollar amount is divided by the purchase price to measure the return.

For example, consider a stock that was purchased for $40 per share at the beginning of the year. Assume that a dividend of $2 per share was paid to the investor and that the stock was sold for $44 at the end of the year. The return on this stock over the year is:

$$\text{Return} = \frac{(\text{Selling Price} - \text{Purchase Price}) + \text{Dividend}}{\text{Purchase Price}}$$

$$= \frac{(\$44 - \$40) + \$2}{\$40}$$

$$= .15, \text{ or } 15\%$$

Since the return on the stock is made up of dividends plus the increase in the stock's price, investors cannot just assess a stock's performance by its dividends. Some firms that tend to pay out a higher proportion of their earnings as dividends have less ability to grow in the future, which may limit the potential increase in the stock price. Conversely, firms that retain (reinvest) most of their earnings pay low or no dividends but are more capable of growing. Therefore, investors who are willing to invest in growth firms that do not pay dividends may benefit from larger increases in the stock price.

Return-Risk Trade-Off for Small Stocks

Some investors prefer to invest in stocks of small firms that have potential for a large increase in the stock price. They may attempt to invest before the firms have had much success, because they can purchase the stock at a relatively low price. If these firms become successful, the share price should increase substantially. Many investors realize that if they had purchased shares of successful growing firms such as Microsoft and Dell Computer when those firms went public, they would be millionaires now. However, for every huge success story, there are many other firms that failed. Investors who invested in these other unsuccessful firms may have lost 100 percent of their investment. Stocks of small firms tend to have potential for high returns but also tend to have high risk. In addition, many stocks of small firms are not traded frequently, which means that investors who wish to sell their shares may have difficulty finding a buyer. This can force the investors to sell the stock at a lower price.

FACTORS THAT INFLUENCE STOCK PRICE MOVEMENTS

The perceived value of a firm (and therefore the stock's price) can change in response to several factors as explained next.

Economic Effects

Any factor that enhances the expected performance of the firm can increase its value. For example, when economic conditions are expected to improve, the firm's performance may be expected to increase, and so should the firm's value. Some firms are more sensitive to economic conditions, as a change in economic conditions affects the demand for some products more than others. A retail store such as Sears is more sensitive to economic conditions than a utility company. Therefore, the stock price of Sears should be more sensitive to economic conditions than the stock price of a utility company.

Market Effects

bullish periods in which there is considerable demand for stocks because investors have favorable expectations about the performance of firms

bearish periods in which investors are selling their stocks because of unfavorable expectations about the performance of firms

A stock's price may ride along with the general trend of the stock market. During some so-called **bullish** periods, there is considerable demand for stocks because investors have favorable expectations about the performance of firms. During other so-called **bearish** periods, investors are selling their stocks because of unfavorable expectations about the performance of firms. As an extreme example, the prices of stocks declined by about 22 percent when the stock market crashed on October 19, 1987. Most stocks declined by a large amount on that day. The crash illustrates how general stock market momentum can influence firms' stocks even when there is no new information about their future performance.

Industry Effects

Stock prices are also driven by industry factors. For example, expectations of future performance in the computer industry may be very favorable in a specific period, while expectations may be less favorable in the steel industry. In the 1997–2000 period, stock prices in technology increased substantially, while stock prices in the airline and tobacco industries were relatively weak. Yet, in the 2001-2002 period, technology stock prices declined substantially.

Characteristics of the Firm

In addition to market and industry effects, stock prices can also be affected by characteristics of the firm. For example, one firm may have better management than others in the same industry, which could result in higher earnings and higher stock returns. Alternatively, a firm could experience a labor strike, which could cause its earnings and stock return to be lower than other firms in the industry. Stock price movements of firms in the same industry vary over time, even though these firms are affected by the same industry conditions.

A given firm may use many strategies that could cause its stock price return to be different from those of other firms in the industry. In general, any strategy that is likely to improve earnings will result in a higher stock price. The stock price of IBM rose after IBM restructured its operations and eliminated thousands of jobs. Investors may have expected that operating expenses (such as salaries) would be reduced as a result of the restructuring.

How Stock Prices Respond to New Information

The price of a stock adjusts in response to changes in the demand for the stock or in the supply of the stock for sale by investors. The price may change throughout the day. For example, stock of Summit Autonomous (a laser vision company) increased by about 45 percent on May 26, 2000, when investors learned that it might be acquired by Alcon (an eye care company). The new information made investors realize that Summit would be valued more highly if it were acquired by Alcon. This caused investors to increase the demand for the stock, which pushed the stock price up. On the same day, the stock price of Progenics Pharmaceuticals, Inc., declined by 69 percent in response to news that its products for cancer treatment were not performing as well as expected.

IDENTIFYING UNDERVALUED FIRMS

Investors recognize that any new information about a firm's performance (especially its earnings) will affect its stock price. Consequently, they would like to anticipate the information before other investors so that they can take their investment position before others become aware of the information. For example, investors may attempt to forecast whether firms are implementing any major policies, such as acquisitions or layoffs. They use such forecasts to estimate future earnings. If their estimate of the firm's earnings is higher than that of most other investors, they may believe the firm is undervalued.

As explained earlier, some investors closely monitor PE ratios to determine whether a firm's stock is undervalued. Consider Firm Z with a stock price of $20 per share and recent annual earnings of $4 per share. This firm's PE ratio is 20/4, or 5. Assume that most firms in Firm Z's industry have a PE ratio of 9, which means that their stock prices are nine times their recent annual earnings, on average. Since Firm Z's stock price is only five times its recent earnings, some investors may believe that Firm Z's stock is undervalued. They may argue that its price should be nine times its annual earnings, or about $36.

Stock Market Efficiency

stock market efficiency a term used to suggest that stock prices reflect all publicly available information

The term **stock market efficiency** is used to suggest that stock prices reflect all publicly available information. That is, the prevailing prices have not ignored any publicly available information that could affect the firms' values. Consequently, stocks should not be overvalued or undervalued. The rationale for stock market efficiency is that there are numerous stock analysts who closely monitor stocks. If any stock was undervalued based on existing information, investors would purchase those stocks. The stock's price would be pushed higher in response to the strong demand by all the investors who

How Much Risk Can You Take?

Investing in the stock market isn't for those with queasy stomachs or short time horizons. The money you've earmarked for emergencies should be in liquid investments with relatively steady returns, such as money market funds. But stocks are the backbone of a long-term portfolio for retirement or other goals that are at least 10 to 15 years away.

This simple, self-scoring risk-tolerance test is designed to help you decide what percentage of your long-term money should go into stocks. As you (and your stomach) become more accustomed to the market's ups and downs, you might want to retake the test. Questions come from VALIC (The Variable Annuity Life Insurance Company) and other sources.

_____ 1. Which of the following would worry you the most?
   a) My portfolio may lose value in one of every three years.
   b) My investments won't stay even with inflation.
   c) I won't earn a premium over inflation on my long-term investments.

_____ 2. How would you react if your stock portfolio fell 30 percent in one year?
   a) I would sell some or all of it.
   b) I would stop investing money until the market came back.
   c) I would stick with my investment plan and consider adding more to stocks.

_____ 3. You've just heard that the stock market fell by 10 percent today. Your reaction is to:
   a) Consider selling some stocks.
   b) Be concerned, but figure the market is likely to go up again eventually.
   c) Consider buying more stocks, because they are cheaper now.

_____ 4. You read numerous newspaper articles over several months quoting experts who predict stocks will lose money in the coming decade. Many argue that real estate is a better investment. You would:
   a) Consider reducing your stock investments and increasing your investment in real estate.
   b) Be concerned, but stick to your long-term investments in stocks.
   c) Consider the articles as evidence of unwarranted pessimism over the outlook for stocks.

_____ 5. Which of the following best describes your attitude about investing in bonds as compared with stocks?
   a) The high volatility of the stock market concerns me, so I prefer to invest in bonds.
   b) Bonds have less risk but they provide lower returns, so I have a hard time choosing between the two.
   c) The lower return potential of bonds leads me to prefer stocks.

_____ 6. Which of the following best describes how you evaluate the performance of your investments?
   a) My greatest concern is the previous year's performance.
   b) The previous two years are the most important to me.
   c) Performance over five or more years is most significant to me.

_____ 7. Which of the following scenarios would make you feel best about your investments?
   a) Being in a money market fund saves you from losing half your money in a market downturn.
   b) You double your money in a stock fund in one year.
   c) Over the long term, your overall mix of investments protects you from loss and outpaces the rate of inflation.

(continued)

recognized that the stock was undervalued. Conversely, investors holding overvalued stock would sell that stock once they recognized that it was overvalued. This action would place downward pressure on the stock's price, causing it to move toward its proper level.

Even if the stock market is efficient, investors differ on how to interpret publicly available information. For example, investors may react differently to information that IBM's earnings increased by 20 percent over the last year. Some investors may view that information as old news, while others may believe it is a signal for continued strong performance in the future. Such differences in interpretation are why some investors purchase a stock and others sell that same stock, based on the same information.

PROBLEMS IN VALUING STOCKS

As just explained, investors buy a stock when they believe it is undervalued and sell a stock when they believe it is overvalued. To decide whether a stock is over- or undervalued, they commonly rely on financial statements provided by firms. In particular, they derive the value of a stock from the firm's reported earnings because earnings serve as an estimate of cash flows. When a firm's revenue is in cash, and its expenses are paid in cash, the earnings are a good measure of cash flow.

Although earnings can be a very useful indicator of a firm's performance, investors must recognize that the reported earnings are subject to manipulation. A firm has some flexibility in the rules it uses when estimating its revenue and its expenses. Thus, it

_____ 8. Which of the following statements best describes you?

    a) I often change my mind and have trouble sticking to a plan.

    b) I can stay with a strategy only as long as it seems to be going well.

    c) Once I make up my mind to do something, I tend to carry through with it, regardless of the obstacles.

_____ 9. If you won $20,000 in the lottery, you would:

    a) Spend it on a new car.

    b) Invest it in a safe municipal bond fund.

    c) Invest it in the stock market.

_____ 10. How much experience do you have investing in stocks or stock funds?

    a) None.

    b) A little.

    c) A comfortable amount.

SCORING: For each a, give yourself 4 points; for each b, 6 points; and for each c, 10 points. Your total score tells you the percentage you should invest in stocks. Put the rest in bonds or other fixed-income investments.

can inflate its reported earnings by using accounting methods that inflate its reported revenue or reduce its reported expenses.

Various accounting methods are used to inflate revenue. For example, if a firm has a multi-year contract with a client, it may record all the revenue in the first year of the contract, even though it receives payment only for the first year. Some firms report all of their sales as revenue even though the cash has not yet been received. If some of the sales are credit sales, the firm may never receive cash from those sales. Sunbeam used this method in 1998 to exaggerate its revenue, which resulted in higher earnings. It sold products with a clause that allowed customers to easily cancel their orders. It then recorded all the orders as revenue even though many of the orders were likely to be canceled.

In the 2000–2002 period, many firms, including Qwest, Gemstar (owner of *TV Guide*), and Xerox, used methods that inflated their revenue. In some cases, the methods used were not illegal, but were misleading. Investors must recognize that the revenue of two firms is not directly comparable, even if the firms are the same size. One firm may use a more generous accounting method, which allows it to inflate its revenue. Normally, a firm that inflates revenue for this year will have an offsetting effect in the future. However, investors who are using the most recent financial statements to assess the firm's future performance may be misled by the inflated revenue estimates.

Firms also have some flexibility when accounting for expenses, which means that some firms underestimate their expenses. One of the most common ways to underestimate expenses is to separately report some types of expenses that will not occur again (such as expenses that result from closing a manufacturing plant). The firm can exclude these from its normal operating expenses. Thus, when it subtracts its normal operating expenses from revenue to estimate earnings, the earnings level will appear to be relatively high.

Perhaps the most publicized example of a firm that underestimated its expenses is WorldCom. In June 2002, WorldCom admitted that it had underestimated its expenses over the previous five quarters by almost $4 billion. Thus, its earnings were substantially overestimated. WorldCom announced that it would revise its earnings for the previous five quarters. However, this adjustment did not help the investors who trusted the earnings reports when they purchased the stock at high prices over the previous quarters. WorldCom's stock declined from $46 per share in June 2000 to less than $1 per share in June 2002. Although WorldCom's stock was already weak in the year before it admitted that it had underestimated its expenses, the stock price would have been much lower if investors had been provided with accurate financial information.

The lesson from WorldCom and other similar examples is that when a firm's expenses are underestimated, its value is overestimated, and its stock price is higher than it should be. Investors who purchase the stock while it is overvalued pay too much for it and ultimately sell the stock for a lower price than they paid for it. The stock's price declines once investors realize that they overestimated the firm's value. Since the financial reports provided by firms can be misleading, investors should use caution when using these reports to value a stock.

Investor Reliance on Analyst Ratings

Many investors make decisions about buying or selling stocks based on ratings by stock analysts, who are supposed to be experts at analyzing stocks. Although some analysts may offer valuable advice, many analysts offer poor advice. Most of the analysts provide very optimistic ratings on most stocks. That is, the analysts are unwilling to discriminate between good and bad stocks. If investors took the analysts' advice literally, they would buy most stocks.

Many analysts are employed by investment firms that are hoping to provide other business for the firms that are being rated. Thus, there is an obvious conflict of interests. Analysts may be implicitly pressured to rate most firms highly. Analysts employed by securities firms are rarely willing to recommend a "sell" rating for any firm that may potentially need consulting services. Consider the case of Enron, which went bankrupt in November 2001. Sixteen of the 17 analysts employed by securities firms rated Enron a strong buy before its problems were disclosed in the media. Thus, if investors are hoping that analysts may be able to detect problems of a firm before the rest of the investment community, they may be disappointed.

STOCK TRANSACTIONS

stock broker a person who facilitates desired stock transactions

Investors who wish to purchase stocks use a **stock broker** who facilitates the stock transactions desired. Brokers receive requests for trades from investors and then communicate these requests to people on the trading floor of a stock exchange (called **floor traders**) who execute the transactions.

floor traders people on the trading floor of a stock exchange who execute transactions

A typical stock transaction order specifies the name of the stock, whether the stock is to be bought or sold, the amount of shares to be traded, and the investor's desired price. For example, one investor may call a broker and request: "Purchase 100 shares of IBM; pay no more than $110 per share." A second investor who is holding IBM stock may call a different broker and request: "Sell 100 shares of IBM at the highest price possible." Both brokers will send this information to the stock exchange. One floor trader will accommodate the buyer, while another floor trader will accommodate the seller. The two traders can agree on a transaction in which 100 shares of IBM are sold for $110 per share.

market order an investor's order requesting a transaction for the best possible price

Market Orders versus Limit Orders

limit order an investor's order that places a limit on the price at which the investor would be willing to purchase or sell a stock

Investors can place a **market order,** which means they request a transaction for the best possible price. They can also place a **limit order,** which puts a limit on the price at which they would be willing to purchase or sell a stock. Examples of a market order are (1) "Purchase 200 shares of General Motors stock at the best [lowest] price available" and (2) "Sell 300 shares of

Eastman Kodak stock at the best [highest] price available." Examples of a limit order are (1) "Purchase 300 shares of Disney; pay no more than $20 per share" and (2) "Sell 100 shares of PepsiCo; sell for no less than $40 per share."

Purchasing Stocks on Margin

on margin only a portion of the funds needed to purchase a stock is in cash

Investors can purchase stocks **on margin,** which means that only a portion of the funds needed to purchase a stock is in cash. Many brokerage firms provide loans to investors who wish to buy on margin. For example, an investor may place an order to purchase 100 shares of Wells Fargo stock at $50 per share. The transaction is priced at $5,000. An investor who has only $3,000 available may borrow the remaining $2,000 from the brokerage firm. There are limits on the amount that investors can borrow, however. Normally, the amount borrowed cannot exceed 50 percent of the amount of the investment.

Types of Brokers

discount brokers brokers who ensure that a transaction desired by an investor is executed but do not offer advice

full-service brokers brokers who provide advice to investors on stocks to purchase or sell and also ensure that transactions desired by investors are executed

Different types of brokers provide services that investors need. **Discount brokers** ensure that a transaction desired by an investor is executed but do not offer advice. Popular discount brokers include Datek, E*Trade, and Ameritrade. **Full-service brokers** provide advice to investors on stocks to purchase or sell and also ensure that transactions desired by investors are executed. Popular full-service brokers include Merrill Lynch and Morgan Stanley.

Commissions on Stock Transactions

commission sales fee

Brokers charge a **commission,** or sales fee, to execute a stock transaction. The commissions charged by full-service brokers are typically higher than those charged by discount brokers. Commissions are sometimes set according to the number of shares traded. For example, a commission of $50 might be set for transactions involving 100 shares, $60 for transactions involving up to 300 shares, and $80 for transactions involving up to 600 shares. Other discount and full-service brokers set their commissions according to the dollar value of the transaction. For example, some discount brokers may

Exhibit A.3

Websites with Online Trading Information

American Stock Exchange	http://www.amex.com
Fidelity Investors	http://www.fid_inv.com/brokerage/fidelity_plus_brokerage_acc.html
Quick and Reilly	http://www.quick-reilly.com
E*Trade	http://www.etrade.com
Charles Schwab	http://www.schwab.com
Merrill Lynch	http://ml.com
Datek	http://www.datek.com
Ameritrade	http://www.ameritrade.com

charge about 1 percent of the stock transaction value, while full-service brokers may charge about 3 to 8 percent of the stock transaction value.

Many stock transactions are now executed online through online brokerage websites (see Exhibit A.3). The commissions for these trades are very low, such as $10 or $20 per trade.

Investors typically purchase stocks in **round lots,** or multiples of 100 shares. They may also purchase stocks in **odd lots,** or less than 100 shares, but the transaction cost may be higher.

round lots multiples of 100 shares

odd lots less than 100 shares

STOCK EXCHANGES

The main stock exchange in the United States is the New York Stock Exchange (NYSE). The NYSE has a trading floor where traders exchange stocks. Many traders represent brokerage firms and execute the transactions that their customers desire. Other traders execute transactions for their own accounts. The trading resembles an auction, as traders selling a stock attempt to receive the highest possible price. Each trader may serve as a buyer for some transactions and a seller for others.

Many of the largest firms in the United States (such as Procter & Gamble, IBM, and General Motors) have their stocks listed on the NYSE. Firms that list their stocks on this exchange must satisfy various requirements on their earnings, size, the number of shareholders who own their stock, and the number of their shares outstanding. They also must pay fees to list on the exchange. More than 1 billion shares are traded per day on the NYSE.

Some firms list on other exchanges in the United States, such as the American Stock Exchange, the Midwest Stock Exchange, and the Pacific Stock Exchange. Each of these exchanges also has a trading floor. The listing requirements to list a stock on these exchanges are not as restrictive. Consequently, many smaller firms that might not meet the NYSE requirements can list their stocks on these stock exchanges.

Over-the-Counter Market

In addition to the exchanges just described, there is also an over-the-counter (OTC) market. The OTC market is most commonly used by smaller firms, some of which do not meet the size requirements to trade on the NYSE or American Stock Exchange. The stock transactions on the OTC are executed by traders through a telecommunications network rather than on a trading floor. There is a computerized network within the OTC for firms that meet specific size and capital requirements, called the **National Association of Security Dealers Automated Quotation (Nasdaq).** This system provides immediate stock price quotations. The network allows transactions to be executed without the need for a trading floor. Stocks of about 5,000 firms are traded on the Nasdaq. More than 1 billion shares are traded daily in the Nasdaq market. Nevertheless, the market value of these trades is less than that of the NYSE, because the transactions on the NYSE are larger. Although most firms listed in the Nasdaq market are smaller than those listed on the NYSE, some (such as Microsoft and Intel) are very large. Many technology firms are listed in the Nasdaq market.

National Association of Security Dealers Automated Quotation (Nasdaq) a computerized network within the OTC for firms that meet specific size and capital requirements

Regulation of Stock Exchanges

insider trading transactions initiated by people (such as employees) who have information about a firm that has not been disclosed to the public

insider information information about a firm that has not been disclosed to the public

The Securities and Exchange Commission (SEC) was created in 1934 to regulate security markets such as the stock exchanges. It enforces specific trading guidelines to prevent unethical trading activities. For example, it attempts to prevent **insider trading,** or transactions initiated by people (such as employees) who have information about a firm that has not been disclosed to the public (called **insider information**). Consider an executive of an engineering firm that has just completed a contract to do work for the government that will generate a large amount of revenue for the firm. If the executive calls a broker to buy shares of the firm, this executive has an unfair advantage over other investors because of the inside information that has not yet been disclosed to the public.

INVESTING IN FOREIGN STOCKS

U.S. investors can also purchase foreign stocks. When foreign stocks are not listed on a U.S. exchange, the U.S. broker may need to call a broker at a foreign subsidiary, who communicates the desired transaction to the foreign stock exchange where the stock is traded. The commissions paid by U.S. investors for such transactions are higher than those paid for transactions on U.S. exchanges.

American depository receipts (ADRs) certificates representing ownership of a stock issued by a non-U.S. firm

Many of the larger foreign stocks are listed on U.S. stock exchanges as **American depository receipts (ADRs).** An ADR is a certificate representing ownership of a stock issued by a non-U.S. firm. Examples of the more popular ADRs are British Airways and Sony.

INVESTING IN MUTUAL FUNDS

Mutual funds sell shares to individual investors and use the proceeds to invest in various securities. They are attractive to investors because they employ portfolio managers with expertise in making investment decisions. Thus, individual investors can place the responsibility of investment decisions with these portfolio managers. Second, individual investors with a small amount of money (such as $500 or $1,000) can invest in mutual funds. In this way, they can be part owners of a widely diversified portfolio with a small amount of money.

net asset value (NAV) the market value of a mutual fund's securities after subtracting any expenses incurred

open-end mutual funds funds that stand ready to repurchase their shares at the prevailing NAV if investors decide to sell the shares

closed-end mutual funds mutual funds that are sold on stock exchanges

The **net asset value (NAV)** of a mutual fund is the market value of the fund's securities after subtracting any expenses incurred (such as portfolio manager salaries) by the fund, on a per-share basis. As the values of the securities contained in a mutual fund rise, so does the mutual fund's NAV.

Types of Mutual Funds

Open-end mutual funds stand ready to repurchase their shares at the prevailing NAV if investors decide to sell the shares. Conversely, shares of **closed-end mutual funds** are mutual funds that are sold on stock exchanges.

growth funds mutual funds that invest in stocks of firms with high potential for growth

Most mutual funds tend to focus on particular types of securities so that they can attract investors who wish to invest in those securities. For example, **growth funds** invest in stocks of firms with high potential for growth.

income funds mutual funds that invest in stocks that provide large dividends or in bonds that provide coupon payments

international stock funds mutual funds that invest in stocks of foreign firms

Income funds invest in stocks that provide large dividends or in bonds that provide coupon payments. **International stock funds** invest in stocks of foreign firms. Each mutual fund has a prospectus that describes its investment objectives, its recent performance, the types of securities it purchases, and other relevant financial information.

Load versus No-Load Mutual Funds

load mutual funds open-end mutual funds that can be purchased only by calling a broker

no-load funds open-end mutual funds that can be purchased without the services of a broker

Open-end mutual funds that can be purchased only by calling a broker are referred to as **load mutual funds.** The term *load* refers to the transaction fees (commissions) charged for the transaction. Other open-end mutual funds that can be purchased without the services of a broker are referred to as **no-load funds.** These mutual funds are purchased by requesting a brief application from the mutual funds and sending it in with the investment.

expense ratio for a mutual fund, expenses divided by assets

All mutual funds incur expenses that result from hiring portfolio managers to select stocks and from serving clients (mailing fees and so on). The **expense ratio** (defined as expenses divided by the assets) of each mutual fund can be assessed to determine the expenses incurred by each mutual fund per year. Some mutual funds have an expense ratio of less than .5 percent, while others have an expense ratio above 2 percent. The expense ratio is provided within the mutual funds prospectus. Since high expenses can cause lower returns, investors closely monitor the expense ratio.

KEY TERMS

Investing in a Business

Recall from Chapter 1 that you were asked to identify a firm that you would invest in if you had funds to invest. You were asked to record the price of the firm's stock at that time. Now, you should close out your position. That is, determine today's stock price (which is quoted on the Yahoo! website and many other websites). Estimate your return on the stock as follows:

1 If the investment period is about three months, one dividend payment would have been made. Divide the annual dividend per share (which you recorded when you selected your stock) by 4 to determine the quarterly dividend per share (D).

2 Estimate the return (R), based on today's selling price (S), the purchase price (P) you paid at the beginning of the term, and the quarterly dividend (D):

$$R = \frac{S - P + D}{P}$$

3 This return is not annualized. If you wish to annualize your return, multiply R by ($12/n$), where n is the number of months you held your investment. Compare your results with those of other students.

To determine how well your stock performed in comparison with the stock market in general, determine the percentage change in the S&P 500 Index over the term. This index represents a composite of stocks of 500 large firms.

Offer explanations for the stock performance of your firm. Was the performance driven by the stock market performance in general? Was your firm's performance affected by recent economic conditions, industry conditions, and global conditions? How? Was its performance affected by specific strategies (such as restructuring or acquisitions) that it recently enacted? Discuss.

The Coca-Cola Company Annual Report Project

Questions for the current year's annual report are available on the text website at **http://madura.swlearning.com.**

The following questions apply concepts presented in this chapter to The Coca-Cola Company. Go to The Coca-Cola Company website (**http://www.cocacola.com**) and find the index for the 2001 annual report.

Questions

1 Using the shareholder information in Coca-Cola's annual report or the business section of a major newspaper, find the stock symbol for The Coca-

Cola Company. What is The Coca-Cola Company's stock symbol?

2 On what stock exchanges is The Coca-Cola Company traded?

3 Go to **http://hoovers.com** and locate the NEWS CENTER. Key in The Coca-Cola Company in the space provided, click on "Search," and review the recent news stories about the firm. Summarize any (at least one) recent news story about The Coca-Cola Company that applies one or more of the key concepts within this appendix.

Appendix B: Careers

This appendix suggests methods that can be used to make college and career decisions.

CHOOSING A COLLEGE

People who decide to pursue a college degree must also select the proper college or university. For those who will be working while pursuing the degree, the choice of a college may be dictated by the location of the job. For others who have the flexibility to relocate, several criteria are worth considering. The first step is to identify the colleges that offer a degree in the main field of interest. College catalogs (available at many libraries) should be reviewed to compare the courses offered. Then, each college that offers a degree in the desired field can be more closely assessed to determine the course requirements, possible elective courses, and minor fields available. Other factors such as tuition and location should also be considered. Several colleges offer a degree in any given field.

Some colleges are more prestigious than others, which can be important in attaining a good job. Colleges' reputations tend to vary, however. One college may have a strong program in one field but a weak program in others.

For people who plan to find a local job, the college does not need to have a national reputation. Specialized jobs are scarce in many college towns, however. Therefore, even if the college is not nationally recognized, it should be reputable from the perspective of potential employers who may hire its graduates.

When considering colleges, obtain information about the admission criteria, cost, reputation, types of majors offered, job placement data, and financial aid. Guidance on selecting a college is available at various websites, including the following:

Website	Offers:
http://www.collegexpress.com	Advice on applying, student life, comparison of private versus public schools
http://www.finaid.com	Advice on applying for loans and scholarships
http://www.savingforcollege.com	Information by state on tax-exempt saving and tuition programs

CAREERS

Some of the more critical career decisions are (1) choosing a career, (2) deciding whether to pursue a career or an additional degree, and (3) determining how to pursue a particular career.

Choosing a Career

Students who prefer to work for a firm rather than start their own businesses must decide what type of job and size of firm would be ideal for them.

Type of Job

A person's salary and level of job satisfaction will depend on the type of job selected. College students should seriously consider this decision before they select their major to ensure that they will have the educational background required for the type of job they desire.

Information about various types of jobs can be obtained by reading the job descriptions associated with particular job listings. Several websites including the following provide useful job listings:

Website	Offers:
http://www.hotjobs.com	Job listings by category; featured companies
http://www.careermag.com	Job listings by profession
http://www.brassring.com	Job listings for high-tech firms; career advice
http://www.monster.com	Job listings in the field you specify
http://www.career.com	Career advice

Salaries   Although students should not necessarily choose the major that results in the highest salary, they should at least be aware of salary differentials before they select a major. This type of information is available at most large libraries and on various websites including the following:

Website	Offers:
http://www.hotjobs.com	Salaries for various job positions
http://www.careermag.com	Salaries for various job positions
http://www.monster.com	Salaries for various job positions

Job Satisfaction   Job satisfaction must also be considered when choosing a career. The job satisfaction level for any given career varies among people. Thus, people may not know whether they like a particular type of job until they have worked at it. This is a major dilemma because it is difficult to properly assess job satisfaction without on-the-job experience, which normally occurs after graduation. To measure your present level of job satisfaction, go to **http://www.hotjobs.com**.

Size of Firm

In addition to the type of job, people must determine whether they wish to work for a small or large firm. There are some obvious differences. Some commonly cited advantages of working for a large firm are more prestige, more training, and more opportunities for advancement.

Working for a small firm also offers advantages, including more attention from higher-level management and more diverse responsibilities. Also, fewer promotions are necessary to achieve a higher-level management position.

The advantages listed here do not apply to all large and small firms, as each firm has its own characteristics. Thus, it is strongly recommended that students apply for particular jobs at both small and large firms. The interviewing process may provide more insight into the differences between small and large firms.

CAREER VERSUS ADDITIONAL DEGREE

Students who receive their associates degree are faced with a decision of whether to pursue a bachelor's degree or a full-time career. Students who receive their bachelor's degree must then decide whether to pursue a master's degree or a full-time career. Both decisions involve weighing an additional degree versus a career. The following discussion suggests some factors to consider when making these decisions.

Although the appropriate decision varies among students, some general guidelines deserve consideration. Students should conduct a cost-benefit analysis of the decision to pursue an additional degree. Some of the more obvious costs are tuition, the forgone income that could have been earned by working instead of going to school, and the forgone on-the-job experience that could have been earned by working instead of going to school. Some possible benefits of pursing an additional degree are more marketability in the job market, a higher starting salary, and greater potential for promotion.

The costs and benefits of attaining an additional degree can vary significantly among majors. In addition to the costs and benefits just identified, other factors also deserve to be considered. For example, some people may need a break from school and prefer to begin their career right away. Others may perform best in school by continuing their education while the previous coursework is still fresh in their minds.

It is often suggested that people get more out of an additional degree if they work full-time for a few years and then return to school. The on-the-job experience may allow for a greater understanding and appreciation of coursework. Such a strategy can have a high cost, however. It is difficult for people to feel motivated on a job knowing they will quit in a few years to pursue an additional degree. Students who are thinking about graduate school can obtain information about finding a graduate school and practice tests for graduate admission tests at **http://www.collegejournal.com.**

Pursuing a Career and Degree

A popular compromise for those facing the career-versus-degree dilemma is to begin a career and pursue the degree part-time. Many firms will even pay an employee's tuition if the coursework could enhance the employee's performance on the job. This strategy allows people to obtain a degree without giving up the income and on-the-job experience they would forgo if they pursued a degree full-time. The disadvantage is that it may take five or more years to achieve the degree part-time. In addition, taking coursework at night after a long day on the job can cause fatigue and stress.

An extra degree does not automatically guarantee immediate success. The number of people receiving bachelor's and master's degrees has increased dramatically in recent years. Therefore, competition for existing jobs can be fierce even with additional education. An additional degree can be especially marketable when it complements existing skills. For example, many engineers have pursued master's degrees in business administration so that they can pursue management-level positions at engineering firms.

Internships

Some firms offer internships that enable students to gain on-the-job experience while pursuing a degree. Information about internships may often be found on a firm's website. In addition, many colleges have internship programs designed for various majors. For example, a specified number of business majors may work at local firms each semester under a college's internship program.

Internships provide many benefits to students. First, students may receive college credit for internships at some colleges. Second, internships may enhance students' understanding of coursework by allowing them to recognize how the theory in the classroom is applied in the real world. Third, internships enable students to learn more about a particular career. Thus, they either reinforce the students' desire to pursue a particular major or career or make the students realize that they need to rethink their major or career plans.

Fourth, some students receive letters of recommendation from the firm where they worked. When they complete their degree, they have experience along with an endorsement from the firm where they interned. This type of letter of recommendation is very valuable because it describes performance in the workplace and thus can complement other letters of recommendation that focus on performance in the classroom.

Finally, internships allow employers to assess interns for future job openings. The information firms obtain from observing an intern's work habits is often more useful than information obtained from a job interview. Some interns ultimately are offered jobs at the firms where they interned. Numerous firms, including AT&T, Apple Computer, and Boeing, frequently hire interns.

These obvious benefits have made internships very desirable. Consequently, many more students apply for internships than the number of internships available. For more information about internships, go to **http://collegejournal.com.**

PURSUING A CAREER

The key steps in pursuing a career are as follows:

▶ Applying for a position

▶ Creating a résumé

▶ Interviewing

▶ Planning a career path

Each step is discussed in turn.

Applying for a Position

After determining the type of job desired, it is necessary to identify prospective employers that may have job openings in that field. The want ads in the local newspapers may identify firms in the local area that have openings. However, local want ads will not provide a complete listing of companies that wish to fill positions. Some companies do not advertise openings but simply select from their applicant file to fill positions. For this reason, a worthwhile step is to submit an application to any firms that may potentially hire for the position desired. Very little effort and expense are required to submit an application.

People can improve their chances of being recruited by sending an application in response to an ad, asking friends with jobs to provide referrals, joining associations, conducting a job search on the Internet, and using the college placement service. They might even consider using employment recruiting firms, although these firms normally do not deal with entry-level positions. People who are very interested in a particular job may revise their résumé to fit that job. They could elaborate on any past work experience that is directly applicable to the job.

When students apply for a job, they should send a cover letter along with a résumé. Exhibit B.1 provides an example of a cover letter. Although many formats can be used, the main purpose of the cover letter is to identify the job position desired and explain how one's qualifications fit the job position. Students pursuing a career should contact the college placement center, which may invite representatives from firms to speak about careers. Firms also conduct interviews of students at many placement centers.

Exhibit B.1

Example of a Cover Letter

1022 N. Main Street
Tallahassee, FL 32306

June 9, 2003

Mr. Raymond Jones
President
Jones Manufacturing Co.
550 East 1st Street
Orlando, FL 32816

Dear Mr. Jones:

[State the specific job you are pursuing.]

I noticed that you have a job opening for a tax accountant. I just recently earned my accounting degree from Florida State University. I worked as an intern at Mega Accountants, Inc., in its tax department. Much of the intern work focused on tax accounting for manufacturing firms. I believe that my educational and intern experience has prepared me for your tax accountant position. I have enclosed my résumé, which provides more details about my education and intern background.

[Describe when you are available for work and how you can be reached.]

I am available for work immediately. Please call me at 999-555-1234 if you would like to interview me. I can be reached at that number during the morning on any day of the week. I look forward to hearing from you.

Sincerely,

Robert Smith

Robert Smith

Exhibit B.2

Career Placement Services on the World Wide Web

Career Mosaic	http://www.careermosaic.com
Career.Com	http://www.career.com
America's Employers	http://www.americasemployers.com
Career Web	http://cweb.com
Monster.com	http://monster.com
JobTrak.com	http://www.jobtrak.com
Monster Campus	http://www.studentcenter.com
College Grad Job Hunter	http://www.collegegrad.com

Many people are unable to identify the ideal job for which they are qualified. Nevertheless, this does not prevent them from applying for jobs. The human resources department of each firm can determine whether the applicants are qualified for various positions.

An important factor in managing employees is hiring the right people in the first place. During the past few years, the number of career placement services on the World Wide Web (WWW) has skyrocketed. Several of these services are listed in Exhibit B.2.

Applying for a job is normally the easiest part of pursuing a career. Some people apply at one or two well-known firms and wait to be called. This can be a frustrating experience. People who are willing to consider several firms for employment are more likely to obtain a job. Even if a specific firm is most desirable, it is worthwhile to at least apply for a position at several firms.

Creating a Résumé

A résumé should normally be included with an application. Various résumé formats are used, and no format is perfect for all situations. Most résumés for people pursuing entry-level positions are one page long. An example of a typical résumé format is shown in Exhibit B.3. Whatever format is used, the résumé should be designed to describe any characteristics that enhance job skills. The job objective states the desired job position and can be tailored to fit the firm where the application is sent. The education and employment background should be listed in reverse chronological order (most recent experience listed first). Specific details that support job qualifications can be described in this section.

For more information about building a résumé, go to the following websites:

Website	Offers:
http://www.hotjobs.com	Post your résumé
http://www.careermag.com	Résumé builder
http://www.career.com	Résumé services
http://www.monster.com	Résumé advice

Exhibit B.3

Example of a Résumé

Résumé

Robert Smith
1022 N. Main Street
Tallahassee, FL 32306

Job Objective: Entry-level accountant

Education: Florida State University, Sept. 1999–May 2003, B.S. in Accounting received May 2003; grade point average = 3.1 on a 4-point scale.

Work Experience: Intern at Mega Accountants, Inc., April 2002 to April 2003.

☐ Assisted tax accountants in compiling information submitted by clients to be used to file their tax returns.

☐ Researched previous tax court cases to provide information needed to answer clients' specific tax questions.

☐ Met with prospective clients to explain the tax services offered by the firm.

Lantern Grocery Store, March 1999 to March 2002.

☐ Responsible for ordering stock, monitoring deliveries of stock, and placing stock on shelves.

Professional Organizations: Treasurer of the Accounting Association at Florida State University, member of Business Club.

Extracurricular Activities: Volunteer for Salvation Army, Intramural Sports (Baseball and Basketball).

References: Provided upon request.

---

self-scoring exercise

Evaluating Your Résumé

Once you create a draft of your résumé, ask a friend to evaluate it based on the following criteria.

	Evaluation	Suggestions
Clearly communicates your experience?		
Clearly communicates your skills?		
Clearly communicates your potential?		
Clearly communicates your comparative advantages over other applicants?		
Length of résumé		
Clearly communicates how you could benefit the firm?		
Focus of résumé		
Grammar in résumé		

Interviewing

Firms conduct interviews to evaluate applicants more thoroughly. Various characteristics, such as the applicant's personality, cannot be evaluated from résumés alone. Personal interviews allow firms to assess these characteristics. Many firms screen applications and résumés to identify a pool of qualified applicants. Then the qualified applicants are interviewed to determine the optimal applicant for the position. Although strong qualifications on a résumé enable an applicant to be interviewed, they do not guarantee a job. A person who interviews well may be preferable to one with a stronger résumé who interviews poorly.

Firms design most interviews to provide the applicant with additional information about the position and to determine the following:

1 Is the applicant neat and presentable?

2 Would the applicant get along with customers?

3 Does the applicant have good communication skills?

4 Does the applicant have a genuine interest in the position?

5 Would the applicant work well with others?

Applicants cannot prepare for all possible questions that may be asked during an interview, but they should at least prepare for some of the more obvious types of questions that may be asked:

1 Why do you want to work for our company?

2 What do you know about our company?

3 Why do you plan to leave your present employer?

4 Why should our company hire you?

5 What are your strengths?

6 What are your weaknesses?

7 What are your salary requirements?

8 When would you be ready to begin this job?

Although applicants cannot guarantee the outcome of the interview, a few simple but critical rules should be followed:

1 Dress properly.

2 Be on time.

3 Send a follow-up thank-you letter to the persons who interview you.

What to Ask in an Interview   A person who is being interviewed is normally allowed time to ask questions about the firm that is conducting the interview. These questions may be just as important as the applicant's answers in determining whether the job is offered. The questions show the applicant's interest in the firm and intelligence about the job. Some possible questions are:

1 How much interaction is there between this position and related divisions?

2 How much responsibility is delegated by the supervisor of this position?

3 What is the typical educational background for this position?

4 Who is involved in the performance evaluation for this position?

5 To what extent does the position involve public relations or contact with customers?

A second set of questions would ask for more details about the position, which could show the interviewee's competence in the area. These questions would vary with the type of position, but a few examples can be provided:

1 What type of computer is used in the department?

2 Which companies are your key suppliers or customers?

3 What are the projected sales for the division over the next year?

Although asking questions can be valuable, the applicant must recognize the amount of time allocated for the interview and make sure that the interviewer has sufficient time to ask questions. For more information on how to interview, go to **http://www.hotjobs.com.**

Planning a Career Path

Even after a job is offered and accepted, career decisions must be made. On-the-job experience may affect the desired career path. Aspiring to a position above the present position is natural. The planned career path to that

business online

An excellent source of career information on the web is the Career Center at **www.monster.com**. This site offers résumé writing services, virtual interviews, salary reports, and much more.

Courtesy of TMP Interactive Inc. d/b/a Monster.

www.monster.com

position may involve either a series of promotions within the firm or switching to a different firm. Although planning a career path is a useful motivator, the plans should be achievable. If everyone planned to be president of a company, most plans would not be achieved. This can cause frustration. A preferable career path would include short-term goals, since some ultimate goals may take 20 years or longer. Setting short-term goals can reinforce confidence as goals are achieved.

WORKING FOR A FIRM VERSUS OWNING A FIRM

During the course of a career, many people wonder whether they should continue working for a firm or start their own business. Some people recognize the potential benefits of owning their own firm, such as being their own boss or the potential to earn a high level of income. However, the decision to start a business requires an idea for a product or service that will generate sufficient sales. A successful business also requires proper planning, production, marketing, and financing decisions, as explained throughout the text. Some general guidelines for developing a successful business, which apply to most firms, are listed here:

1 *Create a product (or service) that the market wants.* A new business is typically created when the owner recognizes a product or service desired by customers that is not being offered by a sufficient number (or by any) existing firms.

2 *Prepare for adverse conditions.* An owner of a business should have enough financial backing to prepare for adverse conditions, such as a decline in economic growth or more intense competition. Even if the business is based on a good product (or service) idea, it may experience weak performance in some periods because of factors beyond its control.

3 *Capitalize on new opportunities.* A business should use a flexible strategic plan that adjusts in response to new business opportunities. Businesses that remain flexible are more likely to capitalize on new opportunities.

4 *Ensure customer satisfaction.* The long-run success of many businesses is based on the quality of a product, which leads to customer satisfaction.

5 *Ensure employee satisfaction.* When owners of businesses create conditions that satisfy employees, they motivate employees to perform well and also avoid a high level of employee turnover.

6 *Promote the product.* A good product will not sell unless the market is aware of it. Promotion may be necessary to ensure that the market is informed about the product.

Appendix C: Answers to In-Text Study Guide

Chapter 1

True/False
1. False (p. 5)
2. True (p. 6)
3. True (p. 7)
4. False (p. 8)
5. False (p. 9)
6. False (p. 10)
7. True (p. 14)
8. True (p. 15)
9. True (p. 15)
10. False (p. 16)

Multiple Choice
11. (e) (p. 3)
12. (c) (p. 4)
13. (e) (p. 4)
14. (e) (p. 4)
15. (e) (p. 5)
16. (b) (p. 5)
17. (b) (p. 6)
18. (c) (p. 6)
19. (a) (p. 7)
20. (b) (p. 8)
21. (a) (pp. 10–11)
22. (e) (p. 13)
23. (d) (p. 13)
24. (c) (p. 13)
25. (b) (p. 13)
26. (b) (p. 13)
27. (a) (p. 13)
28. (a) (p. 13)
29. (e) (p. 14)
30. (a) (p. 15)
31. (d) (p. 15)
32. (d) (p. 16)
33. (a) (pp. 16–17)
34. (b) (p. 16)
35. (c) (p. 17)
36. (c) (p. 17)
37. (e) (p. 18)

Chapter 2

True/False
1. False (p. 36)
2. False (p. 37)
3. False (p. 37)
4. False (p. 37)
5. False (p. 41)
6. True (p. 41)
7. True (p. 42)
8. True (p. 43)
9. True (p. 43)
10. False (pp. 46, 48)
11. True (p. 54)

Multiple Choice
12. (d) (p. 35)
13. (c) (p. 36)
14. (e) (p. 36)
15. (b) (p. 36)
16. (b) (p. 37)
17. (a) (p. 37)
18. (c) (p. 37)
19. (a) (p. 37)
20. (d) (p. 39)
21. (a) (p. 39)
22. (b) (p. 39)
23. (b) (p. 40)
24. (c) (p. 40)
25. (d) (p. 41)
26. (d) (p. 42)
27. (a) (p. 42)
28. (a) (p. 43)
29. (a) (p. 44)
30. (c) (p. 46)
31. (c) (p. 48)
32. (b) (p. 48)
33. (c) (p. 51)
34. (a) (p. 53)
35. (c) (p. 54)
36. (a) (p. 54)
37. (d) (p. 55)
38. (a) (p. 55)

Chapter 3

True/False
1. True (p. 70)
2. True (p. 70)
3. True (p. 71)
4. False (p. 71)
5. False (p. 75)
6. True (p. 77)
7. True (p. 82)
8. False (p. 85)
9. False (p. 86)
10. False (p. 87)

Multiple Choice
11. (b) (p. 65)
12. (a) (p. 67)
13. (e) (p. 69)
14. (d) (p. 70)
15. (b) (p. 70)
16. (c) (p. 71)
17. (a) (p. 71)
18. (b) (p. 71)
19. (c) (p. 71)
20. (e) (p. 71)
21. (d) (p. 71)
22. (b) (p. 71)
23. (e) (p. 71)
24. (b) (p. 73)
25. (a) (p. 73)
26. (d) (p. 73)
27. (c) (p. 74)
28. (b) (p. 75)
29. (a) (p. 76)
30. (e) (pp. 76–77)
31. (e) (p. 77)
32. (c) (p. 77)
33. (b) (p. 78)
34. (b) (p. 78)
35. (d) (p. 79)
36. (c) (p. 79)
37. (d) (p. 82)
38. (d) (p. 84)

Chapter 4

True/False
1. False (p. 105)
2. False (p. 106)
3. True (p. 106)
4. True (p. 107)
5. False (p. 108)
6. False (p. 109)
7. False (p. 109)
8. True (p. 114)
9. True (p. 120)
10. True (p. 121)

Multiple Choice
11. (c) (p. 105)
12. (c) (p. 106)
13. (a) (p. 107)
14. (d) (p. 107)
15. (b) (p. 108)
16. (c) (p. 109)
17. (a) (p. 109)
18. (a) (p. 109)
19. (e) (p. 110)
20. (c) (p. 114)
21. (b) (p. 115)
22. (c) (p. 115)
23. (e) (p. 116)
24. (a) (p. 116)
25. (a) (p. 116)
26. (b) (pp. 117–118)
27. (a) (pp. 117, 119)
28. (c) (p. 120)
29. (a) (p. 120)
30. (e) (pp. 120–121)
31. (c) (p. 121)
32. (a) (p. 122)
33. (b) (p. 122)
34. (d) (p. 123)
35. (b) (p. 123)

Chapter 5

True/False
1. False (p. 133)
2. False (p. 135)
3. False (p. 135)
4. True (p. 136)
5. True (p. 136)
6. True (pp. 139–140)
7. False (p. 140)
8. False (p. 140)
9. True (p. 141)
10. True (p. 147)

Multiple Choice
11. (b) (p. 133)
12. (a) (p. 134)
13. (d) (p. 134)
14. (b) (p. 134)
15. (d) (pp. 134–135)
16. (a) (p. 135)
17. (b) (p. 135)
18. (a) (p. 136)
19. (d) (p. 136)
20. (c) (p. 137)
21. (e) (p. 137)
22. (c) (p. 137)
23. (c) (p. 139)
24. (c) (p. 139)

25. (a) (p. 140)
26. (d) (p. 140)
27. (a) (p. 141)
28. (b) (p. 143)
29. (d) (p. 143)
30. (b) (p. 143)
31. (e) (p. 144)
32. (c) (p. 145)
33. (d) (p. 146)
34. (b) (p. 147)
35. (a) (pp. 147–148)

Chapter 6

True/False

1. True (p. 158)
2. False (p. 161)
3. True (p. 161)
4. False (p. 166)
5. True (p. 167)
6. False (p. 172)
7. False (p. 173)
8. True (p. 174)
9. True (p. 174)
10. False (p. 175)

Multiple Choice

11. (e) (p. 156)
12. (c) (pp. 158, 161)
13. (c) (p. 161)
14. (d) (p. 163)
15. (a) (p. 164)
16. (d) (p. 164)
17. (b) (p. 164)
18. (c) (p. 165)
19. (c) (p. 167)
20. (a) (p. 167)
21. (a) (p. 168)
22. (b) (p. 168)
23. (e) (p. 169)
24. (b) (p. 170)
25. (c) (p. 172)
26. (a) (p. 172)
27. (a) (pp. 172–173)
28. (b) (p. 173)
29. (a) (pp. 176–177)
30. (d) (p. 178)
31. (c) (p. 182)
32. (d) (p. 183)
33. (b) (p. 183)
34. (d) (p. 183)
35. (a) (p. 183)

Chapter 7

True/False

1. False (p. 202)
2. False (p. 203)
3. True (p. 203)
4. False (p. 206)
5. True (p. 209)
6. True (p. 212)
7. True (p. 210)
8. False (p. 213)
9. True (p. 215)
10. False (p. 216)

Multiple Choice

11. (b) (p. 202)
12. (b) (p. 203)
13. (a) (p. 204)
14. (a) (p. 205)
15. (c) (p. 205)
16. (e) (p. 206)
17. (c) (p. 206)
18. (e) (p. 206)
19. (b) (p. 208)
20. (c) (p. 209)
21. (d) (p. 209)
22. (a) (p. 210)
23. (e) (p. 210)
24. (b) (p. 213)
25. (c) (p. 213)
26. (e) (p. 213)
27. (b) (p. 215)
28. (d) (p. 216)
29. (e) (p. 216)
30. (e) (p. 217)
31. (d) (p. 217)
32. (d) (p. 217)
33. (c) (p. 217)
34. (b) (p. 219)
35. (d) (pp. 220–222)

Chapter 8

True/False

1. True (p. 232)
2. True (p. 232)
3. False (p. 234)
4. False (p. 234)
5. True (p. 236)
6. False (p. 237)
7. False (p. 244)
8. True (p. 244)
9. False (p. 246)
10. True (p. 248)
11. False (p. 248)

Multiple Choice

12. (c) (p. 231)
13. (b) (p. 232)
14. (a) (p. 232)
15. (a) (p. 232)
16. (b) (p. 233)
17. (e) (p. 233)
18. (c) (p. 233)
19. (d) (p. 233)
20. (e) (p. 235)
21. (d) (p. 236)
22. (c) (p. 236)
23. (b) (p. 236)
24. (a) (p. 237)
25. (b) (p. 237)
26. (b) (pp. 237–238)
27. (a) (p. 238)
28. (c) (pp. 238–239)
29. (c) (p. 240)
30. (e) (p. 241)
31. (b) (p. 241)
32. (a) (p. 242)
33. (c) (p. 243)
34. (b) (p. 244)
35. (d) (p. 245)
36. (e) (p. 246)

Chapter 9

True/False

1. True (p. 260)
2. True (p. 264)
3. False (p. 265)
4. False (p. 267)
5. False (p. 269)
6. False (p. 270)
7. True (p. 271)
8. False (p. 275)
9. True (p. 276)
10. True (p. 285)

Multiple Choice

11. (d) (p. 259)
12. (d) (p. 259)
13. (a) (p. 260)
14. (e) (p. 262)
15. (a) (p. 264)
16. (d) (p. 265)
17. (c) (p. 265)
18. (c) (p. 265)
19. (b) (p. 266)
20. (d) (p. 267)
21. (a) (p. 267)
22. (a) (p. 268)
23. (c) (p. 269)
24. (b) (p. 270)
25. (e) (p. 270)
26. (c) (p. 270)
27. (d) (p. 272)
28. (b) (p. 273)
29. (b) (p. 274)
30. (c) (pp. 274–275)
31. (b) (p. 276)
32. (d) (p. 279)
33. (c) (p. 281)
34. (e) (p. 284)
35. (a) (p. 284)
36. (d) (p. 285)

Chapter 10

True/False

1. False (pp. 306–307)
2. False (p. 308)
3. False (p. 309)
4. False (p. 309)
5. False (p. 310)
6. True (p. 312)
7. True (p. 314)
8. False (p. 314)
9. True (p. 314)
10. True (p. 322)
11. False (p. 324)

Multiple Choice

12. (a) (p. 305)
13. (a) (p. 306)
14. (d) (p. 306)
15. (d) (p. 307)
16. (e) (p. 307)
17. (a) (p. 307)
18. (c) (p. 308)
19. (b) (p. 309)
20. (d) (p. 310)
21. (b) (p. 311)
22. (d) (p. 312)
23. (a) (p. 314)
24. (e) (p. 314)
25. (c) (p. 317)
26. (c) (p. 318)
27. (d) (p. 318)
28. (e) (p. 319)
29. (c) (p. 319)
30. (b) (p. 319)
31. (b) (p. 320)
32. (b) (p. 320)
33. (c) (p. 320)
34. (c) (p. 322)
35. (b) (p. 322)
36. (e) (p. 322)

Chapter 11

True/False

1. False (p. 334)
2. True (p. 334)
3. True (p. 334)
4. True (p. 334)
5. True (pp. 339–340)
6. False (p. 346)
7. False (p. 347)
8. True (p. 351)
9. True (p. 351)
10. False (p. 352)

Multiple Choice

11. (a) (p. 334)
12. (a) (p. 334)
13. (c) (p. 334)
14. (a) (p. 334)
15. (a) (p. 334)
16. (a) (p. 334)
17. (b) (p. 335)
18. (e) (p. 335)
19. (c) (p. 337)
20. (d) (p. 337)
21. (e) (p. 340)
22. (c) (p. 342)
23. (d) (p. 343)
24. (a) (p. 344)
25. (e) (p. 345)
26. (b) (p. 345)
27. (d) (p. 346)
28. (a) (p. 346)
29. (c) (p. 347)
30. (a) (p. 350)
31. (c) (pp. 351–352)
32. (e) (p. 352)
33. (c) (p. 355)
34. (b) (p. 356)
35. (d) (p. 356)
36. (e) (p. 356)

Chapter 12

True/False

1. False (p. 379)
2. True (p. 380)
3. True (p. 382)
4. False (p. 384)
5. False (p. 384)
6. True (p. 384)
7. False (pp. 385–386)
8. True (p. 393)
9. True (p. 396)
10. False (p. 398)

Multiple Choice

11. (d) (p. 380)
12. (d) (p. 380)
13. (b) (p. 382)
14. (c) (p. 382)
15. (b) (pp. 383–384)
16. (b) (p. 386)
17. (e) (p. 386)
18. (d) (p. 387)
19. (a) (p. 387)
20. (b) (pp. 388–389)
21. (b) (p. 389)
22. (e) (p. 391)
23. (c) (p. 392)
24. (a) (p. 393)
25. (a) (p. 393)
26. (e) (p. 394)
27. (b) (p. 394)
28. (c) (p. 395)
29. (d) (p. 396)
30. (d) (p. 396)
31. (a) (p. 397)
32. (d) (p. 398)
33. (e) (p. 398)
34. (b) (p. 398)
35. (c) (p. 399)
36. (a) (p. 400)
37. (c) (p. 402)
38. (d) (p. 403)

Chapter 13

True/False

1. False (p. 417)
2. False (p. 417)
3. True (p. 418)
4. True (p. 420)
5. True (p. 421)
6. False (p. 422)
7. False (p. 423)
8. True (p. 424)
9. True (p. 430)
10. True (p. 431)

Multiple Choice

11. (d) (p. 415)
12. (c) (p. 415)
13. (a) (p. 416)
14. (b) (p. 417)
15. (b) (p. 417)
16. (c) (p. 419)
17. (c) (p. 420)
18. (d) (p. 420)
19. (e) (p. 421)
20. (d) (p. 421)
21. (d) (p. 421)
22. (c) (p. 421)
23. (b) (p. 421)
24. (a) (p. 422)
25. (e) (p. 425)
26. (b) (p. 425)
27. (a) (p. 426)
28. (b) (p. 428)
29. (e) (p. 428)
30. (a) (p. 428)
31. (b) (p. 430)
32. (a) (p. 430)
33. (a) (p. 431)
34. (b) (p. 432)
35. (d) (p. 434)

Chapter 14

True/False

1. False (p. 445)
2. True (p. 444)
3. True (p. 446)
4. True (p. 453)
5. False (p. 451)
6. False (p. 454)
7. False (p. 459)
8. False (p. 459)
9. True (p. 461)
10. False (p. 462)

Multiple Choice

11. (d) (p. 443)
12. (a) (p. 444)
13. (d) (p. 444)
14. (a) (p. 445)
15. (c) (p. 445)
16. (b) (p. 446)
17. (d) (p. 446)
18. (c) (p. 446)
19. (c) (p. 447)
20. (a) (pp. 447–448)
21. (b) (p. 450)
22. (e) (p. 451)
23. (c) (p. 453)
24. (a) (p. 455)
25. (b) (p. 455)
26. (d) (p. 456)
27. (e) (p. 456)
28. (b) (p. 456)
29. (e) (p. 457)
30. (e) (p. 458)
31. (b) (p. 459)
32. (a) (p. 459)
33. (e) (p. 459)
34. (a) (p. 461)
35. (d) (p. 462)

Chapter 15

True/False

1. True (p. 481)
2. False (p. 482)
3. True (p. 482)
4. False (p. 483)
5. False (p. 485)
6. False (p. 487)
7. True (p. 488)
8. False (p. 489)
9. False (p. 489)
10. False (pp. 491–492)
11. True (p. 493)

Multiple Choice

12. (d) (p. 482)
13. (b) (p. 482)
14. (c) (p. 482)
15. (c) (p. 483)
16. (e) (p. 483)
17. (e) (p. 484)
18. (b) (p. 485)
19. (e) (p. 485)
20. (e) (p. 485)
21. (b) (p. 485)
22. (e) (p. 486)
23. (c) (pp. 486–487)
24. (a) (p. 487)
25. (b) (p. 487)
26. (d) (p. 488)
27. (e) (p. 490)
28. (a) (p. 490)
29. (a) (p. 490)
30. (c) (p. 492)
31. (e) (p. 493)
32. (a) (p. 494)
33. (c) (p. 494)
34. (d) (pp. 497–498)
35. (d) (p. 499)
36. (b) (p. 499)

Chapter 16

True/False

1. False (p. 507)
2. True (p. 508)
3. True (pp. 508, 511)
4. False (p. 509)
5. True (p. 511)
6. False (p. 510)
7. True (p. 514)
8. True (p. 516)
9. True (p. 519)
10. False (pp. 522–524)

Multiple Choice

11. (e) (p. 507)
12. (a) (p. 507)
13. (d) (p. 508)
14. (d) (p. 508)
15. (a) (p. 510)
16. (d) (p. 510)
17. (d) (p. 511)
18. (b) (p. 511)
19. (a) (p. 512)
20. (c) (p. 513)
21. (a) (p. 513)
22. (c) (p. 514)
23. (e) (p. 515)
24. (e) (p. 518)
25. (e) (p. 519)
26. (b) (p. 519)
27. (b) (p. 520)
28. (e) (p. 521)
29. (d) (p. 521)
30. (b) (p. 522)
31. (e) (p. 523)
32. (c) (p. 524)
33. (c) (p. 524)
34. (b) (p. 524)
35. (a) (p. 524)

Chapter 17

True/False

1. False (p. 539)
2. True (p. 540)
3. True (p. 543)
4. False (p. 545)
5. False (p. 546)
6. False (p. 547)
7. False (p. 547)
8. True (p. 549)
9. False (p. 551)
10. True (p. 555)

Multiple Choice

11. (b) (p. 540)
12. (a) (p. 541)
13. (b) (p. 541)
14. (d) (pp. 541–542)
15. (c) (p. 543)
16. (d) (p. 543)
17. (c) (p. 545)

18. (c) (pp. 545–546)
19. (a) (p. 547)
20. (e) (p. 551)
21. (b) (p. 551)
22. (e) (p. 551)
23. (e) (p. 551)
24. (a) (p. 552)
25. (b) (p. 553)
26. (a) (p. 554)
27. (e) (p. 554)
28. (e) (p. 554)
29. (c) (p. 555)
30. (e) (p. 555)
31. (d) (p. 555)
32. (b) (p. 555)
33. (d) (p. 555)
34. (b) (p. 556)
35. (a) (p. 557)

Chapter 18

True/False

1. True (p. 581)
2. False (p. 582)
3. True (p. 584)
4. True (p. 585)
5. True (p. 593)
6. False (p. 593)
7. False (p. 596)
8. False (p. 598)
9. False (p. 598)
10. False (p. 598)

Multiple Choice

11. (e) (p. 581)
12. (c) (p. 581)
13. (d) (p. 581)
14. (d) (p. 582)
15. (a) (p. 582)
16. (c) (p. 582)
17. (b) (p. 582)
18. (e) (p. 583)
19. (c) (p. 584)
20. (c) (p. 584)
21. (a) (p. 584)
22. (b) (p. 585)
23. (a) (p. 585)
24. (d) (p. 587)
25. (d) (p. 587)

26. (e) (p. 588)
27. (e) (p. 59)
28. (d) (p. 591)
29. (a) (p. 591)
30. (b) (p. 592)
31. (e) (p. 592)
32. (c) (pp. 594–595)
33. (d) (p. 596)
34. (b) (p. 597)
35. (e) (p. 597)
36. (a) (p. 597)
37. (d) (p. 598)

Chapter 19

True/False

1. False (p. 610)
2. False (p. 612)
3. True (p. 613)
4. False (p. 616)
5. False (p. 617)
6. True (p. 618)
7. False (p. 619)
8. True (p. 620)
9. False (p. 625)
10. True (p. 626)

Multiple Choice

11. (a) (p. 609)
12. (e) (p. 610)
13. (a) (p. 611)
14. (b) (p. 611)
15. (b) (p. 612)
16. (a) (p. 613)
17. (c) (p. 613)
18. (a) (pp. 613, 616–617)
19. (a) (p. 615)
20. (a) (p. 615)
21. (d) (p. 615)
22. (d) (p. 616)
23. (d) (p. 617)
24. (c) (p. 617)
25. (c) (pp. 617–618)
26. (b) (p. 619)
27. (d) (p. 620)
28. (c) (pp. 622–623)
29. (e) (pp. 623–624)
30. (e) (p. 624)
31. (c) (p. 625)

32. (b) (p. 625)
33. (b) (p. 626)
34. (e) (p. 626)
35. (e) (p. 626)

Chapter 20

True/False

1. False (p. 635)
2. True (p. 635)
3. False (p. 636)
4. True (p. 637)
5. True (p. 638)
6. True (p. 638)
7. False (p. 639)
8. True (p. 641)
9. False (p. 642)
10. False (p. 645)
11. True (p. 647)

Multiple Choice

12. (a) (pp. 635–636)
13. (d) (p. 636)
14. (b) (p. 637)
15. (c) (p. 637)
16. (e) (p. 637)
17. (b) (p. 637)
18. (a) (p. 638)
19. (a) (p. 638)
20. (c) (p. 638)
21. (e) (p. 638)
22. (c) (p. 639)
23. (d) (p. 639)
24. (d) (p. 640)
25. (b) (p. 640)
26. (b) (p. 641)
27. (b) (p. 641)
28. (c) (p. 641)
29. (a) (p. 641)
30. (a) (p. 642)
31. (e) (p. 642)
32. (a) (p. 644)
33. (b) (p. 645)
34. (b) (p. 646)
35. (c) (p. 646)
36. (a) (p. 648)
37. (e) (p. 651)

Glossary

A

accounting summary and analysis of the firm's financial condition

accounts payable money owed by a firm for the purchase of materials

accounts receivable management sets the limits on credit available to customers and the length of the period in which payment is due

across-the-board system a compensation system that allocates similar raises

active resistance occurs when users type in bad data or repeatedly crash a new system to make it unusable

actuaries persons employed by insurance companies to forecast the percentage of customers that will experience the particular event that is being insured

advertising a nonpersonal sales presentation communicated through media or nonmedia forms to influence a large number of consumers

affirmative action a set of activities intended to increase opportunities for minorities and women

agency problem when managers do not act as responsible agents for the shareholders who own the business

agents marketing intermediaries that match buyers and sellers of products without becoming owners

aggregate expenditures the total amount of expenditures in the economy

alpha testing during systems development, the process of making the new application available to a carefully selected subset of sophisticated users; done when the application approaches full functionality

American depository receipts (ADRs) certificates representing ownership of a stock issued by a non-U.S. firm

antivirus applications programs that detect and remove viruses

appreciates strengthens in value

artificial intelligence (AI) a field that focuses on developing computers that can perform tasks traditionally associated with biological intelligence, such as logical reasoning, language, vision, and motor skills

assembly line a sequence of work stations in which each work station is designed to cover specific phases of the production process

asset anything owned by a firm

auditing an assessment of the records that were used to prepare a firm's financial statements

autocratic a leadership style in which the leader retains full authority for decision making

automated tasks are completed by machines without the use of employees

autonomy divisions can make their own decisions and act independently

B

balance of trade the level of exports minus the level of imports

balance sheet reports the book value of all assets, liabilities, and owner's equity of a firm at a given point in time

bandwidth the amount of information a network can carry

basic accounting equation Assets = Liabilities + Owner's Equity

bearish periods in which investors are selling their stocks because of unfavorable expectations about the performance of firms

benchmarking a method of evaluating performance by comparison to some specified (benchmark) level, typically a level achieved by another company

best-efforts basis the investment bank does not guarantee a price to the firm issuing securities

beta testing during systems development, the process of testing a fully functional version of the new application with a wider group of users than was used for alpha testing

board of directors a set of executives who are responsible for monitoring the activities of the firm's president and other high-level managers

bond mutual funds investment companies that invest the funds received from investors in bonds

bonds long-term debt securities (IOUs) purchased by investors

bonus an extra one-time payment at the end of a period in which performance was measured

bookkeeping the recording of a firm's financial transactions

boycott refusing to purchase products and services

brand advertising a nonpersonal sales presentation about a specific brand

brand loyalty the loyalty of consumers to a specific brand over time

branding a method of identifying products and differentiating them from competing products

break-even point the quantity of units sold at which total revenue equals total cost

bugs errors in software code

bullish periods in which there is considerable demand for stocks because investors have favorable expectations about the performance of firms

business plan a detailed description of the proposed business, including a description of the product or service, the types of customers it would attract, the competition, and the facilities needed for production

business responsibilities a set of obligations and duties regarding product quality and treatment of customers, employees, and owners that a firm should fulfill when conducting business

business risk the possibility that a firm's performance will be lower than expected because of its exposure to specific conditions

bylaws general guidelines for managing a firm

C

call feature provides the right for the issuing firm to repurchase its bonds before maturity

capital long-term funds

capital budget a targeted amount of funds to be used for purchasing assets such as buildings, machinery, and equipment that are needed for long-term projects

capital budgeting a comparison of the costs and benefits of a proposed project to determine whether it is feasible

capital gain the price received from the sale of stock minus the price paid for the stock

capital structure the amount of debt versus equity financing

capitalism an economic system that allows for private ownership of businesses

carrying costs costs of maintaining (carrying) inventories

casualty insurance protects a firm against potential liability for harm to others as a result of product failure or accidents

centralized most authority is held by the high-level managers

certified public accountants (CPAs) accountants who meet specific educational requirements and pass a national examination

chain a retailer that has more than one outlet

chain of command identifies the job position to which each type of employee must report

chain-style business a type of franchise in which a firm is allowed to use the trade name of a company and follows guidelines related to the pricing and sale of the product

charter a document used to incorporate a business. The charter describes important aspects of the corporation.

closed-end mutual funds mutual funds that are sold on stock exchanges

co-branding firms agree to offer a combination of two noncompeting products at a discounted price

commercial banks financial institutions that obtain deposits from individuals and use the funds primarily to provide business loans

commercial information service an interorganizational system that provides a packaged assortment of information services to customers (subscribers)

commercial paper a short-term debt security normally issued by firms in good financial condition

commission sales fee

commissions compensation for meeting specific sales objectives

common stock a security that represents partial ownership of a particular firm

communism an economic system that involves public ownership of businesses

comparative advertising intended to persuade customers to purchase a specific product by demonstrating a brand's superiority by comparison with other competing brands

compensation package the total monetary compensation and benefits offered to employees

competitive advantage unique traits that make a business's products more desirable than those of its competitors

composition specifies that a firm will provide its creditors with a portion of what they are owed

compressed work week compresses the work load into fewer days per week

computer program a collection of step-by-step instructions to the processor

computer virus a program that attaches itself to other programs or computer disks

conceptual skills the ability to understand the relationships among the various tasks of a firm

conglomerate merger the combination of two firms in unrelated businesses

connectivity the ability of a firm's computer systems to work together to permit the flow of information throughout the firm

consumer markets markets for various consumer products and services (such as cameras, clothes, and household items)

consumerism the collective demand by consumers that businesses satisfy their needs

contingency planning alternative plans developed for various possible business conditions

contribution margin the difference between price and variable cost per unit

controlling the monitoring and evaluation of tasks

convenience products products that are widely available to consumers, are purchased frequently, and are easily accessible

corporate anorexia the problem that occurs when firms become so obsessed with eliminating their inefficient components that they downsize too much.

corporation a state-chartered entity that pays taxes and is legally distinct from its owners

cost of goods sold the cost of materials used to produce the goods that were sold

cost-based pricing estimating the per-unit cost of producing a product and then adding a markup

cost-push inflation the situation when higher prices charged by firms are caused by higher costs

coupons a promotional device used in newspapers, magazines, and ads to encourage the purchase of a product

craft unions unions organized according to a specific craft (or trade), such as plumbing

creditors financial institutions or individuals who provide loans

critical path the path that takes the longest time to complete

current assets assets that will be converted into cash within one year

customer profile Characteristics of the typical customer (based on gender, age, hobbies, and so on)

cyclical unemployment people who are unemployed because of poor economic conditions

D

debt financing the act of borrowing funds

debt-to-equity ratio a measure of the amount of long-term financing provided by debt relative to equity

decentralized authority is spread among several divisions or managers

decision support systems (DSS) computer models that are used to improve managerial decision making

decision-making skills skills for using existing information to determine how the firm's resources should be allocated

decline phase the period in which sales of a product decline, either because of reduced consumer demand for that type of product or because competitors are gaining market share

decreasing term insurance provides life insurance benefits to a beneficiary that decrease over time

defensive pricing the strategy of reducing a products price to defend (retain) market share

deintegration the strategy of delegating some production tasks to suppliers

demand schedule a schedule that indicates the quantity of a product that would be demanded at each possible price

demand-pull inflation the situation when prices of products and services are pulled up because of strong consumer demand

demographics characteristics of the human population or specific segments of the population

departmentalize assign tasks and responsibilities to different departments

depreciates weakens in value

depreciation a reduction in the value of fixed assets to reflect deterioration in the assets over time

derivative instruments instruments whose values are derived from values of other securities, indexes, or interest rates

design the size and structure of a plant or office

direct channel a producer of a product deals directly with customers

direct foreign investment (DFI) a means of acquiring or building subsidiaries in one or more foreign countries

discount brokers brokers who ensure that a transaction desired by an investor is executed but do not offer advice

distributorship a type of franchise in which a dealer is allowed to sell a product produced by a manufacturer

divestiture the sale of an existing business by a firm

dividend policy the decision regarding how much of the firm's quarterly earnings should be retained (reinvested in the firm) versus distributed as dividends to owners

dividends income that the firm provides to its owners

downsizing a reduction in the number of employees

downsizing an attempt by a firm to cut expenses by eliminating job positions

E

earnings before interest and taxes (EBIT) gross profit minus operating expenses

earnings before taxes earnings before interest and taxes minus interest expenses

economic growth the change in the general level of economic activity

economies of scale as the quantity produced increases, the cost per unit decreases

electronic business (e-business) or electronic commerce (e-commerce) use of electronic communications, such as the Internet, to produce or sell products and services

electronic data interchange (EDI) an interorganizational system that allows the computers of two or more companies to communicate directly with each other

employee benefits additional privileges beyond compensation payments, such as paid vacation time; health, life, or dental insurance; and pension programs

employment test a test of a job candidate's abilities

empowerment allowing employees the power to make more decisions

enterprise resource planning (ERP) systems software programs that automate all of a firm's business procedures and support the flow of information across departments

entrepreneurs people who organize, manage, and assume the risk of starting a business

equilibrium interest rate the interest rate at which the quantity of loanable funds supplied is equal to the quantity of loanable funds demanded

equilibrium price the price at which the quantity of a product supplied by firms equals the quantity of the product demanded by customers

equity the total investment by the firm's stockholders

equity financing the act of receiving investment from owners (by issuing stock or retaining earnings)

equity theory suggests that compensation should be equitable, or in proportion to each employee's contribution

espionage the process of illegally gathering information

esteem needs respect, prestige, and recognition

excise taxes taxes imposed by the federal government on particular products

exclusive distribution the distribution of a product through only one or a few outlets

expectancy theory holds that an employee's efforts are influenced by the expected outcome (reward) for those efforts

expense ratio for a mutual fund, expenses divided by assets

exporting the sale of products or services (called exports) to purchasers residing in other countries

extension provides additional time for a firm to generate the necessary cash to cover its payments

external recruiting an effort to fill positions with applicants from outside the firm

F

family branding branding of all or most products produced by a company

fashion obsolescence no longer in fashion

federal budget deficit the situation when the amount of federal government spending exceeds the amount of federal taxes and other revenue received by the federal government

Federal Reserve System the central bank of the United States

file servers in a network system, one or more machines that store and provide access to centralized data

finance companies financial institutions that typically obtain funds by issuing debt securities (IOUs) and lend most of their funds to firms

finance means by which firms obtain and use funds for their business operations

financial accounting accounting performed for reporting purposes

fiscal policy decisions on how the federal government should set tax rates and spend money

fixed assets assets that will be used by a firm for more than one year

fixed cost the cost of production that remains unchanged regardless of how many units are produced

fixed costs operating expenses that do not change in response to the number of products produced

fixed-position layout a layout in which employees go to the position of the product, rather than waiting for the product to come to them

flexible manufacturing a production process that can be easily adjusted to accommodate future revisions

flextime programs programs that allow for a more flexible work schedule

floor traders people on the trading floor of a stock exchange who execute transactions

flotation costs costs of issuing securities; include fees paid to investment banks for their advice and efforts to sell the securities, printing expenses, and registration fees

forward contract provides that an exchange of currencies will occur at a specified exchange rate at a future point in time

forward rate the exchange rate that a bank will be willing to offer at a future point of time

franchise an arrangement whereby a business owner allows others to use its trademark, trade name, or copyright, under specific conditions

franchisee a firm that is allowed to use the trade name or copyright of a franchise

franchisor a firm that allows others to use its trade name or copyright, under specified conditions

free-rein a leadership style in which the leader delegates much authority to employees

frictional unemployment people who are between jobs

full-service brokers brokers who provide advice to investors on stocks to purchase or sell and also ensure that transactions desired by investors are executed

full-service retail store a retailer that generally offers much sales assistance to customers and provides servicing if needed

G

Gantt chart a chart illustrating the expected timing for each task in the production process

general partners partners who manage the business, receive a salary, share the profits or losses of the business, and have unlimited liability

general partnership a partnership in which all partners have unlimited liability

generic brands products that are not branded by the producer or the store

gigabytes billions of bytes

gigahertz (GHz) one billion cycles per second

going public the act of initially issuing stock to the public

gross domestic product (GDP) the total market value of all final products and services produced in the United States

gross profit net sales minus the cost of goods sold

growth funds mutual funds that invest in stocks of firms with high potential for growth

growth phase the period in which sales of a product increase rapidly

H

hard drive sealed magnetic disks that provide secondary storage in a computer

hardware the physical components of a computer

hedge action taken to protect a firm against exchange rate movements

hierarchy of needs needs are ranked in five general categories. Once a given category of needs is achieved, people become motivated to reach the next category.

horizontal merger the combination of firms that engage in the same types of business

hotelling (just-in-time office) providing an office with a desk, a computer, and a telephone for any employee who normally works at home but needs to use work space at the firm

human resource manager helps each specific department recruit candidates for its open positions

human resource planning planning to satisfy a firm's needs for employees

hygiene factors work-related factors that can fulfill basic needs and prevent job dissatisfaction

I

importing the purchase of foreign products or services

incentive plans provide employees with various forms of compensation if they meet specific performance goals

income funds mutual funds that invest in stocks that provide large dividends or in bonds that provide coupon payments

income statement indicates the revenue, costs, and earnings of a firm over a period of time

indenture a legal document that explains the firm's obligations to bondholders

independent project whose feasibility can be assessed without consideration of any others

independent retail store a retailer that has only one outlet

individual branding the assignment of a unique brand name to different products or groups of products

industrial markets markets for industrial products that are purchased by firms (such as plastic and steel)

industrial unions unions organized for a specific industry

industry advertising a nonpersonal sales presentation about a specific industry's product

industry demand total demand for the products in an industry

inflation the increase in the general level of prices of products and services over a specified period of time

infomercials commercials that are televised separately rather than within a show

informal organizational structure an informal communications network among a firm's employees

information systems include information technology, people, and procedures that work together to provide appropriate information to the firm's employees so they can make business decisions

information technology technology that enables information to be used to produce products and services

initial public offering (IPO) the first issue of stock to the public

initiative the willingness to take action

injunction a court order to prevent a union from a particular activity such as picketing

inside board members board members who are also managers of the same firm

insider information information about a firm that has not been disclosed to the public

insider trading transactions initiated by people (such as employees) who have information about a firm that has not been disclosed to the public

institutional advertising a nonpersonal sales presentation about a specific institution's product

institutional investors financial institutions that purchase large amounts of stock

insurance companies receive insurance premiums from selling insurance to customers and invest the proceeds until the funds are needed to pay insurance claims

intensive distribution the distribution of a product across most or all possible outlets

interest rate swap a derivative instrument that allows a firm to swap fixed interest payments for payments that adjust to movements in interest rates

internal auditor responsible for ensuring that all departments follow the firm's guidelines and procedures

internal auditors specialize in evaluating various divisions of a business to ensure that they are operating efficiently

internal recruiting an effort to fill open positions with persons already employed by the firm

international licensing agreement a type of alliance in which a firm allows a foreign company (called the "licensee") to produce its products according to specific instructions

international stock funds mutual funds that invest in stocks of foreign firms

international unions unions that have members in several countries

interorganizational systems (IOS) employ computers and telecommunications technology to move information across the boundaries of a firm

interpersonal skills the skills necessary to communicate with customers and employees

intrapreneurship the assignment of particular employees of a firm to generate ideas, as if they were entrepreneurs running their own firms

introduction phase the initial period in which consumers are informed about a product

inventory control the process of managing inventory at a level that minimizes costs

inventory management determines the amount of inventory that is held

job analysis the analysis used to determine the tasks and the necessary credentials for a particular position

job description states the tasks and responsibilities of a job position

job enlargement a program to expand (enlarge) the jobs assigned to employees

job enrichment programs programs designed to increase the job satisfaction of employees

job rotation a program that allows a set of employees to periodically rotate their job assignments

job satisfaction the degree to which employees are satisfied with their jobs

job sharing two or more persons share a particular work schedule

job specification states the credentials necessary to qualify for a job position

joint venture an agreement between two firms about a specific project

just-in-time (JIT) a system that attempts to reduce materials inventories to a bare minimum by frequently ordering small amounts of materials

labor union an association established to represent the views, needs, and concerns of labor

Landrum-Griffin Act required labor unions to specify in their bylaws the membership eligibility requirements, dues, and collective bargaining procedures

layout the arrangement of machinery and equipment within a factory or office

leading the process of influencing the habits of others to achieve a common goal

leasing renting assets for a specified period of time

leveraged buyout (LBO) the purchase of a company (or a subsidiary of a company) by a group of investors with borrowed funds

liability anything owed by a firm

liability losses financial losses due to a firm's actions that cause damage to others or to their property

limit order an investor's order that places a limit on the price at which the investor would be willing to purchase or sell a stock

limited liability company (LLC) a firm that has all the favorable features of a typical general partnership but also offers limited liability for the partners

limited partners partners whose liability is limited to the cash or property they contributed to the partnership

limited partnership a firm that has some limited partners

line of credit an agreement with a bank that allows a firm access to borrowed funds upon demand over some specified period

line organization an organizational structure that contains only line positions and no staff positions

line positions job positions established to make decisions that achieve specific business goals

line-and-staff organization an organizational structure that includes both line and staff positions and assigns authority from higher-level management to employees

liquid having access to funds to pay bills when they come due

liquidation value the amount of funds that would be received as a result of the liquidation of a firm.

liquidity a firm's ability to meet short-term obligations

liquidity management the management of short-term assets and liabilities to ensure adequate liquidity

load mutual funds open-end mutual funds that can be purchased only by calling a broker

local area network (LAN) a system in which individual workstations are directly connected by network cabling to the file server

local unions unions composed of members in a specified local area

lockout prevents employees from working until an agreement between management and labor is reached

mainframe (multiuser) system system architecture that uses a single central computer that performs data processing for all users in the organization

management the utilization of human resources (employees) and other resources (such as machinery) in a manner that best achieves the firm's plans and objectives

management by objectives (MBO) allows employees to participate in setting their goals and determining the manner in which they complete their tasks

managerial accounting accounting performed to provide information to help managers of the firm make decisions

managers employees who are responsible for managing job

manufacturing arrangement a type of franchise in which a firm is allowed to manufacture a product using the formula provided by another company

market coverage the degree of product distribution among outlets

market order an investor's order requesting a transaction for the best possible price

market share a firm's sales as a proportion of the total market

marketing means by which products (or services) are developed, priced, distributed, and promoted to customers

marketing intermediaries firms that participate in moving the product from the producer toward the customer

marketing research the accumulation and analysis of data in order to make a particular marketing decision

massively parallel machines experimental computers with many CPUs that operate simultaneously

materials requirements planning (MRP) a process for ensuring that materials are available when needed

matrix organization an organizational structure that enables various parts of the firm to interact to focus on specific projects

maturity phase the period in which additional competing products have entered the market, and sales of a product level off because of competition

megabyte millions of characters

megahertz (MHz) one million cycles per second

merchants marketing intermediaries that become owners of products and then resell them

merger two firms are merged (or combined) to become a single firm owned by the same owners (shareholders)

merit system a compensation system that allocates raises according to performance (merit)

middle management managers who are often responsible for the firm's short-term decisions

mission statement a description of a firm's primary goal

modems devices that permit the digital signals inside computers to be transmitted over lines designed primarily for voice communication

monetary policy decisions on the money supply level in the United States

money supply demand deposits (checking accounts), currency held by the public, and traveler's checks

monopoly a firm that is the sole provider of goods or services Describe the responsibilities of firms to their employees.

motivational factors work-related factors that can lead to job satisfaction and motivate employees

mutual funds investment companies that receive funds from individual investors and then pool and invest those funds in securities

mutually exclusive the situation in which only one of two projects designed for the same purpose can be accepted

N

National Association of Security Dealers Automated Quotation (Nasdaq) a computerized network within the OTC for firms that meet specific size and capital requirements

national unions unions composed of members throughout the country

negative reinforcement motivates employees by encouraging them to behave in a manner that avoids unfavorable consequences

net asset value (NAV) the market value of a mutual fund's securities after subtracting any expenses incurred

net income (earnings after taxes) earnings before taxes minus taxes

net present value equal to the present value of cash flows minus the initial outlay

net profit margin a measure of net income as a percentage of sales

net sales total sales adjusted for any discounts

network operating system software that handles the communications between machines in a network

network system system architecture that connects individual microcomputers together in ways that allow them to share information

news release a brief written announcement about a firm provided by that firm to the media

no-load funds open-end mutual funds that can be purchased without the services of a broker

Norris-LaGuardia Act restricted the use of injunctions against unions and allowed unions to publicize a labor dispute

notes payable short-term loans to a firm made by creditors such as banks

O

obsolete less useful than in the past

odd lots less than 100 shares

on margin only a portion of the funds needed to purchase a stock is in cash

one-level channel one marketing intermediary is between the producer and the customer

open-book management a form of employee involvement that educates employees on their contribution to the firm and enables them to periodically assess their own performance levels

open-end mutual funds funds that stand ready to repurchase their shares at the prevailing NAV if investors decide to sell the shares

operating expenses composed of selling expenses and general and administrative expenses

operational planning establishes the methods to be used in the near future (such as the next year) to achieve the tactical plans

optimization models computer models that are used to represent situations that

have many possible combinations of inputs and outputs

order costs costs involved in placing orders

organization chart a diagram that shows the interaction among employee responsibilities

organizational structure identifies responsibilities for each job position and the relationships among those positions

organizing the organization of employees and other resources in a manner that is consistent with the firm's goals

outside board members board members who are not managers of the firm

outsourcing purchasing parts from a supplier rather than producing the parts

owner's equity includes the par (or stated) value of all common stock issued, additional paid-in capital, and retained earnings

P

par value the amount that bondholders receive at maturity

participative a leadership style in which the leaders accept some employee input but usually use their authority to make decisions

participative management employees are allowed to participate in various decisions made by their supervisors or others

partners co-owners of a business

partnership a business that is co-owned by two or more people

passive resistance occurs when users uncomfortable with a new system overstate difficulties associated with learning the technology

patents allow exclusive rights to the production and sale of a specific product

penetration pricing the strategy of setting a lower price than those of competing products to penetrate a market

pension funds receive employee and firm contributions toward pensions and invest the proceeds for the employees until the funds are needed

perquisites additional privileges beyond compensation payments and employee benefits

personal selling a personal sales presentation used to influence one or more consumers

physiological needs the basic requirements for survival

picketing walking around near the employer's building with signs complaining of poor working conditions

planning the preparation of a firm for future business conditions

policies guidelines for how tasks should be completed

political risk the risk that a country's political actions can adversely affect a business

positive reinforcement motivates employees by providing rewards for high performance

predatory pricing the strategy of lowering a product's price to drive out new competitors

preferred stock a security that represents partial ownership of a particular firm and offers specific priorities over common stock

premium a gift or prize provided free to consumers who purchase a specific product

press conference an oral announcement about a firm provided by that firm to the media

prestige pricing the strategy of using a higher price for a product that is intended to have a top-of-the-line image

price skimming the strategy of initially setting a high price for a product if no other competing products are in the market yet

price-elastic the demand for a product is highly responsive to price changes

price-inelastic the demand for a product is not very responsive to price changes

prime rate the rate of interest typically charged on loans to the most creditworthy firms that borrow

private liquidation creditors may informally request that a failing firm liquidate (sell) its assets and distribute the funds received from liquidation to them

private placement the selling of securities to one or a few investors

privately held ownership is restricted to a small group of investors

privatization the sale of government-owned businesses to private investors

procedures steps necessary to implement a policy

producer brands brands that reflect the manufacturer of the products

product a physical good or service that can satisfy consumer needs

product differentiation a firm's effort to distinguish its product from competitive products in a manner that makes the product more desirable

product layout a layout in which tasks are positioned in the sequence that they are assigned

product life cycle the typical set of phases that a product experiences over its lifetime

product line a set of related products or services offered by a single firm

product mix the assortment of products offered by a firm

production control involves purchasing materials, inventory control, routing, scheduling, and quality control

production efficiency the ability to produce products at a low cost

production management (operations management) the management of a process in which resources (such as employees and machinery) are used to produce products and services

production process (conversion process) a series of tasks in which resources are used to produce a product or service

production schedule a plan for the timing and volume of production tasks

profit sharing a portion of the firm's profits is paid to employees

program evaluation and review technique (PERT) a method of scheduling tasks to minimize delays in the production process

promotion the act of informing or reminding consumers about a specific product or brand

promotion the assignment of an employee to a higher-level job with more responsibility and compensation

promotion budget the amount of funds that have been set aside to pay for all promotion methods over a specified period

promotion mix the combination of promotion methods that a firm uses to increase acceptance of its products

property extension provides additional time for a firm to generate the necessary cash to cover its payments

property insurance protects a firm against the risk associated with the ownership of property, such as buildings and other assets

property losses financial losses resulting from damage to property

prospectus a document that discloses relevant financial information about securities and about the firm issuing them

protective covenants restrictions imposed on specific financial policies of a firm

prototype a working system with limited functionality

public accountants accountants who provide accounting services for a variety of firms for a fee

public offering the selling of securities to the public

public relations actions taken with the goal of creating or maintaining a favorable public image

publicly held shares can be easily purchased or sold by investors

pull strategy firms direct their promotion directly at the target market, and consumers in turn request the product from wholesalers or producers

push strategy producers direct their promotion of a product at wholesalers or retailers, who in turn promote it to consumers

Q

quality the degree to which a product or service satisfies a customer's requirements or expectations

quality control a process of determining whether the quality of a product meets the desired quality level

quality control circle a group of employees who assess the quality of a product and offer suggestions for improvement

quota a limit on the amounts of specific products that can be imported

R

random access memory (RAM) space in which information is temporarily stored in a computer

ratio analysis an evaluation of the relationships between financial statement variables

rebate a potential refund by the manufacturer to the consumer

recession two consecutive quarters of negative economic growth

reengineering the redesign of a firm's organizational structure and operations

reinforcement theory suggests that reinforcement can influence behavior

reminder advertising intended to remind consumers of a product's existence

remote job entry systems interorganizational systems that allow the user to interact directly with a company's internal systems

restructuring the revision of the production process in an attempt to improve efficiency

return on assets (ROA) measures a firm's net income as a percentage of the total amount of assets utilized by the firm

return on equity (ROE) earnings as a proportion of the firm's equity

return on equity (ROE) measures the return to the common stockholders (net income) as a percentage of their investment in the firm

right-to-work allows states to prohibit union shops

risk the degree of uncertainty about a firm's future earnings

round lots multiples of 100 shares

routing the sequence (or route) of tasks necessary to complete the production of a product

 S

S-corporation a firm that has 75 or fewer owners and satisfies other criteria. The earnings are distributed to the owners and taxed at the respective personal income tax rate of each owner.

sabotage the malicious destruction of information by a perpetrator

safety needs job security and safe working conditions

salary (or wages) the dollars paid for a job over a specific period

sales manager an individual who manages a group of sales representatives

sales promotion the set of activities that is intended to influence consumers

salvage value the amount of money that a firm can receive from selling a project

sampling offering free samples to encourage consumers to try a new brand or product

sampling randomly selecting some of the products produced and testing them to determine whether they satisfy the quality standards

savings institutions financial institutions that obtain deposits from individuals and use the deposited funds primarily to provide mortgage loans

scheduling the act of setting time periods for each task in the production process

seasonal unemployment people whose services are not needed during some seasons

secondary market a market where existing securities can be traded among investors

secured bonds bonds backed by collateral

segments subsets of a market that reflect a specific type of business and the perceived quality

selective distribution the distribution of a product through selected outlets

self-actualization the need to fully reach one's potential

self-insurance a firm insures itself by creating a fund to cover any future claims

self-service retail store a retailer that does not provide sales assistance or service and sells products that do not require much expertise

sexual harassment unwelcome comments or actions of a sexual nature

shareholder activism active efforts by stockholders to influence a firm's management policies

shopping products products that are not purchased frequently

shortage the situation when the quantity supplied by firms is less than the quantity demanded by customers

social needs the need to be part of a group

social responsibility a firm's recognition of how its business decisions can affect society

socialism an economic system that contains some features of both capitalism and communism

software programs that determine the specific tasks a computer will perform at any given time

sole proprietor the owner of a sole proprietorship

sole proprietorship a business owned by a single owner

span of control the number of employees managed by each manager

specialty products products that specific consumers consider to be special and therefore make a special effort to purchase

specialty retail store a retailer that specializes in a particular type of product

spot exchange rate the exchange rate quoted for immediate transactions

staff positions job positions established to support the efforts of line positions

stakeholders people who have an interest in a business; the business's owners, creditors, employees, suppliers, and customers

stand-alone system system architecture consisting of one or more computers that function independently

statistical analysis a computer model that applies statistical principles to understanding relationships between data and certain outcomes

stock certificates of ownership of a business

stock broker a person who facilitates desired stock transactions

stock market efficiency a term used to suggest that stock prices reflect all publicly available information

stock mutual funds investment companies that invest funds received from individual investors in stocks

stockholders (shareholders) investors who wish to become partial owners of firms

store brands brands that reflect the retail store where the products are sold

strategic alliance a business agreement between firms whereby resources are shared to pursue mutual interests

strategic plan identifies a firm's main business focus over a long-term period, perhaps three to five years

stretch targets production efficiency targets (or goals) that cannot be achieved under present conditions

strike a discontinuation of employee services

structural unemployment people who are unemployed because they do not have adequate skills

supervisory (first-line) management managers who are usually highly involved with the employees who engage in the day-to-day production process

supply chain the process from the beginning of the production process until the product reaches the customer

supply schedule a schedule that indicates the quantity of a product that would be supplied (produced) by firms at each possible price

surplus the situation when the quantity supplied by firms exceeds the quantity demanded by customers

system architecture the basic logical organization of a computer

systems development life cycle (SDLC) an approach to system development that involves decomposing a system into its functional components

T

tactical planning smaller-scale plans (over one or two years) that are consistent with the firm's strategic (long-term) plan

Taft-Hartley Act an amendment to the Wagner Act that prohibited unions from pressuring employees to join

target market Customers who fit the customer profile

tariff a tax on imported products

teamwork a group of employees with varied job positions have the responsibility to achieve a specific goal

technical skills skills used to perform specific day-to-day tasks

technological obsolescence inferior to new products

technology knowledge or tools used to produce products and services

telemarketing the use of the telephone for promoting and selling products

tender offer a direct bid by an acquiring firm for the shares of a target firm

term insurance provides life insurance for a policyholder only over a specified term and does not build a cash value for the policyholder

terminals devices that combine the functions of a monitor and a keyboard

time management the way managers allocate their time when managing tasks.

times interest earned ratio measures the ability of a firm to cover its interest payments

top (high-level) management managers in positions such as president, chief executive officer, chief financial officer, and vice-president who make decisions regarding the firm's long-run objectives

total quality management (TQM) the act of monitoring and improving the quality of products and services produced

trade deficit the amount by which imports exceed exports

trademark a brand's form of identification that is legally protected from use by other firms

Treasury bills short-term debt securities issued by the U.S. Treasury

two-level channel two marketing intermediaries are between the producer and the customer

U

underwriting syndicate a group of investment banks that share the obligations of underwriting securities

underwritten the investment bank guarantees a price to the issuing firm, no matter what price the securities are sold for

universal life insurance combines the features of term and whole-life insurance; specifies a period of time over which the policy will exist, but builds a cash value for the policyholder over time

unlimited liability no limit on the debts for which the owner is liable

unsecured bonds bonds that are not backed by collateral

upward appraisals used to measure the managerial abilities of supervisors

V

variable costs costs that vary with the quantity produced

variable costs operating expenses that vary directly with the number of products produced

variety retail store a retailer that offers numerous types of goods

venture capital firm a firm composed of individuals who invest in small businesses

vertical channel integration two or more levels of distribution are managed by a single firm

vertical merger the combination of a firm with a potential supplier or customer

video conferencing holding meetings between remote sites using sound and

pictures transmitted over telecommunications links

virtual reality display techniques that combine computerized sights, sounds, and sensations to create a sense of actually "being there"

W

Wagner Act prohibited firms from interfering with workers' efforts to organize or join unions

"what-if" analysis a computer model that generates different potential business scenarios to answer questions

white knight a more suitable company that is willing to acquire a firm and rescue it from the hostile takeover efforts of some other firm

whole-life insurance life insurance that exists until death or as long as premiums are promptly paid and has a cash value to which the policyholder is entitled

wide area network (WAN) a system in which telecommunications technologies are employed to connect pieces of the network

work station an area in which one or more employees are assigned a specific task

workgroup software network software that provides a broad array of user-friendly features, such as electronic mail, document management systems, and work-sharing systems

working capital management the management of a firm's short-term assets and liabilities

work-in-process inventories inventories of partially completed products

workstations in a network system, individual computers that access the software and data on the file server

Y

yellow-dog contract a contract requiring employees to refrain from joining a union as a condition of employment

Company Index

Subject Index

to employees, 71–75, 87–89
to the environment, 80–82, 85, 87–89
to stockholders, 75–78, 87, 89
Restructuring, 280, 284
Resumé, 689–691
Retail store, 427–428
chain, 427
full-service, 428
independent, 427
self-service, 428
variety, 428
Retailer, 418–419, 427–431, 460
mail-order, 429
website, 429
Retained earnings, 46, 50, 488, 507, 514, 517
Return on assets, 494–498
Return on equity, 48–50, 142–143, 495–496, 498, 522
Return on investment, 48
Return on stocks, 674
Right-to-work, 364
Risk, 35, 51, 57, 142, 176, 185, 609–627, 656, 677
Risk management, 609–627, 656
Robinson-Patman Act, 71
Round lot, 681
Routing, 272–273

S

Sabotage, 593
Safety needs, 306–307
Safety skills, 350
Sales manager, 462
Sales presentation, 453, 459
Sales promotion, 454, 463, 655
Sampling, 278
Savings behavior, 536
Scheduling, 220–221
S-corporation, 39
Screening applicants, 336–337
Seasonal unemployment, 107
Secondary market, 517
Segment, 143–146, 148–149
Self-actualization, 307
Self-scanning, 146
Sexual harassment, 73
Shareholder activism, 77
Sherman Antitrust Act, 71
Shortage, 116, 118
Site, 262–265, 643, 653
evaluation matrix, 263–264
selection, 263–264, 637–638
Social needs, 306–307
Social responsibility, 65, 68, 78, 85, 88, 89, 647, 652
Social values, 384
Socialism, 172–175
Sole proprietorship. *See* Proprietorship
Span of control, 236, 240
Spot exchange rate, 183
Staff position, 241
Stakeholders, 4, 23, 65, 68

Stand-alone system, 585–586
Standardization, 420
Statistical analysis, 583
Stock, 5, 67, 76–77, 233, 342–345, 385, 444–445, 488, 490, 507, 514, 517, 524, 556–557, 567, 569, 647, 670–683
exchange, 517
market efficiency, 676–677
offering, 48, 515–516, 567
options, 342–345
Stockbroker, 679–680
commissions, 679
discount, 680
full-service, 680
Stockholders, 5, 7, 23, 40–41, 44–45, 49, 69, 76–77, 210, 233, 342–345, 482, 490, 514–515, 524, 647
Strategic alliance, 167, 170, 185
Strategic plan, 204, 207, 213, 215, 231, 305, 636–637, 647, 653
Stretch targets, 280
Strike, 136, 367–368, 675
Strong dollar, 178, 180–182, 185
Supervisory management, 202
Supplier, 69, 169, 175, 178, 181, 268, 269, 519–520, 616
Supply chain, 285
Supply of loanable funds, 532–537
Supply schedule, 115–118
Surplus, 116
SWOT analysis, 147–148
System architecture, 581
Systems development life cycle (SDLC), 591

T

Tactical planning, 204, 208
Taft-Hartley Act, 364
Target market, 16, 18, 22, 56, 382, 385, 459–460, 464, 654
Tariff, 167
Tax, 44–46, 56, 163, 173, 176–177
Tax incentives, 262
Teamwork, 204, 309, 320, 323
Technical skills, 215, 217–218
Tender offer, 567
Terminal, 587
Theory X, 309, 313
Theory Y, 309, 313
Theory Z, 309, 313
Time management, 219
Times-interest-earned, 493–497
Top management, 202, 211, 239
Total quality management (TQM), 276–277, 638, 649
Trade barriers, 169
Trade deficit, 168
Trade restriction, 165
Trademark, 53–54, 393
Training, 318, 350
Transportation decisions, 422
Treasury bill rate, 615
Treasury bills, 555, 615

Two-level channel, 418
Tying arrangement, 71

U

U.S. Commerce Department, 10
Underwriter, 516
Underwriting, 518–519
Underwriting syndicate, 518–519
Unemployment, 107–108, 110
rate, 108–110
cyclical, 108
frictional, 107
natural, 107
seasonal, 107
structural, 108
Unethical decisions, 66–68, 77, 79, 83
Union. *See* Labor union
Unlimited liability, 37
Upward appraisal, 356

V

Variable costs, 281–283, 399–402
Vending machine, 430
Venture capital, 515–516
Venture capital firm, 515–516
Vertical channel integration, 431–432
Video conferencing, 597
Virtual reality, 597
Volume discount, 268
Voting rights, 515

W

Wagner Act, 364
Warehousing, 430
Warning labels, 68
Warranty, 147
Weak dollar, 178, 181–182
White knight, 569
Wholesaler, 417–419, 430–431, 459–460
Wide area network (WAN), 588
Workflow processing, 646
Work station, 260
Workgroup software, 588
Working capital management, 555
Workplace space, 262, 267
Workstations, 587

Y

Yellow-dog contract, 364

Additional Photo Credits

Part Opener Images

Part I, page xxxvi: South-Western/Thomson Learning

Part II, page 102: PhotoDisc, Inc.

Part III, page 198: PhotoDisc, Inc.

Part IV, page 302: Digital Vision

Part V, page 376: Digital Vision

Part VI, page 478: PhotoDisc, Inc.

Part VII, page 576: Digital Vision

Chapter Opener Images

Chapter 1, page 2: Getty Images

Chapter 2, page 34: South-Western/Thomson Learning

Chapter 3, page 64: PhotoDisc, Inc.

Chapter 4, page 104: South-Western/Thomson Learning

Chapter 5, page 132: South-Western/Thomson Learning

Chapter 6, page 156: Associated Press

Chapter 7, page 200: PhotoDisc, Inc.

Chapter 8, page 230: South-Western/Thomson Learning

Chapter 9, page 258: South-Western/Thomson Learning

Chapter 10, page 304: South-Western/Thomson Learning

Chapter 11, page 332: The Image Bank

Chapter 12, page 378: PhotoDisc, Inc.

Chapter 13, page 414: South-Western/Thomson Learning

Chapter 14, page 442: South-Western/Thomson Learning

Chapter 15, page 480: South-Western/Thomson Learning

Chapter 16, page 506: South-Western/Thomson Learning

Chapter 17, page 538: PhotoDisc, Inc.

Chapter 18, page 578: PhotoDisc, Inc.

Chapter 19, page 608: South-Western/Thomson Learning

Chapter 20, page 634: South-Western/Thomson Learning